MW00777097

SIDDUR
HATEFILLAH

THE JEWISH PRAYER BOOK

Philosophy, Poetry, and Mystery

Siddur Hatefillah

THE JEWISH PRAYER BOOK

Philosophy, Poetry, and Mystery

Eliezer Schweid

Translated and with an
Introduction by
Gershon Greenberg

BOSTON
2022

Library of Congress Control Number: 2022934567

ISBN 9781644698655 hardback
ISBN 9781644698662 Adobe PDF
ISBN 9781644698679 ePub

Book design by Kryon Publishing Services
www.kryonpublishing.com
Cover design by Ivan Grave
On the cover: photograph(s) of Har Rephaim synagogue courtesy of member,
Rabbi Marcel Marcus

Published by Academic Studies Press
1577 Beacon Street
Brookline, MA, 02446, USA
press@academicstudiespress.com
www.academicstdiespress.com

To the blessed memory of my three friends, who really knew prayer, of the synagogue Har Rephaim in Jerusalem: Reb David Farkas, Reb Yehoshua Cohen, and Reb Yosef Ben-Or, from whose example in prayer I learned what *devekut* ("attachment" to God) is and how the intention of the heart is expressed in song, directly and simply.

שלומות,

אלי שביד הלך היום לעולמו. שבע ימים ומעש.
היה צלול ופעיל עד ימיו האחרונים,
וזכה לצעוד בדרך חייו האחרונה ללא סבל,
מוקף במשפחתו האוהבת.

הלוויה תתקיים ביום חמישי, בשעה 11:00 בבוקר,
בבית ההספד "קהילת ירושלים" בהר המנוחות בירושלים.

חייו היו ברכה גדולה. זכרו - ברכה ומצווה.

יוקי

Yehoyada Amir
January 18 2022

Contents

Translator's Acknowledgements

My debt of gratitude is essentially to my teacher Eliezer Schweid *z"l*, who with his wife Sabina have welcomed me in their Jerusalem home on Rehov Yishai for nearly half a century—from the time I was a student in the Department of Jewish Thought at the Hebrew University of Jerusalem to the years when I served there as visiting professor. Beyond a place of learning and meeting point for a constellation of Israeli scholars and artists, their home has been a lifeline out of my academic and cultural solitude in Washington, DC.

I am not a translator by profession, but when the opportunity to translate *Siddur Hatefillah* into English arose during an evening visit, I leaped at the opportunity. It is a text that has the potential to provide thousands in the diaspora with new comprehension of prayer (notwithstanding Jewish sectarianism, indifference, and instinctive resistance)—one nourished by the understanding of the leading historian of Jewish thought of the generation, whose life and work have been a crucible of the Israeli experience.

Reminiscences about my own life of prayer interspersed my work on the translation, along with thoughts of those who have helped me to pray: my beloved and learned father Morris Greenberg *z"l* (Brooklyn, NY); my teachers Eugen Kullmann *z"l* (Annandale-on-Hudson) and Jacob Taubes *z"l* (Berlin); my sister Rayla Temin (Madison, WI); my Israeli family members Eliezer Schwimmer *z"l*, Mosheh Rosenblum, and Arik Shilo (Petach Tikvah), Pinhas Mendelovitch (Tel Aviv), Tsvika Symon (Jerusalem); my colleagues Dani Michman (Elkanah, Dnipropetrovsk), Naftali Loewenthal (Jerusalem, New York), and Yohanan Petrovsky-Shtern (Jerusalem); and my students Marcel Marcus (Berlin) and Hayim Weiser (White Oak, MD).

There are also many at Kesher Israel Congregation and Chabad in Washington, DC, who have enriched my worship. Among them are Dan Brandenburg, James Cleeman, Norm Eisen, David Epstein, Eliezer and Gideon Halbfinger, Shua Hecht, Bernardo Hirschman *z"l*, Lindsay Kaplan, Lew Kest, Dan Klein, Gerard Leval, David Levin, Alyza Lewin, Kurt Maier, Chip Manekin, Allan Mendelsohn, Michael Perkins, Howard Rosen, Eliyahu Roumani, Hyim Shafner, Levi Shemtov, Leon Wiesenthal, and Herman Wouk *z"l*.

The citations from the *siddur* are from *The Koren Siddur, with Introduction, Translation and Commentary* by Rabbi Sir Jonathan Sacks (Jerusalem: Koren

Publishers, 2009). They are indicated by the letter K in parentheses following the citation. Those from the Hebrew Bible are from the *JPS Hebrew English Tanakh. The Traditional Hebrew Text and the New JPS Translation—Second Edition* (Philadelphia: The Jewish Publication Society, 2000). A glossary and index have been added to Schweid's text. Schweid often uses quotation marks as form of emphasis, some of which have been reproduced in the translation.

I received partial financial support for publication from the American University College of Arts and Sciences Mellon fund.

I am indebted to Lenny Levin, veteran translator, who has checked the entire translation and made many helpful suggestion.

I have been blessed throughout the translating process with the presence in my soul of our son Ariel Moshe, and my beloved wife Erika Weinfeld z"l— whose unexpected death in Jerusalem deprived us of sharing the joy of bringing the spirit of her endeared Eliezer and Sabina Schweid to the shores of America.

Gershon Greenberg
Washington, D.C.

Translator's Introduction: Eliezer Schweid as Worshipper in the State of Israel

A Call to Faith and Prayer

Eliezer Schweid, a person of faith, authored *Siddur Hatefillah* to address, and call for, faith through prayer. In "Faith Confronting the Experiences of our Age," he cited Buber's distinction between "faith in" ("a life-tendency and holistic form of relating to existence") and "faith that" ("holding in trust certain views concerning existence"). It enabled him to examine faith in itself objectively, from within faith:

> . . . to identify myself as a believing person, to examine my faith "in itself" as an existential response, to discover its origins, and to come back and examine after the fact the connection between this faith and the objective kind of knowledge on which it relied and the methods of verification proper to such knowledge. Thus I was able to enter into the circle of faith—experience that I had previously contemplated as an outsider . . . from a distance that had appeared unbridgeable. For one can only understand faith if one has faith oneself. As an existential response, faith is only susceptible of objective observation from within.[1]

Schweid understands faith to be related to hope. Faith is rooted in primal life experience (*ḥavayah*).[2] Like faith, hope is a self-sufficient power of life, derived from humankind's hidden network of unknowable forces of energy of life and creativity. They come from God; hope's power to "borrow" from the future is derived from a transcendental source.[3] Faith is also tied to morality. Faith's source and center is God, the first source of all reality, including morality, which will become fully manifest with redemption. If one acts towards God in faith, one can trust that God will act in accord with one's moral expectations. If one fulfills one's moral obligations to God, the source of all morality, morality will manifest itself objectively in the world—God being the source of all reality.[4]

Faith finds articulation through prayer. With creation, God infuses the human body with the ability to speak, and speech enables prayer. Faith and prayer both flow from primal life experience (*havayah*) sourced in God. Prayer erupts out of the soul-breath's (*neshamah's*)[5] attachment (*zikah*) to God. In prayer, the "I" (*Ani*), which embodies body and soul, addresses God as *Atah* (You)—such that the human being is the *Ani* to God (*Atah*), and God is the *Ani* to the human's *Atah*. The words of prayer "speech-act" God's presence in the world, in faith and in hope—and thereby serve to actualize the moral potential of the world in objective reality.[6]

But faith, along with morality and prayer, is shaken by the traumatic reality of the Holocaust, postmodernism, and developments in the State of Israel. As to the Holocaust: Nazism created a region for itself in the heart of humankind, Schweid tells us, a manifestation of demonic evil in an anti-human, anti-godlike form of "human existence." It threatened faith, for faith sought to have morality blend with objective reality—paving a path towards redemption under God. With the Holocaust, it appeared as though divine providence, which was rooted in the ethical foundation of faith, lost the last shred of empirical being. Faith toppled, and the moral quest for redemption, which was enabled by faith, was shaken. However, the Holocaust did not in fact destroy faith, or its potential ties to morality as objectively real. Schweid writes that even in the face of the Holocaust, believers

> were able to enlist the reserves of moral energy that were neces-
> sary in order to resist, to survive, and to look forward in hope,
> solely on the basis of their tottering faith. If they were to give
> up on it, they would be giving up on the hope of life and on life
> itself. They refused. The need for faith became for them the
> source of its validity.[7]

Schweid's *Siddur Hatefillah* offers an interpretation of prayer, which can guide the Holocaust survivor's worship.

Second, there is the threat posed by postmodernism. For Schweid (as formulated by Ari Ackerman), postmodernism represents a consumerist ideology and hyper-capitalist approach that opposes any limit to competition as unfair and anti-liberal. It views culture as another product to be chosen and consumed by individuals—not as a vehicle for forging a shared group consciousness. And postmodernism subscribes to an individualistic neoliberal philosophy, according to which the state is a framework for the self-realization. Finally, while advocating a multicultural society, it criticizes ideologies concerned with social solidarity and collective good for limiting human freedom. The universe of postmodernism, it follows, is antithetical to faith. For faith involves an orientation where one sees oneself as part of something larger; derives a feeling of certitude through relationships. For faith, hope in the future is achieved through confidence in the goodness of the other.[8] By presenting an interpretation of prayer that draws from scriptural, historical sources and analyzes the texts of worship theologically, philosophically, and experientially, *Siddur Hatefillah* presents a counterpoint to the postmodernist mindset.

Third, there is the challenge of bringing to bear the *raison d'être* of the State of Israel. Following a brief period of moral reconstruction and progress after World War II, Schweid explains, world morality underwent a precipitous decline—which, given the technological power now available, pointed to destruction even greater than that of the Holocaust. Materialism and egoism were overwhelming morality—along with its covenantal structure between God and the human being. The sprouting of the redemption (Prayer of the Chief Rabbinate upon the State's creation), the actualizing of moral ideals through the Jewish state, the governmental vessel for "communal justice in the light of Israel's prophets" (Declaration of the Establishment of the State of Israel) had yet to take place. The promise of the ingathering of exiles, uniting the people in the Land of Israel and restoring justice and righteousness for redemption had yet to be fulfilled. To realize their hopes for redemption and that of humankind, communities and synagogues had to renew the covenant upon which the nation of Israel was founded.[9] Schweid writes:

> Before any progress can be made in achieving covenantal morality through the state to any limited degree, the people of Israel needed a redemption in the State in the sense of "Return us to the days of old." (Psalms 77:2). . . . The event of prayer as a life-experience (*havayah*) of faith, love and sanctification, not only educates one for redemptive spiritual, moral ascent. As an anticipation of the future, it is also a symbolic gesture of redemption.[10]

The Personal Impetus

From a personal, scholarly perspective, the time had also come for Schweid to study prayer. Given his interest in all periods of the history of Jewish thought in its various dimensions, it was inevitable that prayer would sooner or later become a *desideratum*. Once he completed his work on the philosophy of the Bible (2004), which dealt with the scriptural sources for prayer, and then on the seasonal festivals, he was ready to explore the philosophical ingredients of the *siddur*—treating it as an additional chapter in the history of Jewish philosophy.[11]

Praying had long become essential to his life. Eliezer Schweid was born in Jerusalem to parents who had arrived in the Land of Israel with the Third Aliyah. His mother had grown up in a *mitnagdic* (Orthodox, non-Hasidic) home, but did not believe in God. His father, educated in a Hasidic household, prayed privately, as an individual. They went to synagogue as a family only on Yom Kippur, but his father also took him to a Yemenite synagogue in Meah She'arim for *Simḥat Torah*. It was there that he had his first serious encounter with prayer, and felt the joy of those who knew its secrets. But he did not share the experience, and did not dare to pray himself. Over time, however, he was drawn by his father's finding individual refuge in prayer, and he discovered the "secret of the secret of prayer": the ability to pray emerged from a need to do so, which burst forth from the depths of the soul. Faith and the need to pray flowed from the same source.[12] Schweid's life with prayer began to take shape during his years in the *kibbutz*, which opened ways for him to celebrate the sacred holiday tradition in the secular environment with which he identified. After arriving in Jerusalem for university study and raising a family, his need for the communal life that he experienced in the *kibbutz* was filled by the synagogue. Fellow worshippers at the Har Refaim synagogue in Abu Tor taught him about the inner meditation of prayer—enabling him to pray with enlivened emotion. And soon, Schweid wanted to understand the words of his prayers.[13]

Approaching Prayer: Experience and Philosophy

Siddur Hatefillah explores prayer's philosophical dimensions—specifically analyzing those prayers that process philosophical *mishnayot* into the language of worship. Those who pray, according to Schweid, also reflect about prayer in language that expressed philosophical ideas—providing them with direction and giving feedback in terms of ideas.

Schweid holds that it would be impossible to exclude subjective considerations in the study of philosophical texts. The scholar unavoidably interacts with the text, and there is always some degree of subject-object synthesis. Thus, with *Siddur Hatefillah*, Schweid's personal prayer found its way into reflection, and relates dialectically to philosophical ingredients found in the prayer texts. While the inner circle of the "subject" (prayer) relates to the outer circle of the "object" (prayer), the outer circle of the subject (philosophy) relates to the inner circle of the object (philosophy). Or: prayer and philosophy interrelate as concentric circles that continually replace one another.[14]

The pages of *Siddur Hatefillah* reveal the deep religiosity of Schweid's own worship. His relationship with God, rooted in an aboriginal soulful identity with God, is one of love. It unfolds individually, historically, metahistorically, and cosmically. His prayer is filled with Torah and framed covenantally, that is, in terms of the material relationship between God and humans in historical and metahistorical context. His mindset is anchored in redemption—which alone makes creation meaningful. The potential realization of redemption provides hope and trust that chaos and sin will eventually subside. Schweid experiences redemption individually on the Sabbath day and as a member of the Jewish people towards the end of the weekday *Shemoneh Esrei*. At these moments, he finds relief and assurance vis-à-vis the postmodern world as well as the State of Israel and the Jewish people—which appears to be overwhelmed by the chaos that has escaped God's ordering of the world.[15]

The Origin and Nature of Prayer as Contained in *Siddur Hatefillah*

As expressed in the mythic language of Hebrew scripture, when God created the universe He separated it into heaven and earth. His spirit nevertheless remained instilled within the earth, setting the stage for earth and heaven to ultimately become one, once again. This required overcoming the chaos (by God and human beings together), which had eluded God's ordering of the world.[16] The book of Genesis defined the destructive void, which preceded creation as an evil essence, and complete being as a good essence. Consciousness of self and its divine source was the highest good and identified with complete being. Death, the negation of life and self-consciousness, was evil.[17] As expressed in the *Kiddush* of the eve of the Sabbath, the human being perfected everything created earlier.[18] When God created the primal man, He exhaled His *ruaḥ* (spirit) into the man's nostrils. This became the *neshamah*, the soul-breath, the extension of the spirit, which is extended into the blood as spiritual soul (*nefesh ruḥanit*). During night-time sleep, the *neshamah* extracts itself from the *nefesh ruḥanit* and body to be with God, before returning to the person at dawn. The *neshamah* assumes the form of the *Ani* (the "I"). Born out of body and soul together, the *Ani* enables the human being to participate, in human terms, in the ongoing cosmic ordering of chaos—from the original division between the heaven and earth (creation) all the way to their reintegration (redemption).

The pure and sacred *neshamah* remains inseparably attached to God—for which Schweid uses the term *zikah* (love-bond). This *zikah* expresses and manifests itself in a dialectical manner: God is the *Ani* to the human being's *Atah*, and the human is the *Ani* to God's *Atah*. As to the categorical difference between infinite God and the finite human being: Schweid explains that the *zikah* was possible because God knows the mystery of the attachment. God traverses and envelopes it, reconciling the division—just as He traverses the mysterious separation between heaven and earth to reveal Himself in history. The substance of *zikah* is the love between God and the human being. Enveloped by God, it dissolves the asymmetry between the finite (man) and the infinite (God). As with the *neshamah*, the *zikah* is reborn daily at dawn.[19]

God externalizes His thought about creation with speech, and He infuses the ability to speak into the human body.[20] In turn, speech supplies the potential for verbal prayer. By revealing His name (*Yod-Hay-Vav-Hay*) to those who serve Him and are committed to His *mitzvot*, God provides the key for the actualization of prayer.[21] Prayer is nourished by the *zikah* (love-bond). It erupts from out of the *zikah* deep within the worshipper, when self-consciousness awakens the *neshamah*. The *Ani*, the form assumed by the *neshamah* (the bearer of the *ruah* from God), did the praying. Prayer necessarily flows from God and man together—such that only after the words of prayer emerges from the *neshamah*, and only after God has opened the worshipper's lips for prayer and the words of prayer have taken human form, can they be apprehended by the one who prays. The *Ani* neither anticipates the outpouring of prayer, nor controls it.[22]

Schweid explains how the words of prayer provide definition, form, and substance to the loving content of *zikah*. The worshipping *Ani*, as self-conscious subject, reflects intellectually (this is the *sekhel*) about the meeting between body and soul (out of which the *Ani* was born). The *Ani* both rises up before God (who is the *Anokhi*) and bows humbly before Him. It also overcomes doubt in God's presence and praises Him for His creation as an expression of His goodness, and his desire for everything good for the human beings.[23] Further, the *Ani* can purify itself of sin and thereby enable the worshipper to participate with God in the cosmic displacement of chaos and evil. Once purified, the soul reengages with God in mutual love. This prepares the human being to be fructified by God, and to participate productively in completing His creation.[24]

Having now probed the *Ani* who prayed, the eruption of prayer from the *zikah* of the *neshamah* with God, and the psychological-theological dynamics underlying Jewish prayer, Schweid addresses the psychological-emotional dimensions, which moved the *Ani* to address God and inspired the loving dialogue. Namely, *devekut* (adherence to God and ascent to a level of mystery) and *kavanah* (intentionality). Insofar as he was created in God's image, the human being could sanctify himself, and *devekut* provided the means. It intensified the experience of God's en-spiriting the human being with *neshamah*—to a point where en-spirited *nefesh*, that is, the *neshamah*, blended with God's humanly en-souled spirit in unifying love. The two spirits adhered to one another—the spiritual soul blended and unified with its source, the spirit of God. *Devekut* was not passive—as if one had to be pulled up towards God. It was an active choice, based upon intellectual knowledge and the understanding that God's path alone enabled the realization of one's destiny. *Devekut* with, and to, God on the spiritual level resembled the physical adherence of husband and wife to one another to be one flesh; for the husband to fructify his wife and for her to be fructified by him. *Kavanah*, the reflection upon God's mysterious unity, emerged from, and accompanied *devekut*. It enabled the release of God's spiritual influx (*shefa*). The high priest served as paradigm. As he uttered the *Shem Hameforash* on the Day of Atonement with *devekut* and *kavanah*, his thought unified into absolute concentration upon, and commitment to, his creator.[25]

Prophecy and Prayer

Schweid's *Siddur Hatefillah* includes an inquiry into the (meta)historical origin and development of the divine-human *zikah* during the era of the prophet—much of the literature of the *siddur* having been drawn from the scriptural texts of prophecy. The prophets constituted an historical and metahistorical turning point and vessel for actualizing the *zikah*, also understood as love between God and the people of Israel. The individual prophet's hierophanic experience channeled the *zikah*, which was naturally universal to humankind, into the particular history of God's chosen nation. It enabled the prophet to make God's *mitzvot* known, narrowing the distance between God (infinite) and the human being (finite).[26]

With the hierophany of the prophet, God enabled the human being to understand His revealed wisdom from the divine perspective itself. God's wisdom and His objectively real creation were identical, and His revelation was inherently true. The transmission of divine, absolute truth to the limited human *sekhel* (intellect) was mysterious—but as with *zikah*, here God traversed the mystery and instilled transcendent truth into the intellect and insight. The prophetic experience was a composite of human and divine aspects. While the prophet knew that the message he conveyed was not self-derived, and unavoidable, and that God provided a trans-human ability to understand His thoughts and desires, the prophet nevertheless retained independent feelings, consciousness, and free will. The composite enabled the prophet to transmit divine, trans-human content of compassion, rebuke, and consolation in human terms—as well as God's secret name (*Yod-Hay-Vav-Hay*) to the people.[27]

The content of the prophet Moses's hierophany was the Torah, which constituted the substance of the *zikah* and made Torah available to the people of Israel. The Torah's articulation of the *zikah* produced words for prayer. In turn, the words provided a means for the individual to purify the soul, by overcoming the sins, which obstructed human participation with God in their endeavor to overcome chaos.[28] Synagogue worship enacted the prophet-Torah connection, making it present and real. Reading the text enacted the worshipper's love for, and closeness to, God; and brought the ancient prophetic content into the here and now. The content was internalized by the audience, with each participant sharing it equally.[29]

Siddur Hatefillah: The Jewish Prayer Book—Philosophy, Poetry, and Mystery focuses on the *Keriyat Shema* cluster of prayers recited on the Sabbath, and the weekday *Shemoneh Esrei* (*Amidah*), both of which articulate the people of Israel's covenantal obligations and hopes for redemption. The *Keriyat Shema* verbalizes and enacts the loving relationship, which grounds the covenant and draws the event of God's ancient liberation in the ancient past into the present (*Ga'al yisrael* in *Tzur Yisrael*), precipitating future liberation. The *Amidah* details the path of righteousness and justice towards salvation (*Go'el yisrael* in *Re'eh Be'onyeinu*).

The Creation of the World and Loving God: Recitation of the *Shema* (*Keriyat Shema*)

Schweid explores the philosophical dimension of the *Keriyat Shema* cluster of prayers (*Le'el Barukh* through *Tzur Yisrael*) as an articulation of the *zikah* with God that stands at the center of the cosmic reconciliation of world-creation. This cluster evokes God's creation of light and order, overcoming darkness and chaos, and His exhaling His sacred spirit into the human being for the *neshamah*. It enunciates and enacts a loving relationship with God as a context for overcoming sin, and the divine-human partnership in the struggle between good (tranquility) and evil (suffering), which transforms history and metahistory into redemption. The cluster includes the liberation of the children of Israel from Egypt—an enduring metahistorical event and a *prolepsis* of redemption.

Specifically, *Le'el Barukh* (the first blessing) testifies to God's creative activity, overcoming chaos as the light of creation streamed through the universe—an activity that discloses itself daily. The stream of light makes God's spirit present, and is shared with humanity in the form of *neshamah*. With *devekut* and *kavanah*, the worshipper can apprehend the progression of light and spirituality towards the comprehensive illumination of God's kingdom—when the original light of the universe will be transformed into the light of redemption.[30]

Ahavah Rabbah (the second blessing) introduces a loving dialogue into the metahistorical arena. It articulates God's love for the people of Israel, who enact it. Drawing from a point of union between the human being and God, enveloped by God, the worshipper asks God for Torah and the ability to understand and follow; and to enable him to focus the heart on the loving God and on substantiating the human-divine process towards unification. Trust in God facilitates one's love, and declaring the trust makes it actual. The content of the *Ahavah Rabbah* is dialogical: the worshipper asks God to perpetuate His love, while God expects the human beings to love Him—which is possible because of God's overwhelming love. Out of mutual affection, the worshipper is able to ascend to God. *Ahavah Rabbah* ends with the expression of the closeness to God and praise of Him, which comes with *devekut*.[31] Having ascended to a level where coalescence with God was achievable, the worshipper can now proclaim God's oneness.

The worshipper does so with the declaration "*Shema yisrael adonai eloheinu adonai eḥad.*" Recited while seated, the passage simultaneously enacts the exaltation of God and lowers the human ego—lessening the asymmetry between the finite human and the infinite divine, as well as between lower earthly personality and higher spirituality. The *shefa* (influx) of God's loving spirit streams into the worshipper, intensifying their *zikah*. The worshipper pronounces and reflects upon each of the nouns (*yisrael, adonai, eloheinu, adonai*), contemplates the transition from one to the other, and concludes with the adjective "one," blending the components into a single concept. Once unified in the thought of the worshipper, they enable the worshipper to aspire towards (a humanly undefinable) higher unity with God. The following phrase, "*Barukh shem kevod malkhuto,*" explicates God's oneness by testifying to God's role as creator of all.[32]

The *Ve'ahavta*, which comes next, returns the worshipper to loving dialogue. God's oneness enables His human creations to unite heart (physical life; blood in the veins), soul, spiritualized *nefesh, sekhel* (intellect and insight), *tevunah* (reason), and remaining human resources, to love Him. Also, to instill them with love and then elevate the love to God through *kavanah* and *devekut.*[33]

The *Vehayah Im Shamo'a,* which follows, provides form and content to the dialogue: study of and obedience to Torah. This evokes the descent of divine *shefa* into nature, intensifying the illumination of the earth. Were love and Torah to be neglected, eclipsing light, nature itself would yield to chaos. *Vayomer Hashem* introduces tangible forms for remembering the covenant and Torah commandments. It also introduces the event of divine liberation of the children of Israel from Egyptian slavery, with its everlasting significance.[34]

With *Emet veyatziv venakhon . . . al harishonim,* the worshipper affirms the surety of God's dominion over the generations of humankind. That is, along with the metahistorical path for creation to redemption, historical events unfold under divine auspices.[35] Finally, *Ezrat Avoteinu* and *Tzur Yisrael* usher the love between God and the human being, which was located in the drama of creation, into the realm of redemption. Facing disaster at the exodus, trapped between Egyptian tyranny behind them and the waters of the red sea in front, the children of Israel were redeemed. Their trust in God and their love for Him tapped both into His redemptive role in history and the redemption at the end of history as implied by the light of creation.[36]

In essence, the *Keriyat Shema* cluster of prayers sets the stage for the metahistorical drama of God's relationship to the universe and humanity's place within it. It outlines the (metaphysical) relation between creation and redemption, and the worshipper's ascent for a higher dialogue of love with God, whereby the finite personality lowered itself. The dialogue and aspirations toward union with God, filled with Torah, are central ingredients of the redemptive process. They advance the people of Israel on their covenantal path to salvation.

Creation and Redemption Meet. The Sabbath *Keriyat Shema*

Sabbath celebration brings future salvation into the present and anticipates the kingdom of God. When recited on the Sabbath day, the *Keriyat Shema* draws the worshipper into the closing of distance between creation and redemption.

The Sabbath day originated with the manna in the desert, when daily allotments doubled every sixth day, because there would be no distribution on the seventh. The people followed this procedure, trusting that the manna would not spoil over the night between the sixth and seventh days. On the seventh day, they were liberated from reliance upon, and concern about, labor (enacting God's respite from His labors of creation) and increasing possessions. When God created the world, He instilled a spiritual longing on earth to blend with heavenly spirit, and the Sabbath was a *prolepsis* of their coalescence. Redemption entered home and synagogue in the form of the *Shekhinah* (God's indwelling presence), leaving time-space matters behind. Thus, the Sabbath interrupted the passage of time, to join the world before time (when heaven and earth were one) and the end of history.[37]

The ritual components included lighting candles on the eve of the Sabbath—replacing the dwindling natural light outside with sacred light within the home. The act marked a boundary between the weekday's secularity and temporality, and the Sabbath's sanctity and eternity. It signaled the extraction from time for worship in the context of creation-redemption. The *Kiddush* at the start of the first Sabbath meal condensed the six days of work during the week with a declaration of its having been completed— closing the distance between past and present. The *Kiddush* also evoked the creation of the human being as a perfection of everything created earlier, as well as the liberation from Egypt and the overcoming of the chaos (evil), which infiltrated the created world.[38]

The *El Adon* hymn of the Sabbath *Shaḥarit* (morning) service expresses and enacts the worshipper's participation in the Sabbath day as a *prolepsis* of redemption, and ascent to heaven. Its content describes how God renews His illumined creation daily, overcoming chaos. God's providence is not a function of historical activity but of the metaphysical process of creation vis-à-vis redemption, and He stands by His people as He participates in their struggle— even in exile. As the universe is God's creation, the struggle will end in victory. For his part, the physical earthbound worshipper ascends to God in terms of intellectual contemplation and rational reflection.[39] At the end of the Sabbath, the *Havdalah* candles simultaneously symbolize the passage from Sabbath rest to renewed labor—and from the sadness of the Sabbath's departure to hope in the coming of the Messiah.[40]

Thus, the *Keriyat Shema* cluster centers on the *zikah*-rooted loving dialogue between the worshipper and God, filled with Torah, against the background of God's creation which implies redemption. On the Sabbath, the dialogue unfolds at the border between creation and redemption, in an eternal present that includes past and future. The dialogue is initiated by God, who traverses the mysterious relation between infinite and finite and resolves the asymmetry. In this eternal moment, which interrupts time, creation meets redemption. The *Ani* can extract itself from time and ascend to a higher love for God.

Participating in the Redemptive Process: The Eighteen Benedictions (*Shemoneh Esrei*)

The content of the *Shemoneh Esrei* centers around overcoming sin and revitalizing the covenantal relation with God—and thereby contributing to the *rapprochement* between heaven and earth. The *Amidah*'s nineteen (not eighteen) blessings traverse the path from patriarchal prehistory to the founding of the nation of Israel to messianic redemption. The potentially sanctified relation between the Jewish people and God enables them to partner with God in displacing chaos and evil (sin) with spirituality and goodness—narrowing the heaven-earth divide, and widening the path to redemption.[41]

The *siddur*, Schweid writes, "embodied the meaning of the exilic condition."[42] The *Amidah*'s first six blessings, from (1) *Barukh Atah* to (6) *Selah Lanu*, are about the exiled individual. The first blessing (*Barukh atah* through *magen avraham*) identifies God as the God of the patriarchs (Exodus 3:6). The worshipper affirms that God approaches His people lovingly, expecting love in return and observance of His commandments so as to advance redemption.[43] In the second blessing, from *Atah gibor* through *meḥayeh hametim*, the worshipper addresses his beloved God as the creator. With the help of humankind, God will overcome chaos, renew the process of creation, and finally establish His kingdom. In the third blessing, *Atah Kadosh*, the worshipper anticipates and affirms redemption. Then the sanctified people of Israel will ascend to the sacred God, as God descended from His sacred Tabernacle—illustrating the fact that His holiness was greater even than His might. The worshipper challenges God to renew and complete creation with redemption—with the human being, who creates in His image, sharing in the renewal. Then the worshipper affirms that the *mitzvot* specified in the Torah make his sanctification (overcoming sin and materialism) possible.[44] *Atah Ḥonen* (blessing 4) praises God for bestowing the practical knowledge needed for sanctification.[45] With *Hashiveinu Avinu* (blessing 5) the worshipper, committed to sanctifying life by means of the *mitzvot* provided by God, turns to God with a request for compassion. The suffering of exile weakens the Jew, with one sin following another. God's compassion is needed so the worshipper can be released from this process, repent, and engage fully in Torah. Insofar as no sin can be totally undone (having taken place, it cannot be thrust back into non-existence), God will, indeed, have to create the sinner's soul anew. Schweid stresses that the entire procedure (self-sanctification, overcoming sin, observing *mitzvot*, possessing practical knowledge, asking God for compassion and to renew the soul) was possible only because of the original *zikah*'s ongoing presence.[46] In *Selaḥ*

Lanu (blessing 6) the worshipper reiterates his role in the sanctification process, specifically, regretting sin, acknowledging that the sin need not have happened, and assuming responsibility. He pleads with God to reveal Himself from out of His hiddenness and provide an opening for the individual to strive to recreate himself.[47] The next blessing relates to the nation as a whole. *Re'eh Be'onyeinu* (blessing 7) addresses the afflictions of the people of Israel and pleads for God to open Israel's exilic history to redemption.[48] *Refa'enu* through *Bareikh Aleinu* (blessings 8 and 9) are pleas to God to heal the sickness (physical and psychological), which come in sin's aftermath. Once health is restored to the people and their environment, they can participate actively in paving the way to redemption.[49] *Teka Beshofar* (blessing 10) sets the stage for God's gathering His people from dispersion. *Hashivah Shofeteinu* introduces the four stages of redemption: (1) restoration of judges upon reestablishing sovereignty (blessing 11);[50] (2) vengeance against Christians who blamed Jews for Jesus's death (his blood atoning for humankind's sins) (*Velamalshinim*, blessing 12);[51] (3) ingathering of the dispersed by the righteous shepherd (*Al Hatzaddikim*, blessing 13); and (4) God's return to rule Jerusalem to prepare the throne of David under divine *aegis* (*Velirushalayim*, blessing 14).[52] The following blessing (*Et Tzemaḥ*, blessing 15), seeks to advance the renewal of David's kingdom, and the onset of redemption.[53] *Shema Koleinu* (blessing 16) is a plea to God to enable the worshipper to participate fully in accelerating the onset, and then to share in the reality of Jerusalem's restored Temple. The worshipper describes his own ascent to God and His redemption as he climbs up to the highest "rung" of the "ladder" to the above. He beseeches God to fulfil His promise to Solomon, return to the restored Temple, and receive His nation's prayers. By this point, the worshipper has traversed the path from the ancient patriarchs, to establishing the nation through exile, and then to redemption. Now, upon the highest rung of the ladder, resting on earth and reaching into heaven, the soul completes the ascent. At the present moment, past enters the future. Time, physicality, and the intuitive and intellectual aspect of *neshamah* and the *sekhel* have been transcended. The ascendant worshipper gives himself to God, as God, descending from His Tabernacle, receives and draws the worshipper towards Himself.[54] The seventeenth blessing, *Retzei Adonai* through *shekhinato letzion*, dwells on giving oneself to God in positive terms (by contrast, the *Kedushah* [*Na'aritzekha venakdishekha*] dwells on separating soul from instinct and defilement).[55] It renews God's return to the Temple and worship in the Temple. *Shefa* is released and revitalizes life. The worshipper ascends to God, and God descends to the human being. Heaven and earth are unified once again.[56] Assured of creation's renewal and imminent redemption, the worshipper rises above the distress and evil of exile and enters into a timeless, sanctified reality.[57] *Modim Anaḥnu* (blessing 18) offers gratitude to God as the source of physical and spiritual existence.[58] *Sim Shalom* (blessing 19), following the *Birkat Kohanim*, which has enacted Temple worship in the present moment, describes God's response to the worshipper's quest for redemption—that of *shalom*: the completion of creation (*shelemut*) upon the decisive conquest of evil and chaos. That is redemption.[59]

While the *Keriyat Shema* cluster of blessings enunciates the *zikah* source and dialogue of love between the worshipper and God and the ascent to God, the *Amidah* describes and enacts the individual and national roles in bringing creation and redemption together. The former is about articulating and enacting the intimate connection between God and the people of Israel, emphasizing its function in the redemptive process. The latter is about the stages in this process. It sets the stage with a description of the patriarchal beginning of metahistory and its salvational culmination (blessing 1). The worshipper affirms God's presence (2 and 3); the ability to overcome sin (4); the need for God's compassion and help (5 through 9); and the stages of redemption itself (10–14). The worshipper then offers a blessing to accelerate redemption (15) and enters directly into the realm of redemption (16). Finally, he describes God's presence at redemption (17) and expresses gratitude to God for completing creation with the defeat of evil and bringing creation into redemption (18–19).

Concluding Statement

In Eliezer Schweid's dialectically structured analysis of prayer, the "subject" is the religious experience of prayer, surrounded by philosophical reflection, and the "object" is the philosophical content, expressed in prayer. His study of prayer emerged against the background of some seven decades of philosophical inquiry (he began reading philosophy at twelve). *Siddur Hatefillah* delves into the nature and content of prayer. It articulates how God has created the world in light, and how His creation involved the developing rule of order over chaos (evil). The human being shares in God's *ruaḥ*, and a *zikah* between God and the human being is set in place. The *zikah* has assumed national identity through prophecy and gained substance with Torah. Prayer affirms and articulates the *zikah*, with God-given speech and access to God's name. Invested with *devekut* and *kavanah*, ascent to God is possible—as

God descends to the worshipper. With *zikah* at the root, God overcomes the asymmetry between Himself and the human being. Out of love, the division between finite and infinite is overcome—actually from God's perspective and potentially from human's.

Thus, the *Keriyat Shema* cluster brings to life a scene of cosmic creation and the illumination shining through it, into which the worshipper enters for loving dialogue (rooted in the *zikah* with God). The words that enunciate the experience blend with the experience itself. They crest with a declaration of God's oneness, drawing the worshipper towards it—albeit never to be one with the God, who has traversed their difference. That is, as part of creation, human beings could strive towards sharing in creation's perfection with redemption— and do so without losing themselves in their coalescence. The pursuit of self-perfection and perfection of the world is a shared process between the human being and God, covenantally structured, and guided by Torah. When recited on the Sabbath, the loving dialogue takes place at the meeting point between creation and redemption, and outside of time.

The scene created by the *Shemoneh Esrei*, running from the patriarchs to Messiah, is metahistorical-historical rather than cosmic. Within this arena, the worshipper articulates and enacts participation in restoring heaven-earth unity. The enactment requires overcoming the sin that belongs to the chaos, which eludes God's creation and order. For this, God's compassion is needed— the exilic suffering weakens the Jew, and recovery requires outside help. Having uttered words about overcoming sin and sharing the goal of cosmic *rapprochement* with God, the worshipper enters the scene of redemption itself—where he ascends to God and God descends from heaven to him. As the *Keriyat Shema* focuses on love at the center of the covenant, the *Shemoneh Esrei* focuses on the moral personification of the covenantal relationship—both equally instrumental in the covenantal path to redemption.

Eliezer Schweid, the leading historian of Jewish thought of our generation and dedicated educator in the State of Israel, has been troubled by the condition of faith in a universe transformed by the Holocaust, and then infected by postmodernism. He has been concerned with the State of Israel's stalled progress on the morality-paved path to redemption. In his eighth decade of life, he committed himself to understanding Jewish prayer, and publishing *Siddur Hatefillah* to educate and guide his fellow Israelis and even world Jewry. Its message of faith and prayer, with their mysterious root, is delivered to a post-Holocaust, postmodern world, and to a State of Israel in danger of squandering its legacy. As such, he has carried on the tradition of Israel's ancient prophets, who served as the first vessels of the act of prayer.[60]

Endnotes

1   Eliezer Schweid, "Faith Confronting the Experiences of Our Age," trans. by Leonard Levin, in Eliezer Schweid, *The Responsibility of Jewish Philosophy*, ed. Hava Tirosh-Samuelson and Aaron W. Hughes (Leiden: Brill, 2013), 51–95.

2   Leonard Levin notes that Schweid drew the term *ḥavayah* from Aaron David Gordon, who used it for life-experience as distinct from objective, scientific knowledge. Schweid, "Faith Confronting the Experience of Our Age," 59n.

In his essay on the philosophy of the *siddur* according to Eliezer Schweid, Hanokh ben Pazi points to Gordon's centrality to his perspective: the *siddur's* life is manifest not only in terms of its being a book for guiding Jewish life—including prayers and life cycle ceremonies—but because it is a book that continues to be alive and to develop. The various prayers brought together in the book echo historical events in the history of the Jewish nation, granting life to the changes and the winds of the time, including those of the new nation. Turning attention to the *siddur* as a book reveals the richness and the variety it contains, which often deviates from legalistic, traditional, or renewed organizing. For the *siddur* as a book includes chapters of study, of recitation, guidance, and behavior, gathering a variety of study, jargons, and as many layers as possible. The *siddur* includes Rambam's principles of faith alongside possibility to study the "Chapters of the Fathers" or recite *taḥnunim* through chapters of the Psalms. Schweid's perspective addresses several subjects of great importance. Perhaps the most important is the relationship to "worship." The idea that the activity of prayer is an activity of "labor" emphasizes the existence of the human being as a laboring one. Thus, Schweid recognizes the contribution and value that the Zionist movement places on the concept of "labor," of realizing thought in practice in the pioneering life. The connection between the worship of traditional prayer and the value of labor, in the interpretation of A. D. Gordon, grants spiritual religious significance to labor and to pioneering activity. Along with this, Schweid identifies the importance of Maimonides's Thirteen Principles of Faith in the *siddur*, to popularize (in the positive sense) their philosophical significance. The special version in the *siddur*, and that of the special *piyyut* dedicated to them, bring Maimonides's philosophical ideas about God into spiritual-communal translation addressed to the wider community. Hanokh Ben Pazi, "Hafilosofiyah shel hasidur be'ikvot eliezer shvayd," in *Iyunei tarbut: Halikhot hithadshut haḥayim hayehudi'im bemishnato shel eliezer shvayd*, vol 2, ed. Yehoyada Amir and Yossi Turner (Jerusalem: Carmel, 2020), 13–45.

3   Schweid, "Faith Confronting the Experiences of Our Age." Idem, "Faith: Its Trusting and Testing—The Question of God's Righteousness," in Eliezer Schweid, *On Personal and Public Concerns: Essays in Jewish Philosophy*, transl. and ed. by Leonard Levin (Boston: Academic Studies Press, 2014), 88–89. Originally published in Eliezer Schweid, *Lehagid ki yashar hashem: Hatzdakat elohim bemaḥshevet yisrael mitekufat hamikra ve'ad shpinoza* (Bat Yam: Tag Publishing, 1994). Ari Ackerman, "Eliezer Schweid on Secularity, Humanism and Religious Faith," presentation at "Hahagut hayehudit vemeḥkarah: Yahadut ketarbut, bikoret haḥiloniut vehadat veparshanut hamekorot. Seminar ḥokrim vehogim al mifalo shel eliezer shvayd bemisgeret hakongres ha'olami hashivah-esrei lemada'ei hayahadut," August 2017, Jerusalem. See also Eliezer Schweid, *Hayehudi haboded vehayahadut* (Tel Aviv: Am oved, 1974), 96–104; and Eliezer Schweid, "Mahi emunah?," in Eliezer Schweid, *Emunat am yisrael vetarbuto* (Jerusalem: Sh. Zaks, 1976), 1–67 as cited by Ackerman.

4   Schweid, "Faith: Its Trusting and Testing."

5   Schweid, *Siddur Hatefillah*, 425. Levin notes that *neshamah*, which he translates as "soul breath," can be used monistically, to mean the manifestation of life that is observed in respiration, and experienced as conscious awareness; or dualistically, to mean the life-principle that

can surround death and become manifest as pure spirit. Schweid allows for either interpretation. Schweid, "Faith Confronting the Experience of Our Age," 61, no. 5.

6 Schweid, "Faith Confronting the Experience of Our Age"; idem, *Siddur Hatefillah*, 42, 70–71, 78–81, 93–96, 104–112, 150, 393.

7 Schweid, "Faith Confronting the Experiences of Our Age," 82.

8 Ackerman, "Eliezer Schweid on Secularity, Humanism and Religious Faith," 6 n12, 9.

9 Schweid, *Siddur Hatefillah*, 424–425.

10 Ibid.

11 Eliezer Schweid, *Siddur Hatefillah: Filosofiyah, shirah umistorin* (Tel Aviv: Am oved, 2009). Schweid began to speak of prayer in his *Li'hyot ben ha'am hayehudi* (Tel Aviv: Eked, 1992), 45–88. See also idem, "Hameyahalim litefillah," in *Emunat am yisrael vetarbuto* (Jerusalem: Sh. Zaks, 1976), 96–108; idem, "Hatefillah—Ketzad hi na'anet?" (unpublished ms., 2009); idem, *Hafilosofiyah shel hatanakh biyesod tarbut yisrael: I'yun basipur, behora'ah uvehakikah shel hahumash* (Tel Aviv: Yediot ahronot, 2004). Schweid, *Sefer mahzor hazemanim* (Tel Aviv: Am oved, 1984).

12 Schweid, *Siddur Hatefillah*, 13.

13 Ibid., 9–17. Author's discussions with Schweid at his Abu Tor home, Jerusalem, August 2017 and 2018.

14 Schweid, *Siddur Hatefillah*, 25. At the same time, when I presented his interpretation at the August 2017 World Congress of Jewish Studies, Schweid told me emphatically, that, when he sang in the synagogue, he was not philosophizing. Author's discussions, Abu Tor. Schweid's views about subjectivity appear to have played a role in his decision as incoming department chair at the Hebrew University. He changed the name from "Department of Hebrew Philosophy and Kabbalah," created by Gershom Scholem, to "Department of Jewish Thought" and included modern Jewish philosophers. Scholem had set modern Jewish philosophy aside, alleging that it could not be studied objectively, because there was insufficient distance and historical perspective. See Schweid, "Hora'at hafilosofiyah shel herman kohen bimedinat yisrael: Haba'ayah veha'etgar," unpublished presentation at the international conference "The Actuality of Hermann Cohen in Israel at the Hundredth Anniversary of Cohen's Death" (Jerusalem, May 8, 2018).

15 Schweid, *Siddur Hatefillah*, 25, 144, 420–425.

16 Ibid., 107.

17 Schweid, "Hatefillah—Ketzad," 9.

18 Schweid, *Siddur Hatefillah*, 360.

19 Ibid., 42, 70–71, 78–81, 93–96, 104–109, 111–112, 150, 393.

20 Ibid., 73.

21 Ibid., 393.

22 Ibid., 70–71, 78–79, 95–96, 107, 150.

23 Ibid., 95.

24 Ibid., 75, 85, 91, 94, 101, 107, 316, 339.

25 Ibid., 412–415.

26 Ibid., 396.

27 Ibid., 74–75, 83–85, 308–309.

28 Ibid., 118.

29 Ibid., 54–57.

30 Ibid., 145–149.

31 Ibid., 150–151.

32 Ibid., 151–152.

33 Ibid., 152.

34 Ibid., 152–154.

35 Ibid., 153–155.
36 Ibid., 143–144.
37 Ibid., 126, 358–361, 372, 375, 415.
38 Ibid., 359–371.
39 Ibid., 402–406.
40 Ibid., 388.
41 Ibid., 388.
42 Ibid., 199.
43 Ibid., 163–164.
44 Ibid., 174–178.
45 Ibid., 183–188.
46 Ibid., 188–192.
47 Ibid., 192–202.
48 Ibid., 202–214.
49 Ibid., 215–219.
50 Ibid., 234–236.
51 Ibid., 236–238.
52 Ibid., 239.
53 Ibid., 239–242.
54 Ibid., 242–245.
55 Ibid., 247.
56 Ibid., 249–250.
57 Ibid., 251–254.
58 Ibid., 257–261.
59 Ibid., 254–257.
60 A personal note: Schweid's *Siddur Hatefillah* brings together his sacred and secular learn-
    ings (see, for example, ibid., 46)—and is naturally accessible to the Hebrew-speaking Israeli
    public arena. In America (speaking as one who lives in both Jerusalem and Washington,
    DC.), *Siddur Hatefillah* is likely to be needed at least as urgently as in Israel. There, the secu-
    lar and religious are split apart, and postmodernism dominates. Notions such as the ego's
    yielding to a *zikah* with God, that prayer erupts from within, and is threaded by messianic
    hope, are foreign. And the Hebrew language of prayer has been marginalized.

Author's Preface: My Path to the Jewish Prayer Book (*Siddur Hatefillah*)

All theoretical research in the humanities has its personal perspective. The study, the inquiry, and the teaching all come from having an interest and a feeling of urgency whose source is the tradition in which the researcher was educated. My desire to participate as an educator in transmitting the cultural legacy of the Jewish nation has motivated my writing my many works in the field of "Jewish thought" over the generations. My perspective has been existential: grappling with the deepest problems of the Jewish nation in the modern and postmodern eras on the philosophical-historical level, for which educators entrusted with transmitting the legacy in one of the most difficult and revolutionary periods in the nation's history must search for solutions. In my opinion, as these matters fall to all researchers and creative thinkers of Jewish studies, I saw no need to shed light upon them in the opening of my book.

But in coming to research and analyze the *Siddur Hatefillah*—the Jewish prayer book—so as to disclose the philosophy concealed in it and its poetic forms of expression, I feel the need to speak first about my personal path to prayer. The desire to write a book of theoretical inquiry into the prayer book has engaged me for many years. I still did not feel completely prepared for this unique theoretical enterprise after I published my book, *The Jewish Experience of Time: Philosophical Dimensions of the Jewish Holy Days* (Hebrew: *Maḥzor Hazemanim*), dealing with the prayers of Rosh Hashanah and Yom Kippur. Only after I published my theoretical research on the thought of the Hebrew Bible, constituting the "written Torah," did I feel ready to deal with the *siddur*—one of the most important educational creations of "oral Torah."

Considered historically, the present book is integral to the chain of my research into the history of the philosophy of the Jewish religion, from the biblical period until today. The book constitutes an additional chapter in the history of Jewish thought—that of the era of the *Mishnah*, between the Babylonian exile and the exile of Rome. Permanent prayers were created for use in the synagogue, which took the place of the First Temple which had been destroyed, and continued to act as a center for divine worship through the days of the Second Temple. The essential prayers at the basis of the *siddur*—the morning blessings focused on faith, the *Keriyat Shema* (Recitation of the *Shema*) focused on love, and the *Shemoneh Esrei* (Eighteen Benedictions) focused on holiness—were all established by the sages of the "Great Synagogue" following the first return to Zion. The prayers were amended in the days of the Yavneh sages, following the destruction of the Second Temple, and by sages of the court of Rabbi Shimon ben Gamaliel the Second, following the collapse of the Bar Kokhba revolt and the beginning of the Roman exile. These became the permanent prayers, which are repeated daily, weekly, monthly, and annually. I found that these prayers contained complete literary creations expressing systematic and crystallized religious thought, from which the religious philosophy of the sages of the *Mishnah* may be extracted.

However, when we are speaking of prayer texts designed to express feelings and meditations of faith, of love and of holiness of individuals who must speak in terms of "I" and "we," in which alone it is possible to express subjective meditations in their substance, the investigating researcher and his students are obliged to adapt their approach to this spirit. A personal-existential, vital text necessitates a personal-existential relationship to it. A praying person authored these texts, and the writing is his prayer. Because of this, only someone who studies and has interest in composition in order to internalize the composition in his prayer, can study and have interest in what is we have here—namely, a prayer text, not a text of lyrical poetry or of philosophical or halakhic (legalistic) inquiry. This is the special difficulty in teaching students who have not acquired the habit of prayer prior to studying it. This is also the source for the unique experience we enjoy, when we study it by means of internalizing it as prayer: the experience of discovering the inner, existential depth—which without prayer remains silent. But in order to overcome this difficulty and give voice to the prayer experience, reliance upon personal experience is necessary.

What was my path to prayer? I was born in Jerusalem to parents who made *aliyah* to the Land of Israel in the 1920s as pioneers of the Third Aliyah. Their worldview was Zionist-socialist, but they differed from the parents of most of my friends who belonged to the same *aliyah*, insofar as they had shaken off materialistic Marxism. My parents' educational message centered on ethics and spiritual values, and this came to expression especially in their relation to the heritage of the Jewish culture that had been created in the diaspora. My parents were not among those who negated the diaspora, or delegitimated the creation of this special culture of the Jewish people in the thousands of years of exile. To the contrary: they identified with the heritage of their nation, and its courage in standing up for its truth. With their *aliyah* to the Land of Israel, they wanted to continue the chain—not sever it. Accordingly, they defined themselves as "free thinkers" rather than "secularists."

This distinction was exact. A Jew who defined himself as "secular" retreated from the sacred and viewed it as a superstition or as some sort of intellectual and emotional servitude. A Jew who, by contrast, defined himself as "free" viewed himself as having no duty to institutional *Halakhah* when it came to anything related to spiritual life. But he was, by choice, obligated to the values of truth and justice that were sanctified in the legacy of the generations. The experience of the sacred, as an ethical and spiritual value, was important to my parents. They shared it on Sabbaths and holidays—not publicly in their synagogue but in their home, in their private domain.

My mother grew up in a religious home of *Mitnagdim* (non-Hasidic Orthodox Jews), my father in a religious home of *Ḥasidim*. Both expressed their "free-ness" by looking upon their inclination to the sacred as something internal and personal—to which they were entitled as individuals. We went to the synagogue as a family only once a year, on Yom Kippur. My parents fasted the entire day and were careful to light the memorial candle in memory of their parents. They went to the synagogue on the eve of the holy day to hear the *Kol Nidrei* prayer among the congregation of Israel, because they felt that prayer had a sacred national value. My mother explained to me the reason for her refraining from reciting the prescribed prayers. It was on account of the awe and reverence that she felt for her mother, who was a true believer. Since she did not believe in God as did her mother, she could not pray as her mother. She felt that if she prayed, she would be committing a lie in her soul and a slight to her mother's faith. My mother, for her part, preferred to express the feelings of the sacred in her heart in lyrical poetry—which she loved and learned by heart. When it came to the *Kol Nidrei* prayer, recited "with the sinners" on the eve of Yom Kippur, she said that, in her eyes, the event amounted to a census—in which all the children of Israel were counted and testified that they belonged to the congregation of Israel.

My father, by contrast, a poet educated in a Hasidic home, was in his way a believer who prayed individually. In fact, he never stopped praying. But he did not need to do this in a synagogue. When the spirit moved him in his home, at work, and during meals, in particular, when he arranged hikes with his children in the open country of Israel, with soulful enthusiasm he would sing the prayers he knew from his parents' home. He had a clear tenor's voice and he sang the melodies of the Sandz *Ḥasidim*. He also did this at the family table at the Sabbath eve meal. In addition to the synagogue on the eve of Yom Kippur, he used to take his children to the Yemenite synagogue, which stood in the Meah She'arim neighborhood, for the *Shaḥarit* of *Simḥat Torah*. He celebrated his birthday on this day and was filled with joy, with much song, and dancing with the Torah. This was my first encounter with world of prayer. I felt how the joy of prayer influenced those who knew its secret, but I did not possess the secret. I saw Jews praying and I was impressed. But I did not pray myself. I did not dare. The partition my mother spoke about also frightened me. I remained dumbfounded, at the edge, drawn and disappointed at one and the same time.

In the days when I and my brother published writings by my father Tzvi Yisrael Schweid (the poet, storyteller, and translator), I discovered the way in which he prayed the prayer of the individual, instilled with faith—truly in the recesses of his soul—when he wrote his poems. Let me cite as a signpost one of his prayers—to me the most beautiful of all. It revealed to me the depth of his faith and his talent for prayer. To me, his prayer seemed a sublime example of the prayer of the individual; an individual whose sphere moved outward from the synagogue because of his way of life—which opened to secularity. The primary essence of his prayer had been directed to being rescued from the secularity in which he was immersed, against his will, so that he could return to pray because he felt God's nearness. This is a unique prayer, written in the style of a psalm. But the request expressed would surprise both the religious worshiper and the secular worshiper, who believed that prayer was designed for requests directed to rescue from trouble, for a happy life. My father's true request was to be worthy once again of God's nearness. To address this need, he was ready to ask God for punishment to purify and refine the soul.

> For the leader on the harp. A hymnal song.
> My God, do not pity me, and do not turn your ear from my
>   entreaties.
> I feared your staff, and my feet did not hearken to the voice of
>   your reason.
> For I was a rotted leaf and I carried the autumn lament in
>   my heart
> While the kindness of your light shone upon the earth and its
>   fullness.
> Look, my God, I am not as a bird waiting silently and seeing the
>   first glow of the sun,
> But like a flowering stalk I have surrendered my soul to the winds
> And have sunk into the pit of confusion. Selah.

Have no pity my God; do not pity me, my God,
For I would react amiss to the abundance of your compassion.
For my days have been an eternal Sabbath, and my soul had
declared perpetual fallow
To the point that I set dogs to guard for me at the threshold of
my storehouse
And wild trees clustered at the gates of all my happiness.
Therefore, send Your fire to my heart and inflame my bones.
My soul will recoil from the flaming of Your rage.
With the dawn, my tears will flow with the joy of morning
And in the evening hours, I will send my longings as a fledgling
between the branches to its mother.
To You, God, to You and Your punishment and Your hard hands
Until my heart will be awakened at the sunrise, until my head
will be stirred to the heights of Your benevolence.

The prayer of my father taught me the secret of the secrets of prayer: the ability to pray emerged from the need to pray, which burst forth from the depths of the soul. The faith that responded to the need flowed from the same source. Prayer is not conditional on "religiosity" in its motivational sense, nor in "faith" in the dogmatic sense. Rather, in the innocent heart of the person who knows that his intellectual abilities do not entitle him to use natural surroundings and the community of his neighbors for egoistic, selfish well-being. To the contrary, they place a duty upon him, whose source is the will to live, a will that permeates the universe—whereby everything that maintains life and its productivity is "good," and everything that injures life is "bad." A person is obliged to the divine will, which maintains his existence, welfare, and productivity in the universe, and therefore to God's command to do good with all His creations. In this connection, I will introduce a poem from the poetry of a contemporary of my father, who influenced me in the same way:

And so, it also happens in these our days
That a human being will rise up and pray
And the person does not expurgate himself, nor return in
teshuvah (penitent return)
Like so many in these days
But before he gave his heart to the true gathering house of the
ancients
To have a prosthetic heart placed in its stead

And this heart beat as did the heart of a human being
Since then and forever, and every year
The heart would also still pray
And would not be ashamed.[1]

But from my mother's inability to pray the prayers that her mother prayed—
even though she wanted to transmit her legacy to us—I learned that parents
transmit to their sons and daughters only what they realize themselves for
their own needs. If they want to transmit something, they must find their
personal way to realize for themselves what they want to transmit. In truth, I
observed what my parents observed. Like them, I fasted on Yom Kippur. Like
them, I went to synagogue on the eve of Yom Kippur to hear the *Kol Nidrei*
prayer. For my own part, I added listening to the *Ne'ilah* prayer as the day
closed, and the sounding of the *shofar* at the conclusion.

I emphasize the words "to listen"—I went to the synagogue as an
observing guest, not as a participant. I admit that: I always left with a feeling
of disappointment, even when the one who led the prayer did so well and the
congregation was attentive. I felt that by experiencing prayer as an observer,
I did not experience what worshippers experienced; the prayer's external
impression touched me in the sense of experiencing a performance. Worship in
a Jewish synagogue is national and all worshippers are called on to participate in
carrying it out. As the ability of most worshippers was far from the sort of perfect
artistic expression liable to impress the outside assembly of listeners, anyone
coming to the synagogue as an observer is necessarily disappointed—until one
reconsiders and becomes one of the worshippers in the *minyan* (quorum) and
participates in its assembly.

Before this happened, I still had to traverse a rather long path. This
happened when I went for training in the Galilee, and then when I participated
in the founding of Tzora, a *kibbutz* in the Jerusalem corridor. I became a member
of the committee for culture and training, and responsibility for cultural life
included attending to the commemoration of Sabbaths and festivals. This
was a daunting issue that perplexed the *kibbutz* movement throughout its
development. The working life in the *kibbutz* was difficult, hard, and permeated
with petty concerns. It created a great thirst for elevating the spirit, a thirst that
was evident when it came to the culture of Sabbaths and festivals. But this was
closed to the members because it was "religion," and was also deficient because
it was shaped in exile. Those who overcame the desolation of the Land of Israel
needed different prayers. As the *kibbutzim* were inclined towards Marxism
at first most sought a solution in the proletarian culture of the workers'

movement—parades, nature celebrations, and dancing the *Horah*—which elevated the experience of realizing the dream. But these substitutes could not fill the role of a tradition that shaped the way of life and that enabled each and every individual and family to express themselves and elevate themselves. Most members of the *kibbutzim* were, like my parents, educated in religious homes, against which they rebelled. With nostalgia, they remembered the joy of the Sabbath and holidays that they had enjoyed in the "mournful exile." When families increased and descendants were born, most came to the conclusion that they needed to create a new *kibbutz* tradition. It would translate the language of traditional Judaism into a communal national language, with its values, worldviews, and pioneering goals.

This decision raised the most difficult problem of all: how do we translate expressions of sanctity into secular language? It became clear immediately that celebration required sanctity. It was impossible to ascend to sanctity without the existential gestures of blessings and prayer. But was it possible for a strictly secular person to express God's name in blessing and prayer? It was obviously possible to rely on societal-national ideology and bless in the name of the "nation" and in the name of the "society." But people who remembered the prayer-experience from which they benefitted in childhood knew—like my father and like the poet Yitzḥak Landau—that the experience of sanctity expressed the spirit's yearning for something beyond the life of the body; for a trans-earthly entity, which constituted the source of life. There were holidays, especially Rosh Hashanah and Yom Kippur, where the moral content seemed most relevant to the *kibbutz* society, which sought to realize the social ideal and fulfill the *mitzvah* of "love your neighbor as yourself." But the sole path for observing these festivals, whose essence was repentance and atonement, was synagogal prayer.

Wrestling with the issue of sanctity in the experience of the *kibbutz* holiday was to some extent resolved during the pilgrimage festivals, especially Passover. I will cite a paradigmatic example of converting prayer into a gesture of poetic, artistic expression, enabling metaphorical use of religious symbol: the Passover service of *Kibbutz* Yagur. It relied on the liturgical, artistic-national creativity of Yehudah Sharett. He created an alternative for public prayer through choir singing, which elevated the public beyond itself. The artistic perfection that the choir could achieve, even when it was made up of individuals who did not have voices of professional singers, was truly comparable to the style of singing of prayer. This was the secret of the influence of this wondrous creation of conducting the Passover Seder, which was widespread in the *kibbutz* movement. But the problem was not resolved, because only a rare ḥalutzic musical personality like Yehudah Sharett could transform a *kibbutz* community into an artistic choir. Moreover, we set the table for the Passover Seder once a year, and prepared for it the entire year. But how was it possible to experience the sanctity of the Sabbath on a weekly basis? How do we replace personal prayer, which was a matter of standing for judgment before God on Rosh Hashanah and Yom Kippur?

While struggling with these problems, I left to study Judaism at the Hebrew University and embarked on the path I chose as a creative scholar. When I lived on the *kibbutz* I had a community, but not yet a family. When I left for study in the city I raised a family, but missed a community. Two interlaced problems arose from this turn of events. From my parents' home, I knew that full family life expressed itself in designating and bequeathing a legacy. But I did not want to go back to what appeared to be a mistake by my parents. They bequeathed to me the yearning for prayer and blessing, but not the instruments for realizing it. My wife thought so as well. Together, we began to form the family custom of welcoming the Sabbath and celebrating the holidays. It quickly became clear to us that the tradition that shaped a way of life in the family required the support of a community. The importance of a unified community as an "assembly of the covenant," as basis for the Jewish way of life, was known to me from my education in the pioneer youth movement, which prepared me for the life of the *kibbutz* community. The nation of Israel is a nation of communities. The communities are the vital foundation for shaping ways of life and patterns of the nation's culture. This fact is not only the result of Jewry's dispersion among the nations, but the result of forming the nation as a covenantal community as legislated by the Torah. I will not go into the subject at length here, as it is the content of the first chapter of my book. In terms of my personal path, when I came to the city two things became clear to me that were two sides of the same coin. First, the absence of a community, in a public that defined itself as secular. Second, the central role of the synagogue and the experience of prayer in the *minyan*—representing the collectivity of Israel—for maintaining and guiding the covenantal community in the Jewish people. I therefore understood, first, that the disintegration of the traditional community due to the sociological process which privatized modern society, and to an even greater extent postmodern society, was the source for the threat of atomization and loss of identity that lay in wait for the nation of Israel from within. Second, the formation of social groups as covenantal communities within the economic-social reality created by technological civilization was possible only by means of spiritual attachments of joint responsibility—the existence of which was made possible by the synagogue. A *kibbutz* version of the community based upon common labor could not retain a position in an economy inclined to particularism and egoistic competitions. With this, the deep truth of which my mother spoke when she described Yom Kippur as a day of taking stock, in which all individuals belonging to their nation congregated together, became clear to me. These words applied not only to Yom Kippur, but to every Sabbath and every holiday. Their fulfillment lay not just in "listening to prayer" but in "making prayer heard" to collective Israel.

The synagogue we chose in the neighborhood in which we lived opened its doors to me, and the assembly of worshippers opened its heart to me. I found friends among them, and I dedicate this book to their memory. I was able to pray, only by virtue of the fact that their worship taught me about the inner meditation of prayer. Only by benefit of my ability to pray with living emotion, have I been able to write this book—in the hope of showing a path and opening a threshold for all those who, like me, seek a way into congregational worship.

Endnotes

1   *The Poems of Yitshak Landau* (Jerusalem: Mossad Bialik, 1973), 104–107.

Introduction
The *Siddur* (Jewish Prayer Book): Its Sources, Goal, and Theological Basis

The Substance of Worship before the *Siddur* Came into Existence

The *siddur*, or Jewish prayer book, is a halakhic composition—a document with legal standing in Jewish law. It contains the text of permanent prayer of communal synagogues—the meeting houses of Jews for the worship of God—as commanded by scripture. Specifically, three times a day: at daybreak, the time for *Minḥah* (afternoon), and evening. The *mitzvah* (command) to worship God is in effect every day in that order. The Torah also distinguishes between the six days of labor—those days of the week when the people are commanded to labor for their own needs—and Sabbaths, holidays, and seasons (*mo'adim*), which are dedicated to the worship of God. On certain days of each holiday and festival, the Torah prescribes an additional service, according to the particular theme of the day. The *siddur* was prepared by scholars of oral Torah, following the order set by scripture for worshipping God in the Tabernacle and after that in the Temple of Jerusalem.

The worship of God in the Tabernacle and Temple revolved around performance of sacrifices and offerings at the altar. The children of Israel were commanded to perform sacrifices of several kinds: to atone for their sins; to acknowledge the abundance and blessings which God bestowed on them; and to sanctify themselves and to rejoice before God with mandated feasts. The sacrifices were accompanied by ceremonies that conveyed these intentions. The children of Israel brought sacrifices appropriate to their possessions, which were considered blessings from God and His gifts to the human beings. That is, by providing the sacrifice from the best of one's possessions, a person gave to God from the fruit of his labors and gave of his produce to praise God at the gates. Since the human beings theselves—their body and soul—were created by God who gave them life, providing a sacrifice from the blessing that God gave symbolized recognition by the people who sacrificed that they owed their life to God, and that they were commanded to give their life to God. They did this by means of worship: by reciting God's praise, by publicizing God's name and the command to serve Him, and by sanctifying God's name by observing all the *mitzvot* directed to improving God's world and glorifying His kingdom.

The sacrifices were raised upon the altar by priests who served in the Temple. Priests were also considered a "gift"—which the nation gave of its own accord to God as a sign of gratitude. Originally, every family was commanded to consecrate its firstborn son, who "opened the womb" of his mother (the first progeny to which she gave birth) to serve God ("Consecrate to Me every first born; man and beast, the first issue of every womb among the Israelites is Mine" [Exodus 13:1]). The narrative of the "binding of Isaac" (Genesis 22) established the foundation of the priesthood in the place where the Temple would rise up in the future, by symbolically embodying the substance of the sacrifice and its significance for the relation between the human being and God. By means of the "binding," Isaac was given to God as a human offering (*olah*), to be consecrated to service in the name of Abraham's family—for Isaac was considered the firstborn son of Abraham ("for he is your seed" [Genesis 21:14]). To memorialize this command, we observe the *mitzvah* of "redemption of the son" until today.

After the sin of the calf, God took all the children of the tribe of Levi to serve in His Tabernacle, and afterwards in the Temple. Aaron, considered the firstborn among the sons of the tribe of Levi, and his sons, officiated. The Levites were considered an equal exchange for the totality of all the firstborn of Israel at the dedication event of the Tabernacle (Numbers 3:40–51). In order for Aaron to officiate as high priest, Moses slaughtered a ram, arranged it on the altar, and sprinkled Aaron the priest and his sons with oil and blood that was on the altar in a symbolic gesture that recalled the "binding" (Leviticus 8:30). This reemphasized that the sacrifice that a person offered to God for forgiveness and atonement for sin should be from the best of the gifts granted to him by God. The sacrifice was a symbolic giving of oneself to God, expressing gratitude to God, and the obligation to worship Him.

The sacrifices had several aims. The most important of all was atonement for sins, in order to return to a life of purity and sanctity, both ethically and nationally. Also, to become worthy to continue enjoying God's gifts and blessings—without which we would not be able to live, let alone deserve happiness. For the purpose of atonement, the person who brought the sacrifice from his possessions placed his hand on the head of his offering (Leviticus 1:4) and confessed his sins. He thus "placed" his sins on the head of the sacrifice, which represented him symbolically. The priest slaughtered the sacrifice, arranged its limbs upon the altar, and raised the sacrifice in the eternal flame burning on the altar. In this way, God took the sacrifice to Himself symbolically. The eternal fire was a wondrous fire that descended from heaven at the dedication of the Tabernacle of Testimony, erected by Moses and the children of Israel in the desert. It resembled the fire that burned in the bush in the sight of Moses and was not consumed.

In sum: a person cannot, actually, give God anything that was not God's from the start. The human being is himself a gift of God and remains God's property. Because of this, only the priests who sanctified themselves to God were permitted to accept the person's sacrifice in His name and slaughter it. Only God Himself could accept the sacrifices given to Him by His command, and raise them to Him. In this way, the ascent of the sacrifice in God's fire towards heaven was itself a sign that the sacrifice was desired, and that the sins of the sacrifices were expiated by the blood of the sacrifice given to God, and that the person was forgiven. The priests kneeled, and the Levites sang hymns of gratitude and praise, accompanied by musical instruments. The people who entered the sanctuary to be seen before God responded with the hymns familiar to us as the Psalms. They rejoiced before God, eating from the additional sacrifices that were offered for this purpose—as if they were feasting with God at His table. This expressed the life of the entire nation of Israel as a kingdom of priests and a holy nation, as compared to the rest of nations.

The Historical Establishment of the *Siddur*

Following the destruction of the Temple, congregational houses of prayer were established in the Babylonian diaspora. They were intended exclusively for prayer, because when the Temple was established on the Temple Mount in Jerusalem, the priests and the prophets prohibited the performance of sacrifices in God's name in any place other than the Temple. Prayer also took place in synagogues in the Land of Israel, after sacrificial worship was renewed in the Second Temple in the days of Ezra and Nehemiah. When the Temple was destroyed for a second time, and it became clear that its construction was a vision for the messianic "end of days," scholars in Yavneh maintained that it was necessary to designate a single, obligatory version of prayer in all synagogues, in order to prevent the division of the nation. The best guess of accepted research, which is supported by literary sources from the tradition of Oral Torah, indicates that the consolidation of the *siddur* as we have it today resulted from an ongoing process, which essentially has not yet concluded. The beginning of its canonization came with the men of the "Great Synagogue" founded by Ezra the Scribe in the days of the return to Zion. Continuing the canonization was the responsibility of the court of Rabban Yohanan ben Zakkai in Yavneh, following the destruction of the Second Temple. A more inclusive continuation was conducted by the court of Rabban Shimon ben Gamaliel the Second, in the aftermath of the shocking failure of the Bar Kokhba revolution and following the separation from Judaism on the part of Jesus of Nazareth's disciples, and the establishment of the Christian church which maintained that it was the true successor of Israel in its position as chosen nation and kingdom of priests.

As said above, daily sacrifices were replaced by daily prayer. In the *siddur*, sacrifices are recalled in an educational manner. It expresses the desire for the Temple and renewal of sacrificial worship. But in practice, the heart's depth as expressed by confession, blessing, gratitude, and praise, replaced the sacrifices themselves, in accord with the oral Torah sages' interpretation of the prophet's words, "Instead of bulls we will pay [the offering of] our lips" (Hosea 14:3). The order of performing sacrifices was converted into the order of prayers recited on weekdays, Sabbaths, holidays and festivals in the synagogue, defined as a "small Temple," and this is the custom until today. The prayer-text was not established all at once. It grew through a lengthy and extended process of transmission, adhering conservatively to its sources, but it was also open to changes taking place in the situation of the Jewish people among the nations, to the influence of surrounding cultures, and to changes in the nation's state of mind, thoughts, and tastes.

The ongoing process of creating and editing the *siddur* became identified with observing the *mitzvah* of prayer in the congregations of Israel. It was a congregational life-experience, which continued periodically: from week to week, month to month, year to year. As long as the people remained faithful to Torah and observed the *mitzvah* of serving God daily through prayer, the creation of the prayer text continued to develop. The repeated recitation invited spontaneous creativity. The worshiper who prayed properly sought to express his feelings, thoughts, and images with the words on his lips as he spoke them, as he pronounced and expressed the words with his lips. One of the early Greek philosophers said that it was impossible to step in the same river twice. Similarly, it is impossible to pray the same prayer twice. The very same worshiper expressed his feeling and thoughts each time anew, in a moment that was unique. The words are the same, but the emphasis and indication are an actuality that cannot be duplicated.

The renewal of the actuality of prayer in the cyclicality of time has influenced the written text. When the distance between the written words and the feelings and reflections of the worshipper in daily life reaches a point where the worshipper no longer feels that traditional prayer and texts provide an adequate expression, the conservative leaning of religious leadership is compelled to submit and agree to the creation of new prayers. At times there was an addition, at times new prayers replaced the first permanent prayers. In this way, the basic seed of the prayer has been preserved, while there have also been changes and expansion from generation to generation; a continuous, yet varied expositional creation.

It is impossible for this process to reach a conclusion, as long as synagogues stand in place and worshippers come to pray with feelings of inner need. The *siddur* is therefore a work of standardizing textual versions, which worshippers are charged with reviving by expressing feelings, images, and thoughts of interest to them—with the intention to understand the written words, strengthen them, and identify with them. It can be summed up in this way: a general plan for the *siddur* was created by means of designating the recollection as a tradition. Foundations for its structure were put into place; contents of oral and written Torah streamed in; and principles and methods of application were defined. But with respect to statements of emotional and intellectual contents, prayer was constantly becoming and flowing continuously from present to present. This is a prominent literary fact, which the *siddur*'s editors and those who disseminated it in each generation did not conceal. Like the trunk of an ancient tree, one can distinguish various vital strata in the *siddur* that has reached us, documenting eras when thirst was stirred and new sources of inspiration came forward to respond to the thirst. The sources of inspiration enriched the prayer any time it was about to freeze into some routine formulation, which no longer fit the congregation's spiritual path. The renewal expressed itself not only in the addition of new *piyyutim* (liturgical poems) which created new connections between, and new perspectives on, the sources, but also in expanding the original formulations, which did not move from their place. It did so by enriching the forms of recital, and thereby the various meanings attributable to the original formulation.

From the literary perspective, the *siddur* is an anthology with a permanent, even homogenous, compartmentalized textual structure. *Siddurim* of different communities certainly have differing versions, but the very fact that these versions exist affirms the assumption of a unified original source from which they are all derived. For the differences between the *siddurim* of different communities are minor matters of style and not substantial, as far as the essential prayers are concerned. The differences are more substantial when it comes to later additions, such as the different sorts of *piyyutim* and accompanying explanations. By means of these differences, literary strata in the *siddur* document the history of Jewish thought as a continuous and varied web of ideas, which are not unified into one "system" but united around a defined axis.

This has been a source of special interest for inquiry in research about the philosophical component in the *siddur*, from two perspectives. First, the *siddur* is a composition about which all the people of Israel—men and women, elders and children—have in fact been educated and which they have internalized. Because of this, more than any other work in the tradition of Torah and *Halakhah*, the *siddur* has united the Jewish people and distinguished them in terms of spiritual life: values, ethics, faith, adherence to sacred sources, consciousness of the covenant, consciousness of common destiny, and the longing to realize the destiny of redemption together. Question: what is Judaism—not only in terms of the reservoir of books and documents in the literature, in archives and remnants of material culture, but from the perspective of the actual experience and practice of Jews? Answer: the "book shelves," which have been studied and learned over and over in the elementary *ḥeder* (primary classroom) and the more advanced *beit midrash* (house of study) and yeshiva (religious academy) as an obligatory Torah tradition. The most popular book on these shelves, the one that changed the most and has been most internalized by all classes of people, is the prayer book of the synagogue—which includes all members of the congregation. Also, this: more than any other composition, the *siddur* reflects the unity of Judaism as a special spiritual universe. It does so in terms of its continuity and its development as an ongoing tradition over the course of generations—from the time the people of Israel began to be called the "Jewish nation" (in the days of the Babylonian exile and the first settlement in Zion) and until today.

The *Siddur* as an Expression of Philosophical Reflection

The question addressed in this book is this: is philosophical thought expressed in the texts themselves, as shaped by legalistic provisions in the *siddur*, such as to constitute a reflective dimension to prayer? Is there a philosophical dimension to the *siddur*, as a thoughtful and focused literary and artistic creation, identifiable as a philosophy of Jewish prayer? Are there reflections found in the *siddur*, which define and interpret the substance of prayer according to its varied aspects and contents; which differentiate between proper and improper prayer; which determine its vital role from the perspective of the worshiper, and from the perspective of God who commanded worship of Him through prayer; which explain the matter of *kavanah* (intentionality) in prayer, and delve into how prayer is heard?

Wrestling with these questions is not something new. Jewish religious-philosophical thinkers, a number of whom contributed to the content and form of the *siddur*, have engaged with this subject of study in their theoretical expositions. There are many systematic philosophic studies that focus on prayer as a subject of inquiry. These explorations are included, for example, in *The Book of Doctrines and Beliefs* of Rabbi Saadia Gaon, *Duties of the Heart* of Rabbi Bahyah ibn Pakudah, *The Kuzari* of Rabbi Yehudah Halevi, *The Guide for the Perplexed* and *Book of Knowledge* of Moses Maimonides, and others. In modern times, thinkers have delved into and expanded upon the subject in the face of the challenge of scientific rationalism—which related to prayer as to a childish gesture bordering on self-deception. In particular, we will cite the philosophy of prayer by philosophers of faith—such as Samson Raphael Hirsch, Hermann Cohen, Harav Avraham Yitzhak Hakohen Kook, Franz Rosenzweig, Mordecai Kaplan, and Abraham Joshua Heschel. Systematic speculative efforts have also come to expression in specific philosophical interpretations of the *siddur* text.

The *novum* of this book is both methodological and substantive. It is not written as an interpretation of the *siddur*, nor as an independent philosophical inquiry into the substance of prayer. Rather, it locates texts in the *siddur* that have two sorts of philosophical dimensions: (a) the processing of religious-philosophical teachings in the language of prayer, and (b) prayers expressing philosophical ideas in prayer's special language, which the worshiper intends to reflect upon in order to direct the prayer, and through which afterwards flows the feedback for which the worshipper hopes.

Presenting the subject in this way requires an explanation of the concept of "philosophy" as used in our discussion. Obviously prayer texts, which are written for the entire people of Israel, are not "professional" philosophical texts. As to paraphrases by professional philosophical authors—for example, *piyyutim*, which reflect Maimonides's "principles of faith"—they are not written in professional language and are not designed for deep conceptual probing. Clearly, in our discussion we cannot use the widespread definition of philosophy employed by the academic discipline of professional philosophy. The *siddur* is an ancient literary composition, which renews itself progressively but remains tied to its early roots. It is stabilized by the halakhic-legalistic discipline, a special sort of wisdom that interprets the *mitzvot* and teachings of the written Torah and applies them to ways of life. The legalistic (halakhic) discipline has also been applied to the *siddur* by means of expressions that are imprinted in texts, based on the premise that these texts directed worshippers to feel the feelings and think the thoughts that embody awe of God, love of God, and total commitment to faithfully observing His *mitzvot*.

Thus, the *siddur* has a special identity, which was created between the legalistic discipline that shaped it, and the philosophy instilled into its texts in terms of educational discipline. The declared goal was to bequeath to all members of the Jewish people a view of the world that actually shaped the experience of a universe reigned over by God for the benefit of all creatures, amid the nation's difficult and painful encounter with real life in the present, a reality conceptualized as exile within exile—where the people were uprooted from their land of birth into a civilization dominated by evil. This was a difficult encounter, often a bitter and painful relationship, between a worldview grounded in faith in God who created the world and led it for the good, based upon a historical memory shaped by Torah sources and raised to the plane of the myth of leaving slavery for freedom, and a direct view of reality as experienced by the nation.

This encounter provided synagogal prayer with its special meaning of spiritual elation. The sanctification of prayer elevated the worshipper above the plane of life in double exile to the plane of the life of myth. Myth explained the collective course of history within history, as a story that included ascents and descents but had a clear and defined destiny from the beginning—the final redemption, the exodus from slavery to freedom. It was impossible to achieve the realization of this destiny without the direct intervention of God, the creator and the redeemer. But this intervention was conditional upon the entire nation's readiness to worship God in faith, by keeping His commandments. We will find that in the course of observing the *mitzvot* of worshipping God in the synagogue, the nation would almost experience the complete redemption for which it longed, especially on Sabbaths and holidays.

These matters are, in effect, the philosophical-legalistic (halakhic) basis, which shaped the Jewish prayer book as an educational book for the Jewish nation in exile. From this perspective, there is no substantive difference between the philosophy of Plato and Aristotle, the fathers of Greek philosophy—which became the classical philosophy of western culture—and legalistic wisdom of the Jewish *talmid ḥakham* (master scholar) who shaped the *siddur*. The philosopher and the *talmid ḥakham* are both educators, and their wisdom is the wisdom of education (pedagogy in the Socratic sense). The difference between these sorts of philosophy is rooted in the points of departure of their inquiries which shaped their foundation. The philosophy of Plato and Aristotle is anchored straightaway with means of learning and thinking of the person himself: sense, imagination, intellect, and reason. Philosophy opens with theoretical understanding of the realities in nature and in natural culture. After this, it seeks to know the sources and the causes that bring about and shape these sorts of reality and set their laws. This quest brought Plato and Aristotle to the concept of God—which Greek philosophers understood as absolute intellect—insofar as God was the cause of all being, the cause of being's existence as such, and the cause of the lawfulness which maintained existence and thereby its purpose. By contrast, the wisdom of the Jewish scholar has been anchored in the Torah, given as prophetic revelation of the word of God who was true and whose word was true. Therefore, the divine speech which sounded the word provided proof of the authenticity of God's instruction. This was so, even if the person did not know how to fathom it with his faculties of knowledge—because the human intellect, which emanated from God, was not absolute intellect. Differences in the educational emphases followed. Plato and Aristotle viewed the study of divine truth as a path of identification between human intellect and divine intellect. In their eyes, reaching that high level was the aim of human perfection and happiness. Against this, Jewish scholars viewed the aim of human being as that of internalized knowing and deep understanding of Torah wisdom, which brought one to observe the Torah's *mitzvot*. The aim of the human beings and their perfection, therefore, was not a matter of ideas—of knowing truth for its own sake—but rather of *mitzvot*, whose observance would improve life and increase light over darkness and good over evil in this world. In other words, the wisdom of the philosophers was based upon knowing which was confirmed by the instrument of human knowledge, whose goal was knowing for its own sake. The wisdom of Torah was based upon faith in the authority of prophetic revelation and its goal of "improving the world" (*tikkun olam*). This is a substantive difference, and a mutual disqualification could follow. But careful examination of these two wisdoms in their entireties shows that, despite the differences, they are two paths breaking forth to the same absolute truth. They have a wide common denominator and are therefore suited to complete each other's deficiencies.

In an introduction to the discussion about prayer, it would be impossible—nor is there a need—to enter into that discussion at length. It is enough for us to point out that, in the thinking of the prophets and the rabbis, faith in God and in His word is not a capricious decision. It is rather the understanding that human beings find in the depths of their intellect and affirm with the same instruments of knowledge which are used by philosophy; human beings have no other means of knowing and understanding. We find that scholars of Torah and scholars of philosophy agree in defining concepts of intellect, reason, knowing, evaluation, and will. Even more, philosophers and scholars agree that intellect and reason distinguish the human being from all living creatures in nature, and that their source is God insofar as He is the cause of all reality and purpose.

The Place of Prayer *vis-à-vis* Different Genres of Literature of the Hebrew Bible

The common denominator between philosophy and Torah wisdom is especially pronounced with regard to subjects where the essence of the respective discussion is based upon direct experience of human beings in the world. This delineation includes prayer, insofar as it is a mode of action opposite to prophecy. In prophecy, God turns to human beings and commands them. In prayer, human beings turn to God and express their feelings, thoughts, and requests. Prophecy teaches them the wisdom whose subject are the ways of God's governing creation in its various strata—including that of the civilization, which they are commanded to establish on the basis of nature, in order to realize the will of their creator. Prayer is an expression of human beings anchored in the experience of his life in the face of the obstacles and difficulties they encounter in their yearning for the well-being assigned to him by God. With prophecy, God commands the the human being. With prayer, the human being wants to influence God to fulfil his expectations and hopes. In sum: in prophecy, God reveals the wisdom of His leadership of human beings, in order that they fulfill the task assigned to them as creature created in the very image of God. As such, human beings are suited to understand the perspective of God's wisdom, even though they could not learn about that wisdom by themselves from observing a reality they do not control. Prayer expresses human wisdom, as anchored in the experience of human life and creation.

This distinction is expressed in the Hebrew Bible by means of grading levels of authority associated with different genres of literature, which are gathered in it: Torah, Prophets, and Hagiographa (*Ketubim*, "Writings"). The books of the Torah (Genesis through Deuteronomy) include the wisdom of God in His relation to creation and to the human being within creation, as revealed in singular manner to Moses as "man of God." This designation grants sublime status to Moses's prophecy, singular and eternal and distinct from the prophecy of all prophets thereafter. Moses was worthy of "face-to-face" prophecy. In the introduction, we will not delve into the full philosophical significance of this connotation. It is enough to determine that Moses's words are identified as the words of God Himself, without addition or subtraction by Moses. His perfect intellect was able to change the "language" of God Himself (which ordinary humans cannot interpret while remaining alive) into a language that regular human beings were suited to hear, learn, and understand. The unique level of Moses's prophecy expresses itself in the authoritative legislation given to him alone. According to this view, legislation is identified with creation, which is an exclusively divine role.

The books of the Prophets represent the wisdom of divine leadership on the second level of authority. It is not legislation, but rather the application of legislation as "statesmanship," and as guidance for a specific time. The prophets had no legislative authority, but rather the authority of correct guidance according to conditions of time and place that underwent ongoing changes. In the books of the Hagiographa, by contrast, human wisdom—accrued over the course of encounters with real conditions of change progressing in nature, civilization, and culture—is gathered in an effort to realize the precepts of the Torah. This is practical wisdom. It is accrued, as said, through human instruments. But this wisdom endeavors to realize God's will, and from this perspective it draws inspiration from God ("the holy spirit"). We will be satisfied with these distinctions. For our subject, the inclusion of prayer in the Writings as a kind of wisdom of human artistry is what is important. This refers especially to the book of Psalms attributed to King David. He was not a prophet, rather a poet by God's grace, a devotee of God, graced with the inspiration of the "holy spirit" as poet and as king of Israel.

The Freedom that is Slavery, Worship of God versus "Idolatry"

The first theoretical question to be discussed in an introduction to the *siddur,* is the Torah's laying a foundation where prayer is included among the *mitzvot* conceived as "service to God." Prayer, as said, is the turn on the part of the human being to God, to express to God one's feelings, thoughts, and one's existential, physical, soulful, and spiritual needs. We saw that the platform in the Torah upon which prayer grew consisted of the *mitzvot* that require serving God with sacrifices, offerings, and contributions. In this context, the substance of prayer is the service a person is obliged to render—just like citizens of a state are obliged to serve the king. This understanding of the substance of "service" (*avodah*) is liable to be seen as its being identical to the "service" that the idolaters of Egypt, Babylonia, and Canaan rendered to their deities. There, presenting sacrifices, offerings, and contributions resembled providing food and property to satisfy the deities' selfish needs. Apparently, it was from here that the distinction also emerged between the *avodah* (service as labor) performed during the week to satisfy one's needs and those of the household, and the *avodah* (service of worship) to God on Sabbaths and festivals. Is this so? Is it not known clearly and in advance that the God who created everything did not lack anything and did not need the gifts of His creatures? If so, why were the *mitzvot* connected to divine-human relations defined as "service to God" (*avodat ha'elohim*)? And how would prayer fulfill that role? In sum: in what is the difference between the understanding of the "service to God," the one and unique, creator of the universe and its king, and service to idols who are only the work of the human beings, anchored?

This is a central theoretical subject for the wisdom of the written and oral Torah. Clearly, the distinction between the Torah's wisdom and the teachings of idolatry is essential to this subject. It is easy to see that we are speaking here not only of the distinction between faith in one God versus faith in a multiplicity of deities, but that between a unique and holy God, a trans-natural God, and idols, which represent earthly forces of nature; and thereby between opposing forms of divine-human relation. In the narrative of the exodus from Egypt and the event of enacting the covenant between God and Israel at Sinai, this deep and inclusive distinction comes to sharp expression in the paradox of human freedom. The Torah of Moses identifies human freedom precisely as a commitment to be a servant of God. Human beings become free in their relation to creation, in relation to themselves, and to other people only when they voluntarily make themselves servants of God.

What is the solution to the paradox of freedom defined as servitude (*avdut*)? The beginning of the solution is implicit to the recognition that serving God is a deep need of human beings. God commands worship. By doing so He responds to human need—because human beings know in the depth of intellect and reason, which God instilled within them, that their selfhood is expressed in their relation of being bound to their God. Accordingly, God does not coerce their service but commands it. This is the deep difference between command (*mitzvah*) and coercion. A *mitzvah* is not fulfilled unless the person chooses it voluntarily. It is fulfilled out of recognition that it calls for what is good and proper in the inclusive, objective sense of what is good and proper for all human beings, all creatures, and for the universe created by God. Only in this sense is it good for God Himself—for God identifies with the good of His creatures and the good of the human being who serves Him, inclusively.

This is the deep difference between service (*avodah*) where human beings are commanded to serve the one and single God, creator of the universe and its king, and service that idols force upon their servants for their selfish benefit. Those servants maintain their service, hoping that if they fulfil the needs of the idols and their wishes, the idols will reward them by fully satisfying their selfish needs, for which they rely on idols: the fall of rain it its season, success of the harvest and its ripeness, help in war against enemies, and everything that follows. These are utilitarian relationships. According to the prophets, they emerge from the idol worshippers' egoistic characteristics. They created images of their idols with their own hands and assigned human instinctual character to the forces of nature that they worshipped.

From this emerges the belief of the prophets and scholars of oral Torah that serving God by keeping His *mitzvot* with total commitment, similar to the commitment of slave to master, guarantees the person's true freedom. In other words, when a person carries out activities in order to satisfy natural urges, when he regards the satisfaction of his urges as being to his benefit, success, and well-being, he becomes a bonded slave to his inclinations and appetites. He thereby becomes a slave to the inclinations and appetites of humans stronger than him who succeed in controlling him, his property, his strength and abilities. But when a person acts according to God's precepts, knowing that the *mitzvot* are intended for the benefit of all His creatures, the human being among them, he chooses the path of truth and righteousness. He frees himself from the fateful force of his urges—and from the chains of fear that enslave him to the will of tyrants—be they human beings stronger than he, or powers of nature that he imagines as deities.

The book of Exodus describes the event of the Egyptian exodus in this fashion. This is an exodus from slavery to freedom—not in terms of breaking the chains of external slavery alone, but also in terms of liberation from the chains of slavery of the soul, out of a longing to establish another regime, one opposed to Pharaonic tyranny and based upon the law of the covenant, which God made with His people at the foot of Mount Sinai by mutual agreement.

The paradox of freedom that exists as servitude to God out of choice and free will is anchored in absolute faith. As opposed to impulses of the Pharaonic tyrants and their idols, which are shaped in the tyrant's image and likeness, the true God does not rule in order to satisfy His selfish inclinations. He leads His world and all His creatures for their benefit. It follows that only when human beings serve God voluntarily, and make the effort to serve God by realizing God's goal in creation, do they choose authentic good and their true happiness.

How, then, does worshipping God with sacrifices, gifts, offerings, praises, and adorations serve the goals of God in creation? The answer to this question deepens the understanding of the essence of the freedom acquired through servitude to God as king of the universe. The first issue to consider in researching the commands regarding service of God in the written Torah is this: the intention of true service to God through sacrifices, gifts, and offers is not to satisfy the needs of the God who commands these sacrifices, gifts, and offerings. Rather, first and foremost, it is to maintain the institution of the priests and the Levites. By means of this institution, the nation relates to God as its king, and God relates to the nation as His assembly and His army. Thereby, the needs of the nation and all its sons and daughters to be judged by God, to atone for their sins, and to rejoice before Him, are satisfied. All of these are, therefore, existential human needs that can be satisfied solely by devotion and commitment to the worship of God. This deep understanding of the needs of the human, as a creature created in the image of God, discloses a new, deeper understanding of the concept of freedom. From the perspective of human beings as naturally selfish animals, freedom is identified with the ability to take everything they desire for themselves—from nature around them, and from all of nature's creations including their neighbors and friends. The Torah, however, views this understanding of freedom as slavery to compulsive urges. The Torah identifies human freedom as the ability and readiness to give to creation, to give to neighbors and friends, and to give to family, community, and nations. By doing so, one thereby gives the best of one's substantial produce to God—a produce that flows from the blessing of creativity with which God graces creation, and especially the human being created in His image.

Serving God, therefore, consists of the contribution (*terumah*, "that which is raised") that human beings give from the best of their produce, which they draw from God's blessing. Through it, they are themselves raised toward God, sanctified, and liberated from their sins, which emerged out of instinctual egoism. They come closer to God and behave towards all those dependent upon them as God behaves towards them. They will give and bestow blessing, so as to be worthy of the ongoing blessing emanating from God to all of His creatures. This is the major difference between serving God and serving idols, and it applies equally to sacrificial worship in the temple and to prayer worship in the synagogue. As stated, idol worshippers pay to the idols—whom they created in their own image and likeness—the dues that they are forced to pay to them, so that the idols can enjoy themselves and compensate those who serve them by satisfying the needs connected with them, and worshippers can continue to provide services to them. But worship of the God who creates the world and reigns over His universe outside Him is intended to elevate the human being to a moral and spiritual height. Only by reaching it, does the human being, as a creature created in God's image, become worthy and ready to receive the blessing that God wants to bestow upon the world. This understanding of the role of the service of God with sacrifices is what enabled its conversion into prayers of the synagogue—which is strengthened through the contributions of the congregants who worship in it, together with all their components. As we will see below, prayer reconstructs the soul's longing to elevate, to contribute, to be sanctified and to sanctify, to bless and be blessed, and to bring abundance to the whole world.

Let us return to the matter of the role of philosophy as a component of the Jewish book of prayer. We saw that the *siddur* was composed as an anthology of various authors over the course of generations. It includes compositions by prophets, rabbinic sages, and various poets who were active in various places and times, and is influenced by various cultures. The principles of compilation are guided by Jewish law, and some of them follow a particular philosophical direction as we pointed out earlier. Clearly, though, research based on compositions included in the *siddur* does not disclose one single teaching in them, but rather portions of many different teachings, conceived within general boundaries set by written and oral Torah: chapters from the wisdom literature in the Hagiographa (especially the Psalms); scrolls intended to be read on the three pilgrimage festivals and on Purim and *Tishah b'Av*; chapters from the Pentateuch and the prophets (the *Keriyat Shema*, portions read from the Torah, and Haftarot); chapters from the midrashic literature (especially the *Shemoneh Esrei* prayers, a strictly midrashic text, but also the morning blessings, and the blessings combined with the *Keriyat Shema*); *piyyutim* anchored in philosophical and kabbalistic literature from much later generations; and also additions reflecting changes in the Jewish national destiny in modern times (such as dirges about the Holocaust), prayers of thanksgiving and Independence Day, and prayers for the army and the State of Israel. Our discussion will focus on the texts that contain philosophical content adapted to prayer-text language, or anchored in philosophical thought upon which the text's full meaning relies.

Are all of these inquiries, joined together into a consistent treatise, to be defined as a philosophy of the Jewish prayer book? The readers themselves will answer this, on the basis of their critical observations.

1

Worship of God and the Process of the Sacred Congregation's Formation and Expression

Service of God as a *Mitzvah* Fulfilled Essentially in Community

The worship of God is a symbolic action that expresses recognition of the believer's obligation to reciprocate to his creator for the gift of his life and for God's favor and benevolence. How can a created creature reciprocate to his creator, who lacks nothing for Himself and whose creation is an act of benevolence that comes from the desire to benefit the other? The prophetic answer is that the human being is created in order to fulfil the designated mission commanded to him by God: to complete creation, with humans within it. Carrying out this mission, through the *mitzvot* commanded by God Himself with the intent of benefitting His creation, is the service which reciprocates God's benevolence with human benevolence.

This prophetic response frees the believer from the isolation of a self-centered creature struggling for his well-being. The *mitzvah* to serve God through fulfilling the mission to complete the creation addresses each individual as a singular personality, who in this capacity is a cell integrated into the social collectivities that comprise the created universe. As such, a person can worship his creator and fulfill his mission only when he maintains the societal, familial-communal, national, and natural relations as part of which he was created. The root of this religious insight, implanted within the human being, is disclosed by examining the development of individual personality from one's natural potential. The human being is born as a weak animal, unfit to exist alone. Human attributes of the person are an inherited potential, which can be developed only in a society that provides protection, educates the individual in its cultural legacy, and opens an arena for individual creative expression. Only through nourishment by the cultural legacy of the society in which one is reared and educated does one become a believer who knows his mission in the world and his obligation to his creator.

We cannot, therefore, determine what precedes what in serving God. Is the first stage recognizing the existential obligation to praise God and His will? Or is it the individual's yearning to integrate into the community and to be good by its standards? These two relations are conditional upon, and complement, one another. It should be stressed that, from the beginning, a youth comes to discern his self as that of a unique "I," by means of belonging to the family, community, and nation preceding him. They form not only a chance gathering of many people different from him, upon whose good will he depends. Rather, he feels that he is bound to them internally. Along with him, they form a collective entity bearing consciousness of a communal "I"—which preceded him and all individuals around him—and would go on to exist forever without him. His successors will perpetuate his belonging to the collective entity of the future—just as he perpetuates his parents' and grandparents' belonging to the collective reality of the present.

The Political Significance of Service of God during Jewry's Settlement on Its Land and in Exile

We cannot develop these anthropological assumptions any further, but they are essential for understanding the worldview that came to expression in the *siddur*. It follows from this that sociological and political research of the worshipping community must precede research into the ideological content and the forms of its expression. Prayer is the creation or sustained continuity of a *zikah* with God, and it draws nourishment from the *zikah* which establishes the individual human being.

As stated in the introduction, the Temple was designated to unify the tribes of Israel into a nation, based on the political covenant that the people of Israel made with the God of Heaven—the one God, creator and guide of the universe, supreme over the gods of all nations. According to prophetic teaching, earthly existence is ruled by a hierarchy of divine powers. All are subservient to the God of Heaven, the one creator God, sovereign over His creation. This is a political covenant. The early kingdom of Israel was built upon its basis, and relations to the kingdoms of nations surrounding the kingdom of Israel were determined by this covenant. Among the nations, each served one of the gods constituting a hierarchy of natural powers subordinate to the God of Heaven. The nation of Israel differed from those nations, insofar as the sovereign deity chose this nation directly, to be its national God. The merit of its patriarchs—Abraham, Isaac, and Jacob—stood the nation in good stead, because in their deep intelligence the patriarchs recognized the supremacy of the God of Heaven. The patriarchs chose to worship Him and testify before the nations about His sovereignty over heaven and earth. By merit of this, God chose the seed of the patriarchs to be His "special nation" (*am segulah*) (Exodus 19:5; Deuteronomy 26:18).

The *segulah* ("special cohort") is the society of the servants who carried out the word of the king, who accompanied Him as He appeared before His subjects to elevate Him, shed splendor on His glory, and bear witness to His power and ruling authority. The nation of Israel was chosen, then, to be the "special cohort" to the God of Heaven in His manifestation as King of the Earth. To fulfil its mission, the nation was commanded to be a "kingdom of priests and a holy nation" (Exodus 19:6) to God. The nation that ministered before God was to bear witness by its service, and by the success that it earned because of its loyal service, that no powers of nature, and surely no deities created by humans for themselves out of haughtiness to rule instead of God, ruled the land, but rather the God of Heaven alone. Therefore, when the nation of David served God faithfully, God "rested" in its midst, protected it and blessed it with productivity of the land and productivity of its spirit.

This is the ideational foundation upon which worship of God rested in the Tabernacle, which the nation built when it left Egypt, and then in the Temple in Jerusalem—thereby effectuating its existence as a "kingdom of priests and a holy nation." When the people gathered in the Tabernacle and then in the Temple and worshipped God through the mediation of the priests who represented the nation, God's *Shekhinah* descended from heaven to earth, and His blessing flowed to the nation—again, through the priests. Let us note that this myth gave symbolic expression to a political reality: in the Jerusalem Temple, the Israelite nation stood before its sublime king, in counterpart to the other peoples who stood before their human kings while bragging about their divine attributes.

The uniqueness of Israel among all the nations in serving a trans-earthly God created an exceptional political problem—which became clear when the people of Israel left the desert to settle the land. On account of its wars with its enemies when it reached the land, the nation also needed a king of flesh and blood to unite it and stand at the head of its army—like all the nations around it. Samuel, the prophet-priest, responded to this request (I Samuel 8).

He proposed a solution to the problem of double sovereignty, which created a tension between the exalted King who ruled over the forces of creation, and the human king who claimed sovereignty for himself over the nation. According to Samuel's solution, the human king would be chosen by the nation's elders on the one hand; and by God through the prophet and high priest on the other. The king was to submit to God—with submission expressed by the supremacy of the laws of God's Torah over the capricious will of the human being. However, over the entire period that the kingdom based on Samuel's legislation existed, only a few kings stood the test of limiting their sovereignty. Against the background of intrigue created among priests, prophets, and king, on the one hand, and between these and the nation's elders on the other, the kingdom of David and Solomon split into two opposed kingdoms, and then the two collapsed—first the kingdom of Israel and then the kingdom of Judah. The people were uprooted from their land and exiled into Babylon.

This complex conception of the kingdom of Israel is reflected in the ceremonial hierarchy of the Temple—the high priest, the priests, Levites, and Israel—and in the societal-political hierarchy—the king who was subordinate to God, the elders, and the people. Each sacerdotal and social class had its defined areas of responsibilities and tasks, whether in the secular *avodah* (labor) that sustained and maintained the people, or in the sacred *avodah* (the Temple service) that united them before God.

The memory of this hierarchy is preserved in the Jewish prayer book, which was composed after the destruction of the kingdom and the Temple, after the loss of the nation's political independence in its land, its uprooting, and the beginning of dispersion into the diaspora and exile. Usually, when a nation's kingdom and temples are destroyed, let alone when a nation is exiled from its land and scattered, the people assimilate and disappear within two or three generations. This is what happened to the tribes of the kingdom of Israel after they were exiled by the king of Assyria. But the people of the kingdom of Judah did not relinquish their unity, which was based upon the eternal covenant with God. This covenant was made in the desert, before the people entered their land. Maintaining the covenant was perceived as a condition for the success of their settlement, for their well-being, and for continuing in the land. In a fundamental sense, the covenant—whose authority obligated the nation on one hand and God on the other—did not rest on the people's settlement in the land, but rather on their desire to inherit it. Because of this, the covenant's authority did not diminish even when God kept His word as communicated through the prophets, and punished the nation for breaking His covenant. To the contrary: the punishment, which reflected God's zealousness for His nation, testified that God did not relinquish His kingdom. He rather sought to educate His people. We see that the people remained obligated to Torah, and God remained obligated to them, even after they were uprooted and exiled from their land. This explains the fact that, precisely following the punishment of having to leave for exile, the people returned to their God without mediation by a king of flesh and blood. They adhered to their Torah and were ready to fulfill their duty as God's special cohort—hoping that in time they would be redeemed and return to their land, their kingdom, and their Temple. This was the incentive for the rise of the prophetic idea of *teshuvah* (repentance, return) in two senses—(1) the people's return to their God, and (2) the return of God to His people—as the conceptual axis of the worship of God in the synagogal prayers that would replace the sacrificial worship of God.

The communal synagogue, defined as "the little temple," was established to maintain the worship of God in exile in the absence of the Temple—which could only be established in Jerusalem by the free people settled on their soil. Sacrificial worship, offerings, and priestly dues on produce (*terumah*) were replaced by worship and Torah study for its own sake. But people in the synagogue were also required to adapt their worship to the socio-political reality of their situation in exile. The *siddur*—the book of prayer—was created for the synagogue, and therefore reflects the societal-familial and political structure of the congregations that replaced the state. The "sacred congregation" took the place of the sacred kingdom, and in this capacity the synagogue represented the entire nation and its members wherever they were exiled. Standing before God in their worship at the same time and with the same prayers, recitations, and blessings—and sanctifying God's name as His nation's king on the one hand, and sovereign over the nation and the universe on the other—all congregations united into one collective entity. In gathering to worship God, each congregation was considered to be an *edah* (assembly), symbolizing the unity of *klal yisrael* (collective Israel). It was a symbolic-spiritual rather than administrative unity, to be sure, but by means of this unity, the Jews have succeeded in preserving their existence as a nation over the course of thousands of years of exile. This spiritual unity is what returned them to their land of birth to establish their kingdom anew, when it became necessary for the continuity of their existence as a nation.

The Norms Defining the Communal Nature of Prayer

The legalistic norm defining the connection between the communal-ceremonial mode of action of prayer and its content is twofold. Firstly, almost all prayers and blessings are recited in the language of "we" and not in the language of "I." Each and every individual is commanded to pray for himself, and the prayer is to express his feelings, thoughts, requests, and intentions. But the individual is required to include himself in the community, and the local community is to include itself in *klal yisrael*, worshipping and blessing God as its king in the name of, and for the sake of, the collective through the language of "we." Secondly, the correct performance of the liturgy (namely, oral recitation expressing the intent of each worshipper individually and all worshippers together), in order to be worthy of God's response to His nation's request, relies upon gathering a *minyan* (quorum) and the presence of the Torah scroll, which symbolizes the covenant made between the people and their God at Sinai. All this together enables the worshippers to turn directly to God in the language of "You" (*Atah*), as God their king who is present to the worshippers by means of the Torah.

The *minyan* consists of at least ten adult males. This is the legalistic definition of the concept of assembly (*edah*), as a collective unity directed to a simple purpose. Ten is the first composite number, which, as a complete unit, contains all the basic numbers that comprise it. Each number from one to ten is enumerated by its particular name: one, two, and so forth. But the number ten is also a basic number. It completes the order, and summarizes all the particulars, and transforms them into a second basic collective number. It is included in the hundreds, and the hundreds in the thousands, and the thousands in the tens of thousands. The number ten is therefore a symbolic, mathematical presentation of the idea of the collectivity based upon the covenant—in the sense that the covenant is a voluntary unity of independent human beings into a collective entity: family, congregation, nation. It is notable that the unity based upon the covenant does not swallow the particulars that constitute it, and does not blend them into a homogenous body. To the contrary: the first step in enacting a covenant is the ritualistic cutting of the sacrifice (see Genesis 15:9–21). Its symbolic significance is the distinctiveness of each individual as a free personality, possessed of will and choice; a personality with ability to take responsibility to obligate itself to others and require obligation towards itself in exchange. The second step in enacting a covenant is the affirmation of the independence of each of the individuals, and honoring their rights, or the part of all individuals entering the covenant voluntarily. On this basis, by means of the collective (*klal*) which is based upon and represented by the chosen leadership, the independence of each individual is recognized and authorized by all those entering the covenant. In this way, the individuals who enter the covenant constitute a collective unit, which relates to other collective units, as a collective "I" to a collective "You," by means of representative institutions and leaders.

Entry into the covenant is a free undertaking. On the one hand, entry is voluntary on the part of the individual participants, by choice and agreement. On the other, once the covenant has been enacted, it obligates all to realize its goals—to each other and to the institutions they establish. Mutual testimony sets and maintains recognition of the obligation. All those who join the covenant enter actively into the organized framework, which is the gathering of the assembly. It operates according to laws legislated in the "Book of the Covenant" on the one hand, and according to direct democratic agreement by all participants on the other. In this organized framework, all families and clans (through their elders) are designated to make decisions at any time as needed, to testify to one another about their decisions, and thereby to validate their agreement to work together according to covenantal law. The families and clans are thereby also sworn before God their king, their legislator, and judge. By means of convening and providing testimony, they maintain the assembly. From then on, if one of them breaches his commitment to his neighbor or to the entire assembly, he is punished—by the assembly's selected institutions on the one hand, and by God on the other—for he broke his oath to his king and betrayed his covenant. In sum, by its actions, the assembly is the collective nation-state or communal entity—namely, meeting as an established political framework, in which the assembly makes its decisions in all areas of its activity and realizes its goals and mission.

To continue the discussion, a distinction is to be made between the different functions of the assembly, whether as a governmental or as a communal phenomenon. When the assembly gathered to decide and to carry out decisions touching on the people's life and earthly, economic, political, and cultural life of the nation settled in its land, it established the societal and political institutions of the government, those designated to function according to the basic law of the Torah. In parallel, in the diaspora, the community establishes local congregational institutions on the basis of the autonomy that the gentile kingdoms grants them—in the lands where the latter are interested in the contribution of the Jews to the economy, various professional services, and to the state. When the assembly gathered in the Temple in Jerusalem to worship God, it constituted the "kingdom of priests" ministering to God when the nation was settled in its land. In parallel, in the diaspora, it establishes the symbolic representative "sacred congregation," which gathers in the synagogue for prayer, and in the house of study alongside the synagogue for Torah study.

The Concept of Assembly and the Distinction between State and Communal Norms

The community and the communal synagogue were created under exilic conditions. But the roots of these two institutions, state and communal, were fastened into the cultural–historical memory that established Israel as God's special cohort. The source for this unique image is the myth of the double covenant made at the foot of Mount Sinai, before the God who revealed Himself to His nation atop the smoking mountain and gave the nation His Torah. Let us remember that, according to the narrative in Exodus, the eternal event took place at the foot of Mount Sinai against the background of the nation's exodus out of Egyptian slavery and into the desert. This was on the way to inheriting the Promised Land, and to establishing the government whose king was God and the sanctuary in which He would reside. Also to be remembered, is that according to this narrative, God did not force Himself upon the nation. He rather proved His love with the act of redemption, and on that basis He offered—and the nation accepted—His kingship.

This political outlook created a blend between the principle of a democratic rule and the principle of a monarchical rule. The monarchical rule serving the benefit of the nation is expressed by the rule of divine law revealed in the Torah. The monarchy is embodied in the rule of the law that God enacted in His Torah for humankind—which is distinct from the law imposed upon all creation from within creation. For indeed, the human being who is created in the image of God is required to obey Him out of his free will.

As creator, God is king, both in the sense that His creation is His absolute possession that cannot be expropriated, and in the sense that createdness is impressed upon His creatures. By contrast, human soul (*nefesh*) emanates from God's spirit. Because of this, human beings are not compelled to act in accordance with their physical nature—so long as their souls are not spoiled by the evil of their physical inclinations. They are commanded to live according to the law given to them in their covenant with God. If they sin, they will be punished. If they obey voluntarily, they will realize their freedom—for they will have acted for their own good and the good will be their reward. This, then, is the basis of the blend between democracy and monarchy, as embodied in the idea of the covenant.

According to the narrative in Exodus, the assembly was instituted in Israel with the descent of its tribes into Egypt, but slavery undid it. We learn about this from the beginning of Moses's mission of redemption. Moses's first step was to gather the assembly, where he and his brother Aaron would be chosen as representatives of the nation to negotiate with Pharaoh in the people's name about their exodus from Egypt (Exodus 4:29–31). The political significance of this step is noteworthy. The gathering of the assembly to decide what it wanted, was itself the beginning of the exodus from slavery to freedom. This voluntary step by the nation was the absolute condition for the nation's redemption. God said that He would redeem His people from slavery by activating the powers of creation, which He ruled—given the fact that the nation was not itself strong enough to fight against tyrannical slavery. But God's action did not release the people from demonstrating their desire to participate in the redemption effort. If the nation did not liberate itself from the fear of its oppressors, it would never emerge to freedom—even if the prison gates were to burst open for the people from the outside. In other words, redemption is not an event from the outside, not a forcible removal of chains and collapsing of walls. Essentially, it is a spiritual process of liberating the personal and national will. At the same time, God's struggle with Pharaoh was an internal struggle between the desire for freedom and the desire to enslave the nation and each and every individual within it. This process entails suffering. Only a people prepared to suffer for its freedom, to confront its suffering and overcome it, is worthy of its freedom.

According to the Exodus narrative, the nation was required to participate in its redemption—at least by openly expressing its agreement with the mission of Moses and Aaron and its readiness to bear the initial consequences of the mission. Pharaoh's response to the demands of Moses and Aaron to release the people from his land had worsened the conditions of slavery, and brought about capitulation by the nation's elders to the conditions of slavery imposed by Pharaoh. Moses was compelled to fulfill the mission in God's name, without the participation of the assembly. The assembly had to be prepared a second time, before the enactment of the covenant at the Sinai revelation—so that Moses could stand before God in the name of the nation, and execute the covenant between God as sovereign and the nation as a collective entity choosing Him freely.

The Sinai covenant was enacted in the desert in anticipation of settling in Canaan; in this respect, exile preceded settlement in the homeland. The unification of the community into an assembly according to Torah law, gathered around the Tabernacle of Testimony, also preceded the unification of the people as a state around the Jerusalem Temple. Organizing the assembly around the Sanctuary in the desert provided the ideal model for establishing the community around the synagogue as a "small temple" (Ezekiel 11:15) when the people exiled from their land returned to the "desert of the nations" (Ezekiel 20:35), and sometimes fell into the deep pit of violent slavery.

Nevertheless, the rabbis found an essential difference between the slavery in Egypt, and the exile that grew increasingly darker. Even when the exiled nation fell for a second and third time into the pit of slavery, the first redemption was not at all annulled. The prayer book designates this in a blessing that bridges the *Keriyat Shema* and the *Shemoneh Esrei*:

> With a new song, the redeemed people praised Your Name at the seashore. Together they all gave thanks, proclaimed Your

kingship and declare: The Lord shall reign forever and ever. Rock of Israel: Arise to the help of Israel. Deliver, as You promised, Judah and Israel. Our Redeemer, the Lord of hosts is His name—the Holy One of Israel Blessed are You, Lord, who redeemed Israel. (K:106, *Shirah Ḥadashah, Tzur Yisrael*)

Note the past tense in the blessing. The blessing designates that the redemption endured from then until today and would remain so forever—even in exile.

How so? The answer of the rabbinic sages to the question appears in another section of the *siddur*, in the *midrash* cited in the beginning of the Passover *Haggadah*: "From the beginning, our fathers were worshippers of alien gods, but now the All-present has brought us close to Him for His worship."

The meaning of this theological-historical determination is clarified by the prayer in the second blessing of the *Keriyat Shema*:

> You have loved us with great love, Lord our God,
> And with surpassing compassion
> Have You had compassion on us.
> Our Father, our King,
> For the sake of our ancestors who trusted in You,
> And to whom You taught the laws of life,
> Be gracious also to us and teach us.
> Our Father, compassionate Father, ever compassionate,
> Have compassion on us.
> Instill in our hearts the desire to understand and discern,
> To listen, learn and teach, to observe, perform and fulfill
> All the teachings of Your Torah in love.
> Enlighten our eyes in Your Torah
> And let our hearts cling to Your commandments.
> Unite our hearts to love and revere Your name,
> So that we may never to ashamed.
> And because we have trusted in Your holy, great and revered name,
> May we be glad and rejoice in Your salvation.
> (K:468, *Ahavah Rabbah*)

The deeper explanation of these words is that God's love for His nation was expressed in the granting of the Torah, which shaped the good and upright way of life. All who practiced Torah with a full heart lived a life of freedom, filled with joy. Exile cannot annul the love that is answered with love, or the freedom and joy of serving God according to his *mitzvot*. The people were exiled with the Torah during the second exile, and continued to maintain the Torah in exilic lands. While kings of the nations could enslave the bodies of the nation's people, they could not enslave their soul and spirit. As long as the members of the nation worshipped God by obeying His commands, they were free citizens of the realm of God. Therefore, when the people worshipped their God in exile, they built a life of hidden inner freedom—until the day would come when the kingdom of God would be revealed on earth before all peoples. Israel would return to the land and establish God's sovereignty and His Temple therein.

The Roles of the Community in Exile: The Relation between the Kingdom of Heaven and the Kingdom of the Nations

Let us return to the exilic community. From the sociological-political perspective, the community was a fully functional system. It organized itself locally at the initiative of exilic groups when they arrived at their temporary dwelling places, according to rights (privileges) granted them by ruling powers of the nations. The nations provided protection for the Jewish settlement, in order to benefit from skilled services by Jews with expertise. The financial, material considerations of communal life existed within the political framework, which the assembly (the gathering of all the *ba'alei batim*—the responsible parties—of the community) shaped according to regulations that the assembly enacted for itself. This followed the example of how Moses proceeded with Jethro's advice, before the event of granting the Torah at Sinai—but here in the framework of traditional Jewish law (*Halakhah*) and by agreement of the authorized rabbinic court. The community's secular work, which supported and maintained it from the economic, communal-cultural, and political perspective, was also conducted within the framework of these regulations. It did so by means of traditional Jewish law—while recognizing the need to adapt to economical, sociological and political conditions of the hospitable nations, their laws and their governance.

In this connection, it should be emphasized that the relationship of *Halakhah* to material civilization, and to the rules of creativity and service which maintained civilization, was positive as long as *Halakhah* was employed for good and responsible life—also, as long as the civilization did not make the satisfaction of material needs the highest goal of human life, but regarded the satisfaction of those needs as means towards a spiritual goal. Given this framework, *Halakhah* encouraged the incorporation of Jews into roles in economy, management, government, and state service in the states into which they were exiled. The operating halakhic principle here was: "The law of the state is the law." It is based upon distinguishing between what is in the category of "law" (*Din*)—which comes from proper fulfillment of the state's positive roles, roles that the Torah recognizes to be vital—and what falls under "robbery (*Gezelah*)." We find that in states where the government passed the test of ethics and legal justice, Jews who observed *Halakhah* conducted themselves as citizens who observed the law of the government that protected them. They saw no contradiction between loyalty to the state and to Torah laws, which rendered them citizens of the Kingdom of Heaven—which was higher than earthly kingdoms.

The *siddur* expresses accord between the kingdom of heaven and the kingdom of earth by addressing God as *melekh malkhei hamelakhim*, literally: "king of the kings of kings, the Holy One Blessed be He" (from *Shalom Aleikhem*, recited on the eve of the Sabbath). This is a monarchical title that represents the following hierarchy: the emperors of the major empires (Babylonia, Persia, Greece, and Rome) saw themselves as the "kings of kings," and the deity exalted above them was the "king of the kings of kings." Moreover, as in our time Jews in Israel recite the blessing for the State of Israel in the synagogue after reading the Torah, those dispersed in exile have always recited—and still recite today—a blessing for kings and heads of nations who rule and provide protection for the communities.

It should be emphasized that, according to written Torah and the *Halakhah* of oral Torah, there is a substantive and qualitative connection between the earthly means of human civilization and the moral-spiritual purpose designated for the nation of Israel. This connection does not allow for absolute distinction between the secular and sacred realms of the same state. To explain: when secular labor satisfies physical needs, so that a person can commit himself with all his might to the life of spirit in which he sees his higher purpose, secular labor is also sanctified. Thus, the children of Israel are commanded to work, each at his occupation, during the week to support themselves and their households, just as they are commanded to rest on the Sabbath and dedicate themselves to serving God. This means that the human being also serves God when he "works the ground" to establish and maintain a "settlement" (civilization) upon it—which is a condition for human life. As long as one does one's work faithfully and honestly, and remains responsible not only to one's own benefit and to that of and to one's family, but to one's friends, neighbors, and community, these activities are considered service to God.

Those who study the *siddur* will find explicit expression of these norms. The hierarchy of roles of the community: rabbis, scholars, priests, Levites, *gabbaim* (sextons), *parnassim* (communal executives), householders, males and females, sons and daughters—all find their place in the community in the right order. All are honored as members of the covenant (*b'nai brith*) according to status and mission in the community. At the same time, the difference between sacred worship and secular labor is preserved. The "roof" of the first "story," that of the functioning secular community, is the "floor" of the second story, the functioning of the sacred community. This is indicated through commandments regulating the moral relations between person and person. These commandments are basically about righteousness (*tzedakah*) shaping the texture of individual relations within the family, between families, and between all friends and neighbors who are members of the community according to the principle of "And love your neighbor as yourself—I am the Lord" (Leviticus 19:18). The emphasis on the authority that is binding, "I am the Lord," establishes unambiguously that love of neighbor is not detached from God's love for all humankind, created in His image. God's love for human beings as His children obliges them to return their love to Him, which includes love for one another. In their relation to God, they are all brothers. The Torah hangs the existence of the great principle included in the *Keriyat Shema* ("You shall love the Lord your God with all your heart and all your soul and with all your might" [Deuteronomy 6:5]) upon this great principle.

The *Mitzvah* of Righteousness as the Societal Basis of the Sacred Community

But the *Halakhah*, which is intended to be implemented in act, is not satisfied with great principles. In order for activities to be implemented, the principles need to be detailed. The detailed *mitzvot* that join love of God to love of neighbor are those of righteousness, which consolidate and shape the community's image both in terms of the texture of individual relationships between its members, and in terms of their relation to the congregation of Israel.

Let us first emphasize that the *mitzvot* of righteousness are considered to be absolute duties—both in the written Torah and in the *Halakhah* of oral Torah. To be sure, they are not to be enforced by a court. We expect them to be observed out of recognition and agreement—although they are absolutely binding in terms of enforcement as commands of God and the "judgment of heaven." The community does not punish the person who does not observe them; God punishes him—in this world and the next. In this regard, there is also the pressure of public opinion. A person desiring to preserve honor in the eyes of the community, wealthy or poor—even if in need of charity—commits himself to observing these *mitzvot* to the extent possible. This recognition is also expressed in prayer, and with emphasis. Already in the morning blessings, we observe symbolically the *mitzvah* of Torah study. Then we observe the blessing that accompanies that *mitzvah*, and study a halakhic *midrash* from the *Mishnah*—so that the obligation before God on behalf of relatives and neighbors is fixed into the worshipper's consciousness so as to become part of the order of his day:

> These are the things whose fruits we eat in this world but whose full reward awaits us in the World to Come:
> Honoring parents; acts of kindness; arriving early at the house of study morning and evening; hospitality to strangers; visiting the sick; helping the needy bride; attending to the dead; devotion in prayer; and bringing peace between people—but the study of Torah is equal to them all. (K:10; *Eilu Devarim, Shabbat* 127a)

Anyone astonished that this *mishnah* is chosen for observing the *mitzvah* of Torah study and its blessing should pay heed to the emphasis that the *Mishnah* places on the connection between the essential *mitzvot* of righteousness and worship of God—to which a person's reward both in this world and the world to come is related.

These words express the connection between the concept of *tzedek* (justice), as an attribute of legal truth, and the concept of *tzedakah* (righteousness, also charity). Justice is what any person claims from his allies; that is, the rights coming to him which those allied to him as individuals and community are obliged to provide, in exchange for the obligation he accepts to maintain their rights. The attribute of *tzedakah* for the poor—those suffering various forms of deprivation such as loss of property, loss of sources of earning, orphans, the bereaved, widows, the handicapped, the sick, and those who fall captive—is determined on the basis of this definition. This is the obligation placed upon neighbors and their community to restore someone who falls from a status proper to him, as a covenantal partner created in God's image, to his proper status as a *ba'al habayit* (householder)—someone able to stand independently and carry responsibility for himself, his family, his community, and his nation. Because of this, all are obliged to give charity, to the extent they are able (up to the point of injuring their independent standing)—just as all have the right to receive charity as needed.

The written Torah defined those norms as equal to the *mitzvot* that the rabbinic sages described as "*mitzvot* dependent upon the land"—that is, *mitzvot* whose observance was a condition for continuing the nation's settlement on its soil. The basic assumption of these *mitzvot*—the assumption that includes them among those for serving God—is that true mastery over possessions is that of their creation. Thus, all lands of the earth are the possession of God, who created them and are a possession that cannot be expropriated. In other words, human beings do not have the right of absolute possession of their property. What they maintain for their work of shaping materials of creation into secondary form is to be considered a gift, which God gives to all His creatures: species of plants and animals, with the human being at their top. All of these were created on condition that they support themselves as needed, and contribute to each other for success and happiness. According to the Torah, this just allotment—following the principle of "to each creature according to need"—can be implemented if each of the creatures, including human beings, takes for itself only what it needs, and does not try to deprive the other. No one should strive to control all the resources and possess them. To the contrary, each should enhance the environment and contribute to it.

Animals maintain this principle reluctantly. Even the strongest animals of prey are limited and cannot take for themselves more than what the environment provides for them. Animals are drawn to others of their species to help them. The battle for survival between creatures of nature creates a balance among them, which enables their survival and development. Not so with humans. They create instruments and invent strategies anchored in knowledge. This enables them to develop an increasing ability to control various resources that are not necessary for instantaneous existence. For this reason, humans are likely not only to rob the portions of all other beings, but to transform those beings themselves into "resources"—that is, to use them as food or as slaves. This is how the special talent of creativity with which the human being is blessed turns into a curse. The egoistic inclination upsets the natural balance that has prevailed in their environment and among themselves. With this, their environment and society are destroyed by overexploitation, murder, oppression, controversy, and war.

It follows from this that human survival in nature and the survival of civilization are conditioned upon the observance of the laws of morality. These are not anchored in the physical and instinctual nature of the person, but rather in his rational nature, which confers on him freedom of choice both on the basis of deliberation and on the basis of setting limits on himself and not only on his surroundings. In this regard, the great problem in which the human being is caught is the conflict created between impulses of natural instinct and deliberations of moral reason. As such, it is impossible to rely on human reason alone. A higher authority is needed to enforce laws on human beings, laws whose observance is necessary for human existence in an orderly society and a civilization of service.

The Torah's legislation in these matters is based upon the assumption that God, as ruler of heaven and earth, apportions to each nation a land to inherit, in which to live and work, flourish and create. God does not transfer absolute ownership to nations, but rather only the right to use its resources on the condition that they would live in it according to the law of justice given to them in the earlier covenant, that of Noah and his sons, which was enacted when the waters of the flood abated. The land remains the possession of God. It is loaned to nations and individuals on the condition that they honor the rights of their neighbors; the earth and its growth; the beautiful animals living upon it; individuals, families, clans, and the tribes that compose the clans—all equally. Within the framework of this divine policy, God gave the land of Canaan to Israel as a legacy, because its original inhabitants did not observe the conditions for their settlement in the land and lost their right to it. Obviously, this condition would apply more stringently to the children of Israel. Were they to take the path of the Canaanites and sin against God, they would lose their right to the land and be punished severely. Based on this stipulation, the Torah instructs the children of Israel not to infringe on the settlements of the people with the right to be there, on the one hand, and to distribute the land of Canaan equally, according to the tribes, clans, and families, on the other. In this way, all could support themselves by working the soil of the land—with mutual respect of rights according to the law of the covenant.

The negative *mitzvah* (that is, a legal restriction) that follows from this outlook is that no tribe should attempt to control the property of another tribe, and the same with each clan and family. It follows from this, that even if the head of the family sells his property to others, or sells himself into slavery on account of economic failure or various debilities, there is an obligation to liberate him in the year of the *shemitah* and to return all properties to their original owners at the Jubilee. From here we come to the corresponding positive *mitzvah* (that is, a legal injunction): since God apportions the right of each person to support himself honorably from the resources of the land that God created, the wealthy who succeed in their work are obligated to share with the poor who do not succeed, and grant to the poor what they deserve. This is *tzedakah* for the poor. It coincides with the concept of right (*zekhut*). Each poor person has a right to receive *tzedakah* from his wealthy neighbors and friends, so as to receive the portion that God commanded to him from his land's harvest. We emphasize that this is an absolute right according to the Torah principle, "that your kinsman may live with you" (Leviticus 25:36). The principle is applied in the *mitzvot* of gleaning, forgotten sheaf, corner of the field, and poor man's tithe, and to general support of the poor with money and its equivalent—until the poor are restored to the situation that they deserve by right.

The *mitzvot* that depend upon the land (laws of debt release, Jubilee, gleanings, forgotten sheaf, and corner of the field) were obligatory for the people only when they were settled in the land. But the *mitzvah* of *tzedakah*, in its normally inclusive sense according to the rabbinic version of "all Jews are responsible for each other" (*Shevu'ot* 39a), also applies in the diaspora. We can assert that this obligation has received even more emphasis in the diaspora, where it changed into an absolute condition for the people's basic existence in exilic circumstances. According to the words of the literary prophets, which are quoted a great deal in the *siddur*, observance of laws of justice (*tzedek*) and *tzedakah* in Israel is a condition of the nation's redemption and return to settle on its soil: "Zion shall be redeemed with justice [*mishpat*] and they that return of her with righteousness [*tzedakah*]" (Isaiah 1:27). The *halakhah* of *tzedakah* was developed in Israel on this basis. It is detailed in various sources (see especially Maimonides, "Laws of Gifts to the Poor" [*Hilkhot matanot le'aniyim*] in the *Mishneh Torah*), and is applied and observed in communities of Israel as a basis for the sacred community.

Testimony for this is also found in the *siddur*. Among the blessings recited after the reading of the Torah, there is also this blessing—whose established, practical aim stands out:

> May He who blessed our fathers, Abraham, Isaac and Jacob, bless (*name*, son of *father's* name) who has been called up in honor of the Torah, and in honor of Shabbat (on *Yom Tov*: "and in honor of the festival"). As a reward for this, may the Holy One, blessed be He, protect and deliver him from all trouble and distress, all infection and illness, and send blessing and success to all the work of his hands (on *Yom Tov*: and may he merit to go up to Jerusalem for the festivals), together with all Israel, his brethren, and let us say: Amen. (K:508, *Mi Shebeirakh*)

The Synagogue as Communal Institution

From here, we come to the role of the synagogue as a communal institution. Prayer is obviously the principal function of the synagogue. But in its capacity as a gathering place (*beit keneset*), prayer is not the only function. In order to function as a house of prayer proper to serve God according to the content of the *siddur*, the synagogue first needs to function as a gathering house for the assembly, both for the sake of its very existence and activity as an assembly, and for the sake of maintaining the web of interpersonal and interfamilial relations among the members of the assembly. The members of the assembly are covenantal partners and friends who bear responsibility for one another, take interest in one another, and participate in one another's lives and events—in moments of sorrow, failure, and mourning, as well as in moments of joy, success, and honor. This concerned participation of members of the worshipping community in one another's troubles and joys comes to expression in prayer itself, whether in the *Mi Shebeirakh* ("He who blessed our fathers") blessing following the ceremony of reading the Torah or in prayer itself as a form of expression. For prayer includes not only the turn of the unified assembly to God, but the turn of worshippers to one another in an ongoing effort to establish the experience of the "we"—which is required by prayer for God to respond. They should not refrain from the effort!

We can apprehend the deeper meaning of this determination, if we compare the experience of gathering in the Jewish synagogue with that in the Christian church. In the church, people gather for lofty prayer and personal confession. Prayer is implemented by the priest, the choir, the organ, and by the formation of architectural space, pictures, and sacred statues—all of which together create the experience of exaltation and elevation to God, who is worshipped with sanctity. By contrast, the synagogue is, first of all, a place to convene for different activities, including social pastime on Sabbaths, holidays; and individual celebrations such as circumcision, *bar mitzvah*, and marriages. During prayer, we indeed expect that all those present avoid conversation. But before and after prayer, and from time to time during it, the worshippers converse—be it about daily matters, the meaning of the weekly Torah portion being studied, or about the significance of personal and communal problems on the agenda.

This results from the fact that, beside prayer, the assembly gathers to discuss all its concerns in the synagogue—such that it is impossible to set a partition between the various tasks. When the assembly convenes, it discusses its concerns, and also prays; or prays and also discusses its concerns. Either way, when people come to the synagogue to pray, they are happy to meet the assembly, neighbors and friends, guests and those returning from travel. They show interest in one another, honor one another, provide news, converse, confirm claims of privileges, mark the events of mourning, trouble, and celebration. Serving God does not reject such topics as profane; it extends to them a sanctified status—whether by integrating them into the ceremony or through blessings and various honors.

The synagogue's space and its furnishings are appropriate for a variety of tasks and the *siddur* is, first of all, adapted to the passages between them. First, the assembly congregates at the designated time, and attends to completing the *minyan* and to preparing whatever is necessary. This includes appointing a *shaliah hatzibur* (representative of the public; that is, a prayer leader); wrapping oneself in the *tallit* and, for weekday *Shaharit*, donning the *tefillin*. The transition from this phase to prayer itself is regulated. After wrapping the *tallit* and donning the *tefillin*, individuals enter into the spiritual process of prayer reciting the morning blessings among themselves; and by reciting the psalms that at one time had accompanied the daily sacrifice in the Temple. When this semi-organized recitation ends, the prayer leader rises and stands before the Ark, affirms that a *minyan* has gathered and that those assembled are ready to pray, and signals that he wishes to begin. He opens with silent prayers, asking that he succeed in his mission and that he curry favor before God and before the congregants whom he is about to lead in prayer. Only after these preparations, does he turn to the congregants to recite the Half-*Kaddish* and proclaim "*Barekhu et adonai hamevorakh*" ("Bless the Lord, the blessed One," K:454), so that the audience can unite and pray with him. This is a structured social process, which is spontaneous on the one hand, and established custom on the other. The individuals become a congregation when they respond to the call of the *Barekhu* and bless God in the third person with "*Barukh adonai hamevorakh le'olam va'ed*" ("Bless the Lord, the blessed One, forever and all time" (K:454)—not as with most blessings, where the prayer is composed in the second person. That is, their response is still testifying to the individual's readiness to worship God before the congregation. In this way, the entry into the assembly and the entry into prayer belong to a single double-faceted mode of action.

Establishing the Sacred Congregation as a Central Component of the Prayer

The *Kaddish* recitation, in its various forms, acquires special importance in the context of establishing congregational worship. This prayer, which is recited in Judaic-Aramaic—the people's daily spoken language at the time when this text was created—is repeated and modified several times in the course of the worship. At times it is shortened; or there are various additions in transitioning from one portion of the worship to what follows, as a kind of punctuating event.

My view is that it is not a regular prayer recited by all worshippers together in a turn to God, but recited by the *shaliaḥ hatzibur,* or mourners of the worshipping congregation, as a declaration of faith in God and affirmation of His sovereignty, of the righteousness of His judgment and fairness of His conduct regarding the nation of Israel until its future redemption. The worshipping congregation hears, validates and affirms by responding with *"Amen."* This is speech about God as bearing witness to worshippers who believe in Him, speech that only indirectly requests God to stand by His word and rescue His people—including every individual. At the same time, this is an existential expression that confirms that the individual reciting the *Kaddish* belongs to the congregation, and the consciousness of the unity of the worshipping congregation. Such is the role played by the recitation of the *Kaddish,* in transitioning from one portion of worship to what follows. That is, before we begin the new portion of prayer, we renew the recognition of the individual and the desire for his dedication to God in prayer—such that the intensity of standing together in prayer does not weaken due to its length.

In other words, the primary role of the *Kaddish* is the recitation of readiness for, and alertness to the worshipping assembly. As to being astonished that mourners are commanded to stand together in a *minyan* to say *Kaddish* for relatives who have died: the explanation is to be found in the congregational function. The mourners' concentration in prayer obliges them to transcend their private sorrow, which is liable to become crushing and to absorb them in an alienating bitterness. Mourning has the character of distancing one from life and sharing in death—removing one from the world and society. It is said in Psalms: "The dead cannot praise the Lord, nor any who go down into silence. But we will bless the Lord, now and forever" (Psalms 115:17–18).

The mourner's heart is bitter. He is absorbed in the agonies of death. How could he praise God? As a consequence, those around him are inclined to distance themselves from him—as the friends of Job were alienated because of his dejected appearance and the outcries over his disaster. The *Kaddish,* which the mourner recites, and the congregation's response of *"Amen,"* together overcome the obstacle that is liable to weaken the entire assembly's feelings of sharing in the worship of God. The remedy is for the mourner to stand amid the assembly, receive the yoke of heavenly sovereignty upon himself, and justify the judgment. By so doing, he returns to belong to the holy congregation standing before God, serving and praising Him. The sacred congregation encourages the mourner towards it and consolidates anew by responding *"Amen."* In this way, the mourner returns to the course of responsibilities that apply to every Jew in the assembly. He thereby returns to his normal life and is consoled.

The Ceremony of Renewing the Covenant in the Torah Reading

We now come to the central event in establishing the worshipping assembly and its sacred function: the ritual of Torah reading during the Sabbath and festivals (with shortened versions also performed on Mondays and Thursdays). Let us begin by describing the ceremonial context. Emissaries of the congregation stand alongside the Holy Ark, which holds the congregation's Torah scrolls. They remove the curtain, open the doors of the Ark, and remove the Torah scroll, which is dressed in splendor with a royal crown on top. The presentation of the Torah, in all its royal splendor in the presence of the sacred congregation, symbolizes the appearance of God as king of His nation. It brings to mind the meaning of the ritual as symbolizing the journey of the camp of Israel in the desert, with the Tabernacle carried in the center; a pillar of fire going before Israel, directing the path, and a pillar of cloud gathered behind, to protect the Tabernacle from pursuing enemies. The Bible further describes the scenario with the words recited in the synagogue in the Torah procession:

> When the Ark was out, Moses would say:
> Advance O Lord!
> May Your enemies be scattered.
> And may Your foes flee before You.
> (Numbers 10:35)

The citation recalls the journeys of the camp of Israel in the desert under God's leadership. The citation that follows recalls God's appearance as king over His nation in its sanctuary, once the people were settled in their land.

> For instruction shall come forth from Zion,
> The word of the Lord from Jerusalem.
> (Isaiah 2:3)

After that the congregants accepts the yoke of sovereignty with the blessing: "Blessed is He who in His holiness gave the Torah to His people Israel" (K:498, *Barukh shenatan*). On certain holidays, the congregation responds with the biblical passages, which describe how God revealed Himself to Moses when He gave him the two Tablets of the Covenant after the sin of the golden calf: "The Lord! The Lord! A God compassionate and gracious, slow to anger, abounding in kindness and faithfulness, extending kindness to the thousandth generation, forgiving iniquity and transgression, and sin" (Exodus 34:6–7). With these sentences the congregants welcome the countenance of God, which is present "upon" the Torah—symbolizing His sovereignty over the nation. This starts the royal journey. The congregation opens the path and honors the Torah and the God who gave it. The journey concludes by placing the Torah on a table raised upon a platform in the center of the synagogue—both above the congregation and in its midst. The Torah's cover and ornaments are removed, and the Torah is opened at the place indicated for reading. Individuals of the congregation are now merited with ascent up to the Torah, to bend over to bless and read it with the pointer, to hear and take the Torah's words to heart.

In the procession, the feeling of awe for the royalty is expressed by lifting up the Torah, and by keeping one's distance from it. The feeling of love is expressed in the reading. The dialectical duality stands out with these two dimensions: nearness within distance—like the nation standing at the foot of Sinai in fright, before the revelation of divine, absolute power; and distance within nearness—Moses enacting a covenant between the nation and its God by reading the book of the covenant in the nation's very midst when he descended from the mountain with the scroll of the book. The symbolism of black letters on white parchment, as black fire upon white fire, now leaps out to the eye of the reader and to the one who ascends to the Torah. This recalls the boundary that Moses marked around the mountain, on which God revealed His word from behind the covering of the cloud of smoke. The revealing was simultaneously covered, and the covering was simultaneously revealed.

The chosen individuals are called to the Torah one by one, by their names and those of their fathers to testify to their lineage. The *Ba'al hakore* (the reader), who knows how to chant the words of Torah according to their prescribed intonations and with a sweet voice, begins the ceremony of reading. He understands how to call up and to instruct those who ascend to the Torah, and through them the entire congregation, which maintains the Torah scroll open before it. All pay attention to the oral recitation, while also reading the text themselves.

The ceremonial meaning of this event distinguishes it from a routine lesson whose goal is theoretical-educational rather than ceremonial. The recitation is addressed to individuals, who are connected by their relation to their affiliated congregation, to unite them in the participatory event. It joins together and unites the individuals in the presence of Torah on the one hand, and edifies them by their internalizing the Torah's teaching on the other. To this end, the weekly portion is divided into seven (or four) small portions and the requisite number of readers is called up to the Torah in the proper order: first a *Kohen* (one of the priestly clan), next a Levite, then a scholar or honored Jew. After them, prominent members of the community—each according to the level of honor. Each individual adult in the congregation is eligible for an *aliyah*, according to this order—in exchange for which he contributes a gift to the congregation, according to ability, to help strengthen the synagogue.

As said, the ceremony of reading the Torah embodies the transition from the Torah's appearing externally to revealing its internality. This carries out the transition from the royal appearance of the Torah above the congregation to the elevation of the congregation to the Torah. The congregation is called upon to internalize the words of the Torah, to live with it and to maintain what is said in it: "For they are our life and the length of our days" (K:244). With this, each ascender to the Torah offers a blessing at the conclusion of the reading of his portion, in his own name and that of his congregation: "Blessed are You, Lord, our God, King of the universe, Who has given us the Torah of truth, planting everlasting life in our midst. Blessed are You, Lord, giver of the Torah" (K:506, *Barukh atah adonai eloheinu melekh ha'olam*).

Let us pay attention to the blending of the principle of divine sovereignty and the principle of democratic assembly expressed in this ceremony. In the order of their ascent, those who ascend represent the hierarchy of the assembly's leadership—the *Kohen*, the Levite, the scholar of Israel, and the ordinary lay participants. Each is a personality standing under his own authority, contributing to the synagogue with his presence and activity, and stating his opinion about any topic the assembly needs to decide upon and carry out. By doing so, they all symbolize, ratify, and invigorate the communal hierarchy and strengthen also authority outside the synagogue. In our opinion, the level of the honor of each member is not determined by the power one has, but by the activity and leadership one contributes to the congregation, and by the responsibility one assumes for the congregation's maintenance and functioning. Notably, granting the honor establishes the leadership as serving the assembly, and thereby serving God—not the assembly as serving the leadership.

This is the educational message of the congregational prayer gathering: all Jews are equal before God in terms of their duty to contribute to the assembly devoted to serving God, but each is unique according to his lineage, qualification, and ability. The measure of duty and the ability of each individual to contribute to the worshipping assembly is a divine commandment and a blessing for the individual—and makes each individual, according to his singularity, a channel of spiritual flow to collective Israel. The hierarchy does not annul the equality of the individuation of the members of the congregation before God. Each member, with all his talents, is a unique individual who realizes himself in his designated relation to God and to the collective. All members listen respectfully to the public reading of the Torah, even if they are competent to recite it with its intonations by themselves. They all recite the same blessing at the start of their reading and at the conclusion. They all are blessed and share blessing and honor personally with their family, relatives, friends, congregants, and collective Israel. They thereby pledge a contribution to the synagogue and to charity to the extent of their ability. When they return to their seats among the assembly, they are worthy to shake hands, expressing the gratitude and appreciation of the congregation. Here we have a social process with the double meaning of receiving the yoke of *mitzvot* before God, and of close personal integration into the worshipping congregation.

After reading the Torah portions, the *Haftarah*—a chapter from the prophetic books—is similarly chanted. The custom of the *Haftarah* concludes the reading, just as the *afikomen* concludes the celebratory Passover feast in a form that both adds and completes. The *Haftarah* relates to a particular teaching or commandment in the Torah portion, which it illuminates with the light of words recited appropriate for the moment. It reminds the congregation, firstly that the *mitzvah* in the written Torah is to be kept as having meaning for every time; and secondly that all parts of the Torah, despite differences between them, are directed to the same eternal truth—to be reviewed over and over, because the Torah contains everything.

Following the *Haftarah* and its blessing, we arrive at the climax of the ceremony: the symbolic renewal of the eternal covenant made at Sinai. One of the congregants is honored with the lifting of the scroll above himself and above the congregation. All the individuals point to the scroll and testify in unison: "This is the Torah that Moses placed before the children of Israel, at the Lord's commandment, by the hand of Moses" (K:512, *Vezot Hatorah*). This sentence actualizes the obligation that the nation's ancestors accepted upon themselves at the foot of Mount Sinai, on their own behalf and on behalf of all generations of their descendants, when they said "All the things that the Lord has commanded we will do" (Exodus 24:3)—for the Torah is the same Torah and its eternal truthfulness is forever obligatory. No other doctrine that claims to be the Torah of God could annul the Torah.

As we proceed in our inquiry, we will address the performative components of the ceremony, in terms of organizing congregational life based upon volunteering—but out of recognition of absolute duty. To begin, let us finish presenting the framework. The Torah scroll, which is crowned, is carried above the heads of the congregants in a celebratory procession. Standing in front, the prayer leader calls out: "Let them praise the name of the Lord, for His name, His alone, is sublime" (Psalms 148:13). The congregants respond with an answer from the Psalms:

> His splendor covers heaven and earth.
> He has exalted the horn of His people
> For the glory of all His faithful ones,
> Israel, the people close to Him.
> Hallelujah
> (Psalms 148:13)

The procession of honor returns the Torah from the platform in the center of the synagogue to the Holy Ark, which stands at the wall facing in the direction of Jerusalem. The congregants clear a path and pay honor to the Torah and to the procession that carries the scroll, and calls out the text that was recited at the conclusion of each stage of the journey in the desert, upon entering the encampment:

> And when it halted, he would say:
> Return, O Lord,
> You who are Israel's myriads of thousands.
> (Numbers 10:36)

> Advance, O Lord, to your resting place;
> You and Your mighty Ark!
> (Psalms 132:8)

The recitation closes the cycle. We return the scroll to the Ark and close the Ark with the curtain, while listening to the passages in praise of the Torah:

> Her ways are pleasant ways,
> And all her paths, peaceful.
> She is a tree of life to those who grasp her,
> And whoever holds on to her is happy.
> (Proverbs 3:17)

> Take us back, O Lord, to Yourself,
> And let us come back;
> Renew our days as of old.
> (Lamentations 5:21)

The Political Significance of the Ceremony of *Aliyah* to the Torah

The closing verse of the ceremony is taken from the conclusion of the scroll of Lamentations (5:21). It expresses the political significance of the ceremony of *aliyah* to the Torah: the nation's return to the place designated for it in the kingdom of God on earth, by means of God's return to His nation and the nation's return to God. The ceremony recalls the mutual responsibility, where the nation is not only obligated to God, but God is obligated to His people, with God's obligation to His nation coming first. The people who knew that in daily life each individual, and the congregation as a congregation, were liable to become distanced from the covenantal obligations and to sin against them, expressed their desire to return to God by keeping the commandments of His Torah—so that God would return to them and help them succeed in their path. *Teshuvah* and renewal of the covenant meant the same: if we return to be for God what our forefathers were to God at the foot of Mount Sinai, God would renew His obligations and have our ways succeed as in earlier times. But the congregation also comes and reminds God of the absolute non-equivalence between Him and human beings. This non-equivalence first obligates God. God is to keep His obligations to the people as He did with the exodus from Egypt. In order for the suffering nation to overcome its disasters and despair, and be able to return to God, He is obligated to first advance His salvation and bring the people to Him, making it possible for the people to return.

This complex consideration of relations between the people and their God is indicative of the historical pattern that shaped the ceremony of Torah-reading in the synagogue. Earlier, we recalled the covenantal event that took place at the feet of Mt. Sinai -but regarding its significance for the history of covenantal renewal over the generations from then until now. It includes an entire series of convocations at great turning points in the nation's history when the covenant was ratified anew. All of them are brought to mind in the prayer ritual, whether directly in the performative act of reading the Torah or in the many allusions in the prayer texts themselves. First, let us return to the established mythological example, which historical events of renewal emulate. From the story in Exodus (chapters 19-24) we learn that after organizing the assembly according to Jethro's advice, the nation was sanctified at the feet of the smoking mountain. Moses ascended the mountain, and then descended to warn the people a second time not to come too close to the demarcated line at the feet, because of the danger. Moses re-ascended the mountain, covered by a veil of smoke, clouds and with blinding lightning. God reveals Himself from behind the covering and by means of it. His voice breaks forth from above the smoking mountain, like a terrible *shofar* sound, frightening to the soul. The people feel the awe-imposing divine presence, but they cannot understand the message concealed in the awesome voice. Only Moses understands, and he translates for the nation in his own voice. The Ten Commandments, the fundamental precepts of the covenant subsequently made among the children of Israel, and between them and God, are heard from Moses's lips. As testimony to the making of the covenant, the commandments are engraved into stone tablets. Moses is entrusted with placing them in the Ark of Testimony in the Tabernacle, which the entire assembly of Israel is commanded to erect through its contributions.

The Ceremony of the Covenant on Mount Sinai

The event of God's revelation on the mountain was introductory, and the covenant itself was yet not enacted. The people were terrified, frightened, and could not bear the awesome voice. This made it impossible to enact the covenant, which was supposed to testify to voluntary commitment by free men, and be annulled were any sort of coercion to be involved. The people asked Moses alone to represent them before the God who revealed Himself on the mountain, and then returned to the encampment—which was at a distance. Moses, who expected this mode of action, remained alone before God uphill. First, he was commanded to build an altar of stone at the foot of the mountain under the open sky, around which the covenant would be enacted. For the same purpose, he received ritual and civil laws, which the people would need for their governance after enacting the covenant, for the length of the journey to inherit the land of Canaan. Moses wrote these laws on a scroll and came down so the people could conduct the ceremony of the covenant and participate without feeling threatened. The ceremony began by having the youth of Israel, the firstborn of all the nation's families, erect the altar at the foot of the mountain. This detail has a political meaning, and it calls for explanation. Moses was sent by God's command to establish an administration of free men, as substantively distinct from the idolatrous, tyrannical regime of Egypt. Remember, in Egypt the priests were a special class, with administrative authority based upon inherited great economic power. The ordinance of the Torah of Moses annulled such status and added, by way of contrast, that priests would not constitute a class with power that did not come from the people. As such, the priests became flesh of the flesh of the people, and they would represent the people according to their will. The solution arrived at was the selection of all the nation's firstborn to be priests. The people contributed their firstborn as gifts to God (as Abraham contributed his firstborn Isaac, and Hannah her firstborn son Samuel to serve the nation as priests). It was only after the sin of the calf that members of the tribe of Levi were chosen to serve as priests instead of the firstborn, and this was a reward for their role in suppressing the nation's idolatrous revolt. But a symbolic representation was maintained by numbering the priests according to the number of firstborn of the nation at the exodus from Egypt, as well as through the commandment to redeem the firstborn (*pidyon haben*) before the priest (see Exodus 13:11–13). This symbolism is also evident in the stipulation that priests not own their land and property, and that their earnings and service would depend upon contributions of the people who served God through the priests.

In the ceremony of the covenant made at the feet of Mount Sinai, Moses raised the sacrifices upon the altar built by the youth of Israel. He proclaimed the laws, which had been put into writing on the mountain, to the attentive assembly now gathered around the altar. They answered in unison: "All that the Lord has spoken, we will faithfully do" (Exodus 24:7). Moses then collected the blood of the sacrifices in basins, and emptied it over the people on one side, and on the altar representing God on the other. This symbolism connected the nation with God, after the ceremony of enacting the covenant. It was performed by dismembering the sacrifices, to express the unity drawn from mutual obligations of free men (Exodus 24).

The ceremony of the covenant at Sinai concluded with a celebration, with meat from the sacrifices raised upon the altar. Moses and Aaron, Nadab and Abihu—the sons of Aaron—and seventy elders of Israel representing the assembly rose to eat a mandatory meal before God, as partners of His covenant. When the ceremony was over, Moses ascended the mountain to receive the Tablets of the Covenant and the plan for erecting the Tabernacle of Testimony as a sign of God's *Shekhinah* amid the nation, to lead it as its king, from contributions by the children of Israel.

The Ceremony of Renewing the Covenant in Anticipation of Entering the Land

The Tabernacle was built with contributions by the people, according to the plans presented by God to Moses on the mountain, and the ceremony of enacting the covenant was the first example of worshipping God in the Tabernacle and later in the Temple. When the people left for exile and the synagogue replaced the Temple, synagogue prayer emulated worship in the Tabernacle—which was perceived as a symbolic representation of Mount Sinai journeying with the people to their land. God guided the people in their path with a pillar of fire in front of them and a cloud behind. When they encamped, God observed them, overseeing their worship of Him; or He descended to the people in a cloud as He had descended upon Mount Sinai to speak with Moses and to continue to command him. The Tablets of Testimony, which Moses accepted on the mountain, were carried in the Holy Ark, which remained hidden behind a curtain in a room of the Tabernacle. The altar was erected in the courtyard, under heaven, from which God looked upon the world—the heavens articulating His glory without speaking words. Significantly, the affinity between the Tabernacle and synagogue is clearer than that between synagogue and Temple. When the Tabernacle was built, Moses met with God in front of the Ark of Testimony. The cloud descended upon the Tabernacle, as it had descended upon Mt. Sinai. The voice speaking to Moses was heard from behind the veil, as it was heard on Mount Sinai from behind the cloud that covered the "crevice of the rock." Moses received the instructions of God, wrote them on the scroll, and taught them to the nation in order to lead it on the path of Torah. The ceremony of the *aliyah* to the Torah, described above, emulates this symbolically—obviously, in different historical circumstances.

Sacrificial worship in the Tabernacle and the Temple, as said, maintained the covenant through ongoing renewal. When the people reached the final stations in the path of desert wandering, a need arose to renew the covenant itself—in order to adapt it to the era of the possession of the land of Canaan. The nation was required to take stock, draw lessons from its past experience, learn its duties, and anticipate the difficulties it would encounter in its war with Canaanite nations immersed in idolatry. The lesson of the peoples' failures in the desert sounded an alarm about the growing danger—whether that of opposition by Canaanite nations to Israel's possessing their land or that of idolatrous nations seducing the people to sin against God as they did—where God would withhold His help, the nation would fail, and the people, like the Canaanites, would ultimately be evicted from the land.

The transition in the nation's condition at the end of the campaign to settle may be summed up by three outstanding changes. First, the people who left Egypt and stood at the feet of Mount Sinai died in the desert. Only three remained to testify to the earlier event: Moses, Joshua ben Nun, and Caleb ben Jephunneh. A new generation arose, one educated in freedom. The fathers of this generation obligated themselves in its name, so that from the perspective of God the covenant made in the past remained firm and binding. God did not appear a second time to renew it. The ritualistic ceremony of enacting the covenant remained in force and did not change. At the same time, the young generation, which did not stand at the feet of Sinai, had the right and duty to accept the covenant as free men. Second, the time had come for Moses to relinquish his leadership, and for Joshua to assume leadership instead. Third, the phase of conquest and possession in the lands east of the Jordan was completed. The young generation proved that it was ready for its role—whether in terms of the strength of its spirit, or in terms of ability to fight and win. But the episode of seduction by the daughters of Moab proved that this generation was not immune when faced with the temptation of idolatrous worship.

The covenant ratified in the wilderness of Moab reflected these two perspectives regarding the nation's situation: The nation was free and prepared for war, and it was impossible to curb its desire to leave the desert for the land of settlement any longer. But Moses knew that it was impossible to ensure that the nation would not sin upon being victorious—as the Canaanites had sinned after they settled in their land. Moses prepared the ceremony of the covenant on the basis of a twofold recognition: he spoke to the people, as one addresses free men who are prepared to take responsibility for their lives. But he admonished and warned them about the serious dangers of idolatry, which lay in wait for them, and the bitter consequences they entailed. This was a desperate effort to avoid the sin and downfall which would result from the sin. Deep in his heart, Moses knew that the first settlement in Canaan would fail, and that only after the nation's return to God, and to its land after exile from it on account of its sin, would the time come for its successful settlement.

The first convocation for renewing the covenant took place in the wilderness of Moab, as we said. It is documented in the last book of the Pentateuch, the book of Deuteronomy—which in rabbinic language is called the *Mishneh Torah* ("second Torah," hence in Greek *deutero-nomos*). The book's innovation *vis a vis* the four preceding books is articulated by its name. It was designed "to repeat" (*leshanot* < *shnaim*, "two") the founding convocation of Sinai and also "to inculcate" (compare the word *Mishnah*, which designates the Oral Law learned by repetition) its content, so as to teach the basic eternal instructions of the Torah in depth, and, at the same time, to renew what needed to be renewed in order to apply the *mitzvot* of the Torah in conditions of settlement. We have before us an account of the event in which the second Torah was actually given. It extended and applied the first, and subsequently came to be called by the name "oral Torah."

The book of Deuteronomy is the book of the renewed and changed covenant. It documents Moses's status within his people in a form other than that of his standing at Sinai—not as a prophet but as a teacher who instructed his people orally, and as a scribe who then put what he taught into writing. At the climactic conclusion of the ceremony, Moses deposited the Torah—which had been created orally and placed into writing in the sight of the nation—into the Ark of the Covenant alongside the Tablets of the Covenant. He commanded the priests, Levites, and the nation's elders to study this Torah and teach the Torah's precepts in the changing conditions of the time. Only at the end of the book of Deuteronomy did Moses return to his initial role as a prophet standing next to God, above his people. He recited the poem *Ha'azinu* (Deuteronomy 32:1–43) and engraved it upon the people's hearts as a testimony and as a serious warning. As a teacher, Moses stood amid his people and spoke to them face to face—because teaching placed words upon the heart of the student to be internalized as a component of spiritual personality, flowing from love, not from fear. The teacher needed to be friendly, to understand and to persuade, to warn by coaxing and to make entreaties about the danger of sin and the temptation of idolatry out of concern for the welfare of the people and their well-being in their land. Towards this end, the nation needed to accept the Torah, as a living teaching, and to opt for it with the power of its choice for life and good. This is how the Torah is presented in the ceremony of *aliyah* to the Torah in the synagogue.

Moses's words began with bringing up the lessons of the past. He emphasized the importance of historical memory for the nation's existence, because memory contained the guarantee that the people would not forget their mission, would not deny their covenant, and would not lose their identity. This is the model adopted by prayer. We think about the many commemorations of the people's history—from Egyptian slavery to complete redemption in their land—which fill the *siddur*, especially on Sabbaths and holidays. Moses told those of the nation who did not stand at the foot of Sinai about the event of enacting the covenant, and how amazing it was. He emphasized that the commitment of their forefathers also applied to them. But he also saw the need to emphasize the difference between the first convocation at Sinai, whose eternality brought the nation out of the constraints of nature and necessitated that it be a one-time occurrence; and the second, historical convocation at Moab, where God did not appear, but was present to the nation through His Torah. Appropriately, Moses taught the Torah, which he had received in the past as prophet, teacher, and scribe, while the ratification of the covenant was expressed by the people's committing themselves to study and review the Torah and to internalize it, so that it should be active in the soul of each and express the identity of each in feeling, thoughts, and deeds—not only from external submission to the authority of the *mitzvot*. The *siddur* also fulfills that role, by means of instruction and ceremonial study.

The Command to "Gather the People": Renewing the Covenant over the Generations

As said, we are speaking of the second covenant, the one at Moab, which renewed the authority of the first covenant. The second covenant is also the first, in the sense of its being an applied covenant, directed to its time. In order to understand the meaning of this distinction we refer to the words with which Moses concluded the ceremony of ratifying the covenant, after selecting Joshua, after reading the book of Deuteronomy to the attentive nation, and after writing and presenting it to the Levites for deposit alongside the Ark of the Covenant for a testimony as eternal as the Tablets of the Covenant.

> And Moses instructed them, as follows: Every seventh year, the year set for remission, at the Feast of Booths, when all Israel comes to appear before the Lord your God in the place that He will choose, you shall read this Teaching aloud in the presence of all Israel. Gather the people—men, women, children, and the strangers in your communities—that they may hear and so learn to revere the Lord your God and to observe faithfully every word of this Teaching. Their children, too, who have not had the experience, shall hear and learn to revere the Lord your God as long as they live in the land that you are about to cross the Jordan to possess. (Deuteronomy 31:10–13)

The instruction included in these words is clear. Moses commanded those who followed his path to renew the covenantal event in every Sabbatical year with a "congregational" event. He did this in order to bring all generations of Israel into the covenant, not only by renewing the agreement and the commitment of "All that the Lord has spoken, we will faithfully do!" (Exodus 24:7), as is expressed through obedience to instructions by leaders and elders of the nation, but by in-depth study of the words of the Torah. In this way each individual of Israel—men, women, and children—would know, internalize, and conduct themselves according to the Torah in all their activities.

Was the instruction of this book, to renew the covenant at the proper time in each generation, carried out in Israel after the conquest of the land of Canaan? The accepted assumption of historical research is that the *mitzvah* of assembling the congregation came later, and was not implemented before the return to Zion in the days of Ezra and Nehemiah. Therefore, the inclusion of this commandment in the book of Deuteronomy was "oral Torah,"—put into writing after the days of Moses, when it became necessary. It was attributed to Moses, as the one who gave God's people the Torah, together with whatever flowed from it over the generations. There were, however, four additional ceremonial instances of renewing the covenant, recounted in the historical books of the Hebrew Bible in the generations from Joshua to Ezra and Nehemiah, responding to the needs of historical moments: (1) at the end of Joshua's days (Joshua 24); (2) at the end of Samuel's days (I Samuel 10) when the need to select a king over Israel with all nations became clear; (3) in the days of Josiah (II Kings 22), after the long period of the rule of kings who "did what was displeasing to the Lord" (I Kings 16:25); and finally (4) in the days of Ezra and Nehemiah upon the completion of the walls of Jerusalem, following internal and external troubles. These events were all connected and resembled one another. They also resembled the first event documented in *Mishneh Torah* (Deuteronomy) (the book of the Torah, which wholly fulfilled the role of a "book of the covenant" that also related to the needs of the time). But the final ceremony in the days of Ezra and Nehemiah had special importance in terms of influence on Jewish prayer. We will therefore describe it in detail.

The "Congregational" Event: Renewal of the Covenant in the Days of Ezra and Nehemiah

As in the last days of Joshua, Ezra and Nehemiah regarded the partly political achievement of building Jerusalem and the renewal of Temple worship as the conclusion of one era and the beginning of a new one. To be sure, the exile did not end. Exilic conditions also prevailed in the Land of Israel, and were more difficult than those in Babylon, because the kingdom of the House of David was not renewed. But the messianic "end" appeared near: the Temple worship in Jerusalem was renewed—again at the initiative of Cyrus, King of Persia, who was considered to be the ruler of the entire world he had succeeded in conquering. Corrective measures were urgently required for the coming times, with respect to the governance and leadership of the nation. As in the Moab wilderness, there was a need to renew the covenant, and to inculcate the lessons of Deuteronomy, in which innovations needed for the time had been collected, thereby closing this book as written Torah and laying it as a foundation for the oral Torah, collated for the sake of another era in the book of the *Mishnah*.

Below, we bring the description of the event in the book of Nehemiah.

> When the seventh month arrived—the Israelites being [settled] in their towns—the entire people assembled as one man in the square before the Water Gate, and they asked Ezra the scribe to bring the scroll of the Teaching of Moses with which the Lord had charged Israel. On the first day of the seventh month, Ezra the priest brought the Teaching before the congregation, men and women and all who could listen with understanding. He read from it, facing the square before the Water Gate, from the first light until midday, to the men and the women and those who could understand; the ears of all the people were given to the scroll of the Teaching.

> Ezra the scribe stood upon a wooden tower made for the purpose, and beside him stood Mattithiah, Shema, Anaiah, Uriah, Hilkiah, and Maaseiah at his right, and at his left Pedaiah, Mishael, Malchijah, Hashum, Hashbaddanah, Zechariah, Meshullam. Ezra opened the scroll in the sight of all the people, for he was above all the people; as he opened it, all the people stood up. Ezra blessed the Lord, the great God, and all the people answered, "*Amen, Amen,*" with hands upraised. Then they bowed their heads and prostrated themselves before the Lord with their faces to the ground. Jeshua, Bani, Sherebiah, Jamin, Akkub, Shabbethai, Hodiah, Maaseiah, Kelita, Azariah, Jozabad, Hanan, Pelaiah, and the Levites explained the Teaching to the people, while the people stood in their places. They read from the scroll of the Teaching of God, translating it and giving the sense; so they understood the reading. (Nehemiah 8:1–8)

What followed relates how the people cried and mourned when they heard the words of the Torah. They understood how many of its laws they neither knew nor observed. But Nehemiah, Ezra, and the Levites encouraged the people to celebrate the day with joy: "He further said to them, 'Go, eat choice foods and drink sweet drinks and send portions to whoever has nothing prepared, for the day is holy to our Lord. Do not be sad, for your rejoicing in the Lord is the source of your strength'" (Nehemiah 8:10). The next day all the householders, along with the priests and the Levites, gathered as one assembly to study Torah. This time they learned the *mitzvot* of Sukkot. After they observed the *mitzvah* of Sukkot as written in Deuteronomy (*Mishneh Torah*), they also observed the *mitzvah* of "assembling the congregation" as cited above. As Joshua had been appointed as a leader in the ceremony of teaching Torah to the people in the event described in Deuteronomy, the Assembled congregation in the days of Ezra and Nehemiah concluded with the ratification of the Covenant of the Pact around the new leadership. First, the younger scribes read a special prayer in writing, which appears to be a creation by Ezra the Scribe. The prayer, which paraphrases Moses's opening words in Deuteronomy, outlined the history of the covenants that God made with His people, from the days of Abraham to the present event, outlining the failed attempts to carry them out and citing the punishment for breaking a covenant. The people who gathered in the assembly heard this and repented. Their repentance was expressed in renewed commitment in terms of taking on those obligations that needed to be fulfilled at the time for renewing the Temple worship. The heads of the assembly and its elders signed the pact. Its content was as follows: your sons shall not marry foreign women; your daughters shall not marry foreign men; you are to obey the Sabbath properly, with regard to forbidden labor and activities dealing with the satisfying of earthly needs; you are to raise contributions to strengthen the Temple, and for orderly maintenance of Temple worship; you are to offer first fruits from year to year, and contribute all the tithes that are written in the Torah.

We now direct the reader's attention to the following: despite the renewal of the worship of God in the Temple from the first days until the arrival of the returning Jews to Jerusalem, gatherings of the people, ceremonies of study, and renewal of the past did not take place in the Temple. Rather outside it, in an area in front of the water gate. The organizational framework for carrying out these *mitzvot* was the assembly, which gathered in the area in front of the water gate. Ezra the Scribe brought the Torah, read it to the people, and explained it with the help of his select students. Ezra persuaded all members of the nation as they stood together, each and every one, to assume the Torah's *mitzvot* upon themselves. The area in which the ceremony took place provided the spatial framework. The people contributed a wooden tower for the ceremony, and Ezra stood upon it and led the people in reading. In effect, the square facing the water gate was transformed into a synagogue, adjoining the Temple and facing it.

Enacting the "Covenant of the Pact" was itself a fulfillment of a *mitzvah* of the Torah that Ezra had read aloud and explained. The fact that Ezra did not play the part in the ceremony that Moses had, is instructive. Ezra did not function as the executor of the covenant. This teaches us that the execution of the covenant had political significance, and, for that reason, its initiator was the minister Nehemiah, who at this time filled the role of Joshua at the side of Moses. The difference between the days of Moses and the days of Nehemiah was decisive. Nehemiah was not chosen by the people and was not chosen by God. He was an official of the Persian government, a lay individual but pious, representing the authority of the Persian king, who initiated the worship of the God of Heaven in the Temple on behalf of the united Persian government. The political significance of this fact is very clear. Renewal of Temple worship did not symbolize the renewal of the nation of Judah's earthly political independence. To the contrary, the Persian government insisted that there was to be no sign of renewing political independence in any of the convocations for worshipping God in the Temple, and insisted that everything would take place under its protection and in its name.

This testifies to the fact that those who returned to Zion remained in exile, even in their land. Entangled there in great difficulties, they complained about being "in great distress" at the opening ceremony in which the Covenant of the Pact was concluded. They felt exiled in their land under the rule of foreigners, while their situation in Babylon was much better, both economically and politically. These facts are key to understanding the content and character of the Covenant of the Pact. It was not a governmental pact, but a congregational one. It was enacted in something resembling a synagogue, and not in a Temple. The great similarity between the ceremony documented in the book of Nehemiah and the ceremony of *aliyah* to the Torah, as customary today, is derived from this. The latter ceremony fills the same role, whether from the symbolic perspective of representing the nation before God outside of the Temple, or the practical responsibilities necessary for proper observance of the *mitzvah* of the worship of God in the synagogue.

Directing Communal Life: From Theory to Practice

Finally, let us focus on the practical aspect of the ceremony of reading the Torah in the synagogue. Its societal importance is highlighted by its institutional role. The ceremony defines the position of each individual and family in the social system in terms of their respective status, obligations, and tasks. From this perspective, the ceremony of reading the Torah, which reconstructs the event of renewing the covenant, is a matter of presenting oneself for the census by assembling before the king who oversees the assembly. Or, in the words of the well-known *piyyut* recited on Rosh Hashanah and Yom Kippur: "As the shepherd seeks out his flock" (Ezekiel 34:12). The ceremony is understood as a sort of census in which each individual stands in his place, ready to fulfill his role and pass a test. In this way the formalism representing the hierarchy of the leadership, and its functioning on the symbolic level, acquires practical meaning in directing the general way of life in the community. The ceremony itself expresses this function insofar as the synagogue's *gabbai* (originally, treasurer or senior officer) sets in motion the machinery of responsibilities of each member of the congregation, according to his importance and ability to contribute to strengthening the synagogue, its activity, and the peace of the community—so that the community can fulfil its moral-spiritual mission.

The details are a matter of custom in the synagogues of various communities—and there is no need to include them in this discussion. The principle is common to all synagogues in all communities: the distribution of honors connected with the *aliyah* to reading the Torah, with the blessings said in the name of those having *aliyot*, are efficient mechanisms for inducing contributions on the one hand, and for demonstrating the authority of the spiritual and practical leadership on the other. The response of the community as an assembly to situations and events, which shape the personal life cycle of its sons and daughters, is annexed to these functions. These situations and events are understood as an inseparable portion of the life-texture which constitutes and develops the congregation: the recitation of the *Yizkor* prayer for Jewish martyrs who died in sanctification of the name; praying for the health or members of the congregation and their relatives; words of gratitude and praise for being rescued from various disasters; expression of gratitude for good deeds; and, finally, ceremonial and celebratory marking of rites of passage in the biographical journeys of members of the congregation: marriages, circumcisions, naming newborn daughters, entering under the yoke of *mitzvot*. The congregation regards all these instances not only as personal-familiar events that are important to the members, but events that are central to the community's experience. Through them, the congregation relates to its history and to the history of its people—and preserves the continuous memory of generations of inherited legacy. The congregation is built upon the formation of new families, the birth of children, their education, their maturation, and their beginning to assume responsibility for realizing the congregation's mission and taking responsibility for maintaining the congregation and its welfare. The moral and legal covenant, which establishes and maintains the congregation, is laden with existential meaning of neighborly and interpersonal relations, by means of the ceremonial and festive markers. This covenant comes to expression in the entire texture of relations that build the congregation on both secular and sacred levels.

2

Prayer as a Form of Primal Expression of the Human Soul

The Lord God formed man from the dust of the earth. He blew
into his nostrils the breath of life, and man became a living being.
(Genesis 2:7)

The permanent prayer of the *siddur* is a product of the exile, yet its materials
are drawn from all strata of the creative canon of the Jewish people, and above
all from the Hebrew Bible. As said above, the service to God that was originally
ordained by the written Torah focused on sacrifices, offerings, and libations.
The words that fall under the definition of prayer—the confessions, blessings,
praises—accompanied them and interpreted their meaning. More important
is the fact that personal prayer is documented in the narratives of the Bible, and
takes precedence over sacrifices as a direct expression of the relation between
the person, conscious of his created existence, and his creator, understood here
as his father and his king. Personal prayer documented in the Hebrew Bible
erupts from the person's heart in moments of crisis. Prayer is a direct outcry,
necessary and primary, and as such takes precedence over sacrifices—which
accompanied prayer in an effort to gain God's favor with deeds that He
commanded through His priests and prophets.

The origin of personal prayer as an existential gesture grows out of
awareness of a mutual existential *zikah* between the person and God. This
consciousness rests on an anthropological outlook particular to the Bible,
embodied in the biblical myth of creation, whose presence in the *siddur* is
most palpable. It is already referenced in the "Genesis" chapter of the *siddur*:
the morning blessings (*Birkhot Hashaḥar*) are recited when a person awakens
at dawn from sleep, to find the world before him as a renewed creation and
to find his soul within his body, ready to fulfill the day's responsibilities. As
with the act of creation, God again breathes soul-breath (*neshamah*) from His

spirit into the body of the person who was asleep and awakens him to a life of Torah and the labor bound up with it—by means of which he becomes uniquely human.

According to the myth of Genesis, the human being is similar in physical terms to all animals. Like them, his body is kneaded and shaped from the earth—which is permeated by the powers of primeval chaos. The human is unique in terms of his intellectual soul (*nefesh sikhlit*), which God breathes into him from His spirit. This is the deeper meaning of the description of the human being as created "in His image" (Genesis 1:27). The meaning of this definition of the mutual *zikah* between God and the human being calls for detail. The creation myth in Genesis distinguishes the body (the arrangement of fleshly organs by means of which the human being is nourished, grows, procreates, senses, feels, steps, and acts) from the soul (*nefesh*, the power of life that activates these organs within the body). The myth applies this distinction to all animals and even to plants. But it applies a different substance to the human soul, by virtue of which the body also stands erect on two feet, exalted so as to have a comprehensive view from on high, and by virtue of which his hands are enabled to produce artistic work, and his face takes on a joyful and glowing expression. From additional statements in the Bible, it emerges that for every creature, "the blood is the soul" (Deuteronomy 12:23). We learn from this that the true soul of animals is a material substance that comes from the earth, and that animals are moved by instinctual energy stored in the powers of the chaos, which preceded creation and from which the earth was created. Not so with the human being. The determination that "the blood is the soul" does apply to the human, but only in relation to life activities shared with animals. For the human body is not awakened to a life of consciousness before God breathes *nefesh* or *neshamah sikhlit* (intellectual soul) into it, the source for which is the spirit erupting out of the depths of the divine substance. Delving into the details of the creation story, we learn that by means of this spirit—which began to hover over the waters of chaos—God "created," "made," and "formed" the bones, substances, plants, and animals. He at first reflected upon them in His thought, but externalized them by means of their impression upon materials of chaos, as a supreme artist. And He granted life and existence to His creations, by themselves, separate from Him.

What is meant by the picturesque depiction of God's bending down to the inchoate human being, fashioned from the dust on the ground, stirring him into independent life, indeed to independent consciousness, by breathing the creative spirit (*ruaḥ*) into his nostrils to enable him to start breathing? The answer is hidden in the two words, *nefesh* and *neshamah*.

They are derived from the first movements of life, the inhalation (*neshimah*), drawing inwardly from the spirit outside (*ruaḥ*); and exhalation (*neshifah*), the outward emission of the spirit from within. By means of the exhalation of God's spirit, the human obtained the soul, and was awakened to exhale and after that to inhale, independently. With that, God granted the human being a degree of spiritual life, which is expressed in thought, will, and ability to act. By doing this, the human being becomes similar to God—which is the deeper meaning of the expression "in the image of God, He created him" (Genesis 1:27). To be precise about the meaning of "image" (*tzelem*), this expression does not attribute to the human being the same abilities as those of God's spirit. It only brings the human being near to God and comparable to God in terms of abilities that emulate those of God on an external level. The intellect, the will, and the creativity of the human being are secondary and based upon the first creation, which God created earlier. In other words, the human being knows how to shape substances, which God created, into likenesses and instruments, which the human conceives in his intellect. But the human being is not able to acquire independent life for them. The human beings' limited abilities make them into creators-cultivators of the life around them, to fit their needs. In this way they becomes the "rulers" of the earth. The human phenomenon symbolizes the deity to the sight of animals, who do not have the intellect to know the hidden essence beyond the created universe—as do human beings. To reemphasize, even in their role as rulers of the earth, human beings are not authorized, and are not able, to take the place of God. They are commanded to rule on God's behalf and according to His word. The goal of the rule granted to them by God is not, therefore, to satisfy physical needs, which are similar to those of the animals. Rather, it is to do God's will according to His commands—which are intended for the good of all His creatures. In other words: as rulers, the human beings are commanded to serve earthly creation for its benefit and for themselves within it. They are not to reign like some tyrannical, exploitative lords. Obviously, they have the ability to try to do so, and to take a stand of pseudo-authority during a certain era. With respect to the relationship between human beings and God, having been created in God's image, human beings become the only creatures whom God approaches to converse with them. They are capable of providing feedback of love, awe, and honor to God. Also, they can participate voluntarily, together with God, in completing creation to the extent God intended when He created it—albeit this activity is fraught with danger lest their divine-like qualities would incline them to revolt against God and undermine God's labors.

Prayer: Completing the Incomplete Creation

The inclination to sin and revolt established the phenomenon defined in the Hebrew Bible as "idolatry." The central idea in the monotheistic worldview comes from this: the one and only God, whose power directed for the good of the external entities that He created out of His benevolence was absolute, did not succeed in creating a perfect universe to suit His original idea. To be sure, He did succeed in creating the heavenly universe and establishing a perfect eternal kingdom for Himself. But the creations of the earthly universe did not achieve the level of perfection God intended. They were subject to the cycle of birth, development, decay, and death. The cause of this failure is not a deficiency of divine ability, which is in itself absolute, but rather the quality of the physical material taken from earth, which provides independent existence to the creatures, outside the plan of the creator. The powers of chaos, which preceded the creation of the earthly universe, were dark and blind; they came into conflict with one another and destroyed one another. They refused to accept any fixed form or fixed law—even though they yearned to come into being and to exist as independent entities identified as such. In creating the earth, God took it upon Himself to redeem the powers of chaos from the destructive evil latent in them. This was a mighty endeavor to impose the good rules, which shaped the perfect forms that arose in God's thought, upon the powers of chaos. But note: God's intention was for their good. He was not out to suppress the autonomy of those powers, but to provide them with instruments for expressing their latent positive power, and in this way redeem them by raising them to the good. This is a lengthy process. While possible to advance in the direction of perfection, it is doubtful that it would actually be achieved.

These matters clarify the quality of the existential relation between God and human beings—of which prayer is the reflective expression. God needs human beings to complete His work of creation. God emanated the human soul from His spirit. He did so for man to acquire self-conscious intellectual identity for himself, in which voluntary creative ability for improvement of self and surrounding creation (the earth, plants, animals) was latent. God was moved by the understanding, that if earthly creatures themselves participated in the effort to arise and conquer the evil which made them sin, the possibility would be created for material beings to rise to the level of perfection intended for them by God.

It follows that, despite the absolute difference between God and the human being, and despite the infinite distance between them, they needed one another in order to achieve their common goal. Despite the profound, absolute difference disclosed between God and the human being, there remained a measure of equality between independent personalities, who have established a covenant obligating them to each other in mutual responsibility, to realize a common goal. Hence the high status of the human being and the nearness to God—despite the human's being an earthly animal. Therefore, according to the myth of creation in the Bible, the status of the human being is higher than that of heavenly angels, for angels did not have their own will and did not create anything. Only about the humans is it said, that God loves them and is zealous for them. That is, God needs human love and their participation in His work.

With this, we return to prayer as a gesture that expresses and maintains the special relation of love between God and the human being. In the context of the anthropology of the book of Genesis, prayer is human feedback to God. While prayer is not mentioned in the myth of creation, the relation that underlies prayer is described with great clarity in its second chapter. It explains the ideational meaning of the *neshifah* (exhalation) of the spirit of God into the nostrils of the human being. When an animal exhales air (*ruaḥ*) from its lungs, this is only a material blowing. It makes sounds with which the animal can express feelings and physical desires. The animal cannot articulate words that express thought. When God exhales His spirit from Himself, He speaks. Speaking is the externalizing of thought and expression of desire, which go out from the desiring subject to realize his thought in acts. Let us recall that the entire process of creation documented in Genesis 1 is anchored in speech. God meditates over creation with His deep, absolute intellect. God commands creation with His utterances. The spirit of God, which externalizes His word, hovers over the face of the waters of chaos. The spirit "makes" the substances, over which God meditates. He disperses their ideas as seeds to fructify the waters of creation.

"And whatever the man called each living creature, that would be its name" (Genesis 2:19)

The human being was created in a unique way. Its description provides the ideational meaning of God's infusing the spirit of God into man. For the significance of spirit in the ideational sense is that God bestows on the inchoate body of the human being, the ability to speak, which includes the capacities of thought and will. The human being is made into a spiritual creation—a creation that speaks, reflects, wants, creates, and knows God as its creator and sovereign from the inner depth of its soul. Human beings are able to understand intellectually what God commands them, and what their mission is—and even how to respond to God with feedback expressing love, independent will, and yearning for good and well-being.

Based on this understanding of the exhalation of *neshamah* (soul-breath) into the human body, we should explain God's invitation to the human being to name God's creatures—which He created with His words. God invites the primal man to name himself and also his wife, who was created with him to be his helpmate. Calling himself and his wife, with a name expresses the self-consciousness of the primal man and of his wife as creatures who existed for their own sake and who were capable of reflecting upon themselves. Calling creatures of creation by name grants the human being a certain mastery. But here too it is appropriate to emphasize the limitation. Human beings are not made to rule over earthly creation. God does not provide them with the ability to create with speech, or with the ability to change the character of something created. The names, with which humans call substances and creatures, suit their attributes and rules of character, which are created by God. The name defines the independent substance of any creature—which is really also the name from the creature's own perspective. Therefore, by means of the name, or by means of having knowledge of the creature latent in its name, human beings can unlock the potential of each creature according to its inherent character, and achieve good or bad aims of interest to them. With regard to the subject of prayer, it is important to note here that the words of the prayer are also said with knowledge of the true name of God Himself, that of *Yod-Hay-Vav-Hay*— the name that reveals the special power through which God creates and leads creation. Only the prophet, to whom God Himself reveals His name and the way to pronounce it, is able to know God's name. The intention is to enable the prophet to call to God to hear and rescue him when in trouble. As we will see below, the worshipper makes use of this secret—which is handed down by the prophets. The worshipper knows God by His name; he calls to Him by His name. If he calls Him with all His soul and might, he will be answered.

Something essential emerges from this, which will help to understand the efficacy of prayer recited with proper intention (*kavanah*) and with knowledge. Human speech to animals, to other human beings, and to God has the power to shape reality. As stated, human speech does not create and cannot change the character of the created beings. But it does influence their will; it rules the relation of one to the other and to the person who knows the creatures for better or worse. From this comes importance of telling the truth and distancing oneself from the lie, in the teaching of the prophets. True speech establishes a truthful relation between a person and his fellow, between a person and his natural surroundings, and between a person and God. Lying speech creates bad and corrupt relations. It is clear from this that prayer, as feedback of speech from the human being to God, is profound wisdom with the ability to shape the relations between a person and God, his neighbor, and the world around him. Hence, prayer that uses proper terms with right intention has the power of actions. Something else may be learned from the narrative of the creation of the human being in Genesis 2: the ability to speak is a quality that God implanted in the human being at his creation. This ability is transmitted by heredity, from parent to progeny, but study and instruction are required to articulate and develop it. Distinct from the rest of creations in the world, man is a creature who requires education, direction, study, and experience, in order to develop the abilities and necessary attributes to fulfil his mission in creation. God plants a garden—a protected place where special conditions for growth and education prevail— in which humans are to settle and prepare for independence. Towards the same end, God assigns the human beings "to till it and tend it" (Genesis 2:15). Only after that does God have them face an educational test. It examines whether or not the human being had already achieved mastery over himself, so as to be able to rule in his garden and to confront the evil implanted in him and in his environment by himself. These understandings explain the goals and the obligations which emerge from the relation between God and the human being. God, the creator of humanity, is also its first educator. God directs the paths of all human beings, and teaches each of them the rules of life for becoming an independent person (*ish*), for bearing their own responsibilities, and for developing the desire to to help God in mending His world (*tikkun olam*) and the understanding of how to do that.

Prayer as an Instrument of a Human Being's Education

Prayer is a central instrument of the human being's lifelong educational process, and, as we will see below, educational achievement is the prime measure of prayer's effectiveness. We ask: can prayer change the situation of human beings in their society and the world? A positive response comes from understanding that prayer is self-education, which influences the behavior of the worshipper in all areas of his life. If a person prays with authentic knowledge of his desire to be good before God, the prayer bears fruit in realizing the beneficial mutual bond (*zikah*) between the worshipper and God, and draws God's blessing to the worshipper. In the same measure, prayer changes the worshipper into a blessing for his family, neighbors, and nation. By doing so, prayer exalts and improves his life. Two spiritual activities that manifest the two-way bond between God and the human being in the foundational dialogue between them have already been alluded to: prophecy and prayer—prophecy as the divine educator's instructing and commanding speech to the human being, and prayer as the response of the human being, who longs to carry out his mission and be worthy of wellbeing, to God.

To be sure, these two gestures, which depend upon and complement one another, are documented in narratives about the nation's patriarchs, teachers, and rulers. In the course of our discussion of permanent prayer we will present events of the prayer of the patriarchs and of Moses and the prophets that have been taken as necessary models of prayer. Concerning the subject of this chapter, let us recall the primary source that the *siddur* incorporates and from whose language it borrows means of expression. It is the book of Psalms, traditionally attributed to David, King of Israel, the pious poet. His personal prayer accompanied him throughout his wandering paths and all his struggles. But given prayer's priority as an expression of the human soul, we run into the basic problem that engaged those who fixed permanent prayers, their creators and editors. What is the efficacy of prayers that are not expressions of personal awakening in unique situations where people feel the need to turn to God, cry out to Him, and confess to Him? What is the efficacy of texts fixed by prayer-experts for recitation at regular times and in a regular order, to which the worshipper is to adapt, and through which the worshipper is to express his thought and feeling? It is clear that in order to achieve this, a person has to adapt his soul to prayers created by others, according to norms suited to their knowledge about what God wants a person to say, and even directed to what a person should say to be worthy of response. Is such prayer at all possible? Especially if intended for the entire public, and not just for expert worshippers who pray on behalf of the public?

This is a deep and difficult problem. On the legal level, it raises doubt as to whether the fixed prayers recited in the synagogue are a fitting substitute for sacrifices. That is, whether sacrifices and the prayers express the same gesture of service to God, and whether the same result can be expected. Sacrifice is a gift, which a person gives to God from the best of his property, and from the fruits of the ground which he works by the sweat of his brow, in gratitude for the benevolent love that God renders by creating the person, the earth, and its resources; and for the blessings of rain, dew, and other conditions for success. Were these to stop, creation would revert to nothingness and chaos. God the creator, who possesses the entire world, surely does not need the gifts themselves. While idolaters believe that idols also require necessities such as those which nourish human beings and are enjoyed by them, the one and only God of the Bible did not create the world to satisfy His own needs, but rather to express His benevolent love and to receive feedback and gratitude for, and acknowledgement of, His unqualified goodness. God commands human beings to sacrifice the best of their property and the fruit of the ground to Him, as an expression of their love and his readiness to give to the God who creates everything. In doing so, they become worthy to atone for their sins and to straighten the path for their own good, amid the totality of the creation that provides them sustenance. By doing so, they provide satisfaction to God; they find favor, they elevate desire, they atone for their sins, and renew God's desire to pour His blessings upon them.

To be sure, such a presentation needs to express love and good will. A presentation to God under force and pressure, out of fear, is not considered authentic, nor would it have influence for the good. In practice, however, there is objective value to the presentation of sacrifice. It establishes an order, which is itself correct and proper. Accordingly, it is not only possible that the presentation of sacrifices be commanded and the presentation defined according to established norms, but it is even necessary for it to be commanded so that the person may know what the good deed is that God desires, and how God's desire is fulfilled by the good deed—in a way that the deed is not derived from the human's egoistic requests. That is, the deed should be performed in the name of God and not for the sake of the worshipper expecting something good in return.

If so, it is not only possible but necessary to fix the times, nature, quality, quantity, and manner of sacrificial worship of God, as Moses was commanded on Mount Sinai. This is not so with prayer, where words are said that need to flow from the heart and to enter into the heart. Only when prayers are said from the heart so as to enter into the heart, do they carry the weight of a deed in which a person gives himself to God through commitment to His *mitzvot*. Is it therefore possible to replace sacrifice with prayer? More precisely, is it possible to replace regular sacrificial worship in the Tabernacle and Temple with regular prayer scheduled in the synagogue?

There is an ongoing controversy about this among scholars of oral Torah. Some scholars respond negatively, because authentic prayer partaking of sanctity has to erupt from the depths of the human soul; this depends upon an internal awakening—over which a person has no voluntary control. If we probe the depth of the opposing claim of the scholars who decide in favor of the obligation of regular prayer, we will argue that they do not differ as to the essence of that claim, but rather insist on the necessity of a substitute for permanent service of God. Also, the turn to the worship of God in the synagogue, gathering together and maintaining ceremonies properly, fell within the parameters of divine service in terms of observing God's *mitzvot* for its own sake—provided that the worshipper would strive to pray with an understanding of the words and in agreement that the words obligated him. From this, a distinction is deduced between automatic rote observance, which does not fulfill one's obligation, and intentional, mindful prayer, which is articulated through standard patterns of expressive behavior that can be learned by imitating model "prayer leaders": expressive body movements, proper recitation, melodies. In all these ways, the worshipper is able to stir his soul to the point of identifying it with the words recited as self-expression of the soul.

But this is a learned art. It necessitates original and innovative creativity as manifest in the open-ended process of the arrangement of the *siddur* and its formation. From this perspective, we have a literary creation before us that is exceptional, that preserves an established, solid foundation—but is never closed. It adapts itself continually to changing circumstances and conditions. It does so through interpretation on the one hand, and by addition and subtraction on the other, parallel to the development of the canonical creativity by the people of Israel over the generations through its written and oral Torah.

Who is the "I" Who Prays?

As said, permanent regular prayer is artistry anchored in deep sensibility. Understanding this sensibility requires further probing of the thought that authentic prayer flows from the stirring of the internal part of the worshipping soul, and that a person does not have voluntary control over his soul and its desires, any more than over the life processes of his body. For the soul, which emanates from God's spirit and, like the body, is shaped by God, has a life that is concealed from the sight of the human's intellectual "I." This life is anchored in an inner regularity of processes of the body and the soul's reflections. Only God knows them and only God rules them. The worshipper represents himself as "I" or as "we" before God as the original "You" and original "He." The "I" who worships is known to itself as a singular, actual being for whom there is no substitute. But who, essentially, is this "I"? Is it the body of the worshipper, known to him? The soul? The answer in the Bible, as in the *siddur*, is far from clear about the matter. In it inheres a great mystery, which is disclosed to God alone. We will see that, according to the Genesis myth, the "I" is born and renews itself in a reciprocal relation between the particular human body defined by the particular soul, which the body is appointed to serve, and the particular soul defined by the body, which the soul is appointed to serve by enlivening it. Consequently, the body constitutes the boundary to the "I," which knows itself beyond its physical activities, and the soul constitutes the boundary to the "I" which knows the body that serves it. This means that the intellectual "I" of the human being is an intellectual reflection on the encounter between the soul and the body. For only when they act as one do they define one another as two aspects of the same entity. This also means that there is an ongoing tension between the two entities, where they limit one another and strive to overcome and dominate one another. This is the true meaning of the struggle between the "good tendency" which comes from the soul, and the "evil tendency" which comes from the body, in the depths of the "I" and its identity. From this perspective, the role of prayer is to reinforce the good tendency and to atone for sins caused by the evil tendency.

This is the source of the paradox that prayer mediates. From the external perspective of an individual human being, looking at the mirror of creation, the distance between God and the human being appears to be infinite. How could the worshipper, as an ephemeral being, claim the ability to speak to the eternal God, and that God would pay attention? From the inner experience of the "I," the soul is joined to God, and God is intimately present to the soul—to the extent that nothing is hidden from God's sight. Hence, even if human beings cannot know God, they know with absolute certainty that God knows the human beings, sending them allusive dreams and true intuitions, and resting His holy spirit on them. If worshippers dare to pray to his God in the language of "I–Thou," it is because God turns to them and commands them in the same language.

It follows that prayer is created within the internal dialogue which takes place at a point of connection between God, who breathes His spirit into the human being, and the soul, which is separated from God's spirit upon entering the body. It is not the self-conscious "I," which utters the prayer. It uses the lips only for reciting the prayer. The "I" itself finds the prayer when it is playing musically by itself within the human soul, which is nourished from its hidden depths. These depths are bound to God as the source of the soul's inspiration. Before the "I" opens the lips to recite the poem, the "I" does not know the words it will recite. It is only when the "I" hears the words as it leaves the lips that it knows that it intended them—or more precisely, that the soul so intended them. Do the words that burst forth from the lips of the poet-worshipper belong only to the "I"? Or are they the words of God, as He opens the worshipper's lips and brings out from them the words of praise for God?

"O Lord, You have examined me and know me" (Psalms 139:1), David said, in one of the hymns of the Psalms into which he poured his soul, as an infant at its mother's breast, and unveiled the mystery of his poetic inspiration:

> O Lord, You have examined and know me.
> It is beyond my knowledge;
> It is a mystery; I cannot fathom it.
> Where can I escape from Your spirit?
> Where can I flee from Your presence?
> (Psalms 139:2–7)

We have before us, first of all, the power of the internal experience, explaining to nonbelievers the source of the worshipper's absolute certainty, not only that "there is a God," creator of the universe, its king and leader, but also that the hidden and awesome creator, who imposes fright when He reveals Himself in natural phenomena, relates with love to all His creations, small and large, and to each and every human being individually. Because of this, each human being is invited to turn to God, as a person to his neighbor, or son to the father who begat him, in the intimate language of "I–Thou."

For David, the reality and nearness of God are neither conjecture, intellectual deduction, nor faith in its epistemological sense—rather, an absolute certainty. It is impossible to doubt it, because it is impossible to separate from the reality of the relation experienced in the innermost part of the soul. Try to distance yourself, and you will find that distance and denial are impossible:

> If I ascend to heaven, You are there;
> If I descent to *Sheol*, You are there too.
> If I take wing with the dawn
> To come to rest on the western horizon,
> Even there Your hand will be guiding me,
> Your right hand will be holding me fast.
> If I say, "Surely darkness will conceal me,
> Night will provide me with cover,"
> Darkness is not dark for You;
> Night is as light as day;
> Darkness and light are the same.
> It was You who created my conscience;
> You fashioned me in my mother's womb.
> (Psalms 139:8–13)

David's prayer erupted from an internal experience. Its quality and substance cannot be described externally, and certainly not defined conceptually. The prayer can only be embodied verbally-musically and descriptively-symbolically, so that the reader who repeats and expresses its words as his own speech would thereby draw forth a soulful-physical movement, which rises as an emotional-conceptual wave. This is exactly the experience of prayer as it is occurring.

We will present in this connection the personal prayer that constitutes the first example of the psalm genre in the Hebrew Bible. This is the prayer of Hannah, standing before the Tent of Meeting before Eli the High Priest to pray for a son. She dedicated the son in advance to God so that he could officiate as a priest before God in the name of his people—thereby making her desire the desire of God, and the desire of God her desire:

> Now Hannah was praying in her heart; only her lips moved, but her voice could not be heard. So Eli thought she was drunk. Eli said to her, "How long will you make a drunken spectacle of yourself? Sober up!" And Hannah replied, "Oh no, my lord! I am a very unhappy woman. I have drunk no wine or other strong drink, but I have been pouring out my heart to the Lord."
> (I Samuel 1:13–15)

Eli the High Priest, present at the event, was attentive to Hannah's words. He knew from the words that her prayer was being answered: "'Then go in peace,' said Eli, 'and may the God of Israel grant you what you have asked of Him.'" (I Samuel 1:17). How did he know this? From his knowledge that a prayer, which was said as a pouring out of the soul, flowed from God who had awakened the prayer, for God had already made her will His will.

This is also the key to understanding the paradox of permanent prayer. If the person has truly internalized the prayer, it overcomes the infinite distance between God as creator and king of living things, and God as attentive to all creation in His world—as expressed in the psalm:

> Who is like the Lord our God,
> Who, enthroned on high,
> Sees what is below, in heaven and on earth?
> He raises the poor from the dust,
> Lifts up the needy from the refuse heap.
> (Psalms 113:5–6)

These words are based on the same biblical anthropology memorialized in the daily *Shaḥarit.*

Accordingly, by way of concluding, we introduce the first blessing of the morning, word for word:

My God,
> The soul You placed within me is pure.
> You created it, You formed it, You breathed it into me,
> And You guard it while it is within me.
> One day You will take it from me,
> And restore it to me in time to come.
> As long as the soul is within me,
> I will thank you,
> Lord my God and the God of my ancestors,
> Master of all works, Lord of all souls.
> Blessed are You, Lord,
> Who restores souls to lifeless bodies.
> (K:6, *Elohai, neshamah*)

This blessing is the mother of the several blessings following it, which accompany the worshipper's becoming acquainted anew with the progression of all the day's tasks, duties, and appointments.

3

Torah and Prayer: The Problem of Love and Sin in the Relations between God and the Human Being

Prayer from out of the Human's Self

As said, prayer is the human response to God's call to the human being, mediated by prophecy. The general call of God to Israel and to mankind is the Torah. Human beings are required to learn and perform the Torah's precepts, which maintain the bonds between the human being and God and the bonds between human beings. It follows that the essential response expected of human beings to God's call is to study Torah and perform its *mitzvot*. What does prayer add to this? As we will see below, the *siddur* also includes studying words of Torah with the intention of knowing them for their own sake and enacting them—but, in a ceremonial form expressing the substance of soulful commitment to study and to act. In other words, the response expressed by prayer implies an additional dimension of obligation beyond mere study. This dimension is the act whose intent is to express the soul-to-soul bonds, the emotional-intellectual gesture, in which the mutual existential bond between God and the human being is implicit: the feeling of honor; moral valuation; recognition of obligations; the embrace that discharges love.

This deepens what was said in the earlier chapter about God's expecting human beings to respond to God's command in a way other than that of angels who carry out God's word automatically. Angels, as said, do not have independent will. They act as God's emissaries, identifying totally with His will, which is impressed upon them. By contrast, God favors human beings with selfhood. Humans have their own intellect, knowledge, and will. They are also zealous about their independence. As will be seen below, they are liable to flaunt their independence before God, to be prideful of their achievements and to refuse God's command. From God's perspective, God expects human beings to respond to His love from out of their own selfhood and love, and from knowing that what is good in God's sight is also good from the human perspective. With this, a twofold obligation comes to expression: the obligation to keep God's command out of humility and the obligation to realize the independent identity emanated by God to the human being, through readiness to be a "helpmeet for him [God]" (Genesis 2:18). The combination of these two obligations is the paradoxical recognition that servitude to God is the highest level of human freedom—while revolt against God is, for human beings, enslavement to their egoistic inclinations, casting disaster upon them. That is, human beings realize their selfhood when they give to the world, to others, and to God from out of their creative productivity. In doing so, they emulate their creator and walk in God's path—but not when they seek to take for themselves anything they can get their hands on, from the world and from other human beings.

The Prophets—Translators of God's Word to the People

This general determination applies to all humans. It applies to a greater extent to the children of Israel, who accepted the Torah upon themselves as covenantal partners with each other and with God. It applies to an even greater extent to the prophets, especially to Moses, who is called "servant of God" by God and by himself in the Torah. Who is a servant? A person who commits himself to the work placed upon him by his master, as though he has no concern, opinion, or desire of his own. Ordinary people are liable to view prophets of this stature as an earthly sort of heavenly ministering angels, that is as emissaries charged with transmitting God's word to human beings as they hear it from God's mouth, without addition or subtraction, and accepting with love the misery and suffering bound up with fulfilling their task. For most humans, and even the children of Israel, would be inclined to hide themselves from the divine call, to avoid God's commands—and to view the prophets who remonstrate against them about this as their enemy.

Understanding the role of the prophet from their own perspective distinguishes them substantially from angels. Angels are not emissaries and do not know how to teach others. They resemble perfect mechanisms that carry out the will instilled in them by God. Moses and the prophets, by contrast, need to teach other human beings the words of Torah, which come directly from God's mouth and which ordinary people are incapable of learning by themselves, in a language they can understand—because the language of spiritual expression is beyond them. This means that prophets are favored with a superhuman attribute granted by God: to understand divine thoughts and desires concerning human beings, as God thinks and desires, with their human intellect, and to translate them into human language.

It is clear from this that the prophets do not transmit God's word itself. They transmit their understanding of His words out of fidelity to the truth revealed to them. The truth is comprehensive and absolute, objective and devoid of subjective bias, because the creator's knowledge of His creation, including that of the human being, is identical to what God creates with His thought and will. The possibility that a human being would understand divine thought with his human intellect is, accordingly, a matter which is inherently mysterious. Only God, who knows the secret of creation, knows the secret of disclosing what He knows to others. The prophets, including Moses who was the greatest of all, were not capable of knowing how God infused His truth into their intellect. The prophets knew only—and with absolute certainty— that they themselves did not think up this truth on their own; and that if the thought infused in them was directed by God Himself, they could not deviate from it. In this sense, it is possible to say that God imposed His word upon the prophets. On the other hand, in order to fulfill their mission, prophets were required to identify themselves with it willingly. With this, we return to the paradox of servitude to God, which liberates the prophets from all other servitude to which human beings are routinely inclined to submit—whether servitude to other humans, to physical inclination, or to the inclination of pride and egoistic self-isolation. This is servitude to absolute truth and justice—and not to the tyrannical egoism of some absolute ruler. It is, therefore, according to the prophets themselves, freedom of the highest level, a level emulating that of the God who would never lie and never disappoint—because lying and disappointing contradict His essence.

Freedom at this high level expressed itself in the exemplary behavior, which the prophets publicly manifested—whether as transmitters of God's words, or by enacting them (that is, as leaders who carried direct responsibility for their people's fate). Clearly, in order to do this they were required to exercise independent deliberation, and to use their human intellect to decide about the proper form for applying God's word and His *mitzvot* to earthly realities. As all humans, they understood this reality with the instruments of their knowledge and wisdom. Let us note that by assuming the yoke of the responsibility of leadership upon himself, the prophet stood before God—again, Moses is the exemplary illustration—mostly in agreement but sometimes in opposition. The opposition is manifested in the difference between the way in which God judged human deeds based upon His truth as the creator, and the way in which the prophet judged humans, keeping in mind the limits of human ability to pass the test of divine truth and justice—for which reason the prophet knew that he was unable to demand and to receive from human beings what God demanded and received from him.

The Prayer—Standing before God in Judgment

The dispute liable to be disclosed between God's command and the rationale of the leadership of the prophet is expressed in situations such as those where the prophet entered into judgment before God on the basis of His Torah laws. We note that this is the primary form of prayer as it appears in biblical narratives. The term *tefillah* (prayer) derives from *pelilim* (litigation). Its concern is standing before God to be judged for one's deeds—obviously, with the wish to emerge worthy of God's blessing that grants life and well-being. Most people who seek judgment before God know they have sinned, whether intentionally or unintentionally. They come for judgment, in order to confess their sins and be worthy of forgiveness and atonement—based upon their regret and God's compassion and consideration of their capacities on the one hand, and their promise to endeavor not to sin again on the other. This is the primary and essential concern of prayer: confession of sins, assuming responsibility for them, expressing regret, supplication, and the promise not to sin again. When it comes to prophets—the rare individuals who demonstrate lofty levels of overcoming the evil tendency that inclines toward sin—prayer assumes a reverse meaning: that of entering into judgment on the basis of the values of God's Torah, to protest against the decrees of God's judgment that He brought against His people according to the standards of His zeal for absolute truth and justice, without considering the limited abilities of people of flesh and blood. God created human beings as they are, and knows that He did not grant them the ability to adhere to His *mitzvot* all the time. Blame for human sins falls partly upon the God, who created humans without the ability to avoid sin absolutely. This obligates God to have a degree of compassion—especially when speaking of humans who have wittingly accepted His covenant. God is obligated to have a degree of compassion for them—not only from their perspective but from His own as well; from the perspective of His glory as the king who rules with truth and justice.

Moses entered into judgment with God with such protest, at least four times over the course of his life. The first time was when he prayed at the theophany of the burning bush. He prayed then for himself, with the understanding that God had placed him in a role that exceeded his human ability. Only in stages, and after extended negotiations, did Moses become convinced that his duty was absolute, that God selected him precisely because He knew that Moses alone was capable—and therefore, obligated—to bring His people out of Egyptian slavery to freedom. At the same time, Moses was convinced that he could trust in God as God trusted in him; and that God would be with him and intervene so that his mission would succeed (Exodus 3–4).

The second time that Moses entered into judgment with God was when he took it upon himself to continue the struggle with Pharaoh who stubbornly continued to enslave God's people and aggravated the conditions of their slavery instead of liberating them. The people, groaning under the misery of worsening slavery, blamed Moses. He vindicated his suffering people before God, and also received a response—that as the struggle with Pharaoh continued the people would no longer suffer, because of the plagues that God would inflict upon the Egyptians (Exodus 5).

The third time Moses stood for judgment before God, he was required to assume responsibility for leading the people after the sin of the golden calf. In this way, he could rescue them from the destructive anger of a zealous and vengeful God (Exodus 32).

The fourth time Moses stood for judgment before God, he received the two tablets and was required to lead the nation himself, according to the ordinances of the Torah. Moses was no longer solely a prophet who transmitted the ordinances in the name of God who reigned directly over the nation. Rather, like a human king, he filled the roles of judicial authority and political and military leadership by himself, according to the ordinances of Torah and by emulating the attributes of God's leadership—but also according to his understanding of the situation of his people and his own responsibility. The reason for this was that God recognized that the people were unable to adhere to responsibilities coming from His direct leadership. Only Moses, as the human leader representing God, could lead the people to their well-being. This consideration was also expressed symbolically with the tablets given to Moses to replace those that he smashed because of the sin of the calf. The tablets were no longer written by God Himself, but by Moses who heard them from God's lips (Exodus 33).

This fourth time, there was a far-reaching change in the relationship between God and His people, and also, necessarily, in the relation between

Moses and God on the one hand, and between Moses and the people on the other. If we probed the details in the narrative describing this change, we would be convinced that as God made His will the will of Moses, to the same extent Moses made his will that of God. As a consequence of this change in the status of Moses, the "Torah of God" was also called by his name, "the law of Moses my servant" (Malachi 3:22). From our perspective it is important to emphasize that the prayer, which Moses prayed in that hour of contending with God regarding his standing as leader and the fate of his people, became one of the basic models of prayer for inclusion in the *siddur*, especially for Yom Kippur.

These matters return us to in-depth inquiry into the problem of the relation between Torah, as the word of God, and prayer, as a response expressing the mutual relationship with God from the human perspective. We note that feeling the need to pray in the sense defined above—that of entering into judgment with God, whether in order to earn forgiveness and atonement, or in order to protest against divine judgment—testifies to a conflict within the human soul. This conflict necessarily changes into an internal conflict in the relationship of God to the human being—one in which, according to the rules of covenantal partners, mutual obligation unites them despite the absolute distance that separates them. The essential goal of prayer is thereby defined as an effort to reduce this emotional-intellectual conflict from both sides.

From the human perspective, this conflict is anchored in the exceptional creation of the human being as a physical animal whose soul is breathed into the body by God's spirit. We see that this composition creates a confrontation between the longing stamped in the depth of the human soul to respond to God out of love and identity, and the opposing longing stamped in it by the strength of the soul's tie to the body to preserve its distinct independent identity. The blessing, which emanates repeatedly from God's spirit into the human soul for it to blossom, resolves the conflict through the harmony of love. But the path to harmony imbued with love is one of suffering and hard work, marked by encounters with painful obstacles. The love resolves the conflict but does not remove it once and forever. In the cycles of human life, a need to resolve it is stirred over and over again. The two covenantal partners, bound together in love and struggle, are required to take part in the effort to resolve it—so that the human being succeeds in carrying out the human mission, and God can reward the human with His blessing.

What Is Love?

According to the view of the Torah, love from God's side is the desire to bring about the blossoming of the human being. This love is expressed in the descent of rain and dew, in the warmth and light of the sun, and in the wonders of nature, with which the human being is blessed along with the rest of animals. But the human being is blessed even more by the granting of the Torah, which aids the blossoming of the human spirit with creations of moral and legal wisdom and practical wisdom. Human love to God is the desire to be fructified by God and is expressed in the study of the wonders of creation and its powers on the one hand, and the study of Torah and keeping its *mitzvot* on the other. In the language of prayer, this understanding of the concept of love comes to expression in the hymn that opens the book of Psalms:

> Happy is the man who has not followed the counsel of the wicked,
> Or taken the path of sinners,
> Or joined the company of the insolent;
> Rather, the teaching of the Lord is his delight,
> And he studies that teaching day and night.
> He is like a tree planted beside streams of water,
> Which yields its fruit in season,
> Whose foliage never fades,
> And whatever it produces thrives.
> (Psalms 1:1–3)

Parallel to the love of the human being and God is the love between husband and wife. The husband's love is the desire to know his wife and to fructify her; and the wife's love is the longing to know her husband and to be fructified by him in order to give birth together to progeny in their image. This image emanates from the image of God, which is impressed within them. When we examine the love being realized between husband and wife, a conflict surfaces between longing to be helpmates to the other, and the libidinal urge to sin one against the other, against themselves, and against God through lustful domination, born entirely of egoism and cunning exploitation.

Love as Opposed to Lust: The Case of Adam and Eve

This sentence returns the reader to the creation myth of the book of Genesis, to the chapter describing the conflict between the longing of love and the urge to sin—the sin of the husband and wife against God on the one hand; and the sin of husband against wife on the other. The reference is obviously to the episode about the test that God set for Adam and his wife Eve, mother of all living, before the "tree of knowledge of good and evil," and before the seductive snake lying in wait for them at its foot.

God's love for Adam and his wife is expressed by the planting of a garden east of Eden and inviting the couple to enjoy all the fruits of the garden, including those of the "tree of life." We note that, in the language of prayer, the "tree of life" symbolizes Torah, as stated in the verse chanted at the conclusion of the ceremony of Torah reading: "It is a tree of life to those who grasp it, and those who uphold it are happy" (K:512, *Etz Ḥayyim*). Thus the wooden spindles around which the Torah scroll is rolled are called *atzei ḥayyim* ("trees of life"). God's love is also expressed in His instruction warning man and his wife against eating from the "tree of knowledge of good and evil," because the sin of death was tied to it. Nevertheless, it is clear that God set a test for the innocent couple—which they necessarily failed the first time, because they were able to understand the reason for the prohibition only after eating from the tree's fruit. Moreover, the warning before the test was more provocation than deterrent. From the dialogue with the cunning snake, symbolizing the mindset and evil inclination of the husband and wife, it appears that the warning provoked them to transgress the prohibition no less than did the enticing fruit. It is impossible to think that God, who planted the tree in His garden and also created the snake beneath the tree, did not know in advance the result of the trap that He effectively set for His beloved couple in creating the tree and the snake, and by warning Adam and Eve about them.

The story of the temptation in the Garden of Eden tells of a double conflict in God's relation to Adam and Eve, in their relation to God, and in Adam and Eve's relation to each other. In each case, it is a conflict between love and a sin that generates its opposite—hatred, jealousy, the fierce desire to punish and avenge—which takes place in the curse that befell the relations between the man and his wife and in the cursing of the land. We note: if love is the desire to fructify and be fructified, the curse of the couple and the land expresses the desire to uproot, to make desolate, to destroy, and to annihilate. This expresses death, with which God threatens the first couple: if they eat of the forbidden fruit, they will sin and bring this curse on themselves.

Why did the man and his wife go ahead and eat the fruit of the forbidden tree? It was pleasant to look at, it was provocative, and it promised intense sensuous enjoyment. But this is only the external part of the explanation, pointing to the human animal's disposition to greed and hedonism. As with all animals, humans crave things that satisfy the primary physical needs of life: eating, drinking, aromatic air, pleasant sounds, and sexual intercourse. But more than with other animals, who are not endowed with intellectual understanding, the satisfaction of human needs of vital bodily functions does not satisfy the yearning for enjoyment. This yearning changes from a mere means to a supreme need-in-itself, which enslaves the soul. In the end, this higher need damages the health of the body, which is exploited by the yearning. Everything that appears "pleasant" (promising sensible enjoyment) draws the human to enjoy it—even before one examines whether it is really needed or useful, or possibly injurious. This is the basic meaning of "knowledge of good and evil" learned by experience. It is only after the activity takes place that it becomes clear that something which appeared outwardly enticing was in truth inwardly evil—whether in terms of physical health or in terms of moral-psychic wholeness. The couple's sensuous giddiness, which came after tasting the intoxicating fruit, opened their eyes to see that they were naked. The delicate hint included in this symbolic expression is sufficiently clear. The couple that used to stride naked in the garden perceived the hidden, guileful meaning of their nudity. They revealed their sexuality and the wonderful sensuous enjoyment to be derived from it. Their craving was inflamed. They ravished one another in an endeavor to use one another sexually in order to intensify their egoistic pleasure—and not out of a desire to fructify one another in the manner of lovers. They understood immediately that they had sinned against each other. For they had betrayed their duty to be a helpmate to one another. From all this—from the shame that befell them on account of the nudity that lay bare their disgrace; from the blame they cast upon one another and upon the snake who revealed only what was on their mind; and from what is narrated in what followed—we learn that only after the sin and punishment, after putting on clothes and covering their snake-like nakedness, did Adam and his wife "know" each other as a loving couple and beget children in their image and likeness.

"Desirable as a source of wisdom" (Genesis 3:6)—The Delight of Knowing Good and Evil

The temptation of sensuous pleasure is the first half of the explanation. But let us complete the dialogue with the cunning snake lying in wait at the foot of the tree. It teaches why God's warning had the opposite effect on Adam and his wife than was intended. In this connection, it is notable that beside the fact that the fruit appeared "to be good for eating" and "a delight to the eyes," it also appeared to the wife to be "desirable as a source of wisdom." The expression's intention is explained by the words of the snake, which expressed in an amplified voice the suppressed reflections of the wife and husband. "Behold

God seeks to prevent them from tasting the fruit of the tree, which appears more attractive than any other fruits of trees in the garden—both to the sense and to the intellect! God does so to prevent them from having the knowledge to distinguish between good and evil by themselves—God kept that for Himself, so that His advantage would require them to obey and serve Him."

There is a double irony hidden in the serpentine reasoning. In hearing the words of the cunning snake, it seems to the innocent couple that, in fact, the snake already knew how to distinguish between the good, apparent in the fruit of the tree, and the evil expressed in the divine prohibition. The reader already knows that this thought attests to its opposite, because it is based on error. It is clear from this that God's warning, which rested "innocently" on that erroneous assumption—that the innocent couple knew how to distinguish between the good of keeping God's command and the evil of the path of capricious physical yearning—was therefore designed to teach the innocent couple how to distinguish between good and evil. But they could learn about this only through the trial, by being enticed to violate the prohibition, and concluding that the illusion of the physical senses did not suffice, and that humans required wisdom and knowledge, the source for which was God's Torah and not their own sensuous experiences.

What then, moved the couple to violate the prohibition? Why were they tempted to think that God's warning was to their detriment? The simple answer is the suspicion in their hearts that God sought to rule over them capriciously and to suppress their independence. Clearly, the source of this suspicion was psychological and physical. The deep source was the desire of the couple, created in God's image, to realize their distinctive independence completely; to stand totally under their own authority; to bring to bear all their physical and spiritual abilities, and to enjoy them by themselves and without sharing their pleasure with others. This is what they wanted to acquire by means of their being "like divine beings who know good and bad" (Genesis 3:5). This means that sin did not come solely from the natural inclination to satisfy bodily pleasures, but rather principally from the urge for psychological independence. God also implanted this urge in the human being, as He implanted the physical "evil inclination" for human use. But God made the proper realization of these drives dependent upon the love, which fructified and was fructified, which emanated and provided, which expressed selfhood by means of the creativity latent in it. Importantly, this love could not act by means of utilitarian egoism, which sought to take everything for itself; which gave only to get more; and which exploited and destroyed everything around it—in the end, the egoistic self itself.

As the scriptural narrative continues, we learn the following: the impulse of the human self to yearn for divine absoluteness, expressed by craving for control, utility, and sensual pleasure for its own sake as the highest expression of well-being, is the source of sinful idolatry. It dominates human civilization with hubris, which maintains that we should not be satisfied with the status of being created in God's image, but be like God and rule instead of Him (the Tower of Babel narrative). Idolatry is a complaint against loving the fecund and fructifying God which is expressed in the Torah that teaches human beings the laws of life: to work the soil; fructify it as in the Garden of Eden; live upon it in justice and in peace for the benefit of all humans, animals, and earthly creatures. As the scriptural narrative continues, God responds to the spread of idolatry that dominated humanity by enacting the covenant with the patriarchs, who chose to keep faith with Him in love. In God's covenant with the patriarchs, God obligated Himself to raise a people for Himself from their seed, who would serve Him and testify to His sovereignty until the time would come for it to be revealed on earth for all to see. Until then, the conflict between Israel and the nations would continue and intensify. Against this background, the conflict would also continue within the nation of Israel, when the pseudo-success of idolatrous nations—compared with Israel's suffering—tempted the people of Israel to fall into the sin of idolatry like all the others.

The prayer that has entered into the *siddur* expresses the struggle of God's exiled nation with its mission. Like all human beings, its members struggle with the inclinations that lead them to sin; but as members of the chosen nation, they also struggle with the suffering bound up with fulfilling its mission. Because of this, the people are thrown between two attractive forces. The first consists of God's love for them and their love for God, which are expressed on the one hand by the granting of Torah; and on the other by studying it and keeping its *mitzvot*. And the second of their longing for earthly well-being like all humans and peoples, which they indeed deserve as all humans, but which leads them to sin as it does with all humans. In the Jewish prayer book, the divine call for love and Israel's response of love is represented in the *Keriyat Shema* and its blessings. The *Shemoneh Esrei* prayer represents standing for judgment before God for a life of well-being and honor, but cleansed of sin. These are the two major axes, around which the world of prayer revolves from day to day and through the whole variety of Sabbath, holidays, and festivals.

4

The "Name and Kingship" Blessing as the Fundamental Rubric of Standing before God in Prayer

Awakening for Prayer and the Gestures Accompanying It: Standing Up and Bowing

The conceptual definition of prayer is the turn to God out of awakening on the part of the worshipper. This means self-awakening, even when moved by God's *mitzvah* to pray to Him daily at set times and in a set manner. In its all-embracing legal code, the Mosaic Torah distinguishes between *ḥukkim* (ordinances, rulings) and *mitzvot*. *Ḥukkim* are performative duties, prohibitions, and principles of behavior imposed upon all humans equally by authority of the community's legitimate government. The practical meaning is that the established legal system of the community imposes *ḥukkim* on its individuals, and takes no consideration of opposition for any reason. *Mitzvot*, by contrast, are not imposed by the community, because their goal is not achievable unless they are kept voluntarily and they bring about feelings of awe, love, and desire to do good in the eyes of God and the human being. Prayer to God is not a *ḥok*, but a *mitzvah* to be kept for its own sake, in order to express awe for the glory of the creator and the love of the creature for Him.

Self-awakening is the expression of the need for relation with another. As such a need, prayer is instilled with the expectation of response. But its primary goal is attained by externalizing feelings that articulate the bond to God with symbolic gestures, speech, and singing. It is our opinion that these expressions, especially the symbolic gestures, articulate the prototypal need that gives birth to prayer: the need to feel loving closeness to God; to be privileged with His illuminating presence. The response to this prototypal need is the relation that is realized in the articulation of prayer—which represents the physical-psychological personality coming together, as in the verse "all my bones shall say" (Psalms 35:10). The reference is, first of all, to the gesture of rising to stand before the lofty and sublime God, in an expression of respectful closeness. To understand the meaning of this gesture, let us remember that standing erect is the primary expression with which the human infant manifests the spark of consciousness that sets it apart from the animals around it—as a creature created "in His image, in the image of God" (Genesis 1:27). The infant imitates the adults around it, standing erect on both its legs, extending its full height above the ground, looking straight forward and up, freeing its hands for expression and creative tool-making, and expressing joy over its great achievement with a beaming smile. When the adult who is conscious of the human advantage over animals wants to turn to the *Anokhi* ("I am") who is higher than all humans, more so than humans are higher than the animals—for it is He who has conferred on humans their uniqueness and superiority—he does so by standing, an act laden with symbolic meaning, and then by bowing forward. Bowing is a symbolic gesture with double meaning. It begins with standing erect, which projects self-value and the respect man demands for himself from the creatures around him. Then, by bowing back toward the ground, it shows humility before God, who is higher than the human being and emanates His glory to the human being. Standing, which is ascending towards the *Anokhi*, the highest authority, is a step of coming close in order to negotiate with Him and express love for Him. Bowing is a gesture of distance, which expresses awe for the glory. They are two opposing gestures, but complementary rather than contradictory.

The Name

The gestures of standing and bowing express a person's relation to God as king and father. Regarding this, let us look into the meaning of the name *Elohim*. In terms of etymology, it is derived from EIL (איל), a root meaning overwhelming power. The name *Elohim* expresses the understanding that the divine "I am" (*Anokhi*), which it signifies, is the single bearer of sovereign power who has overcome chaos and darkness, who has created and renews the creation of creatures, establishes laws, who judges and rules. The name *Elohim* was given to *Anokhi*, the creator, by the human beings. Human beings discover the name *Elohim*, which discloses expressions of the sovereign power, by observing the environment of which humans are a part and upon which their life depends. Human beings discern the activity of many different powers around them, which appear at first to be competing with, and confronting, one another. But after that, discerning people discover the wisdom hidden in the wondrous harmony, which unifies the multiplicity and differences and transforms them into a totality. Then they understand that all environmental powers fulfill the many missions of the one ruling *Anokhi*, the divine "I" who has created the totality and renews it with the cycle of birth, maturing, old age, and death, which cycle eternalizes the unity of the totality, generation after generation. This is how human beings invented the name *Elohim*. It points to the unity that activates the many powers of nature towards the same eternal goal of overcoming death and evil with life and goodness.

The worshipper who calls to the divine "I" (*Anokhi*) and unites the many powers of nature by the name *Elohim*, expresses amazement at the wisdom revealed in the natural order; recognition of human dependence on the natural order; and gratitude to the divine "I" who controls the granting of human life and well-being. With regard to our subject of prayer: it is important to emphasize that the divine "I" does not identify Himself with the name *Elohim* when turning, for His part, to humans with whom He wants to establish a relation— requiring them to do His will and provide Him with feedback of gratitude for His benevolence.

Understanding the meaning of the name *Elohim* explains the full significance of the description of the human being as a creature created in the image of God, while emphasizing the absolute difference between creator and creature. "*Elohim*," Maimonides said, was a "homonymous word" (*Guide of the Perplexed*, I, 2)—a word that applied to different objects that shared a defined similarity to which the homonym pointed. When we say the name *Elohim* we refer to legislative function, judgment, and governance, as attributes that identify the divine "I," who is called by that name from the perspective of humans under His authority. In the continuation of his discourse, Maimonides showed that the Bible also called angels, judges, and human rulers by the name *Elohim*. The name *Elohim* was thus an adjective common to all those with legal authority. Thus, it is possible to say that the human being is created "in the image of *Elohim*" ("You will be like divine beings who know good and bad," Genesis 3:5)—without attributing the divine essence to humans.

But is the name sufficient for the needs of prayer? Prayer is the stance of the human worshipper before the divine "I" who rules the human—out of a self-awakening where the worshipper seeks to feel the divine person Himself apart from His functions. The worshipper also seeks to influence God's judgment.

But above all, the goal is to form a substantial relationship between the human being and God, despite the absolute differences between the level of the divine "I" and the human "I." How can a mortal creature, who knows that a human is absolutely nothing when compared to God, create an interpersonal bond with God and speak to Him in the "I–Thou" language—the language in which God has breathed His spirit into the amorphous mass of the human body and infused it with life? Clearly, such a relation becomes possible only if it is the sovereign will of God Himself. It needs to be preceded by a turning of God to the human being, expressing this will and inviting the human to a personal meeting. In other words, the possibility of prayer depends upon the turning of God to the person whose prayer God desires; whom God permits to turn to Him, and to whom God will transmit the name by which He identifies Himself when He turns to the creatures who know Him.

This is, then, the problem that the image of turning to the divine "I," the creator, "mentioning the Name and the kingship of God" (*beshem ubemalkhut*) comes to resolve. Let us return to the extensive theological discussion in the Bible and rabbinic literature, which is also reflected in the *siddur*: God appears to humans who know Him, and who attribute to Him many different and sacred names. In the *siddur*, this theology is epitomized in clearest form in the philosophical poem, the Song of Glory (*Shir Hakavod*), which we customarily sing at the end of the *Musaf* prayer of the Sabbath morning service to express gratitude for the elevation of the spirt of the worshippers who are concluding the service: "I will sing sweet psalms and I will weave songs, to You for whom my soul longs" (K:570, *Ane'im Zemirot*). According to this poem, God appeared to those who loved Him with many descriptive terms, in keeping with the variety of situations that awaken human beings to pray.

The images appropriate to the various situations are as inexhaustible as the multiplicity of the situations themselves. The prophets, and the liturgical poets who followed their example, enriched the treasury of these similes from renewed life experiences. By means of these experiences, the feeling of intimacy and trust of the worshippers—who needed to place in their sight the appearance of the personality to whom they turned to glorify, praise, seek out, and thank—is stirred and expressed.

However, as we saw above, there is not enough in these similitudes for prayer which is a matter of standing for judgment before God and His people. For the sake of prayer, the nation's ancestors, prophets, priests, bards, scholars, and liturgical poets established standard descriptive names representing different aspects of the manifestation of God as king and father. The most widespread appellation is *Elohim*, to which the descriptive names *Adonai* (Lord) and *Shaddai* (Almighty) were added in the Hebrew Bible. But these, too, conveyed the impression of the manifestation of the divine "I" who created and commanded in the presence of humans, by means of the sights of creation and events of history, so that they too were insufficient to identify the divine "I" Himself. The only name that identified Him essentially and uniquely was the name by which He represented Himself to the prophets, priests, and Torah sages, and through them to all the people—by which they become "knowers of His name" (*yod'ei shemo*), people worthy to turn to Him in the language of "I–Thou." The reference is to the name written with the letters *Yod-Hay-Vav-Hay*. It is explained in the sentence that simultaneously reveals and conceals, in the event of the burning bush which is not consumed: *Ehyeh-Asher-Ehyeh* (Exodus 3:14).

This takes us back, beyond the narrative of Moses's revelation, to the narrative of creation—in particular to the occasion of Adam's being asked to name the creatures created by God. From this narrative we learn about the relationship of identity assumed in the Bible between the substance of entities and the name that signifies the singular quality of each entity. Based upon this assumption of identity, "knowers of the [true] name" of the entity identified by the name can relate to its identity. When it is a living creature, they can bring it into a relationship with them by using the sound that calls it by name.

Human beings experience this when they call one another by each other's true name—that is, the name with which the person identifies. It is the name given to the person by the parents who gave birth to him in the presence of God who breathed His spirit into him—and therefore the person identifies with it. Therefore, whenever a person hears his name from out of the lips of another, the person turns his head, identifies himself before the one calling him, and pays attention to the caller's words. In this way, conversation develops between individuals who know each other's names. The true divine name functions similarly—the name by which the divine "I" identifies Himself when He turns directly to the persons whom He wants to bring close to Him and to command. Obviously, there is an essential difference between the treatment of the name that identifies the divine "I" Himself and the treatment of names that identify human persons. The difference is expressed thusly: Even after the name of the divine *Anokhi* is transmitted to the prophet, and after the prophet transmits the name to his people, chosen to serve God, the name remains a secret in terms of the form of its pronunciation and its deeper meaning. Only the external, general, and vague meaning of the name is expressed in the combination of the letters *Yod-Hay-Vav-Hay*. It is the absolute "existent" (*hoveh*), the "I" that is the source of all existence (*havayah*)—the nature of which human beings are not able to grasp. The internality of the name, which is the correct form of its pronunciation and the symbolic meaning inherent to the name, thereby remains hidden to ordinary human beings. It is clear that even the prophets and high priests, who knew how to pronounce the name and to relate to its symbolism, were unable to know and to understand how this name influenced God Himself, when He responded (or refused to respond) to the turning by "knowers of His name."

This depth of knowing the name of the divine *Anokhi* is explained in the narrative of God's revelation to Moses at the event of the burning bush that was not consumed. The Israelites who were able to turn to Him in prayer did not know—and therefore were not privileged –to pronounce His name aloud. They read the combination of letters they saw and directed their feelings to Him. But their lips pronounced only one of the combination's abbreviations (*Yod-Hay*; *Yod-Hay-Vav*; *Yod-Yod*) or they absorbed it into one of His standard descriptive appellations (*Elohim, Adonai*). Only the prophets and the high priest knew and were privileged to sound the name aloud, at an appropriate event and in a proper form as commanded to them in the Torah.

The *siddur*'s formula *Barukh atah adonai* ("Blessed are You, [*the divine Name*]") is its way of turning to the divine "I" addressed as "You." This is part of the formula referred to as *beshem ubemalkhut* ("with Name and kingship"). This is the legal version established based on God's words to Moses at the same awesome event.

> Moses said to God, "When I come to the Israelites and say to them, "The God of your fathers has sent me to you," and they ask me, "What is His name?" What shall I say to them?" And God said to Moses, "*Ehyeh-Asher-Ehyeh*." He continued, "Thus shall you say to the Israelites, '*Ehyeh* sent me to you.'" And God said further to Moses, "Thus shall you speak to the Israelites: The Lord, the God of your fathers, the God of Abraham, the God of Isaac, and the God of Jacob, has sent me to you:
>
> This shall be My name forever,
> This My appellation for all eternity.
> (Exodus 3:13–15)

The last words in this passage are the prophetic prooftext that God wanted the children of Israel to pray to Him with the name *Ehyeh*. God promised that when they turned to Him with this name and with feelings of sanctity and purity and with refined thought, He would turn "His face" to them and bless them.

These words clarify the opening text of the turning to God in the *siddur*. The opening is permanently fixed, and the continuation varies only in terms of the specific topics about which we pray. The general form is a blessing, opening with a direct turning to God Himself by the proper name that identifies Him, and adding the descriptive appellations *Elohim* (God) and *Melekh* (king): "Blessed are You, Lord our God, King of the Universe" (K:506, *Barukh atah adonai*). The following text, which has different versions, is either a reference to a *mitzvah*, which the worshipper is about to perform so that God will respond to him, or reference to one of God's works or activities for the benefit of all the creatures he created, for the benefit of all human beings, for the nation of Israel, and for a certain community or a certain person who prayed to Him.

The Blessing

The subject that remains to be clarified is the preference for the form of the blessing as a formula for turning to God—for this preference should be at first sight be very surprising. The worshipper comes to ask for a blessing by God, but stands up and proceeds to bless God, as if a created creature could bestow a blessing on its creator! It would be easy to argue that preference for the form of the blessing for turning to God in the *siddur* (as distinct from the formulas of prayer in the Bible) flowed from the need to change worship of God with sacrifices and offerings into synagogal prayer. According to the rationale for worshipping God, the human being is required to give God some of himself, of his property, from the abundance of blessings that God has bestowed on him; to express the commitment making him worthy of the blessing that God would continue to bestow on him in the future. This is the general assumption: when the human being sought to receive something from another human being—from the king, ministers, parents, and neighbors—he stirred their good will towards him with a gift of himself or from the best of his property. By doing so, he demonstrated recognition of the duty and the good, and his deserving of grace. It is clear from this that when he was required to change the sacrifices into words, he had to find a gift that expressed itself in words—and this was the blessing.

What then, is the blessing? This question also returns the reader to the chapters about creation in the book of Genesis. God created all creatures. After

He tested them and found that they were good, He blessed them with the blessing to live by their own power. This is manifest in their ability to be fruitful and multiply—that is, the ability to grant the gift of life, and the qualities that maintain life, to their progeny. The blessing's content, as such, is the gift of life and the qualities of life, which are unique to each species among creation. This gift of the creator will continue to be possessed by the species. The species will be able to transmit the gift to its progeny, as long as the progeny will continue to endeavor to be good and worthy in the sight of God.

The blessing delegated to human beings is of course unique. It singles them out from among all creatures of the earth as the one creature made "in the image of God." This blessing is expressed not only by the spiritual qualities unique to the human beings, but also by their abilities—to derive from the earth and all its creatures the abundant fecundity that is latent in them, and to benefit the earth and all its creatures by increasing their fecundity. This blessing dwells upon human beings and maintains them at this special level. Their true happiness, which is expressed in their contribution to the world and to the God who loves His world, depends upon this blessing. Therefore, it is renewed as recompense for human effort to walk in the path of God and bestow blessing upon the world. Beyond this, the person who is good in the eyes of God is worthy to bequeath to his descendants the blessing he inherited and expanded through good deeds, as inheritance and legacy. This is the secret of the blessing with which the forefathers blessed their descendants, when their time came "to be gathered to their kin" (lehe'aesef el avotehem, see Genesis 25:17 et al.). Their children kneeled before them with an expression of readiness to continue their mission. They placed their hand on the head of their children and transmitted the blessing to them—which their children earned through a prayer to God, the source of the blessing—for them to keep among their descendants; each one according to his worthiness. As such, the blessing is maintained by the descendants as long as they make the effort to be good and to be worthy thereof.

According to the narrative of the book of Genesis, after the flood Noah earned the blessing that was given to Adam. Noah bequeathed it to his worthy sons Shem and Japheth, but did not transmit it to Ham, father of Canaan, who had sinned gravely against Noah. Instead, Noah gave him a curse (the opposite of a blessing). Abram the Hebrew chose to serve God in a generation of idolatry's dominance and therefore earned the blessing of the highest of all levels of blessing of which the human being was worthy:

The Lord said to Abram, "Go forth from your native land and from your father's house to the land that I will show you.

> I will make of you a great nation,
> And I will bless you;
> I will make your name great,
> And you shall be a blessing.
> I will bless those who bless you
> And curse him that curses you;
> And all the families of the earth
> Shall bless themselves by you."
> (Genesis 12:1–3)

The uniqueness of the promise given to Abraham is expressed by his stature as a prolific and fructifying person. He, by himself, would be a blessing to all the environs of life through which he would pass. He would serve God and thereby fulfill a mission to all humankind. Abraham bequeathed the great designated promise to his son Isaac, who was worthy thereof. Isaac passed it on to Jacob, who was worthy thereof. Jacob passed it on to all his children, each one of them according to his distinctive stature and trait. From the children of Jacob on, all the people of Israel became inheritors of the special blessing promised to the forefathers—obviously, as long as they passed the test that God placed before them of loyalty to their mission; keeping God's commands, and being worthy and deserving of the great promise containing God's love for His chosen nation.

The reason for establishing the blessing as the central form of prayer becomes clear from these considerations. As said above, prayer is recited while bowing—equivalent to kneeling before God to receive the blessing hidden in God's loving presence. But according to the prescribed format of prayer, the person begins by blessing God in order to be worthy of His blessing, and this process raises the question: how can the human being bless God, who is the source of the blessings with which humans are to be blessed? The answer to this question is given in the precise formulation of the text of the blessing cited above: the worshipper does not, like God, say "I will bless You" (*avarekheka*), but rather "Blessed are You, O God" (*Barukh atah adonai*). The exact meaning is that the human being turns to God, calls Him by His Name, and describes God as "blessed" (*barukh*) and as the source of all blessings expressed in the creation of a universe with its multitude of all the creatures; with its nourishment, its continued existence, and its independent productivity as manifest in its ongoing renewal. Does the worshipper thereby give something of himself to God? The positive answer is anchored in the two dimensions of the emotional intent expressed in the "Blessed are You" text. The first of these dimensions is relating to God through the expression of love in response to God's love. Responsive love is the feminine desire to be fruitful from the male desire that fructifies, thereby confirming the divine desire that longs to do well by all creation. The other dimension is relating to God through the gesture of feminine love that longs to receive the seed, to be fertilized by it, and to give birth; this is the readiness to contribute to God from one's self—as the woman contributes of herself to the man, to enable him to produce. This means that in saying "Blessed are You" (*Barukh atah*) the human expresses readiness to be fruitful from God and become a blessing for all that surrounds him. Moreover, by expressing readiness to thrive from God, the person increases the internal influx flowing from the deep essence of the fructifying God—just as the woman, by being attracted by the man in order to be fruitful by him and become pregnant for him, increases the influx that he bestows upon the world through her.

The form of the blessing as a central rubric therefore confers on prayer the meaning of loving encounter. In it, each side contributes its fertility to the other, and together they contribute to themselves, their family, community, nation, to humanity, and in general to creation, which renews and enriches.

5

Establishing the Covenant of Faith between the Individual Human Being and His God

The *Shaḥarit* Prayer

The daily prayer rite according to the *siddur* consists of three services: (1) morning (*Shaḥarit*); (2) afternoon (*Minḥah*); and (3) evening (*Arvit*, plus the prayer recited as a person goes to bed to sleep). This division accompanies the Jew, guiding him over the course of the day from awakening to going to sleep. It does so with ceremonial documentation, bringing to mind the transitions between the different life-functions in the temporal cycles of day and night, as well as those of the week (Sabbath), the month (beginnings of the month) and the year (holidays and festivals). The daily prayer cycle is also divided into three portions in terms of content. The focus of each is an experiential-reflective topic special to it, although the topics flow from each other, shaping the personal and communal consciousness of each Jew, and defining his values, goals, and destiny.

The most complete and developed display of these topics is to be found in the *Shaḥarit* (morning) prayer. *Shaḥarit* may be seen as the essential prayer in terms of importance, quantity, and depth. It reflects the ever-new return of the Genesis event and raises it to the worshipper's consciousness. Creation renews itself every morning with the shining sun ("Let there be light"—Genesis 1:3), expelling the darkness and shadows that arise from the depths of primeval chaos as yet not totally subdued. The creation of the human being is also renewed every morning, upon awakening, as expressed by the image of God breathing His spirit into the human being and returning the soul to the human body to revive it. Every morning human beings prepare themselves in their homes and synagogues for the experiences that await them with the labors of the day.

The three large sections of prayer recited in the morning are: (1) the *Birkhot Hashaḥar* (Blessings of the Dawn); (2) the *Keriyat Shema*; and (3) the *Shemoneh Esrei*. In terms of the subjects, these sections can be described in the following way. (1) The *Birkhot Hashaḥar* include wrapping oneself in the *tallit* and donning *tefillin*. This is designed to renew the covenant of faith between each singular Jew, as an individual situated among his people, and the one God, singular and unique, who is also the deity of all humans whether they know Him and keep His commandments or not. (2) The *Keriyat Shema* is designed to renew the covenant of love between the people of Israel, as individuals who constitute the assembly of the nation that is chosen to be God's treasure, and the one singular and unique God. (3) The *Shemoneh Esrei* prayer is an encounter of judgment before God. It is designed to renew the covenant, whereby prayer comes to realize the *mitzvot* between individuals who constitute the assembly chosen to serve God; each one by himself, and all together as one nation, and their one, singular, and unique God.. This covenant includes the individuals who know God according to His Torah, the God who knows the individuals, and the individuals who know themselves in their effort to serve Him and be good in His sight, cleansed of sin and adhering to Him—whether through divine-human *mitzvot* (between a person and God) or interpersonal *mitzvot* (between one person and another).

The Morning Blessings (*Birkhot Hashaḥar*): The Individual Recognizes God and Declares Faith in Him

With regard to the philosophical ideas laid as the theoretical foundation of the *siddur*: the theme of the *Birkhot Hashaḥar* (Blessings of the Dawn) is that of knowing God and having faith in Him. Expression of that faith is an intellectual-emotional gesture shaping the consciousness of each individual Jew's identity. The text of these prayers is couched in the first person singular, with references to the individual "I"—to the particular individual created in the image of God. He is singular and unique, because in terms of his identity as an individual in his own eyes and in terms of God his creator, he is unique and without substitute.

Understanding the meaning of faith in God as a foundational experience shaping the individual's personal identity first requires clarity about the relationship between knowing God—that is, knowing with certainty that there is a God who creates, legislates, commands, and governs—and believing in Him. According to the Torah of Moses—as contrasted with the Christian doctrine—these are two intellectual-rational gestures that rest upon one another but are not identical. Knowing the reality of God is a matter of intellectual cognition. It is based upon internal and external observation—on feelings, on the one hand, and on perceptions, images, and concepts, on the other. Faith in God is an intellectual volition based upon the moral certainty that God is good; that He wants what is good for the human being, created in His image; that He oversees and rules the universe that He created with righteousness, benevolence, and compassion and that because of this, the human being can be reliably certain that if he obeys the commands of God and walks in His way, he will succeed, enjoy well-being, and realize his promise. At the same time, daily experience demonstrates that in a reality permeated with evil—in the earthly universe—the righteous are rarely compensated and the evil ones rarely punished. Faith—in the sense of having confidence as expressed in freely chosen obedience to the *mitzvot* of God, out of readiness to do good for its own sake—therefore shapes the individual's ethical identity, whether in his own sight, in God's sight, or in the sight of human beings around him.

These factors reveal the deep difference between human beings, *qua* human, and the rest of creation: The human being is possessed of a knowing intellectual soul, willing and choosing, which makes him into an individual person (*ish*). He is not only the object of the God who knows him, but also an independent subject shaping his ethical identity through his relationship to his environment—which he is capable, to a certain extent, of shaping according to his needs and values. The term "intellect" (*sekhel*) is derived from "observation" (*histaklut*). It means knowing, in the sense of mirroring objects in the "I," which considers them in terms of its own needs, values, and goals. The ability to mirror objects and carry their image and form in internal memory is anchored in the ability to create a distance between the knowing "I," as an independent subject, and the subject's intuitions and feelings, which represent external and internal objects before it. As such, observation is "reflection," which mirrors the objects of the senses and the emotions, and through them also the intellectual activity that mirrors itself—and by doing so, becomes self-conscious. This is the significance of the distinction between the unmediated intuitions and feelings of animals, and human intellectuality. Only the human being, who knows that he knows, is able to achieve the creation of abstract concepts, which define objects by comparing them according to the sensory qualities that identify them.

It is easy to see that the subjective "I"'s consciousness is anchored in the intellectuality of the human being: The "I" is the self-identity of the *nefesh* (soul) as mediated by the intellect, which grants the soul its self-recognition and self-value. The intellect, one of the functions of the human soul, delineates the boundaries that separate its own body-and-soul from the entities around it. The intellect identifies these entities as others ("not-I") and is thereby changed into subject—which relates to itself and to its environment from its perspective and from out of itself. On this basis, the "I" demands that all subjects around it recognize it as a free subject with self-value (respect) and not solely as an object to be utilized. Thus, it also shapes its relationship to its environment, which is composed of different types of "not-I." These include the human "you" (a different subject turning to me); the "he" (a different subject who does not turn to me); the "this" (an object—an entity lacking self-consciousness, which is not identified by itself but solely by subjects around it); and the "those" (several objects of different species lacking self-consciousness, which are not identified by themselves but rather by the subjects around them, which compare objects with one other—and by doing so distinguish between them). The self-conscious "I" likens its existence as a living subject, sensing and feeling, recognizing, working, and creating, to a purposeful property. From this perspective, the "I" is a singular, unique, living creator whose value is embodied in evaluating itself and in its sacred relation to itself. In this sense, it has no substitute.

But when the "I"—which is conscious of itself as subject—experiences the world outside it, the world of "not-I," and discovers its dependency upon that world's resources, creatures, and other humans, it experiences discrepancies between pleasure and pain, good and evil, and between truth and falsehood. The "I" is forced to come to the opposing recognition, that from the objective perspective (the viewpoint of those who see the "I" from beyond it, which is also the perspective of the "I" when it sees itself as it sees others and as others see it) the "I" does not exist only of itself and for itself. It follows that the objects of its relationship, subjects as well as objects, do not exist only of themselves and for themselves. Rather, they are created, or come into being, or are born out of another, sovereign entity, or by means of it. Therefore, they are not eternal but temporal. They are not able to know by themselves whether their souls existed before they were born, and if so—how, by what means—and to where their souls would go upon their death.

The knowledge that there is God, who created them by breathing His spirit into the human beings' lifeless matter; and the belief that it is God who will gather the human beings' souls into "eternal Life" (*tzeror ḥayim*; literally, "bundle of life") after death, comes from the reflection of the "I" about its source and its end. Belief in the God who is known to human beings in this way becomes the single solution open to humans, to the problem latent in the contradiction between the recognition that there is absolute value to human life and recognition that each person is born at a certain time and will die in the future, and to the mystery enveloping human life from both ends. All these ideas rest on the foundation of the biblical creation narrative. Adam and Eve knew the reality of God as their creator; and in their youth (prior to sin) they also believed in God and obeyed His commands. They hid from God (they denied God's reality) only after they sinned. They sinned after their belief that God wanted what was good for them was shaken, and when they stumbled upon their sexual maturation, and were tempted by the intoxicating seduction of sensual pleasure—which bore the danger of spiritual-ethical death.

The narrative of creation assumes, clearly, that anyone born in the image of God knows in the depth of the soul that God is present, that God leads his life and determines his fate—and believes in Him. Also, there is the knowledge that when a person falls into great trouble, there is no other refuge than turning to God to be rescued. But the experience of life on earth places the human being before the continual test of choosing between good and evil, between righteousness and sin—and thereby between faith in God and denying Him. This is because, when stumbling into the evil which permeates earthly creation, many people come to wonder whether the good and beneficial God who lives in the person's soul, the God of whose glory the heavens speak, and whose wisdom they express, is but a deceptive illusion created in the depths of the human soul that longs for well-being. Prayer to God bursts forth from the recesses of the human soul, when the human being is caught in such doubt and seeks to restore the innocent faith experienced in youth. This is the great paradox: the certain knowledge that God is present, and the recognition that it is possible to believe in Him, are the conditions that make prayer possible. A person in whose heart the need for prayer is awakened is compelled to renew the certainty of his knowledge and the innocent faith of his youth. He needs to return to the first point of his life and to change the middle path into a recurring beginning. This is the function of the *Birkhot Hashaḥar*, the blessings of the dawn.

The *Birkhot Hashaḥar*: Acknowledgement and Gratitude

The first statement that the *siddur* places on the lips of the worshipper when he awakens from his sleep for a new day distills the deliberation about the subject of knowledge and of faith with lucid simplicity: "I thank You, living and eternal king, for giving me back my soul in mercy. Great is Your faithfulness" (K:4, *Modeh Ani*).

The utterance that opens the *Birkhot Hashaḥar* is not a blessing but rather an acknowledgement. The Hebrew word *hoda'ah* (acknowledgement) has a double meaning. It has the same root as *vidui* (confession), and in that sense is the declaration of one's recognition of a compelling truth—hence, "acknowledgement." But it is also related to *todah* (thanksgiving), and in that sense it is the expression of gratitude to God for the benevolence He renders to the person awakening from sleep—in essence, his return to life. On a deeper level it expresses thanks to the creator for the gift of the particular life of the person offering thanks for the privilege that falls to his lot—to become a living "I." In contrast to the standard blessing formulas recited in the language of "we," the *Modeh Ani* is recited in the language of "I" from the lips of each and every worshipper by himself—and not yet as part of the *minyan*. If we look into the continuation of the *Birkhot Hashaḥar* we can ascertain that the blessings woven into this section of the *siddur* are recited according to the familiar rubric in the language of "we," while the emotions and the reflections are expressed in the language of "I." In this way the "we" type of blessing actually expresses the thoughts and feelings of each particular worshipper included in the "we." But each worshipper blesses in his own name. Similarly, the blessings and the ceremonies (wrapping oneself in the *tallit* and donning the *tefillin*), which are within the category of the *mitzvot* unique to the people of Israel, are recited in the language of "I"—representing the worshipping individual as a person created in the image of God and His likeness. Humanity is the most encompassing and yet the most particularized circle of identification, and on its basis the children of Israel identify themselves as a collective entity chosen to serve the God of humankind and carry out the mission directed to it. Identity as a Jew does not remove the individual from one's human identity; it rather deepens and elevates it. As individuals, Jews are equal to all members of the human species—and their affiliation to their nation is a communal form that is universally human. It is only their entry into the Sinai covenant and acceptance of the *mitzvot* of the Torah upon themselves that distinguishes them as a chosen nation. The belief in the one and only God, creator and governor of the world, which is the condition for the selection of their nation but hangs upon the choice of each individual, is an emotional-intellectual experience on the level of the Jew's identity as a person. Therefore, when each individual awakens from his sleep, he becomes aware again of the soul that is returned to him. He returns, first of all, to his humanity, and he sets his faith, which is to distinguish him, upon this all-human basis.

How does God appear in the thought of the person who awakens from sleep and expresses gratitude (*"modeh"*) for the renewal of his life? What is

God for him at that moment? God is the source of eternal, enduring life infused from above into all creatures of creation and, at their center, into all humans who know they were created in His image. At the same time, God is the "living and eternal King" (K:4). His gift, for which the worshipper expresses gratitude, is double. First, it is "giving me back my soul in mercy" (K:4). The second aspect of the gift is expressed in the phrase "great is Your faithfulness" (K:4). The gratitude is, first of all, for the gift of life. The one who gives this gift of life, and by means of it grants selfhood and particularity to the human being, is the generous "personality" upon which, and upon whom alone, every creature— the human more than all the others—can rely to stand by him, to nourish, and sustain him; to give him shelter and rescue him from all trouble and distress. The creator expresses Himself in His creation, and had He not wanted His creation to be what it was, He would not have created it like it did when it came from His hands. Because of this, "great is Your faithfulness" (K:4).

Let us look closely at the personal narrative embodied in the thanks for the gift of life at dawn. When a person goes to bed at night, he entrusts his soul into the hands of his creator. This shows that sleep, in the eyes of the person who goes to bed, resembles a sort of temporary death—in terms of the disappearance of self-awareness of the "I," and absence of the person's knowing that he is alive and existing. To where could the soul, which knows itself in its relation to the body, disappear during sleep? To where does the self-knowing intellectuality turn, when it ceases to be related to its body? There is one real answer to both of these questions: the soul that was breathed into the body from God's spirit longs to return to its source. When it separates from the body during sleep, it returns to God and knows the God who gave it. Indeed, the body does not die during its sleep. Rather, its life contracts into the physical functions, which are anchored in the soul, the life-principle identified with the body's blood. When the person awakens from sleep and becomes acquainted anew with his intellectual soul, his humanity returns to him. If he looks closely into the meaning of this experience, it becomes known to him that he does not control his soul. This is because, at its source, the soul is not his, as it seems while he is awake—rather, the soul belongs to God who has breathed it into the human.

The return to one's existence as the "I," to the "I" known to itself, is therefore not automatically obvious. The soul does not return to its body by its nature or by the nature of the body. To the contrary, the natural place of the soul is in the spirit of God who gave it. The soul returns and connects to the body, to become its intellectual life, only by the will of God. This is the benevolence that God renders to the human beings. It follows that only God's kindness and loyalty to the human beings guarantee that, with the dawn, they awaken and return to live the life known to them. This is said explicitly in the conclusion to the poem *Adon Olam* as the morning prayer continues:

> Into His hand my soul I place when I awake and when I sleep.
> God is with me, I shall not fear; body and soul from harm will
> He keep.
> (K:22, *Beyado afkid ruḥi*)

After the grateful worshipper completes his prayer, he leaves home and the synagogue for the day's labors. Then the trials begin, which expand and increase his frustration as disappointments and troubles come to him—which are liable to upset his faith. It is therefore good for him to remember the acts of benevolence that he experienced as he awoke from sleep. Hundreds of expressions of gratitude recited in the language of blessing, after donning the *tallit* and *tefillin*, come from this concept. The benevolence of God—who grants him life to him every day, continually, and along with this traits and abilities to confront life-challenges—is expressed in every one of these gifts. The grateful worshipper attends to each one of them: the call of the rooster that awakens the person at dawn; the discovery that all parts of the body function properly; the ability to stand up erect, to move, to see, to hear, to sense, to taste; proof that the essential resources of life are present: the air for breathing, the water for drinking, the bread to eat, the house that protects, the light and warmth of the shining sun. The grateful worshipper, who has returned to life in this radiant God-given world, raises all of these to consciousness in the language of gratitude. These ought to allay all the doubts and perplexities that come from its many deficiencies, so as not to forget what is essential: life, with its conditions and resources, given to him. Were it not given to him, he could not invent it. This is also consolation for all the deficiencies he encounters. More than to any other creature, the human being is given the ability to cope with them, overcome them, and, even if only a little, to correct the deficiencies of creation and thereby become a helper to himself—and to his creator.

The *Birkhot Hashaḥar*: A Daily Ceremony of Betrothal

The *mitzvot* of wrapping oneself in the fringed *tallit* and donning the *tefillin*, after washing the hands for the sake of purity, and the blessings that accompany these ceremonies—are symbolic *mitzvot* of memory. They are intended to remind the person stirring from sleep about faith in his creator, from a specific, additional perspective unique to him as a person and as a Jew. God gave all human beings the instruction (*torah*) of the children of Noah, and the Torah to the children of Israel. Wrapping in the *tallit* and donning the *tefillin* came to perpetuate the covenant of Sinai from one's particular perspective, the perspective that relates to the soul of each individual of Israel over the generations.

The people of Israel were commanded to remember the Sinai covenant as a fortress for their faith. It is remembered not only as a national experience, but as an experience of each individual as a human being. The foundational myth of the oral Torah was that the souls of all Israel stood at the foot of the mountain, at a moment when time ascended to the plane of eternity. This meant that the event—which established the nation like a betrothal covenant ratified by the souls of all individuals of Israel over the generations and by God—was stored in the depths of memory of each individual of Israel. What was a betrothal covenant? Originally, it was a public event, documented and witnessed, in which a man and woman in love committed themselves to remain faithful to one another. At the foot of Sinai, God betrothed the souls of the people of His nation, "as a covenant for all time" (Exodus 31:16). The betrothal ceremony between man and wife was arranged under the canopy, with a ring placed on the extended finger of the bride. Being wrapped in the *tallit* symbolizes entry beneath the canopy. Donning the *tefillin* is a ceremony of consecration and communion. Let us remember that the soul of the person in relation to God, who fructifies the person with the spirit of His holiness, plays the feminine role. So, too, did the nation of Israel (called *keneset yisrael*, "the congregation of Israel") as it entered into worship of God. In this spirit, the rabbinic sages interpreted the Song of Songs as a song of covenantal betrothal between *keneset yisrael* and its God. The congregation of Israel was Shulamit, the beloved and the bride. Since each individual of Israel was a "member of the covenant" (*ben berit*), he was betrothed personally to his God. That is, if one remained loyal to one's God, one would find that God was loyal to him.

We will not go into particulars about the symbolism of being wrapped in the fringed *tallit* and donning the *tefillin*. These are known to each individual of Israel who has prepared himself for the ceremony of assuming the yoke of the *mitzvot*. It is sufficient to deal with the principle summarized in the worshipper's words as he winds the strap of the *tefillin* around his extended finger, in the manner that a bride extends her finger to receive the betrothal ring from the hand of the groom:

> And I will espouse you forever:
> I will espouse you with righteousness and justice,

And with goodness and mercy,
And I will espouse you with faithfulness;
Then you shall be devoted to the Lord
(Hosea 2:21–22)

The winding of the band of the *tefillin* around the extended finger symbolizes the act of the groom (God) who places the ring of betrothal on the extended finger of the bride who desires to consecrate herself to him. The worshipper, quoting the words of the prophet Hosea who developed the symbolism of the bond between God and His nation as a bond between man and wife, does not recite these words to God, but rather recites to himself the words of God who sanctifies the worshipper's dedicated, humble soul to Him. In this way, the covenantal betrothal is interpreted as a covenant of faith: "And I will espouse you with faithfulness; then you shall be devoted to the Lord."

After becoming wrapped in the *tallit* and donning the *tefillin* come the morning declarations of gratitude cited above. One may see in them processes of identifying the "I" before God in the midst of one's life-surroundings, in preparation for fulfilling the tasks of one's day. The worshipper first returns to a much broader and clearer articulation of the ideas of the *Modeh Ani*—although the emphasis is different:

My God,
The soul You placed within me is pure.
You created it. You formed it, You breathed it into me, and You guard it while it is within me.
One day You will take it from me,
And restore it to me in the time to come.
(K:6, *Elohai, neshamah*)

The worshipper speaks here of his soul, his relation to his soul, and the relation between the soul and God. The soul breathed from the spirit of God into the body was in itself pure, because it came from a pure source. This assertion is doubly significant. The purity of the soul, which emanated from God's spirit, is the basis of a person's glory as a human being, because from the perspective of the soul's relation to its divine source, the soul of every person, including sinners, remains forever pure and deserving of life and happiness. On the basis of this assumption, the covenant of faith between God and the human soul endures forever. But that purity also places a heavy responsibility on human beings—not only before God who breathed their souls into them, but before the souls placed within their bodies—which are borrowed from God and remain in their original relation with God even when placed in a body. It is as if the soul is claimed from both sides. The human being is obliged to preserve the purity of his soul and not soil it with sins that are liable to kill it. The prayer for God to help the human beings to believe in Him and to remain loyal to Him flows from that double responsibility—because the body's inclinations, over which humans do not have complete control, turned him to sin against God, against himself, and to betray God!

On the basis of all this, faith in God from the human side means not only reliance based on trust. It also means consciousness of the obligation to deal with one's inclinations, overcome them, and rein them in. Since God's way of helping human beings maintain the purity of their souls is the Torah, which teaches them the ways of life, the worshippers should be thankful for the granting of Torah and recognize that their faith is tested in terms of their obligation to live according to its *mitzvot*. First of all, they are to keep the *mitzvah* to study, understand, and inculcate the Torah. They are obliged to take it to heart so that it—and not their inclinations—would direct their actions. Since bodily appetites turn the soul to immerse itself in the pursuit of its pleasures, the worshippers ask for God's help with strengthening the soul to overcome their appetites so they can commit themselves to studying Torah and deriving spiritual pleasure from it—as appropriate to the human being created in God's image: "Please, Lord our God, make the words of Your Torah sweet in our mouths and in the mouths of Your people, the house of Israel" (K:8, *Veha'arev Na*).

This passage includes the blessing: "Blessed are You . . . who has commanded us to engage in the study of the words of Torah" (K:8). For the blessing not to be said in vain, one now has to fulfill the *mitzvah* of studying Torah. The *siddur* offers the worshipper chapters of written and oral Torah related to several *mitzvot* that are especially important in terms of guiding a proper way of life. A Jew is commanded to commit himself to these daily, to the extent he is able, because the good person's promise is realized by them. Torah study is the most important of them all, and is "equal to all others," even though study is not action, while Torah is fulfilled only by action. Study that brings about internalization identifies the human soul with the *mitzvot* of the Torah and in this way moves the soul to observe the appropriate *mitzvot* at all times and in every place. After these essential words of Torah come the blessings of gratitude, which relate to the person's identity and shape the circles of belonging and habits of behavior of each individual Jew as a human—that is, from birth.

The gratitude portion of the *Birkhot Hashaḥar* is said in the first person singular ("I"), beginning with "the soul You placed within me is pure" (K:6,

Elohai, neshamah), moving through "who has not made me a heathen" (K:26, *Shelo asani goi*), and ending with "who removes sleep from my eyes and slumber from my eyelids" (K:30, *Hama'avir sheinah*). The same is the case with the request for God to extend His help to the worshipper and rescue him from sins, mishaps, and failures over the entire course of his life. Such requests are generally made in the language of "we." But at the conclusion of *Birkhot Hashaḥar* a second version is offered, which repeats the request in individual language. We have said that faith is an individual gesture. Additionally, meritorious deeds and sins are actions of individuals, for the only real existence is of individuals and particulars—each itself an embodiment of the species and of the human collective that reared it: each human embodies humanity in himself, and each Jew embodies in himself the nation of Israel. The twice-repeated request of *Yehi Ratzon* ("May it be Your will")—one in the language of "we" and one in the language of "I," emphasizes this understanding: what was permissible and proper for the individual to request for himself as "I" is proper for every human as human, and for every Jew as Jew, to request for himself as a singular unit.

To summarize: the axis of every blessing, confession, and request discussed above is faith, with the meaning of loyalty and authenticity: the loyalty and authenticity of God *vis-à-vis* the human being and the loyalty and authenticity of the human *vis-à-vis* God. Loyalty and authenticity are mutually related terms, both designating an obligatory relation to the other, which is conditioned upon the relation of that other to its other. The declarations of gratitude in the morning blessings recall the conditions and abilities that God gave to the human being for the sake of his life and happiness. They demonstrate God's concern for His creatures, and especially His chosen humans. These conditions and abilities were set at creation, and testify that God was loyal to all His creatures, each according to its needs. The worshipper is called upon to become convinced that there are sufficient resources in creation to satisfy the needs of all living creatures. God provided each of His creatures with the conditions, abilities, and instruments for acquiring what was needed for nourishment, habitation, development, propagation, and self-defense. God gave the human being the most and the greatest abilities, because with his intellect the human knew how to create suitable life environs for himself. If human beings kept God's commandments and shared the life-conditions and resources under their control fairly, they would all be able to live happily and honorably. This is the most inclusive and concrete evidence that God is loyal to all His creatures and is worthy of their trust.

6

Principles of Faith

Three Declarations on Foundations of Faith

The Jewish prayer book is not satisfied with documenting the direct experience of life. It adds a theoretical, systematic layer: reliance upon scientific and metaphysical truths that respond to doubts, the source of which is systematic, scientific, and philosophical thinking. These truths—the product of scientific philosophical encounter with doubts in order to defend the faith that was under attack—seek to base faith on a systematic worldview, inclusive and unified, an objective worldview in the sense of obliging every human being of intellect and reason to recognize its axioms. The goal, as stated, is to defend the faith that is under attack, but by doing so faith itself comes to be charged with broader meaning. The axioms discussed in the area of faith in God and God's relation to the world and human beings are metaphysical. They are the product of deep research, which seeks to discover what is hidden and what is beyond the external appearance of things. To this end, skilled systematic thinking is required, of which only a few are capable, and when we direct research to subjects of faith, we probe exalted areas of knowledge at the border of the ability of the understanding of human intellect and reason.

Even skilled individuals have difficulty in researching those areas of knowledge, and their integrity and pursuit of truth leads them to wonder whether the human being can achieve absolute certainty based solely on research. Could the human being, who acknowledges the limit of his intellect, know with certainty what God knows as creator? If the great talented individuals are stymied, how much more so their students, and the people who are asked to rely on their instructions without the ability to affirm them intellectually? What could bridge this abyss between researched metaphysical truth and the human intellect and reason's ability to understand and evaluate?

The answer is: the faith that rests upon authoritative instruction anchored in the religious institution—which rests upon the divine Torah revelation that established it. The conclusion is that only mutual confirmation between systematic scientific and theoretical research and authorized religious instruction—resting upon the authenticity of divine revelation at its basis and the reliability of its instructors and teachers—can bring the certainty that this is the one truth and that there is no other. One can trust that it will direct the believer to serve God and keep His commandments, so as to find grace and benevolence before Him.

In other words, not only faith in God is required at the scientific and theoretical stage of developing religious thought, but also faith in what the human being knows about God, His will, His knowledge about the world and the human beings, His ability as creator, and His relation to the human beings as the chosen of creation. The role of principles of faith is to offer truths to the collective of believers, upon which their religion bases faith in God, His Torah, and His leadership, so they would accept those truths on the basis of trust in their authorized teachers—even if they were not capable of verifying them or understanding them fully by themselves. As those who adhere to the Torah of Moses and observe its *mitzvot*, they are required to acknowledge these truths to themselves, their community, and their nation, out of understanding that these truths are the bedrock of their identity as Jews—the bedrock upon which the community identifies itself as a community, and the nation as a nation, and maintains its ways of life that rest upon Torah. We have before us a broadening of the concept of a faith, which is liable to be problematic. This concept changes into a certain kind of incomplete knowing, out of knowledge that is incomplete. As such it rests upon a certainty, the source of which is not in the substantive clarity of knowledge, but rather the proven authority of its source: God himself, the prophets who spoke in His name, or the scholars ordained to teach the Torah.

This conceptual development in the *siddur* is represented by two poetic works added to the morning blessings—*Adon Olam* and *Yigdal*—and by a third composition that we are accustomed to sing at the conclusion of the weekday *Shaḥarit* prayer: the Thirteen Principles of Faith (*"Ani ma'amin bi'emunah shelemah"*—"I believe with perfect faith . . .," K:202, *Ani Ma'amin*). These three works are based on the principles of faith articulated by Maimonides in his interpretation of chapter 10 of *Mishnah Sanhedrin*, providing a kind of legal norm to determine the boundaries of belonging to the congregation of Israel as organized into its communities. Deviation from them would constitute heresy, for which the proponent is excluded from collective Israel.

The Context for the Formulation of Maimonides's Principles of Faith

From the perspective of the Torah's written and oral tradition up to the Middle Ages, the formulation of the *mitzvot* of faith as a legalistic norm which defined belonging to the community, and through it to the Jewish nation, was a revolutionary innovation. Maimonides endeavored to find support for it in the *Mishnah*, but actually this was part of the general reform he successfully applied to the rabbinic establishment in dealing with the cultural and political challenges of his age (the twelfth century). His motivations were political on the one hand, and cultural-spiritual on the other, and the two perspectives were interwoven. The spiritual motivations came from developments in the religious thought of Judaism, Christianity, and Islam, which followed from the encounter between their scripture-based traditions (the biblical legacy of Judaism, the New Testament of Christianity, and the Koran of Islam), and the political, scientific, and theoretical legacy of Greece and Rome. These two sources, the religious and the secular, had a vital role in the development of civilization and of western culture in the medieval period. This development awakened an urgent need to resolve conceptual contradictions between the ancient pagan scientific-philosophical legacy of Greece and Rome, and the monotheistic legacy of the western medieval religions, on the metaphysical, ethical, and political level. This assumed a common denominator which enabled an interpretation that closed the distance between them. It integrated the truths that resulted from scientific and philosophical research whose authenticity was empirical and intellectual, with the truths of the religious Torah based upon divine revelation that the religious institution transmitted on the basis of self-ascribed authority based on the proven prophetic message of its founders.

The institutional motivations to define principles of faith emerged from encounters between the three monotheistic religions—Judaism, Christianity, and Islam. Each claimed ownership of the absolute truth, as ascribed to its prophet, and required every human being to accept it and commit to maintaining it in its beliefs, thoughts, and rituals. Each one of them sought a synthesis with the legacy of Greece and Rome appropriate to it, in its own way, while rejecting the syntheses of the competing religions. Considered retrospectively, however, the three competing religions influenced one another, and were forced to accept their coexistence on the basis of their common relation with Jewish scripture—each with its own interpretation—until God Himself would resolve the controversy at the "end of days."

Judaism had the advantage of dependence upon the heritage common to it and its daughter religions. Internal theological causes obliged its two "daughters" to tolerate Judaism's existence under their rule, insofar as they relied on its legacy. The advantages of Christianity and Islam, on the other hand, were the numbers of their followers and their imperial status. They were the religions of the majority that ruled the lands of western culture. The Jewish religion under their rule was the barely tolerated religion of a small, dispersed, and conquered nation. In order for this small nation to be able to maintain its standing in the struggle forced upon it, Jews were forced to integrate into the material civilization of the lands of their exile. That is, Jews were pressured to appropriate scientific-philosophical, economic, and political enlightenment, in order to contribute to the cultures of the lands of their exile, a contribution that would make granting permission to settle and earn a living, even become wealthy, among Christians and Muslims, mutually worthwhile. But along with this, Jews had to avoid assimilation and absorption by means of strictness in keeping the *mitzvot*, which distinguished them from their neighbors in terms of faith, ritual, and way of life. In its way, the rabbinic leadership of the Jewish nation, which was organized and consolidated in its communities, imitated Christian leadership—whether in terms of its institutions or in terms of the dogmatic theological formula of "principles of faith." This imitation was intended for the leadership to endure controversy imposed upon it, and to convince its believers that it was proper, even worthwhile, to endure the trials imposed upon them and the lurking temptation to change their religion, and to strengthen their faith, and, when the time called for it, to "sanctify the Name of Heaven" (that is, undergo martyrdom), when refusal to change their religion meant death and great suffering.

The work of Maimonides in this area is, as said, revolutionary. It set off arguments between different religious movements that arose among the Jewish people. Did Judaism have principles of faith in its Torah sources? Did it need such principles? If the answer was affirmative, what were the principles and how could their truths be demonstrated? And finally, how was the concept of faith to be understood, and the relation between faith and understanding and intellectual knowledge? Perhaps the controversy itself testified that the formulation of principles of faith was needed at the time, for without it, the unity of the religious communal institution and the unity of the people could not be preserved. This would explain why Maimonides's teaching concerning the principles of faith was accepted, and why it made its way into the *siddur*—not in its full philosophical version, but as adapted in liturgical poems addressed to religious feeling. The advantage of Maimonides's version is its legalistic style, which was anchored in the sources of oral Torah, and his unsurpassed legal authority ("from Moses to Moses, there arose none like Moses")—despite the stormy controversy that erupted around his philosophy.

Between Knowing God and Believing in God?—The Morality in Creation

To comprehend the developments involved in understanding the concept of faith underlying Maimonides's formulation of principles, it is appropriate to return to the Torahitic-prophetic concept of faith and probe it. Above, we dealt with the connection and the distinction between knowing God and having faith in Him. According to the written Torah, the human being knows God from an external and an internal perspective. The external perspective is that of recognizing the sublime wisdom, which was invested in the orders of creation. The orders of creation balance out the many powers that create, in the course of their confrontation, a coordination which testifies that the creator imposed His purposeful laws upon those powers. In the speeches of the prophetic books and in the Hagiographa, especially in the Psalms, we find lofty and enthusiastic descriptions of the splendor of nature. All of them express admiration for the wisdom that has unified opposites, that has subdued the powers of chaos and created a world intended for the good and the beautiful. It would be impossible to refute this as testimony to God's moral motives in His creation, and His concern for each detail, large and small, among the particulars of creation. We thus find that "the heavens declare the glory of God" (Psalms 19:2), a glory that is expressed itself in His wisdom, goodness, and beauty—and they testify to His loyalty, and oblige faith in Him.

The depth of the thought that supports the faith in the wisdom, benevolence, and the beauty of creation is expressed in the Torah idea that the laws, which God laid down for creation, overlap with the laws of morality. These laws identify the good with existence and with coordination between parts of reality; and evil, with chaos and destruction of reality. We will find in the Hebrew Bible many clear expressions of the idea that creation was basically moral in its foundation. Because of this, by breaking laws of morality in communal life and in their relation to creatures of creation, human beings bring about creation's revolt against violators of its laws. Creation does not reconcile with the evil done within it. It rather protests against the evil and endeavors to vomit it out. Thus God cried out to Cain, "Your brother's blood cries out to Me from the ground!" (Genesis 4:10), for the red blood (*dam adom*) came from the earth (*adama*) from which the body of the primal man (*adam*) was created, and the human body would be gathered into it at death. The prophets also repeatedly warned the people of their nation that their sins would have the earth of the land vomit them out as it vomited out the sinful nation of Canaan. Clearly, recognitions of such truths were, in the eyes of the prophets, concrete testimony that God was the legislator and righteous judge, and that He was to be trusted to render good to the good, bad to the bad, and to keep His promises.

In addition to the morality impressed upon creation, the nation of Israel had a special source of faith: that of God's word in His Torah. Also, all the people of Israel were present at the event of His royal revelation at Mount Sinai, when He gave His people the ten sacred commandments. With them He set Israel apart "to be His treasured people" (Deuteronomy 7:6). The rabbis asserted in a mythic manner that the souls of all the children of Israel, until the end of all the generations, were present at the event of enacting the covenant at Sinai. But the biblical narrative of the covenantal gathering also testified that at this event, the children of Israel obligated all future generations. For this purpose, they received the Tablets of Testimony, and the Torah in which the divine revelation was documented. Accordingly, anyone who studies the Torah assiduously, and applies its *mitzvot* in his time—it is as if he stands at the feet of Mount Sinai and receives the Torah which is revelation itself, interpreted by its teachers according to the tradition that began at Sinai and transmitted authentically from generation to generation. To this was added the certainty that emerged from the believer's looking into the depth of his soul. Human beings were created in the image of God and the divine spirit; thus the "holy spirit" from which the soul was breathed into the primal man resides within them. If all people can understand the word of God directed to them, this is because "the spirit of His holiness" dwells in the soul of every person—so long as they do not corrupt their soul's path and do not totally darken the soul with sins.

Opposite the knowledge of the presence of God, His will, and His word, which establish faith, an abyss is disclosed between divine revelation as the God of compassion, grace, long-suffering great benevolence and truth, and the experience of human life in creation. As a consequence of their existence as bearer of intellect and self-consciousness, all people come to know in their maturity that they are temporal and ephemeral creatures. They were born, mature with difficult struggles, and expect the death that lies in wait for them. Every lack, every mishap and blemish, every sickness and handicap signifies and symbolizes death, and, in their eyes, death is the extremity of evil. God does not guarantee human beings eternal life on this earth. The day will come when he will not awaken with dawn to live in his world. God does not assure human beings against poverty, enemies, or sickness. God does not even assure human beings against the trouble that their neighbors among their fellow citizens are liable to cause them. All these experiences upset faith. They might even cause revolt, heresy, and denial, especially among those who succeed, by merit of their abilities, talents, and strength, to achieve a certain (temporary!) control of their surroundings—for then it seems to them that "their strength and power of their hand" (Deuteronomy 8:17) would help them more than God's promises.

The fact that the sinners and evil ones succeed in terms of the strength of their rule, wealth, glory and pleasure is liable to convince people that morality does not rule creation and that God is not a righteous judge, or that He is indifferent to the fate of the creatures He created. That is why the evil ones succeed and the righteous suffer and only rarely experience well-being. Because of this, even the Torah describes the success of the righteous and their rescue from the distresses of life as a miracle—as opposed to something expected according to set orders of creation.

Were we to raise these conclusions to the level of objective scientific observations, we would say that in the created world, necessary and mechanical rules, determined in advance, are in control. These rules are not purposeful and are indifferent to ethics. Even the instinctual and sense-based longing of a person for survival and well-being is necessary and not subject to ethical choice. This teaches the human to obey the laws of creation and the laws of his physical instincts, to adapt to them and have them adapt to him, in order to succeed and be worthy of well-being. If divine powers shaped this reality, these powers ("the gods") are clearly not ethical. They are egotistical and materialistic and pursue pleasure and control. In order to find favor in their eyes, it is necessary to satisfy their appetites, to entice, and to bribe them. This is the idolatry against which the Torah struggled with all the power of persuasion.

How, then, does the Torah respond to the difficulties that arise from the experience of human life? The essential answer is that the laws of creation, legislated by God in His wisdom, are ethical. But they still do not rule with absolute control over the earthly universe. The powers of chaos, which are also the source of physical energy for creatures of creation, are not subdued. They are sources of evil of different kinds, including the human inclination to idolatry. Human beings are called to rule over themselves and over creation, in order to help God realize His will, by means of the humans' improving themselves and their culture. This is the ongoing test that they are required to pass, adhering to doing good for its own sake, according to God's *mitzvot*—even if all humans, righteous or wicked, are doomed to suffer from the deficiencies and blemishes in creation until they are corrected, and God's dominion—hidden from the eyes of most people who cling to idols—would be revealed to the eyes of all.

If so, what is the compensation for the righteous who suffer? How does the justice, which God is obliged to administer, take place? How does God justify their faith in Him? The answer implicit in the claim that the pious will reap their reward in the world to come, when their souls return to God, is hinted at in several places in the Hebrew Bible—although not explicitly. The reason lies in the prophets' belief that redemption—which is conditional upon victory over idolatry, as well as ascendancy of the Noahide rules among humankind and the *mitzvot* of the Mosaic Torah among the people of Israel—was a task to be realized in this world and in the present, and not in the distant future. On the basis of this thought, it is also clear that the requirement for every person to commit to improving himself, his neighbor, and his culture, despite the suffering, is not likely to be accepted by most humans without bringing them to a deeper understanding that the substance of doing good for its own sake, out of love for God and adherence to God, is authentic well-being and worth all the suffering.

The designated answer to the problem of the reality of evil in creation gives active meaning to faith. The human reliance on the protection promised in advance by the good God who rules the world is not enough. Routine, passive observance of the *mitzvot* of Torah also does not guarantee that the human beings will succeed in seeing good in their world. Therefore, the believers are called upon to prove by their deeds as well, and not only by expressing their feelings and thoughts, that God is worthy of faith. The believers are required to keep the commands of God; to improve themselves and their surrounding through them. Also to strive to demonstrate by their ethical achievements, which flow from obedience to God's will, that justice and good are the purpose that God strives to realize with human help. Towards that end, the pious person is required to exemplify commitment to the good, to righteousness, and benevolence for their own sakes, without asking for reward, and to recognize that "the reward of *mitzvah* is *mitzvah*." That is, the well-being of the pious identifies with the good that the *mitzvah* brings to the world. Confronting the gap that opens up between what ought ideally to be and what really is, including evil, faith itself changes into the willful power that brings about deeds that bridge the gap which is liable to bring on heresy. In the language of the rabbinic sages, the true believers are the people who make their will as the will of God. They are the people who imitate God's governing traits, as documented by the Torah. They demonstrate, through their readiness for self-sacrifice, that God rules the earth by means of those who do His will, who believe in Him. These are deeds defined by the rabbinic sages as "those which sanctify the name of heaven in public," in terms of models of faith. If all humans would emulate them, the people of Israel would be redeemed from their suffering, and humanity would be released from its sins and from the troubles which come to humanity because of them.

Survival Mindset *vis a vis* Believing Mindset in Israel's History

The call to the nation of Israel to believe in God in this active sense is exemplified in the Bible in narratives of the nation's patriarchs in Genesis and in the story of the exodus from Egypt in Exodus. They are also the source on which the *Siddur Hatefillah* draws. Moses was called to fulfill his destiny as the redeemer of his nation. Facing the bush burning with fire, we see Moses struggling with the gap between the condition his nation deserved in light of God's promise to the patriarchs, and the suffering of its slavery; between his human ability to fulfill the task of the redeemer, and the power he had to activate in order to fulfill that task. Moses was persuaded to accept his mission, which was too heavy for a human to carry, only after God assured him, saying "I will be with thee" (Exodus 3:12). That is, by His sovereign strength, God would fulfill the task of the redeemer. Moses would be the prophet, the human voice who brings the word of God to the nation and Pharaoh, to know what they were required to do by themselves.

Moses's first step in fulfilling his mission was to gain the nation's trust, in anticipation of the struggle with Pharaoh over its leaving for freedom. This was the initial act required of the nation for its redemption. The nation was to stiffen its resolve, and liberate its soul from slavery—which was expressed in fear of the tyrannical ruler that changed into fear of assuming responsibility for a life of freedom. The people were required to participate in the struggle by organizing themselves and by taking the initiative to turn to Pharaoh with the demand to let them worship their God in the desert. With this, they had to disclose their readiness to suffer for their freedom as long as Pharaoh opposed it and sought to increase the weight of his yoke on the slaves who were rebelling against him. When he arrived in Egypt, Moses first stood before the congregation of his people and asked for their trust in God and in him, and for them to elect him and his brother Aaron as their representatives. The people, who were desperate, trusted, and empowered Moses to represent them before Pharaoh, with his demand, "Let My people go" (Exodus 5:1). But the nation's trust faded fast when Pharaoh refused to liberate the nation and made its yoke heavier.

After the crisis of confidence, Moses and Aaron were forced to take a stand by themselves before Pharaoh in the name of God, and not in the name of the submissive nation that did not dare to liberate itself psychologically and to endanger itself. By their personal example, Moses and Aaron sought to reconstruct the confidence of the nation, which was a condition for the success of their mission—no less than subduing the pagan stubbornness of Pharaoh. Despite their human frailty and isolation, they dared to stand before the tyrannical ruler. He could kill or imprison them without difficulty, but he did not dare. Why? Because the fear of God fell upon him. So, when Pharaoh's resistance was broken, and the time arrived for the exodus into the desert, the nation was asked again to participate. Leaving the house of slavery had to be done by foot, and going out on its way supplied and equipped. In the desert, the nation had to take responsibility for its future, as was the essence of freedom. The condition for that, obviously, was trust in God and in Moses who would lead the nation through the desert into its land. And it was clear from the start that when the nation reached its land it would have to conquer it, settle it by force, and take responsibility for it before God. In order to do this, the people went out into the desert, once equipped to do so.

In this instance as well, there was a pattern of confidence becoming temporarily inflamed, and then quickly extinguished in the face of a new and different experience at this time. The people who witnessed the plagues, which God wondrously brought upon Egypt without hurting the nation itself, trusted in and went out after Moses into the desert. But when the people stood before the Red Sea and saw the Egyptian army pursuing them, the confidence evaporated, and regret and disappointment replaced it. The reason is obvious. According to the established orders of creation which appeared irrevocable, their rescue from the huge army which rose up against them, appeared absolutely impossible. Flight into the desert was also not possible. Only a miracle of direct divine intervention could rescue the nation from destruction. The people, who had already witnessed God's ability to subdue the nature of creation so as to bring them out of the house of slavery, were not certain that God would intervene and rescue them this time as well.

This was a natural, human form of thinking and behavior. It followed from conditions of the existence of human beings in creation and from characteristics of the soul whose source was tied to the human body. The human beings' existential tendencies inclined them to rely on essential established laws of creation, and not upon divine intervention which was conditioned upon a person's ethical behavior. This intervention was not certain, and therefore impossible to rely upon in advance. One could acknowledge it only retroactively. Again, the gap opened between what ought to be in ethical terms (a person's rescue) and what reality presented in terms of creation's necessary laws. In order to bridge the gap, confidence was required to enable the nation to dare to tread into the stormy sea. This time only isolated individuals were confident and entered into the sea, yet the entire nation was rescued by their merit. Based on this, it was said of the children of Israel after the splitting of the sea, the rescue of the nation and the destruction of the Egyptian army, "The people feared the Lord, and they had faith in the Lord and in His servant Moses" (Exodus 14:31).

In what follows, we will see that even the faith acquired through such a great miracle did not hold for long. When the nation was finally rescued from the tyranny of Pharaoh, it stumbled into the next hindrance, resolution through the path of nature also appeared to be totally impossible. How was it possible to provide a large nation with water and food in the desolate and barren desert? Could God also intervene in this situation and bring water and nourishment to the 600,000 souls who had left Egypt? The people came up against this question immediately, after they were released from the waters of the Red Sea and turned to the desert. They were immediately overcome by thirst, but when they reached the closest wells of water it became clear that the water was bitter. From where would the sweet water come, to quench the thirst of the nation? The people despaired again and regretted their agreement to leave the house of slavery, where there was plenty of water and food. To their thinking, slavery, where it was possible to live, was better than freedom that brought death. That is, the nation sought again to rely on natural conditions, which were certain, and even to become enslaved by them. They declined to trust in divine intervention, which now had to be day to day and continual, not one-time, until they reached the land they were to inhabit. Could a person who was enslaved to his physical nature and to the nature that surrounded him, trust in ongoing miracles?

Moses found a miraculous way to sweeten the bitter water, and the people had confidence in him once again. But the same test repeated itself immediately when it came to the narrative of the descent of the manna. Insofar as the manna came as an educational experience, it had special conceptual significance. Its appearance was tied to an important *mitzvah* in which faith in God was embodied as an eternal sign—the *mitzvah* of the Sabbath. The nation complained that it had no food in the desert, and God received the complaint and promised unnatural nourishment. The people were not accustomed to it, and did not understand its substance and source. This was again a faith-dependent wonder. This time, the nation was required to prove that it deserved to have a miracle done for it, by showing faith. It was commanded to gather the divine gift, for which it did not labor, strictly according to norms which were stipulated for its status as a united nation in desert conditions. The first norm was for every man and woman to gather the portion necessary for them and the members of their family for one day only. This assured the equal justice which united the nation, and the frugality required in desert conditions. Gathering for the next day, on the other hand, was forbidden. These two requirements collided with the natural inclination of human beings who were struggling for survival in nature: to take as much as possible for themselves, much more than they truly needed, and hoard for the next day. For who knew if, on the day after, they would have the opportunity they had today?

Imposing limits on gathering the manna tested the nation's trust in God and in Moses. The people were required to rein in their inclinations and trust that God would provide food for them, day by day, if they observed His *mitzvot*. It would be natural for the people not to obey, not to trust, and to take as much as possible and hoard for the next day. But anything gathered beyond the needed and allowed allocation spoiled. The people were therefore convinced that they had to concede, maintain equality, and be content with the day's portion, for that was the "nature" of the manna. But then God commanded the people to gather food on the sixth day for two days, for the Sabbath—when it was forbidden to work for one's livelihood. Now the people were asked to believe the word of God from the mouth of Moses, that the manna which previously spoiled, would not spoil at this time because it had no independent nature—it "listened" to the will of God. Of course, the people found it difficult to accept these words in faith, until experience demonstrated their truth. If the nation wanted to maintain itself in the desert, it was forced to believe.

The experience with the manna was intended to accustom the people to a life of trust. That is, to live based on the understanding that fulfilling the *mitzvot* of ethics and service which God commanded was a necessary condition for success in earthly life, rather than satisfying the natural instinct for survival. This also explained the connection between the narrative of the descent of the manna and its gathering and the observance of the Sabbath—which was later established as a sign of the covenant between God and the nation. On the Sabbath day, the nation was forbidden from doing any work for livelihood, even when settled in its land. On this day, it had to be satisfied with what it prepared the day before. It had to regard the nourishment it had prepared as a gift of God, in which all members of the nation were equal.

The people had to believe that if they conducted themselves according to the *mitzvot* of God and refrained from all work, their nourishment would be assured in the coming days as well. The experience tied to the descent of the manna is repeated every week on the Sabbath day. Especially because of this, the Sabbath is considered the most wonderful gift of God to the nation after it left the house of slavery: a day of true freedom, a day of liberation from the burdensome concern for livelihood, when one could dedicate oneself to the worship of God that emanated moral and spiritual blessing.

In order to be worthy of this one day in which the vision of freedom was realized, each individual of Israel was required to pass a test, and overcome the inclination that tempted him to work more so as to earn more and become richer. The individual had to cease working and, along with this, cease being anxious—knowing that it was not his work in the field and factory that determined whether there would be sufficient product. Rather, it was his readiness to daily observe applicable commandments that was determinative. We could argue that even today most human beings see the demand to keep Torah laws as a test, which is difficult to pass. For the law requires people to lose what they would earn from another day of work, and halt the daily demands for their products. In this respect, the freedom tied to the prohibition of work is, in their view, deemed to be religious oppression. They defend their "freedom" to work for their livelihood on the Sabbath day as well. We thus find that the Sabbath respite is a sign of faith, which resolves the gap between the ideal and the real, through voluntary activity that expresses the commitment to do the will of God.

Until now, we have dealt with the concept of faith in the thought of the written Torah. The concept of faith as active will to bridge the gap between the ideal and real through loyal observance of God's *mitzvot*, in order for Him to reign over the world and improve it according to His will, and not only as passive reliance on God's help, does not blur the distinction between knowing God's reality and faith in Him. The knowledge that God is present, that He creates the universe and wants what is good and possible for it, is grasped as a sure truth based on the human experience of nature's splendor, on the Torah that teaches the human beings the laws of the righteous life, and on the knowledge that the soul is a gift of God. The feeling of the need to formulate principles as *mitzvot* of faith emerges from the undermining of this direct certainty. In order to restore this certainty to its full strength, faith needs to be drawn more deeply into the arena of knowing, and knowing deeper into the arena of faith, until they became two sides of the same coin. In order to know, research into creation is needed to disclose its secrets. In this way, the human being understands the wisdom and the divine will which are expressed in creation, and becomes convinced that all is directed towards the goal of betterment and overcoming the powers of chaos. It is also necessary to research prophetic revelation and its paths, especially to understand how the prophet arrived at the certainty that it was God who spoke to him, and what enabled those who heard his message to distinguish between true and false prophecy. In addition, it is necessary to research the human soul in depth, the manner of its connection to the body, and especially the connection between physical and intellectual processes. The great problem is that research obliges placing methodological question marks, which temporarily suspend the conviction regarding the authenticity of Torah instruction, or the way to interpret the instruction, until the research is completed. All knowledge that was considered previously as a sure message lesson based upon institutional authority of the prophets and rabbis is in this way made into the object of critical thought aspiring to objective knowledge. If so, to what extent is the person permitted to trust in the results of his research? Clearly, regarding these results as well, the question of faith—upon which certainty of the decision that the conclusions of research are authentic and the reality is as they depict it—is paramount.

The determination of the principles of faith includes the instruction of the prophecy of Moses on the basis of the authority of divine revelation on the one hand, and the results of a person's research on the other. This combination is a vital need, both from the perspective of the religious institution, in order to shore up its authority, and also from the perspective of the community of believers, in order to grant them the certainty that its members did not err on their path in darkness like the blind. They needed to be convinced that their perceptions were not the mere imaginings of their heart, but reality; that they know their path, paved by the religious institution, truly leads them to their well-being. The research is so vital, because of controversies among various religions and the different spiritual movements within each.

Thirteen Principles of Faith that Distinguish Judaism from Christianity and Islam

Against this background, let us examine Maimonides's version of the thirteen principles of faith. As said above, the aim of Maimonides as a halakhic authority was to set boundaries for belonging to the Jewish community and its Torah-religious framework—by responding to three fundamental questions. (1) What were the ideational norms, which by complying with them, a Jew (a person born to Jewish parents and thereby belongs to the Jewish people) identifies himself with Judaism? (2) In what did the distinction between identity with the Torah of Judaism and identity with idolatry, Christianity, and Islam consist? (3) What was the absolute advantage of Judaism over idolatry, Christianity, and Islam in terms of proving its authenticity? What made Judaism into the single, true religion? Why was it proper for a Jew to remain faithful to his Torah, despite the misery it caused him in the life-conditions of his nation's exilic existence under Christian and Muslim rule? But before examining Maimonides's answers to these three questions, let us first attend to a prior problem. How did Maimonides understand the concept of faith, and in what sense did he think that it could be commanded? The importance of this prior clarification lies in the fact that the difference between the Torah of Moses and idolatry, Christianity, and Islam, as well as the rabbinic establishment's claim that the Torah of Moses was authentic while the teachings that deviated from it were false, are anchored in a basic difference between the Torah of Moses and the teachings competing with it. This was a difference in terms of understanding the substance of faith and the way it was properly conferred upon human beings.

Let us formulate the problem, as Maimonides encountered it. When he came to formulating the principles of faith for the Jewish religion he adopted— by means of a considered change—a conceptual rubric that was foreign to the halakhic legal tradition customary in Israel, but original and established in the Christian religion. It is clear that such a revolutionary step, taken in order to distinguish Judaism from Christianity and Islam, and not in order to bring them closer, had to involve a careful formulation of the differences between these religions, first of all from the perspective of the essence of faith and the role of the principles.

Christianity separated from Judaism when it established a universal church on the basis of the truth of a mysterious event, which in the prophetic and rabbinic worldview was not only absurd but constituted heresy. This is because it contradicted the Mosaic Torah's view regarding the relation of God to the human being and to creation, and distorted the faith in the unity of God and His uniqueness, which was integral to His absolute holiness. Study of the New Testament regarding all the teachings attributed to Jesus directly conveys that he was a Jew loyal to Torah and to Jewish law, as taught by the School of Hillel. He did not intend to preach to gentiles, but rather turned to his people, especially to the poor and the suffering. He extended help and compassion, and heralded the imminence of the salvific "kingdom of heaven." It was not he who established the Christian church, which separated from the nation of Israel, but rather his disciples and apostles, headed by the apostle Paul (in Hebrew, Saul), born after the death of Jesus. These apostles established Jesus and his tidings in the center of their worldview, which emphasized faith in a savior as the highest value, and upon this they founded the church. The apostles attributed to Jesus the status of "Son of God" not in a metaphoric but in a substantive sense—which in the eyes of the sages of Israel was gross idolatry. The apostles maintained that, as a Son of God, Jesus brought death on the cross upon himself in order to atone for the sin of the first Adam and the sins of all his successors who were born from Adam in sin—and therefore unable to be redeemed from sin by their own power. The church fixed these articles of faith as norms requiring acknowledgment (dogmas), by virtue of recognition of the authority of the church. People were obligated to believe (and to confess) the truths of these dogmas—in which inhered a mystery above human intellect and understanding. For by means of this faith the person adhered to the savior Son of God, and was saved from original sin to enjoy an eternal spiritual life in the world to come.

The source for the idea of original sin—that the first Adam, who was created in "the image of God," sinned the sin of fleshly desire, and on account of this was expelled from the Garden of Eden to work the cursed earth with the sweat of his brow—was the Torah of Moses. But there is a decisive difference between the traditional Jewish explanation and the Christian interpretation of this topic. According to the Christian interpretation, creation was at first entirely spiritual and only after the sin of Adam and Eve did it sink into the abyss of material physicality—from which all sins and evil were derived. The conclusion emerged from this, is that as long as human beings lived on earth as physical creatures, they would be immersed in sin. Redemption from sin depended upon transcending the physical universe. This was too difficult for the human beings to do by their own powers. Only God could return the human beings to their spiritual existence prior to sin, and this was the messianic mission of Jesus, Son of God. He was born of a woman of flesh and blood with a pure body, in order to die a physical death upon the cross to atone, by his grace, for the sin of the first Adam. His divine soul did not die, of course, but rather ascended to heaven, back to God his Father. With this, humanity's journey of redemption began, by means of selecting between human beings who believed in the savior and who by their faith were worthy of eternal life in the world to come, and sinners who did not believe and who would be punished with eternal suffering. According to Christian church doctrine, only after the selection was completed, would Jesus appear again on earth. He would return the earth and all its creatures to their first spiritual height, and this would be the complete redemption. That the church was an institution of priests, appointed to represent the Son of God on earth, was derived from this doctrine. Its first task was to call upon humankind as individuals, beyond their national attachments, to belong to the church, to hear its gospel message, to believe in it, and to accept its sanctity and rituals. By merit of their faith, they would be worthy of purification and atonement of the soul, which suffered from the sin that adhered to them against their will, as long as they were immersed in their lustful body. Its second, and loftiest, task was also to be remembered: to prepare all humanity for the second appearance of Jesus upon the earth, in order to bring final redemption. Towards this end the church was to make every effort, with all means at its disposal, to persuade all humanity, of all nations, to believe in its tidings and to accept its sanctity. The relationship of the Christian church to the Jewish nation, which continued to hold onto the "Old Covenant" (Old Testament) and refused to acknowledge the teachings of the "New Testament," was determined by this aspiration. Through this, the nation of Israel was made into the sinful chosen nation. On the one hand, the church was in principle obliged to punish Israel. On the other, it was to convince Israel to accept the message.

A difference in kind emerged from this, between the Torah of Moses and the doctrine of the Christian church. According to the doctrine of the church, redemption from sin was not achieved through practical *mitzvot*, which repaired the human being and repaired the world, but rather by faith alone, as a profession of absolute certainty that the tidings of Jesus were true, and would be fulfilled in the future—even if the experience of life on earth appeared to refute this, and even if the story of Jesus's redemptive appearance seemed impossible according to the fateful regularity that ruled nature. Human beings, who relied on their intellect and reason based on earthly experience, therefore denied the church's tidings of faith and ridiculed it. It is no surprise, therefore, that the church responded that the person's very tendency to rely on his intellect, which rested upon physical experience, was itself a sin and even the archetypal sin. The believer who relied on the testimony of the church, which was supported by the Son of God himself, was therefore asked to resist this temptation, and to tell himself that his sinful intellect led him astray in order to imprison him in the chains of his sin and prevent his redemption. It was forbidden to rely on one's intellect. Or more precisely: his original intellect, which was impressed upon him by the creator, obliged him to rely instead on the doctrine of the church, whose foundation was authoritative by divine revelation. As such, faith was defined as suprarational knowledge, which annulled every contradictory rational claim in advance. This was the truth, even if no human intellect in this world understood the causation hidden in it. In this way, faith was grasped as a voluntary decision that flowed from the power of the soulful aspiration to be redeemed from sin. As such, faith was made into a salvific power.

All these considerations made clear the essence of the concept of dogma. The church established verbal formulas, which documented the mysterious narrative and explained its theological significance authoritatively. The believers had to rehearse the words, sanctify them, and affirm the truth embodied in them by concentrating the powers of their souls not in an effort to understand the words intellectually, but in an effort to trust that they were true, and that the truth was expressed in the salvation promised by them. Only by defining faith in this way was it possible to command, even punish, those who denied the truth publicly—of course, for their good, in order to redeem them as well from the sin of no-faith.

We return to Maimonides's doctrine of Jewish principles of faith according to the Torah. In his opinion, the concept of faith and the definition of its principles in Christianity were idolatrous—that is, false. As a philosopher, Maimonides defined the concept of faith of the prophets anew, on the basis of the Aristotelian epistemology. According to this doctrine, the process of intellectual understanding passed through three stages. The first stage was sense perception and imagination. The second stage was conceptual abstraction. The third stage was internalization, in the sense of identifying intellect with concept, with a clarity that left no ambiguity or doubt. The last stage was described as intuitive enlightenment. It concluded the process of "discursive" thinking, with the decisive affirmation that the process included the pleasure of achievement. Maimonides identified intuitive enlightenment with faith, in the sense of final decision that the concept—or the theory—was true. It followed that faith was the perfection of knowledge, and it is understandable why Maimonides was convinced that the Christian concept of faith was wrong. In his eyes, it was simply deception, by means of which the priests of the church tried to lead the masses of the people after them in blind obedience.

The Contradiction in Maimonides's Very Attempt to Harness Intellect for Faith

Maimonides's critique of the doctrine of Christian faith raised a problem also regarding his attempt to formulate intellectual principles as commandments of faith. If faith is the perfection of knowing, apprehended by critical thinking by a well-tested method, how is it possible to command it? Could a person believe in what he does not believe on the basis of knowing? That is, can he believe what he did not learn, did not verify, did not understand, or was not convinced of? Is there value to a verbal profession of the truth, even if it is correct in itself, if the person who acknowledges it does not arrive at knowing it fully? From the philosophical-rationalist viewpoint of Maimonides, the answer to this question is negative. There was no way to bypass the process of knowledge. Faith was possible only when the process of logical thinking was concluded successfully. Maimonides agreed, therefore, that only consent to truths that teachers of religion knew to be true and could prove to be true would be commanded. But the teachers also knew that, on the one hand, most human beings were not capable of reaching such truths by themselves because of intellectual limitations, and on the other, knowing these truths was vital to their well-being. The moral and political precepts that lead to the improvement of humans and repair of their world were based upon that knowledge. What was required, therefore, was for human beings to believe in such truths in their opaque formulation, whereby they understood the literal meaning—so they could recognize their absolute duty to keep *mitzvot* whose moral logic was understood by every upright person. By means of this, they would advance to the degree of which they were capable, depending on their intellectual and moral level, to a clearer understanding of metaphysical truths (divine science), which embodied the eternal happiness of the human being.

It is clear from this, that the teachers' instruction of the principles of faith as commandments was meant to include not only external profession of truth based on trusting the rightness of teachers who knew the truth, but also observance of the moral and ritualistic symbolic *mitzvot* that relied on this truth and expressed it, and also of the educational effort of each believer to advance the process of recognizing the truth—each according to one's level. In his philosophical work *Guide of the Perplexed*, Maimonides gives an account of the thought process that can bring every person to a certain level of understanding metaphysical religious truth. He viewed prophets as exemplary teachers who knew how to draw all their students closer to ascend the ladder of knowing God in order to observe His *mitzvot*. But this is a deep subject for study, which does not enter into the framework of this discussion. Important for our concern is only its principle: the gradual negation of erroneous concepts (or phase-by-phase negation of idolatrous views), and defining the goal of the intellectual effort asked of the believers—realizing their portion in the world to come, in the community of Israel as rooted in this truth. This is, obviously, the role of the formulation of the principles of faith. It represents the stages of ascent from truth to truth, up to the encounter with the metaphysical knowledge of divinity.

The legal basis of Maimonides's doctrine of the principles of faith can be found in *Mishnah Sanhedrin* 10:1: "All Israelites have a share in the world to come. And these are they that have no share in the world to come: He that says that the doctrine of the resurrection of the dead is not from the Torah, and he that says that the Torah is not from heaven, and the Epicurean." The relevance of this Mishnaic teaching to the formulation of the doctrine of principles is inherent to the definition of several views, the denial of which excludes a person from the "community of Israel." This is not stated explicitly in our *mishnah*. All that is stated is that those who deny the three views "have no share in the world to come." That is, they belonged to the category of "a Jew who sinned." The reason for this is clear, and the fact that Maimonides closed his eyes to the difference between negating a share in the world to come and exclusion from the community of Israel, testifies to the substance of the reform that he suggested in his commentary on the *Mishnah*. According to the traditional *Halakhah*, belonging to the community of Israel was determined on the basis of belonging to the people. A person born a Jew was born into the covenant of the nation, and he was obligated to keep the *mitzvot* of the Torah, but it was impossible to strip him of his Judaism, even if he cast off the yoke of Torah and *mitzvot* and denied God and His Torah. Maimonides ignored this restriction by means of logical inference. If "all Israelites have a share in the world to come," those who had no share in the world to come had left the community of Israel. He made the promise of a share in the world to come contingent on each individual's belonging to the community. In this capacity, each person had a share in the world to come by the strength of the Sinai covenant between God and His nation. In this way, Maimonides emphasized the aspect of religious institutional (ecclesiastical) association over the aspect of national association. On the basis of this opinion (that chosenness was conditional upon acceptance of Torah and obeying its *mitzvot*), he rejected the view of Rabbi Yehudah Halevi: that the selection of Israel issued from a genetic attribute, which bestowed a superhuman level of existence to the children of Israel. According to Maimonides, the selection of Israel was expressed solely in the acceptance of Torah and in keeping the *mitzvot*, and in terms of belonging to the human species, there was no difference between Jew and gentile.

Grouping the Thirteen Principles

We come to the formulation of the principles. The *Mishnah* detailed three views, which, if denied, brought expulsion from the community of Israel—and they read: "They have no share in the world to come"—in an order ascending from light to heavy. (1) The one who says: "The [doctrine of the] resurrection of the dead is not from the Torah." This statement is attributed to the Christian who holds the view that only Jesus brought the redemptive knowledge of resurrection of the dead to the world, by his death and ascent back to heaven. But one may also understand this view as a more general claim, according to which the Torah of Israel does not know of the soul's survival after death, and this is a denial of the share in the world to come entirely. (2) "And he that says that the Torah is not from heaven," actually denies obligation to all *mitzvot* of Torah, the observance of which makes one worthy of a share in the world to come. How, then, would a denier of Torah be worthy of this share? Let alone: (3) "the Epicurean" who denies the reality of God—knowledge of whom and observance of whose *mitzvot* are the share of the world to come? In this form, the *Mishnah* delineates three truths commanded by Torah which, according to Maimonides, are conditions for belonging to the assembly of Israel and its community: the reality of God, Torah from heaven, and resurrection of the dead.

But Maimonides was not satisfied with this general and vague formulation of the *Mishnah*. As a philosopher, he delved into the meaning of each of these truths as related to the Torah's comprehensive worldview. Knowing that God truly existed required critical observation into the substance of this determination, that is, the meaning of the concept of God. It is not enough to say the correct word. It is necessary to ask what the one who is saying it is describing in his thought. Because if the speaker is not a philosopher, who arrives at this concept out of systematic study of the reality of which God is the cause while recognizing that God is the metaphysical cause of this reality; if he just repeats, like a parrot, a verbal formulation that surpasses his understanding—it is absolutely clear that he is not describing the true concept of God in his thought. If so, he has an erroneous, sensory image—for example, of a king sitting on his throne, or of a compassionate father. That is, he grasps God in anthropomorphic images, and this is an error, which leads astray. One must be cautious about this—because it is liable to bring sinful, idolatrous views and deeds.

The same applies when it comes to the two other insights: Torah from heaven and resurrection of the dead. Maimonides was aware of the fact that dealing properly with this stumbling block was possible only through systematic learning—each person of Israel according to his ability and level. But in order for all the people of Israel with a share in the world to come to attend to their obligation to endeavor to learn and inquire so as to arrive at authentic knowledge of the principles of faith according to their ability, it is necessary to present the components and connections through which one can advance and come close to this knowledge. Thus Maimonides built his system of principles around the three insights which the *Mishnah* enumerates, employing them as the axes demarcating three groups of principles—which together constitute a systematic progression of thirteen views, and flow from one another like a ladder on which to climb from physical reality as understood by everyone to metaphysical reality, which obliges effort of deep research—from the light to heavy.

The first group of principles relates to the concept of divinity. (1) God exists, but not as a reality similar to human existence. (2) God is absolute unity, which is in no way divisible into multiplicity; there is no unity in the universe like His unity. And this constitutes His absolute uniqueness. (3) God is intellectual-spiritual being, and not material. God does not have a body and has no physical attribute or function. (4) God is "primordial"—that is, eternal without beginning or end. He is beyond space and time, and therefore nothing preceded Him and nothing will come after Him. (5) There is a hierarchy of spiritual and material entities between God and the human being. God acts on earth by means of them, but prayer needs to be addressed directly to God Himself and only to Him. This means that it is forbidden to ascribe divine attributes or status to entities which mediate between God and the human being. This is so even if the intention is to arrive at God by means of them, because they are closer to human understanding. Maimonides's view is that idolatry began in that form. Since the inclination to idolatry is natural, it had to be strictly forbidden. As such, Maimonides intended to establish a clear partition between faith in pure unity (monotheism) and idolatry. He also pointed to the system of study by means of which each person of Israel is suitable to coming close to the truth, even if he is not a philosopher: the negation of all idolatrous, false, or erroneous thought about God. When we distance ourselves from error, we come close to the truth.

The second group of principles, which revolves around the principle of "Torah from heaven," includes the following. (1) God commands human beings through the prophets. The words of the prophets, which proved that God sent them, are true. (2) Our teacher Moses was the greatest of the prophets, for God spoke to him face to face. His prophetic status was unique; no other prophet like him has come or will come. (3) The Torah that Moses gave to Israel was "Torah from heaven" in the sense that it is entirely the words of God to Moses, and through Moses to the entire nation of Israel. All of it is obligatory truth, in its general rules and in its particulars. (4) As Moses was the greatest of prophets, and since the truth that God teaches is eternal, and it is impossible that it should change, one should examine the authenticity of the mission of other prophets according to their loyalty to the Torah of Moses. It is clear from this that it would be impossible for a prophet to arise with an alternative Torah of truth for human beings. In other words, any pretension of a prophet who would arise after Moses to offer an alternate Torah to humanity is a lie. Maimonides thus decisively rejects both the claim to the authenticity of the New Testament, which established Christianity, and the claim to truth of the authenticity of the Koran, which established Islam. Only the Torah of Moses is authentic, the Torah which the nation of Israel bequeaths from generation to generation, word for word.

The third group of principles also includes everything that Maimonides viewed as placed in the foundation of faith in "resurrection of the dead." (1) God knows with an unchanging knowledge all the deeds of human beings, without denying their freedom of choice. (2) God oversees human beings with an individual providence. That is, He judges them according to their good and bad deeds. He recompenses good deeds with good, and punishes evil deeds according to His absolute attribute of justice. (3) Through His prophets, God promised that when the time comes when Israel would be worthy of redemption, the king messiah would come. He will redeem Israel from the yoke of the nations, return Israel to its land, and establish His kingdom according to the laws of Torah. This will be the complete redemption. We again emphasize that Maimonides described the coming of the messiah as a political-historical event, which had no supernatural dimension. It was tied to the victory of the Jewish religion over idolatry, Christianity, and Islam. (4) Without connection to the coming of the messiah, God promised in His Torah that the souls of the righteous who died would return for resurrection and will receive their good recompense in this world. This principle is mentioned in the *Mishnah*. Clearly, the explicit legalistic obligation that issued from this was to include this principle among the principles of faith. But from the standpoint of the Aristotelian doctrine of the soul, to which Maimonides subscribed, an event such as the resurrection of the dead was not possible.

Critical claims against Maimonides emerged already during his lifetime. It was thought that he heeded to the *Halakhah* only for appearance. His full message could be understood only by accountable philosophers like him. Simple children of Israel would accept the encouragement they needed for their belief that they would receive the full reward owed to them in earthly form— which is how they understood this reward. The opinion that, as a philosopher, Maimonides did not believe in the resurrection of the dead was strengthened by the fact that in his *Sefer Hamada* (Book of Knowledge) included in his great legalistic composition, *Mishneh Torah,* he did not repeat this principle. Maimonides's opponents added that even in his *Guide to the Perplexed,* where three sections were actually dedicated to the three parts of his doctrine, this principle did not arise and was not discussed. Maimonides was forced to write a special composition, his "Letter on the Resurrection of the Dead," to explain his stance. But even here he did not succeed in persuading his critics. On the other hand, this should be noted: from the halakhic perspective, which is based upon the *Mishnah,* belief in resurrection of the dead was the basis upon which Maimonides formulated the obligation to believe in the group of principles which discussed the existence of God as leader, legislator, judge of justice, who awarded all humans according to their deeds. From the societal-political viewpoint, for which he formulated all his thirteen principles, this was the most important group of principles. It had to be understood and to be convincing from the viewpoint of each person of Israel. This group of principles was the ultimate motivation for observing the *mitzvot* of Torah, including the *mitzvah* of faith. Those principles led the person step by step to understand the supreme purpose of the *mitzvot*: knowing God and walking in His way. If so, the principle that is discussed in "Resurrection of the Dead" affirmed that the attribute of justice with which God leads human beings is absolute, and that justice will be fully realized in the future at the end of days, in a way beyond our knowing.

The first group of principles was of highest importance, from the perspective of the purpose set for the human being. According to Maimonides, this is perfection in terms of knowing the truth about the universe as a unified and eternal entirety—as God its creator knows it. Every person in Israel is to strive towards this goal according to ability. The importance of the last group of principles is first in instrumental terms. Certain knowledge of it awakens and moves all individuals to be diligent in Torah study and keep its *mitzvot* for their well-being. The middle group of principles bridges between the sublime and distant goals, and the direct and close means, for they include the path: Torah study and observance of its *mitzvot.*

Each Jew begins with the first group of principles through a process of education. The students learn by recognizing the authority of their parents and teachers, who want what is best for them and demonstrate this by their actions: that if they study Torah and keep its *mitzvot,* they will come to their good reward. The teachers allow the students to understand the substance and quality of reward in their own way—be it childish or vulgar. In this way, the capable students arrive at knowledge of the Torah and understanding its substantive value in terms of their well-being in their adult lives. In this way they rise to the knowledge of the second group of principles, which is tied to the granting of Torah and to recognition of its superiority over any other doctrine. As they proceed, this raises them to the metaphysical knowledge that is the perfection of spiritual success and well-being: a share in the world to come, of which the righteous are worthy while still living in this world. It should be emphasized that, according to Maimonides's view, no one can achieve perfection in knowledge of truth (as God knows it). Were a human to achieve such knowledge, his intellect would be identical with the divine intellect. Since such a height is withheld from human beings, all are equal in the sense of being infinitely distant from that goal—even though they are not equal in terms of positive achievement. They are also equal insofar as they realize their destiny and are worthy of well-being by persevering on the infinite path to their goals, and insofar as they are commanded to strive and advance on the path of truth and not be satisfied with what they already learned and understood. Only when human beings strive towards more exact and complete understanding of their knowledge regarding God, do they come closer to His truth and become illumined by it. When they conclude that they already have the perfect knowledge with which one could possibly be satisfied, they miss their target, they mistake the partial for the complete and transform the divine truth they acquired into idolatrous error. In other words, people grasp the divine truth as long as they are on the path to it. This is the depth of Maimonides's understanding regarding the concept of faith: infinite striving towards perfect knowledge.

These issues relate to Maimonides's doctrine of principles in their original formulation, which was made for the purpose of educational study. The poetic versions found in the *siddur* were also composed for the sake of education—not through classroom study, rather through ceremonial acknowledgment, which awakens feelings that bring faith and what issues from it. The abstract ideas are represented in metaphors that accentuate meaning in terms of emotional impetus to adhere to the ideas, delve deeper into their meaning, and to do what the ideas obligate: feelings of belonging to the chosen community, which is sheltered in God who is truth and in His Torah that is the doctrine of truth; the feeling of existential trust, which this shelter provides to those loyal to Torah; and especially the trust of individuals who are good and desirable in the eyes of the community, good in the eyes of their spiritual leaders, and good and worthy in the eyes of God. Also represented is the feeling that they are walking on the path of truth, which will bring them to their destined aim, and by virtue of that effort they will receive the good reward—partly in this world, and essentially in the world to come.

7

The *Keriyat Shema*: The Covenant of Love between God and His People

The Tie of Love and Sanctification of the Covenant Expressed by the *Keriyat Shema*

The two essential components of the *Shaḥarit* (morning) and *Arvit* (evening) prayers are the *Keriyat Shema* (Recitation of the *Shema*) and the *Shemoneh Esrei* (Eighteen Benedictions). The *Keriyat Shema* is not a prayer in the narrow sense of the word. The term *keriyah* as used in this context has two general meanings, each including the other. The worshipper reads (*korei*) three passages from the Pentateuch (from Deuteronomy and Numbers), in which God calls (*korei*) to the children of Israel across the generations through the lips of His prophet Moses, who also represents his people (using the language of "we"), exhorting them to hear God's voice, love Him by means of studying His Torah, and internalize His Torah and keep its *mitzvot*. The desire to repeat the "reading" or "call" daily and to obligate oneself to respond to it with all one's soul and with all one's might issues from absolute divine authority. This authority imposes awe and awakens love, which embodies itself in the call heard by the entire nation at the foot of Mount Sinai. It is heard in the depth of the soul of each person who recognizes and knows that he is created in God's image and is also a Jew who remembers his going out of Egypt with God's strong hand and outstretched arm, out of God's love for His people and all their children across the generations.

The addressee of the call that echoed from Sinai is self-evident. The first passage is in the language of "I–Thou." The "I" is the God who speaks through the mouth of Moses, who was elevated from among his people to be God's voice. The "Thou" (singular of "you") is the nation, which Moses represents before God. But it is possible to interpret the call in two ways, a command directed to the nation as a single gathered entity, and a command directed to each one of the nation. It makes sense that it was directed to both the nation and the individuals, as components of the nation. Both passages that follow are in the language of "I—you" ("you—all," plural). Again, the "I" is God who speaks through the lips of Moses who stands above the nation; "you—all" is the nation. But one could interpret the "you—all" either as a call to the many who are gathered, or as a call to each one of them separately, on the basis of one's inclusion in the many who are united. We will see, that in contrast to the morning blessings, the *Keriyat Shema* is directed to individuals as members of the chosen people, the nation loved by God who loves each one of its sons and daughters. It is a special love, which distinguishes them from other human beings and other nations, and a love that God claims from each one of them with all their soul and all their might.

The reason for the different form of address between the *Birkhot Hashaḥar* and the *Keriyat Shema* is clear from the above. The Torah is the book of the covenant, which God made with His people at the foot of Mount Sinai, for them to be His treasure. After that, the same covenant was ratified a second time in the desert of Moab on the way to the settlement of the tribes of Israel in Canaan. Then, a fifth book was added to the four books of the covenant, which were written over the forty years of the nation's wandering: the book of Deuteronomy. The writing of this book, defined as a "second Torah" (*deuteronomos*; in Hebrew: *Mishneh Torah*) began with Moses in the Moab desert. But it was destined to be written over the long era of Jewish settlement in the land of Canaan, during the sequence of events of renewing the covenant in the days of Joshua, Samuel, and Isaiah. It was completed by Ezra the Scribe in the period of the return to Zion. After the book of Deuteronomy received its final form, the writing of the Torah, which renewed the covenant, continued with changing times as the "oral Torah," comprising the *Mishnah* and the two versions of the Talmud and their interpreters. The ceremony that ratified the earlier covenant and applied it to the present is perpetuated in synagogues from Sabbath to Sabbath, on holidays and festivals, and also on Mondays and Thursdays, in symbolic form, emulating the founding ceremony that took place in the days of Ezra the Scribe. But in addition to that ceremony, renewing the covenant by a local community representing the nation, the rabbis instituted the recitation of *Shema* every morning and evening, in which each Jew sanctified himself to the covenant as an individual within the larger community.

Listen Israel (Shema yisrael) as Testimony to Faith in God and His Uniqueness

The *Keriyat Shema* also has a central position outside the synagogue, as the consecration of individuals within their nation, as an expression of the identification of the members of the people of Israel with their nation and their Torah. For this purpose, the first sentence in the first paragraph was marked off from what follows, in order for the congregation to respond with the words: "Blessed be the Name of His glorious kingdom for ever and ever" (K:98). The recital of this sentence thereby received the status of a *mitzvah* in itself: to remember the difference between the one and singular (*yaḥid*) God of Israel, who is the God of all the universe, and the gods of the nations and their idols. The sentence "Listen, Israel, the Lord is our God, the Lord is One" (K:98) is made into a proclamation. When recited out loud, each individual in Israel testifies that he worships God alone and listens only to Him. This distinguishes the individual from idol worshippers, even in difficult times when one was forced to encounter their hatred and envy. It also calls on him to memorialize and remind himself that the one and only God is the true God who rules over heaven and earth. Accordingly, even if the children of Israel were few in number compared to the nations that ruled over them, they were sheltered under God's wing—and this assured them that God would defend and rescue them.

These words explain the juxtaposition of the *Keriyat Shema* and the *Shemoneh Esrei*. From the perspective of the human being who knows his smallness *vis-à-vis* God's greatness, prayer to God in I–Thou language becomes possible solely on the basis of an earlier address by God through the prophet, to the nation and its members, inviting them to turn to Him in their time of trouble. Towards this end, God revealed His name to the nation, and promised that if they call His name in holiness and heartfelt intention, they will be worthy of God's attention and response. As such, the *Keriyat Shema* repeats God's address to the members of His people, to command them to love Him, and to assure them that it is proper for them to love Him, for He loves them especially and has even proved His special love for them through deeds.

As we will see below, the three paragraphs included in the Recitation of the *Shema* identify the Torah with God's expressing Himself to His nation, which is made present any time Torah is read aloud and heard, and identify the nation's love for God with studying the Torah, internalizing it, and keeping its *mitzvot*. The feeling of love itself is being conscious of the meaning of the act of love. The lover wants to express that feeling as a direct relation of respect, wonder, and yearning for the personality present before him, through the voice he hears. This is the feeling that each individual is to express when he unites with his God by reading His words aloud, while turning to the "You"—who addresses the individual through the words of the scriptural text. This intimate turn is a sort of embrace of lovers. In order to be worthy thereof, the following is required: ascent from the level of the feeling of faith, of trust that God will rescue the one who believed in Him from all evil if he did His will, to the level of trust where the substance of nearness to God redeems and shelters the believing soul from all injury by the evil in the body—for not even physical pain damages the soul or distances it from the God who breathed the soul into the body and returns the soul to him in the future.

This level of faith is expressed most explicitly in the third blessing, recited after the three scriptural passages of the *Shema*. It reminds the worshippers— and they in turn, so to speak, remind God—of the great singular event, which decided the fate of Israel when it left Egypt and faced the Red Sea. God redeemed His nation (note the past tense) in a form that would stand for the generations:

> [*Emet Veyatziv*]
> The Lord, your God is true—
> And firm, established and enduring, right, faithful, beloved,
>   cherished, delightful, pleasant,
> Awesome, mighty, perfect, accepted,
> Good and beautiful
> Is this faith for us for ever.
> (K:474)

> [*Ezrat Avoteinu*]
> From Egypt You redeemed us, Lord our God,
> And from the slave-house You delivered us.
> All their firstborn You killed,
> But Your firstborn You redeemed.
> You split the Sea of Reeds and drowned the arrogant.
> You brought Your beloved ones across.
> The water covered their foes; not one of them was left . . .
> (K:476,478)

> [*Tzur Yisrael*]
> Rock of Israel! Arise to the help of Israel.
> Deliver, as You promised, Judah and Israel.
> Our Redeemer, the Lord of hosts is His name,

The Holy One of Israel.
Blessed are you, Lord, who redeemed Israel.
(K:478)

What does this passage seek to express, by speaking in the language of the absolute past ("who *redeemed* Israel") about the present and the future? It establishes that any trouble to come to Israel after this event—whose memory would serve as an eternal monument from the past amid the changes of time—would attest to how the children of Israel ascended at that hour—when the dawn of a new day arose in Israel's history among the nations—to a level above that of their Egyptian exile, a moment when it was said of them, "they had faith in the Lord and His servant Moses" (Exodus 14:31). At that hour, they were worthy to be exalted as one nation to a level of faith that could endure any disaster, persecution, slavery, and failure to come in the future. The people of Israel would not degenerate again to that low level in Egypt, when slavery oppressed the free soul. In this sense, the children of Israel were redeemed once and for all. This is the power of faith that they achieved when they saw the miracle of full salvation taking place at the shores of the sea, and yet did not occur with the plagues which had earlier struck in Egypt. The threat of catastrophic tyranny was eradicated forever when the king, his ministers, and his entire army drowned. The children of Israel would now stand as free people when they faced future trials, and be required to bear the responsibility of free people, in the sense of believing in themselves and in their ability to confront future challenges, since God would stand by them. This trust is their redemption, which lifts them from the level of those who feared God to the level of those who love Him.

Yotzer Hame'orot (Creator of Heavenly Lights)

The theme of redemption, articulated explicitly in the third blessing, is already inherent to the first two blessings that introduce the *Keriyat Shema*. The call to love can only be heard by believers on a level higher than that expressed in the Morning Blessings (*Birkhot Hashaḥar*), and they rise to it in two ways. The first is the blessing to God as the "creator of heavenly lights," as they express His love for all creatures. The second is the blessing to God as the grantor of Torah to His nation, insofar as the Torah expresses the love to Israel as a chosen nation to be His treasure. The thinking that gave birth to these two blessings in their continuity and in their mutual relation is articulated in Psalms 19 (this psalm is also included in the *Pesukei Dezimra*—the "verses of song"—for Sabbaths and holidays, recited between the Morning Blessings and the main prayers):

> The heavens declare the glory of God,
> The sky proclaims His handiwork.
> Day to day makes utterance,
> Night to night speaks out.
> There is no utterance,
> There are no words,
> Whose sound goes unheard.
> Their voice carried throughout the earth,
> Their words to the end of the world.
> He placed in them a tent for the sun,
> Who is like a groom coming forth from the chamber,
> Like a hero, eager to run his course.
> His rising-place is at one end of heaven,
> And his circuit reaches the other;
> Nothing escapes his heat.
> The teaching of the Lord is perfect,
> Renewing life;
> The decrees of the Lord are enduring,
> Making the simple wise;
> The precepts of the Lord are just,
> Rejoicing the heart;
> The instruction of the Lord is lucid,
> Making the eyes light up.
> The fear of the Lord is pure,
> Abiding forever;
> The judgments of the Lord are true,
> Righteous altogether,
> More desirable than gold,
> Than much fine gold;
> Sweeter than honey,
> Than drippings of the comb.
> Your servant pays them heed;
> In obeying them there is much reward.
> Who can be aware of errors?
> Clear me of unperceived guilt,
> And from willful sins keep Your servant;
> Let them not dominate me;

Then shall I be blameless
And clear of grave offense.
May the words of my mouth
And the prayer of my heart
Be acceptable to You,
O Lord, My rock and my redeemer.
(Psalms 19:1–15)

The psalm is divided into two parts. In the first half the heavens are described, with the sun at their center. The sun rises at dawn, when the first ray of light marks the horizon at the ends of the dark earth, and touches the edges of the firmament which began to shine—this is the proper time for the *Birkhot Hashaḥar* and the beginning of the time when the *Shaḥarit* morning prayer may be said. From there, the sun moves through the sky until the completion of its trajectory at the western edge (the fixed time of the *Arvit* evening prayer). In the language of visions, the heavens praise the glory of God to all creatures of the earth, but especially to the human beings created to rule it. They praise in the language of pageantry—"There is no utterance, there are no words" (Psalms 19:4)—that is, in a language understood by all creatures and not only by human beings. All feel the greatness of the God who created them, His wisdom, and His providence, which rules over the creatures immersed in the temporal cycles—time that the sun measures as it moves around creatures from its dwelling place in eternal heaven.

The poet who recites the praise of God focuses his glance, and that of those who recite his psalm, on the sun that illumines the day with its power—by itself, when its light waxes and obscures the light of the minor luminaries, the moon and the stars, which appear only at night when the sun sets. During the day, the sun reigns as sovereign over the expanse of heaven and symbolizes the God who created the sun and fixed it as "ruler over the day" (Genesis 1:18). In its ascendancy, as a "bridegroom coming out of his chamber," the sun testifies without speech or words to the sovereignty of the Lord its creator, whose creation conquered darkness and overcame chaos, and who conquers and overcomes anew daily. But when the poet passes to the second half of the psalm, he replaces the language of the silent visions with that of symbolic words, which symbolize and define. The sun, which emerges as a bridegroom coming out of his chamber, is replaced by the Torah, which could be compared to the sun. Not with respect to all of creation, but with respect to human beings who hear the word of Torah, which is the word of God Himself, who legislates good rules for human beings just as He impressed His laws by might of His sovereign will on the universe He created. The rules of creation, symbolized by the movement of the sun, were therefore imposed upon His creatures so as to overcome the powers of chaos, which rebel against the will of God, while the rules of the Torah, its laws and *mitzvot*, are not directly imposed but established as conditions for the success and well-being of human beings. God expects that humans will receive them voluntarily, impress them upon their heart and intellect out of understanding, and observe them as free men, and not as forced or coerced. If so, the Torah, like the sun that illumines and warms the body, will illumine the human intellect and open the eyes of the human spirit, establish good orders of life, teach the laws of righteousness, fight against sins and injustice, and awaken feelings of awe and love towards God. In these ways the Torah makes those who study it and keep its *mitzvot* worthy of a life of productivity, well-being, honor, and peace. With this, the Torah expresses the love, which flows from God to all creation, to humanity in general and to His nation in particular. The poet concludes the psalm with the prayer of the individual to his God, that He might show him the path of faith, pardon him from unintentional sins that are due to limited human vision and weakness of human will, rescue him from the hands of the cunning evil ones who are liable to lure him away from the righteous path, guide him on the path of innocence and integrity, and turn His ear to his prayer.

The first two blessings of the *Keriyat Shema* are directed to the same sources of love-bearing faith. The first blessing relates to God as creator He expels darkness with the command, "Let there be light" (Genesis 1:3). He separates light from darkness and day from night; who has created the major luminaries (sun and moon) and minor luminaries (stars) to illumine the earth, day and night while clearly distinguishing between them, has, by means of these luminaries, fixed the orders for times for days, weeks, months, and years, as well as holidays, festivals, and seasons; and has established the firmament of heaven as the roof-dome to the temple of the earth, over which He rules, through the luminaries that He set in it.

"Who forms light and creates darkness, makes peace and creates all" (K:88, *Yotzer or*)

But understanding the meaning of the first blessing requires attention to the fact that it does not relate directly to the narrative of creation but rather hints at it through the words of the prophet:

> I am the Lord, and there is none else.
> Beside Me there is no god.
> I engird you, though you have not known Me,

So that they may know, from east to west,
That there is none but Me.
I am the Lord and there is none else,
I form light and create darkness,
I make weal [peace] and create woe [evil]—
I the Lord do all these things.
(Isaiah 45:5–7)

The interpretation of these verses requires identifying the person to whom the words "I engird you though you have not known Me" were addressed. The intention is explicit in earlier passages, not cited above, which reference Cyrus, the king of Persia, upon ascent to the throne of his kingdom. Cyrus carried out a decisive task by facilitating the return to Zion in the days of Ezra and Nehemiah. He called for volunteers from among the exiles of the kingdom of Judah to return to Jerusalem and rebuild the Temple to the God of Heaven, which had been destroyed by Nebuchadnezzar, king of Babylon. Cyrus testified that he did so because the "God of Heaven," who chose Israel to minister to Him as His treasure, commanded him to rebuild His Temple, which had been destroyed in Jerusalem, and serve Him there in the name of all nations of the worldwide empire that Cyrus succeeded in uniting under him. The words of Isaiah appeared in this context as a prophecy, which informed Cyrus that the "God of Heaven" chose him. Cyrus's ascent to kingship instead of Belshazzar King of Babylon, who was declared unfit because he profited from the holy vessels that Nebuchadnezzar had confiscated from God's Temple—according to the will of the God of Israel to punish His nation for its sins—obligated Cyrus to repair the destroyed Temple, return the holy vessels to their place, and to offer thanks to the God of Heaven and serve Him.

This relationship to Cyrus explains the surprising proclamation that God was the creator not only of light but also of darkness, not only of good and peace, but of evil. This is a confrontation with the Persian faith, according to which there are two parallel powers, darkness and evil on the one hand, and right and good on the other, battling one another over creation. At times, darkness and evil overcame light and goodness, at times it is the other way around. The prophet Isaiah established the doctrine of unity in opposition to this dualistic idolatry: The one and only God ruled over creation in its entirety from above and not from within it, and there was no god other than He. As such, the light and darkness, the good (wholeness [*shelemut*] of reality, or peace [*shalom*]) and evil (the power that separated and destroyed wholeness, the chaos) were not original and independent sources. God created them by Himself and ruled them with the might of His will, to achieve His goal in creation by gradually overcoming of the powers of darkness and evil—for they too were a requirement of creation. To emphasize: according to the prophet Isaiah, the chaos was also created by God, who assigned it a positive role in creation. Darkness was not only the absence of light, and evil was not only the absence of the good. Darkness and evil were wild, original unrestrained powers, from which creation itself evolved. Creation gave shape to matter, which was an independent, vital source of creation, as well as the source of the human ability to choose between responding to God's *mitzvot* or avoiding them. For this reason, Isaiah replaced the word "good" (*tov*) with the word "peace" or "wholeness" (*shalom*), expressing the reciprocal complementarity between the wild, material powers and God's wise rules of creation towards which God strove, in His ongoing struggle to renew creation, to rule it, and perfect it.

The *siddur* uses passages from Isaiah and interprets them in what follows in the spirit of the words of the prophet who proclaimed the rule of the one and only God of the universe:

> Blessed are You, Lord our God,
> King of the Universe,
> Who forms light and creates darkness,
> Makes peace and creates all.
> In compassion He gives light to the earth and its inhabitants,
> And in His goodness continually renews the work of creation,
> day after day.
> How numerous are Your works, O Lord.
> You made them all in wisdom.
> The earth is full of Your creations.
> He is the King exalted alone since the beginning of time—
> praised, glorified and elevated since the world began.
> Eternal God.
> (Psalms 104; K:88, 90, *Barukh atah adonai eloheinu melekh ha'olam*)

In the end, the *siddur's* citation of Isaiah is not exact. Instead of "creates evil" it says, with simple inclusiveness, "and creates all."

The "all" also is to include darkness and evil. But in prayer addressed to the faithful of Israel, the *siddur's* authors were careful not to present God as having created evil directly. In place of this expression, which was liable to lead innocent believers astray and make them err, the *siddur* emphasizes another idea, which relates to the meaning of the blessing said when the dawn illumines: God renews creation every day, when He has the sun shine in the east, remove the darkness, lift the shadows, and reveal the sight of fresh creation, which awakens to life at the very moment that the human beings, too, awaken, find their souls anew in their bodies, and rise afresh, ready for the day's work in assisting their creator in renewing His creation and in perfecting it.

With this blessing, the worshipper experiences morning, on the one hand as a revelation of God's power and sovereign wisdom, and on the other as renewal of powers that God Himself instills in him to actively create, renew, and fructify. The highest and most complete faith emanates from this double experience, based upon internalizing the words of Torah and its *mitzvot*, and upon the joy and light, with which words of Torah, "sweeter also than honey, than drippings of the comb" (Psalms 19:11), fill the worshipper's heart. The words bring him near to his creator and stir him to go out to meet the travails of the day, trusting that he will succeed in his activity if he keeps the creator's *mitzvot*. Thus, as Torah's instruction and command express God's love and "compassion" (the Hebrew *raḥamim* [compassion] connotes the mother's love for her progeny, the fruit of her womb [*reḥem*]) to His people, so Torah study and keeping its *mitzvot* express the love of the people for God, who has fructified them with His teaching and precepts, which are designed to cause the blessing of fruitfulness to rest on all their good deeds.

The rise of faith to this level of *devekut* (adherence) to God is expressed at the end of the prayer, which looks beyond the daily renewal of creation to the gradual convergence to the goal of perfection and peace, towards which God strives with the help of His treasured nation. When the hoped-for time comes, the dawn of a new day will shine in the history of Israel among the nations. "May you make a new light shine over Zion, and may we all soon be worthy of its light" (K:94). The new light, which will shine on Zion, will be the peace and good which should overpower the darkness and evil forever. Creation will reach its perfection. With this expectation, the worshipper passes from the blessing intended for each individual of Israel, as one person created in the image of God, to the blessing directed uniquely to the nation of Israel, which made humanity worthy by keeping the *mitzvot* of God's Torah and becoming a "light of nations" (Isaiah 42:6).

Ahavah Rabbah (Abundant Love)—the Love of God for the People, and the Love of People Dependent on the Love of God

In the first blessing, God's love and compassion for His creation are expressed in the language of symbolic pageantry. In the second blessing, God's love for His people is expressed with clear and open words.

You have loved us with great love, Lord our God,
And with surpassing compassion
Have You had compassion on us.
Our Father, our King,
For the sake of our ancestors who trusted in You,
And to whom You taught the laws of life,
Be gracious also to us and teach us.
Our Father, compassionate Father,
Ever compassionate,
Have compassion on us.
Instill in our hearts
The desire to understand and discern,
To listen, learn and teach,
To observe, perform and fulfill all the teachings of Your Torah
in love.
Enlighten our eyes in Your Torah and let our hearts cling to Your
commandments.
Unite our hearts to love and revere Your name,
So that we may never be ashamed.
And because we have trusted
In Your holy, great and revered name,
May we be glad and rejoice in Your salvation.
(K:96, *Ahavah Rabbah*)

Two emphases in this utterance stir the attention of the worshipper. They interpret the essence of the love as a mutual, non-symmetrical relation between creator and creature, between that on high which descends and that below it, which longs to ascend to the above; between the fructifier needing the fructified so as to give birth through it, and the fructified needing the fructifier to be able to give birth. First, the worshipper who expresses his love to God sees in God's love for him a benevolence that he does not deserve. But that benevolence will become his right, if he responds in love to the love of God directed to him, as the seed of Abraham, Isaac, and Jacob. This is emphasized in the statement that the source of God's love for Israel is "for the sake of our forefathers who trusted in You." Ancestral merit is the merit of their love for God, which preceded God's love for them, out of which He chose the nation. Since the patriarchs chose God, God chose them and chose their seed. The clear message of this statement is that the children of Israel would merit the love that God in His benevolence would initiate, if they responded to Him as their father. The matter depends on them alone.

But the second emphasis seems to say the opposite: the worshippers see their choices, their voluntary response to the love of God, as dependent not only on themselves but also on God. To be precise, we find this is the essential content in the utterance of love from the human side: the help, which people who love God as God loves them seek from God, is that God will persevere in His love for them and thereby help them to persevere in their love and express it in all their deeds. This expectation from the human side is necessitated by the difference between the divine creator and the human creature. For God's love is a continuation of creation, and the love by the created is a continuation of having been created. The love of God for His creatures therefore has to precede His expectation that His creatures will love Him—while the love by the creature for the God who has created it has to come after its knowledge that God loves it. This means that the very ability and desire to love are given to human beings through God's love for them. God's love stirs the creature to step outside of its self and extricates itself from the prison of egoistic physical inclination in which human beings are immersed since their birth in bodies shaped from the dust of the earth, and still permeated by powers of chaos which are imprisoned in their destructive blindness. Only when God instills reason and intellect in the human heart; the will and ability to study and learn; the will and ability to hear God's voice and fulfill His commandments; the will and ability to adhere to the word of God; the will and ability to unite with Him and exist only for Him in body and soul—only then can human beings activate their will and their choice, and overcome the blind inclination and egoism that chain them. With these words we have defined faith on its highest level ("for the sake of our ancestors who trusted in You"), which is the beginning of love, because love is already dependent upon faith out of the inclination of yearning towards the future.

Like the first blessing, the second ends with faith that the love of God is a great promise. If the Jewish people would respond to this love with readiness to keep the *mitzvot* of Torah, the nation and its members will merit the day of their redemption, settled in their land in peace. Peace would rule within the nation, and between it and the nations around it, and this would ensure its permanent security:

And because we have trusted
In Your holy, great, and revered name,
May we be glad and rejoice in Your salvation.
Bring us back in peace from the four quarters of the earth
And lead us upright to our land.
For You are a God who performs acts of salvation

> And You chose us from all peoples and tongues,
> Bringing us close to Your great name for ever in truth,
> That we may thank You
> And proclaim Your Oneness in love.
> Blessed are You, Lord,
> Who chooses His people Israel in love.
> (K:96, *Ahavah Rabbah*)

The conclusion to the *Ahavah Rabbah* blessing directs the worshipper to the sublime expression of love as a gesture of complete dedication (*devekut*, adherence). This is the preparation for the spiritual act of love, which is an act of the soul parallel to the physical-soulful love between man and wife in their copulation and unification. This term expresses the gesture of joining, almost to the point of a unifying blending: "and they shall be one flesh." But let us insist on the boundary that differentiates love as mutual relation from love as a conquering desire, which enslaves and swallows the other to the point of nullifying it into the physical or spiritual character of the one who swallows it. The desired unification is neither swallowing, nor being swallowed, but "uniting" (*yaḥdut*). That is, the persons who unite with one another give themselves to each other willingly and do not force themselves on each other against their will. In the coupling of husband and wife, man fructifies his wife, and his wife receives his seed into her womb out of longing to be fruitful and deliver offspring in their semblance and the image of herself and her husband. The unity takes place not by means of transforming the bodies and souls of the separate parents into a single body-soul, but as the fruit of their act of love, which is the body-soul of their infant children who blend their heredity within it. After that, the union is expressed as the common legacy, which is the love of the parents who created the child in the womb of its mother, and after that, as the embrace of the child's family. Thus it is also with the gesture of adherence and unity between the people of Israel and God. The expectation of ascent to a higher level transitions the worshipper from the second blessing to the *Shema* itself, whose initial verse is defined as a unit of its own—a gesture of unification expressing response to the divine call: "Listen, Israel: the Lord is our God, the Lord is One" (K:38, *Shema yisrael*).

The unity of the God who created the human being obligates the human to unify the powers of his soul, to unite his body with the soul, and to love God with all his heart, soul, and might. "Heart" means the feeling of physical life, identified with the flow of the blood in the veins. "Soul" means the spirituality of the soul of the human being, created in the image of God, his intellect and reason; and "might" means all the property of the human being in addition to his soul—the body and the instruments, which serve it by satisfying its needs. In order to unite with his creator and dedicate himself to Him, the worshipper is called upon to activate all components of his personality together and ascend and commit himself to God, in order that God descend to him, and fructify him with His word. The worshipper expresses his readiness with a posture of obeisance (the *Keriyat Shema* is said while sitting), in words that exalt his God over him: "Blessed be the Name of His glorious kingdom for all ever and all time" (K:38). Then the *mitzvah* is read and heard, which includes all the *mitzvot* of the Torah in terms of their lofty purpose: "Love the Lord your God with all your heart, with all your soul, with all your might" (K:38, *Ve'ahavta et adonai*).

Can love be commanded? Is love an act of choice? The answer that we hear from this divine commanding utterance is decisively positive. God commands His love but does not force it, because force—whether by external coercion or inner necessity—is the opposite of love. The explanation comes immediately, asserting that love is a voluntary gesture: "These words which I command you today shall be on your heart." This is love for God "with all your heart." "Teach them repeatedly to your children"—this is love for God "with all your soul." "Speak of them when you sit at home and when you travel on the way, when you lie down and when you rise. Bind them as a sign on your hand, and they shall be an emblem between your eyes. Write them on the doorposts of your house and gates" (K:38, *Ve'ahavta et adonai*)—this is love for God "with all your might" (K:38, *Ve'ahavta et adonai*). What is, then, the matter (word) around which the comprehensive effort focuses, that unites the powers of body and soul? "These matters [*devarim*, words]," which are the Torah of God, His commandments, laws, and judgments. If so, these matters, or words, are like the husband's seed that fructifies the wife, who is consecrated unto him to bear and give birth to their children and to unite with him in them. The "placing" of these matters, or words, upon the heart is the *zikah* of love between the children of Israel and God. Their internalization and dissemination, inculcating them into the children and applying them in deeds that bring blessing to the Jews and the world, are the streaming and the absorption of the fructifying emanation—similar to the physical seed, except that the seed of Torah is directed to a soulful-spiritual creativity, which is then expressed in the labors of the person who brings abundance to the world.

The second paragraph of the *Shema* presents the *mitzvah* of love from its negative side, that of "do not do." The wife who has unified with her husband to bear his children consecrates herself to him. This consecration is expressed in absolute continence—that is, in the absolute prohibition to love another man and surrender to him. Like her, the Jew is also bound—in the *zikah* of his love for God. The covenant of Torah places a serious prohibition upon him: not to deviate from the worship of God and worship other gods. As written in the Ten Commandments: "You shall have no other gods besides Me. . . . You shall not bow down to them or serve them. For I the Lord your God am an impassioned God." (Exodus 20:3–5). Straying from God, to worship other gods, is described with the word "jealousy," as an act of prostitution and adultery whose gravity in the Torah is equal to that of murder. According to the second paragraph of the *Shema*, every Jew is required to overcome blind physical desire and the lustful egoism of the human animal. The human animal is attracted to anything that gives it pleasure. It commits itself only to its pleasure for its own sake. The human beings' egoistic inclination grows stronger together with the material abundance and prosperity that they achieve for themselves in exchange for their work at home and in the field. When they become rich, they are not satisfied with fulfilling their physical needs as necessary. They rather yearn for more and more without end, and do not know satisfaction. Therefore, when people become rich, the power of the temptation of pleasure for its own sake grows stronger, as does their confidence that they alone, with their ability, might, and strength, have achieved this wealth. They no longer depend upon others or even upon God, because in order to maximize their pleasures they endeavor to liberate themselves from all their responsibilities and become enslaved to their inclinations and to the material factors upon which their satisfaction depends.

According to the Torah, this is the source of idolatry, about which God warns His people. In the second paragraph of the *Shema*, God warns about the danger that, should the people of His nation merit the abundance promised them in the land flowing with milk and honey in exchange for worshipping God, they would be liable to be captivated by egoistic tendencies. The result would be cessation of the abundance, because in bitterness, the children of Israel would not acknowledge God's blessing, and instead would imitate the idol worshippers whom God drove out before them, and thank idols for their blessings. Punishment would not be long in coming. The abundance would cease, and the nation would be uprooted from its land and be enslaved by their conquerors. Israel's longevity in its land depended, therefore, on observing the *mitzvot* of Torah—as called for above: with all their heart, with all their soul, and with all their might.

"To make tassels on the corners of their garments" (K:100, *Ve'asu lahem*)

The third paragraph of the *Shema* includes a *mitzvah* that was already cited in general language in the first passage, but in this third passage it is the main point.

Its goal is explained as a means for fulfilling what is stated in the first and second paragraphs: fixing the memory of the covenant between God and His people and each of God's children externally. As stated in the morning blessings, this covenant is comparable to the covenant of marriage between man and wife. It is symbolized by a tangible *mitzvah*, connected to a person's body through his clothing. Its function is to remind him of the sanctity of the covenant, so that he does not stray from his God out of lust, or neglect observance of God's *mitzvot* out of laziness. This refers to the *mitzvah* of the fringes (*tzitzit*), which are at the corners of the *tallit* (prayer shawl) that the worshipper wraps around himself: This is in addition to placing the *tefillin* on the forehead, at the place of the human intellect, and on the arm next to his feeling heart; and to affixing *mezuzot* to the house and its gates. These are *mitzvot* of memory, which are recalled in the two earlier paragraphs. The *tzitzit* and wrapping oneself in the fringed *tallit* are a tangible sign of memory—from which it is impossible to dispel the knowledge that a Jew is bound to observe all God's *mitzvot* and walk in their way.

The *Shema* in its entirety is recited after the worshippers have wrapped themselves in the *tzitzit* and placed the *totafot* (frontlets) of the *tefillin* on the forehead and on the left arm facing the heart, while reciting the morning blessings. This is a halakhic principle of "we bless the *mitzvah* and straightaway perform it" (*over lekiyuman*), lest it be a "blessing in vain" (*berakhah levatalah*). This *Halakhah* can be learned from the third passage of the *Keriyat Shema*— and is perhaps the special ideational message included in it. A person does not discharge his own obligation to perform a *mitzvah* by studying it, but rather by carrying out the *mitzvah* through deeds, which testify to the internalization of the *mitzvah*. The emphasis on the deed is repeated two and three times in this passage: "The Lord spoke to Moses, saying: Speak to the Israelites and tell them to *make* tassels on the corners of their garments . . . and remember all the Lord's commandments and *keep* them. . . . Thus you will be reminded to keep all My commandments, and be holy to your God" (K:100, *Vayomer Adonai*). In other words, the Torah was given so the Jews would do its *mitzvot*. They were not only to live according to its directives; they were to enliven the Torah itself in deeds. We will return to this emphasis in our discussion of the *Shemoneh Esrei* prayer: "To keep all My commandments, and be holy to your God" (K:100). The deeper significance of the *Keriyat Shema* is not strictly about learning and study; it is rather that of a symbolic gesture of ritual action, which unifies the worshipper's personality in its standing before God. When the worshiper reaches the concluding paragraph of the recitation, he brings his prior action together with his learning, and thus experiences his learning and prepares himself to recite the third blessing.

At the conclusion of the *Keriyat Shema* (which is recited while seated!), the worshipper stands up for the Eighteen Benedictions (*Shemoneh Esrei* prayer, also called *Tefillat Ha'amidah*, or prayer while standing). The gesture of standing is a dramatic emphasis, which accords special importance to the *Shemoneh Esrei*. One can see it in the culmination of uniting the person with God up to the height of holiness, in which the stances of God and the human being in their dialogue are reversed. In the *Shema*, God calls the person, who recites audibly and listens by placing God's words on his heart. In the *Shemoneh Esrei*, the person speaks and God listens to his words, and the person is answered. This is an ascent of the lovers of God to the position of equality with God—as created in God's image and consecrating oneself to God. This is the very highest level achieved by human beings, by merit of God's love for them and their love for God.

8

The Poetics of the *Shema* and the *Shemoneh Esrei*

Prayer as a Halakhic Undertaking of the Scholars of Israel after the Destruction

A study of the *Keriyat Shema* and its blessings as a complete literary unit reveals a well-developed conceptual and formal logic. Its goal was to satisfy the Jewish person's need to pray to God while fulfilling the obligation of "serving God" under exilic conditions. This was a halakhic undertaking with which scholars of Israel dealt, beginning in the days of the return to Zion in the days of Ezra and Nehemiah, with the same creative tools they used to bring out the oral Torah relating to changing temporal conditions, as distinct from the timeless written Torah. The question was: What is proper for a Jewish person to say before God? How can he say it, so that when God hears his request that He "who hides His face" from His people will return and be revealed to them, He will return and redeem His people within the prison of their exile and then from the prison itself, as He redeemed them when they left Egypt?

This definition of the literary and legal undertaking assumes that prayer is an art, that is, a special wisdom which we cultivate by combining two sorts of consideration in two areas. The first is the area of authoritative instruction anchored in the written Torah and its interpretation through oral Torah up to that time in order to say what is proper and desirable in the eyes of God. The second is the area of the life experience of the nation of Israel in its exile, in order to say what is necessary for the life of the present and in order for the nation to maintain its mission as a chosen nation facing the experience of the life of exile, with its distresses on the one hand, and temptations on the other. The exile established the "stump" (Isaiah 6:13) of the nation, which remained faithful to Torah in its encounter, not only with the loss of political independence and the destruction of the Temple that symbolized God's presence amid His nation, but also in the face of the animosity of the religions that dominated the gentile states into whose midst Israel was exiled—and further, in the face of temptation of assimilation into national cultures with impressive achievements in many areas.

A comprehensive turn occurred in the social, political, and cultural conditions of the people who, following exile, were called "the Jewish nation." Some norms of divine worship established in the written Torah were inapplicable to, and not feasible for, living in the new reality, and others could be actualized only by applying their basic values differently. For this, not only new interpretations were required, but new methods of interpretation that would be able to bridge the great gaps between the old and the new—and do so without changing the Torah that was given at Sinai and was binding for the generations in terms of its essential value and continuity of instruction and study. Otherwise, there would be a need to define both the foundational value and the supportive and applicable wisdom anew. How was this to be achieved? The path that fit best in the area of prayer was to look beyond the norms of the *mitzvot* of Torah to exemplary lives, those of the nation's patriarchs, priests, elders, and kings, as documented in the Hebrew Bible, and learn how they dealt with new challenges of their time—given that the merit of these personalities helped to rescue the nation in times of trouble.

The nation's patriarchs, its prophets, priests, elders, and sages carried out two complementary tasks simultaneously. They brought the word of God and His *mitzvot* to the people. They also represented the people before God, and brought their cry to Him. More than once, when it appeared as though God was testing those figures themselves, and also their nation, with difficult tests that were too much for human power, they did not retreat from challenging God. Their loyalty to God, whose word was true and whose judgment was just, obligated them, from their perspective, to express what was in their hearts and remain faithful to their people, who, in their view, were suffering not only because of their sins, but also because they were righteous and loyal to the *mitzvot* of their God. At moments of crisis in their leadership, in difficult situations where they could not accuse their people, or could not reconcile themselves with the severity of punishment which God decreed for them as if they sinned, they protested against heaven. At times, they revolted against the misery which God decreed for them with the mission He placed upon them, feeling that it was beyond their human ability. In these situations, they prayed. They also litigated with God, and asked Him for the justice and compassion to which he bound Himself in the covenant He made with His nation. These events served as examples, which the authors of the *Keriyat Shema* and the *Shemoneh Esrei* cited and emulated in the prayer they authored for their people.

The systematic approach with which the sages of oral Torah crystallized the *Shema* and the Eighteen Benedictions testifies to the level of their craftsmanship. It demonstrates that, despite the additions and changes in the various versions of the *siddur* text over the generations, these prayers are an original creation, created as a complete text, which expanded and was adapted over several stages, from the days of the Great Synagogue to those of Rabban Shimon ben Gamaliel the Second after the suppression of the Bar Kokhba rebellion.

The Literary Structure of the *Keriyat Shema*

We saw that the *Keriyat Shema* is a well-thought-out combination of three excerpts of written Torah. They were chosen carefully, to create a thoughtful and instructive sequence. Its recitation is a ceremonial experience which combines teaching, internalizing, and expression of identity, to be expressed in course with the observance of *mitzvot* between human beings, and between the human being and God. Those who recite the paragraphs of the *Shema* "affirm the unity" of God in thought, striving to grasp the absolute singularity of God. It distinguishes between Him as creator, and the creation constituting the entire universe which unites within itself a multiplicity that subdivides endlessly. The worshippers recite the *mitzvah* of "Love the Lord your God with all your heart" (K:98, *Ve'ahavta et adonai*), and elevate the feeling of love in their hearts in a gesture of devotion, inculcating the positive and negative *mitzvot* that express love, and pledging themselves to remember and observe them. They kiss the fringe, mentioned in the last paragraph of the recitation, as a sign of memory. By doing so, they combine the carrying out of the *mitzvah* with its study, and thereby realize the pleasure which fills them by keeping the *mitzvot* of Torah that express love. They are convinced that these *mitzvot* are neither a burden nor any imposition, but rather a matter of spiritual pleasure. To summarize: textual recitation is not only a matter of learning and intellectual internalization but actual experience of what is learned, and a dramatic acting-out before God who is present symbolically in the Holy Ark.

The sages composed three blessings to accompany the three paragraphs taken from the Torah, two introductory passages and a closing one. The third blessing is comprised of two parts: the part that concludes the recitation, attesting to the obligating truth which is internalized by the recitation, and the part constituting an introduction to the *Shemoneh Esrei*. It does so by recalling the memory of the foundational event when all the children of Israel rose as one to the highest degree of faith in God and in Moses. By doing this the worshippers, as members of the assembly (the *minyan*), draw the ancient event—the encounter between the children of Israel and their father-king in heaven—into the timeless present, in which the event returns and takes place daily and forever, as if the worshippers were now standing on the other shore of the Red Sea and seeing the enemies who have been pursuing them, drowning in its depths. Then straightaway, with the sublime feeling of being rescued by faith, they pass to the *Shemoneh Esrei* prayer—also called the *Amidah* (the standing prayer, contrasted with the *Shema*, which is recited while sitting). This well-thought-out literary structure testifies that an experiential sequence was planned from the *Keriyat Shema* to the *Shemoneh Esrei* as two parts of a single creation. Within this, a structural balance is created between the two blessings that introduce the *Shema* and relate to it, and the third blessing which is divided into two parts, the closing and the opening.

If we examine the literary materials from which the blessings of the *Keriyat Shema* are shaped (which we did earlier by way of example, in analyzing the content of the blessings), we arrive at a similar literary discovery. The content of the blessings is drawn from the Torah, the prophets (especially Isaiah), and the Hagiographa (especially the Psalms), and so reflect essential ideas of the Torah passages that are recited. We are not speaking here of God's word to the nation but of the response of the nation's prophets and its writers to the divine call. We have before us an arrangement based upon theoretical wisdom, developed by the faculties of human knowledge of Israel's rabbinic sages to plumb the depths of divine wisdom, which had been revealed to Israel in prophetic teaching, and to apply and maintain this human wisdom amid changing reality.

This literary creation appears to reflect the instruction of written Torah, quoted literally, in the exegetic mirror of human wisdom drawn from the life-experience of the nation, alongside the prophetic teaching which is cited with its exegetical understanding on the lips of the Israelite people as words with which they express themselves, so they may meditate what is proper to meditate and feel what is proper to feel when standing before God to serve Him and receive His blessing and help. The wisdom by means of which this literary and legal-canonical undertaking was carried out was, as said, the same general wisdom by means of which the sages of the *Mishnah* and Talmud brought the oral Torah out of the written Torah—that is, the wisdom called *midrash*.

The *Midrash*

What is *midrash*? We will answer this question by applying it. The Torahitic source for the wisdom of the *midrash* is the *mitzvah* that directed judges in Israel to carry out righteous judgment according to the ordinances of Torah and its laws. This *mitzvah* was expounded a number of times in the Torah. The most detailed reference is in the law that directs judges about how to adjudicate their judgment of individuals or whole groups in Israel who betrayed God and His Torah and served other gods. The punishment for such a serious charge was death, and therefore the Torah placed great responsibility on judges to clarify the truth completely and remove all doubt. It was forbidden for them to be swept away by their emotions. They were forbidden from adjudicating on the basis of one witness's testimony, which could not be compared with another. They were forbidden to receive testimonies without examining their trustworthiness or to determine judgment by simplistic application of language of general law to a certain particular event. The Torah formulated the instruction thus: "You shall investigate and inquire and interrogate thoroughly. If it is true, and the fact is established . . ." (Deuteronomy 13:15). The concept of *midrash* is derived from the principle of "you shall investigate." What, then, is the Torah's intention with this instruction?

First, we pay heed to the fact that the verb "You shall investigate" (*vedarashta*) is the first in a series of three verbs: "you shall investigate" (*vedarashta*), "and inquire" (*vehakarta*), "and interrogate thoroughly" (*vesha'alta heitev*). All refer to the same theoretical goal, but if the Torah needs all three, and in this order, they are not synonymous. Each one adds a special meaning clarifying the general meaning of the first verb. The general intention is sufficiently clear—the investigation, the inquiry, and the interrogation are necessary to clarify the authenticity of the writ, and to decide whether and how to apply the Torah judgment. For this purpose, the verb "and inquire" (*vehakarta*) is added to "and investigate" (*vedarashta*), and the verb "and interrogate [thoroughly]" (*vesha'alta*) is added to "and inquire" (*vehakarta*). The applicable meaning of "and investigate" (*vedarashta*) is the simplest and the clearest.

The judge paid close attention to the words of the witnesses, and endeavored to conjure up a realistic depiction of the reality described in front of his eyes. If the judge was trained to do this in a professional manner, he discerned various difficulties: missing links, contradictions, ambiguous statements, and the like. Accordingly, he needed to ask witnesses to complete their testimony and provide details, and by doing so also illuminate and disclose how the information they provided reached them. From hearing or seeing? If from seeing, what were the circumstances of their finding themselves at the place? We have a sequence of questions which, if asked systematically while comparing the words of the witnesses, constitute "investigating" to disclose what is hidden behind each of the testimonies. Is it trustworthy and given without ulterior motive? What are the circumstances that constitute the context for the events under discussion? What are the motives and intentions of those who did the deeds and of those who provide testimony? And finally, do the Torah ordinances that relate to such deeds apply—and to what extend do they apply to the event being adjudicated? All this is included in the scriptural instruction "and inquire."

If we attach together the results of the various directions and areas of research, we come to the general instruction, "and investigate." The aspect of "do not do" leaps out to the eye. "Investigate" is a command of restraint. We are speaking here of a very serious charge—doing something that could cause serious damage to the entire nation. Precisely because of this, a verdict is liable to change quickly into something more serious than the sin itself— innocent people would be punished, while witnesses who provided false testimony and were really guilty would emerge as innocent. This would be a legal wrong opposed to the Torah's axioms, no less than the worship of other gods. Moreover, in all legal matters, the Torah requires that righteousness not only be achieved, but be seen as such—and with such a serious matter, which touches the entire nation, all the more so. The people have to be convinced that righteous judgment took place, and not an act of zealotry coming from lust for power by false witnesses or judges.

"Investigate" is, as such, a command to act with precision, trustworthiness, and consistency, according to the rules of legal wisdom—whose directing principle is "justice, justice shall you pursue" (*tzedek tzedek tirdof*) (Deuteronomy 16:20). The emphasis of this law is two-fold. (1) "Justice, justice" is opposed to simulated justice at which we arrive when the deliberation is hurried and superficial, and general law is applied to a particular, unique act. (2) "Shall you pursue" (*tirdof*) is a command referring to a consistent and diligent effort to arrive at full clarity, even if this entails great difficulties and great commitment. The matter of "the pursuit" of truth explains the instruction of "investigate." It is forbidden to adjudicate on the basis of the initial depiction provided by the witness, which is necessarily superficial. This means that it is also forbidden to accept testimony in terms of passive attentiveness. Testimony is a description, which expresses the observational tendency of witnesses. It results from the intention to ascribe special meaning to the depicted facts. The judge, who is required to be objective, is obliged to free himself of any emotional connection to the sort of activities under adjudication. He is to disclose critical activism (regarding the testimony and regarding himself simultaneously) with the intention to reveal the truth—and not only in terms of the description but also in terms of the meaning anchored in the intentions of the doers, and in the consequences of the acts. From the perspective of the professional judge, this is the greatest difficulty. It requires not only deep research but deep and critical contemplation about outcomes, so as to provide the outcomes with objective interpretation. The objective interpretation is what is significant about the act being adjudicated in the eyes of the judge of all judges.

This is the meaning of "investigate" as a general instruction. According to this, *midrash* is the critical process of research and exegesis, which strives to decipher the meaning of the actions and facts to which Torah relates. But they need to be researched with the human instrument of knowledge on the one hand, and with instruments of ordinances, laws, and *mitzvot*, whose source was divine wisdom, on the other. In order to apply those ordinances, laws, and *mitzvot* to the real lives of human beings, they need to be explained with the same instruments as those for human research and interpretation. That is, to interpret the divine ordinance and law with human instruments of thought, in light of the reality which humans create; and for which they are responsible and are required to apply.

We saw that the Torah instruction from which we learned the definition of *midrash* is a legal one. But *midrash* is used to clarify all areas of activity, thought, and knowledge taught by the Torah as God's word placed upon humans—who had to understand it in their own way. Moreover, as a literary text, the *midrash* is not satisfied with suggesting conclusions, but sums up the essence of the thought process that brings about these conclusions. In this process the meaning of the conclusions and their authenticity is discerned and proven. The learner is required to internalize its essence and thereby study the path to be taken in his independent thought. In this form, *midrash* can be used not only for the needs of law and legislation or for the needs of learned study, but also for prayer. The worshipper, who is judged by God and at times brings God to judgment, relies on Torah as the book of the covenant that documents the nation's obligation to God, and God's obligations before the nation. He is required to say to God what is proper and desirable to say before Him, in order to justify himself and find grace and benevolence before Him. Indeed, the substance of prayer is the same deliberation in which he engages in proper self-reckoning before God. In this way, one's prayer constitutes *midrash*. It lays bare the deep reflection about the Torah and the depth of one's personal, soulful experience, the expression of which brings relief.

The Midrashic-Literary Structure of the *Shemoneh Esrei* Prayer

The *Shemoneh Esrei* prayer is the second half of the literary text that comprises it and the *Keriyat Shema*. It too constitutes an example of midrashic creativity, based upon the literary materials of the Hebrew Bible and upon an interpretative look into the recesses of the human soul. Like the *Keriyat Shema*, it constitutes a single and original literary creation complete in terms of structure, thoughtful-experiential development, and style. Overall, it is a profound, accomplished expression of the monotheistic religious worldview with which the sages of the *Mishnah* sought to educate their people during exile.

What, then, is the monotheistic religious philosophy, as uttered in the *Shemoneh Esrei* through the instruments of midrashic expression? Let us open the deliberation in this chapter with the first two benedictions. They constitute the opening of this prayer, in the sense of the worshipper's standing before God his judge. We will quote passage by passage from the blessings, indicate their sources, and explain the meanings to be gleaned from them.

First Blessing: Blessing of the Forefathers

The first blessing opens with "Blessed are You, Lord, our God and the God of our fathers, God of Abraham, God of Isaac, and God of Jacob" (K:108, *Barukh atah adonai*). We already indicated the source—the documentation of the event of God's revelation to Moses at the burning bush that was not consumed, in the book of Exodus, chapter 3. At that event, God revealed to Moses the name with which the children of Israel could turn to Him in distress. But what is the meaning hidden in this? It is explained by analyzing the conversation between God and Moses about his mission.

Moses shepherded the flock of Jethro in the desert, and as if by chance he came to the appointed mountain where in the future he would enact a covenant between God and His nation based on the Torah, which was to be given and received at the same event. God revealed Himself to Moses by means of the bush that flamed with a mysterious fire, which burned of itself—and was not a burning of ignited material. Moses's talent as a prophet was revealed in his alertness. He saw the wonder and was stirred to look closely, to understand its source and its meaning. Then he heard the answer to his question, in the form of a serious warning not to come closer than needed, and not to try to see what was forbidden to humans, because it was beyond their understanding. He was to take off his shoes and lower his gaze, because it was a holy place. Instead of approaching and looking, he was to be vigilant and listen to the voice speaking to him from within the vision. The place Moses reached was "holy ground." We will need to explain the meaning of the concept of "holiness" when we come to the third blessing of the *Shemoneh Esrei*; at this point, we should focus on its behavioral implications. Moses was cautioned to show the humility proper for a person of flesh and blood standing before the sovereign power of his God. Humility consists in the acknowledgement of an absolute authority, binding without limit. It is also the expression of unlimited readiness to hear and obey. This is a preliminary message, which pertains directly to the worshipper, who enters the circle of holiness that encompasses the Ark of Testimony—in which the Torah through which God revealed Himself to His people rests. Humility is a dialectic of standing before God out of a combination of love, the attraction to know in order to internalize, and awe—standing back before that which is loftier than human insight, out of recognizing the absolute distance between God and human beings. God bridges the distance with His love for human beings, and human beings bridge it with their love for God.

In the course of the prophetic discourse between God and Moses about his mission, Moses asks:

> "When I come to the Israelites and say to them, 'The God of your fathers has sent me to you,' and they ask me, 'What is His name?' what shall I say to them?" And God said to Moses, "*Ehyeh-Asher-Ehyeh.*" He continued, "Thus shall you say to the Israelites, '*Ehyeh* sent me to you.'" And God said further to Moses, "Thus shall you speak to the Israelites: The Lord the God of your fathers, the God of Abraham, the God of Isaac, and the God of Jacob, has sent me to you:

> This shall be My name forever,
> This My appellation for all eternity."
> (Exodus 3:13–15)

The meaning of Moses's question is as clear as necessary. He would have to demonstrate to his people that he spoke the truth. The God of their fathers was not revealed to them in their distress until now. They felt that He forgot them and abandoned them to their slavery. Moses had to demonstrate, therefore, that they were indeed remembered by the God of their forefathers, and that He sent His prophet to them. Towards that end, Moses had to prove that, indeed, the God of their fathers was revealed to him and sent him. Also, that the tidings on his lips were authentic, because their liberation from the mighty power of the pharaonic ruler by their own power and that of Moses and Aaron did not seem to be reasonably possible. Knowledge of the hidden name of God, the name by which He presented Himself which enabled turning to Him and stirring Him to rescue the people was the proof required. But God's response to Moses's question was not really clear. It had to be deciphered.

God's response to Moses's simple question was not in one sentence, but spread into three phrases which embodied a process of deep reflection. The first phrase was God's way of identifying Himself before Moses himself, in its initial words: "'I am,' He said, 'the God of your fathers, the God of Abraham, the God of Isaac, and the God of Jacob'" (Exodus 3:6). This name related to Moses, and it meant: "Behold, I am your God, as I was the God of your father who transmitted this knowledge to you. He learned it from the mouth of his fathers, as a testimony to the memory which established your people, the memory of the covenant which God made with the patriarchs about their seed." This determination explained why the sons were bound to see their God in the God of their fathers and to hearken to Him. God thus identified Himself before Moses, first as the God of his father Amram, from whom Moses heard the initial testimony; and secondly as the God of the fathers of Amram—from whom Amram received the tradition which he transmitted to Moses as his seed, which was the seed of their fathers.

Moses was satisfied with this name, and did not ask for more, because the divine "I" was speaking to him directly at that moment—and there was no greater certainty than the wondrous divine presence itself. But Moses knew that his people, who were living in slavery, would not be satisfied with his testimony, and so he asked about the hidden name. The second response followed: "And God said to Moses, 'Ehyeh-Asher-Ehyeh.' And continued. Thus shall you say to the Israelites, 'Ehyeh sent me to you'" (Exodus 3:14). This statement is composed of two statements, and there is a certain tension between them. The first statement is not heard as an answer to the question, but rather an evasion, even a rejection. It was as if God sought to say: "I do not have some hidden name of the sort you are asking about—that is, a name like the personal name of a person which signifies him, so that anyone who knows it can grab hold of him, and turn him towards him, and at times even force him by means of the name to do his will. The gods of Egypt had such names, and used them to perform wonders, which reinforced their rule." Here, the reference is clearly to wonders

like those that God wrought, with obvious irony, by afflicting Moses himself—
by way of demonstrating that Moses could not perform these wonders and then
undo them—in order to be able to show them to his people of little faith.

Meanwhile, God said of Himself: "'*Ehyeh* (I am)' what I want to be. And I
respond only to those I wish, because they deserve it or because I promised to
do so to his fathers who deserved it." Only as a second thought, does God say
to Moses that it is possible to use *Ehyeh* as His name, with its exact meaning,
that of a voluntary creative power. It is not within the bounds of existence fixed
firmly within itself, but rather an eternal existence directed to the future and
expressed by deeds that will shape the future and thereby reveal the creative
presence of its leader.

This meaning is invited by the comparison between *Ehyeh* as a name, and
God's words to Moses in response to His earlier question: "'Who am I that I
should go to Pharaoh and free the Israelites from Egypt?' and He said, 'I will
be with you; that shall be your sign that it was I sent you. And when you have
freed the people from Egypt, you shall worship God at this mountain'" (Exodus
3:11–12). The immediate interpretation of these words is: "It is incumbent on
you to accept your mission, and go out on the path based on the foundation of
the faith that I, who am sending you, will be with you as I am with you today.
Also, if your people want to be redeemed, they are obligated to accept your
mission out of faith in Me and based upon My promise to your fathers and to
them through you, such that they are bound to worship Me in this place. For
this purpose, they will be liberated from the yoke of Pharaoh. For my might
is greater than his might, and my authority is greater than his authority." This
was the response that God presented to test Moses, and it was intended to be
presented to test Israel as well. If the people believed that God sent Moses to
bring them to Mount Sinai to worship Him, they would be redeemed. If they
did not believe, they would not be redeemed. For God's authenticity was tested
by God's turning to the future that He had promised to the patriarchs regarding
their seed, which He then promised again to their seed.

We note that it was as the God of the future that God had revealed Himself
to the fathers of the nation, and first of all to Abraham: "The Lord said to Abram,
'Go forth from your native land and from your father's house to the land that I
will show you. I will make you a great nation, and will bless you; I will make your
name great, and you shall be a blessing'" (Genesis 12:1–2). And we learn in the
"covenant of the pieces":

The word of the Lord came to him in reply, "That one shall not
be your heir; none but your very own issue shall be your heir."

He took him outside and said, "Look toward heaven and count the stars, if you are able to count them." And He added, "So shall your offspring be." And because he put his trust in the Lord, He reckoned it to his merit. Then He said to him, "I am the Lord who brought you out from Ur of the Chaldeans to assign this land to you as a possession." (Genesis 15:4–7)

All is about promise for the future, the distant future that relates directly to the event in which Moses stood before the bush burning with fire: "And He said to Abram, 'Know well that your offspring shall be strangers in a land not theirs, and they shall be enslaved and oppressed four hundred years; but I will execute judgment on the nation they shall serve, and in the end they shall go free with great wealth'" (Genesis 15:13–14).

To summarize: on the basis of God's concern for the future, on the basis of which the patriarchs and their seed were asked to believe in God, *Ehyeh* is the name God gives to Himself in relation to His nation, whose time for redemption has now come. From the words of the "covenant of the pieces" we are permitted also to draw the meaning of the connection between the name with which God identifies Himself before Moses, "The God of your father, the God of Abraham, the God of Isaac, and the God of Jacob" (Exodus 3:6), and His identity in terms of His relationship to Moses and His nation, expressed by the name *Ehyeh*. We arrive at the conclusive answer. With the name that God placed on Moses's lips to place on the lips of the nation, the name *Ehyeh* changes into *Yod-Hay-Vav-Hay* (YHVH—the He who will be), who relates to the nation in particular as the God of their fathers, the God of Abraham, the God of Isaac, and the God of Jacob. This name relates to the people—to them obviously, because of their being chosen conditioned upon their believing in the future when they will have the opportunity to actualize their eternal destiny. This is the intention of the command, "This shall be My name forever, This My appellation for all eternity" (Exodus 3:15).

Against the background of the inner tie between God's revelation to Moses because of his mission and the revelation of God to Abram in the "covenant between the pieces," which foresaw the mission and promised it, let us continue our inquiry into the first blessing. It opens with the name revealed to Moses and concludes with "the Shield of Abraham." The phrase "The great, mighty, and awesome God" follows first. As expected, it is also a quotation—this time from Moses's words at the end of his way as the nation's leader:

And now, O Israel, what does the Lord your God demand of you? Only this: to revere the Lord your God, to walk only in His paths, to serve Him, and to serve the Lord your God with all your heart and soul, keeping the Lord's commandments and laws, which I enjoin upon you today, for your good. Mark, the heavens to their uttermost reaches belong to the Lord your God, the earth and all that is on it! Yet it was to your fathers that the Lord was drawn in His love for them, so that He chose you, their lineal descendants, from among all peoples—as now the case. Cut away, therefore, the thickening about your hearts and stiffen your necks more. For the Lord your God is God supreme and Lord supreme, the great, the mighty, and the awesome God, who shows no favor and takes no bribe. (Deuteronomy 10:12–17)

The citation of Moses's words in the *Shemoneh Esrei* prayer recalls Moses's warning to the people of his nation who at that moment faced an event of the great future—the settlement in the Land of Canaan. The attributes "the great, the mighty, the awesome" are placed in the mouths of worshippers in every generation, insofar as they are the seed of their forefathers chosen by God from among the nations, out of love for them and expecting that they would keep His commandments for their own benefit. This does not fall under the category of "calling by name," but that of acknowledgement. The worshippers are reminded of, and acknowledge their obligations to worship the God who chose them and drew them near, for their own benefit. For God was the greatest of the great, the mightiest of the mighty, the most awesome of all those who intimidated sinners who did not take the path of God. The worshippers know that everything depends upon God, and that He does not depend on them or any other divinity. He is the sovereign who does His will to complete His work—which is still not perfect and never will be. As such, no creature, small or large, has a way to divert God's judgment. It is impossible to bribe Him or deceive Him. It follows that recognition of His greatness, His might, and His awesomeness, distinguishes Him from gods of all other nations, just as this recognition distinguishes Israel from all of them. The gods of all nations who, in fact, are various powers implanted into creation, and in this capacity are subject to their creator, are gods only in relation to the peoples who believe in them. In relation to their creator, their sovereign, and to His chosen nation of Israel, they are not gods, and it is forbidden to worship them.

The importance of remembering the words of Moses at the moment of standing at worship before God is clear. The worshipper who stands before God to be judged by Him is bound to know and to remember all that, because he has to be truthful about himself and his deeds. For only by saying and acknowledging the truth can he be saved.

The continuation of the blessing completes the message: "God Most High, who bestows acts of loving-kindness and creates all, who remembers the loving-kindness of the fathers and will bring a Redeemer to their children's children for the sake of His name, in love" (K:108, *Barukh atah adonai eloheinu ve'elohei avoteinu*). These sentences are also directed to the future, when that which was promised to the fathers' seed would be realized. But what is their source? First, the words of Melchizedek, king of Salem and priest to *El Elyon* ("the supreme God") to Abram, "when he returned from defeating Chedorlaomer and the kings with him" (Genesis 14:17), and Abram's response to his words: "Blessed be Abram of God Most High (*El Elyon*), Maker of heaven and earth; and blessed be God the Most High, who hath delivered thine enemies into thy hand. . . . And Abram said to the king of Sodom, 'I have lifted up my heart unto the Lord, God most high, Maker of heaven and earth'" (Genesis 14:19–20, 22). Second, the words of God to Abram after his great victory over the kings who captured Lot, the son of his brother and after he declined to take for himself from the plunder: "Fear not, Abram, I am a shield to you; Your reward shall be very great" (Genesis 15:1).

This is to teach that the reward for Abram's good deed, to be given by God in the future, is beyond the value of any reward he could receive in the present from the kings he rescued. It follows that the worshipper who turns to God by merit of being a seed of the patriarchs and by means of the special name, which makes the God of the fathers into his God; who knows His greatness, His might, and His awesomeness; and who is ready to observe His *mitzvot*, will be answered as was Abraham, and God will shield him as He shielded Abraham.

Second Blessing: Revival of the Dead

The second blessing is clearly continuous—in thought and in language—with the first: "You are eternally mighty, Lord [ADNY]. You give life to the dead and have great power to save" (K:110, *Atah Gibor*). This sentence, the sources of which we will discuss below, ends with a gesture that illustrates its intention by pointing to a constant, continuous experience of life, which all humans witness.

During the summer months, when rain does not fall in the Land of Israel, we say "He causes the dew to fall" (K:110, *Atah Gibor*). In winter months, when rain falls, we say "makes . . . the rain fall" (K:110, *Atah Gibor*). This embodies the might of the God who resuscitates the dead—here, the dry seeds hidden in the dust of the earth. For the dew in the summer and the rain in winter enliven the dry and withered vegetation and the animals nourished by it. The blessing now continues the line of thought of the opening sentence, describing God in His might—

> He sustains the living with loving-kindness,
> And with great compassion revives the dead.
> He supports the fallen, heals the sick,
> Sets captives free,
> And keeps His faith with those who sleep in the dust.
> Who is like You, Master of might,
> And to whom can You be compared,
> O King who brings death and gives life,
> And makes salvation grow?
> Faithful are You to revive the dead.
> Blessed are You, Lord, who revives the dead.
> (K:110, *Atah Gibor*)

What is the connection between the first blessing and the second blessing? Why does the author of the prayer choose to emphasize the attribute of "mighty" from among the three attributes with which Moses crowned God? The answer is to be found in the first source cited in this blessing, in this case in the prayer of Jeremiah the prophet who gives concrete form to his faith in God and His salvation in deed, nearing the time of the destruction of Jerusalem and the Temple of God standing within it. From the perspective of Jeremiah, a prophet of God and representative of His nation, this was a moment of serious testing. The nation was likely astonished, as was Jeremiah, at the might of his God who saw the destruction of the Temple and city and did not prevent it.

> The word that came to Jeremiah from the Lord in the tenth year of King Zedekiah king of Judah, which was the eighteenth year of Nebuchadnezzar. At that time the army of the king of Babylon was besieging Jerusalem; and the prophet Jeremiah was confined in the prison compound attached to the palace of the king

of Judah. For King Zedekiah of Judah had confined him, saying, "How dare you prophesy: "Thus said the Lord: I am delivering this city into the hands of the king of Babylon, and he shall capture it." (Jeremiah 32:1–3)

At the same time, God commanded His prophet to perform a surprising deed: to redeem a field with full value from Jeremiah's cousin Hanameʾel—a *mitzvah* carried out immediately by the prophet, and thereby testifying to his trust that the disaster about to take place did not result from the weakness of the God of Israel, as compared to the gods of Babylon, but rather precisely from the sovereign might of God, who does only what He wants done in the distant future, beyond the near future which is already determined.

The explanation of the matter was that salvation would grow from out of the depths of an imminent catastrophe:

> But after I had given the deed to Baruch son of Neriah, I prayed to the Lord: Ah, Lord God! You made heaven and earth with your great might and outstretched arm, Nothing is too wondrous for You! You show kindness to the thousandth generation, but visit the guilt of the fathers upon their children after them. O great and mighty God whose name is Lord of Hosts, wondrous in purpose and mighty in deed, whose eyes observe all the ways of men, so as to repay every man according to his ways, and with the proper fruit of his deeds! You displayed signs and marvels in the land of Egypt with lasting effect, and won renown in Israel and among mankind to this very day. You freed Your people Israel from the land of Egypt with signs and marvels, with a strong hand and an outstretched arm, and with great terror. You gave them this land that You had sworn to their fathers to give them, a land flowing with milk and honey, and they came and took possession of it. But they did not listen to You or follow Your Teaching; they did nothing of what You commanded them to do. Therefore you have caused all this misfortune to befall them. (Jeremiah 32:16–23)

The fact that the opening of the second blessing alludes to the prayer of Jeremiah is demonstrated by its addressing God as *Adonai* (spelled ADNY)— for Jeremiah addressed God in that language. The reason for bringing this source to mind becomes clear when we read it. Every Jew who prays to God to ask for help in his distress, and in that of his people after the destruction of the Temple and the city, resembles Jeremiah who saw the might of God in His uncompromising zealotry, destroying His city and His temple because His people sinned against Him. But nevertheless, the signs and wonders, which God performed in taking His nation out of Egypt, still stand "even unto this day" (Deuteronomy 3:14) along with the promise to bequeath His land to His nation, to settle there forever. Therefore, Jeremiah trusted that the might of *Adonai*, which was revealed in the punishing of His nation. This punishment demonstrated the might of God, who would later redeem His nation, and return it to its legacy.

Still, attention is properly paid to the difference between Jeremiah's prayer and the second blessing of the *Shemoneh Esrei* prayer. In the *Shemoneh Esrei* prayer, the relationship does not raise only the problem of faith in the future against the background of the nation's great catastrophes, but rather, the general human-personal problem as well, the problem of every worshipper facing the evil encountered in creation—death, and all the signs that portend it: disasters, hunger, and illness. Jeremiah responds with the *mitzvah* of redeeming the field, which he fulfills despite anticipation of imminent exile, and with his prayer, in which he prays to the almighty God, to whose might—not, heaven forbid, to His weakness!—he attributes the expected destruction and exile. After the destruction, in face of the disasters visited upon him in his personal life, the worshipper seeks to disclose, in all these manifestations of evil, a testimony to the might of God who wages war against them—for God does not stop bestowing dew and rain upon the face of the earth, and renewing all of creation to remedy, maintain, and enliven it. This is the source of the confidence that God will conquer the evil and be victorious in the future.

In what follows, this understanding is drawn from the cited sources—in an act of midrashic patchwork throughout the second blessing. Let us present them in the order in which they are cited.

A. Who is this coming from Edom,
   In crimsoned garments from Bozrah—
   Who is this, majestic in attire,
   Pressing forward in His great might?
   It is I, who contend victoriously,
   Powerful to give triumph.
   Look down from heaven and see,
   From Your holy and glorious height!
   Where is Your zeal, Your power?
   Our yearning and Your love

Are being withheld from us!
(Isaiah 63:1, 15)

B. The Levites said, "Rise, bless the Lord your God who is from eternity to eternity: 'May Your glorious name be blessed, exalted though it is above every blessing and praise!'

C. 'You alone are the Lord. You made the heavens, the highest heavens, and all their host, the earth and everything upon it, the seas and everything in them. You keep them all alive.'"
(Nehemiah 9:5–6)
The Lord deals death and gives life,
Casts down into *Sheol* and raises up.
(I Samuel 2:6)

D. The Lord supports all who stumble, and makes all who are bent stand straight. (Psalms 145:14)

E. A Psalm of David: Bless the Lord, O my soul. . . . He forgives all your sins, heals all diseases. He redeems your life from the pit. (Psalms 103:1, 3)

The text of the second blessing is composed of these citations, in its duration up to its conclusion. They represent a number of essential prayers, which are cited separately in central places in the *siddur*: the prayer of Jeremiah, the prayer of Isaiah, the prayer of Ezra the Scribe, the prayer of Hannah, and the psalms of David. All express the theological idea that confirms the faith of worshippers before God, who have confidence in His might: the source of evil in the world are the forces of chaos, which permeate creation, and which God fights to overcome. The human being is created in God's image to help in His struggle against the forces of chaos. For the sake of this destiny, the people of Israel were chosen as special to God. The evil, from which humanity in general and Israel in particular suffer, follows from the great struggle that takes place mainly among and between great cultures. This is the fateful struggle between people and nations who hearken to the will of God and idolaters who refuse to do so. It actually takes place within each of the cultures, including the culture that the people of Israel built in its land, based on its obligation to God's Torah. But they did not adhere to it; they sinned and were punished and exiled. The agony from which humans of all nations suffer, and the nation of Israel in particular, comes therefore from the war in which they participate. God fights in it as the hero, so that all humans and creation will recognize Him and hearken to His *mitzvot*. It is clear that the sinners whom God punishes see the weakness of God in the ongoing evil of the creation, including the evil they suffered as punishment for their sins. On account of their evil inclination and wickedness, their eyes are clouded from seeing the truth, which is revealed to prophets and leaders of Israel who are faithful to Torah—that the suffering results from their guilt, because of which the pious also suffer. But the pious know the truth, and along with the suffering they see God's benevolence being revealed in the renewal of life, and they have confidence in Him.

The pious have no doubt that in the future God will overcome, and His kingdom will be established in the land. Then everyone, including those who suffered and died in the struggle, will see the great victory, the victory of good over evil, of life over death, health over sickness, satiety over hunger, happiness and joy over misery and trouble. Therefore, they pray to merit the great recompense, and they offer praise about it.

9

The *Shemoneh Esrei* Prayer: The *Kedushah* (Sanctification) and *Ḥaninat Hada'at* (God as Giver of Knowledge)

Might and Sanctity as Symbols of the Bond between Creator and Creature

The attribute "mighty," with which the worshipper addresses God in the second blessing of the *Shemoneh Esrei* prayer, is one of the aspects of divine sanctity. "Holy" is higher than "mighty," insofar as it is more than an attribute of God as leader and judge of His universe. It suggests transcendence, beyond the aspect of relationship to the world He created. "Holy" is one of the attributes of God's essence, by means of which God wants to appear to His creatures as ruler in order to let them know how He relates to Himself and to them, and how they are to relate to each other, and to Him when they come to stand before Him to serve Him and make requests of Him. This is a mutual relationship between persons who attach their self-identities to mutual recognition—that is, *zikah* (correlation, bond). *Zikah* is more than an external relationship between persons who view themselves as existing only for themselves. *Zikah* is a non-symmetrical attachment between persons who are joined to one another causally or purposefully—such that each of them defines the identity of his fellow from his perspective. Such is the *zikah* between husband and wife, between father and mother and their progeny, king and subject, and between master and slave. Therefore, only in the *zikah* with the human being whom He created does the *Yod-Hay-Vav-Hay* emerge from the absolute isolation prior to creation and anonymity. Otherwise, there is no one to know, appreciate, and affirm Him, and to be made into God's creatures.

The deep significance of this view, which is alluded to in the teaching of the prophets and made explicit in the words of the *Mishnah* and Talmud sages, is the recognition that despite the infinite gap between the God who created and the human who was created, they stand face to face with one another in dependence upon creation and mutual recognition. Indeed, were there no human being, a creature with reason and knowledge like that of God, with the ability to know His creator, YHVH would not be God. From here follows God's love for the human being, which changes into "jealousy as cruel as the grave" (Song of Songs 8:6) when the human betrays Him and serves one of His creatures or makes himself into God instead of Him.

In the chapter about creation, the Genesis narrative describes God as an artist who expresses Himself, revealing His wisdom, His will, and creative energy through His creation. As an artist, He separates His creations from Himself after completing them. He removes Himself from them, and lets them exist by themselves. The unique greatness of God as an artist is expressed in His ability to grant independent life to His creatures by means of laws that He implants in them. As God's creatures who act and are acted upon according to the laws which God implants in them, they remain solely His possessions, and He rules over their life and death. God aspires to assure their fidelity to their formal essence, to the laws and the destiny He set for them according to their place in the entirety of creation. But since His creations, especially humans, have independent lives and are activated not only by God's laws but by terrestrial matter which does not observe laws—from which material the body is fashioned—God's laws do not assure the permanence of their original formal essence. Over time, His creatures suffer corruption and decay, become sick and die, and so require oversight and supervision and ongoing renewal through their descendants. The work of creation is, as such, perceived as a phased process of formation, disconnection, and joining in a relation of power and wills between the Creator who rules and the creatures who are ruled by Him. Since each wants to be separate and sufficient unto itself, yet needing the other for this, an extreme tension is created between them. There is a yearning for reconciliation but it generates conflicts.

From His perspective, God is that being who is set apart and exists of Himself and for Himself, and He creates His world out of the necessity of his emanating "nature," which seeks feedback assuring His absolute power. The created world, confronting Him, and especially the person who is gifted with intellect and reason, yearns to be "as God," separate and acting by himself. But by power of that same isolation, the human being and God need (*zekukim*, a word related to *zikah*) each other: God—so as to receive feedback of the obedience, recognition, and praise that make Him God; and the human being—so as to continue to be blessed with the special properties that God bestows on the human. The attribute "holy" (*kadosh*) raises the internal tension between God and the human being to the consciousness of God on the one hand, and of the human being on the other. This attribute challenges God to renew and complete His creation, and challenges the human being to imitate God in His relationship to the creation He rules. As such, the human being yearns to be as God, to merge together or compete with Him—but humans can only make peace with their dependence and find their completeness in it. God is the *Kadosh*—the Holy One—by Himself, while human beings can only "sanctify themselves" to God, and elevate themselves to God in an effort to purify their souls of materiality and serve Him according to His *mitzvot*, and by doing so, achieve a certain level of *kedushah* relative to other people who did not purify and did not serve God with the same intensity.

Sanctity (*Kedushah*) and Sanctification (*Hitkadshut*)

With this, we come to defining *kedushah* (sanctity, holiness): absolute separateness from materiality permeated with evil, which is possible only for one whose power is absolutely independent, and which comes only from oneself. But as opposed to the primordial chaos which is permeated with evil, disorder, darkness, and death, sacred power is the absolute affirmation of perfect being and constitutes the source of all creatures who are good in the eyes of their creator, and thereby a model for creatures to emulate to their best ability.

This definition is found in the language of scripture in the central section of the book of Leviticus, which is actually dedicated to the norms of sanctity in relations between God and the human being—whether on the ritual-symbolic level of worship of God, or on the ethical level of one's relations with one's neighbor and other creatures of creation. This section includes a second version of the Ten Commandments, in a different order, from the perspective of relations of sanctity and sanctification between God and the children of Israel. It starts: "The Lord spoke to Moses, saying: Speak to the whole Israelite community and say to them: You shall be holy, for I, the Lord your God, am holy" (Leviticus 19:1–2). According to this opening passage, human beings are not set out to be holy by themselves. They are not likely to isolate themselves absolutely from the physical and material, which are permeated with the powers of chaos, which from the ritual perspective contain *tum'ah* ("impurity" arising from contact with death and corruption) and from the moral perspective, evil—disrupting the boundaries of law that aims at the perfection of reality and its continued existence. But since humans are created in the image of God and are worthy—as were the children of Israel—to enter into a covenant with God and receive His Torah, they are suitable to sanctify themselves to God and are therefore commanded to do so.

The question immediately arises: how can human beings, who are not holy from their creation, sanctify themselves? The answer: by means of observing God's *mitzvot*, whether on the moral or on the ritualistic level, because these *mitzvot* separate the human soul from the impurity and evil with which it comes into contact through his body. Another question in this regard is this: Is the human body shaped from earth suitable for sanctification? This question carries essential importance in the encounter between Judaism and Christianity—which comes to emphatic expression in the pages of the *siddur*. Christianity assumes that once primordial Adam sinned, he was no longer suitable to sanctify himself and be purified, for he was essentially impure and sinful. In Judaism, by contrast, according to oral Torah the recognition took root that the body of the human being, created "in the image of God," was not in itself impure; it received impurity through contact with forces of chaos and their creatures. Therefore, the human being required purification (*taharah*) as a condition for sanctification of the soul. In this sense, the purification of the body constituted a connection to sanctity.

The basic assumption of the Torah is therefore that sanctification improves human beings by realizing their spiritual destiny, which distinguishes them from the rest of God's creations on earth. As creatures of physical appetites, the aspiration to sanctity places human beings in a continual state of testing, which is impossible to pass with perfect success. The people who serve God, who aspire to be sanctified, are required to emulate God in the attribute of "might" that they manifest in their struggle with evil. It is up to the human beings to return to "conquer" their inclinations, especially the sexual inclination, the inclination for eating, and for glory and rule. The proper way to do this is by sanctifying the human inclinations for the good purposes for which they are designed by God: begetting children in the likeness and image of their parents, satisfying bodily needs to the extent necessary for health, conducting a well-ordered community, observing the boundaries that distance one from impurity and from seeking pleasure for its own sake. With this, we return to the third paragraph of the *Keriyat Shema*, which speaks of the obligation to remember all of God's *mitzvot*.

"To keep all my commandments, and be holy to your God" (K:100, *Va'yomer adonai el mosheh*). The emphasis is on the deed, which comes from knowledge and understanding, because the doing is what shapes the bonds of moral and ritualistic life among human beings and between them and God. As such, it separates human and animal experience, and brings the human being closer to the divine experience.

Sanctity (*kedushah*) and sanctification (*hitkadshut*) are expressed in activity and behavior according to norms that are binding from the moral and ritualistic perspective. But the emphasis on "and do them" means that, essentially, the *mitzvot* are forms and levels of being. Sanctity appears and becomes present as an absolute power, so that those who behold and feel it are unable to disregard it. It inspires a fear, which forces a "distancing," while at the same time draws one close to it out of adoration—which is the highest form of committed love. Sanctification is the result; it is an exaltation to a level of being that awakens in people, who have not achieved it, a feeling of awe and admiration for those who have achieved it. To return to the simile of God's revelation, which Moses beheld in the fire burning in the bush: an isolated fire, inflamed by itself and radiating light and incandescence from within to everything around it. Moses, of flesh and blood as all humans, could not withstand the power of the light and incandescence radiating from the holy flame—which was other than of earthly materiality. Moses felt, and knew, that if he satisfied his desire to come one step closer than permitted, he would burn. If he looked into the center of the flame for a moment, he would go blind. But the fire that burned in the bush and radiated light on everything around it was designed so that Moses would see that if he came as close to the boundary as allowed, he would be sanctified. This is the twofold dynamic of nearness-and-distance, which embodies within itself the internal tension of the *kedushah*—which at times awakens the same feeling of awe on the part of the people who sin, so that they recognize their sin and long to be sanctified out of it.

Moses's stance before the bush burning with flame is a simile, an archetype, by means of which a number of central events are explained, where the connection between God and His prophets, priests, and nation is experienced. Let us first recall the theophany on Mount Sinai, and then the dedication of the Tabernacle of God in the desert. The wondrous fire, which symbolized the presence of God in His sanctity, appeared in both. The fire of the bush, it appears, was connected to the first light, where God appeared as creator of His world. The flame, which burned of itself and radiated light and incandescence that overwhelmed all other lights, symbolized the direct manifestation of God, the eternal *Yod-Hay-Vav-Hay*, in action. Notably, this view of the manifestation of sanctity as a creative force embodies a well-known internal contradiction: the power that creates is simultaneously the power that destroys, when the closeness between it and the creature who is separated for the sake of its independent existence becomes too close, and the partition separating them is breached. From here comes the radical duality in the relationship between God the "Holy One" to His world, which is emphasized to the point of the contradiction in the phenomenon of God on Mount Sinai as a jealous God who seeks revenge against His enemies but who acts benevolently towards the thousands who love Him.

Might and Sanctity—The Punishment That Maintains the Covenant

These determinations explain the tie between the attribute "mighty" and the attribute "holy." The words of Jeremiah contain the explanation: God destroys and ruins not only His enemies, the idolaters who fight against Him, but also His nation which has entered into covenant with Him, and His Temple and city, for sinning against Him. From the human perspective, revenge against His nation and His Temple appears to be at odds with God's own interest: the gentiles and idolaters viewed the destruction of God's Temple as their victory and that of their gods—both over the nation of Israel and over its God. But the God of Jeremiah did not shrink before the idolaters' error, for the time of their accounting would yet come. God demanded that his people recognize and know that it was not their enemies who punished, destroyed, and exiled the nations, nor the deities and idols that the enemies worshipped. It was rather their almighty God who punished them, such that their enemies, who were indeed His enemies, were but an axe in God's hand. Knowing this is to know simultaneously that God's zealous vengeance against His nation expressed His great love, and that as the magnitude of punishment expressed as destruction increased, so also the consolation of salvation would increase, when its time would come.

If so, God's taking revenge against His people does not annul the covenant He made with its patriarchs for the sake of their seed, nor does it annul the promise to redeem them forever. To the contrary: it is the condition for keeping the covenant and keeping to the promise. Jeremiah demanded that his people know this from the strength of the higher affirming power, whose existence he felt and knew as permeating deeply into the avenging divine power. God does not obliterate His people with the vengeance that flows from His love, but when one "hand" destroys the generation that sinned against Him, the other "hand" rescues the young generation for the future. Therefore, Jeremiah recalled in the words cited above the signs and wonders of the Egyptian exodus as signs that existed and stood also in his generation and for all generations. He even cited what was said in the Ten Commandments, as engraved on tablets and placed in the Ark of the Covenant in the Holy of Holies in God's Tabernacle in the desert; and thereafter in the Temple built in Jerusalem: "For I the Lord your God am an impassioned God, visiting the guilt of the parents upon the children, upon the third and upon the fourth generations of those who reject Me, but showing kindness to the thousandth generation of those who love Me and keep My commandments" (Exodus 20:5–6). For Jeremiah, not only did vengeance not contradict benevolence. It revealed itself from the depths of benevolence, and benevolence emanated from the depths of vengeance. For God, "holy" is the one attribute that turns continuously as a flaming sword. Those upon whom it acts determine its consequences on the basis of their righteousness and sin.

God's might in punishing His sinful nation and destroying its Temple and city upholds His commitment to His nation and as such does not annul the nation's selection as "a Kingdom of priests and a holy nation" (Exodus 19:6). To the contrary, it is the ratification of the covenant, and is designed to purify the nation of its sin, restore and sanctify it, and thereby uphold the nation's commitment to the patriarchs with regard to their seed. God's sanctity therefore expresses itself in the absolute veracity, devoid of motive, of God's judgment. Also in the resolution that expresses itself—insofar as the decision of God's will is, at the same time, its own realization—in the activity that shapes the reality in the orders of life and creation of humans, which God seeks to improve through His law. In summary: the "veracity" of God's judgment over His creations in His world, especially over humans, and His chosen nation, defines both His existence above the world (His "transcendence") and His "residing" (*Shekhinah*) within His world as king. As such, the might of God radiates His sanctity as it appears to the world and humanity.

God's sanctity is not cited in the second blessing. But the indirect relationship to it is disclosed when we compare Jeremiah's words about God's might to the narrative of the punishment that God inflicted on the sons of Aaron the priest, when they offered "alien fire" on God's altar during the dedication of the Tabernacle in the desert—contrary to God's command. The sin was innocent, and of good intention. They should have expected that the holy fire, the fire that burned in the bush beheld by Moses at the foot of Mount Sinai, would descend from heaven to earth and devour the sacrifices. But the sons of Aaron were anxious that the wondrous fire would not descend at its time, and that God's name would be profaned along with the name of His priests, and He would be ridiculed in the sight of the people. This anxiety testified to lack of faith, and it caused the priests to deviate from their own human authority: it was forbidden for humans to do anything that God alone was authorized to do. That was the severity of the sin of offering the "alien fire," and it was aggravated precisely because the sinners were priests chosen by God Himself to minister to Him. The divine response was immediate and zealous. The divine fire burst forth and killed the two sons of Aaron in the sight of their father and the entire nation: "Then Moses said to Aaron, 'This is what the Lord meant when He said: Through those near to Me I show Myself holy and gain glory before all the people.' And Aaron was silent" (Leviticus 10:3). Divine might is expressed here in strict and proportional judgment—measure for measure—upon His priests, in His Tabernacle, and in the sight of His people. And yet, this time the scripture does not use the attribute of the might of God, but rather His attribute of holiness.

"We will sanctify Your name on earth, as they sanctify it in the highest heavens" (K:112, *Nekadesh et Shimekha*)

The text of the third blessing of the *Shemoneh Esrei,* in the version designed for the prayer for each individual to pray before the repetition of the *Shemoneh Esrei* (in which the cantor or prayer leader—*shaliaḥ hatzibur*, representative of the community—repeats all the blessings aloud), is very short: "You are holy, and Your Name is holy, and holy ones praise You daily, Selah! Blessed are You, Lord, the holy God" (K:114, *Atah Kadosh*). This text acknowledges that God, who is present to the worshipper, symbolically represented by the Torah scroll which rests in the Holy Ark, is holy, and the "name" of God which the worshipper uses in turning to Him is holy. This is succinct language, and it is not possible to suggest a definite citation as a source. One could bring tens of references from the words of the Torah, prophets, and writings attesting to God's being holy, and His name being holy—that is to say, that extra caution is required both in expressing and writing it. Let us recall in this connection the third of the Ten Commandments, even though the word "holy" is not mentioned there: "You shall not swear falsely by the name of the Lord your God; for the Lord will not clear one who swears falsely by His name" (Exodus 20:7). The matter of sanctity is hinted at in the warning and also in the punishment for bearing God's name in false oaths, promises, or declarations. Doing so is a form of desecration of the holy, and equating sublime value with light matters.

From this we understand why the *Kedushah* blessing, which refers to God's holiness, is recited after recalling the *Gevurot*, which praise God's might.

The blessing is called for by the consciousness awakened in the worshipper, who is approaching the moment of judgment, when dread of the judge of truth—before whom there is no preferential treatment, and who is zealous and vengeful against His enemies—falls upon him. The worshipper is bound to sanctify himself, and the act of *hitkadshut* (sanctification) actually occurs when the worshipping congregation reaches the third blessing of the cantor's repetition of the *Shemoneh Esrei*, which is recited aloud with active participation by the entire congregation.

The recitation of the blessing aloud is preceded by a dramatic ceremonial sequence—for the public proclamation of God's holiness is an intense experience. The prayer leader calls to the congregation as someone speaking in its name before God: "We will sanctify Your name on earth, as they sanctify it in the highest heavens, as is written by Your prophet; And they [the angels] call to one another saying" (K:112). The last sentence is a citation from the prophet Isaiah. The congregation and the cantor echo it, and by doing so assume the role of the angels as described by the prophet, as if at that moment they are angels of God, reciting: "Holy, holy, holy! The Lord of hosts! His presence fills all the earth!" (Isaiah 6:3; K:112). The prayer leader continues and recites in descriptive language which changes on his lips to a call to his congregation: "Those facing them say 'Blessed'" (K:112). The response again is also a citation from the words of the prophets—this time, Ezekiel, and the congregation with the *shaliah tzibur* continue as if they are the angels being described: "Blessed is the Lord's glory from His place." (Ezekiel 3:12). The prayer leader continues to chant, "And in Your holy Writings it is written thus," as the congregation with the prayer leader responds: "The Lord shall reign for ever. He is your God, Zion, from generation to generation, Hallelujah!" (Psalms 146:10; K:112. The *shaliah tzibur* concludes with: "From generation to generation we will declare Your greatness, and we will proclaim Your holiness for evermore. Your praise, our God, shall not leave our mouth forever, For you, God, are a great and holy King. Blessed are You, Lord, the holy God" (K:112, *Nekadesh Et Shimekha*).

The comparison between the short version of the prayer of the individual by himself with the longer version recited by the worshipping congregation gives concrete form to the function of the longer version. The shorter version expresses an idea upon which the worshipper is required to reflect actively in his thought, whereas the longer version is an act in which body and soul of the worshippers are united—by means of which they ascend to a height of reality where they not only reflect upon holiness but experience it. In order to appreciate the depth of the experience we present the two prophetic sources which shaped the ceremony as an event of really standing before God's throne in His eternal sanctuary "in heavens above"—the first source from the words of Isaiah and the second from Ezekiel. Both are prophetic visions, in which the prophets consecrated themselves to their mission:

> In the year that King Uzziah died, I beheld my Lord seated on a high and lofty throne; and the skirts of His robe filled the Temple. Seraphs stood in attendance on Him. Each of them had six wings: with two he covered his face, with two he covered his legs, and with two he would fly.
>
> And one would call to the other,
> "Holy, holy, holy!
> The Lord of Hosts!
> His presence fills all earth!"
> (Isaiah 6:1–3)
>
> Then a spirit carried me away, and behind me I heard a great roaring sound: "Blessed is the Presence of the Lord, in His place," with the sound of the wings of the creatures beating against one another and the sound of the wheels beside them—a great roaring sound.
> (Ezekiel 3:12–13)

In these two visionary events, the prophets stand before God's throne, facing the angels of glory who surround it, and sanctify the God who is elevated above His throne and above them. The worshippers cite the words of the angels who sanctify God, and imitate them by standing straight and erect on their feet, resembling the angels as described elsewhere by Ezekiel (Ezekiel 1:7). The meaning of the visionary parallel is clear: the children of Israel sanctify God in the synagogue, which is the "small sanctuary" (*mikdash me'at*) which replaced the Temple that now stands in ruins, just as angels sanctify God "in the heavens above." By so doing, human beings elevate themselves to the extent possible for humans on earth (and to the people of Israel in their exile) to the level of sanctification that enables them to stand before God who sits in His sanctuary in heaven, to praise and glorify Him, to bless Him and be blessed by Him. In this way, the convocation of prayer in the synagogue reckons with the disaster of the destruction and exile. When the earthly sanctuary was destroyed and the earthly kingdom was annulled, the sanctuary of heaven and the holy kingdom of heaven remained standing forever. In this way, the children of Israel can imagine standing before God in His sanctuary, even while in exile.

Graciously Bestowing Knowledge (K:114, *Atah Ḥonen*)

Further study of the blessings of the *Shemoneh Esrei* in their proper order draws attention to the fact that the two events of sanctification emulated by the worshippers in the third blessing are taken from prophetic visions. Isaiah and Ezekiel, one in Jerusalem and the other in Babylon, ascended in their visions to the eternal palace of God in heaven, and intermingled with the angels of heaven, so as to receive the task (the mission) which only they, as children of Israel, could fulfill, as Moses did in his time: to reprove the sinful people, warn them about imminent destruction, and lead them to rescue. This is the goal of their sanctification, similar to the goal of Moses's sanctification at the event of the burning bush. From here, we learn about the elevated place merited by the person who sanctifies himself to his God by virtue of coming as close as one can come to God to serve Him: to know God and to know His *mitzvot*. Knowing this path, therefore, is the condition for being rescued and redeemed from exile, and is the first general request that is proper for the worshipper to make. The worshipper needs the additional knowledge that is necessary for keeping the *mitzvot* of Torah amid the difficult reality of exile—whether for his own sake as an individual, or for that of his community and nation. In the condition of exile the response to this request is bound up with great difficulty. Perhaps this is the reason for citing the vision of Ezekiel who still had the merit to receive prophecy, even though he was on foreign, exilic soil. For at that moment, the time when prophecy would end because of the *hester panim* (hiddenness of God's face), which necessarily occurred with the destruction of the Temple and the kingdom, was already near.

What, then, replaced prophecy? The answer is hinted at in the language of the fourth blessing: the inspired wisdom, which emanated to scholars of oral Torah by merit of their diligence in Torah learning and their delving into it, to draw from it the instruction necessary for their time. This request is made in succinct, yet well-considered language: "You grace humanity with knowledge and teach mortals understanding. Grace us with the knowledge, understanding and discernment that come from You. Blessed are You, Lord, who graciously grants knowledge" (K:114, *Atah Ḥonen*). The opening is not stated in the language of request, but rather in language of a reminder to God about His path with human beings since they were created: "Bestowal of knowledge" is what made the animal, designated to become a human, into a human. It determined the human's destiny in creation. What is knowledge (*da'at*)? By comparing the use of the word in different biblical contexts, we can conclude that knowledge is the ability to act and conduct oneself according to reasonable understanding (*de'ah*), based upon knowing the needs and life-conditions of the human beings. And what is *ḥaninah* (gracious bestowal)? It is a giving that does not issue from the merit of the recipient or from the duty of the giver, but rather from the fact that the recipient finds favor in the eyes of the giver, and the giver has compassion for him and wants to act for his welfare. As such, this is the wisdom of the worshipper that expresses itself in his humility. Since God already generously bestowed knowledge upon him in the very fact of his existence as a human, the worshipper knows that knowledge is not a right he deserves according to justice. Rather, by expressing the request to know more about God's *mitzvot* and His Torah, the human finds favor in God's eyes; and God will be gracious to him as is His way.

Next comes the request, with specification of the sought-for addition to the aptitude for knowledge, which God already graciously bestowed: *de'ah* (knowledge), *binah* (insight), and *haskel* (intellect). By studying the wisdom literature in the Hagiographa and especially in the book of Proverbs, we learn that *de'ah* is knowing, defined with regard to different subjects learned by the person through his *da'at* (thinking aptitude). It reaches the state of *binah*, which is observation that distinguishes between attributes, qualities, causal connections, and goals. It evaluates the benefit and damage, good and bad, which emerge from them. *Binah* brings about *haskel*, which is proficiency in the application of *de'ah* and *binah* to acts that enable the human beings to derive benefit and good from them.

The fourth blessing does not cite sources, but is based on them. We recalled wisdom literature above, primarily the Proverbs. We now add the source from which we learn that the request for knowledge of a certain type is the request proper for a person to make when standing before God, to find favor in His eyes, and to have all proper requests that he directs to God fulfilled. The reference is to the request that Solomon (the wisest of all men, and traditionally the author of the book of Proverbs) made of God, while walking to Gibeon to perform a sacrifice in the name of God, once he would sit on the throne of his father, when he was consolidating his rule:

> In Gibeon the Lord appeared to Solomon in a dream by night; and God said: "Ask what I shall grant you." Solomon said, "You dealt most graciously with Your servant my father David,

because he walked before You in faithfulness and righteousness and in integrity of heart. You have continued this great kindness to him by giving him a son to occupy his throne, as is now the case. And now, O Lord my God, You have made Your servant king in place of my father David; but I am a young lad, with no experience in leadership. Your servant finds himself in the midst of the people you have chosen, a people too numerous to be numbered or counted. Grant, then, Your servant an understanding mind to judge Your people, to distinguish between good and bad; for who can judge this vast people of Yours?"

The Lord was pleased that Solomon had asked for this. And God said to him, "Because you asked for this—you did not ask for long life, you did not ask for riches, you did not ask for the life of your enemies, but you asked for discernment in dispensing justice—I now do as you have spoken. I grant you a wise and discerning mind; there has never bene anyone like you before, nor will anyone like you arise again. And I also grant you what you did not ask for—both riches and glory all your life—the like of which no king has ever had. And I will further grant you long life, if you will walk in My ways and observe My laws and commandments, as did your father David." (I Kings 3:5–14)

The circularity expressed in Solomon's words and in God's response is instructive. Solomon greatly revealed his heart's understanding when he responded properly to God's query with a response which included all desires of the heart. Had he asked to satisfy those desires without asking for the knowledge to enable him to complete his mission as king, leader, and judge of his people according to God's instruction, he would not have been answered. But since he asked with wisdom and demonstrated that he was worthy, God granted him the knowledge and understanding he requested. We learn from this, that prayer is wisdom: it is the knowledge of what is proper to request, and the manner in which the request should be made, if it is to find favor in God's eyes and be answered. We learn that the first request, upon which all else depended, is for the knowledge and understanding by means of which a person can complete the mission he is to carry out in the world. We can learn from this, that the knowledge and understanding requested are the ability to distinguish between good and evil in order to improve, and to follow the paths of God properly, as they are commands in the ordinances and laws of Torah. By walking on this path, a person acquits himself before God and all his requests will be answered to his benefit.

By probing the special version the sages formulated for this blessing for the evening prayer at the close of the Sabbath, we can speak to the connection between this blessing and the *Kedushah*, on one hand, and the blessings that immediately follow, on the other.

> You grace humanity with knowledge and teach mortals understanding. You have graced us with the knowledge of Your Torah, and taught us to perform the statues of Your will. You have distinguished, Lord our God, between sacred and profane, light and darkness, Israel and the nations, and between the seventh day and the six days of work. Our Father, our King, may the days approaching us bring peace; may we be free from all sin, cleansed from all iniquity, holding fast to our reverence of You. And Grace us with the knowledge, understanding and discernment that come from You. Blessed are You, Lord, who graciously grants knowledge. (K:260, *Atah Ḥonen*)

10

The *Shemoneh Esrei* Prayer— Requests by the Individual in the Assembly: *Teshuvah* (Repentance) and Forgiveness

The first three blessings of the *Shemoneh Esrei* prayer are recited in the language of "we" (*anaḥnu*), language denoting the *minyan* that worships as a single assembly. The children of Israel were chosen as one assembly, insofar as they were the "seed of Abraham, Isaac, and Jacob," who received YHVH as God to be "special to Him," and God would be known in the world by their name. Therefore, only as a single assembly are they sanctified and compared to God's pure angels, who always enact His word. But the fourth blessing, the request for knowledge, begins a series of the six requests in the *Shemoneh Esrei*, which are requests by all the individuals who compose the assembly, regarding their eeds.

The connection of these blessings-of-request to the individuals is a khic (legal) determination, the logic of which is relevant. The knowledge de into the property of the public by means of individuals who study ternalize the wisdom of Torah. The wisdom of Torah is of course the l legacy to collective Israel, but individuals are the ones who study and e it, to the extent of their abilities and skills, and apply and teach the ich expands increasingly by means of the individuals to their entire an conclude from this, that while the collective—the nation—as entity is prior to the individuals who constitute it in terms of tion, individuals are prior to the collective in terms of learning, rpretation, and renewed creativity. This determination is also basis of the source from which the language of the *Ḥonen* as borrowed, which is the personal request of Solomon, wisest of men, who had the intelligence to request wisdom as an instrument to serve him in fulfilling his essential task as king in Israel, to judge his people righteously. Like Solomon, it is appropriate for the worshipper to have the intelligence to ask for knowledge as an instrument for preparing his request to God, his king and judge, in a form to assure willing acceptance. Accordingly, on the basis of knowing the path of prayer suitable to its goals, five personal requests are formulated whose fulfillment is necessary for the life and happiness of every person of Israel, whether in terms of satisfying life-needs, or in terms of the *mitzvot* for which the person as member of the assembly of Israel bears responsibility.

We can also learn from this, that God's response to personal requests by one of the assembly of Israel is conditioned also by knowledge of the things which God, as creator of all creatures, gives to His creatures out of love for them. It is appropriate and good in God's eyes to request them. It is also conditioned by the question: What is the proper way for a person to ask, such as to demonstrate that he is good and deserves an answer? Knowing this provides the worshipper, when he prays, with a feeling that God expects the request and will respond. This was a legalistic rationale and was defined by Rabban Gamaliel the son of Rabbi Yehudah Hanasi in his striking aphorism: "Do His will as if it were yours, so that He may do your will as if it were His" (*Pirkei Avot* 2:4; K:646). This wise statement is exemplified by the five requests in the *Shemoneh Esrei* prayer, which come after the request for knowledge. We start with the two requests that begin the path—the request for *teshuvah* and that for forgiveness (*seliḥah*).

On Return (*Shivah*) and Penitent Return (*Teshuvah*)

A person gifted with knowledge knows, when he stands before divine judgment, that as a person of flesh and blood whose heart is "evil from his youth" (Genesis 8:21), he has surely sinned against *mitzvot* that are between him and God, and violated *mitzvot* that are between him and his fellow, if not maliciously then unintentionally, and if not intentionally then by inattention and out of weakness. It follows that the privilege of standing before one's God in prayer, and making personal request, depends upon one's psychological readiness to repair what was perverted by evil deeds, so as to make oneself worthy to ask for good for oneself, and to be answered for the good.

> Bring us back, our Father, to Your Torah,
> Draw us near, our King, to Your service [*avodah*],

Lead us back to You in perfect repentance.
Blessed are You, Lord, who desires repentance [teshuvah].
(K:114, Hashiveinu)

The will of the worshipper to return in complete teshuvah to the path of Torah and avodah (service) from the sins he committed is expressed in this version of the request. But the form of its expression, as a request to God to respond to the worshipper and to return the worshipper to Him, but not as a gesture of return (through confessing, expressing regret and readiness to rectify), embodies a puzzling paradox. Does the teshuvah to God's Torah, the teshuvah to serve Him, and the complete teshuvah from sins committed by the worshipper, depend upon God's will to return him to His Torah, which has already been given, and to God's service, which was already known to all members of Israel? Is teshuvah (in the sense of return or repentance) not one of those mitzvot whose observance depends upon human will—for which purpose God graced him with free choice? Does God also rule the free will of the human, and direct him towards sin or righteousness?

The question could be answered cleverly, with an answer containing a grain of psychological truth, which makes the prayer into an art of "finding favor" in the eyes of God. Clearly, one who says "Bring us back, our Father" expresses, by these words, one's desire to return and thereby to direct the heart of God to relate to one's sins with the attribute of compassion as a father to his wayward son—rather than with the attribute of judgment, as king to a slave who sinned against him. The father hopes for the return of his beloved son to him, not only because he is concerned about him, but because he yearns for his son and needs him—even though the son has sinned against him. In other words, while the plea "Bring us back, our Father" posits God's call to the human beings as the precondition for their repentance, it simultaneously embodies the act of teshuvah in a gesture of endearment, akin to a son who sins against his father and is punished with expulsion from him, and who then asks for compassion so the father would listen to his regret and call him to return from his exile.

These words contain a grain of psychological truth, but they do not remove the theological quandary. Let us study the version of the request in detail. It expresses the will to return to the Torah and to serve God. But the ability to do this depends upon a specific act asked of God so that worshipper could do God's will. To what act, which God alone can perform, are the words directed? How is God supposed to "return" the worshipper to the Torah? What is the worshipper missing that enables him to fulfill his wish to return? The only answer has to be about removing some obstacle or some deterrent, which God Himself had placed on the path to return to Him. Something extraordinary happened, constituting a partition between God and the assembly of Israel—which God on His part alone can remove.

Hashiveinu ("Bring us back")—Precondition for *Nashuvah* ("We shall return")

What was the event? The answer to the quandary is to be found in the source quoted in the text of the request. It is the prayer of Jeremiah the prophet, in the name of his people who survived the disaster of the destruction of Jerusalem, the kingdom of Judah and the Temple—at the conclusion of the lamentations of the scroll of Lamentations:

> Gone is the joy of our hearts;
> Our dancing is turned into mourning.
> The crown has fallen from our head;
> Woe to us that we have sinned!
> Because of this our hearts are sick,
> Because of these our eyes are dimmed:
> Because of Mount Zion, which lies desolate; Jackals prowl
> over it.
> But You, O Lord, are enthroned forever,
> Your throne endures through the ages.
> Why have You forgotten us utterly,
> Forsaken us for all time?
> Turn us back, O Lord, to Yourself,
> And let us return
> Renew our days as of old!
> For truly, You have rejected us,
> Bitterly raged against us.
> Turn us back, O Lord, to Yourself,
> And let us return;
> Renew our days as of old!
> (Lamentations 5:15–22)

We find at the conclusion of the passage cited above the request that is expressed in the fifth blessing of the *Shemoneh Esrei: Hashiveinu* ("Bring us back") as a precondition for *Nashuv* ("Let us return")—but against the background of the event that explains it: the destruction of Zion, with jackals prowling amid the ruins. The destruction expressed God's abandoning His nation; it expressed His loathing of His nation, and His destructive wrath. God returned to His heavenly eternity, and hid His face from His nation—immersed in depths of distress and despair. This was the reason for the prophet's request, in the name of the remnants of his exiled people, to return to serve God as in earlier days, and to find favor in His eyes. But in order for the remnant to be able to return from the sins—on account of which they were punished and whose rectification was a condition for their redemption—God needed to return them to Him, and do so by means of a sign of the easing of their situation to the extent of enabling them to regain strength and return to an orderly life, so that they would be protected from the animus of the cruel enemy into whose midst they were exiled. Only by means of such a change in their situation, while still in exile, would they feel that God no longer loathed them, was not wrathful, and did not hide His face. Only then could they return to Torah and service, as a path of return to God. To understand the depth of the feeling of the remnants that God must remove the obstacle He placed on their path before they could return to Him, it needs to be remembered that at the conclusion of the lamentation over the destruction of his land, government, Temple, and nation, Jeremiah spoke in the name of the younger generation, which had survived the destruction. They were the children who, like him, were innocent victims. The punishment was recompense for the sins of their fathers, while they, the youth, had not sinned—indeed, they could not sin because of the cruel blows, which fell upon them. If, despite this, they were ready to return to Torah and service, hoping that by doing so they would return to their land, city, government, and Temple, this would be justice for them before God. They had the right, not only to ask, but to claim from God those rights owed to them by the power of the covenant, which had not been annulled. They deserved a sign of graciousness, they deserved God's easing the suffering and opening a threshold of hope of being redeemed. For otherwise, how could they return to faith as the condition for the psychological ability to observe the *mitzvot* of Torah and serve in the right spirit—and not in rote fashion?

Remembering the passages of Lamentations positions the worshipper, such that he is included, in his request, along with the remnant of his nation suffering from the destruction. The void created in the nation's life was still not filled—although that was not because of sin. The request to return to Torah and worship is, therefore, a request to return to being good and proper in the eyes of God and worthy of hoping for an imminent return to Zion—for which a good sign was also required of God.

Teshuvah in a Reality That Does Not Include Atonement Sacrifice

But not even these matters resolve the great problem which the prayer for return encounters in the context of destruction and exile. The theological depth of the problem is expressed by the question: in a situation where prayer has to replace serving God in the Temple, is there a path to return from sins committed by the nation in the past, and which individuals continue to commit? Does the gate of "atonement," which is the condition for *teshuvah*, remain open? Did not the destruction of the Temple, which prevented serving God with sacrifices, close the nation's path of return to God, the Land of Israel, Jerusalem, and the Sanctuary, which was shut, once and for all?

What was the essential role of the sacrificial service in the Temple, the absence of which was felt by the nation? The "Book of Priests," which is the book of Leviticus, enumerates several types of sacrifice, which filled different functions in the life of the nation. These included eating kosher meat at the Sabbath, holiday, and festival feast—and providing kosher meat for priests and Levites as reward for their service. But the most important role of the sacrifice had to do with the need to atone for the sins of the children of Israel, cleansing their souls from the pollution of trespasses committed due to their inclinations. Sacrifice purified and sanctified their souls, so they could continue to serve God by keeping all His *mitzvot*. This would realize their destiny, for their own benefit as well as that of their entire surrounding, in terms of good health, abundant earnings, and peace.

The problem which the *Hashiveinu Avinu* request came to deal with- enabling the worshipper to request forgiveness and redemption, and after that health, earnings and peace- was the exchange for sacrifice offered by synagogal prayer to atone for the nation's sins. A terrible trap was created regarding "measure-for-measure" punishment for the nation's trespasses—at that time it was impossible to atone for sins with sacrifices alone. The nation was deprived of the path taught by written Torah for the nation to atone for sins, preventing the possibility of returning to Torah and service in order to rectify what had gone wrong. The question posed, and simultaneously answered by "*Hashiveinu Avinu*," was this: how could the exiled children of Israel, who yearned to return to their land, city, and Temple, rectify the perversion, sanctify themselves, and serve God in exile, while they remained saturated in the pollution of their ritualistic and moral sins?

The *Shemoneh Esrei* prayer came to pave an alternative way to atone for sins and crimes. Also in this regard, the expression of God's response was required as a precondition—for this was not at all an easy problem. From the Torah's perspective, it was a critical problem whose solution was a condition for the ability of the chosen nation, treasured by its God, to survive in exilic conditions and continue thereby to fulfill its mission. From what did this critical problem come? From the importance that the Torah ascribed to atonement for sins, as a condition for fulfilling Israel's destiny to become a "kingdom of priests and a holy nation."

The Moral Perspective of the Possibility of Atonement

The basic assumption of the Torah's doctrine of the human is that human beings, created in God's image, and granted knowledge and reason, are responsible for all their deeds, good or bad. A person of healthy mind and spirit is not permitted to evade responsibility for deeds that damage relations between human beings, and between the human being and God, by claiming to be compelled to sin by some external or internal force more powerful than his moral will. Even in the most difficult circumstances of life, even if forced to pay a heavy price for righteousness, humans can avoid sinning. But the Torah also acknowledges that human inclination, evil from youth, weakens the moral will and clouds one's rationality, and thereby precludes the real possibility for a person to always be rescued from the trap of sins that lies in wait at every step. Sometimes humans stumbled into sin unintentionally, sometimes unknowingly, and sometimes out of temporary weakening of the power of judgment in the face of pressure or very great temptation. The book of Ecclesiastes states: "For there is not one good man on earth, who does what is good, and does not sin" (Ecclesiastes 7:20). Clearly, the failure of sin is an everyday reality for most humans, who are not heroes of moral will.

This observation about human nature and examination of its significance against the background of the providential status that the Torah assigns to humans—to rule the land in the name of God for the good of all its creatures and their improvement—raises a serious problem in terms of God's ability to realize His goal in creation with human help. If a way is not found to overcome the moral weakness of the creature created in God's image and appointed to be the elect of creation—a creature who joins divine spirit with material physicality so as to sanctify it—the ability of the creature to fulfill the role placed upon him to improve himself and to improve creation would be annulled.

The reason is obvious. Sins and crimes have an accruing character. Every sin and every crime impacts the environment and the person who has committed them. The sins satisfy the sinners' evil inclination. Because of this, they increase the appetite to sin, until the sinners' ability to rule over their inclinations and to choose their path is completely annulled, and they become slaves to sin. In such a situation, the sins "infect" the pure soul. The soul fills up with feelings of guilt, as well as despair and anger. For if the person has no way to be purified and liberated from feelings of guilt which paralyze on the positive path of doing good, these feelings will increase the tendency to sin more and more, in order to hide the crime, and to release one's anger towards God—an anger that puts one into a situation from which there is no exit. Such anger moved Job's wife to advise her suffering husband: "Blaspheme God, and die" (Job 2:9).

Apparently, for the Torah, there was only one way to resolve the distress of human existence. This was to provide human beings with a second opportunity to return and to choose good even after they have chosen evil—that is, to enable them to repent, to desire the contrary—and thereby annul their prior choice and its consequences. In other words, the distress could be resolved only if it were possible for the committed sin to be considered an error—which one could rectify if one became convinced that one erred, and that what was done did not express one's true desire.

These matters explain the vital necessity of the concepts of atonement and forgiveness with regard to rectifying the God-man connection against the background of God's knowing, that He placed a mission upon the human beings which was necessary for creation, but which exceeded their abilities as physical creatures. Clearly, this raises a difficult moral problem. The return of free choice with regard to a sin that has already been committed means the erasure of everything that was done, with all its consequences, and annulling the sin as if it has never been committed. Is this within the range of possibility?

One possible answer is that there are sins, whose damage to the human soul and those around him is light and passing. They can be rectified by doing good to compensate for them. But even such sins cannot be erased from the memory of those around the sinner, as if they were never done, let alone serious sins whose consequences cannot be annulled, such as murder or causing physical or psychological damage. The conclusion which scripture draws from this, is that human beings by themselves are unable to atone even for a sin someone committed against them, let alone for their own sins against others. Even if they take responsibility for their actions, bear punishment, and endeavor to the best of their abilities to rectify the damage they have caused, they cannot annul what has been done and the guilt that has ensued. Obviously, their moral responsibility is to do everything they can to rectify, and discharging this obligation is the condition for atoning for their sins. But only God, as creator of the human beings and the universe, can atone for and erase the sins and the crimes as if they had not been done. How? By renewing His creation and renewing the human soul into which He breathed from the breath of His spirit—and insofar as the soul emanated from the breath of His spirit, its original purity remained. This was expressed by David's words in the Psalms: "Fashion a pure heart for me, O God; create in me a steadfast spirit" (Psalms 51:12).

The conclusion to be drawn from the above, is that for atonement of human sins to take place, rectifying action is necessary from the side of the sinful person, and atoning activity from the side of God. From the side of the humans it requires decisive expression of wanting to give themselves to their creator, to be worthy of Him, and keep His commandments. From the side of God it requires responsiveness, which creates a pure heart for the human beings, and renews the right spirit for them to do God's *mitzvot*. From here, we come to the subject of sacrifices. Chief of these is the performance of the "sin offering" (*ḥatat*), where a person offers the best of his herd to God. During this act, the person confesses his sins and symbolically transfers them from himself to the sacrifice, which he sacrifices to God; an act that expresses symbolically the absolute desire of the sacrificer to commit his soul to God by keeping His *mitzvot*. The symbolic identification between the sacrificer and his sacrifice is created through the "confession," while placing hands on the head of the sacrifice. The Torah states: "For the blood is the life" (Deuteronomy 12:23). Pouring the blood of the sacrifice onto the altar symbolizes the blood of the sacrificer—as if it is being poured upon the altar. As such, the sacrificer "expiates" or "purifies" the altar from the sins that have encumbered it. The fire of God, which burns upon the altar, consumes the sacrifice and its blood which is entirely purified, so as to raise the smoke to heaven, satisfying the God who has compassion and forgives. The sins are then forgiven and erased, the person's soul is purified and renewed, and becomes as it was when it was breathed into the body of the person at birth.

"What need have I of all your sacrifices?" (Isaiah 1:11)

A critical inquiry into this ceremonial symbolism properly raises moral questions, which need not be detailed. A partial excuse for these difficulties can be found by comparing the view of the Mosaic Torah on the role of sacrifices in relations between the human being and God with the views of idolatry—in the era in which offering sacrifices were considered the principal mode of service of the human being to God. According to the views of idolatry, the sacrifices were a gift designed to bribe the idols, who could eat and drink like human beings, so they would be well disposed towards those who sacrificed to them and would bestow their benevolence upon them. The Torah rejected this view with derision and anger. It interpreted sacrifices as an act of atonement, which reflected a psychological human need to come close to God, in order to keep His commands. With this, the Torah accorded spiritual significance to the service of sacrifices, whose principle was the feeling of giving oneself to God, of coming close so as to feel God's presence—from which compassion, love, and blessing pour forth. But the difficulty remained, because, according to the spiritual-moral assumptions of prophetic teaching, God did not need human gifts. Not only did God neither eat nor drink as humans do; He did not "smell" the smoke of sacrifices or become appeased by them. God became appeased only by the observance of His *mitzvot*.

On account of satisfying the human need to sacrifice and come close to God, the prophets went along with the service of sacrifices. But they stipulated that the sacrifice was to express authentic feeling of regret for sins, and sincere desire to make an effort to avoid them, as well as loyal readiness to commit to God and to bring this commitment to actual—and not merely ceremonial—expression with acts of righteousness and benevolence. It was clear, however, that the wealthy among the people corrupted the service of sacrifice and transformed it into a "technique," which enabled them to continue with their acts of extortion, oppression, deceit, greed, and lewdness; and then atone to satisfy God and thus get rid of feelings of fear of punishment; to celebrate happily and start a new cycle of sins.

A powerful controversy erupted about this between most of the priests, for whom sacrificial service was important in itself, and the prophets, whose opposition grew increasingly and expressed itself in prophecies about the approaching destruction of the Temple: In their view, the Temple changed from a place of holiness to a place of idolatrous defilement.

> Hear the word of the Lord,
> You chieftains of Sodom;
> Give ear to our God's instruction,
> You folk of Gomorrah!
> "What need have I of all your sacrifices?"
> Says the Lord.
> "I am sated with burnt offerings of rams,
> And suet of fatlings,
> And blood of bulls;

And I have no delight
In lambs and he-goats.
That you come to appear before Me—
Who asked that of you?
Trample My courts
No more;
Bringing oblations is futile,
Incense is offensive to Me.
New moon and sabbath,
Proclaiming of solemnities,
Assemblies with iniquity,
I cannot abide.
Your new moons and fixed seasons
Fill me with loathing;
They are become a burden to Me,
I cannot endure them.
And when you lift up your hands,
I will turn My eyes away from you;
Though you pray at length,
I will not listen.
Your hands are stained with crime –
Wash yourselves clean;
Put your evil doings
Away from My sight.
Cease to do evil;
Learn to do good.
Devote yourselves to justice;
Aid the wronged.
Uphold the rights of the orphan;
Defend the cause of the widow.
(Isaiah 1:10–17)

Considered carefully, these words do not oppose the substance of sacrificial offering. Indeed, it is an essential *mitzvah* of Moses's Torah. Opposition would have meant negating the institutional role of the priests and negating the role of the Temple as a place of pilgrimage of the people of Israel, thereby negating the satisfaction of the psychological need of the children of Israel to feel, as all human beings, the nearness of God to them—and perform acts for Him expressing commitment and their longing to find favor in His eyes. The intention of the prophets was, therefore, to emphasize that when sacrifices were raised upon the altar and the sacrificers ate meat and celebrated a lifestyle based upon extortion, theft, murder, lewdness, and crass materialism, they missed the original goal of sacrifice, contradicted it, and transformed the sacrifices from holy symbolism into an abomination. Only if the sacrificers make a real effort to rectify their paths, only if they were careful not to violate the prohibitions of the Torah and also to observe the positive precepts of justice, righteousness, and benevolence, could sacrifices be considered as authentic service to God, bringing about atonement, purity, and holiness. Clearly, the transfer of emphasis from sacrifices to acts of righteousness and benevolence changed sacrifices into a subordinate, ceremonial matter, and essentially superfluous. When these words of rebuke were stated by the prophets, as a citation from the mouth of God Himself, it was understood that sacrifices were given to the people of Israel to satisfy a human need. God had no desire for them. God wanted the human being himself, and not by means of ritualistic symbolism but by means of observing His *mitzvot*—specifically, those *mitzvot* that touched upon moral relationships between human beings. Clearly, therefore, in the view of the prophets, it was not the offering of sacrifices in itself that atoned for sins. Rather the effort to avoid sinning and to rectify sins committed by trespassing serious prohibitions by-over against this-observance of the essential positive precepts, which are the *mitzvot* of righteousness and benevolence.

The above is reinforced by the following text, which scholars of oral Torah determined to be read as the first *Haftarah* of the Day of Atonement:

Cry with full throat, without restraint;
Raise your voice like a ram's horn!
Declare to My people their transgression,
To the House of Jacob their sin.
To be sure, they seek Me daily,
Eager to learn My ways.
Like a nation that does what is right,
That has not abandoned the laws of its God,
They ask Me for the right way,
They are eager for the nearness of God:
"Why, when we fasted, did You not see?
When we starved our bodies, did You pay no heed?"
Because on your fast day
You see to your business
And oppress all your laborers!

Because you fast in strife and contention,
And you strike with a wicked fist!
Your fasting today is not such
As to make your voice heard on high.
Is such the fast I desire,
A day for men to starve their bodies?
Is it bowing the head like a bulrush
And lying in sackcloth and ashes?
Do you call that a fast,
A day when the Lord is favorable?
No, this is the fast I desire:
To unlock fetters of wickedness,
And untie the cords of the yoke
To let the oppressed go free;
To break off every yoke.
It is to share your bread with the hungry,
And to take the wretched poor into your home;
When you see the naked, to clothe him,
And not to ignore your own kin.
Then shall your light burst through like the dawn
And your healing spring up quickly;
Your Vindicator shall march before you,
The Presence of the Lord shall be your rear guard.
(Isaiah 58:1–8)

The fast on Yom Kippur is the sacrifice that the person makes of his body, to God. He does so by afflicting himself, but in the view of the prophet this sacrifice does not atone, unless preceded by acts of righteousness and benevolence, with total recognition that this is a person's obligation before God.

With these moral considerations in mind, the literary prophets, especially those who prophesied towards the onset of the Babylonian exile or soon thereafter, spoke of the requirement "to return" to God, "to return" to His Torah, and "to return" to keeping His *mitzvot*, for this was the single way to avoid imminent punishment. After the punishment came, as they prophesied, that remained the only path of appeasing God, for Him to return His nation to Him, and for Him to redeem it. It follows from this that the concept of *teshuvah*, which the *Shemoneh Esrei* prayer needed as an alternate path to atone for the nation's sins after the Temple destruction, was drawn from the prophets. Nevertheless, it should be emphasized that neither the concept itself, nor the legal ceremonial norm that gives it concrete form, were mandated either in the words of Isaiah, Jeremiah, or even Ezekiel, or in those of the rest of prophets whose prophecies were spoken after the destruction and exile. As a legal norm, *teshuvah* developed on the basis of the words of the prophets, especially Isaiah and Jeremiah, when prayer became the principal path of serving God in the synagogue after the destruction of the first Temple. It was concretized through three emotional-reflective gestures, accompanied by actions: confession, expression of regret, and request for forgiveness from those injured. These actions were an effort to rectify the iniquities to the extent possible, and accept a definitive decision to make every effort not to sin again.

But did these emotional-reflective gestures, and the acts that confirmed them in interpersonal relations, bring about atonement in the full sense? Were they able to erase the sin which took place, and its consequence? We already clarified the matter of negative *teshuvah*. Atonement remained an act that God alone could perform, in response to the request of the worshipper who returned in repentance to God's Torah and service. That is, the matter of atonement remained dependent upon the direct relationship between the person and God. In this sense, it was a ceremonial-ritualistic matter, carried out in exile by prayer in the synagogue. The scholars of oral Torah, like the prophets, also did not annul the *mitzvot* of sacrifice even after the Second Temple was destroyed. To the contrary, they preserved the memory of the service in the Temple as a precious remembrance, an object of longing and of the heart's desire for "return as in the days of old."

The rabbis thus taught that one should pray for the return of the service in the Temple in Jerusalem. We will see below that this request was also included in the *Shemoneh Esrei* prayer as the climax of the coming messianic redemption. Towards this end, the rabbis meticulously ensured that recalling the sacrificial service should become a permanent part of the prayer regime. They established the recital of the legal procedures of the sacrificial worship in the Temple in the morning, afternoon, and evening prayers, which were the times when the sacrifices had been offered in the Temple. They included the request to renew the service of God of the Temple as a permanent component of the liturgy for Sabbaths, festivals, and holidays, and they added many liturgical poems that described the order of service and glorified its splendor and value.

In this way, the *siddur* prayer service embodies the meaning of the exilic condition in which the people of Israel lived. Exile is a condition of *hester panim* (hiddenness of God's face). In the absence of the Temple, even when the nation is not persecuted, the distance between the nation and God remains actual for the people. Prayer alone bridges the distance, through living memory. Giving voice to the memory carries the emotional power of intimate nearness—which the original experience in the Temple could not create. There is another paradox, coming from the encounter with the extraordinary situation of the nation of Israel among the nations: the nation that was chosen to be God's treasure is forced to keep its mission as an exiled nation, an oppressed and disgraced people among the nations. If in the pre-exilic era the prophets viewed the Temple as a place which sacrificial service to God made sinful to the point of being abhorred by God, from the perspective of exile the memory of the sacrificial service was idealized. The memory was abstracted from the physical, and changed into a refined spirituality by the power of aesthetic imagination—which can be experienced through mystical ascent even in exilic conditions.

Confession

This brings us to the question of the essence of repentance as a psychologically purifying and atoning mode of action, which can serve as a ceremonial alternative to offering sacrifices in the Temple. The primary ceremonial element that can be transferred from the sacrificial service and adapted to the language of prayer for the need of atonement, is confession. As a component of the ceremony of raising the sacrifice upon the altar, the confession functioned as a symbolic transfer of sins of the person who performed the sacrifice to the sacrificial animal—while in the sixth benediction of the *Shemoneh Esrei*, the confession is a component of the conversation taking place between the person and God. The first and essential task of the confessional prayer is reflective. The worshipper recites his sins to himself, he raises them to critical understanding, to his knowing, and to his comprehension, and in so doing he spells out to himself the existential significance of his deeds, as they affect his relationship with all the members of his congregation, as well as his relationship to God. The fear of judgment falls upon him and he places the punishment he deserves before his eyes and justifies it. By doing so, he assumes responsibility for the deed. The responsibility is expressed in the feeling of guilt on the one hand, and in the incentive to work to rectify his trespasses on the other. The natural tendency of human beings is to conceal their sins, deny them, and pretend that they have not sinned, or to rationalize the sin by placing responsibility upon others—primarily those who had sinned against them and to whom they have only given payback. In this way, however, they only deepen their sins in the eyes of their judge, and increase the punishment they rightfully deserve. Therefore, elevating the sin to judgmental consciousness, comprehending its seriousness, and taking responsibility for it, are the necessary conditions for repentance and atonement. This is because recognition of guilt and taking responsibility are expressions of the original moral will in the soul of the human being who was created in God's image to do good and abhor evil. That is, they are expressions of the will to change the decision of the prior will, which has sinned willfully, into error which can be atoned through *teshuvah*.

Regret, which is the depth of feeling of guilt, follows the gesture of confession. The person feels the pain over the pain he caused to another being, the shame before the other who was caused to suffer and before all who knew and would know. That gives him the strength to denounce the deed. Regret also includes the strong desire that the act of sin had never been committed; even that the drive or temptation that brought it on would not have become manifest, because the shameful evil which needed to be overcome and uprooted, was embodied in that drive. Notably, when it comes to anything touching the relations between the human being and God, the sorrow of regret is the worst punishment for the person who regrets, because he is punishing himself. Perhaps this also embodies the good energy to rectify and exonerate the sinner in the eyes of his judges—if following the regret there is a bold decision to do everything to rectify, and absolutely avoid any such act in the future. To be sure, true regret does not allow a person to forgive himself for his sin. But it does express a deep need for forgiveness, and it makes the regretful person worthy of pardon by those who can forgive: first of all, on the part of those injured; and beyond them on the part of God, the creator of beings whom He loves. The forgiveness of God, therefore, atones for and erases the sin as though it had not been committed, and renews the spirit of the worshipper to do only good.

The blessing "Return us, our Father" (*Hashiveinu Avinu*) is, therefore, an address to God, for Him to "reveal His face" to His children, for Him to return from out of the depths of His hiding His face in which they were immersed in their exile. But the act of *teshuvah* itself is experienced in a request-blessing that follows: "Forgive us our Father, for we have sinned. Pardon us, our King for we have transgressed; for You pardon and forgive. Blessed are You, Lord, the gracious One who repeatedly forgives" (K:116, *Selaḥ Lanu*). This blessing contains two elements of the gesture of *teshuvah* described above: the confession ("for we have sinned . . . for we have transgressed." (K:116, *Selaḥ Lanu*), and the regret, which is expressed in the request for pardon, mercy, and forgiveness. This text of the blessing contains the rich tone of scriptural passages, especially from the latter prophets and a number of psalms, where there are a great many passages testifying that God is merciful, compassionate, and forgiving. But it appears that the text of this prayer depends especially on two central events of prayer, and upon prophetic counsel. The central events include: (1) God's revelation to Moses in the cleft of the rock after the sin of the calf, which is cited frequently in the prayer service, especially for Yom Kippur: "The Lord passed before him and proclaimed: 'The Lord! The Lord! A God compassionate and gracious slow to anger, abounding in kindness and faithfulness'" (Exodus 34:6); (2) the prayer of the Levites at the dedication of the Second Temple, which also appears often in the prayer service—and it echoes God's call to Moses, but comes closer to the language of our blessing: "But You, being a forgiving God gracious and compassionate, long-suffering and abounding in faithfulness, did not abandon them" (Nehemiah 9:17). The prophet's counsel contributes a central expression to the text of our blessing, and thus its importance:

> Seek the Lord while He can be found,
> Call to Him while He is near.
> Let the wicked give up his ways,
> The sinful man his plans;
> Let him turn back to the Lord,
> And He will pardon him;
> To our God,
> For He freely forgives.
> (Isaiah 55:6–7)

These scriptural passages contribute an enriching, deep, and clear tone to the short text in the *Shemoneh Esrei* prayer. But it is clear from the brevity of the text that the request for *teshuvah* and the request of forgiveness are not placed at the center of the prayer. They rather serve as an opening, presenting the worshipper before God in a position that provides him with a pretext to present requests to satisfy the life-needs of all individuals of the exiled nation. Also those of the nation as a collective entity, which has been chosen and now has to fulfill its mission amid the realities of exile which change this mission into a superhuman task. The full expression of the gesture of repentance leading to atonement in the confessional prayer—expressing regret and promising to resolve not to sin again, and pleading passionately for forgiveness—is found in the prayer of the one day considered to be the day of exaltation and supreme sanctity for the people of Israel, namely, Yom Kippur, the Day of Atonement.

According to the ordinance of the Mosaic Torah, Yom Kippur is unique as a day of fasting, and the offering of special sin offerings, and especially the atonement-act of sending away the "goat of Azazel" (Leviticus 16). According to the *siddur* for Yom Kippur, the chapter of Leviticus documenting the *mitzvot* of these sacrifices is read during the *Shaḥarit* prayer, but by way of contrast, the rabbis designated a *Haftarah* reading from the words of the prophet Isaiah, the central passage of which is quoted above. With this *Haftarah*, a great change in the Yom Kippur experience effectuated by the great oral Torah scholars comes to expression— that, from a day of atonement by means of transferring the nation's sins onto the head of a goat sent to death in a place of defilement, to a day of atonement by means of repentance. The lengthy confession found at the center of the Yom Kippur prayer details the sins one was liable to commit. It raises them to the worshippers' recognition, obligating them to take responsibility for their sins and to understand their seriousness and the extent of anticipated punishment. The worshippers, who sacrifice themselves to God by fasting, return to this confessional prayer six times, recited each time in a whisper by each person individually, and then aloud as one assembly. After the confession comes the expression of regret with the request for forgiveness, repeatedly invoking the attributes of compassion with which the God of compassion and graciousness revealed Himself to Moses in the cleft of the rock.

These attributes strengthen the feeling in the worshippers' hearts that their pain is kept firmly in mind and remembered, that their request has been heard, that they have atoned for their sins; that they have been judged for life in a trial before God; and that they can now begin the cycle of their life in the new year, "cleansed from all iniquity and attached to fear of You" (*Atah Ḥonantanu* blessing of the evening *Shemoneh Esrei* prayer for the close of Sabbath and holidays, cited above).

11

The *Shemoneh Esrei* Prayer: Redemption, Healing, and Livelihood

"Who Redeemed Israel" *Vis-à-Vis* "Who Redeems
Israel": The Exiled Nation Remembers Its Redemption

There is a purposeful connection between the prayers for repentance, forgiveness, and redemption. The repentance which brings forgiveness and atonement is the path to redemption: God returns the nation to Himself in a complete *teshuvah*, and the nation returns to God in complete *teshuvah*. With this, God returns to His nation to be its God, to rest His *Shekhinah* (divine presence) in its midst—to take the nation under His protection and to lead it, to be its redeemer. This is the situation of happiness and peace, identified with complete redemption. It can be summed up by saying that in actuality, the completion of *teshuvah* and the returning (*hashavah*) is redemption. This belief comes to expression in the language of the seventh blessing of the *Shemoneh Esrei* prayer—although with the humility of those experiencing the full force of the trials of *teshuvah* in difficult exilic conditions: "Look on our affliction, plead our cause, and redeem us soon for Your name's sake, for You are a powerful Redeemer. Blessed are You, Lord, the Redeemer of Israel" (K:116, *Re'eh Be'onyeinu*).

We recall for the reader that God's attribute, "the redeemer" (*go'el*) of His nation, was cited earlier in the final blessing of the Recitation of the *Shema*, which bridges it to the *Shemoneh Esrei* prayer. But in that blessing, "who redeemed Israel" (*Ga'al yisrael*) is said in the past tense and refers to the great and victorious salvation on the shore of the Red Sea. God, the "powerful savior," exhibited there His strong and victorious arm. God split the waters of the Red Sea, helped the children of Israel pass through the turbulence, and after that caused Pharaoh and his entire army to drown in the depths. Egypt was destroyed, the house of slavery drowned, and Israel, redeemed, sang the song of their redemption from the sea—the song that prophesied the realization of the entire vision of their redemption, when they would settle as a free people in their land, and God would reside among them in His Temple (Song of the Sea, Exodus 15).

When the children of Israel experienced the great salvation at the shore of the Red Sea, they "had faith in the Lord and His servant Moses" (Exodus 14:31). Describing this event of the distant past reminds the assembly of worshippers who live in exile that the song and its vision are forever in force. When they sang the Song of the Sea, history, which unfolded in passing time, embraced timeless eternity. At that moment, the people of Israel ascended as a unified nation to a level beyond one of subjection to Egyptian slavery—even though they realized that maintaining this high level for all individuals would be a difficult assignment and take forty years of desert wandering. An essential change took place in the relation of the nation—as a unity—to God; and in God's relation to the nation. The people left Egyptian slavery as a collective entity. The fear of rule by tyrannical human beings like Pharaoh, and the fear of his army, were now lifted: the nation was convinced that tyrants were ephemeral beings, and that their power turned into absolutely nothing in the face of the true and absolute power of their God. The kingdom of the God whom they served was eternal. Knowing this truth, insofar as they experienced this truth as an eternal moment, the people became free, in a higher and full sense. They served the creator of the world, their creator, to their own benefit, and He was "their savior" (*go'alam*). They understood now that God was the God of the future: "I am that I am." Indeed, they knew that much suffering was to be expected on their path before completing their mission and their vision would come to pass. But in their song at the shore of the sea they experienced the great future. They saw God their redeemer bring them to their land, bequeath it to them, settle them in His city, reside amid them in His Temple, and reign forever. In this sense, they were already redeemed forever, even amid the suffering of exile.

In the seventh blessing of the *Shemoneh Esrei*, the children of Israel address God with the attribute *go'el*, in the present tense. They are again in exile. Their enemies still threaten them on account of their faithfulness to the Torah of their God. But unlike the exile in Egypt, they trust in God who is their redeemer (*go'alam*), and they remind themselves of this before Him: that God should look upon this oppression as He looked upon their oppression in the days of Egyptian slavery; He should fight their battle against the enemies who pursued them as He fought their battle with the army of Pharaoh, which pursued them as they left Egypt; He should rescue them from the danger of destruction at the hand of the cruel enemy as He rescued them in that eternal moment; and

He should open the path for them to return, redeemed, to their land, city, and Temple, as He opened the path before their leaving Egypt.

On the Different Meanings of the Root G'AL

How can we verify that this is the intention of the short and succinct text of this blessing? The answer is again to be found in the sources from which the blessing was drawn. Before we turn to them, we should define the concept of *ge'ulah* (redemption) and the role of the "redeemer" (*go'el*) in Halakhic language. Like many words of scriptural Hebrew, the root G'AL has two opposed meanings, which both focus on the relation of an independent personality to the others among whom this person lives. The essential meaning of this root is positive: a relation of preference, closeness, and benefit. This is expressed in accepting responsibility for, and granting, protection: "to redeem" (*lig'ol*) in the positive sense of extending help in distress; to offer succor for poverty in its different forms; to promote refuge from persecution; and to rescue from menacing attack; and by means of all these to return the other who suffers, to whom something bad happened and who fell from his rightful status, to a good and proper track of life. The opposite meaning is "to discriminate against," reject and distance oneself from, as expressed in removing the responsibility and protection, and abandoning to an evil fate. Clearly, we are speaking of a judgmental relation to the other, a relation anchored in the social attributes of creatures of intellectual consciousness and moral reason. For the feeling of responsibility towards, or releasing responsibility for others, comes from consciousness of the need to rely on the other, and from consciousness that the other feels the same need. It is therefore impossible to receive support from that other without being ready to support him. Would they be attentive to the other's expectations? Would one stand by, or abandon, the other?

The source for the relation expressed by two opposed meanings of the root G'AL is the feelings of belonging and dependence of human beings upon their relatives and friends, and their yearning to control this dependency so as to maintain independence, by converting mutual dependency into mutual support, willingly and lovingly. Against this background, we can define the relation of *ge'ulah* as natural, primary, and as established in relations between human beings insofar as they are bearers of social recognition and feeling. This relation is established naturally between parents and their children who have not yet reached maturity, and between mature sons and their elderly parents, or between man and wife, between neighbors, and between friends who discharge their means of livelihood and defense together, and between leaders who represent the collectivity and individuals who are led by them. This relation is based upon, and defined by, moral and legalistic language in the context of the civil covenant that establishes the family, tribe, congregation, and nation. The civil covenant constitutes the mutual responsibility and defines the parties to the covenant as mutual "redeemers" (*go'alim*). When one of them finds himself in trouble and his power to defend his life and freedom is attacked, the responsibility for redemption falls upon the closest member of the family, neighbor, or closest friend whose position remains strong. The collective—the family, the congregation, the assembly—is responsible for all the individuals and families it includes. In the absence of an individual redeemer, the organized collective is obliged, through the court, to take responsibility for the redemption, and to appoint a trustee who will restore the rights to those injured and return them to their proper position.

The application of this obligation in the Torah is broad and varied. We begin with "redemption of the blood" (*ge'ulat hadam*) in case of murder. The *go'el hadam* (redeemer of the blood) is the person closest, in terms of the blood flowing through his veins, to the murder victim, who has the ability to avenge the murder of the one close to him—for one blood streams through their veins. "The blood is the soul." It cries out from the ground, as did the blood of Abel over the crime done to him. Insofar as it is impossible to rectify the crime by returning Abel to life, the only way to rectify the wrong already committed is to avenge it, measure for measure, as we read in the covenant of the sons of Noah: "Whoever sheds blood of man, by man shall his blood be shed; for in His image did God make man" (Genesis 9:6). The meaning of these words is that the murderer is to pay with his blood for the blood he has shed, so that the proper moral order arranged at creation, that of "justice," is restored. The "redeemer of the blood" is commanded, on the basis of this order, to assume the responsibility upon himself because his blood and that of the one close to him are one, and he therefore cannot find rest for his soul until he fulfills his obligation.

The redemption expressed in this way, as punishment that restores the moral order which had been perverted to its equilibrium, calms the blood of the innocent one who was murdered, and returns him to his dust in peace. By this example, we can attend to the depth of the feeling of belonging of individuals to their families and their nation, to the depth of the feeling of identity among relatives, and to the depth of the claim for justice—which all come to expression in the idea of *ge'ulah*. We should emphasize, nevertheless, that while the Mosaic Torah recognizes the justness of the fierce will of the *go'el hadam* to avenge the murder of someone close to him and to return the moral order to its equilibrium, the Torah criticizes the application of the idea of redemption of blood to an act of vengeance, where judgment is absent. Even if such an act is emotionally just, it does not rectify the trespass, but instead doubles it. The murderer is also a person created in the image of God, and his punishment therefore has to be decided by divine ordinance—that is, by an authorized court, and not by the feelings of human beings. From here comes the obligation to dedicate a number of "refuge cities," to which the murderer can escape from the blood redeemer until his guilt is considered by an authorized court (Numbers 35).

The best-known positive interpersonal act of redemption in the Hebrew Bible, narrated as a paradigm, is the incident of Boaz taking Ruth the Moabite—the wife of Mahlon, son of Elimelech, who had died childless, as his wife. He did so in order "that the name of the deceased may not disappear from among his kinsman and from the gate of his hometown" (Ruth 4:10). Boaz appears as the redeemer in a legal process in which the concept of redemption received its definition. Boaz is a relative of the family of Elimelech. He wants to take Ruth the Moabite as his wife, but his personal desire is not decisive in matters of redemption; it rather required legalistic authorization. Boaz knows there is a closer relative than he, who therefore has priority in terms of obligation to redeem. It is only after the first redeemer is asked, and refrains from exercising his obligation to redeem the legacy of Elimelech, that Boaz "acquires" Ruth as a wife. Along with Ruth, he acquires the legacy of the house of Elimelech, which has no direct legal heirs and is liable "to be cut off" from its clan.

The rectification takes place when the firstborn son of Ruth and Boaz is considered as the son of Mahlon, Elimelech's first son. The right of inheritance of the father's legacy passes on to their firstborn son, in accordance with the Torah's laws. The inheritor will be named after the deceased. He and his family will thereby be spared the judgment of "being cut off" (*karet*) as decreed upon them because of the sin of the family of Elimelech—which abandoned its legacy in Bethlehem, went down to Moab, and assimilated into an idolatrous nation, into which the people of Israel were prevented from marrying.

The story of Ruth and Boaz serves as a paradigm for maintaining the *mitzvah* of redemption and fulfilling the role of the redeemer. Boaz was a powerful man who could redeem, and a righteous one who wanted to redeem—not just for his own benefit, but because he recognized his responsibility to the family of Elimelech. The family of Elimelech sinned and was punished with the judgment of *karet*. According to the law, Ruth was not obliged to stick by her mother-in-law; and out of benevolence she contributed her portion to the redemption of the assimilated family from the doom of being cut off decreed against it—but Boaz performed the decisive act of redemption. Boaz was charitable towards

Ruth, and he completed the mission she had accepted. By doing so, he restored the family of Elimelech to its position among the people. The redemption of the sinning family thereby assumed higher national significance. The family of Elimelech was destined to give rise to David, who would reign over Israel in the future. Boaz's act of redemption redeemed the nation of Israel from the undermining of its possession of its land during the era of the Judges, because that possession was the reason for betrayal by Elimelech's family. Boaz ensured the birth of the messiah, who in the future would redeem his people by establishing the kingdom of Israel, which would stand the test of the special requirements of the Torah's ordinances.

The story of Ruth and Boaz is the paradigmatic redemption narrative about relations between human beings and between God and His people. But the redemption ordinance that applies to relations between human beings is broad. The ordinance is expressed especially in the *mitzvot* that relate to "the poor"—an inclusive term for the weak of the community, especially those where the head of the family, responsible for their protection, dies, leaving its members impoverished by their loss: the orphans, the widows, and also strangers without relatives seeking refuge among the people of Israel. The law of their redemption applies to all members of the community, according to their level of closeness to the impoverished and according to the measure of their financial and social ability to redeem. But if an individual redeemer is not found for them, the responsibility falls upon the community, through its court. The *mitzvah* as spelled out by the oral Torah is to appoint a guardian (*epitropos*) who would care for all their needs, and protect them from exploitation and deprivation of communal rights. From this perspective, every member of the family, the ancestral house, the community, and the nation is entitled to be redeemed by his family, tribe, friends, and nation in times of trouble. Each of these is obligated to fill the role of the redeemer, if their member, relative, neighbor, or friend should fall in trouble, and if one has the strength to redeem the person from it. This is the basis for the laws of charity that the Torah places as a moral obligation upon all the children of Israel. The scholars of oral Torah defined these *mitzvot* as depending upon the land. This group of *mitzvot* included the gleanings; the "forgotten sheaf"; the corner of the field left for the poor; the "tithes" for the poor, priests, and Levites; and others. These *mitzvot* depended upon the land either because their matter related to the produce of the land, which the Torah commanded to be distributed equally among all the families of Israel, or because the settlement of the nation in peace on its land for the long term was conditioned by their observance. The reason is clear: if the people do not abide by justice and equity in their societal relationships, the brotherhood that unites them will collapse—brotherhood being the source of the nation's righteous standing before God, and the source of its strength to withstand its enemies. The land would become destitute; it would withhold its produce, Israel's enemies would overcome them, and they would be exiled from their land.

The Role of God as Redeemer

On the basis of this moral-political perspective, the prophets defined God as *Go'el yisrael*—redeemer of Israel. It should be emphasized in this connection that the original definition of the role of the redeemer assigned to God in relation to His nation is no different than the definition of the role placed upon the heads of families, princes, and kings in relation to their families, tribes, and nations. According to the promise to the patriarchs and according to the Sinai covenant, God is obliged, as father and king, to redeem the nation of Israel any time it stumbles and falls from its proper position among the nations—because of poverty, sickness, defeat in war, conquest by enemies, or falling into the pit of slavery. By authority of His responsibility to the patriarchs, God heard the cry of the children of Israel to Him, from their toil, and decided that the time had come to act as redeemer of His people—to take them out of Egypt, bring them to Him, spread His sheltering protection over them, and grant them Torah—according to which they were to live as a free nation in their land. This is the regular socio-political meaning of redemption: the restoration of the nation to its proper position among the nations, even though God does this with the powers of creation with which He rules directly, whether by means of activating them or of suppressing them.

The act of God's redemption as king of His nation is a permanent component of the way of life as defined by the ordinance of the covenant made between God and the nation of Israel at the foot of Mount Sinai. The meaning of this statement is far-reaching in effect. It is expressed in the legal institutionalizing of the *mitzvot* whose fulfillment by the institutions of the assembly constitutes the organizational foundation for God's leadership as redeemer of His people. The nation experiences this leadership as a permanent component of its daily, weekly, annual, and periodic way of life, in its service to its God. How? By cyclical practices of emending and renewing the moral way of life, based upon justice and truth, in order to restrain the processes of deterioration and corruption, which are unavoidable in reality as defined by traits of the earthly nature and traits of human civilization based upon it. In parallel to the renewal of the earth's creation in cycles of day and night, months, seasons, and years, the Torah commands the renewal of the moral order based upon the justice and equity of interpersonal, socio-economic, and political relationships of the assembly of Israel.

The children of Israel are no different in their inclinational human quality, with its tendency to sin lying in wait for human beings, when it comes to their concern and labor to satisfy their human needs, than the idolatrous nations. Like all other humans, the children of Israel are inclined to the same sins for the same reasons. The societal order that Moses established for his people on the basis of Torah is the best, most righteous, and most efficient one in terms of preserving justice and unity. But even the most perfect order decays, becomes corrupt, and degenerates in the course of being put into practice in the reality generated by a settled society. Humans are equal before God in their rights, but not equal in terms of talent, ability, longing, and destiny, which depend upon conditions beyond human control. Against this background, the inclinations of the human being are manifest in power struggles, which, more than once, are transformed into violent war, even within the same community and the same state.

The unavoidable result is this: not only do sins of exploitation, oppression, and deception need to be atoned for on a cyclical basis (on Yom Kippur, when rectification by the redeemer is also apparent!). The corruptions and perversions of the legal order of life in the economy, society, and state also require atonement. If not corrected, the state of priests, designated to be the example of righteousness and truth, will change into Sodom and Gomorrah, two cities regarded by the Torah as examples of idolatrous evil. Clearly, such a state will collapse, be devastated, and be overcome by its enemies; and when it comes to the small nation of Israel, on its beautiful land—smallest and most lacking in large sources of abundance, and surrounded by a kingdom of idolatry, richer and stronger than it—the destruction would be immediate. Accordingly, the nation's state must pay strictest attention to its rules of *tzedakah*, justice, and truth, and renewal through ongoing recalibration of its socio-economic and political order. This is its redemption from the destruction and uprooting into exile, which ever lie in wait for it.

Redemption through Cycles of Seven

The highest expression of the institution of redemption in the Torah ordinances is the regulation of holidays—especially the weekly Sabbath, the sabbatical year, and the Jubilee. The goal of these regulations is to restore the commonwealth, which the people of Israel will establish on their land, on its proper moral foundations, are isolation from idolatrous, corrupt governments. From this perspective, the redemption is described as "return to the days of yore." Redemption is actualized by means of the fixed sevenfold cycles. It advances through them toward the realization of the appointed vision in its perfection and forever—in a way where every new beginning reflects symbolically the perfection towards which one strives, and enables the nation to experience its realization through symbolic commemoration: six days, and Sabbath on the seventh; six years, and *shemitah* (sabbatical year) in the seventh; seven sabbatical year cycles, and the Jubilee in the fiftieth year.

First, the Sabbath: the children of Israel, the resident aliens who join them, their slaves, and their animals are all forbidden to do any work designed to satisfy their physical needs on the Sabbath. In place of labor for the sake of maintenance, to which the children of Israel are commanded during the six days of the week, it is imposed upon them to dedicate themselves on the Sabbath to spiritual service to God. They are liberated from their burdens, cares, and their competitiveness. They stand before God as an assembly of free people, equal in terms of their rights before God as human beings, and bound to one another as friends. In their service to God on the Sabbath, the assembled community experiences the symbolism of the brotherhood of free men who have been redeemed, not only from the slavery of Egypt, but from the slavery to satisfying the needs of material life—which incentivizes humans to enslave their brethren and to be enslaved to them, to use, exploit, and cheat one another. On the Sabbath, they remember their brotherhood before God, and by doing so, they are redeemed during this day from the distresses of the struggle for existence. They are worthy of true happiness, in both physical-material and spiritual-moral terms (Exodus 20:8–11; Deuteronomy 5:12–15).

During the sabbatical year, the land used by its laborers is returned to the ownership of God its creator, and acquires its right to be renewed, and to renew the fertile powers embodied by it. The entire harvest that grows by itself in the seventh year is removed from private ownership, and anyone in need is permitted to enjoy it as needed. The seventh year is also the year of liberating Hebrew slaves, and their return to their proper status as free individuals in terms of their possession (Deuteronomy 15). During the Jubilee year, all properties—which were originally to be divided equally among all children of Israel, according to family—are returned to their original ownership. All Israelites who were sold into slavery, or to be maids and servants, return to their property, regaining independence in terms of their possessions and the status of free men among the nation.

The year of the Jubilee is signified by the sounding of the *shofar* of the Jubilee, and a later blessing of the *Shemoneh Esrei* prayer will also relate to its symbolism. The great *shofar* announces the coming of the year of the redemption in its collective sense: the socio-political order, based upon the just division of the land of Israel and its treasures, is reinstated. All properties return to the original ownership of God. Obviously, all the debts, enslavements, and injustices, which resulted from unjust distribution by the ruling powers, are annulled. All members of the assembly stand as free men, bonded to original justice in terms of their economic and political abilities and on the basis of mutual responsibility. Thus, they begin the new cycle of national life together, in the hope that this time they will succeed, more than before, in implementing the rules of justice and avoiding the disgraces, perversions, and sins that corrupt all human regimes. Therefore, the year of the Jubilee is identified with realizing the vision of complete redemption (Leviticus 25).

Notably, from the outset, the blueprint of this vision has rested upon the utopian foundation of emulating heavenly order on earth. Is the fulfillment of such a worthy vision possible? The Torah commands striving to actualize that vision in historical reality to the extent possible in the life-conditions of earthly creation, and in the differing circumstances of changing times and places. The prophets of Israel judged their nation, kings, ministers, advisors, and judges by their respective efforts to implement this vision in reality. The prophet Jeremiah determined that God adjudicated the kingdom of Judah for destruction and exile, after the king and his ministers liberated their Hebrew slaves in the seventh year but immediately reversed themselves and enslaved them again (Jeremiah 34:6–22). In this way, the expectation of realization becomes an educational legacy in the *Shemoneh Esrei* prayer, in other prayers, and in scriptural chapters special to Sabbaths, festivals, and holidays. But as we move to study the teachings of the latter prophets, which nourished the entire *Shemoneh Esrei* prayer and the rest of the *siddur*, a distinction is to be added between the Pentateuchal doctrine of redemption and that of the prophets, who prophesized after the destruction of the Kingdom of Israel, when exile under the rule of evil, idolatrous powers changed from threat to bitter reality—followed soon thereafter by the destruction and exile of the people of Judah as well.

Redemption in History and Redemption at the End of Days

The Pentateuchal doctrine of redemption is couched in legal terms and is intended for implementation in concrete historical reality, whereas the doctrine of redemption of the prophets and oral Torah scholars is messianic, in the sense that it is depicted as an ideal vision, whose fulfillment in the reality of history is beyond human ability. As such, it will be fulfilled only in the end of days, when the nation of Israel will be deemed worthy and God will intervene in the order of creation, not only to overthrow the evil forces of reality which enslave Israel, but to create the necessary conditions in creation, and in the civilizations built from its resources, for fulfilling the vision of perfection and peace.

It seems, in fact, that the later prophets of Israel despaired of believing that it would be possible to effectuate gradual advances in relations between Israel and the nations, and in rectifying the nation of Israel's life according to Torah. To the contrary, the prophets saw a rapid decline towards idolatrous evil, which grew ever stronger. Israel sinned repeatedly. Meanwhile, there were successive idolatrous, evil governments, which became more and more powerful, cruel, and tyrannical. In contrast to them, the persecuted nation of Israel—which suffered because of its loyalty to Torah—appeared as a righteous nation that was not punished for its sins but to the contrary, "sanctified the name of heaven" by bearing witness that the "kingdom of God"—as a "kingdom of heaven"— existed and stood forever (*Mishnah Berakhot* 2:5), even if this kingdom was hidden.

But in the face of the visible deterioration in the history of the nation of Israel among the nations, was it possible for humanity to ever fulfill the destiny that God placed upon it at creation? Was it possible for the nation of Israel to succeed in fulfilling its mission among the nations? The prophets of Israel and its scholars—who firmly believed that God assured that the efforts of Israel would at some point bring the redemption of the nation from exile, amid a humankind redeemed from idolatry—concluded that fulfillment would be possible only when God intervened directly into earthly reality as the creator, and changed the rules of creation and its order. He would uproot evil, or transform its powers to the good. He would remove idolatry and its regimes from the world, and uproot sickness and death from the earth. He would redeem His nation, not only by having the walls of the prison of exile collapse, but by returning His nation to its land and to its sovereignty in peace. The people of Israel could bring the fulfillment of this vision closer, by observing the *mitzvot* of Torah. But only God could bring salvation itself, by virtue of His sovereign rule over the power of creation, including transformations and prodigies.

Let us reemphasize that the role of redeemer fulfilled by God in relation to His people with the Egyptian exodus was not of a messianic dimension. God intervened in the order of creation to bring His nation out of slavery, because the nation was incapable of liberating itself by its own power. But the ordinances of creation and its orders did not change, and God laid the task of redemption, in its positive sense, upon His nation. On the threshold of the second exile it became clear that the experiment failed. Was the nation of Israel alone guilty of this? The prophets, who could not compare the sins of their small nation, surrounded by enemies, to the sins of their powerful adversaries, were pressed to recognize from the outset that it was impossible to expect any other result. Out of their trust in the righteousness of a God who would not do a wrong, they concluded that the return of Israel from exile a second time would take place upon God's direct intervention. Israel would be restored not only by defeating powerful enemies, but by bringing the nation to its land, and by settling it without war, and with the agreement of all nations—for ultimately all will formally acknowledge the kingdom of God, and Israel will be acknowledged as His chosen nation. The kingdom of the House of David would then arise anew, exist in peace and quietude, and the earth, which would be redeemed from the powers of chaos, would yield, from itself and effortlessly, all plenitude required for the happiness of the nations. Then, people would no longer sin or go to war.

We find two types of redemption mentioned in the *Shemoneh Esrei* prayer. In the seventh blessing (*go'el yisrael*) we find the redemption of individuals who are persecuted harshly in exile, which is the redemption documented in the Pentateuch. The prayer for redemption in the messianic sense is expressed in the six requests directed to the nation's redemption.

The Biblical Sources for the "Redeemer of Israel" Blessing

Against the background of the concept of redemption, with its two comple-mentary meanings, let us research the sources for the seventh blessing. The first source evidences the definition of the seventh blessing as a personal request in the context of destruction and exile; it is the source for the language of the prior request for *teshuvah:* the book of Lamentations, attributed to the prophet Jeremiah. In its third chapter, the prophet laments the bitterness of his personal fate as prophet of destruction; indeed, he was persecuted by his people because of his difficult mission.

> I am the man who has known affliction
> Under the rod of His wrath;
> Me He drove on and on
> In unrelieved darkness.
> (Lamentations 3:1–2)

Against this background, as his lament continues, the prophet speaks the words that shape the second blessing:

> I have called on Your name, O Lord,
> From the depths of the Pit.
> Hear my plea;
> Do not shut Your ear
> To my groan, to my cry!
> You have ever drawn nigh when I called You;
> You have said "Do not fear!"
> You championed my cause, O Lord,
> You have redeemed my life.
> (Lamentations 3:55–58)

Comparison will persuade us that the language of the blessing overlaps with the last sentence, which should be interpreted in full context. It is clear from the context that this is about personal redemption of the individual Jew, living amid the depth of destruction and exile.

As a prophet, Jeremiah viewed himself as a representative of the entire nation. He identified his suffering with that of his people, but this is not explicit in the passages cited above—which form the essence of the seventh blessing. The identity between the individual prophet and his nation is shown explicitly in the following verses taken from the book of Isaiah:

> Listen, O coastland, to me,
> And give heed, O nations afar:
> The Lord appointed me before I was born,
> He named me while I was in my mother's womb. . . .
> And he said to me, "You are My servant,
> Israel in whom I glory."
> (Isaiah 49:1, 3)

On the basis of this identity, the prophet turns to God as the Lord, the "Redeemer of Israel," in the present.

> Thus said the Lord,
> The Redeemer of Israel, his Holy One,
> To the despised one,
> To the abhorred nations,

To the slave of rulers:
Kings shall see and stand up;
Nobles, and they shall prostrate themselves—
To the honor of the Lord, who is faithful,
To the Holy One of Israel who chose you.
(Isaiah 49:7)

As the prophecy continues, it is not only about the redemption of the individual, but the redemption of the nation from exile:

Thus said the Lord:
In an hour of favor I answer you,
And on a day of salvation I help you—
I created you and appointed you a covenant people—
Restoring the land,
Allotting anew the desolate holdings,
Saying to the prisoners, "go free"
To those who are in darkness, "Show yourselves."
They shall pasture along the roads,
On every bare height shall be their pasture.
They shall not hunger or thirst,
Hot wind and sun shall not strike them;
For He who loves them will lead them,
He will guide them to springs of water.
(Isaiah 49:8–10)

These words of prophecy are spoken with an instructive comparison to the nation of Israel's path as it left Egypt. Let us pay attention: these words include several hints regarding the next blessings of the *Shemoneh Esrei*, which deal with the redemption of the nation, that is, redemption in its messianic sense.

Healing and Livelihood

We pass to the two final personal blessings of request. Let us quote them in full.

[Blessing 8]
Heal us, Lord, and we shall be healed.
Save us and we shall be saved,

For You are our praise.
Bring complete recovery for all our ailments,
For You, God, King, are a faithful and compassionate Healer.
Blessed are You, Lord, Healer of the sick of His people Israel.
(K:118, *Refa'einu*)

[Blessing 9]
Bless this year for us, Lord our God,
And all its types of produce for good.
Grant dew and rain as a blessing
On the face of the earth,
And from its goodness satisfy us,
Blessing our year as the best of years.
Blessed are You, Lord, who blesses the years.
(K:118, *Bareikh Aleinu*)

The connection between these two blessings, or requests, to the previous blessing, "Redeemer of Israel," becomes clear against the background of their sources. The eighth blessing, "Heal us, Lord, and we shall be healed," has two obvious sources. The first source is the story of the waters of Marah, immediately following the song of those redeemed at the shores of the Red Sea:

> They came to Marah, but they could not drink the water of Marah because it was bitter; that is why it was named Marah. And the people rumbled against Moses, saying, "What shall we drink?" So he cried out to the Lord, and the Lord showed him a piece of wood; he threw it into the water and the water became sweet. There he made for them a fixed rule, and there He put them to the test. He said, "If you will heed the Lord your God diligently, doing what is upright in His sight, giving ear to His commandments and keeping all His laws, then I will not bring upon you any of the diseases that I brought upon the Egyptians, for I the Lord am your healer." (Exodus 15:23–26)

The second source is, again, the personal prayer of Jeremiah, prophet of the exiled. It is reproduced in the *Shemoneh Esrei* prayer with a simple change—the language of "we" (*anaḥnu*) in place of "I" (*ani*):

> Heal me, O Lord, and I shall be healed;
> Save me, and I shall be saved;

For Thou art my praise.
(Jeremiah 17:14)

The ninth blessing, "bless this year for us," with its focused concern on the heavenly rain that assures abundant crops, is anchored in several more general sources that ascribe the abundant harvest, which the land provides for its inhabitants, to God's blessing. Let us cite the principal source, upon which all others rely. It is a passage in Deuteronomy, a portion of which is included in the *Keriyat Shema*.

> For the land that you are about to enter and possess is not like the land of Egypt from which you have come. There the grain you sowed had to be watered by your own labors, like a vegetable garden; but the land you are about to cross into and possess, a land of hills and valleys, soaks up its water from the rains of heaven. It is a land which the Lord your God looks after, on which the Lord your God always keeps His eye, from year's beginning to year's end. If then, you obey the commandments that I enjoin upon you this day, loving the Lord your God and serving Him with all your heart and soul, I will grant the rain for your land in season, the early rain and the late. You shall gather in your new grain and wine and oil—I will also provide grass in the fields for your cattle—and thus you shall eat your fill. Take care not to be lured away to serve other gods and bow to then. For the Lord's anger will flare up against you, and He will shut up the skies so that there will be no rain and the ground will not yield its produce; and you will soon perish from the good land that the Lord is assigning to you. (Deuteronomy 11:10–17)

It is easy to see that the ninth blessing not only relies on this source, but draws from it literally.

The sources cited above point to the common conceptual basis of the two blessings that also function as personal request. They also reveal a conceptual connection between these two blessing and the previous one—the belief that God, as a king and a father of human beings in general and of Israel in particular, was a leader-educator. God tests human beings in general, and the children of Israel in particular, by having them confront the inclination to evil that throbs within them, and the evil in their society and in surrounding creation. God sets before them the choice between good and evil. He examines and judges them. He tolerates their sins up to a point, but when the right time comes, he punishes them for their sins and recompenses them well for acts of righteousness and grace, measure for measure—all of this through the powers of creation under His sovereign rule. Thus, God makes justice and equity prevail, and educates human beings to internalize values of justice and equity, to identify with these values, to act in accordance with them as a free people, and to rise to the height that is proper for a creature created in the image of God—so that human beings can complete their mission of rectifying earthly creation. For this purpose, God watches over everything that is done in His earthly universe. He observes the deeds of humankind. He offers His thoughts with love and with strictness—especially when it comes to activities of the children of Israel, who have chosen, and have been chosen, to be His treasure, to help Him in His governance as king-educator of all humanity. So God exercises providential care: He examines, judges, and recompenses for good and for evil, by means of the powers of creation that serve Him as He wills.

It follows clearly from these sources that the two request-blessings, "Heal us, Lord, and we shall be healed" and "Bless this year for us" (K:118, *Bareikh Aleinu*), relate to the two principal instruments of creation with which God governs His living creatures in general, and human beings in particular—of all creatures, human beings are the most sensitive to the life-conditions that creation supplies to them, because they need special conditions of plenitude and stable protection. These instruments are: (1) physical health, as opposed to injurious disease; and (2) plenitude of provisions for physical life as opposed to poverty. Health and livelihood, which are the two most basic conditions for the good life, are the instruments by which God rules His earthly universe. Intellect and reason, with which God favors human beings created in His image, enables them to care for themselves—more so than it is with other living creatures. But not even humans have control over their health and the plenitude of their livelihood, and they rely on God's blessing.

Presenting matters in this way sets the reader before one of the crucial distinctions between the educational path of the Torah of Moses and the path of idolatry. Idol worshippers look for various paths of magic and science to master the causes of health and plenitude, while the Torah of Moses teaches that these paths are false, even though the idolaters may gain some influence by activating the ordinances that God implants in creation. Only the life according to the values of Torah and its *mitzvot* can assure a person of his health and livelihood, and success and physical-material pleasure—all of this on the condition that the person would not make material enjoyment his goal, but only the means for moral-spiritual service to God.

These matters rest upon the foundation of the sources cited above. Let us consider their full educational significance by analyzing the narrative of the liberation of the children of Israel from Egyptian slavery. God, sovereign of creation, struck down Egypt by destroying its natural sources of livelihood and by the diseases He inflicted on it, to the point of the death of its firstborn. Meanwhile, He gave preference to the people of Israel, and watched over their health, their welfare, and their livelihood, and when they left for the desert, He remedied their great afflictions caused by draught and want. He satisfied their need for water and nourishment—even if He doled out these resources and withheld them as a means to educate the people to believe that only by keeping God's *mitzvot* would they be able to live in the desert, and then settle in their land and reside there in conditions of health, plenitude, dignity, and peace.

The final question that arises in this context is: does this mean that the human being does not need, and is not commanded, to do everything within his ability for the sake of his health and livelihood? The negative response, which comes from analyzing the above sources, is unequivocal. To the contrary, human beings are commanded to work for their livelihood, and blessings of plenitude are not maintained without work. Likewise, human beings are commanded to be strict about principles of distancing from sources of defilement that cause sickness and death. They are to use the curative traits of different materials supplied by God for the purposes of their health. But even with diligent, professional work, observance of health principles, and caution regarding sickness and cure, humans will not achieve their goal without the blessing of God, which protects them by means of rain and dew in season, by means of desirable warmth and light, and the rest of conditions needed for health and plenitude. Over these, the human being does not and cannot have mastery; he can only ensure that God will continue His blessings through observance of the commandments, including personal prayer. This prayer is certainly beneficial—because it is God's will to provide humans with the means for health and plenitude, and because he conditions the fulfillment of His will on the human being's acknowledging that His blessing is the source of all of life and happiness.

12

The *Shemoneh Esrei* (Eighteen Benedictions) That Are Really Nineteen: Redemption from Deepening Exile

The Expectation of the Imminent End of Days with
the Return to Zion

Corresponding to the six blessings that consist of requests for redemption by individuals of the nation encountering exile, there now follow six blessings (which have become seven) that consist of requests for messianic redemption of the nation of Israel as the chosen nation. But why is this prayer called *Shemoneh Esrei*—"Eighteen Benedictions"—when there are really nineteen blessings? This riddle goes to the heart of the literary structure of this composition, and testifies to the originally contemplated pattern of the blessings. At a certain stage, the urgency was felt to add another blessing, and to emend the blessing coming after it, but without effacing the original plan. The addition responded to an unforeseen predicament, which resulted in distortion of the original pattern. Those who emended the blessing believed and hoped that this distortion would remain in effect only temporarily. But as time went on, the predicament was not corrected, so that the necessity for the change became protracted and, with it, practical hope changed into utopian aspiration. Because of this, we recite nineteen blessings—while keeping in mind the original intention to have only eighteen of them.

The historical events extending through the exilic era, which continued after the return to Zion in the days of Ezra and Nehemiah; after the renewal of worship in the Second Temple; and even after the establishment of the sovereignty of the Hasmoneans—and deepened and continued after the enforcement of the sovereign house of the Hasmoneans under the Roman

Caesar and after the destruction of the Second Temple—are, apparently, the background for the solution to this riddle, and for understanding the philosophical-religious logic of the anticipation of the messianic redemption, as expressed in the *Shemoneh Esrei* prayer.

The prophets of Israel, who predicted the destruction of the First Temple, and viewed it as the end of days, envisioned, from their anticipatory perspective, a complete redemption that would break forth as the dawn of a new and eternal day in the history of the nation of Israel and of humankind, following the night of destruction. The end of days, as they envisioned it, was supposed to be the end of history and the transition from time to eternity. The God who ruled over the earthly world from the firmament of heaven would reveal Himself upon earth to the eyes of all the world, and would impose His absolute will over all. This would be the great day of judgment. God, judge of the whole earth, would arraign all nations and all individuals in judgment. After the sinners received their punishment, measure for measure, the pious would receive their full reward: the measure of accrued good adjusted for the measure of accrued misery that they had suffered because of the sins of the wicked. The earth would return to the situation of the Garden of Eden, prior to the sin of the first Adam and Eve and the curse over the earthly world because of it. The powers of chaos, which infiltrated the earth, would be tempered, and the evil inclination in the human heart would be raised to good from early on. The nations that had exiled Israel from its land would return the exiled people from all corners of the earth to their land in splendor and glory. The nations would accept the Torah, which would go out from Zion to all the lands; they would beat their swords into ploughshares and their spears into pruning hooks; they would learn war no more. The land would produce its harvest with enough plenitude to satisfy all human needs without hard labor. Together with sins and crimes, sickness and death would also disappear. Jerusalem would be built into a citadel. The Temple would be raised anew on Mount Moriah, and the scion of the House of David would renew the kingdom of Israel. It would obey the ordinances of the Torah, and the scion would rule it as a wise judge—doing just judgment and truth in the name and spirit of God. The House of David would not need to coerce its rule. Rather, a nation of free men would legislate the Torah on the tablet of their hearts. The people would live according to the *mitzvot* of Torah because the *mitzvot* would identify with the nation's nature. All humankind would conduct itself according to that example.

According to the depiction of the great prophets, especially Isaiah, Jeremiah, and Ezekiel, the messianic transformation in the future would take place as a single event, following God's direct intervention, with a sovereign declaration of creation. God's sovereignty over everything will be revealed with all the might of His war against the evil remaining in the world after the original creation of the universe. Jeremiah, who both predicted and experienced the destruction, sent a letter from Jerusalem to the exiles in Babylon and instructed them to strike roots there. He also proclaimed that, at the end of seventy years after Jerusalem's destruction, the kingdom of God over all the nations would be revealed. By subduing the nations, the exiles will be returned to Zion in the splendor of glory and peace (Jeremiah 29:1–20). Indeed, when seventy years passed, the sovereignty of Babylonia collapsed under the weight of its sins, through a political upheaval that elevated Cyrus, king of Persia, to rule.

According to the book of Daniel, this upheaval was punishment for the intoxication of Belshazzar, the last king of Babylon, with sacred vessels stolen from the Temple of God in Jerusalem (Daniel 5). As a consequence, a surprising change came over the world: with the establishment of his rule over the huge empire, Cyrus viewed himself as governing the entire settled world in the name of the "God of Heaven," who stood at the head of the assembly of gods of all nations and united these nations under the earthly king. According to his own testimony, Cyrus received an order from the "God of Heaven" to repair the Temple ruins, return the holy instruments stolen by Nebuchadnezzar, conqueror and destroyer of Jerusalem, and to renew the worship of God by the children of Israel who were chosen to minister to Him in the name of all the nations of the world (Ezra 1).

It appears that Cyrus knew the prophecies of redemption of Jeremiah and Isaiah. He recognized how they related to him, and how the nation of Israel was destined to be "a kingdom of priests and a holy nation," and he decided to return the nation to its land. But it was not to reestablish an independent sovereignty; rather, Israel was to become a nation of priests surrounding the Temple, symbolizing the unity of the empire over which Cyrus ruled—for at that time, Judah was included in Cyrus's world kingdom. Cyrus provided the help necessary to the Jews who responded to his proclamation to ascend to Jerusalem and renew worship of God under the leadership of Ezra, the scribe of the Torah of Moses. It included orders that enabled the ascenders to return in peace to their abandoned property in Judah and begin immediately to rebuild the ruins of the city, establish the Temple, and restore the order of service to its position.

There was no deviation from the order of earthly creation in these salvific acts; but from the perspective of normal behavior of kings of idolatrous power, the salvation was a deviation that appeared miraculous to the children of Israel, a sign of divine intervention that constituted a new direction in history. Indeed, this was a proper beginning of the ingathering of exiles. It was a first step in renewing the kingdom of Israel in the path of peace prophesized by the prophet. One could regard Cyrus's proclamation as the sounding of the great *shofar* that heralded the year of the Jubilee in the messianic sense, the year in which the exiled nation returned to its possession in its land and to its destined position among the nations.

The Return to Zion as Continuation of Exile

It quickly became clear that this was not the logic of historical events. Not the beginning of the end of days, rather only a modest illumination of a new day in history, out of which complete salvation might have developed—but in the distant future and not very soon. First of all, doubt arose as to whether the nation was worthy of complete redemption, because only a relatively few of the exiles responded to Cyrus's proclamation and ascended to Jerusalem under the leadership of Ezra the Scribe. Most of the people preferred to settle in the Babylonian diaspora. The reason is obvious. The Jews who had implemented the commands of Jeremiah in his letter, struck roots in Babylon and enjoyed preferential acceptance there. When the proclamation of Cyrus was heard, Jews were rooted in a rich and developed Babylon, which benefitted from them greatly. Truly, there was no comparison between the conditions of economic and political life of Jews in Babylon, and the conditions that awaited the exiles returning to their impoverished, ruined, and desolate land.

There was another important consideration for preferring the settlement in Babylon, which is hinted at indirectly in the books of Ezra and Nehemiah. Cyrus, and those who continued his line, wanted to renew the Temple worship in Jerusalem in the name of the peoples of their world government, but they did not desire the renewal of the House of David as an independent Jewish kingdom. This strange paradox was created by their ambivalent policies regarding the Jewish people. Already in the days of Nebuchadnezzar, Jehoiachin, the diaspora king from the House of David, was awarded preferential status over the kings of other nations whom the Babylonians ruled while exiling their kings. Jehoiachin's status was extended to his descendants under the rule of the Babylonian line and, after that, under the rule of the Persian line. His descendants were appointed as recognized political leaders of the community of Israel in the diaspora, and they officiated formally as exilarchs—but only in Babylon and Persia. It is striking that Cyrus chose Ezra the Scribe to lead those who moved back to Jerusalem, and thereby prevented the stabilization of a descendant from the House of David at their head. Similarly, afterwards, when the conditions that formed in Judah necessitated providing permanent political and military protection, Cyrus's successor Artaxerxes chose Nehemiah—a Jewish minister respected in his government—as governor. Clearly, this preference prevented the appointment of Zerubbabel, descendant of the House of David, to that role, since he was apt to revolt against the Persian authorities in order to restore his independent government in Jerusalem.

The explanation is that, also from the perspective of political independence, the position of Babylonian Jews was preferable to that of Jews who ascended to the Land of Israel. This combination of factors was already enough to awaken the feeling in the hearts of those ascended—which they openly expressed (Nehemiah 9:36–37)—that despite their success in repairing the altar and in renewing the Temple worship, they were exiles in their own land, and their exile was more difficult than that of their brethren in Babylon and Persia. In addition to economic and political difficulties, there were factors regarding the definition of Jewish identity. The returnees of lineage from Babylon found in the Land the thinning remnant of the nation of Judah, which had not gone into exile. In Samaria, they found the descendants of the Samaritans—forced converts who had settled in the place of exiled tribes of Israel. Naturally, these surviving remnants regarded themselves as proper Jews, and wanted to share in establishing the Temple and in the rights granted by the Persian kings to those who ascended. But the educated and those of distinguished lineage who returned from Babylon did not see the indigenous inhabitants as their equals, because they brought the Torah and traditions of the scribes, who determined the text of the Torah and its interpretation—using the techniques of oral Torah tradition, while confronting and receiving the influence of Babylon's advanced legal and scholarly culture.

This development created an unbridgeable gap between the returnees from Babylon and the remnants who had not been exiled. The latter were rejected by those who ascended as idolaters and total aliens—similar to Canaanites in the days of Joshua and the Judges. As a result of the rejection and the disgrace, they changed from friends into enemies. They did everything they could—including informing on the ascenders to the Persian rulers, and violent attacks—in order to sabotage the reconstruction of the ruins in Jerusalem and in the Temple. For these reasons, the work of building the walls of Jerusalem and the Temple continued with long delays. No wonder that when the returnees succeeded in completing the work after much toil and dedicated the Temple, they viewed it as a pitiful reminder of the magnificence of Jerusalem and the Temple's splendor during their days of greatness—and they cried bitterly (Nehemiah 1–10).

They were, however, consoled by the belief that this was only the beginning. It became clear that it would be necessary to explain anew the lofty visions of the return to Zion as presented by Jeremiah, Isaiah, Ezekiel, and the other prophets, according to the historical realities they experienced. When the future about which the prophets prophesied did come, it was clear that the great and lofty vision was not destined to be fulfilled all at once, but rather gradually, by stages. "Though your beginning be small, In the end you will grow very great" (Job 8:7). Moreover, the staged transitions depended upon the nation's worthiness. That is, history had not yet reached its end, and the trial that Israel had to pass was not yet over. The good end was obviously assured. But how much time would pass, before it would be implemented? This could only be estimated by comparative observation—with great changes still underway in the life of the Jewish nation and relations between it and the nations into whose midst it was exiled.

The Flowering of Apocalyptic Literature

This logic of viewing history gave birth to prophetic literature of a new interpretative sort. In the absence of a king of Israel, the established authority of the prophets also ceased, and, therefore, words of prophetic interpretation were traced to the patriarchs, Moses, and the prophets. Their words spoke in hidden allusions, so to speak, of matters relating to a time long after them. The general goal was to interpret earlier prophecies according to the torrent of events of history, in order to decipher the secrets of the "end" concealed in them, and to determine, according to the logic of the events, when Israel's trial would end, and the kingdom of God would be revealed to the eyes of all nations. The book of Daniel, which is included in the Hebrew Bible, is the best-known representative example of this type of literature—which modern research designates as "apocalyptic" (that is, deciphering secrets of the end of days). Most of these creations were not included in the Hebrew Bible, but were preserved instead as "apocryphal" literature. The task, as said, was to decipher the logic of the development of the redemption on the basis of the prophets' words on the one hand, and of the present events on the other. Since the resolutions proved over and over to be incorrect, the task became complicated and bred great controversies. How could one resolve the ever-deepening contradiction between the prophets' lofty vision of redemption and the future, which unfolded increasingly in history? This could be resolved with relative ease, were reality to prove that history was a process of ongoing advance towards realizing the vision, but in fact, the opposite seemed to be the case. The reality did not look like a gradual realization of supernatural redemption, rather there was a subnatural slide into the depths of *Sheol*. From era to era, intolerable evil was exchanged for worse intolerable evil! Idolatrous powers, which were seeking world rule, rose up and destroyed one another. Greece took the place of Persia, and transgressed even more than Persia; Rome replaced Greece, and transgressed even more than Greece. At the end, the Roman Empire covenanted with the Christian church, which emerged from out of the people of Israel—and by doing so it aggravated the exile in the most extreme way.

Wars between nations succeeded one another, and the relation of idolatrous powers to the nation of Israel, its Torah, and its faith became more tyrannical, cruel, and hate-filled. This was especially so in the Land of Israel, to the point that the Second Temple, like its predecessor, was destroyed—and with a tremendous, immeasurable flood of blood. Did this mean that God, who governed the world from the hidden place of heaven, wanted to unveil the evil that was embodied in the powers of chaos and in the darkest depths of human inclination, in order to uproot the evil completely before the light of world salvation would shine in the world of darkness? Was it precisely the depth of ever-increasing evil that proclaimed the nearing of the messianic redemption in the end of days? Could the absolute climax of darkness and evil signify that redemption would shine immediately thereafter?

Sadducees, Pharisees, Essenes: The Religious-National Split in the Nation

Two interconnected developments marked the worsening of the situation in the exile of the Jewish people among the nations. First, the zealous separatist controversy erupted among the people. Unlike that of the First Temple era, with its division between adherents of the Torah of Moses and the prophets and devotees of Canaanite idolatry, this was a serious division within the religious leadership—all adherents of the Torah of Moses and the prophets. It split them into three spiritual-political movements, differing with one another on the question of the correct way of worshipping God in their time, and of realizing the destiny of Israel among the nations. This question was raised urgently in the face of the political-spiritual challenges posed by conquering idolatrous cultures. These challenges were immeasurably more complex than the challenges of Assyria, Babylon, and Persia in the past. While it was true that these conquering powers sought to impose their faith upon Jews, especially those in their lands, they also justified their rule with impressive material and spiritual achievements. The Jewish exiles were, however, required to engage in a very complicated struggle under the ruling powers also in their own land—for their success in withstanding the test of idolatrous tyranny, which persecuted them with excessive cruelty, depended upon the Jews' ability to absorb the achievements of gentile wisdom into their Torah culture.

From those perspectives, the reality in the Land of Israel after the return to Zion was more difficult and problematic than the reality of exile in Babylon and Persia. Overall, the Babylonian-Persian dispersion was generally easy for Israel. There was tolerance of, and even admiration for, its Torah. Against this background, there was a positive dialogue between scholars of oral Torah and Babylonian scholars, especially in the legal-halakhic area. From the internal perspective, the unity of the people was preserved around the two leaderships that divided authority and complemented one another—even if, now and then, there was friction and conflict in the spiritual-legal leadership of the scribes and scholars, creators of the oral Torah, and the civil organizational leadership of the exilarchs from the House of David who earned recognition of the Babylonian-Persian rulers. It was otherwise in the Land of Israel. There, a serious problem of leadership was created, causing a deep division among the people. The leadership claims of the descendants of the House of David were rejected, and the ruling authority was transferred into the hands of the high priest. This transfer took place after the era of the Persian Jewish governor Nehemiah, causing a division and a zealous struggle between the three parties. Each saw itself as the sole true representative of the Torah outlook, and regarded its rivals as deniers of the Torah's truth and breakers of its yoke. The controversy unfolded against the background of influences initially absorbed from the cultures of Babylon and Persia and then by the cultures of Greece and Rome—whose philosophy challenged the sages of Israel no less than the wisdom of Babylon and Persia. Because of this, there was an ambivalent tug-of-war between the tendency of wary self-seclusion and that of sweeping openness.

The three rival movements created among the Jewish people following the return to Zion were: (1) supporters of the supreme leadership of the priests (the Sadducees); (2) supporters of the supreme leadership of the scribes and scholars, proponents of the oral Torah (the Pharisees); and (3) supporters of the lineage of the House of David (the Essenes). This was a zealous political controversy over the leadership authority, but each movement represented its own exegetical approach—whether toward the *mitzvot* of the Torah of Moses and the prophets, with its paths of implementation; or toward the challenges of the cultures of Greece and Rome that ruled the land following the conquest of Alexander of Macedonia.

The Hasmonean House as Perpetrator of Division

With the ascent of the Hasmonean dynasty, the rivalry of the three movements turned into a permanent, unbridgeable schism. Initially, the revolt against the Greek rulership that had desecrated and defiled the Temple in Jerusalem united most of the people. But the Hasmonean leaders at their head relied for their authority on their status as Temple priests. After the success of the revolt, they could also rely on their command of the army, it was even natural for the Hasmonean leadership to assume the authority of Israelite royalty—although this authority, according to the teaching of the prophets, was promised to the scion of the House of David. This created a zealous confrontation with devotees of the kingship of the House of David, who regarded the takeover of this authority as an act of betrayal. They also rejected the legitimacy of the Sadducee high priests who collaborated with the Hasmonean kings. The Pharisees did not revolt against the rule of the Hasmonean dynasty, but they did not recognize it as authorized by the Torah law.

This legalistic reservation intensified when the last of the Hasmonean brothers to rule identified openly with the Sadducee priests of the Temple in their controversy with the Pharisees—who considered the Sadducees to be Hellenizers. Ascribing that label to the Hasmonean state gave voice to the halakhic view that the Hasmonean dynastic rule had been forcibly imposed upon the people, just as the Greek rule before it. In the mind of the Pharisees, the reign of the Hasmonean dynasty—from the nation's perspective—represented the Greek, and later Roman rule, and operated according to the legal paradigm of Hellenistic reign, which was subject to the supreme rule of the Roman Empire, and acted according to its ordinances. The Pharisaic scholars thus denied the legal authority of the Hasmonean dynasty over the people, and retained that authority for themselves. This meant that according to the Pharisees—and they led most of the people in the Land of Israel and the diaspora—the people of Israel in their Land were in worse exile than in the diaspora because Jewish kings ruled the land in the name of an alien authority, and worship of God in the Temple went according to Sadducean law, which was also "Hellenistic." This meant that, from the perspective of people who followed the paths of Torah according to oral Torah interpretation in the hands of Pharisaic scholars, not only the people but their Torah and their Temple were all captives of the internal enemy, who was subservient to the external enemy.

This was a most tangled, crisis-laden symptom. It appears to have been the catalyst for the violent, revolutionary zealotry which ultimately caused the destruction of the Second Temple. Also for emigration from the land to new diasporas, which emerged within the boundaries of the Greco-Roman empires, since in these diasporas an explicit conflict with Greek and Roman governments—whose focal point was in Jerusalem and the Temple—did not take form.

The loss of the political-legal framework, which had unified the entire nation precisely in its homeland, defined a situation that was incomparably more serious and curious than the exilic situation in Babylon and Persia—and even more than in the new diaspora which arose in the Greco-Roman empires. Precisely in its land, a degrading, oppressive, and corrupt exile prevailed over the Jewish nation—which debased it among the pagan nations that surrounded and ruled it. This situation also had implications for the dialogue that had developed with Greek and Greco-Roman culture. Simultaneously, there was both an attracting dependence and a repelling menace, both a challenge to fruitful dialogue which could have aspired to mutual influence, and an incentive to belligerent defensiveness, striving for separation.

This ambivalence characterized how the two sides related to one another. Ambivalence on the Jewish side was expressed, first, in the struggle of the oral Torah sages against Hellenization—which they saw as encouraging idolatrous values and servile imitation of idolatrous ways of life; and, secondly, in the sages' deep interest in Greek and Roman wisdom—which distinguished itself by the development of sciences, advanced building techniques, progress of civilization, development of the arts, of jurisprudence, of military and governmental administration techniques, and a philosophy that came close to monotheism. Ambivalence on the Greek and Roman side was expressed, on the one hand by the development of ideological hatred of the Jews, their Torah, and beliefs—which reached the intensity of religious war; on the other hand by openness to the faith and moral values of Torah monotheism, which came to expression in the very broad phenomenon of religious proselytism.

This comparison between realities of the Second Temple era, as described above, and those of the First Temple, emphasizes the difference in the form of encounter of the people of Israel with the idolatrous cultures of neighboring peoples. In the First Temple era, the encounter was essentially an internal, rather than external confrontation—a rivalry between those loyal to the Torah of Moses and the prophets, and their brethren who were influenced by the idolatry of the peoples of Canaan. The prophets criticized idol-worship in general, but sought to influence only their own people. The prophets of Israel in the era prior to the destruction of the First Temple left the war against idolatry of ancient peoples to God Himself. They demanded that their people should uproot idolatry only in their own land, lest they become influenced by it.

The contribution of the nation of Israel to the revelation of the kingdom of God among the nations required only exemplary observance of the *mitzvot* of Torah, which would demonstrate the moral superiority of life according to those ordinances, so that over time all nations would follow the light of Torah to come from Zion. But at the beginning of the era between return to Zion and destruction of the Temple, a radical change took place. The war against idolaters turned essentially outward—to the point that even internal struggles also became functions of struggles against the foreign government and its idolatrous culture. With this, the exile became an arena for the struggle between the prophets' monotheistic faith and Greco-Roman idolatry. Each side was invested in this struggle, not only in conquering the other, but in convincing it—as each side sought to absorb its opponent.

This struggle was also of a higher level in terms of the suffering of the persecuted special nation, which was often required "to sanctify the name of heaven publicly" in order to testify that God, who hid His face from the nation, was the true king of the world. But at the same time, there was a higher level also in terms of relations between the nation and its God. The nation's ever-increasing terrible suffering did not come because of its sins. To the contrary, it came because of the readiness of its faithful members, those who stood the test of fulfilling its mission among the nations, to sanctify the name of their God publicly. There was also a higher level in terms of relations between the nation of Israel and the gentiles. Over the course of their wars with Israel, many gentiles came to understand that Israel's Torah was preferable, and that it was the true teaching; that only by keeping its *mitzvot* could one merit true happiness—whether in this world, or in the world to come.

Christianity: The Faction Extracted from the Jewish Nation

The clearest expression of this change in the internal and external relations of the exiled Jewish nation in its land was Christianity. Christianity appeared in the Land of Israel close to the time of the destruction of the Second Temple, as a Jewish messianic movement which broke away from written and oral Torah sources, in the context of the nation's sufferings in its land. But against the background of the failure of this messianic movement to be accepted by the Jewish people settled in their land, Christianity turned, by means of Jews in the Hellenistic diaspora, to gentiles—to redeem them from their sins and the evil in which they were immersed. That is, Christianity expanded the concept of exile. With Christianity, the concept of exile acquired cosmic and universal dimensions: all of humankind, and each and every individual within it, was thought of as being in exile in human existential terms. How? In terms of the descent of the human soul into the abyss of sinful material corporeality.

According to the Christian view, all earthly existence degenerated into exile, in the sense of experiencing the material life of defilement and sin which entered into the world as a consequence of the first Adam's sin. Since human beings were born in sin "in this time," they could not be redeemed from sin by their own power. They needed a Son of God to atone for their sins by his death and redeem them. As a movement born out of the Jewish people, which severed itself from them in order to turn to all humanity, Christianity divided the chosen nation in an unprecedented and very strange way. It defined those Christians leaving their Jewish people as continuers-but-destroyers, as lovers-but-enemies to their chosen nation. And indeed, the new Christians did not tie themselves to the nations who ruled the Greco-Roman empires, they established a "church," whose goal was to unite all human beings as individuals within itself and thereby to make them into the "authentic Israel," "Israel in spirit," superior to those whom they called, from their perspective, "Israel in the flesh."

The Christian church saw itself as the authentic people of Israel. On the one hand, it attributed high theological importance to the recognition of the Jewish nation—the nation of "the old covenant"—within the truth of "the new covenant." On the other, the church blamed the Jewish nation for the murder of the Son of God—on account of its refusal to accept Jesus as Messiah. The significance of this defamation of the image of the Jewish nation, and the significance of the worsening of its destiny among the nations, became clear and began to be institutionalized after the destruction of the Second Temple, especially after the defeat of Bar Kokhba, for it trampled upon the hope that the Temple would soon be established for a third time. The Christians considered the destruction as everlasting proof of their being right. The Jews, for their part, viewed the Christian justification for the Temple's destruction as proof of its betrayal of their people and their Torah.

The significance of the split between rabbinic Judaism and Christianity for the nation of Israel's destiny as a people exiled among the nations became further clarified and established in the days of the emperor Constantine the Great at the beginning of the fourth century according to the Christian calendar, through the covenant negotiated between the Eastern Roman Empire and the Christian church. This was the most severe worsening of the exilic condition, because the ruling church could punish the chosen (or, from their perspective, sinful) nation by degrading and persecuting it, coercing it to "voluntarily" acknowledge the truthfulness of the New Testament and be baptized into Christianity so that its sin would be forgiven by the grace of the "Savior."

Which, then, was the authentic Israel? Who was the Messiah? Whom would the Messiah redeem in the future? This twisted complexity became an obstacle in the path of the development of the messianic redemption, and it is what made the addition of a new blessing-request to the *Shemoneh Esrei* a necessity. After church rule had been established, it was impossible to expect the continuation of the process of the Jewish nation's redemption in the way that had been anticipated from the days of return to Zion and until Christianity's appearance—on the basis of the prophecies of Moses, Isaiah, and Jeremiah—without the dethronement and the ruin of the Christian church. Clearly, the nation of Israel could not do anything about this matter by its own powers, aside from readiness to be strong in its faith despite its degradation and persecution, and to sanctify the name of the true God of Israel amid the nations that persecuted it.

The Expression of the New Conception of Redemption in the *Shemoneh Esrei* Prayer

The blessings of the *Shemoneh Esrei* prayer, which describe messianic redemption according to the sequence of its occurrence, reflect a purposeful theological logic on the one hand, and reliance on the words of Moses and the prophets on the other. The first step, necessitated by the exile which began with uprooting the nation from its land and dispersion among the surrounding nations, was the opposing action: the ingathering of exiles. The tenth blessing expresses this need: "Sound the great *shofar* for our freedom, raise high the banner to gather our exiles, and gather us together from the four quarters of the earth. Blessed are You, Lord, Who gathers the dispersed of His people Israel" (K:120, *Teka Beshofar*). In terms of the order of events, this request first of all obliges a divine proclamation from the prophet's mouth, like the *shofar* blast signifying the beginning of the Jubilee year, so that all gentile nations will hear that the Jewish nation, which is dispersed and exiled among them, is to go out from servitude to freedom, and that God Himself will gather and lead the nation to its land to settle there in peace, by agreement of all the nations.

Consider the parallel between this blessing and the blessing with which the request for personal redemption opens: "Lead us back to You, in perfect repentance" (K:114, *Hashiveinu*). We see that the return of individuals in *teshuvah* turns into the first stage of the redemption of the entire nation, as one collective entity, and is interpreted as the restoration of the nation and its collective return to God. This is *teshuvah* in its national sense—the return to protection under the wings of God which are spread over the nation only when it worships its God in its land, city, and Temple. The expression "ingathering of exiles" connotes return to the land, whether as physical return or spiritual *teshuvah*: gathering out of the dispersion, assembling out of banishment, and unification. Consider the emphasis on the word *yaḥad* ("together") in the blessing for the ingathering of exiles. This word adds the dimension of participation internally, and unifying externally. That is, the ingathering of exiles means not only assembling into one land, but identification as a distinct and unique collective entity. In this way, the return to the land to settle there as a nation also assumes the meaning of *teshuvah* from the sin, which has divided the nation, weakened it, uprooted it from its land, and led it into exile.

This conceptual correlation is explicit in the sources that underlie the blessing, first of all in the end-of-days prophecy attributed to Moses. According to the account in Deuteronomy, this prophecy was uttered close to his death. Moses anticipated the settlement of Israel in its land, the narrative of the succeeding generations, and the end of their state. He knew with complete certainty that the nation would stumble on account of the idolatry of the Canaanite nations; that it would be seduced and would sin against its God; that it would be severely punished and be uprooted from its land, dispersed, and exiled. Nevertheless, Moses assured in God's name that the covenant made between God and His nation obliged God for eternity, and would not be annulled. In the depths of its exile, the nation would remember its God, cry out to Him, and return with full *teshuvah*. The people would receive a response, as they did when they cried out to God in the land of Egypt: "Then the Lord your God will restore your fortunes and take you back in love. He will bring you together again from all the peoples where the Lord your God has scattered you" (Deuteronomy 30:3).

After that, the prophet Isaiah relied on these words of Moses in his vision of redemption: "And in that day, a great rams' horn shall be sounded; and the strayed who are in the land of Assyria and the expelled who are in the land of Egypt shall come and worship the Lord on the holy mount, in Jerusalem" (Isaiah 27:13). In sounding the great *shofar*, which the blessing commemorates, Isaiah is supported by the *mitzvah* of sounding the *shofar* on the Day of Atonement, which opens the year of the Jubilee (Leviticus 25:9). In this way, Isaiah created a parallel between the year of the Jubilee, designated for the internal redemption of the children of Israel in their relation to one another, and their leaving the houses of slavery in gentile lands for freedom. These two redemptions depended upon one another, in the sense that observing the *mitzvah* of the Sabbatical year and the Jubilee were considered conditions for the return of the nation from exile to settling on the land it possesses in righteousness and peace.

This legal determination is explicit in the words of prophecy said by Moses, continuous with legislation regarding the Jubilee in the book of Leviticus. His words parallel his prophecy at the end of the book of Deuteronomy. He sounds a dire warning: should the people not observe the *mitzvot* of Sabbatical year and Jubilee, they will be punished with exile until the number of Sabbatical years and the Jubilees that were not observed will be "compensated for." Then the people will cry out to God, and promise to keep His *mitzvot* in the future. God will respond and proclaim the Jubilee year to be that of the return of His nation to the land of its possession, where it will reside in righteousness and peace (Leviticus 26:27–46). Thus, this blessing of the *Shemoneh Esrei* prayer relates to the two prophecies of Moses through the prophecy of Isaiah. It adds an allusion to the words of Jeremiah, which were directed to realizing the vision of the ingathering of exiles—with reference to the connection between the Jews and the gentiles who enslaved them but would be forced to liberate and return them by their own hands, just as they exiled them by their own hands: "Declare among the nations, and proclaim: Raise a standard, proclaim: Hide nothing!" (Jeremiah 50:2).

Four Blessings of the *Shemoneh Esrei* (10, 11, 13, 15) *Vis-à-Vis* Four Stages of Redemption

The next step in messianic redemption emerges from the first step. In terms of the order of the blessings, this next step is based on Jeremiah's vision of consolation and redemption after the destruction that had already been determined. At the conclusion of his words of consolation, Jeremiah fixes the order of the phases in the realization of the prediction of redemption that will come after the destruction:

> "And I Myself will gather the remnant of My flock from all the lands to which I have banished them, and I will bring them back to their pasture, where they shall be fertile and increase. And I will appoint over them shepherds who will tend them; they shall no longer fear or be dismayed, and none of them shall be missing"—declares the Lord.

"See a time is coming"—declares the Lord—"when I will raise up a true brand of David's line. He shall reign as king and shall prosper, and he shall do what is just and right in the land. In his days Judah shall be delivered and Israel shall dwell secure. And this is the name by which he shall be called: The Lord is our Vindicator." (Jeremiah 23:3–6)

Consider the four phases of redemption as discerned in these visionary words, and their congruence with the phases of four blessings of the *Shemoneh Esrei* prayer, in order: (10, *Teka Beshofar*) the ingathering of exiles ("And I will gather the remnant of My flock out of all the countries to which I have driven them"); (11, *Hashivah Shofeteinu*) the reinstatement of the judges and advisors ("And I will set up shepherds over them who shall feed them"); (13, *Al Hatzaddikim*) the assurance of the peace of the nation under the oversight of the true shepherds, as God will protect the shepherds ("And they shall fear no more, nor be dismayed, neither shall any by lacking, says the Lord"); and finally, (15, *Et Tzemah*) the flowering of a righteous heir of David who will renew the proper government, one of justice in Israel. Consider also that the logic which connects all these steps into a single ladder, identifies redemption with the rule of justice and equity in the nation. By merit of practicing justice and equity, the people would be able to be confident that God would protect them from all their enemies, even before their sovereignty is established. As written in the words of the prophet Isaiah, cited in the eleventh blessing:

I will restore your magistrates as of old,
And your counselors as of yore.
After that you shall be called
City of Righteousness, Faithful City.
Zion shall be saved in the judgment;
Her repentant ones, in the retribution.
(Isaiah 1:26–27)

We learn from the prophecy of Jeremiah that the ingathering of exiles alone will not unite the nation. The nation is also obligated to rectify the iniquity, which caused its dispersion: The division which nullified the covenant made at Sinai between all individuals, families, and tribes to become one assembly, unified and unique. This iniquity is to be rectified through ordinances of righteousness and laws of the truth of God's Torah. In order to be redeemed, the nation is obliged to restore moral and legal unity, based upon the laws of the covenant. All this is contained in the eleventh blessing: "Restore our judges as at first and our counselors as at the beginning, and remove from us sorrow and sighing. May You alone, Lord, reign over us with loving-kindness and compassion, and vindicate us in justice. Blessed are You, Lord, the King who loves righteousness and justice" (K:120, *Hashivah Shofeteinu*).

Consider again the parallel between this blessing and the two following individual requests attached to the request of "bring us back" (K:114, *Hashiveinu*): the request "forgive us" (K:116, *Selaḥ Lanu*), and the request "Look on our affliction, plead our cause" (K:116, *Re'eh Be'onyeinu*). The parallel is highlighted by reference to the prophecies which constitute the sources of this blessing:

A. I will turn My hand against you,

   And smelt out your dross as with lye,
   And remove all your slag:
   I will restore your magistrates as of old,
   And your counselors as of yore.
   After that you shall be called
   City of Righteousness, Faithful City.
   Zion shall be saved in the judgment;
   Her repentant ones, in the retribution.
   (Isaiah 1:25–27)

B. And the Lord will reign over them on Mount Zion. Now and for evermore. (Micah 4:7)

C. And I will espouse you forever:

   I will espouse you with righteousness and justice,
   And with goodness and mercy,
   And I will espouse you with faithfulness.
   (Hosea 2:21–24)

D. That I the Lord act with kindness;

   Justice, and equity in the world;
   For in these I delight.
   (Jeremiah 9:23)

All these prophecies determine that God's sovereignty over His nation will be expressed by obedience to the ordinances of morality and justice of Moses's Torah, and their observance by the people through their leaders. This does not depend *a priori* upon having a monarchical ruler, because until the days of Saul and David there was no king in Israel, and God ruled His nation through His prophets, priests, elders, and judges who kept His Torah. It follows that the substance of redemption was the nation's dwelling on its land in the ways of justice and equity, because behaving in these ways was true freedom, and the optimal way of maintaining freedom was symbolized by observing the *mitzvot* of Sabbath, Sabbatical year, and Jubilee.

Once this order was restored, it would be possible to renew the kingdom of the House of David, and after that to properly renew Temple worship, and then God would return and reside amid His nation, and assure its peace by the power of His rule over all powers of creation. During the return to Zion in the days of Ezra and Nehemiah, the nation began to establish ways of justice and equity. Over time came the divisions and controversies surrounding their interpretations and implementations, and these ultimately gave birth to the Christian heresy. Clearly, as long as internal strife continued, it was not possible to complete the ingathering of exiles and their entry into the land. To the contrary, the emigration from the Land of Israel into the exilic diaspora increased, and there was no possibility of restoring the unity of the nation and of establishing true shepherds to lead all the sheep of their flock in justice and equity. That is, the process of redemption began with the return to Zion, but since the people did not pass the test, the process not only did not advance but reversed itself.

"For the slanderers let there be no hope" (K:120, *Ulemalshinim*)

We now pass to the twelfth blessing. According to most scholars, it was instituted in the days of Rabban Shimon ben Gamliel II following the suppression of the Bar Kokhba revolt. At that point, the possibility of imminent rebuilding of the Jerusalem Temple became nil, and the final push was also given to disconnect Jewish Christians from their people:

> For the slanderers let there be no hope,
> And may all wickedness perish in an instant.
> May all Your people's enemies swiftly be cut down.
> May You swiftly uproot, crush, cast down

And humble the arrogant swiftly in our days.
Blessed are You, Lord,
Who destroys enemies and humbles the arrogant.
(K:120, *Ulemalshinim*)

The deviation of this blessing from the pattern of all other blessings in the *siddur* is evident from the fact that the request contained in it is not positive but negative: the request for God to bring a violent curse upon His nation's enemies. They are enemies of His Torah, and therefore also enemies of His sovereignty, who come from within, from out of the chosen nation itself. Even worse: idolatrous nations that oppressed the nation of Israel in the past were also called enemies of God. But now there was the extremely serious matter of the "sectarian" hatred of the God of Israel. It preceded hatred for their people, and was the reason for it. In other words, the sectarians' hatred for their people came from their blind faith in a false and deceitful divinity, which replaced the God of truth. On account of this, they persecuted the people who remained loyal to the true God with satanic animosity.

These factors justified the deviation from composing a positive blessing. God judges His people with His attribute of might, and is vengeful with extraordinary severity when it comes to their sins. This is precisely because they are His chosen nation. The logic of the law of justice, which He legislates, requires Him to act against His enemies: "For I the Lord your God am an impassioned God, visiting the guilt of the parents upon the children, upon the third and upon the fourth generations of those who reject Me, but showing kindness to the thousandth generation of those who love Me and keep My commandments" (Exodus 20:5–6). Consequently, it is up to God to activate His attribute of vengeful judgment upon these enemies of His nation who have left from within it, and to recompense His loyal shepherds of the nation who observe His *mitzvot*, even when they are persecuted by their enemies for doing so, with the promised benevolence.

The legalistic determination is emphasized by means of the special terminology that the twelfth blessing employs. This refers, first of all, to the terms "wickedness" (*rish'ah*) and "malice" (*zadon*). With these two synonymous words, the Torah of Moses identifies sins of the highest level of gravity—sins committed with forethought, with the intention of doing evil for its own sake. What is the forethought that explains such corrupt intention by human beings who are also created in the image of God? Surely, the evil inclination of the person "evil from his youth" is the cause. But the reference is to its most serious ramifications for the human being's intellectual soul, expressed in the lust to rule and the pride bound up with it. The lust to rule and pride impel a person to compete with God, to try to establish oneself in place of God. But since the person cannot compete with God when it comes to God's attributes of benevolence as creator, he competes with God in the ability to destroy, which his intellect facilitates. In this way he covenants with the evil in the forces of chaos, and transforms good into evil and evil into good.

We are referring, in other words, to the twisted desire to have evil dominate in the universe. Towards this end, evil goes all out to oppress and destroy the pious, who know the truth and are prepared to struggle for it and to sanctify the name of God in the world. Therefore, the blessing requests God to help His nation in its struggle to sanctify His name, and to bring to bear His attribute of judgment against His enemies with full severity and without compassion: to ruin, destroy, shatter, defeat, and disempower; not to have mercy and not to leave any remnant. Because compassion for evildoers means cruelty towards the pious who are persecuted on account of their innocence.

The key to defining the ingredients of the twelfth blessing is to be found in the following conceptions. Who are the "slanderers" in the published version of the *siddur*? According to the Talmudic debate, this blessing is defined as the "blessing of the sectarians" and this definition is affirmed in ancient manuscript versions. Based on this, most scholars are of the opinion that the term "slanderers" replaced the term "sectarians" at the behest of the Christian censors—even though it was possible that the first version included both "sectarians" and "slanderers." Who were the "sectarians"? The legalistic answer is that "sectarianism" is the knowing aberration of belief in the Torah's uniqueness, as interpreted by ordained oral Torah scholars. This is the gravest act of denial, because it exchanges truth for a lie that contradicts it. In this sense, "sectarians" could also refer to the Sadducees. But in this blessing, instituted by Rabban Gamaliel II, it clearly refers to Christians who believed that Jesus, who was taken out to be killed on the cross by the Roman governor, was the Son of God who died in order to atone with his blood for the sins of all humankind, but who, with his death, laid the guilt for his murder on his people. From the Jewish-rabbinic perspective of the oral Torah scholars, this was evil and malice of such gravity that it would be impossible to imagine anything more serious. Clearly, its rise to dominance among the gentiles brought a "reign of malice" (*Uvekhen Tzaddikim*, morning *Amidah* of Rosh Hashanah) to the world, a rule of evildoers who claimed with great insolence that they ruled in God's name for the salvation of humanity. Clearly, as long as they ruled the world and Israel was oppressed under them, the messianic redemption could not come.

"To the righteous, the pious" (K:122, *Al Hatzaddikim*). The Other Side of the Coin

The thirteenth blessing (originally the twelfth) can be explained against that background. We referred to its source in the prophecy of Jeremiah. In it, God is asked to assure the peace of the good "shepherds" whom He would appoint to His people during the era of the ingathering of exiles. God would do this, so the people could settle securely in their land during the stage of advancing the flowering of the "offshoot" of the House of David, who is the "shoot [that] shall grow of the stump of Jesse" and the "twig [that] shall sprout from his stock," as prophesized by Isaiah (Isaiah 11:1), and is the sovereign over God's nation.

Following the "blessing of the sectarians," an exceptional addition is made to the thirteenth blessing in order to balance out the relations of Israel to the gentiles. In addition to the "righteous," the "devout," "the elders of Your people the House of Israel," and the "remnant of the scholars" who, in Jeremiah's words, are the faithful shepherds, the amenders of the blessing added "the righteous converts" and "all who sincerely believe in Your name," to distinguish them from those who do not sincerely believe in the God of truth and righteousness, but in a lying and deceitful God. In the face of the success of the "sectarians" to expand and even rule over the gentiles, crucial importance is attached to the phenomenon of "righteous converts" among the gentiles. The misery that fell upon the members of the chosen nation did not deter the converts from identifying with the Jews in exile, for they were convinced that the God of the exiled nation was the God of truth, and His name was truth. They thus encouraged the people of Israel to believe in the rightness of their cause, even when it seemed to everyone that evil would prevail.

Building Jerusalem and the Davidic Kingship—Next Stages of the Redemption

According to the sequence of the stages in Jeremiah's vision, the stage for the appearance of the kingdom of the House of David had now arrived. But we will see that in what follows, the *Shemoneh Esrei* prayer distinguishes two complementary stages in the process of establishing the sovereignty of the House of David (which is the proper government, as opposed to any other government that the nation might establish). The first is the return of God Himself to Jerusalem to reside therein, rule over it, and prepare the throne for His servant David. Only after that can the descendant of the House of David rule his nation by occupying his throne in its capital city of Jerusalem—not in his own name, as an idolatrous king would do, but rather in the name of God, whom he serves as His devoted servant:

> To Jerusalem, Your city,
> May You return in compassion,
> And may You dwell in it as You promised.
> May You rebuild it rapidly in our days
> As an everlasting structure,
> And install within it soon the throne of David.
> Blessed are You, Lord, who builds Jerusalem.
> (K:122, *Velirushalayim Irekha*)

This is the language of the fourteenth blessing, which is connected explicitly to the blessing which follows, which seeks the establishment of the legitimate government itself.

From where do we learn about the urgency of the blessing that requests God's return to Jerusalem to reside there—as a stage prior to establishing the kingdom of the House of David? The simple and clear answer is that we learn it from the narrative about establishing the government of David in Jerusalem, after God chose it as the capital city of the kingdom of Israel, which united all the nation's tribes (II Samuel 5–7), and then from the narrative about establishing the kingdom of Solomon and the building of the Temple in Jerusalem (I Kings 8). Below, we will argue that these two narratives determined both the order of the blessings of the *Shemoneh Esrei* prayer—from the fourteenth through sixteenth blessings—and their respective content.

The narrative begins with the gathering of all the tribes of Israel before David, who was ruling in Hebron, the capital of Judah, to receive him as their king. As a result of the approbation, David decided to establish his capital in Jerusalem. He conquered it, and in order to make it into the capital of all Israel's tribes, he decided to bring the Ark of the Covenant up to Jerusalem. Let us attend to the details of the narrative, because its essence is testimony to God's refusal to allow David to bring the Ark of the Covenant up to Jerusalem as David decided—given that he was a servant of God and God was the sovereign who ruled over him. To the contrary, David was obliged to show the people clearly that it was God Himself who brought the Ark of the Covenant up to Jerusalem and decided to come and reside there.

This was the purport of the entry of the Ark into Jerusalem when David, the devout king, performed sacrifices at each and every step before the Ark and danced and leaped like a servant before it until its arrival, according to God's order, in the hands of the priests who were selected by God to serve Him at its resting place in the tent prepared by David. The same inversion is exhibited as the narrative continues and the Ark of God is transferred from the tent in the city of David to the Temple that arose upon Mount Moriah. By means of His prophet, God forbade David to build a house in His name. He allowed that only to David's son Solomon, by the merit of peace that prevailed in the land throughout Solomon's days. It appears that God Himself built His house by means of Solomon and his servants, and that the house was sanctified only when God Himself "descended" into it from His eternal height and caused His *Shekhinah* to rest in it. The *Shekhinah* is described as a perceptible presence for the entire nation. Solomon did not dance and did not leap before the Ark, as his father David did. Rather, he offered sacrifices of thanksgiving, he bowed in humility, and—what is essential from our perspective—he prayed at the altar, outside the Holy of Holies and the Sanctuary.

We will deal with the matter of Solomon's prayer and its connection to the *Shemoneh Esrei* prayer, when we get to the sixteenth blessing which relates to it. Here we will refer to the text of the fourteenth blessing, "builder of Jerusalem" (*boneh yerushalayim*). Consider the accord between what is said in the blessing and what is said in the narrative about building Jerusalem as the capital of the nation of Israel. God is asked to return Himself to His city, to reside therein, to build it, and prepare the "throne of David" there. The building of the Temple itself is not yet discussed, rather only the preparation for renewing the kingdom of the House of David—which over the course of time would allow for the building of the Temple and the renewal of worship.

The transition to the fifteenth blessing is smooth, and it is in agreement with both Jeremiah's prophecy and the narrative of the coronation of David's descendant:

> May the offshoot of Your servant David soon flower,
> And may his pride be raised high by Your salvation,
> For we wait for Your salvation all day.
> Blessed are You, Lord, who makes the glory [literally, "horn"] of salvation flourish.
> (K:124, *Et Tzemah*)

The content of the request is clear and obvious. The text, especially the end of the blessing—"who makes the glory [horn] of salvation flourish"—might appear strange, but this is resolved when we look on one hand, at the problem bound up with the coronation of the king who represents the lineage of the House of David after centuries of being cut off; and on the other hand at the prophetic sources that grapple with this problem. This topic is implicit to the scroll of Ruth, which describes the genealogy of the House of David, at the beginning of the era of the return to Zion.

According to the scroll of Ruth, the lineage that connected the family of Judah son of Jacob, patriarch of the kingdom, was severed twice before David's birth. Tamar, Judah's Canaanite wife, renewed the continuity of the lineage for the first time, through a benevolent deed. Boaz and Ruth the Moabite renewed it for a second time. Here, we emphasize the fact that Peretz and Obed were not direct descendants who continued the stem of the kingdom's genealogical tree, but rather were "branches," which sprouted from the root—in parallel to the severed stem. Isaiah prophesied about the renewal of the kingdom of the House of David in "the end of days" in this language:

> But a shoot shall grow out of the stump of Jesse,
> A twig shall sprout from his stock
> (Isaiah 11:1)

Jeremiah used similar language in his prophecy:

> See, a time is coming—declares the Lord—when I will raise up a true brand [literally, "shoot"] of David's line. He shall reign as king and shall prosper, and he shall do what is just and right in the land. In his days Judah shall be delivered and Israel shall dwell secure. And this is the name by which he shall be called: "the Lord is our Vindicator." (Jeremiah 23:5–6)

The "shoot" is also a metaphysical expression directed to the renewal of the kingdom from the root, and not from the stem. Continuous with it, a second metaphor for expressing the renewal of the kingdom is the "horn," which sprouts into glory and splendor. From what source is it borrowed? From the prayer of Hannah, which, at its conclusion, is a prophecy of the appearance of the kingdom of the House of David:

> The foes of the Lord shall be shattered;
> He will thunder against them in the heavens.
> The Lord will judge the ends of the earth.
> He will give power to His king,
> And [give] triumph to [literally, "raise the horn of"] His anointed one.
> (I Samuel 2:10)

If we go back, we will find the image of the sprouting of the horn in the Psalms, attributed to David himself: "There I will make a horn sprout for David; I have prepared a lamp for My anointed one" (Psalms 132:17). This image also appears in the poem that David composed after the death of Saul and David's ascent to the throne of kingship:

> O Lord, my crag, my fastness, my deliverer!
> O God, the rock wherein I take shelter:
> My shield, my mighty champion [literally, "horn of my salvation"], my fortress and refuge!
> My savior, You who rescue me from violence!
> All praise! I called on the Lord,
> And I was delivered from my enemies.
> (II Samuel 22:2–4)

Like David, then, will be the "sprout" who will spring from the root of the House of David, the anointed of God, who will deliver his nation by the strength of salvation granted him by God. To emphasize this point, the image of the lofty "horn" is added to the previous passages, the fighting horn of the gazelle, which is exalted over the splendor of the kingdom. It is joined to the image of the sprouting shoot. Thus is created the poetic similitude that compares the exaltation of the king of the House of David, in its success, to the sprouting of the gazelle's horn.

King Solomon, Founder of Prayer

At first glance, the sixteenth blessing appears to be a summary of the previous blessings. It is a request that all previous blessings be answered:

> Listen to our voice, Lord our God.
> Spare us and have compassion on us,
> And in compassion and favor accept our prayer,
> For You, God, listen to prayers and pleas.
> Do not turn us away, O our King,
> Empty-handed from Your presence,
> For You listen with compassion
> To the prayer of Your people Israel.
> Blessed are You, Lord, who listens to prayer.
> (K:124, Shema Koleinu)

But is this request also an additional stage in the development of redemption? We can bring clarity to this question by connecting to the source of this blessing, which is the prayer of King Solomon when he brought the Ark of the covenant of God up from the city of David, in the sight of all Israel, to place it in its permanent place in the "Holy of Holies" underneath the wings of the cherubs: "The poles projected so that the ends of the poles were visible in the sanctuary in front of the Shrine, but they could not be seen outside" (I Kings 8:8). This, accordingly, is the event to which the seventeenth blessing also related in what followed—namely, the symbolic entry of God into the Temple: "When the priests came out of the sanctuary—for the cloud had filled the House of the Lord and the priests were not able to remain and perform the service because of the cloud, for the Presence of the Lord filled the House of the Lord" (I Kings 8:10).

As to our subject: on this basis it is important to indicate the difference between the event of bringing up the Ark in the days of David and that in the days of Solomon. In the days of David, this was God's symbolic entry into Jerusalem, but only to reside in the tent as in the days of their wandering in the desert—that is, to settle temporarily. In the days of Solomon, God entered into His sanctuary to reside permanently. By doing do, God created an eternal tie between Himself and His nation—by means of the priests, on the one hand, and the king, on the other. For this purpose, the division between the role of the king and the role of the priests was also important. Like David, Solomon offered a sacrifice to God by bringing up the Ark of the Covenant of God, as the Ark remained outside the "Holy of Holies." With the entry of the Ark into the Holy of Holies, Solomon remained outside the sanctuary and outside the Shrine, and consecrated the Temple in the sight of all his people with an official prayer in the name of all Israel and together with all of Israel. This event is described as the establishment of permanent prayer as a form of worshipping God, in which all the people of Israel participate directly; and not only upon their entering the Temple, but wherever they were. Upon God's entry into the Temple to reside there permanently, all of Israel could pray to Him directly. When they directed their faces, from near or far, to the Temple, and when their prayer was recited with sanctity, with ritual, and with moral purity, it ascended straight to God who "resided" permanently in His Temple, in order to spread His protection over the people, hear their prayer, pardon their sins, and bless them.

From the perspective of the *siddur*—the Jewish book of prayer—there is, therefore, double importance to this event. With this, synagogue prayer was also established effectively as a way in which the people could worship God directly, and without sacrifices, to atone for their sins and be blessed.

With this event Solomon, as king, fulfilled his role as "representative of the community" (*shaliah hatzibur*) for all his people. His prayer exemplified the essence of worship, which is to stand in (judicial) judgment before God, in order to return in *teshuvah* and be worthy of atonement and blessing. In his prayer, Solomon asked for atonement and blessing for all members of his people. He showed them the way to turn to God at any moment of individual or group distress in order to be rescued—trusting that God would hear the voice of supplication and listen to their prayer-song:

> Then Solomon stood before the altar of the Lord in the presence of the whole community of Israel; he spread the palms of his hands toward heaven and said, "O Lord God of Israel, in the heavens above and on the earth below there is no god like You, who keep Your gracious covenant with Your servants when they walk before You in wholehearted devotion. (I Kings 8:22–23)

After that opening, Solomon began to pray about himself and requested:

> Yet turn, O Lord my God, to the prayer and supplication of Your servant, and hear the cry and prayer which Your servant offers before You this day. May Your eyes be open day and night toward this House, toward the place of which you have said, "My name shall abide there"; may You heed the prayers which Your servant will offer toward this place. And when You hear the supplications which Your servant and Your people Israel offer toward this place, give heed in Your heavenly abode—give heed and pardon.

> Whenever one man commits an offense against another, and the latter utters an imprecation to bring a curse upon him, and comes with his imprecation before Your altar in this House, oh, hear in heaven and take action to judge Your servants, condemning him who is in the wrong and bringing down the punishment of his conduct on his head, vindicating him who is in the right by rewarding him according to his righteousness. (I Kings 8:28–32)

In the continuation of his prayer, Solomon enumerated various situations in which the people and its member would stand to pray and earn favor before God:

Should Your people Israel be routed by an enemy because they have sinned against You, and then turn back to You and acknowledge Your name, and they offer prayer and supplication to You in this House, oh, hear in heaven and pardon the sin of Your people Israel, and restore them to the land that You gave to their fathers.

Should the heavens be shut up and there be no rain, because they have sinned against You, and then they pray toward this place and acknowledge Your name and repent of their sins when You answer them, oh, hear in heaven and pardon the sin of Your servants, Your people Israel, after You have shown the proper way in which they are to walk; and send down rain upon the land which You gave to Your people as their heritage. (I Kings 8:33–36)

So, too, if there is a famine in the land, if there is pestilence, blight, mildew, locusts or caterpillars, or if an enemy oppresses them in any of the settlements of the land.

In any plague and in any disease, in any prayer or supplication offered by any person among all Your people Israel—each of whom knows his own affliction—when he spreads his palms toward this House, oh, hear in Your heavenly abode, and pardon and take action! Render to each man according to his ways as You know his heart to be—for You alone know the hearts of all men—so that they may revere You all the days that they live on the land that You gave to our fathers.

Or if a foreigner who is not of Your people Israel comes from a distant land for the sake of Your name—for they shall hear about Your great name and Your mighty hand and Your outstretched arm—when he comes to pray toward this House, oh, hear in Your heavenly abode and grant all that the foreigner asks You for. Thus all the peoples of the earth will know Your name and revere You, as does Your people Israel; and they will recognize that Your name is attached to this House that I have built.

When our people take the field against their enemy by whatever way You send them, and they pray to the Lord in the direction of the city which You have chosen, and of the House which I have built to Your name, oh, hear in heaven their prayer and supplication and uphold their cause.

When they sin against You—for there is no man who does not sin—and You are angry with them and deliver them to the enemy, and their captors carry them off to an enemy land, near or far; and then they take it to heart in the land to which they have been carried off, and they repent and make supplication to You in the land of their captors, saying: "We have sinned we have acted perversely, we have acted wickedly," and they turn back to You with all their heart and soul, in the land of the enemies who have carried them off, and they pray to You in the direction of their land which You gave to their fathers, of the city which You have chosen and of the House which I have built to Your name—oh, give heed in Your heavenly abode to their prayer and supplication, uphold their cause, and pardon Your people who have sinned against You for all the transgressions that they have committed against You. Grant them mercy in the sight of their captors that they may be merciful to them. For they are Your very own people that You freed from Egypt, from the midst of the iron furnace. May Your eyes be open to the supplication of Your servant and the supplication of Your people Israel, and may you heed them whenever they call upon You. For You O Lord God, have set them apart for Yourself from all the peoples of the earth as Your very own, as You promised through Moses Your servant when You freed our fathers from Egypt. (I Kings 8:37–53)

Finally, let us also present the promise that was given to Solomon in response to his prayer:

Then the Lord appeared to Solomon a second time, as He had appeared to him at Gibeon. The Lord said to him, "I have heard thy prayer and the supplication which you have offered to Me. I consecrate this House which you have built and I set My name there forever. My eyes and My heart shall ever be there." (I Kings 9:2–3)

We find that the *Shema Koleinu* (sixteenth) blessing relates to all requests of individuals and the nation, which are mentioned in the *Shemoneh Esrei* prayer, but, as the highest rung on the ladder of messianic redemption, it includes the request for God to return to His Temple, to reside permanently among His people, to keep His promise to place His name, His eyes, and heart there, for all time, and to hear the prayers of all individuals and the prayer of the entire united nation. "To hear" means to receive this prayer and be responsive to it with pardon and forgiveness of sins, and with a blessing for the nation and all its individuals. This stage of complete redemption is the great thing sought for at the blessing's end—in brief language: "Blessed are You, Lord, who listens to prayer" (K:124, *Shema Koleinu*).

Thus, the blessing asserts that God "listens to prayer" (*shome'a tefillah*, K:124, *Shema Koleinu*), and in this way turns the request into fact. When the partition of sin, which separates the nation from God in exile, falls, when God returns to reside in His Temple, He will again be "He who hears prayers." Indeed, this is what God said, and what God promised to Solomon at the consecration of His first Temple. By virtue of this promise for the future, the exiled nation has the hope that God will hear its prayer—the prayer of its children, who fell into enemy captivity, and exiles of the present, when they pray from afar in synagogues, downcast and desperate, facing in the direction of Jerusalem and the Temple. If they are worthy and justified before Him, He will respond to them and rescue them. With this, the future and present of those who long for God meet—towards the three blessings that conclude the entire prayer.

13

The *Shemoneh Esrei*— Responding in Anticipation of Complete Redemption

The anticipation of the period of redemption, which intensifies in the concluding blessing of the *Shemoneh Esrei* prayer, is a reflection of the vision of peace and perfection—which the prophets promised for the future to come. They did so by means of their emotional, imaginary, reflective-symbolic ability—ripening the path of worshipping God with supplication, poetry, and singing. The worshipper raises himself up towards God with words of song, of praise and gratitude, and with cantillations of longing and yearning. He is exalted by the wave of his emotions, which rises to a crest. He experiences the expansion of his soul "to the beyond" in feeling and thought, and his exit from the boundary of his self to a spiritual realm beyond the horizon of intuitive-intellectual comprehension, where he savors one-sixtieth of the light, joy, celebration, perfection, and peace for which he longs, and is assured that he will arrive at a future that is beyond all "now," and a space that is beyond all "here."

The spiritual-poetic-prophetic ability to ascend, and to anticipate the realization of the distant future, is implanted into the human being as the creature created "in the image of God," because the soul longs for the source from which it came. The *Shemoneh Esrei* prayer does not define the idea of anticipation, but rather realizes this idea with the poetic gesture to which it ascends at the conclusion. It does so by means of the transition from reciting the request-blessings to reciting the gratitude for the response, which the worshipper experiences while conversing with God in the language of "You" (*Atah*) when he "sets" God before him. From here comes the faith that when the prayer climaxes it "will be favorable" and the worshipper "will find favor" and will be answered.

From the vista attained in the three concluding blessings (17, *Retzei Adonai*, 18, *Modim Anaḥnu*, 19, *Sim Shalom*), the *Shemoneh Esrei* prayer appears as a kind of ladder resting on earth, with its top reaching heaven. Worshippers ascend towards redemption by stages of the request-blessings, until they come as close as possible to the top of the ladder, which they cannot reach as long as the soul is tied to the body. It is as if they extend their hands upward towards the extended hands of God who responds to them, and as if God descends towards the worshippers from distant heavens, beyond conception, as a compassionate father "who, enthroned on high, sees what is below" (Psalms 113:5) with His children. Then God showers on them the blessing of peace, which emanates from His perfection. The double emotional movement of request and blessing is the movement of soulful endeavor of the worshipper, which pushes from below on the one hand, and draws down from above on the other. By means of this, it is as if the worshipper climbs up the rungs of the ladder until he reaches the rung of the seventeenth blessing. At this rung, the requests made to God to satisfy the needs of his servant-children change into an expression of readiness to give oneself to Him, in order for God to draw the worshippers to Him; they will be united with Him in His realm, as His priests, who served Him with sanctity, were united with Him in the sanctuary of the Tabernacle and the Temple. It was so when the high priest cast the blood of sacrifices upon the curtain of the Holy Ark (*Kaporet*), offered the "show-bread" (Exodus 25:30) on the table, placed the candles in the lamp of seven branches, and pronounced the "Tetragrammaton according to its letters" when entering the "Holy of Holies" on the Day of Atonement (Exodus 30:10), in the presence of the cherubs— over whom God revealed Himself in His speaking to Moses.

The idea about "anticipating" the future is identified with the ascent to God who descends from His heavenly Tabernacle towards the human being—by means of observing the *mitzvah* of self-sanctification: "Ye shall be holy, for I the Lord your God am holy" (Leviticus 19:2). In our inquiry into the third blessing ("You are holy"), we have seen that observing this *mitzvah* through purification and refinement enables the worshipper to stand before God, be judged and blessed. From the perspective of the seventeenth blessing (*Retzei*), by contrast, the "sanctification" blessing emphasizes the negative perspective of the person who gives himself to God, the perspective of separation from individual appetite, defilement, and sin, while anticipating the time of redemption is here a positive aspect, an expectation of being united with God.

The Sabbath: Anticipating the Conclusion of Creation

The idea of anticipation is expressed most explicitly in the narrative about creation in the book of Genesis, in the passage dedicated to the Sabbath day, which is recited in the *Kiddush* of Friday night:

> The heaven and the earth were finished, and all their array. On the seventh day God finished the work that He had been doing, and He ceased on the seventh day from all the work that he had done. And God blessed the seventh day and declared it holy, because on it God ceased from all the work of creation that he had done. (Genesis 2:1–3)

According to what is said in this passage, nothing is added to creation on the seventh day. Instead, God "completed" creation with His probing observation, and joined creation to Himself, after He separated it from Himself, through its sanctification. Thus He united, joined, and completed His creation in the way a king completes the chariot designated to carry him when he rises to rule, and the chariot lifts and exalts him with songs of praise. As said in the psalm that concludes the book of Psalms, 150:

> Hallelujah.
> Praise God in His sanctuary;
> Praise Him in the sky, His stronghold.
> Praise Him for His mighty acts;
> Praise Him for His exceeding greatness.
> Praise Him with blasts of the horn;
> Praise Him with harp and lyre.
> Praise Him with timbrel and dance;
> Praise Him with lute and pipe.
> Praise Him with resounding cymbals;
> Praise Him with loud-clashing cymbals.
> Let all that breathes praise the Lord.
> Hallelujah.
> (Psalms 150:1–6)

This is the meaning of the vision embodied in the words "God completed" and "God hallowed," from the perspective of creation. God, who rules over creation, is a paragon for its development, and creation yearns to ascend to Him. God carried out His plans during the days of creation, He impressed His ideas upon materiality, and He emanated to the creation which He created the ability to separate from Him. On the Sabbath He rested. God enthroned Himself upon the chariot of creation, which set itself apart in order to have Him ascend, and was worthy of the praise of all its components in their unity—which is its perfection. But as the narrative of creation continues, and in the narrative of the human history that follows, it becomes clear that on the seventh day God only anticipated the perfection of creation in His vision. In order for creation to be truly perfect, God needed humans to work the earth and build their community and settlement, which would be established according to God's laws. Therefore, the encounter with the forces of chaos continued and still continues. God renews creation every day. The children of Israel, who have assumed the yoke of Torah, are commanded to sanctify themselves for worshipping Him, and every week they anticipate the envisioned perfection of creation on the Sabbath day, "a remembrance of the work of creation" (K:382, *Vayehi Erev*) and the expected of future redemption.

Striving for Desiring (*Retziah*) and Favor (*Ratzon*)

The same gesture of anticipating the envisioned future is given concrete form in the *Shemoneh Esrei* prayer as it approaches its conclusion. In the seventeenth blessing (*Retzei*) the worshipper reaches the highest stage in the process of redemption, which is symbolized by the renewal of worship in the Tabernacle. The worshippers exalt themselves in their worship and they invite God to turn to them from His lofty dwelling, to favor them, and be united with them in His Temple:

> Find favor [*retzei*, literally, "desire"], Lord our God,
> In Your people Israel and their prayer.
> Restore the service to Your most holy House,
> And accept in love and favor [*ratzon*]
> The fire-offerings of Israel and their prayer.
> May the service of Your people Israel always find favor [*ratzon*]
>   with You.
> And may our eyes witness Your return to Zion in compassion.
> Blessed are You, Lord,
> Who restores His Presence to Zion.
> (K:126, *Retzei Adonai*)

Two motifs come to expression in this blessing, which complement one another when combined. The first motif is expressed in the key word that shapes the body of the blessing: the act of favoring or desiring (*retziah*) and the favor, or satisfaction (*ratzon*). God favors His people, and He experiences satisfaction (*sevi'ut ratzon*) from the prayer of the people who worship Him according to His commandment. The worshippers request that their prayer be received and "may it find favor [*utehi leratzon*]—with You" as a proper replacement for the worship performed for God's favor in the Temple. If the worship extracts "favor" (*ratzon*) from God, the worshippers will "find favor" (*ḥen*) in His sight. This means that God will bring the worshippers near to Him, and they will benefit from the essence of His presence, which radiates His goodness. If this happens, their prayer would be equal to the sacrificial worship and the offerings, which were gifts expressing their desire (*ratzon*) to give to God their entire selves and all their possessions. Indeed, the gifts are, in essence, God's, and the human beings only return God's gifts to Him in order to receive them back from Him, purified and renewed. To emphasize, this is the special subject of the seventeenth blessing: it changes the worshippers' request for themselves into a gift from themselves that they wish to offer to God as an expression of gratitude for His benevolence towards them. The gratitude expressed in words of praise and adoration is what exalts them towards God and draws His favor (*ratzon*) towards them to be gracious towards them.

These words explain the concept of *ratzon* (favor). Let us probe the meanings of the expressions "find favor in Your people" and "may [their service] find favor with You." They express a mutual bond, from its two emotional-personal sides. "Favor" is conceived here as an expression of personal need for the response of the other, which expresses the same personal need. With this, the command (*mitzvah*) is distinguished from an order, instruction, or law, which express a one-sided demand for obedience, whether consenting or forced, because the "correct" act as defined by the order is what is essential in the eyes of both sides. Thus, *ratzon* accentuates the importance of the interpersonal relation that emerges from appreciation for the personality of the other, and appreciation for good relations with the other for their own sake. This is so, because the mutual appreciation, and the need for the connection itself, define the act that is commanded and provide meaning to it—so that performing the act out of ulterior motives or extraneous intentions misses the meaning, whether from the perspective of the one who desires (*rotzeh*) or from the perspective of the one who satisfies the desire (*meratzeh*). The request that is expressed in the seventeenth blessing relates to these two perspectives of *ratzon* and to the two personalities who desire (*harotzim*) one another and are desired (*hamitzratzim*) by each other: God who desires the prayer of the human, and the human who prays to Him. To reemphasize: the seventeenth blessing is not another request concerning the worshipper's needs. It is rather an expression of the desire (*ratzon*) to find favor (*ḥen*), to desire (*li-rtzot*), and to placate (*le-ratzot*), pointing to the bond that exists between creator and creature: "Find favor Lord our God, in Your people Israel and their prayer" (K:126, *Retzei Adonai*). That is, look at our prayer not only as a request for You to satisfy our needs, but as an expression of our desire to do Your will, to satisfy You. This matter clearly depends upon Your shining Your divine countenance on us, telling us that we have found favor in Your sight. Therefore, the shining of Your divine countenance is that for which we yearn.

This is the turn that the congregation of worshippers is supposed to experience in nearing the conclusion of the *Shemoneh Esrei* prayer. The worshippers are called on to change their requesting and praying into giving and praising, by reciting gratitude and praise for the effulgence that God pours forth from Himself to the worshippers—always, every day, every hour, and at every moment. Does one need to ask for this? When we offer ourselves up as a gift to God, we know with all our body, soul, and might that God renews His creation every day and that He revives our soul in our body every morning, and provides effulgence to us and to all His living creations. We know well beyond our complaining that if the effulgence which God emanates to the world daily, hourly, and at every moment were to end, the universe would be destroyed and humanity would be lost. Our very existence, in a universe filled with everything its creatures need, is therefore a testimony to the emanation of His goodness and to the force of His benevolence. With this, we can be assured about the future, and this is also the source of our hope that the evil we suffer will disappear in the future. For this is the will (*ratzon*) of God, in His might.

"And may our eyes witness Your return to Zion" (K:126, *Retzei Adonai*)

These words are the basis for understanding the connection between the motif of expressing the *ratzon* in the seventeenth blessing, and the second motif which is emphasized in its conclusion: the return of God to reside permanently in His Temple in Jerusalem as an additional phase of messianic redemption, because by doing so the connection between earth and heaven will be renewed and the kingdom of God will spread and be revealed over all the earth. Solomon's prayer states:

> But will God really dwell on earth? Even the heavens to their uttermost reaches cannot contain You, how much less this House that I have built! Yet turn, O Lord my God, to the prayer and supplication of Your servant, and hear the cry and prayer which Your servant offers before You this day. May Your eyes be open day and night toward this House, toward the place of which You have said, "My name shall abide there." (I Kings 8:27–29)

We learn from these verses that the name of the God who resides in the Temple represents His kingdom on earth. This kingdom is established with the help of "those who see His face"—the priests who serve Him in His Temple on earth as the angels serve Him in heaven.

We learn about the substance of the return of God's name to reside in the Temple, as the final phase of the process of redemption, from the passages in Torah and prophecy from which two of the motifs of the *Retzei* blessing were drawn. These are the disclosure of God's favor towards His nation, and His revelation in the Temple in Jerusalem as the capital of peace for all humankind. Let us start with the motif of the disclosure of the divine favor. Its foundation is in the Torah, in the description of the role of the high priest who represents his people before God to gain God's favor:

> You shall make a frontlet of pure gold and engrave on it the seal inscription: "Holy to the Lord." Suspend it on a cord of blue, so that it may remain on the headdress; it shall remain on the front of the headdress. It shall be on Aaron's forehead, that Aaron may take away any sin arising from the holy things that the Israelites consecrate, from any of their sacred donations; it shall be on his forehead at all times to win acceptance (*le-ratzon*) for them before the Lord. (Exodus 28:36–38)

Our focus is on the double meaning of the expression "to win acceptance [favor] before the Lord." God will be pleased with the unblemished sacrifices which the pure priest, who sanctifies himself for this role, offers Him, and through this God will pardon the children of Israel whom the priest represents. They will find favor before Him, and He will repay them with the recompense due to them. He will forgive their trespasses and bless them. Isaiah expresses the same reciprocal meaning in the description of the vision of redemption, whose climax is the joy of God's uniting with His nation in His Temple.

> I will bring them to My sacred mount
> And let them rejoice in My house of prayer.
> Their burnt offerings and sacrifices
> Shall be welcome [*le-ratzon*] on My altar.
> For My house shall be called
> A house of prayer for all peoples.
> (Isaiah 56:7)

An additional prophecy that is echoed in the blessing strengthens the image of the climax of redemption in the renewal of Temple worship:

> Arise, shine, for your light has dawned;
> The Presence of the Lord has shone upon you!
> Behold! Darkness shall cover the earth,
> And thick clouds the peoples;
> But upon you the Lord will shine,
> And His Presence be seen over you.
> All the flocks of Kedar shall be assembled for you,
> The rams of Nebaioth shall serve your needs;
> They shall be welcome offerings [*al ratzon*] on My altar,
> And I will add glory to My glorious House.
> (Isaiah 60:1–2, 7)

The *siddur* makes frequent reference to the last verse of Psalms 19, cited below. It ties the prophecy about renewing worship in the Temple to prayer, which is offered as worship to God.

> May the words of my mouth and the prayer of my heart
> Be acceptable [*le-ratzon*] to You,
> O Lord, my rock and my redeemer.
> (Psalms 19:15)

The simple intention of this passage is the request that God will find favor with the worshipper's "words of [the] mouth," which are filled with praise for God and His Torah, with fearing Him, and with praise for His laws and ordinance, and that God will accept them as a gift given to Him. For indeed, this gift expresses the obligation to serve Him, to narrate His praises, to witness His kingdom, to observe all His *mitzvot*, and to carry out His mission. In this sense, the gift is like a sacrifice and offering. Let us pass over the basis for these words to the source of the blessing's conclusion, which identifies the return of worshippers to Jerusalem, "Your city" (blessing 14, "Your most holy House" [*dvir betekha*], K:126), "as in the days of old and as in ancient years" (Malachi 3:4), with the higher stage of the redemption of Israel amid humanity, when

> ... instruction shall come forth from Zion,
> The word of the Lord from Jerusalem.
> (Isaiah 2:3)

The topic of redemption in the seventeenth blessing draws upon two prophecies. One is from Zechariah:

> The word of the Lord of Hosts came [to me]:
> Thus said the Lord of Hosts: I am very jealous for Zion, I am fiercely jealous for her. Thus said the Lord: I have returned to Zion, and I will dwell in Jerusalem. Jerusalem will be called the City of Faithfulness, and the mount of the Lord of Hosts the Holy Mount. (Zechariah 8:1–3)

The other is from Malachi:

> Behold, I am sending My messenger to clear the way before Me, and the Lord whom you seek shall come to His Temple suddenly. As for the angel of the covenant that you desire, he is already coming. But who can endure the day of his coming, and who can hold out when he appears? For he is like a smelter's fire and like fuller's lye. He shall act like a smelter and purger of silver; and he shall purify the descendants of Levi and refine them like gold and silver, so that they shall present offerings in righteousness. Then the offerings of Judah and Jerusalem shall be pleasing to the Lord as in the days of yore and in the years of old. (Malachi 3:1–4)

The anticipation of the envisioned renewal of Temple worship "as in the days of old and as in ancient years" (Malachi 3:4) constitutes the worshipping assembly in the present as it looks to the realized vision of the end of days. We compare this delayed present, snatched away from the flowing passage of time because it has been sanctified to God, with the timelessness of *Ehyeh-Asher-Ehyeh*, who from His sublime residence in heaven, assures the perfection of His kingdom and its tranquility at any time and at any moment. This is God's blessing, and human beings can sense it even in the present that is not sanctified and not snatched away from the passage of time, when they think about renewal: about the cyclical renewal of creation, about the cyclical renewal of their life, amid the cyclical renewal of the effulgence of fruitfulness and creativity which ever revitalizes human lives—as God promised in His covenant with Noah and his sons, when they left the ark after the great flood that had reverted the world to chaos:

> So long as the earth endures,
> Seed time and harvest,
> Cold and heat,
> Summer and winter,
> Day and night
> Shall not cease.
> (Genesis 8:22)

When the worshippers exalt themselves to praise God for the gift of their life, they liberate themselves, accordingly, from the distress of their limitations and deficiencies and from the evil that damages them. They experience the great good, which is in the substance of their existence, and in the substance of the creation which sustains them and makes them happy. Indeed, they know and acknowledge that their existence is not an inherent right, but an act of benevolence towards them.

The Eighteenth Blessing: Thanksgiving for the "Good"

With this we arrive at the eighteenth blessing. We know, first of all, that in contrast to the prior blessings this is not a request but a statement of gratitude. The blessing to God at the conclusion of this blessing is not occasioned by God's emanating giving, but by the essence of His existence as the source of all being, the source of all creatures, the source of the spiritual-physical existence of the human being and of His special people. Everything comes from Him, everything returns to Him, everything is His. Therefore, everything is obliged to thank Him for existence.

> We give thanks to You,
> For You are the Lord
> Our God

> And God of our ancestors,
> God of all flesh,
> Who formed us
> And formed the universe.
> Blessings and thanks are due
> To Your great and holy name
> For giving us life
> And sustaining us.
> May You continue
> To give us life and sustain us;
> And may You gather
> Our exiles
> To Your holy courts,
> To keep Your decrees,
> Do Your will and serve You
> With a perfect heart,
> For it is for us
> To give You thanks.
> Blessed be God
> To whom
> Thanksgiving is due.
> (K:128, *Modim Anaḥnu*)

A glorifying gratitude opens the eighteenth blessing, a glorifying gratitude ends its recitation, and a glorifying gratitude concludes it as a blessing which assures that God insofar as He is good, deserves praise befitting only Him. Had He not created human beings out of His great benevolence, and had He not satisfied all their needs, they would not have existed. Indeed, their existence and their ability to know God and to praise Him in truth is the principle and basis of the good, which they already merited as a gift of pure benevolence!

From the perspective of literary structure, the eighteenth blessing is relatively long, so as to counterbalance all the requests to which it relates in an inclusive manner. The blessing hinges on the relationship to the name of God—that is, to the representation of His responsive and beneficial nearness. The eighteenth blessing opens a second time by addressing YHVH, "the God of Abraham, the God of Isaac, and the God of Jacob" (Exodus 5:61), the name that God Himself gave to Moses and to all the children of Israel, so they would call to Him and He would answer them. But this time, the worshippers call upon this name not for the sake of a request, but for the sake of stating gratitude for God's response even before it was expressed: gratitude for God's being that which His name testifies; gratitude for choosing the patriarchs and revealing His name to them; gratitude for promising them to respond to the prayers of their seed after them, "from generation to generation," when they called His name. After the first blessing, which serves as a statement of gratitude, an inclusive gratitude is stated for God's response to all the individual requests made in the prior blessings. How do the worshippers know that they have already received a response? By the fact of their existence and by the fact of their remaining alive, and of standing before God, believing, and trusting in His protection, in His defense, and in His salvation from all the diseases, troubles, and evil decrees to which they are subject in exile. The requests for the nation's redemption are still not answered, and for that, the anticipation, which is in the next blessing, is required. But the conclusion to the eighteenth blessing prepares the response, which concludes the entire prayer. How so? By changing from a blessing that follows a request to praise that, again, relates to God's name. That is, it represents God's presence amid the nation also in exile, and this is the source for the trust that requests for the nation's redemption will also soon be answered. The name of God guarantees this. And a new name is spoken in the conclusion, the name that confirms the guarantee: "Blessed are You, Lord, whose name is 'the good' and to whom thanks are due" (*Ve'al Kulam*. K:130).

From where did the authors of the *Shemoneh Esrei* prayer, and those who recited it over the generations, know that "the good" is the "name" of God? Was this term also recited by a prophet in the name of God Himself? A probing of the sources demonstrates that the answer to this question is negative. The term "good" is an adjective that testifies to perfection and positiveness, and in general is not used as noun. The meaning of the term is explained in the story of creation (Genesis 1). It is said of each and every detail of creation examined by God, "And God saw that this was good" (Genesis 1:17). The meaning of the statement is that it expresses the creator's contentment with the products of His creation. They are good, insofar as they are appropriate to His idea and His intention in creating them. Thus, He set them in His thought and directed them in His will. Since their existence fits their idea, they are good in the sight of their creator and good in themselves, and therefore worthy in the eyes of their creator to separate them from Him, to grant them independent existence and the ability to be fruitful and multiply—"in their likeness and in their image" (see Genesis 1:26, 5:3). By means of this, He Himself earns the praise of His creatures. Since they are living, existing, secure in their happiness before Him, and in His benevolence, He is good. For they did not create themselves, but rather became living creations by His benevolence.

"Good" is the valuation of the perfection of each thing's reality in terms of its fitting the form and purpose designed for it in the thought of its creator or by its nature. In contrast, "evil" indicates factors of injury, deprivation, destruction, annihilation, sickness, and death. This is the basis for determining moral valuation of activities and behaviors in God's Torah. From the moral perspective, the good is the act that maintains and advances the perfection of reality, and evil pertains to what deprives, diminishes, degrades, and destroys reality. On this basis, Moses testified in God's name, concerning God's Torah: "See, I set before you this day life and prosperity, death and adversity. . . . I have put before you life and death, blessing and curse. Choose life—if you and your offspring would live" (Deuteronomy 30:15, 19).

It is easy to see that the gratitude expressed to God in the eighteenth blessing was originally derived from the words of Moses about His Torah, as a Torah of life, and about those who accept its *mitzvot*, who chose life and are worthy of the good. One may therefore conclude that the good is identified with life, which is the highest level of reality of those created on earth. Life is the level of capabilities required to perform independent activity, to feel, to think, to express, and to create. Evil identifies with death, which negates this reality. The worshipper who vigorously experiences life in his prayer brings the experience to glory in his gratitude.

But it follows from this that *a priori*, the term "good" relates to God as an adjective which expresses God's value in the sight of His living creatures, who feel and think, and not as a name symbolizing God's unique character. Many biblical sources testify to this. The most important among them is the documentation of God's revelation to Moses in the "cleft in the rock" (Exodus 33:22). This was after Moses received the two Tablets of the Covenant and requested to know God, so that God would be a model of leadership appropriate to Moses' people. In God's response to this request, to the extent it was possible to respond to the request, He said to Moses: "I will make all My goodness pass before you, and I will proclaim before you the name Lord, and the grace that I grant and the compassion that I show" (Exodus 33:19). It follows from these words, that the knowledge of God to which the human being, to the best of his ability, has access, is knowledge of "all His goodness." This is identical with the entirety of His creation and with His way of directing it to its good. We can recall other passages that document God's being good to those who are good in His eyes, especially in the Psalms. For example, "Good and upright is the Lord" (Psalms 25:8), "Praise Him! . . . for the Lord is good" (Psalms 100:4–5), and many other instances. And even "I declare that Your name is good" (Psalms 52:11), as well as "I will praise Your name, Lord, for it is good" (Psalms 54:8). But even in these passages, which are related to the name of God, the term "good" functions as an adjective, while in the *Shemoneh Esrei* prayer this word changes from an adjective to a name that signifies God Himself from the perspective of His relationship to His creation. Apparently, the name "the Good," which relates to God, is deduced by the author of the *Shemoneh Esrei* prayer, and is deduced again by those who recite it, from the content of the *"Modim"* blessing. God is "the Good" and the statement of gratitude is appropriate to Him, insofar as His goodness denotes His presence to His beneficiary worshippers who know Him by taking the path of His Torah, for their good.

The Nineteenth Blessing: Peace and Perfection

The trust, which is presented as a sign of gratitude, brings the worshippers to the nineteenth blessing, which concludes the *Shemoneh Esrei* prayer with God's positive response to the requests for redemption of the entire nation, with the revelation of God's goodness, and with the worshippers feeling that their requests were already answered, for this is the way of the good God from the perspective of His character:

> Grant peace, goodness and blessing, grace, loving-kindness and compassion to us and all Israel Your people. Bless us, our Father, all as one, with the light of Your face, for by the light of Your face You have given us, Lord our God, the Torah of life and love of kindness, righteousness, blessing, compassion, life and peace. May it be good in Your eyes to bless Your people Israel at every time, in every hour, with Your peace. (K:132, *Sim Shalom*)

What is the source from which this blessing is drawn, by means of which it is shaped into a ceremonial gesture in which the blessing of God for the redemption of the nation is not only requested, but granted? The answer to this question does not require research. The *siddur* responds to it with a citation, which is an essential component of the ceremony under discussion. Prior to starting this blessing, the *Kohanim* (those of the priestly lineage) are called to ascend to the pulpit before the Holy Ark, to wrap themselves in their *tallitot*, and have the assembly hear the priestly blessing as it was recited in the Tabernacle and the Temple, according to Moses's commandment:

> The Lord spoke to Moses: Speak to Aaron and his sons: Thus shall you bless the people of Israel. Say to them:
> The Lord bless you and protect you!

The Lord deal kindly and graciously with you!
The Lord bestow His favor upon you and grant you peace!
Thus they shall link My name with the people of Israel,
And I will bless them.
(Numbers 6:22–27)

The particulars of the ceremony establish the place of the entire prayer in the synagogue as a replacement for the Tabernacle and the Temple, and as a sort of reconstruction of the service which took place in earlier days, to be renewed in the future to come. First of all, the priestly blessing is recited in the language of the individual, but is intended for all the children of Israel. This means that the grammatical singular does not refer to individual persons, but to the nation as one assembly. So it is also in the synagogue. The individuals wrap themselves in *tallitot* over their heads. The *Kohanim* hide their personal individuality in the same way, and stand before their assembly, unified in the name of God. The prayer leader, as emissary of the congregation (*shaliah hatzibur*), recites the words of the blessing to the priests (*Birkat Kohanim*)— as Moses was commanded through the words "and say to them" (*amor lahem*), that is, to Aaron and his children—and the *Kohanim* who stand on the pulpit repeat the text which the *shaliah hatzibur* calls out, which is the original text of the blessing, in a special melody which emphasizes that it is the word of God Himself for the ears and eyes of the assembly. Moreover, this gesture constitutes a dramatic reenactment of the original blessing of the priests in the Tabernacle and the Temple: through extending their hands before the assembly and spreading their palms at the name of God, they "placed" the name of God upon the assembly, for God Himself to bless it.

The final blessing of the *Shemoneh Esrei* prayer thereby reconstructs the original ceremony, and anticipates the renewal of the ceremony in the Temple when the time of complete redemption arrives. The worshippers plead before God and entreat Him to bless them: "Grant peace, goodness and blessing . . ." (K:132, *Sim Shalom*) corresponding to "May He bless you. . . . And protect you!" (Numbers 6:24), from the priestly blessing (K:830, *Yevorekhekha*). With precise detail, the word "grant" (*sim*) echoes the "Thus they shall link [*vesamu*] My name with the people of Israel" (Numbers 6:27). "Bless us, our Father, all as one, with the light of Your face" (K:132, *Sim Shalom*) echoes "The Lord make His face shine upon thee, and be gracious unto thee" (Numbers 6:25) from the priestly blessing. "May it be good in Your eyes to bless Your people Israel, at every time, in every hour, with Your peace" (K:132, *Sim Shalom*) captures the sense of "The Lord bestow His favor upon you and grant you peace" (Numbers 6:26).

Upon hearing these words, the worshipping assembly bows towards the Holy Ark, which symbolizes the sanctuary of the Tabernacle and the Temple. The *kohanim* stand on the pulpit raised above the people who bow before the Holy Ark, wrapped in their *tallitot*, and "place" the name of God upon the heads of the children of Israel as one assembly. As one voice, the people affirm, "May it be Your will" (K:132, *Ken yehi ratzon*).

The prayer is concluded and the blessing that completes it is the request for peace. What is peace? First of all, it is the most common blessing in biblical Hebrew and remains so to this day. When a person meets his relatives or neighbors, or members of one's congregation or country—anyone who is not his enemy—he greets them with "*Shalom*." The word *shalom* here corresponds to the English word "hello," which is related to the word "hale," meaning "healthy." By the way of this greeting, one verifies one's good intention and that of the other; that they have no complaint against one another, or bad will towards one another. When someone departs from people, he blesses them with "*Shalom*," expressing his and their satisfaction at having met, and their mutual good will in the future. "*Shalom*" also expresses good wishes and hope for the other and for all. Those who express good wishes and hope for other people want the best for them. "*Shalom*" is the inclusive vision of the realization of good and happiness, which all humans and humanity hope for, for even though human beings, families, communities, and nations fight each other for sources of sustenance, over rule, and for status of honor, they know that they will reach their goal of happiness and maintain it only through peace. Therefore, when human beings open a conversation with one another—after saying "*Shalom*"—they ask one another, "*Mah shelomekha?*" ("How are you?"—literally, "what is your peace?"). By this, they express interest, attention, and a certain degree of mutual responsibility, because, by the very fact that they come together, they are commanded to make peace with one another, and to be together as one assembly.

The abstract meaning of the concept *shalom* is learned from these usages, and from the etymology of the term. *Shalom* is a condition of perfection (*shelemut*). More precisely, it is the condition in which individuals, who stand independently, complement one another with their positive attributes, talents, and possessions, complete one another's deficiencies with their respective advantages and, once complete, create a family together, a single community able to stand independently, with its members fructifying, strengthening, helping, and maintaining one another, and advancing one another in the realization of their happiness. This picture of a well-functioning society stands in contrast to situations of withering, degeneration, and disease, on one hand, and war, strife, oppression, and exploitation, on the other.

What, then, is *shelemut* (perfection, completeness)? We learn from what is said above that it is the positive relationship between different limbs and different components of the body, and among individuals and groups of individuals who constitute the community together. In this sense, *shelemut* is the conceptual definition, or formal structure, by means of which each creature becomes a unit by himself and contributes to the unity of the community and the natural surroundings, which constitute his source of nourishment and his area of activity and self-expression. The words *shalom* and *shelemut* are not mentioned in Genesis 1, but the terms already explained above—*tov* (good) and *tov me'od* (very good)—include *shalom* and *shelemut*, since saying "good" and "very good" is affirming the existence of a positive, fitting, and reciprocal relation between the thing that is praised as good and the good of the person who praises it on behalf of himself and his surroundings.

We will be persuaded of the accuracy of the identity between evaluating a creature as good and attestation of its perfection if we look again at the passage that defines the Sabbath in these words: "The heaven and the earth were finished, and all their array. On the seventh day God finished the work that He had been doing, and He ceased on the seventh day from all the work that He had done" (Genesis 2:1–2). Completing a creation means that its entirety is unified, and in this capacity it is "very good." The creator can rest from His work on the seventh day, because on that day the entirety is unified by virtue of God's relationship, which affirms and sanctifies. God has finished His work, and it is completed to God's satisfaction with His world, and to the world's satisfaction with Him. This satisfaction will come to expression when the worshippers will recite their praise of God, with obligatory gratitude for His great benevolence. The Sabbath day is a day of wholeness (*shelemut*) and a day of peace (*shalom*). It is a day when we rest from all work—whose role is to deal with negativities and deficiencies in created reality—and the universe celebrates its wholeness by reciting prayers to its creator, thereby anticipating the wholeness and the peace towards which creation strives in serving its creator—for the universe is suited to achieve wholeness and peace only if it yearns for and praises the name of God, and God responds, elevating and establishing His name therein.

The same concept of wholeness and peace is expressed with the creation of the human being, the select of creation, as male and female together. The idea expressed in the creation of man and woman as one is that only by existing as a pair, whose components maintain one another as helpmates, can the male complement the female and the female complement the male. Only if they exist together, can the male and the female multiply and give birth to progeny in their likeness and image—which are, as recalled, in the image and likeness of God—and educate them to wholeness as human beings, according to the Torah that God designated for them. It should be emphasized that, according to the Genesis narrative, the male by himself and the woman by herself are not whole. They are halved. By themselves, they do not have independent existence and God's blessing does not rest on them. Only in their sanctification to one another do they become a single unit of life, inclusive and whole—a family, which builds human society and distinguishes itself from a herd of animals by observing God's ordinances, by which it is shaped. Of course, this is the case as long as their relations are not disrupted by the sins that bring strife among them, replacing the relation of mutual help with one of conflict, coercion, slavery, and exploitation. The covenant of Torah obliges humans to be helpmates to one another, according to the obligations and rights defined by divine ordinance, and it shapes the wholeness of the community from within and assures its peace.

The process of creation described in Genesis 1 fits this concept. God reveals Himself in this process as an artist who instills His wisdom into His creation. The wisdom expresses itself in the act of creation as a formal structure, which is built in a logical order and keeps balanced relations between the various parts of the collective body. Importantly, this order is also correct in the sense of temporal development, because it is the logic of realizing the structure stage by stage, defining its goal and the means to achieving it. God's wisdom is expressed in the laws that sustain and activate the structure of the entire creation as a single totality: heaven and earth, water above and water below, dry land and sea, herbage and grass on earth, illumination in heaven, fish in the sea and birds in the air, animals walking on all fours, and the human being standing erect over them, ruling over them in earthly creation as God rules in heaven. So, God binds earth and heaven in order to make them into one universe.

On the Path to Wholeness

The narrative of creation testifies that the wholeness and peace envisioned by God on the seventh day of creation are visions of the distant future. The celestial firmament is completed in six days of creation and is instilled thereafter with eternal peace. But the earthly universe is only destined for wholeness and peace; it is not yet worthy to realize them. God renews His creation over the cycles of time, and advances it towards its wholeness and peace, but it is still far from its goal. Its perfection depends upon human beings, and its perfection by human beings depends upon perfection by the nation of Israel—through observing the *mitzvot* of God's Torah and serving Him. But as long as forces of chaos permeate creation, neither human beings nor the people of Israel have the power to prevail over them and subdue them forever.

The testimony of the Hebrew Bible reflects several ascents and descents along this path. The first ascent to the heights of wholeness and peace took place at Mount Sinai, in the perfect arrangement that unified all of Israel as one person to receive its Torah. At the same convocation, Israel was given the *mitzvah* of the Sabbath, included in the Ten Commandments. From then on, this *mitzvah* was a sign of the covenant between God and His nation, a model of realization in the present that anticipated the vision of wholeness and peace. But right after this, came the nadir of the sin of the golden calf.

The second upward movement, in preparation of setting out to take possession and find redemption in the land of Canaan, was achieved at the foot of Mount Sinai by the great effort of Moses and Aaron, and the tribe of Levi faithful to them, with the setting up of the Tabernacle through contributions of the children of Israel, and with organizing the entire nation into one assembly, according to tribes. This assembly was arranged as a national army and a workforce around God's Tabernacle, which unified, completed, and instilled peace. The nation's unity was further cemented by the dedication of the Tabernacle. When the ascent reached its peak, the nation was given the priestly blessing, described above. But the second ascent was also followed by failure, with the sin of the spies.

The third ascent is documented in the book of Deuteronomy: it was the convocation for renewing the covenant of Sinai within the community itself. The wholeness and peace, which they realized at that time, are attested by the words of the blessing that the gentile prophet Balaam uttered against his will before Israel:

> Now Balaam, seeing that it pleased the Lord to bless Israel . . .
> As Balaam looked up and saw Israel . . .
> Taking up his theme, he said
> "How fair are your tents, O Jacob, Your dwellings, O Israel!"
> (Numbers 24:1–5)

But this ascent, which helped Israel succeed in settling its land in the days of Joshua, also failed when the nation sinned during the period of the judges.

The greatest ascent of all, which provided the background for instituting the *Shemoneh Esrei* prayer, came in the days of the Temple of Solomon—the king whose name symbolized the kingdom of Israel's condition during its blessed era. The pious king David, the poet of the Psalms who paved the way for the success of his son Solomon's kingdom in Jerusalem, sought to build the Temple in Zion and to transfer the Ark of Testimony from a temporary, itinerant tent into a glorious structure in the city, which he would dedicate in God's name to his kingdom. But the prophet Nathan, in God's name, did not allow David to do as he desired, because David was a man of war and much blood was shed during his campaigns. The permission to build the Temple was promised to his son Solomon, conditioned upon obeying God's Torah, and judging the people according to it. Since for most of his days Solomon— described as the wisest of all men, and true to God and His Torah—judged his people justly, and established good relations with all neighboring nations, the promise was carried out. Solomon was permitted to establish the Temple in which God's name would reside amid His people permanently.

The first chapter of I Kings documents the wholeness of the arrangements, which the wise king introduced in his kingdom, and the internal and external peace, which the nation of Israel enjoyed under him in his time: righteousness and true justice, economic success, glorious building, political success, tranquility, and happiness. The scripture summarizes: "All the days of Solomon, Judah and Israel dwelt in safety, everyone under his own vine and under his own fig tree" (I Kings 5:5). In what follows, the building of the Temple and its dedication are described as the peak of the wholeness and peace that reigned in the days of Solomon (I Kings 8). Solomon's prayer, which, as we saw, constitutes a model for the *Shemoneh Esrei* prayer, brings the experience of ascent to God to its climax. Its conclusion reads:

> When Solomon finished offering to the Lord all this prayer and supplication, he rose from where he had been kneeling, in front of the altar of the Lord, his hands spread out toward heaven. He stood, and in a loud voice blessed the whole congregation of Israel:
> "Praised be the Lord who has granted a haven to His people Israel, just as He promised; not a single word has failed of all the gracious promises that He made through His servant Moses. May the Lord our God be with us, as He was with our fathers. May He never abandon or forsake us. May He incline our hearts to Him, that we may walk in all His ways and keep the commandments, the laws, and the rules, which He enjoined upon our fathers. And may these words of mine, which I have offered

in supplication before the Lord, be close to the Lord our God
day and night, that He may provide for His servant and for His
people Israel, according to each day's needs—to the end that all
the peoples of the earth may know that the Lord alone is God,
there is no other. And may you be wholehearted with the Lord
our God, to walk in His ways and keep His commandments,
even as now."

The king and all Israel with him offered sacrifices before the
Lord. (I Kings 8:54–62)

But even after reaching this peak of perfection, there is a steep descent. Already
at the end of his days, Solomon's heart was not "whole" with his God; and at
the same time there was already murmuring among the nation. The orders
of justice and righteousness were not observed; the unity was shattered, the
kingdom began to come apart, and the neighboring kingdom of Egypt began
to undermine the nation's unity, subvert its power, and endanger its peace.
Following the end of the Solomonic kingdom, the kingdom of Israel was torn
asunder for years. Thus began the great internal and external declines leading
to the destruction of Jerusalem and its Temple, the collapse of sovereignty, and
the Babylonian exile. The *Shemoneh Esrei* prayer, which replaced the sacrificial
Temple service, concludes with the hope of renewing the days of wholeness
and peace of earlier days, as in the days of Solomon. But the vision, which the
Shemoneh Esrei anticipates, is that of the great literary prophets. They foresaw
destruction, experienced it, and hoped for peace as the result of the great
mending of creation—when God would finally conquer the powers of chaos
in creation and in humankind. By means of the ordinances of God's Torah,
righteousness and peace would prevail under God's reign—and there would
be no need to impose them. Therefore there would not be another descent and
decline.

In the days to come,
The Mount of the Lord's House
Shall stand firm above the mountains
And tower above the hills;
And all the nations
Shall gaze on it with joy.
And the many peoples shall go and say:
"Come,
Let us go up to the Mount of the Lord,

To the House of the God of Jacob;
That He may instruct us in His ways,
And that we may walk in His paths."
For instruction shall come forth from Zion,
The word of the Lord from Jerusalem,
Thus He will judge among the nations
And arbitrate for the many peoples,
And they shall beat their swords into plowshares
And their spears into pruning hooks:
Nation shall not take up
Sword against nation;
They shall never again know war.
(Isaiah 2:2–4)

The prophet Isaiah also prophesied about this era:

But a shoot shall grow out of the stump of Jesse,
A twig shall sprout from his stock.
The spirit of the Lord shall alight upon him:
A spirit of wisdom and insight,
A spirit of counsel and valor,
A spirit of devotion and reverence for the Lord.
He shall sense the truth by his reverence for the Lord:
He shall not judge by what his eyes behold,
Nor decide by what his ears perceive.
Thus he shall judge the poor with equity
And decide with justice for the lowly of the land.
He shall strike down a land with the rod of his mouth
And slay the wicked with the breath of his lips.
Justice shall be the girdle of his loins,
And faithfulness the girdle of his waist.
The wolf shall dwell with the lamb,
The leopard lie down with the kid;
The calf, the beast of prey, and the fatling together,
With a little boy to herd them.
The cow and the bear shall graze,
Their young shall lie down together;
And the lion, like the ox, shall eat straw.
A babe shall play

Over a viper's hole,
And an infant pass his hand
Over an adder's den.
In all of My sacred mount
Nothing evil or vile shall be done;
For the land shall be filled with devotion to the Lord
As water covers the sea.
(Isaiah 11:1–9)

This lofty vision documents God's prevailing, with the help of His messiah from the House of David, over the forces of chaos and evil which permeate creation and its creatures. The reformation which will assure that the Jews and their king are wholehearted with God, and God is wholehearted with His people and their king, and every nation is wholehearted toward God and His nation. Then the kingdom of peace will be established, to stand forever. This is the complete messianic redemption—to which the "Great Peace" (*Shalom Rav*) blessing, which concludes the *Shemoneh Esrei* prayer, is directed.

Types of Biblical Poetry as a Source of Prayer

The Language of Poetry *Vis-à-Vis* the Language of Communication

In terms of content, prayer is about humans being judged before God according to the covenantal Torah, expressing the requests that concern their needs for existence, their destiny, and their well-being—as individuals, family members, or members of community and nation. In terms of duties of human beings to God, which are God's expectations of them according to what is said in the covenantal Torah, prayer is their service (worship) to God and also their highest need—whether in terms of the character of the soul, which God breathed into the human body from His spirit, or in terms of the mission for which the human beings were created—the realization of which is their destiny, perfection, and well-being. But as to the form of the experiential expression of these two aspects, as discussed in earlier chapters, prayer is the recitation of "songs and praises" (*Mishnah Sukkah* 5:4) before God. The word "songs" (or "poems," *shirot*) is plural, because prayer comprises poetic texts of various genres. There is the song into which the worshipper pours his soul and expresses his pain, longings, and hopes; there is the supplication in which one pleads for help and "cries out" for salvation; there is the song of thanksgiving in which one thanks God and praises Him for all His goodness and saving power; there is the didactic poem in which one ascends to knowledge of God by internalizing God's teaching and *mitzvot*; there is the historical ode in which one recalls God's deeds as king and father of His nation and all His children as He leads them to realizing their destiny; and there is the mystical poem in which the worshipper, who has united his soul and body in total submission to God, rises up and anticipates the realization of the destiny of his life and his well-being—whether as individual or member of his family, his community, and nation.

The reason why poetry is appropriate to prayer includes the essential aspect of its definition: it is distinct from the speech needed for substantive communication between humans in all areas of life. The language of communication relates to overt reality. It seeks descriptive or conceptual precision, and its topics are generally objects, situations, activities and deeds, desires and longings, deficiencies and accomplishments, problems and their solutions, and challenges that must be dealt with in the present and near future. All of these touch upon the visible exterior of reality. Therefore, the language of communication has a preference for the unequivocal, the one-dimensional, and the aesthetically simple. By contrast, the language of poetry relates, through open, intuitive, and intellectual means, to what is hidden psychologically and spiritually, employing means of conception and means of feedback (understanding, appreciation, will) with which human beings express themselves when they face the challenges of reality. Poetry therefore needs to be multi-dimensional, multi-faceted, complex, and deep, for which it has to activate several means of apprehension and expression at the same time. Poetry uses words in all their expressive, substantive, rhythmic, and resonating capacity, and joins them with music, physical gestures, and dance, in order to attain the expression that epitomizes the feeling and thought in terms of "all my bones shall say" (Psalms 35:10). From the artistic-technical perspective of this distinction, we can say that the language of open communication is essentially indicative or signifying (denotative). The language of poetry is essentially symbolic and imaginative, or imitative (mimetic). In this way it not only describes and interprets the visible, external reality from the personal perspective; it represents the inner world of the soul by means of the impressions of external reality, which are absorbed by the human being's perceptive faculties—either as influence from out of the soul's depths, which are physical and tied to the material, or as inspiration from the soul's heights, which are spiritual and tied to "the spirit of God" from which the soul breathes, or as an encounter between these two sources.

Poetry and Divine Inspiration

As shown in earlier chapters, Jewish prayer is anchored in the Hebrew Bible from two aspects of its content: the aspect of the worshipper who requests and blesses, and the aspect of God who commands the worshippers to serve Him in faith. But when we examine prayer as poetry, so as to understand how it fulfills its various roles, we arrive at the foundation of the spiritual creativity that unifies the different kinds of prayer in the *siddur*. When the various literary-artistic texts—which are apt to foster different philosophical worldviews that might even contradict each other from certain perspectives—serve the needs of prayer, they combine and complement one another. This takes place on a Halakhically valued foundation, which shapes a multi-dimensional and multi-faceted way of life, constituting the distinctive Torahitic spiritual culture of the Jewish people as a unique, treasured nation. It is a foundation based upon the written and oral Torah and dedicated to the worship of God as king and father.

According to the prophetic doctrine of the covenant, which was made by agreement between God and His nation, the wisdom with which God created His world was the source of the Torah and the source of all creativity in the world. By contrast, human wisdom is nourished by observing the created world . It is therefore suited to come near to the wisdom of God—but only to those portions of the divine wisdom revealed in the earthly realm, to which the people of Israel add what is revealed to them in Torah. It follows from these premises that philosophy, which seeks to unite the human wisdom within itself, grasps only the wisdom of earthly creation. There are many hidden matters in philosophy that appear as opposed, as contradictory, while divine wisdom unified opposites and reconciles the contradictions. But even the Torah reveals only a portion, that human beings need to know in order to realize their destiny as creatures created in the "image of God;" and that the children of Israel need to know in order to realize their destiny as a people—and this is essentially the wisdom of ordinances, the laws, and the *mitzvot*, and the morality according to which the human beings conduct themselves properly so as to realize their destiny—whether in terms of ruling the earthly realm or in terms of their welfare and well-being. Poetry, however, with its symbolic-mimetic instruments, flows from divine "inspiration" of the highest possible prophetic type—namely, God's revelation to human beings in His words, or in the visions that He shows to human beings, or from a type of "holy spirit" (see Psalms 51:11) which flows from the internal bond between the human spirit and the spirit that God breathes into human beings. By its means they are suited to be worthy of the illumination in which sparkles the hidden, the wondrous that is behind the veil, which separates the world of human wisdom from the world of divine wisdom.

The assumption that poetry flows from divine inspiration, directly or as internalized, is embodied in the etymological affinity of the two words, *shirah* (poetry) and *hashra'ah* inspiration. This assumption ties poetry entirely to worship of God, even when the poetry expresses earthly experiences. For example, the experiences of nature or of love, or the experiences of war and peace. This, because on the exalted level of poetry these experiences are also connected, directly or indirectly, to the special bond between the human being and God. Another assumption, complementing the first, is that poetry expresses elevated feeling. It lifts souls from their depths and raises them to God, who is their source—and this explains the name that symbolizes its substance. In our time, it is accepted that *shirah* is derived from the root ShYR, meaning speech set to music. But in scriptural Hebrew, speech set to music is called *zemer* and its lyrics are *mizmor* ("hymn" or "psalm")—while *shir* is derived from the root ShRR, from which the word *sharir* (strong) is derived as used in the expression *sharir vekayam* (valid and abiding). *Shirah*, therefore, is a recitation with strength, a firm and abiding recitation because of its fullness, concreteness, and perfection. It is able to perfectly capture the spiritual or historical event it expresses, and whenever we recite the *shirah* with its full resonance, we experience it anew. Insofar as feelings and thoughts (in the nomenclature of scriptural poetry, "meditations"— *hegyonot*) are responses of the intellectual-rational soul to positive and negative challenges, and to the soul's own attractions and obstacles, the poem, which expresses those feelings and thoughts, affirms their positive substance and perpetuates them. The poem thereby expresses overcoming negative challenges of physical-spiritual life, and the achievements that are embodied by creation. In this sense, the poem is a victory over death, sicknesses, distresses, weaknesses, and pain. This is the life of the person who sings, giving expression to his feelings and impressing their stamp on the memory of the poet. Because of this, when the poetic song is sung, it identifies with life itself as it reaches its peak.

The Descriptive Epic Poem Compared with the Poem of the Individual Worshipper

Let us analyze two representative examples. Here is the first one:

> I will sing to the Lord, for He has triumphed gloriously;
> Horse and driver he has hurled into the sea.
> The Lord is my strength and might.
> He is become my deliverance.
> (Exodus 15:1–2)

These are the two opening verses of the Song of the Sea. Let us attend to the verbal structure of these lines, which resembles a rising and falling wave.

God's power, which vanquishes His enemies, is represented by the image of the stormy sea, with its powerful waves, which retreats before the people who are rescued from their tyrants, and returns to drown the pursuant army of Pharaoh with sweeping majesty. The power of the stormy wave, sweeping across the shore and shattering the mighty chariot army, awakens a wave of praising song in the heart of the poet who expresses the great rescue. The fear of certain death, oppressive and mortifying, is reversed. Joy arises from the depths of fear, expressing victory and concretizing wonder. The internal exaltation is an emotional wave, which resembles the waves of the sea. It comes to expression with a word whose resonating power resembles its meaning: *ramah* (height). It has a double meaning: the waves cast the army of Pharaoh from above to below, and lift the nation of Israel from below to above, from the bottom of the sea to the secure shore.

The poet feels his power in the glorious *shir* (song) in his heart, and the *shir* lifts him to his God, who takes his side and redeems him. The opening "I will sing" (*ashirah*) is a mighty accord of feelings, which rise together in a dramatic, visionary narration. It expresses the glorious soulful impulse, which ascends and erupts from the inner depths of the poet's soul as if from the stormy sea. The individual who sings in the language of the individual does not sing in his name alone. The song, which bursts forth from his lips, is that of the entire nation rescued on the shore of the sea. Indeed, the individual sweeps the entire nation along, to sing with him as one person. In this way, a monument of words that preserve the unique moment is created—as if snatched from the flux of time in order to be fixed forever in memory as an eternal present, to which we return in every moment when we remember it. Any time the people remember this event, they will recall not only that the miracle took place, but that it will return and be experienced anew—as if taking place in the nation's present.

The second example presents, by way of contrast to the Song of the Sea, the poem of the individual exiled from his city and Temple because of the circumstances of his life. His heart yearns for the house of God, and pours forth streams of water from its hidden depths. The substantial similitude, which expresses the sorrows of exile in the wailing of powerful longings, is humble, modest, and even intimate, touching the heart with its beauty:

Like a hind crying for water,
My soul cries for You, O God;
My soul thirsts for God, the living God;
O when will I come to appear before God!
(Psalms 42:1–3)

By contrast with the stormy waves in the Song of the Sea, the opening verses of this psalm resound with a lyrical musicality of the trickling of the river waters, whose limpid streaming is represented with a whisper. In contrast to the celebratory joy which calls out with determined assurance, the yearning expresses itself with a question of longing: when? But let us focus on the transformation that takes place in the mindset of the lyric poet when the source of his hidden feelings erupts with pouring of the heart from his whispering lips. The poet expresses his thirst for the living God when he stands as a hart at the streams of flowing water, and their quiet flow changes from an expression of longing to one of consolation. As the water satiates the thirst of the hart who yearns for its hind, the prayer satiates the thirst of the lonely poet for his God. The prayer changes the feeling of loneliness, abandonment, and oblivion in the distance into the consolation of the secure knowledge that God sees into these distances, so that nothing is distant from Him. The poet is now assured that God does not forget His servant who longs for Him, as a son longs for his father:

> Why so downcast my soul,
> Why disquieted within me?
> Have hope in God.
> I will yet praise Him
> For His saving presence.
> (Psalms 42:6)

Thus, the poet scolds his soul in order to console it in its grief. As you are stirred with self-pity over my loneliness and you are cast down, turn your face directly to God who is present in your distress—and you are already rescued!

The Poetical Prose of the Bible: The Transfer of the Myth

We are accustomed to discerning between the instructive, the narrative-historical, and the legal-juristic portions of the Bible. According to this division, the poetry in its different genres constitutes the uppermost layer of creative expression, combined in different ways with the three components enumerated above. From this perspective, the poetry appears as an elevation of narrative, instructive, and legal expression to a higher level of spiritual expression in crucial situations, in which is felt the direct intervention of God, whose very appearance brings about salvation. This is what happened with the exodus from Egypt and the enacting of the Sinai covenant; this is what happened in the days of Joshua and in the days of the judges; this is what happened in the days of Samuel, and what happened in the days of David and Solomon for the good; and at the threshold of the destruction of the kingdom of Israel and the exile of Judah—when it was for bad. The great chapters of poetry that sustain the *siddur*—the myth of the exodus from Egypt; the Song of the Sea; the myth of the Sinai covenant; the myth of settlement and the Song of Deborah; the Song of Hannah; the Song of David and his psalms; Solomon's Song of Songs; the poetry of the great literary prophets; the poetry of Lamentations; the poetry of the prophets of the return to Zion—all these were created at great moments of transition, moments of pride and of humiliation in the history of the people of Israel. That is, they are testimonies to the history of the people as a narrative of development of the unique love relationship between God and His people.

It is understood that, in comparison to such special situations, the spoken and written narrative, instructional, and legal accounts are matters of modest, everyday, and prosaic expression. But this is a relative and not absolute distinction. The fact that poetic passages are integrated organically into the narrative, instructional, and legalistic expositions of the books of the Bible testifies, first of all, that the biblical prose is also permeated, whether in form or content, with poetic qualities. Secondly, the interpenetration of genres shows that the distinction between them is more theoretical than literary-artistic. Actually, texts of different genres are blended into one another, and transitions from one subject to another in each book are continuous and successive. For example, the story of the exodus from Egypt in the book of Exodus begins on the level of myth and continues on the level of epic in the Song of the Sea, integrating these two styles and melding them with the highest poetic quality.

As a general observation, however, all the styles of the books of the Hebrew Bible appear as different varieties of one single style, characterized by a special poetic quality. Let us call this style the historical myth of the Hebrew Bible. Examples of it include the narrative of creation and the history of humanity until the days of Abraham the Hebrew in the book of Genesis, the narrative of the Egyptian exodus beginning with the miraculous appearance of Moses, the ten plagues and the splitting of the Red Sea, the narrative of the covenantal convocation at the foot of Mount Sinai, the narrative of the death of Moses and the beginning of settlement in Canaan and the leadership of Joshua ben Nun. All of these exhibit a genre of elevated narrative poetry, which documents the history of the universe, the history of humankind, and the history of the nation of Israel in their founding, from the point of view of God as creator and as king, who governs and judges.

The prophet-narrator and his listeners learn about themselves from this historical narrative. How did they come to be? Who are they and what is their destiny? To their benefit in realizing their destiny in the creation, they are commanded to internalize the narrative and shape their way of life accordingly. But the perspective from which they experience the narrative and participate in it, is that of creature and not of creator; of children and not the father; of servants, and not the King, of physical human beings who live on earth and not of the God and the host of His spiritual angels who reside in eternal heaven. Human beings lift themselves up in order to experience these foundational events, while knowing that they are situated in the world and therefore do not rule but are ruled. The choice given them as creatures, created in the image of God, is between obedience to the Torah, which explains the lessons of the myth, and refusing the Torah and the myth's lessons. But from God's perspective, the myth is the narrative of the test, whereby humans are examined as to whether they are worthy of the destiny for the sake of which God granted them free choice. Obviously, this is limited freedom, defined conditionally. God does not renounce His sovereignty and does not grant His sovereignty to human beings. He expects that His creatures, who are created in His image, will obey Him willingly. Accordingly, they do not have control over the consequences of their choice, and the single path open before them, which will enable them to preserve the image of God emanated to them and to live as free men, is to obey the Torah willingly, and to heed the lessons that the myth, as foundational narrative, imparts to human beings.

Foundational events are not accidental and are not the products of blind fate. This view, which is transmitted by the biblical narrative, is what distinguishes it from pagan myths. The myth of the Hebrew Bible negates narratives of deities identified with powers of nature who also intervene in human civilization. Instead of this, scriptural myth tells about the one and only God, the sovereign God, the good and benevolent, the creator and renewer of the universe, and His effort to overcome the powers of chaos and to establish His kingdom on earth. Clearly, as sovereign over His creation, He is distinct from the powers that are immanent in creation. He is holy unto Himself, and governs creation as one who determines its order and legislates its laws—as well as the laws of any good human civilization worthy of existence.

The mythic narrative thereby fulfills a primary role in shaping the relationship between God and all humans of all nations, and especially between God and the children of Israel who chose God to be God to them, and not the created forces of nature as did other nations. And God chose them to be a kingdom of priests and a holy nation. Clearly, to understand the full significance of these foundational facts in terms of their shaping the history of humanity and the history of the nation of Israel, human beings and above all the children of Israel are required to see these foundational facts from the perspective of God the creator and ruler. It is clear that only the prophet can impart this vision to them—the wondrous person, raised up from his nation, chosen by God to inform His people, and through them all peoples, about the matter of His kingdom. But even the greatest prophet, who understands the word of God in the way God understands His word and knows how to transmit God's word in the language of His people, is not able to overcome the gap between divine wisdom, which creates, and human wisdom, which is created, or learned from what is created.

For this reason, the scriptural myth makes its way on two parallel planes of narrative, which aspire to be integrated into one another but which touch one another only at rare, climactic moments—such as the splitting of the Red Sea and the Mount Sinai theophany, when the children of Israel succeeded in rising to the grandeur of their destiny. The first plane is that of myth in its pure sense, the plane upon which God appears as the exclusive hero: the creator and founder who battles mightily against the powers of chaos and evil; the one who reigns, and determines the course of His nation's history amid humanity from the founding of Israel as a nation chosen to be His treasure, until realizing its destined redemption; who establishes Israel as a model to the nations to be redeemed with Israel from their sins and sufferings, when God's kingdom will be revealed on heaven and earth. The other plane is that of the historical epic, whose hero is the nation of Israel, the nation heading towards redemption from out of its slavery, and to realize its destiny in its land. Only if the nation will obey and succeed, will the two planes of action coalesce and come together forever.

Accordingly, the historical myth of the Hebrew Bible documents the encounter between God and the human being (in the Garden of Eden narrative) and between God and the nation of Israel (in the narrative of the Egyptian exodus), in which God's wisdom and His will overcome both the powers of chaos, which permeate creation, and the limitations of human nature. In the depths of their human experience, the human being and the nation of Israel experience the revelation of God, which illumine the narrative of their histories from the angle of the eternal, divine perspective. This is a prodigious artistic task. The myth of creation and God's kingship over creation is formulated in order to document, in monumental poetic language, the transtemporal memory that assigns to the foundational events of the past the status of being eternally present. Let us therefore attend to the fact that the foundational events, which comprise the myth, are events that effectuated a comprehensive change in the histories of Israel and the nations for good or ill. They brought about progress in realizing the destiny of Israel among the nations—as with establishing the kingdom of David and Solomon and building the Temple—or retreat from realizing this destiny. From this perspective, the events of the salvation are similar to events of destruction of the kingdom, destruction of the Temple, and leaving for exile. They established a generally new situation in the history of the people in the course of realizing its destiny.

In order to institutionalize these ways of impressing the myth about the nation's rises and declines upon its consciousness, these events are fixed for the generations on the nation of Israel's calendar, by means of the days of the festival (assembly) time (mo'ed), which are days of remembrance. In this way, the yearly cycle of seasons, which represents the time of creation, touches the linear time of history, which advances from past to future, so that history is also transformed into a cycle and past events are experienced in the present. This is the nature of the festivals—the days in which the children of Israel assemble together to experience anew the meaning of events that shaped the reality of the history in which they are immersed, and to internalize them as a portion of each individual's personal-communal experience. During those days the nation exalts itself in anticipation, from the plane of history to the plane of myth, by means of the celebration (ḥagigah), a ceremonial event instilled with song and dance.

The Poetic Technique of Transmitting Myth

How, therefore, does the monumental style of the myth characterize itself? Let us first emphasize that the existent text is used for two purposes, which complement one another: (1) textual reading, which is an artistic (performative) celebratory event ("worship of God" in the broadest sense); and (b) interpretative, institutional study (talmud torah). Textual reading means reading in the full, original sense of the term: not reading what is written with the eyes only, but rather reading out loud, with vocal expression proper to the sounds of the words and the conceptual and syntactical emphases. This adds the mimetic dimension, that is, vocal and physical imitation with facial and hand gestures (gesticulating), which makes perceptible the reflective—emotional and spiritual—movement of the soul, which is beyond the conceptual meaning of the words. In this way, reading with gestures expresses ascents and descents that show excitement or quietness, urgency or forbearance, tension and trembling or relaxation and calm, anticipation or surprise, amazement or certainty. All are part of the presentation of narrative events and the ideas embodied by them. The aesthetic goal is recitation which embodies itself in its expression during a public event. The actual event of reciting the poem itself reflects the original event documented in words as a secondary experience, strengthening it and bringing it close to the image preserved in memory. In the vocal presentation and experience, the musical, rhythmic, and tonal accompaniment is also added to the original event.

The commemorative poetic-narrative style requires a choice of precise words, in terms of compatibility between the words and the depiction—the feeling, the idea, which the words are to express. This requires knowledge of, and special attention to, language—especially to the mimetic, symbolic, rhythmical, and tonal element of every word. The poetics of the commemorative poem require considerable concentration and precision, but also the ability to use symbols and to consider multiple levels of meaning. It forbids the use of vague, empty, or superfluous words. Every linguistic nuance also needs to be deliberate—whether in the use of singular or plural language; or the choice of person—"I," "we," "you" (which in Hebrew has male and female forms, each of which can be singular or plural), "he," "she," or "they"; or tense—past, present inclined to the past, delayed present, present inclined to the future, and future. By means of this, the poet aspires to achieve not only special precision of the description or the expression of the emotion and thought, but also special complexity of resonance of meanings, expressed beyond the denotative meaning of the words, through the connections between words; through pictorial imagery they suggest; and through their musical associations.

In other words, the short, measured and simple sentences, which comprise the poem in developmental sequence, include pictorial, symbolic, associative, and reflective information, which is double and triple the information transmitted in regular communicative texts. The decoding of these meanings requires interpretative study, and the variety of "correct" interpretations from the standpoint of attending to the significance of combining all the words in a sentence, paragraph, chapter, and book is very broad. Especially so, since the message that a reader finds in the poem is conditioned by the reality in which he lives, his time and place. Also, in the ceremonial reading, where performance is an act of interpretation, the complexity creates a feeling of the full presence of the documented situations or events, and in this way, each sentence is captured in the poem not as speech about things in reality, but rather as their embodiment on a special plane of reality that the poem creates for itself between the concrete reality of present circumstances and the imagined reality in memory. For the poem that is being performed is also a present event, which grants memory its concreteness.

Let us return to the poetic syntax. A commemorative poem is constructed with full sentences, equal in length in terms of the number of words and their syllables, and symmetrical, so that they create a unified and harmonious whole. Thus it is with regard to the opening, the recitation, and the closing of each sentence; and thus it is with the rise and lowering of emotion, for each of the emotions corresponds to a situation or a full idea which develops in time and space. In this form, the poem creates an image of a structure built according to plan, in a way required by the structure itself—from the foundations to the walls, and from the walls to the ceiling—in terms of the presentation of the narrative plot that advances towards its goal, or of the instruction striving towards the aim of understanding and conviction. And again, the lines are simple in terms of lexical choice, but complex in terms of narrative, visionary, tonal, emotional, and ideational weight. This complexity is expressed with vocal and musical emphasis.

In architectonic terms, one may compare the syntax of the commemorative poem to building a spacious structure with large stones, like a castle, a palace, or a temple. The "stones," of which the poem is built, are the events of miraculous quality that constitute the myth. Three meanings are unified in the word *nissi* ("miraculous"), which by itself belongs to the special lexicon of the poetic style. According to the original meaning of the word, *nes* is the banner, under which an army gathers and is led to its objective. Its secondary meaning is "miracle"—an event that deviates from the reality which humans experience in the created world and which takes place according to the laws of nature; an event that appears "greater than life" and in this sense is impossible in earthly reality and therefore not to be expected in advance. However, a miracle is an event that is expected, even required from the perspective of its ethical goal, whether speaking of the salvation of the pious who are worthy thereof, or of the punishment deserved by evil ones. From this, the third meaning of the word *nes* is derived—it refers to miraculous events as disclosing the proper order of the world, whether in the sense that they represent the ideal model of proper conduct to be emulated, or in the sense that they demonstrate that God, who alone can enact such an event, is performing His office as king of humankind and king of Israel, and leading them towards realizing their objective.

The Narrative of the Foundational Event

From the literary-conceptual perspective, there are two sorts of commemorative poetry in which scripture renders historical myth as a narrative with God as the main hero. The first sort is the symbolic narrative that depicts foundational events as a memory of the past, in the sense that in the present they already fall under the definition of solid facts that define present life-conditions and determine future developments. But take note: in this very sense, these foundational events stand forever, testify to the wisdom of God who has wrought them, and embody a crucial lesson for creatures—and first of all for the human being, created in God's image, who speaks and understands and provides feedback to God about His creation.

Clearly, the creation narrative is the most prominent example of the foundational myth. The creation is documented in the book of Genesis as a dramatic happening that took place in the past. As far as humans are concerned, this event belongs to a distant past; it is therefore impossible for the creation itself, as an event, to be remembered. The word of God alone can tell about the creation to human beings, through the prophet. Accordingly, in this narrative God is not only the single hero, but also the original narrator. The great masterful question is: how can human beings understand what God narrates about His wisdom as creator? The simple answer: From the perspective of the eternal God, who exists by Himself above the universe He created, creation itself is the speech that expresses God's wisdom and will through externalizing; as is the way of the human artist who expresses his wisdom and will in pictures, sculptures, melodies, and poems. The artist's creation is his language, but in his creation, which flows from human wisdom and will, he imitates the original models of creation and therefore his language is not original. God externalizes His own wisdom and will—which are the sources for His creation. His creation is, therefore, identical with speech, which human beings imitate in their languages. This is the deepest meaning of the description of creation in human language as the speech of God, who says-and-does (because for Him, saying and doing are identical): "And God said, let there be . . . and there was" (Genesis 1:3).

Thus, the myth of creation is created with creation itself—when the human narrator "translates" into imitative human language the divine utterance, which identifies the creation-within-creation, and by means of this language externalizes the wisdom embodied in it, making it accessible to the understanding human being. The information transmitted in the narrative of creation does not, accordingly, relate to the question about how God created the universe. Rather, it seeks to explain what moved God to create the universe and what this intention was in His wisdom when He created it. It also reflects on the language embodied in the order of creation, as a planned and thought-out process—which can be studied from creation's structural logic that testifies to its proper purpose, namely, the progress of reality towards perfection and the good. Finally, the narrative of creation strives to determine the specific message that creation, as divine speech, transmits to the human, and the special response that it requires of the human being, as the creature to whom God speaks, and whose destiny God thereby determines, as His servant and child.

The same mode of inquiry informs the narrative in the book of Exodus, which parallels the narrative of the creation of the human being with the story of the wondrous birth of Moses and his miraculous appearance as savior of his people in the name of God—in the full representative sense of this definition: Moses is a "man of God," "servant of God," the emissary that "God was with." In this capacity, Moses is an exemplary human being, the human who is found to be "good" in the eyes of God from his birth.

The meaning of the matter is that God created Moses for the sake of his mission, and did so with a special intention. The miraculous circumstances of his birth point towards his mission as savior, and notify the people in advance about the promise embodied in him. Through Moses, God Himself would rescue His nation and lead the people to their land. The mission of Moses is essential to God and nation, but the redemption itself is realized on the plane of history, which is the plane of the nation's earthly life. For this reason, Moses had to be born, grow up, be educated, act, and even be tested, sin and suffer as a human being of flesh and blood—and not like a heavenly angel of God who is innocent of all these things. From this perspective, Moses's appearance on the mythic plane as a "man of God" touches his activity as a leader of the nation on the historical plane, and over the course of his entire path he acts as a prophet linking myth and history.

This fact also has an influence on shaping the style of the wondrous narrative on the plane of myth and the style of the actual narrative on the plane of history. In terms of the epic of history, the appearance of Moses symbolizes the ascent of the level of the nation's existence and its status among the nations in terms of its suitability to fulfilling its test as a "special nation" (*am segulah*). In this capacity, the nation is required to function as "kingdom of priests" and rise to a prophetic height. Moses and Aaron are made into models, whom the people are commanded to imitate. All the experiences that the nation undergoes in the desert are destined to educate the people and advance them to this height. When the nation passes the test, it rises to the height of its destiny, and the plane of its history touches the plane of divine myth. This connection expresses, symbolically, that the myth, which prophesizes the future, is to be actualized in past history as well as in future events. For example, the ark in which Moses was rescued, so he could rescue his people, symbolizes on the one hand the ark of Noah in which all humankind was rescued from the waters of the flood, and on the other the ark in which the two Tablets of the Covenant would be placed in the future, as the Ark of Testimony which fulfilled the covenant made between God and His people and assured their redemption. Similarly, the river upon which the ark rested was the water that returned the universe to the chaos of the days of Noah, but also the water that would come out of the barren rock in order to revive the people in the desert, and the rain with which God would fructify the land of Canaan for milk and honey to flow when the nation settled there and kept God's *mitzvot*. The manna, which tasted like ambrosia, symbolizes the sweet fruits of the Garden of Eden, which Adam and Eve enjoyed without labor, as well as the milk and honey that the people would eat in Canaan, their fertile land, if they would keep God's *mitzvot* and not be seduced into worshipping idols.

Similar symbolism can be found in the other portions of the Moses narrative, which have been elevated to the level of myth. Among them are the enacting of the covenant at the foot of Mount Sinai; the narrative of the sin of the golden calf; the revelation in the "cleft of the rock;" after that the narrative of the controversy with Korah and his cohort; and the narrative of the death of Moses, which was as miraculous as his birth. In his death, Moses was stripped of his flesh-and-blood existence. The prophetic spirit, with which God inspired Moses, giving it to him from His spirit, became identified with the Torah, which God gave the nation through him. By means of the Torah, which the children of Israel were commanded to place upon their hearts; to reflect upon day and night; and to follow without deviation, Moses continues to lead his nation on the plane of history across all generations—until the realization of the vision of complete redemption, in which the plane of history will meet the plane of myth forever. Moses leads his nation after his death not as a person of normal flesh and blood but as a messenger of God, as God's angel, who appeared from the plane of myth, conducted his mission on the plane of history, and returned to the plane of myth, when the time came for another leader of flesh and blood—Joshua the son of Nun—to lead the nation, which had already been prepared to accept upon itself full responsibility for its future. Accordingly, it was said of Moses after his death:

> Never again did there arise in Israel a prophet like Moses—whom the Lord singled out, face to face, for the various signs and portents that the Lord sent him to display in the land of Egypt, against Pharaoh and all his courtiers and his whole country, and for all the great might and awesome power that Moses displayed before all Israel. (Deuteronomy 34:10–12)

The Narrative of the Historical Epic

The second sort of poetry, which documents the myth, is the poem that embodies the miraculous event while it is happening. It does so against the background of historical events in the present, in which the people experience great salvation and eternalize it for the generations. Above, we presented the first paragraph of the Song of the Sea. Let us take note that the verse "I will sing unto the Lord" (Exodus 15:1) is speech in the language of the present. Not the present of history, but rather the present of myth, the present that symbolizes the eternity out of which God looks upon the history of nations from their beginning until their end. The miraculous event is grasped in poetry while the event is taking place. From then onward it remains alive and enduring, in the sense that it can return and be introduced into any present by uniting the assembly that sings the poem together, and by bringing out its lessons at any time in order to realize the vision of the future embodied in it.

This understanding is explicit in the Song of the Sea itself, insofar as the song documents the entire narrative of redemption from beginning to end, as a vision that already has been realized: on the shore of the sea, the nation rescued from the army of Pharaoh envisions its difficult path ahead—as if the path has already been completed:

> In Your love You lead the people You redeemed;
> In Your strength You guide them to Your holy abode.
> The peoples hear, they tremble;
> Agony grips the dwellers in Philistia.
> Now are the clans of Edom dismayed;
> The tribes of Moab—trembling grips them;
> All the dwellers in Canaan are aghast.
> Terror and dread descend upon them;
> Through the might of Your arm they are still as stone—
> Till Your people cross over, O Lord,
> Till Your people cross whom You have ransomed.
> You will bring them and plant them in Your own mountain,
> The place You made to dwell in, O Lord,
> The sanctuary, O Lord, which Your hands established.
> The Lord will reign for ever and ever!
> (Exodus 15:13–18)

In other words, by means of the poem the people on the shore of the Red Sea "saw" God's direct leadership; and when they were elevated through Moses to the plane of myth, which prophesized the history, they also saw future history from the transtemporal perspective of God: "For the horses of Pharaoh, with his chariots and horsemen, went into the sea; and the Lord turned back on them the waters of the sea; but the Israelites marched on dry ground in the midst of the sea" (Exodus 15:19). Here we have the exemplary use of one of the instruments of the self-interpretation of the scriptural poem: the ongoing, repeated emphasis of a single word, which becomes a symbolic keyword with multiple meanings that require inspection and decoding. The sea, about which the children of Israel sang the song to God on that day, is presented as a medium of revelation of God's redemptive power. The children of Israel "walked into the midst of the sea." Their walk carries revelational symbolism: they are cut off by the sea from the Egyptian shore which symbolizes their past, and they arrive at the desert shore which symbolizes the future towards which Israel advances from out of the sea, moving to the encampment in the free desert where God alone rules. In Israel's encampment under God's protection, the vision of the nation's redemption is realized. The symbolic image of walking on dry land amid the sea, therefore, epitomizes Israel's entire journey, which on the plane of history will be very long and twisted. A straight line joins the peaks of success where the plane of history, which we experience and expect from the perspective of the people, touches the plane of myth as experienced and expected from the divine perspective. There, according to our perspective, the past which relates to the future as its completion, and the future which relates to the past as its basis, blend together to become an eternal present.

This second form of poetic narrative is, as said, the historical epic. In contrast to the myth, it is a lower genre of narrative poetry, one which describes the historical experience from the human perspective. But it does so on the basis of the faith that the significance of the events—their causes, incentives, and purposes—is directed by divine providence on the basis of the mission for which the human being was created in God's image. In other words, the myth documents events in which God, as creator and sovereign, determines the entities of creation (ontology), its ordinances, and permanent processes of creation. Also the history of human culture conducts itself within the framework of these events. By comparison, the epic documents the encounter between human choice in response to, or refusal of, God's *mitzvot*, and God's will that human beings receive God's mission upon themselves and obey it voluntarily. By means of the encounter between the divine will anchored in divine wisdom, and the human will anchored in human wisdom, decisions are taken which constitute the historical narrative. In the narrative the human witness discloses singular events, in which advance towards the goal is recognized, from among the mass of events that embody the cyclical routine permeated with chance and fatefulness of life that follow the laws of creation. Out of the mass of events which constitute history, the epic selects the singular, innovative events which open a new day in history, and eternalizes them in a "new song."

It is clear from this that the poetic, mimetic quality of the epic differs from that of myth. The epic is "prosaic" from the perspective of the style of documentation, in the sense that it does not come to symbolize, but to narrate what actually happened. Also to interpret what happened according to compliance or non-compliance with the will of God as made explicit in His *mitzvot* on the one hand, and the lessons of the foundational events of the myth on the other.

To skeptical readers who are not convinced in advance that the narratives of the myth and the *mitzvot* of the Torah are reliable revelations of God's wisdom and will, the epic narrative of history in the Hebrew Bible appears as a document of subjective personal observation, mediated by a worldview in which faith in God as creator and leader of the universe is assumed from the outset. But from the perspective of the scribe who documents the things that he himself saw or heard from reliable witnesses, this worldview is the sole true path which is proper in terms of determining the perspective, the emphasis, and the lessons and meaning of the observed events. In the scribe's opinion, this is not his individual worldview, but rather the worldview of the God who revealed Himself to him through His prophets. From this perspective, there is a clear similarity between the style of the myth which documents the miraculous, and the epic which documents events that are considered significant by the historical scribe, which are therefore worthy of remembrance as singular events that are not accidental but represent stages on a continuous path of progress towards the vision determined in advance by God when He created His world.

These considerations apply also to the legislative instructions and *mitzvot* that are integrated into the myth or the scriptural epic. The scriptural narrative does not reproduce formal documents of legislation and law, but rather documents the narration of the legislation and the responsibility to accept it. By doing so, the narrative intends not only to legislate or to enforce, but to represent the binding authority of the legislation and to explain its incentives and the purposes, so as to convince the nation and awaken its will to obey and be worthy of the promised recompense. From this perspective, a text such as the Ten Commandments is more than a formal document that dictates certain laws. With its poetic rhetoric, it embodies the majestic event of its recitation as an inseparable portion of the myth of God's revelation at Sinai. Thus, the words of Torah are read in the synagogue not as a theoretical instructional treatise, but as poetry with musical-celebratory accentuation which engages the worshipping assembly in a lofty experience of renewing the event of the Sinai covenant. On the plane of history, this is what Moses did at the threshold of setting out to inherit the land of Canaan, as documented in the book of Deuteronomy. It is also what Ezra the Scribe did at the time of return from Babylon—as documented in the books of Ezra and Nehemiah. In that event, the performative celebratory ceremony reflects the epic, and the epic reflects the myth.

The three genres of poetry which nourish the *siddur* are the personal and congregational lyrical hymns, mainly from the book of Psalms; the epic novella, exemplified principally in the scrolls of Ruth and Esther; and the prophetic oration. These three poetic genres may be defined as three ways of mediating between the epic plane of history and the miraculous plane of myth. The first type is an ecstasy in song that ascends toward the plane of the myth of the redeemer, from the perspective of individuals who personally encounter experiences of history in which the people are called upon to realize their mission. The second type is a narrative-epic encounter with problems of the nation's existence in exile, in anticipation of the coming redemption. The third type is a memory of God's intervention into His nation's conduct, which takes place on the plane of history from out of the plane of God's heavenly, mythological sovereignty, related through prophets who are God's messengers to His nation. We already saw above that there is a close connection between the *siddur* and these three essential genres of biblical poetry. It is therefore appropriate to discuss each one separately.

15

Between the Poetry of
Prophecy and Prayer

"Who am I that I should go to Pharaoh?"
(Exodus 3:11)—The Definition of Prophecy in
General and the Singular Prophecy of Moses

Prophecy in Israel is defined by the Torah as a form of relationship between
God and the human being; as a spiritual, ethical, and political mission; and as
an institutionalized spiritual leadership whose authority is conferred by the
basic law of the Torah. The definition of prophecy is first included at the event
consecrating Moses for his exemplary mission. At the end of his days, Moses
himself fixed the definition in the book of Deuteronomy (18:15–22), as part
of the legislation which determined the general structure of the kingdom of
Israel that needed to be established after settling in Canaan. According to this
definition, prophecy is the word of God, as the king over all the nations—and in
particular as the king of Israel—addressed to the people He wishes to rule and
command, through a human messenger (as distinct from a heavenly "angel"),
who is authorized to "bring" the word of God as it came from "His mouth,"
without addition or diminution and without change, to the people to whom the
messenger is sent.

According to the book of Genesis, God revealed Himself in His words to
a line of chosen individuals, from Adam to Joseph, but He spoke to them about
themselves and about their future seed. He did not send them to transmit His
word to others, so not a single one of them was called "prophet." The first person
to be called by that name was Moses. His role in connection to God and His
people was defined, as said, in the first revelation to him—in the presence of
the burning bush at the foot of Mount Sinai (Exodus 3–4). The word "prophet"
is used in this narrative not in relation to Moses but in relation to his brother
Aaron, selected to be a "prophet" for his brother, who had difficulty speaking. In
this way, a parallel was created between the status of Moses in relation to God

and His people, and the status of Aaron in relation to Moses and his people. Aaron was to serve Moses and his nation, in the way that Moses was required to serve God and His people.

In the first revelation at the feet of Mount Sinai, Moses was sent to let his people know that God heard their cry, that the time for the nation's redemption had come. Moses was to command the actions which the people themselves were to carry out in order to be redeemed. Parallel to this, Moses was to stand before Pharaoh, and demand in God's name that Pharaoh send the people to serve their God in the desert—outside the area of Pharaoh's kingdom. Following that, when God would compel Pharaoh to obey His commands, Moses would be commanded to lead the nation and bring it to the feet of the mountain from which Moses had been sent. It follows that the goal of the prophetic mission is to enact divine justice in the land by means of judgment of the wicked for punishment and the righteous for salvation; to foretell the divine recompense that will come in the future, both for the evil ones and the pious; and to give instruction of the *mitzvot* which the people are to obey in order to be justified before God and be saved.

From this perspective, the mission of Moses is similar to the mission of all the prophets who arose after him and fulfilled their role within the framework of the basic law that Moses gave to his people. It should be emphasized that, as Moses was the first prophet, the founder, sent to an enslaved nation without effective leadership and without political and military instruments for resistance and self-defense to establish independent life for them, his was a special mission. It was for one time and carried exceptional powers. Implementing them in proceeding further, Moses added the role of king to that of prophet. As said above, Moses was initially sent to prepare the nation for the appearance of its God as savior and avenger, and after that to lead the nation to the desert—a space outside government of human sovereignty, where God alone ruled—and then to the mountain from which Moses was sent and from which God would proclaim His sovereignty over His nation on the basis of a covenant of mutual consent. Moses completed this mission as a prophet, but at the foot of Mount Sinai God placed a supplementary mission upon him: to begin with, to establish the nation as an independent "assembly," which would recognize Moses as its highest judge and representative before God. On this independent foundation, Moses was to sanctify the nation and, as a prophet, bring to the nation the Torah of God, with its ordinances, laws, and commandments, and enact the covenant which obligated the nation *vis-à-vis* God, and God *vis-à-vis* the nation, to keep them.

With these two missions, Moses fulfilled his special role, the role of founder. To be sure, from the perspective of God and from the perspective of Moses as prophet, it was not Moses but God Himself who rescued His nation, led it in the desert, gave the people water to drink and manna to eat, and taught the people the ways of justice and righteousness of free men. In the eyes of God and in the eyes of Moses himself, Moses was but the "mouth" by means of which God made known His will. But from the perspective of the nation, Moses was the savior, the leader, and the legislator. Moses's efforts to correct "the error" of the nation did not succeed—a fact which was finally established when Moses ascended to the height of the mountain to be alone with God, and receive the Tablets of the Covenant and the plan for the Tabernacle. The people, who felt abandoned by their leader, exchanged God's sovereignty for a golden idol. After the event, Moses strengthened the authorities of leadership, the law, and the legislation of the king over his nation—although in the covenantal law that Moses gave to the people in God's name, the prophets who came after him were deprived of such authority.

The reasoning was clear: Moses was selected for his mission in order to establish a kingdom of priests who would be God's treasure on earth. The act of founding is a new beginning, and in this sense it is a revolution that can take place solely through the appropriation of exceptional powers by a strong leader—upon whom the people, in great distress, depend and see as their only hope. Because of this, Moses had great power to enforce his will whenever a controversy arose among the people in the face of internal or external obstacles.

"A prophet from among your own people" (Deuteronomy 18:15): The Role of the Prophet from the Days of Moses and Thereafter

Even if the intention of the leader was to establish a government for free men, the first step—the founding step—had to include elements of enforcement. This was an undeniable necessity. It justified the exceptional powers that the leader assumed for himself, although only for a limited period and as an exception. Once the beginning was over, the nation accepted the basic law, and the institutions needed to apply it were established, there would no longer be place for continuing to concentrate all the powers in one hand—unless the initiator intended to annul the government that had been established, or to change its basic law in order to establish another in its place. Since the government that Moses established was, in his eyes and those of the people, a divine administration whose basic law was that of God, any initiative to annul or change it appeared as a revolt against God, sovereign of the universe. The conclusion emerging from this regarding the mission of prophets after Moses is unequivocal: the Torah of Moses, together with its laws, judgments, and *mitzvot* were established as criteria, according to which the propriety of the claim of prophets sent by God who appeared after Moses whom God sent was measured. If the prophets said anything in God's name that contradicted the Torah of Moses, they would be considered false prophets, rebels against the government, and were to be sentenced to death by the court of the assembly.

Based on this consideration, the Torah of Moses deprived the prophets after him of authority of legislation, interpretation of the law, its application, or enforcement in the name of God. With the establishment of the government of Israel, the authority of practical governance, which was in the hands of Moses, was transferred to the separate authorities of instruction and judgment, the priesthood, and military leadership, which were appointed in the name of the assembly and according to the law of Torah. What, then, was the mission of the prophets and the authority of their instruction? It was to tell the people about their sins and their piety before God; to envision the future that was to take place according to God's will as punishment of the evil ones and as reward for the pious; to admonish the nation, its elders, its priests, its Levites, and kings and to demand that they turn back from sinning; to entreat them to keep the *mitzvot* of God for their own benefit. As advisors to the king, they were to outline, in God's name, a social and political path, which assured the kingdom's loyalty to its destiny as a kingdom of priests of God, and as a holy nation. With this, of course, the happiness of the nation and its peace would be assured.

This definition of the mission opens anew the question about the urgency for the institution of prophecy, especially after the granting of Torah and establishing the government. Why was the prophetic mediation between God and His nation needed, once God's Torah was offered and accepted? Alternatively, how could a person of flesh and blood stand in direct speaking with God, and return to transmit God's word to normal human beings? And if the matter was possible for special individuals, in whom the spirit that God breathed into their bodies achieved a very high caliber, what were the ramifications of their dedication to this mission, for their earthly life and their relations with their brethren, friends, families, tribes, and nation?

In order to answer the first question in a way that could serve as a key to responding to questions which evolve from it, let us return to the event of Moses's consecration before the burning bush, which was discussed above in other contexts. As recalled, God revealed Himself to Moses with a special name, the holiest and most concealed—calling Himself "I shall become what I shall become" (*Ehyeh-Asher-Ehyeh*). A combination of letters, *Yod-Hay-Vav-Hay*, was created on this basis, which were combined to mean "He who will be." Only God can and should pronounce the name "I will become" (*Ehyeh*) in the singular first person in presenting Himself to another, while human beings who have achieved sanctification can pronounce the name "He who will become" (YHVH)—although, clearly, they could not conceive the essence to which the name refers, given its absolute power. Insofar as God is absolute power, which is abstracted beyond all limits of space and time (and therefore, from the human perspective, God was, is, and will be [HYH / HVH / YHYH] simultaneously!), He is holy and awesome, and from the human perspective God embodies an assuring-threatening contradiction. God's power is good, and intended to be beneficial, but every entity He creates and separates from Him is made finite and therefore is destroyed if it comes closer to God than its essence is able to endure. As fire symbolizes God's presence at the bush, and after that at the top of Mount Sinai, smoking, thundering, and sending forth lightning, the power of God is the mother of all creation but also burns and annihilates that creation if it does not maintain necessary distance.

Accordingly, the revelation of God with the name that symbolizes this power casts a terrible fear over the person who comes near the focus of the vision which reveals the name. This explains the frightening voice, which Moses heard when he asked to come closer than he was allowed to have a better look at the sight that appeared to his eyes from afar: "Do not come closer. Remove your sandals from your feet" (Exodus 3:5). Moses was commanded to be satisfied with what he saw from afar. That is, to know that something mysterious was inherent to it; to understand that the mysterious *Anokhi* ("I") revealed to him is directed to him; to hear what the mysterious *Anokhi* had to command to him; to internalize what he heard; to identify with it so as to carry it out—but under no circumstance was he to try to decode the mystery itself. For if he came closer than allowed, he would be blinded and burned.

This profound thought is not presented in a philosophical lecture, but is rather expressed in narrative documentation. In it, we will see an exemplary product of prophetic poetics. It recurs in many examples, especially in the depiction of experiences of consecration of prophets to their prophetic missions. But in fact, all prophecies attributed to the literary prophets belong to this poetic genre. Let us first of all emphasize that, in this genre, the writer is necessarily the prophet who comes to give testimony about himself. Only a prophet can write in this way, as one witnessing his experience—to which we may add the determination that in order to fulfill the role of a reliable document that has the weight of authentic testimony, it has to be written in the mimetic language of the poem whose content reconstructs the personal experience about which the poem comes to bear witness. In our opinion, there is no other way to authenticate the testimony, because other than God and the prophet, no one is present at the meeting between them. All of the prophetic revelations of Moses, including his consecration before the burning bush, are testified to by him; it is he who transmitted the words of God to him in the different circumstances of fulfilling his mission: at the foot of Mount Sinai, in Egypt, on the shore of the Red Sea, on the way to Mount Sinai, atop Mount Sinai, in the cleft of the rock, and after that at the Tent of Meeting and in the Tabernacle above the Ark cover. Moses reports about all these events, and not only this—he narrates the event of revelation to him in the way it happened, and he quotes what God told him. He quotes in the language of poetry, whose literal imitation embodies not only the conceptual content, but also the pathos of the one who commands, warns, admonishes, threatens or reconciles; and the authority that imposes awe, or the compassionate and loving presence. From the perspective of the nation called upon to internalize and be convinced and act, these are essential.

Prophecy: Humility That Brings Elevation

The condition for the continuation of the revelational event before the burning bush is, as said, the gesture of physical distance which embodies consciousness of spiritual distance: humility before God. Humility is the highest spiritual level a person can achieve: the higher the moral and spiritual height is in relation to other humans, the deeper the person's humility before God; and the more conscious he is of the distance which is impossible to bridge between the physical-spiritual being of the human and the absolute spiritual being of God. We learn this from the Torah's testimony about Moses, the greatest of the prophets of Israel and the greatest among its wise leaders: "Now Moses was a very humble man, more so than any other man on earth" (Numbers 12:3). Yet, these words are said about him exactly at the time that his sister Miriam protests against his "elevation" above her and her brother. God, who testifies to Moses's humility before Him, thereby testifies to Moses's greatness. That is, the person more modest than any other human is esteemed above all of them in the eyes of God, on account of his intrinsic worth. Moses knows this, and is supported by it in fulfilling his role as leader. For indeed, he does not himself represent authority, rather the authority of God embodied in His word. This complex idea is also an essential component of the poetics of prophecy. The authority of the prophets in their appearances before kings, ministers, and great priests, comes from this. Their humility before God empowers them "to elevate" themselves above these dignitaries, for they are but of flesh and blood, like themselves.

But, on the other hand, the humility also enhances the prophet's stature before God. The more his humility increases the greater his importance, because God relies on His prophets to fulfill His role as king over His earthly creation. Only a person who accepts this thankless role—one that earns him no gratitude from his people, and especially not from their powerful figures—could fulfill the mission, the goal of which is to mend the world by mending human civilization. Towards this end, God is obliged from His side to bridge the gap, which the prophet cannot bridge from his side. God has to turn to the prophet, show him visions, and have him hear the words with which to instruct the people in an obligatory manner, and convince them that these are not the words of the person who prophesizes, but rather the words of God obligating them. This too is a basic premise of the poetics of prophecy, upon whose foundation the poetics of prayer develops. The form of Moses's stance before the angel who revealed himself to him in the bush that burned but was not consumed—after Moses removed the shoes from his feet and lowered his gaze—is the form of the stance of a person who prays before God. From this perspective as well, it is not by accident that exactly at this encounter God provided the name to Moses through whom His nation can turn to Him in prayer "for the generations."

Humility, as said, is recognition of the true self-worth of a person in relation to God. In such a capacity, it expresses purity of soul and spirit: moral uprightness and intellectual integrity are the two qualities that the prophet needs in his role as God's messenger to His people. They are also the two characteristics to which the worshipper is required to adhere, if he wants his prayer to be answered. The Torah attributes these two qualities to Moses—the pursuit of justice and adherence to truth—even before he becomes a prophet and begins to reach out to his brethren to see their suffering. Just as Moses is later disclosed to be a person who sees wonders that arouse his attention, when he goes out to his brethren he discloses himself as a person who sees injustice and deceit. Most importantly, he is a person for whom the truth that he sees requires him to act to correct the situation, without being deterred by the danger to himself. Moses does not think about himself, but rather about the justice that ought to be done; and when he sees injustice, he feels the responsibility imposed upon him by virtue of the truth he beholds—to correct the injustice, to condemn the wicked one and punish him, and justify and rescue the righteous one. This is the correct way to "be like divine beings who know good and bad" (Genesis 3:5), but in order to become a prophet, Moses has to learn that justice is not entrusted to his heart and intellect, but to the law that God legislates, and that as a human being he should obey the law. On the basis of this knowledge, which is derived from his experience, Moses—in his capacity as a prophet—is to become a person who gives God's law to His people. This is the culmination of his work as a prophet. God Himself appears amid the smoke atop Mount Sinai and legislates the commandments to His people, which constitute His kingdom's basic law. But the people cannot understand the divine voice, and Moses "translates" God's words into human terms, which the nation understands. In so doing, Moses defines the essence of the mission for all the prophets to come after him.—to be trustworthy translators of God's words, which they alone are able to understand.

"I will put My words in his mouth and he will speak them" (Deuteronomy 18:18)

Let us return to the inclusive theological meaning of the stipulation required by the paradoxical existential relationship which exists between the creator and the created: the direct revelation of God to the human being has to be personal and private. It has to take place in total isolation, and in complete secret. The nation to which the prophet is sent cannot verify the prophetic encounter from its own experience, nor what was said to the prophet; especially not the deep truth of the message embodied in the presence of the commanding God. We have dealt with this above. But now we should pay attention to the problem that the prophet is required to confront, because of the singular privacy of direct revelation: How is he worthy of the nation's trust, both in terms of his mission, and in the binding truth of his message? Below we will detail the legal response, which the Mosaic Torah gave to this problem for prophets who followed Moses. But from this discernment it is clear that Moses' legalistic answer not only did not apply to him, as the one who gave the Torah to his people. The prophets who came after him were also granted authenticity. This was by means of an answer—upon which Moses could have relied during his first appearance: the authenticity which flowed from his independent testimony, standing before the nation with God's word in his mouth. He did so, realizing that he, and immediately thereafter his people, knew that God heard his words and judgment; and understanding that anyone who knew that God knew him and judged him could not lie in His name.

Standing before his nation, therefore, the prophet stands in judgment, both before his people and in sight of his God. He knew in his soul that were he not sure that the pure truth was on his lips—which he was forced to express because he was commanded and because his nation's life and well-being depended on it—he would not dare to endanger himself and speak it. Indeed, this significance of the utterance—that it was critical both from the prophet's perspective and that of the people—needed to be transmitted in the form of his stance before the people, and in the form of his speech. In other words: in his speech to the nation, the prophet had to create an authenticity which could not be doubted, and which he himself felt when God spoke to him. This could be achieved only through the participation of his people in his public appearance in the revelatory event which he experienced in secret and privately. In other words, in order to convince his people, the prophet had to reconstruct the event of divine revelation, which motivated him to his mission, in public in the sight of his people.

For a deeper understanding of these words, let us go back and establish that the prophet had no doubt that the God who identified Himself when He addressed the prophet ("I am the Lord") was speaking with him in truth. This was not a sensory imagining, illusion, or deceptive appearance by some other personality. The prophet also had no doubt that the words that he heard, as he understood them at the time, were the words of God. The reason for his certainty was embodied in the power of the revelation, and in the absolute clarity of the truth embodied by it. It would have been impossible for a prophet, who was found to be worthy of revelation, to be mistaken about it when the revelation took place. It would also be impossible to ignore it or deny it. Divine revelation is a comprehensive event, which does not emerge from a person's egoistic anticipations and desires. To the contrary: the revelation takes the person away from the track of his life and alters his life in the face of the truth made known to him. This is the facticity that shapes the consciousness of the prophet anew, in two aspects: the prophet's self-consciousness, and consciousness of his environment and the place that he occupies in it. Such an event, even if it takes place in absolute privacy, cannot be subjective (that is, bursting out of the inner soul of the prophet), it is always objective (emerging out of the authority that has created the reality and knows it as it truly is). The proof for this is simple and clear: the event is indeed private, and only God and the prophet are present in it, but it is not within the scope of a response to the prophet's private needs or quest for his well-being as an individual. To the contrary: this event is opposed to his immediate success and to his immediate well-being as an individual. It is opposed to his proper, private desires outside the bounds of sin. It tears him out of his privacy, for him to act for the sake of God and His nation. The certainty that such a demand is a divine matter, with the meaning of objective truth, cannot be an error, for if the prophet had but the slightest shadow of doubt about its absolute necessity, as is proper for all "scientific" truth, it would have been preferable to be seized by doubt and to retreat from the mission for which he had to radiate authority—not his own, but that of the one who sent him.

Until now, we have been discussing factors that draw an absolute distinction between prophecy and prayer; nevertheless, they constitute a basis for the possibility of prayer. The other side of our findings brings prophecy close to prayer. Moses himself and all the prophets who arose after him dared to negotiate, to raise objections, and to express wishes and even demands before the God who was revealed to them without fear—or even on the basis of the fear that God aroused in them. If God chose them to make known His truth to their people, they were bound to be sincere before God about their attitude to the mission, which He placed upon them. They would be responsible before God, and He would be responsible to them, as befitting members of the covenant. If they had doubts and difficulties regarding their mission, they were bound, and not only entitled, to express them without fear. God was bound to provide a sufficient answer, as we learned from God's revelatory encounter with Moses at the bush.

An additional conclusion emerges from this. The agreement of the prophet to surrender his privacy for the sake of his mission, and to be the "mouth" by means of which God expresses His words to human beings, does not mean that the prophet achieves "unification" with God. Nor does it mean that the prophet loses consciousness of his separate self and his free will. To the contrary: the prophet strengthens them in order to dedicate himself to his mission with all his physical, psychological, and spiritual powers. This too is a paradox, because the independence of the prophet does not contradict the fact that, when God is revealed to him, he knows that it is forbidden for him to refuse the mission that is to be placed upon him. He is bound to it from the onset—but not only from the perspective of his knowing the power of authority of the command, but from the perspective of his knowing himself—as one who is destined to the mission from birth. By examining the words of Moses, we learn that his doubts as to whether he could carry out the mission, a mission that appears to be far beyond the capacity of a flesh-and-blood person like him, comes precisely from this self-knowledge.

"How can we know that the oracle was not spoken by the Lord" (Deuteronomy 18:21)

The greatest obstacle, which not even Moses would ultimately overcome in his lifetime, was expressed in his question about how people could believe that he was sent to them—that is, those who were not present at the encounter when his mission was placed upon him, who did not experience what he did, or see for themselves what he saw. This was the other side of the paradox of the prophetic mission: the prophet's experience and vision were beyond the comprehension of most people, who therefore were conditioned to think that such an experience was above the capability of all humans—meaning that the revelation was not possible, and that Moses invented these things.

Moses anticipated this possibility. He too did not foresee the exceptional event, even a moment before it happened. How, then, could his listeners be convinced that he was sent to them by God? How could they be convinced that his news would make them happy, but also alarm them because of actions they would need to take—actions that would bring them into a course of confrontation with the tyrant who ruled them, whose power was right before their eyes while the power of God who promised to redeem them was hidden from sight. How, then, could they be convinced of Moses's news? As long as it was not actually revealed to them as it was to Moses, they could not rely on it. In other words, in the eyes of the slaves, exodus from under the yoke of the very powerful rule of Pharaoh appeared to be clearly impossible.

Accordingly, when God revealed the content of his mission, Moses questioned its authenticity. Immediately, Moses asked for the hidden name with which God called Himself, the name whose pronunciation elicited Moses's immediate response, and also enabled prayer to God. In fact, Moses's intention with this question was for God to arm him with the ability to enact exceptional "signs," which would demonstrate the authenticity of his mission to his people and the wondrous power of the one who sent him. God did not respond immediately to his request, but by revealing His name as a sign of redemption itself, God assured that the nation would have a controversy over redemption when it would meet Him, in terms of the nation's fitness to bear it and receive God's Torah. Moses therefore had to ask a second time. But even when he received the power that he requested, which he would employ by competing with Egyptian magicians to create wondrous signs; and even when he tested that power on location, he was not entirely convinced that God "would be with him"—that is, that he could prove to his people and to Pharaoh that God sent him to them.

From whence his doubts? From his feeling that he would be unable to prove his authenticity by means of the authoritative power embodied in his speech. With God's answer, that Moses's brother Aaron would be God's prophet and that it would be up to Aaron to assure that God would be with Moses and grant him the ability he felt he lacked, Moses's contentions out of anxiety finally came to an end and he accepted his mission. However, the ongoing narrative testifies that only after the Pharaoh and his magicians on the one hand, and the nation on the other, experienced their own miraculous encounters, and only after God demonstrated the power of His sovereign rule over creation to the people directly, were the children of Israel convinced, for the time, that God sent Moses. But even then, their conviction was not conclusive. Before the army of Pharaoh drowned in the Red Sea, the people did not believe. Nor did they believe before the Sinaitic theophany, when God revealed Himself, by Himself, in the sight of the people and hearing with their ears. And even after this event, the children of Israel did not believe that God was their savior. In what did they believe? That with ability superior to that of the Egyptian magicians, Moses knew how to enact the "signs" of salvation by himself. Because of this, they relied upon Moses alone to lead them in the desert—not upon God who continued to reveal Himself to Moses in the secrecy of his isolated privacy. But for this very reason, the people still could not turn to God and pray to Him directly. They asked for the golden idol, to which they could turn.

"You shall speak to him and put the words in his mouth" (Exodus 4:15). The Prophet as Speaker of the Language of God

It follows that, in addition to the inborn ability to understand the word of God, the prophet needed a rare talent to transmit the word of God to the people, and also the complementary ability to understand, by himself, the sublime word of God, so that he could explain it to ordinary people found to be worthy thereof. They are two separate abilities, but they join together to confront two obstacles: the difference between the divine truth and human wisdom, and the difference between the ways in which God speaks and the way in which people speak. The truth that God knows is original and complete, while the wisdom of created humans is derived from the creation and is necessarily partial, vague, and full of unknowns. As to the manner of expression: it is understood by any knowledgeable person that God does not speak in the language that humans invented on the basis of observing objects around them, in their activities and deeds. The language of God, as the creator of all, is identical to the things themselves—with their essence, activity, and effects. That is, God's language is identical to the symbolism of the objects He creates, which express the wisdom and will of their creator, just as the craftsman expresses his wisdom and his will in his creativity. That is, God speaks through the sights of creation themselves, or through the lofty visions He shows to the prophets and in the higher reason that He rests upon them—so that through the illumination of that higher reason the prophet deciphers the meaning embodied in the sight shown by God and in the sounds He makes audible, in their language, concepts, and images.

We can learn from this, first of all, about the quality of the special inspiration that God rests upon the prophet as he prophesizes. This applies to content—sights, sounds, or "visions," which the prophet envisions, all of which come from God—and to the "illumination," through which the prophet understands his mission and clothes what he understands intellectually with words he can transmit to others. In later religious philosophy, opinions are divided on the question: are prophetic visions a sort of dream, in the sense of impressions by the power of visionary and audible imagination of the human being? Or are they sights of real things in the spiritual, non-material, trans-earthly sphere?

The words of the prophets themselves do not raise this question or give a reflective answer. But the meaning of the term "vision" (ḥazon), in all the contexts in which it appears in the Hebrew Bible, refers to the phenomenon of actual, necessary reality of which the visionary person is certain no less, but perhaps even more, than he is about the actuality of objects that he grasps directly by his senses—when he is in a situation of alertness to the surroundings in which he finds himself. Nevertheless, the visionary person knows that he sees the reality of the vision with the eyes of his spirit, not of his flesh. He knows that this is not the reality of the here-and-now, but rather the reality that will issue from the reality of the here-and-now in the future, even the very distant future; or the reality that constitutes the source of the here-and-now reality in the distant heavens—that is, reality from the level of myth, which embraces everything. God "envisions" the myth from His eternal perspective and willfully grants the ability to envision what He envisions to human beings whom he sends to act, so that the truth of myth is united with the truth of history.

From this issues the prophet's need to prepare himself for fulfilling his mission in terms of the wisdom learned from human experiences as well—either in creation, or in the civilization with which the human being has been entrusted and its history. Clearly, he will not understand the wisdom of God transmitted to him in prophecy without such preparation, nor can he transmit it to other human beings. But even more important is the understanding that the transmission of matters revealed in prophecy is not possible in the same way in which human beings communicate the products of the wisdom of their human observation of creation, of human civilization and its history.

Let us reemphasize: a lecture about things that the prophet envisioned does not transmit the truth envisioned on the level of myth to anyone who does not experience that truth. There is only one way to transmit such a truth in a convincing form, and that is by emulation or by vivid presentation, which tells the observers: what the prophet presents on the stage of history to your eyes is a sort of reality which he envisions with the eye of his spirit as something coming from God. Look closely and give your heart, because the vision of the prophet, which appears "greater" than the reality of history you experienced in daily life, is radical, meaningful, and absolute; while in daily life, one can discern aspects here and there, twists and turns, inconsequence and relativity, which allow people escape hatches for lingering doubts, delusions, and excuses that justify their sins and omissions. Were you to go deeper and discern the reality of "history," known well to you in light of the vision of the prophet, which embodies the word of God, leader of His world, you would argue, indeed, that God's truth which is hidden from your eyes because of its absolute clarity, is the truth that you conceal from yourselves in order to evade its conclusions with your excuses and delusions. In this way, the prophet compels his people to see what they do not want to see but are obliged to see, either in order to be rescued from the great imminent disaster, or in order to be redeemed from the depth of their trouble when it comes.

Here is one wonderful example from among many.

My beloved had a vineyard
On a fruitful hill.
He broke the ground, cleared it of stones,
And planted it with choice vines.
He built a watchtower inside it,
He even hewed a wine press in it;
For he hoped it would yield grapes.
Instead, it yielded wild grapes.
"Now, then,
Dwellers of Jerusalem
And men of Judah,
You be the judges
Between Me and My vineyard:
What more could have been done for My vineyard
That I failed to do in it?
Why, when I hoped it would yield grapes,
Did it yield wild grapes?
"Now I am going to tell you
What I will do to My vineyard:
I will remove its hedge,
That it may be ravaged;
I will break down its wall,
That it may be trampled.

And I will make it a desolation;
It shall not be pruned or hoed,
And I will command the clouds
To drop no rain on it."
For the vineyard of the Lord of Hosts
Is the House of Israel,
And the seedlings he lovingly tended
Are the men of Judah.
And He hoped for justice,
But behold, injustice;
For equity,
But behold, iniquity!
(Isaiah 5:1–7)

The Prophet as Craftsman of Poetic Language

The artistic strategy that the prophet adopts is quite transparent to anyone who reflects on the conclusion of this metaphor, but it hints at a hidden intention, one which becomes increasingly clear as the metaphor proceeds. Thus, it creates the literary tension which persuades the listeners to listen until the end, even if they know in advance that the intention is to upset and shock them, and to admonish them for their sins and threaten them with the punishment they fear but prefer to close their eyes to. This is how the prophet Nathan conducted himself in reproving King David with the metaphor of the poor man's lamb (II Samuel 2:1–10). Isaiah turns his listeners into judges of the parable he is about to narrate to them, by addressing them as "his beloved," rather than as targets of his accusation. But in the course of the narrative it becomes clear, in calculated stages, that the vineyard which "his beloved" planted is a simile to which his listeners are being compared; and that enlisting them as judges has the intention of forcing them to judge themselves as God judges them, and thus to internalize the truth from which they flee but which pursues them to adhere to them.

The narrative skill is expressed in the way the prophet reveals, with dramatic progression, the two referents of the extended simile. Who is "his beloved" who speaks to his people through the mouth of the prophet? Who are "his beloved" when he states, "And I will command the clouds to drop no rain on it" (Isaiah 5:6)? This sentence, which echoes Moses's warnings to his nation given in the name of God several times in his Torah, makes it clear to Moses's listeners who know his Torah that behind the narrator stands the God who sent him. God is the lover, and the beloved is the nation of Israel which was chosen to be God's treasure, but betrayed its mission. The expected, yet surprising rebuke is unsheathed with the speed of a sword. It hovers over the heads of the listeners and strikes its target. The people, who were prepared to justify the word of the prophet as an objective judge, are still ready to hear some difficult and bitter words of rebuke, which openly explain the sins to which the prophet refers, when he speaks in the name of God with the metaphor of the vineyard and the "injustice" that provokes the lover's judgment against his people.

> Ah,
> Those who add house to house
> And join field to field,
> Till there is room for none but you
> To dwell in the land!
> In my hearing [said] the Lord of Hosts:
> Surely, great houses
> Shall lie forlorn,
> Spacious and splendid ones
> Without occupants.
> For ten acres of vineyard
> Shall yield just one *bath*,
> And a field sown with *homer* of seed
> Shall yield a mere *ephah*.
> Ah,
> Those who chase liquor
> From early in the morning,
> And till late in the evening
> Are inflamed by wine!
> Who, at their banquets,
> Have lyre and lute,
> Timbrel, flute, and wine;
> But who never give a thought
> To the plan of the Lord,
> And take no note
> Of what He is designing.
> Assuredly,
> My people will suffer exile
> For not giving heed,

> Its multitude victims of hunger
> And its masses parched with thirst.
> (Isaiah 5:8–13)

With these words, we arrive at the quality of prophecy as an artistic creation that imitates the word of God, which rests upon His prophets and opens the door to prayer. From the poetic perspective as exemplified above, the prophet does not report to his listeners, who see themselves as his judge, about the prophetic revelation he experienced, or about what he was commanded to say. He speaks while the vision is before his eyes, while he is still agitated by the truth he envisions, about the consequences of the deeds of his people and the seriousness of the inevitable punishment. The "Thus says the Lord," which is dispatched from the prophet's lips, cites the words that God wants His people to hear—so they know and understand the truth regarding their deeds, their consequences, and their recompense. Let them judge themselves and understand the necessity of the commandment, which God commands them in order to redeem them from the disaster that they have brought upon themselves. For the prophet knows that his threats in God's name will not influence the people and make them improve their ways until they understand God's judgment and thereby internalize its truth.

These words explain the necessity of reciting the words of the prophets in the poetic language unique to prophecy, which bridges the plane of reality embodied in myth with the plane of historical reality. The prophet needs to embody in words the "excess meaning" that the divine truth invests in them, and thus to force these words to express more than they do in their routine daily context—which is suitable to routine human experience on the plane of historical reality. Only the poetry of rebuke—which knows how to extract from words all the qualities of expression with which they are charged—is capable of doing this, and of using the different possibilities of their interconnecting—whether in terms of conceptual progression or in terms of imagery, symbolism, or emotional expression. Thus, poetry points to excess truth by focusing all these dimensions of expressions in its direction, and thereby creates empathy for the truth whose depth cannot be embodied in the words that point to it:

> You alone have I singled out
> Of all the families of the earth—
> That is why I will call you to account
> For all your iniquities.
> Can two walk together

Without having met?
Does a lion roar in the forest
When he has no prey?
Does a great beast let out a cry from its den
Without having made a capture?
Does a bird drop on the ground—in a trap—
With no snare there?
Does a trap spring up from the ground
Unless it has caught something?
When a ram's horn is sounded in a town,
Do the people not take alarm?
Can misfortune come to a town
If the Lord has not caused it?"
Indeed, my Lord God does nothing
Without having revealed His purpose
To His servant the prophets.
A lion has roared,
Who can but fear?
My Lord God has spoken,
Who can but prophesy?
(Amos 3:2–8)

The difficult truth that the prophet wanted his people, who had sinned against God, to hear, is heard in the first verse. It could have been heard as a routine repetition of Moses's rebuke of the children of Israel, and as such, it would not stir the sinners' conscience. Because of this, the prophet casts his truth in paradoxical form, which indicates then and there the reason why the people deluded themselves into thinking they could evade the imminent punishment as taught by the Torah of Moses. Precisely because this nation, from among all the families of earth, "knew" God—knew, in the sense of coming near to God so as to carry out His mission among the nations, and for God to redeem it from the pit of slavery with signs and wonders—precisely because of this, God would punish the people for their moral sins. When it came to neighboring nations who sinned against Him more than His nation, God nevertheless tolerated their trespasses and they appeared to be thriving despite their sins.

Unbelievable talk? Talk to be disregarded, as the overblown words of a zealous prophet, and not words of truth worthy of God? All the words of the prophet following his warning came to set straight his listeners, who were shocked by the necessity of the truth on his lips. The truth could not be denied, because it was the truth coming from God, and not from the prophet. The prophet himself was crushed by that truth, which he was forced to express, to his own injury and bruising. For he did not remove himself from his people, and he also knew in advance the reaction of his people—that they would not see in him the person who was summoned to rescue them from themselves, but rather, the person who was speaking to bring them trouble. Indeed, the entire intensity of the tragic contradiction between his mission and its outcome, the contradiction in which he and his people were trapped, was implicit in the relation created between the prophet and his listeners, who would sense their guilt reluctantly when they stood before him. Thus, the prophet succeeded in investing words that described routine reality on earth with the excess meaning that he sought to pour into them, as metaphors that concretized the intensity of the truth on his lips, and its absolute necessity. Because only if the truth were to be grasped in this way would it bring the nation to regret, repent, and be rescued from the disaster—which from the prophet's perspective was already a matter of determined judgment which he saw as actually underway.

The Prophet as Critical Authority

Let us move from the examples of the prophetic mission according to Moses to the legal definition of prophecy in the Torah. First, let us determine that, according to the Torah, the prophet's mission was vital also after the granting of the Torah, the nation's acceptance of it, and establishing the kingdom of Israel based on it. The reason for this is implicit in the essential difference between the kingdom of Israel and the kingdoms of the gentiles who worship deities thought of as powers implanted in earthly creation. In the governments of the nations, the human king is sovereign of the realm. He embodies the authority of the king in himself, as a son of the deities, and he bestows the authority upon his son, who will rule in his stead by the rights of birth and heredity. The people, and even the deities, have no legal way to intervene and deprive the king of his right to reign, for as long as he is the ruler he is considered not only protected by the deities, but one of them.

Not so with the kingdom of Israel. It is to be a "kingdom of priests and a holy nation" to God, who is the true sovereign over the kingdom of Israel. The human king is appointed for the needs of the nation, which is in need of human leadership with which it can have daily contact. God agrees to this, on the condition that the king will submit to His Torah and its *mitzvot*, which are renewed according to the changing factors of the time. But remember: according to the Torah, God remains the true sovereign who rules the land directly, by means of His heavenly angels and by means of His control of forces of nature. God therefore determines the destiny of Israel among the nations, and even the fate of the king and his ministers—and because of this, also the destiny of all members of the nation. The question raised by the distinction between kingdoms of gentiles serving idols and deities, and the kingdom of Israel, is this: how can the loyalty of the human king and of the nation to God be assured? How can it be assured that the government will not deviate from the path as prescribed by law? That it will not betray its destiny and not be destroyed?

The experience, which is documented in the history of Israel in the era of the Judges and that of the kingdoms of Israel and Judah until their destruction, proves that, indeed, this could not be assured. God does not compel the nation to keep the law of His Torah, like some tyrant, for the Torah had been accepted as a covenant of free parties. When the nation sins against God and His Torah, God punishes the nation in return, but He requires His people to worship Him of their own will. Together with this, the legislation of Moses has erected several fences of defense and several checkpoints and warnings. Above all, the intention is to effectuate the principle of "separation of powers," as determined by the basic law of the Torah of Moses. The assembly headed by the elders, the priests, and the Levites, and the king and the ministers limit one another. They check and supervise one another, so as not to deviate from the bounds of authority as fixed by the Torah. But this is not sufficient. The inclinations of the administration and the temptation of the idolatrous way of life are liable to overcome these legislative-political balances, and to transform the kingdom of Israel into a kingdom of idolatry and corruption. According to the Torah, the institution of prophecy is founded in order to add a critical authority, which is not dependent on the assembly and its elders, the priesthood, or the monarchy, but upon God Himself. But also—out of concern that the authorities of the assembly and the elders, priests, the kingdom, and the ministers not be injured by the critical authority—lest that authority use God's name to prevail over the nation with tyrannical rule. Keep in mind: such a danger is indeed anticipated by Moses in decisive situations where he encounters rebellion by the people against God and His Torah—whether in the affair of the sin of the calf, or of the spies, or of Korah and Zimri. We shall see that Moses has understood the danger to be anticipated from prophets who depend only upon God and are not obliged to reckon with any factor other than God. Moses's basic premise is that God's sovereignty over His nation is to be identified with the eternal legislation of the Torah, which God gave to His nation in a covenant of free parties. If the enforcement is needed, it is carried out neither by God nor by the messenger He selected, but rather by means of the institutions, to be chosen by the people, subordinate to God's Torah with its righteous ordinances and legislation.

The role and position of prophets who arose after Moses, as critics of the people and their government in the name of God, are defined on that basis. The prophets are commanded to make known to their people, to their leaders, and their king, what God thinks about their deeds, their intentions, and their compliance with their duties of responsibility to their people; how to realize the nation's destiny among the nations; what judgments God has determined for the people; and what He will do if they do not return from their evil path in sufficient time. The Torah obliges the people, the king, and his ministers to listen to the voice of the prophets, who speak in God's name, on the condition that the prophet prove that the word of God is on their lips, because they are commanded to say only what God will place on their lips—yet everything which God places on their lips is without fear, and without the fright of flesh and blood. On the other hand, the Torah does not endow the prophets with the authority or instruments of rule. They are not able to impose their words upon the obstinate, nor defend themselves, should the nation, its leaders, and kings try to silence them or abandon them to the rage of the crowd. God is their assurance. They are to believe in Him, because He is entrusted to punish their enemies with the instruments of His rule of creation. They will suffer, and thereby prove the authenticity of their mission; in the end, they will be rescued and their persecutors will be punished. Indeed, if this promise is fulfilled, it is because there are always those with awe for God to be found among the people—by whose merit the prophet will be rescued.

The legal concretization of the definition of the prophetic mission may be summarized with these provisions of the Torah.

1) Moses's successors in governance of the people, the judge and the king, were commanded to adopt a prophet for themselves who would prove his authenticity. To emphasize: to adopt—and not to appoint. The prophet did not receive payment or any sort of favors. Those were forbidden to him, as he relied on God alone and not on people of flesh and blood—including the king and his ministers. The king was commanded to turn to the prophet whom he adopted for all important matters in governing the nation, and receive the prophet's confirmation in God's name for his decisions. Moreover, the approval of a prophet who was ordained in God's name was also required for appointing the judge or the king, and after that, for appointing their inheritors.

2) The prophet was not ordained by the judge, by the king, or by the assembly. God alone chose His prophet, by planting his ability in him in his mother's womb, by appearing to him and consecrating him. To emphasize: the consecration of the prophet, who responded to God's addressing him, obligated him to God alone and to His Torah. He was to struggle openly against any command and law legislated by the king and his ministers which was not in accordance with the judgment of the Torah, even if it placed him in danger—as happened with the prophet Elijah and Ahab, in the affair of Naboth the Jezreelite (I Kings 21).

3) God's choice of His prophet was expressed in designation from the womb and birth, that is, in "the calling" heard by the prophet in the depth of his soul, or in the address to him by an ordained prophet preceding him, awakening him to his mission in God's name. In practice, there arose around the great prophets, who were known among the nation, societies of students from which prophets then came, who inherited their role. The Torah traditions which prepared them for their roles were transmitted and learned by these societies. In every generation, prophets arose from these societies, and they ordained one another and preserved their independence and their independence of human beings and human institutions, for they relied on God alone.

4) As the event of the sanctification of the prophet was private, since no one other than God and the prophet could testify to it, every new prophet was required to demonstrate the authenticity of his mission. Two ingredients were required as proof—one negative and the other positive. The negative condition was that the word of God to be uttered by the prophet would not contradict what was said and commanded in the Torah of Moses. As such, this limitation needed to be added: the prophet would not interpret the ordinances of the Torah of Moses and its commandments in opposition to the decisions of Torah scholars authorized to interpret it. The positive condition was that the prophet should predict a future event to come as a punishment for sinful deeds by the nation and its leaders against God, and His Torah, and that what he predicted should take place according to his word.

5) The prophet should be free on the part of the nation and its leaders, and obligated on the part of God, to utter all the truth that God placed on his lips without adorning, without concealing, and without changing God's words. This should be so, even if uttering the truth caused the prophet to be hated and persecuted to silence him; even if it meant that his life was in danger because of what he said. The courage to tell

the truth, out of absolute trust that God would fight his fight and protect him, is additional proof, perhaps the most persuasive proof of the
authenticity of his mission.

6) The prophet had no institutional, controlling power—neither political, nor legal, nor priestly, nor military—to help him defend himself
or to impose his word upon the king and the nation. Only the awe of
God could keep him safe, and the threat of punishment from God
Himself could deter his persecutors. The persecutors were then afraid
of the prophet, as Pharaoh and his magicians were afraid of Moses
because they saw that God protected him. But let us reemphasize: the
people and the kings who threw off the yoke of *mitzvot* of the Torah,
or who dedicated themselves to worshipping "other gods," and who
had no awe before God, could disregard the words of the prophets
and persecute them undisturbed—even though, when the time came,
God would take revenge and prove that the truth was on the lips of His
prophets.

In other words, the authority of the prophet is anchored in the truth on his lips,
and this is what imposes the truth upon the nation and its leaders and king—for
their benefit if they abide by it, and to their misfortune if they avoid it. But it
is clear from this, that at times of serious crises in their nation's history, the
prophets are cast into a trial which constitutes a supreme test of their mission. In
such fateful times, most of the people and, above all, the king and his ministers,
are already able to perceive the imminent punishment. But this is the ongoing
obstacle: their responsibility for the imminent catastrophe prevents them from
acknowledging their sins and mending their ways. They refuse to acknowledge
the truth that they already know; to the contrary, they respond with rage against
the critics who accuse them. Unusual courage is therefore required of all the
prophets: the courage to endanger themselves and to sound their truth as
ultimatum and warning. They have to see this as their holy duty, and as long
as it seems to them that there is a possibility to rescue the nation by means of
repentance, they have to continue with their rebuke and warning.

Prophecy between Warning and Consolation

This is the source of the tragic basis to the poetry of the prophets. It reflects
the nation's expected disaster in the personal disaster of the prophets who
anticipate the disaster of the nation and exemplify it. In such moments, the
prophecy, which rages against the nation, turns into prayer and supplication and

asking for compassion—for the prophets themselves and for the nation with whose expected suffering they identify, the signs of which suffering are already revealed and laid bare. Only after the expected destruction takes place in all its terror, and the nation returns with complete *teshuvah* and acknowledges that the prophets are right, can the prophets sound their prophecies of wondrous consolation from out of the depths of their grief.

> The people that walked in darkness have seen a brilliant light.
> On those who dwelt in a land of gloom
> Light has dawned.
> (Isaiah 9:1)

We have before us another example of the poetics of prophetic poetry: the polarized opposition in the passage between extreme conditions of existence, where comparisons between them makes the depth of their experiential significance perceptible: light and darkness, despair and hope, rebuke and consolation, rancor and consolation. The basic opposition embodied in the prophetic experience is accentuated in this way: the transition from the mythic plane of reality, from which comes the inspiration for the prophetic vision, to the plane of history, in which the prophet is bound to fulfill his mission in order that his people see his vision and share it with him, both when the prophet expresses his penetrating rebuke with the threat of punishment and when he expresses his consolation pervaded with happiness—a combination to be experienced in this world only as a dimension of the future, which symbolizes the divine eternity.

> Comfort, oh comfort My people,
> Says your God.
> Speak tenderly to Jerusalem,
> And declare to Her
> That her term of service is over,
> That her iniquity is expiated;
> For she has received at the hand of the Lord
> Double for all her sins.
> A voice rings out:
> "Clear in the desert
> A road for the Lord!
> Level in the wilderness
> A highway for our God!

Let every valley be raised,
Every hill and mount made low.
Let the rugged ground become level
And the ridges become a plain.
The Presence of the Lord shall appear,
And all flesh, as one, shall behold—
For the Lord Himself has spoken."

A voice rings out: "Proclaim!"
Another asks, "What shall I proclaim?"
"All flesh is grass,
All its goodness life flowers of the field:
Grass withers, flowers fade
When the breath of the Lord blows on them.
Indeed, man is but grass:
Grass withers, flowers fade—
But the word of our God is always fulfilled!"

Ascend a lofty mountain,
O herald of joy to Zion;
Raise your voice with power,
O herald of joy to Jerusalem—
Raise it, have no fear;
Announce to the cities of Judah:
Behold your God!
Behold, the Lord God comes in might,
And His arm wins triumph for Him;
See, His reward is with Him
His recompense before Him.
Like a shepherd He pastures His flock:
He gathers the lambs in His arms
And carries them in His bosom;
Gently He drives the mother sheep.
(Isaiah 40:1–11)

With its vivid pictorial images, this poem of consolation anticipates the transformation about to take place in creation with God's appearance as redeemer of His nation. The poem realizes it by means of the dramatic opposition between suffering from punishment for sins, which were already forgiven, and the joy of recompense—the intensity of which matches the pain experienced by the nation, a pain that goes beyond the limit of human endurance. The joy of recompense is symbolized by transformations in creation, which is now freed from the evil that permeated it, to become worthy of God's beneficial presence. "The glory of the Lord" descends upon creation from the heights and the earth becomes a place proper for God's residence, like the eternal heaven from which the glory emanates. But the words are said in visionary pictures, which are boldly expressed by means of sensible intensification of words, which activate the visionary sense of those who hear the prophet. The intensity of their expression is created by their rich tone and dramatic, rhythmic movement, which describe the transformation underway in images belonging to the collective visionary memory of exiles who have been uprooted from their land, whose trauma of uprooting still agitates them.

To summarize: on the basis of what has been said, let us distinguish between two basic stances of the prophet before God and before the nation, and between two essential motifs in his message. (1) The first stance is the position of the prophet before the people as a messenger of God. (2) The second is the position of the prophet before God as a representative of the nation. In his stance as a messenger of God, the prophet tells the truth which God places on his lips, without considering the reaction of his people. As a representative of the nation, he prays both for himself as a messenger and for the nation whose pains he suffers in a very intense way. By doing so, he represents the people before the One who sends him, whose strict judgment exceeds the limit of human endurance. As to the essential motifs of his message, the intention is to give pronouncement to rage and rebuke over the sins of the nation in order to stir repentance, and to offer words of hope and consolation when punishment comes, measure for measure.

The poetics of the prayer of the prophet is exemplified in the *siddur*, and we have pointed to it in detail in the framework of the substantive and poetic analysis of the *Shemoneh Esrei* prayer. We have seen that this prayer is a checkered combination of quotations from the prayers of prophets—in particular, Moses, Isaiah, and Jeremiah. The poetics of the mission is divided around its essential motifs: pronouncement of rebuke and song of consolation. The poetics of these two genres of poetic rhetoric is the openness to the inspiration of the vision, which God reveals and pronounces to the prophet. The openness is to the point of filling his soul and its ascent in the flight of its thought, of determining the soul's will, and the excitement of its feelings to the point that the prophet's will is made as the will of his God, his thought as the thought of God, and his feelings about his people akin to God's feelings about him.

As said above, these words are not to be interpreted as a mystical identification of the prophet with divinity itself, nor as the suppression of the prophet's will, thought, and feeling by means of the force of the will, thought, and feeling of the God who sends him. The prophet does not erase himself before his God; rather, he dedicates himself of his own will. He functions as a "servant of God" in the lofty, positive sense of service in the Torah—as commitment that has the character of a voluntarily accepted mission. This is the status of Eliezer, the servant of Abraham, and that of Moses, who is called "servant of God." In practice, it means that the prophet functions as a mediator who represents God before the people to whom he is sent. But at the same time, he is one of the people—a mediator (medium) representing his people's suffering to God, throughout his destined life as a messenger. Insofar as he has assumed the thankless role—both in terms of what God demands of him, and in terms of his people's attitude toward him—he has acquired for himself the right to quarrel and remonstrate with his nation; even at times to quarrel with his God. This quarrel takes place because of his feelings flowing from the life-experiences imposed by God upon His people who endure expectations and demands that go beyond the limit of the ability of flesh-and-blood humans—including that of fine and good individuals who have demonstrated their desire to do God's *mitzvot*. The prophets' great, essential, and exemplary contribution to the world of prayer flows from that multi-faceted position, for they know how to establish their merit before their creator, and to achieve what they seek in their prayer, not only by merit of their righteousness, but by merit of the duty to which God binds them with their sacrifice. And they know how to represent their nation in their prayers, not only by merit of his being chosen as special by God, but by right of its suffering as the messenger of God among the nations.

The Prophet as Actor on the Stage of Life

The poetics of the prophetic "burden" (*massa'*, also "pronouncement") is, therefore, the poetics of the prophet's functioning as mediator between God and the people and between the people and their God. As mediator, the prophet embodies in his personality, and reflects in his word, the event of God's revelation to him, and the vision he has seen, which has been directly inspired by God. The meaning of this definition becomes clear through the prophet's total commitment to his mission. It is not only about his will, his thought, and his feeling, but rather, as said, about his entire personal, familial, and public life. In his function as mediator of God, the prophet turns into a tragic actor who plays his role on the stage of life itself, as if his entire private and public life were a metaphor that realized and represented the destiny of his nation on the stage of life itself. Through this, he reveals to his people the divine rationale, which determines their destiny. The first demonstration of the prophet's use of his personality as a medium of his mission is, again, provided in the first revelation to Moses before the burning bush. God gives Moses the signs he requested, by demonstrating them on Moses himself. Moses is compelled to recoil from his staff, which turned into a snake, and to remove the leprosy on his hand, which he placed into his chest (Exodus 4:6–8). Anyone who looks into this wonder is forced to understand that it is not Moses who performs these signs, but God, who uses Moses as an actor on the stage of life, to prove that He sent Moses to His people.

The use which God makes of the prophet with the prophet's agreement, as a medium for realizing God's intention, may be learned from the shocking event in which God prevails over Moses to return to Egypt. Apparently, Moses returns to fulfill his mission, but in truth he is as someone returning to his home and relatives with his wife and son because the force of the circumstances compelling him to flee to the desert had subsided. Suddenly, on the border between the desert and the land of Egypt, God threatens to have Moses killed—until Zipporah reconsiders, cuts off their eldest son's foreskin, and casts it at her husband Moses's feet. With this, she acquires Moses as a "bridegroom of blood" for herself. By doing so, she atones for Moses's sin and redeems his soul (Exodus 4:19–26).

The event is destined to prepare Moses for the mission he is commanded to carry out, with all its dangerous implications. He does not return home to be in the bosom of his family. He is deprived of his privacy, and from then on he will live as a representative mediator between God and His nation (the firstborn son of God), and God and Pharaoh (whose resistance will be broken only when God will kill Pharaoh's firstborn). Moses is therefore required to dispatch his wife and son, and to commit himself totally to his mission. And again, it should be said that the substance of Moses's appearance before his people and before Pharaoh and his magicians—when the staff of God in his hands, demonstrating the signs—delivers the principal part of the message, while his words mediated by his brother Aaron are subordinate to it.

These words, said with regard to Moses, pertain also to the appearance of all the prophets who arose after him. Their consecration deprives them of their privacy. More precisely: the consecration also transforms their most intimate privacy—expressed in their relations with their wives and children—into symbols, which reflect the destiny determined by God for His people. Let us recall here the most outstanding events—for example, Isaiah's using his wife the prophetess and the sons born to him as symbols; the redemption by the prophet Jeremiah of his uncle's field at the eve of the nation's exile from its land; the story of the tragic love relations between the prophet Hosea and his unfaithful wife which symbolize the tragic relations between God and His people; and finally, the amazing deeds which Ezekiel is commanded to perform, in order to concretize God's judgment of the exiled people.

Along with this, what stands out in this discussion is the difference between the "earlier prophets" (especially Samuel, Elijah, and Elisha) and the "later prophets," who are the literary prophets. The essential mission of the former is embodied in their deeds, whereas the essential mission of the latter prophets is embodied in the verbal utterances which they committed to writing as a living testimony existing for the generations. From this perspective, their prophecy continues Moses's prophecy, the essence of which is embodied in his Torah that he committed to writing as a scribe—so that any time the Torah's words are recited for the people to hear and to have them understand, the Torah is given to the nation as a present-day gift forever, renewed in all the compelling intensity of its veracity.

As such, the *siddur* uses the written words of Moses and the prophets who came after him in three principal ways. (1) First, it contains the portions of the Torah of Moses that are recited with their melodious accentuation during the public reading of the Torah on Sabbaths and holidays. It will be recalled that, from the ceremonial-symbolic perspective, this is the event in which the covenant between Israel and God, based upon Moses's Torah, is renewed from Sabbath to Sabbath and from holiday to holiday. (2) The *siddur* also contains chapters of prophecy, which are chanted with all their accents as Haftarot to portions of the Torah. Through this, the prophets' application of the word of Torah to the reality of their time is demonstrated. (3) Third, the *siddur* weaves the words of Moses and the prophets, which were said to God in the nation's name, into the prayers themselves. We have seen this in the blessings accompanying the *Keriyat Shema* and in the *Shemoneh Esrei*.

16

The Poetry of the Psalms: Personal-Soulful and Societal-Political Messages

The Psalms—Prayers before the Siddur Came to Be

The book of Psalms is the first book of prayers of the nation of Israel. Most of its hymns are attributed to David, as individual prayers which he composed, sang, and prayed as the holy spirit rested upon him, following different events in his history as king of his nation. According to that tradition of oral Torah, the Levites combined David's hymns, along with additional hymns attributed to several other authors before and after King David, with the sacrificial worship in the Jerusalem Temple. This testimony affirmed the story of the patriarchs of the nation, its prophets, and kings: individual prayer to God when the opportunity offered was acceptable among the people from the days of the patriarchs. It follows that the book of Psalms represents an ancient literary tradition, which is preserved and transmitted from generation to generation in various collections that were arranged and finally unified in the canonical book.

We may derive from the historical narratives of the books of Judges, Samuel, and Kings that the tradition of the hymns of prayer was passed on by two sorts of societies in particular. (1) The Levites, who served in the Tabernacle, and thereafter in the Jerusalem Temple and perhaps also at the local shrines where the people offered sacrifices to God during the First Temple era. (2) The "sons of prophets" who "prophesized" in song, melody, and dance. The tradition of prayer and prophecy also continued in the synagogues that Babylonian exiles established after the destruction of the First Temple. With the return to Zion in the days of Ezra and Nehemiah, this tradition returned to the Land of Israel and became established in Second Temple worship, and also in synagogues, which were built in the land in places far from Jerusalem.

The hymns called psalms thus constituted the primary source for the tradition of the prayer, which was subsequently institutionalized in the *siddur*. But one cannot define the book of Psalms itself as a prayer book comparable to the *siddur*, for it is arranged into five books corresponding to the five books of the Torah, and not according to the order of regular Temple worship. In other words: the book at our disposal in its canonical form is a literary collection of prayers, which are designated by scholars of oral Torah as optional prayers. They express the needs, requests, feelings, and reflections of the individuals, communities, and the people in coping with the trials of their lives at times of distress and pain, of crying out and supplicating; and in times of joy, celebration, exultation of the spirit, and thanksgiving. As in the First Temple era, so too in the Second Temple, the hymns of the book of Psalms were woven into the order of regular worship. By doing so, however, the distinction was not erased between the "worship" (*avodah*) of sacrifices and offerings, which happened regularly, each morning, afternoon, and evening, and the hymns of the Psalms as optional prayers. By themselves, the latter do not belong to "worship of God" according to His commandment, but rather to the category of free expressions of human beings. Thus, even though they are woven into the regular prayers of the *siddur*, they do not, in practice, belong to halakhic requirement, but to custom (*minhag*).

The distinction between regular prayer and optional prayer invited individuals whose souls yearned for the living God and who thirsted for prayer, those who chose the path of the fear of Heaven and devoutness, to increase prayer, whether as individual option or in the synagogue. These individuals regarded the book of Psalms as a sort of *siddur* of optional prayers. In this way, the custom of reciting the Psalms in order, daily and weekly, which spread among the people until today, acquired legal definition. As the need to increase prayer and to be scrupulous about it spread among the people, it was satisfied by adding psalms and collections of psalms, such as the *Pesukei Dezimra* (verses of song) at the beginning of *Shaharit*; saying the "psalm of the day" at the conclusion of the *Shaharit* prayer; the psalms of *Hallel* recited on the holidays commemorating miracles; and the hymns of *Kabbalat Shabbat* (welcoming the Sabbath) to the regular prayer service of the *siddur*. In this way, many of the hymns in the book of Psalms became part of the permanent prayer, because the power of custom that was institutionalized as "ancestral tradition" was even greater than the power of halakhic requirement. However, even the inclusion of psalms in the regular service of the *siddur* did not blur the difference between prayers in the category of obligatory worship and prayer as the worshipper's soulful need, categorized usually as spontaneous "pouring out the heart" of individuals and even the congregation, at times of sorrow and times of joy.

The Artistry of the Poetry of Praise

The name *Tehillim* ("Psalms" or, literally, "praises"), which is the title of the book, has been chosen because most of its hymns are classified in terms of their content and form as songs designed to tell the praise (*tehillah*) of God as loving king and father of compassion and mercy, in order to find favor in His eyes and be worthy of His nearness, protection, and grace. The praise of God, as said, is the overall subject of the hymns in the book, even though the rest of the subjects about which the worshipper praises God is also included in it. From the literary-artistic perspective, the texts collected in the book are songs, which in terms of the art of the song and melody are defined as *mizmorim* (hymns). This classification emphasizes the musical quality of the songs from the perspective of the textual language; from the perspective of the rhythmic tone and balance; from the perspective of accord between the linguistic text and the vocal melody; and from the perspective of accompaniment by musical instruments in accord with each melody— because a melody fits the words of each song, and the accompaniment of each musical instrument fits each melody, and these are cited at the head of every hymn as technical instruction to be carried out. But the traditions which preserved the melodies and the original musical instruments were lost with the destruction of the Second Temple.

From the artistic viewpoint, the hymns are a select genre of poetic artistry in its perfected form that is varied, and the most complete in terms of accord between the content and form. Their goal is to express and provide cathartic and elevating relief to one's existential feelings and deepest reflections. They arise out of soulful attachment between a person and his relatives, friends, and compatriots; between the person and the universe around him, and between the person and God—the creator of the world, and the creator who breathed His spirit into the human being—who is the hidden presence behind all His creations, and within the human soul. As such, God simultaneously disappears into the greatest distance, and is felt as most near. He is the most external entity, and also the most internal—on whom creation depends, and by whom it is renewed. For this, God is glorified—and not only on the lips of the human being, for all of His creatures praise Him with the essence of their existence.

The name of the book, *Tehillim* (praises), is explained by this premise. For the sake of understanding the poetics of its hymns, it is proper to emphasize that their poetry is anchored in the inspiration whose source is in God, in terms of the reverberation of the silent effulgence which flows from Him and renews the life of the soul that God has breathed into the human being. The hymns of Psalms define the inspiration which stirs the soul to rejoice and to sing like the holy spirit that rests upon the poet or throbs within him. This definition makes clear the difference between the song of prophecy and the psalms. Prophecy is the direct speech of God to the human being, while the psalms arise out of a surge of feeling that reveals the ever-pure divine essence hidden inside the soul. Usually, only God knows the hidden depths of the soul. To the human being they only become known at the moments when the poetic wave rises with a longing to return to the divine source and is poured out before God as the weeping of purified sadness or of enthusiastic joy.

The ideational foundation of this understanding will be explained further. But this is the secret of the birth of the psalm in the poet's soul, and the secret of the rising wave of feeling, which culminates with the outpouring of the soul—as in the hymn of David when he was in the Judean desert:

> God, You are my God;
> I search for You,
> My soul thirsts for You,
> My body yearns for You,
> As a parched and thirsty land that has no water.
> I shall behold You in the sanctuary,
> And see Your might and glory,
> Truly Your faithfulness is better than life;
> My lips declare Your praise.
> (Psalms 63:2–4)

Thus the soul speaks to God in its yearning to be liberated from the captivity of its distresses, troubles, and physical pains. Here, the soul can also come to know itself as only God knows it.

> O Lord, You have examined me and know me.
> When I sit down or stand up You know it;
> You discern my thoughts from afar.
> You observe my walking and reclining,
> And are familiar with all my ways.
> There is not a word on my tongue
> But that You, O Lord, know it well.
> (Psalms 139:1–4)

Prayer as a Personal Response to Divine Providence

There are two theological premises at the foundation of the poetics of "outpouring of the soul" before God as the human being's response to the call of God. The first premise is anchored in the prophetic experience. The fact that God reveals Himself to human beings to command them testifies that God exercises providential care over His world, and principally over human beings, and among them especially over the people of Israel and each individual Jew—insofar as they have accepted His *mitzvot* upon themselves and anchored their obligation to serve Him in the covenant of Torah. Obviously, this premise makes prayer possible not only as "service" (*avodah*), which is needed by God ("higher need," *Menaḥot* 64a), but as the embrace, which is needed by the person.

The concept of "providence" presupposes that God, as creator, knows all His creations and wills what is good for them. But God's knowledge and will are not like the knowledge and will of the human being. With God, knowledge and will are "prior" to creation. God created His creatures by means of His knowledge (wisdom). We learn this from the book of Genesis, and it follows from that narrative that all parts of creation come to be what they are through God's knowledge of them, and through God's will that they would be such. The essential difference between the knowledge and will of God and the knowledge and will of the human being in terms of their roles also follows from this. God creates His creatures according to their need, and not His own need in the human sense of the concept of need. God does not lack anything and does not depend upon any source outside Himself. The single need that God satisfies for Himself with creation is like the needs of an artist who creates, where the emanation wells up from within him and expands outwardly to express him. This self-expression is a need in a sense opposite to that of lack, and it produces an additional positive need—that there should be another who receives the emanation, who will benefit from it, and will provide him feedback. In the positive sense the need is, therefore, the desire to give and not to take, and in its depth the need is for a disclosure of ability. We use the metaphor of the artist whose ability comes from divine inspiration, for, in practice, the ability to create is original and absolute only in God. Only God can give not only from Himself, but Himself, in order to create the other who lives for himself and is able to receive what is given to him, to appreciate it, and to rejoice over it.

With these words, we delve into the depths not only of the concept of the revelation of God to human beings, but also of the concept of the human response which expresses itself with praise of God. From God's perspective, praise is feedback, which attributes value to His creation as expression of His goodness and benevolence. Let us note that the judgments of "good" and "benevolent" pertain to objective valuation, only if the valuation is two-sided—from the side of the grantor and from the side of the recipient—so that the gift which the recipient receives enables him to reciprocate to the one who gave it to him, of himself, with a similar creative feedback. In other words: The creative giving is good to the giver because it is good to the recipient, and it is good to the recipient because it is good to the giver. This applies, first of all, to God's perspective in His relation with creation, but the two-sidedness of the relation makes this principle applicable to the human being as well. This is the deeper meaning of the praise which God expects from the human being. The human being feels that he expresses his entire self in the praise, and he thereby merits greatest closeness to God, who has given him his life and the creative potential that is embodied in it. In other words, as poetry and as creation, praise is by its nature the highest expression of life of the human soul.

The Providence Imparted by God to His Creation

In this way, God's providential care over His world is conceived as a model that human beings are commanded to emulate in their relations to the creatures of creation, insofar as human beings have been chosen to rule over other creatures for their good—even if human beings depend upon the other creatures for their own existence. There are implications to their mutual overlapping dependency, not only for understanding God's direct relation to all the creatures big and small which He created with specific intention for each, but also for the relations among the creatures themselves which exercise care for one another. From this perspective, the world is a hierarchy of mutual bonds between lower and higher creatures. The higher creatures oversee those beneath them, while the lower creatures serve those above them. We find that every creature in the world is overseen by God, whether directly or through creatures above it, and oversees those beneath it. In this way, they exist one for the other, and only in this way do they maintain God's intention for them to achieve well-being for themselves, but do so together according to the quality of righteousness, and not of one achieving at the cost of the other.

This hierarchy is described in the book of Genesis through the seven-day order of creation. The first creations are the heaven and the earth. The heavens, meaning firmament, provide purified and permanent material foundations for the higher world. The earth, meaning dry land, provides a soil-based foundation, neither pure nor permanent, for the lower world, permeated by chaotic powers opposed to the will of the creator who has imposed law and order upon them. But the two worlds are connected to each other through the sun, the moon, and the stars, which God fixed in the firmament of heaven to "rule" (to oversee in His name) over the earth; through the pure waters which God rains upon the earth to fructify it; through the wind with which God causes to blow over the earth to enliven its creations; and through the light and warmth of the sun which provide conditions for growth, development, and orientation on earth. Through all these means, the heavens and their retinue oversee the earth— while they testify that God created them and is exalted over them. They serve God when they fulfill their mission, and thereby justify their supremacy.

The story of creation points to the arrangement of its becoming, without explaining it. The book of Psalms reflects complete creation through the renewal of the cycle of its seasons, and thereby emphasizes the significance of the hierarchical relation between heaven and earth:

> For the Leader. A Psalm of David.
> The heavens declare the glory of God,
> The sky proclaims His handiwork.
> Day to day makes utterance,
> Night to night speaks out.
> There is no utterance,
> There are no words,
> Whose sound goes unheard.
> Their voice carries throughout the earth,
> Their words to the end of the world.
> He placed in them a tent for the sun,
> Who is like a groom coming forth from the chamber,
> Like a hero, eager to run his course.
> His rising-place is at one end of heaven,
> And his circuit reaches the other;
> Nothing escapes his heat.
> (Psalms 19:1–7)

We have before us a description in words, in voice, melody, and music; a depiction of reality speaking "voicelessly" through the appearance of objects of creation. Their appearance elucidates these objects much better than any narrative. Offered to us is the vision of the immediate presence of heaven and earth themselves. The poet of the psalm sees and hears the symbolic reality with the eye of his spirit and experiences its meaning. God oversees by means of the rule of heaven over earth—which the image of the sun travelling over the world symbolizes. Just as the sun illuminates the earth, God sees it; and just as nothing is hidden from the heat of the sun, nothing is hidden from divine judgment. Indeed, in the second half of this hymn, the sun symbolizes the Torah of God, which is the embodiment of divine providence itself—for providence illumines to the human being the moral path to the life of well-being and of honor upon the earth.

But the narrative of creation in the book of Genesis does not end with the general oversight of the relation between heaven and earth. It continues with a description of the hierarchical order among the creatures of the earth: the plants according to their species, animals according to their species, and the human being. Again, we find that with each one of them, the lower creature precedes in the order of creation the creatures made from it, which it bears and maintains. The plant species are nourished by the earth and by the rain which irrigates it, and they nourish the animals according to their species. The animals according to their species are nourished by vegetation, and by means of what grows from the earth and the rain. The human being, exalted above animals, is also like them, nourished by vegetation as well as by animals who also help him in working the land. In exchange, the human being rules over the plants and animals and bears responsibility that they should fructify, multiply, and satisfy all their needs. The human is commanded to work the land and guard it; similarly, the animals, which eat the plants, also spread their seeds and even benefit the land; and, similarly also, the plants fructify the earth (*adamah*), mother of all life, including the human being called by its name (*adam*).

Here too, the book of Psalms describes, in words and sentences of imagery and tone, the sights which are the sensory-emotional presence of the world itself for the poet who observes it from within it as part of it—although he is singular in the exceptional ability to know and to understand and to judge. "Bless the Lord, O my soul" (Psalms 104:1)—this is the singular opening, which lays the basis of the psalm of praise through the address of the "I" to its soul; that is, through the soul's gazing into itself in order to express the impression that God's creation impressed upon it and stirred excitement within it.

> Bless the Lord, O my soul;
> O Lord my God, You are very great;
> You are clothed in glory and majesty,
> Wrapped in a robe of light;
> You spread the heavens like a tent cloth.
> (Psalms 104:1–2)

This describes the discovery that arises from the reflection of the poet's seeing the external universe in the internality of the soul: the light of the sun symbolically "wraps" God's appearance in a "garment" which reveals Him in the world, and the soul feels God's presence behind this garment in God's relationship to the soul as part of God's creation.

> He sets the rafters of His lofts in the waters,
> Makes the clouds His chariot,
> Moves on the wings of the wind.
> He makes the winds His messengers,
> Fiery flames His servants.
> He established the earth on its foundations,
> So that it shall never totter.
> You made the deep cover it as a garment;
> The waters stood above the mountains.
> (Psalms 104:3–6)

But in the next verse, there is a change from the images of God's presence in the world to a direct turning to Him. From then on, the poem is the soul's response to God who reveals Himself to the soul in visions symbolizing His creation and oversight. It does so step by step, opening with visions of the sea and land, and continuing with animals, plants that nourish the animals, and the human who feels the blessing that flows from the presence of God and His ruling activity:

> They fled at Your blast,
> Rushed away at the sound of Your thunder,
> —Mountains rising, valleys sinking—
> To the place You established for them.
> You set bounds they must not pass
> So that they never again cover the earth.
> You make springs gush forth in torrents;
> They make their way between the hills,
> Giving drink to all the wild beasts;
> The wild asses slake their thirst.
> The birds of the sky dwell beside them
> And sing among the foliage.
> You water the mountains from Your lofts;
> The earth is sated from the fruit of Your work.
> You make the grass grow for the cattle,

And herbage for man's labor
That he may get food out of the earth—
Wine that cheers the hearts of men
Oil that makes the face shine,
And bread that sustains man's life.
The trees of the Lord drink their fill,
The cedars of Lebanon, His own planting,
Where birds make their nests;
The stork has her home in the junipers.
The high mountains are for wild goats;
The crags are a refuge for rock-badgers.
He made the moon to mark the seasons;
The sun knows when to set.
You bring on darkness and it is night,
When all the beasts of the forests stir.
The lions roar for prey,
Seeking their food from God.
When the sun rises, they come home
And couch in their dens.
Man then goes out to his work,
To his labor until the evening.
How many are the things You have made, O Lord;
You have made them all with wisdom;
The earth is full of Your creations.
There is the sea, vast and wide,
With its creatures beyond number,
Living things, small and great.
There go the ships,
And Leviathan that You formed to sport with.
All of them look to You
To give them their food when it is due.
Give it to them, they gather it up;
Open Your hand, they are well satisfied;
Hide Your face, they are terrified;
Take away their breath, they perish
And turn again into dust;
Send back Your breath, they are created,
And You renew the face of the earth.
May the glory of the Lord endure forever;

May the Lord rejoice in His works!
He looks at the earth and it trembles;
He touches the mountains and they smoke.
I will sing to the Lord as long as I live;
All my life I will chant hymns to my God.
May my prayer be pleasing to Him;
I will rejoice in the Lord.
(Psalms 104:7–34)

The psalm-hymn portrays the broad and vital picturesque canvas sheet, which presents the two sorts of oversight. (1) First is the direct oversight of God over all creatures of the universe, and over each one of them, small and large. (2) The second is the oversight of creatures one over the other. Also, the psalm testifies to the wisdom of God, who united His world with mutual bonds among His creatures. God the creator uses oppositions anchored in powers of chaos which permeate the earth, in order to create the inexhaustible richness of creations that compensate for one another's lacks. In this way, He changes chaos into totality, and confrontation into harmonious accord. The reflection of this totality in the soul, which imagines and feels, enables it to participate, as part of creation, in creation's poetry, which rises and breaks forth from all creatures of life. These sing without uttering words. The human soul responds also to the poetry of the silent sights, and gives voice to them in its poetry, with words that express observation and reflection in tone and music fraught with feeling—the source for which is the inspiration of the spirit that God breathes into the human being. In this way, the human soul adds its singular praise!

The Poem in Praise of Human Beings who Rule over the Creatures of the Earth

As we learned from Psalms 19, the hierarchy of the universe is the example that the Torah of God presents and interprets for human beings, as a model to be emulated in their domains. As creation is obedient to the laws which God implants in it, human regimes are commanded to obey the laws of the Torah, which God commands to humans and their societies, cultures, and domains. In this way, divine oversight expands in its orderly arrangement, and applies itself to relations between human beings, the creatures whom God has graced with free choice, in accordance with the wisdom they acquire by observing creation. For this reason, the law of God, singular for human beings, obliges them according to His commandment, but the law is not imprinted within them. The imprinting is to be made by them, as they internalize the law and identify it with their wisdom and will. This is a double charge: (1) upon the nation and the empires as collective entities, and (2) upon all individuals, individual families, and individual communities, each one separately. Insofar as each human individual is created in the image of God, he merits his own well-being for himself within the sphere of family, congregation, and nation, and is commanded to choose his own good, proper to him, within all the spheres of his relations. Expressed in this way is the response of the nations and of all their families, communities, and individuals to the singular oversight of God which applies to them. In this way, an interpersonal societal and political hierarchy of moral oversight is also created. It is based upon covenants, whose primary example is the covenant that God made with Noah and his children, to observe their seven commandments and thereby accept the sovereignty of God. In this way, God oversees all human beings. He oversees Israel especially, through the legislation of the Torah based upon the sacred Ten Commandments.

In light of all this, God's supervision over human beings in general and over Israel in particular can be identified with the law of the Torah, as is stated in the second half of Psalms 19 (of which the first half was cited above):

> The teaching of the Lord is perfect,
> Renewing life;
> The decrees of the Lord are enduring,
> Making the simple wise;
> The precepts of the Lord are just,
> Rejoicing the heart;
> The instruction of the Lord is lucid,
> Making the eyes light up.
> The fear of the Lord is pure,
> Abiding forever;
> The judgments of the Lord are true,
> Righteous altogether,
> More desirable than gold,
> Than much fine gold;
> Sweeter than honey,
> Than drippings of the comb.
> Your servant pays them heed;
> In obeying them there is much reward.
> Who can be aware of errors?
> Clear me of unperceived guilt,

And from willful sins keep Your servant;
Let them not dominate me;
Then shall I be blameless
And clear of grave offense.
May the words of my mouth
And the prayer of my heart
Be acceptable to You,
O Lord, my rock and my redeemer.
(Psalms 19:8–15)

In terms of content, the words in the psalm cited here are not a conceptual supplement to what is said in the Torah of Moses. In the Torah the words are from the mouth of God, while in the psalm they express understanding which emerges from human beings themselves. As such, they change from prophecy to prayer. Let us bring testimony from an additional psalm:

For the leader; on the *gittith*. A psalm of David.
O Lord, our Lord,
How majestic is Your name throughout the earth,
You who have covered the heavens with Your splendor!
From the mouths of infants and sucklings
You have founded strength on account of Your foes,
To put an end to enemy and avenger.
When I behold Your heavens, the work of Your fingers,
The moon and stars that You set in place,
What is man that You have been mindful of him,
Mortal man that You have taken note of him
That You have made him little less than divine,
And adorned him with glory and majesty;
You have made him master over Your handiwork,
Laying the world at his feet,
Sheep and oxen, all of them, and wild beasts, too;
The birds of the heavens, the fish of the sea,
Whatever travels the paths of the seas.
O Lord, our Lord, how majestic is Your name
Throughout the earth!
(Psalms 8:1–10)

This psalm is the hymn of praise to God placed on the lips of human beings, to thank God for the status He bestowed upon them to be rulers of the creatures of the earth. When human beings lift their eyes above and compare themselves, in their physical smallness, to the celestial bodies which rule over the powers of earthly creation, they know that they are not worthy of the honored status which God emanates upon them with His blessing: "Be fertile and increase, fill the earth and master it; and rule the fish of the sea, the birds of the sky, and all the living things that creep on earth" (Genesis 1:28). The continuation of the hymn relates directly to this verse. But the recital of thanks and praise to God for His lofty benevolence comes to justify the status of the human in the world, because it proves that human beings are destined to this height by merit of their true superiority—their soul, which God breathed into them. By merit of this soul, the human being knows God and becomes a partner in the dialogue with God. In this way, the hymn of praise to God who oversees His people is made into a hymn of praise to human beings, whom God has promoted to oversee themselves and the earthly world beneath them.

What message then, emerges from the praise of the humble human being who knows how to praise God? We discover it in the closing of the psalm, which repeats the opening phrase: "O Lord, our Lord, How majestic is Your name throughout the earth" (Psalms 8:10). The praise of God at the close of the psalm adds to the praise expressed in the beginning. At the opening of the poem the poet, who represents the human being, beholds the praise of God's name in the revelations of creation which state His praise without saying so in words. At the close, the poet adds the praise of the human being expressed in the poem to the praise derived from the sight of creation. By doing so, the poet testifies to the greatest benevolence of all, in which God sets His human creature apart, preferring him even over the heavens and all their hosts—the trait of spirit, which God has breathed into the human being from His spirit. It is the trait of speech that commands and creates, in which God is praised over all creatures of creation. By means of this trait, the human becomes God's partner in dialogue. With these words, the psalm gives the answer to its own riddle: what makes the small and (physically speaking) ephemeral creature greater than the heavens, the moon, and the majestic eternal stars? Answer: the spirit of speech, which God has implanted in the human beings, by means of which God has made him ruler of the creatures of the earth—not above them, but rather from within them!

"Though the wicked sprout like grass" (Psalms 92:8). The Question of the Justice of Providence in the Psalms

The oversight ability, which God grants to the human being as ruler over the creatures of the earth, can be identified as an expression of the special providence of God over the human being who, in God's name, oversees the creations of the earth. But how is God's unique oversight of the humankind actually known? This question has distressed especially those believers who are loyal to God's Torah, those who stand humbly before Him, ready to observe His *mitzvot* at all times. Their faith is strengthened as they consider the wisdom of creation and they reflect the poetry of creation in their song, which utters praise of the creator. But their life experience as humans in the creation itself, and more so in the society of their species, places them before another reality—the reality of malice and evil which annul the Torah of God and upset the moral, societal, and political order, and transform it into tyrannical evil. This reality appears to contradict the belief that God sees, oversees, and rules His earthly world, as He rules the eternal heavens.

This chastising difficulty is the perplexing problem in the book of Psalms. It seeks to resolve it in such a way as to maintain belief in the oversight of God over His world and human society, by explaining the hidden wisdom in God's way of leading His creation to its good goal. Let us bring one of the best-known psalms included in the *siddur*, which offers a solution to this difficulty:

A psalm. A song; for the sabbath day.
It is good to praise the Lord,
To sing hymns to Your name, O Most High,
To proclaim Your steadfast love at daybreak,
Your faithfulness each night
With a ten-stringed harp,
With voice and lyre together.
You have gladdened me by Your deeds, O Lord;
I shout for joy at Your handiwork.
How great are Your works, O Lord,
How very subtle Your designs!
A brutish man cannot know,
A fool cannot understand this:
Though the wicked sprout like grass,
Though all evildoers blossom,
It is only that they may be destroyed forever.
But You are exalted, O Lord, for all time.
Surely, Your enemies perish;
All evildoers are scattered.
You raise my horn high like that of a wild ox;
I am soaked in freshening oil.
I shall see the defeat of my watchful foes,

Hear of the downfall of the wicked who beset me.
The righteous bloom like a date-palm;
They thrive like a cedar in Lebanon;
Planted in the house of the Lord,
They flourish in the courts of our God.
In old age they still produce fruit;
They are full of sap and freshness,
Attesting that the Lord is upright,
My rock, in whom there is no wrong.
(Psalms 92:1–15)

The psalm argues with the evil ones, who are sure that their pseudo-achievements—their wealth, riches, sensual comforts—in themselves devoid of meaning and ephemeral, demonstrate that there is no divine oversight. The land is given over to the powerful, the cunning, the cruel, because might over one's fellow is right. The poet, who represents the pious ones, knows that they too are dumbfounded and perplexed by the success of the evil ones and they suffer at their hand. Where is the rule of God's justice in creation, if precisely those who violate His *mitzvot* appear to be happy, while those who observe them are persecuted and oppressed? But the poet is firm, not only in his faith in God, but in the superiority of his spiritual well-being which is ongoing and not ephemeral. His inspired wisdom shows him the hidden future, already in the depths of the present; but it is open to anyone knowing his creator's intention and the vision that God strives to realize. The poet understands what is hidden from the superficial and short-sighted wicked ones. They see only what their cravings show to them and fall into the trap which God, who oversees His world for the good, sets for them. How? The poet compares evil ones to the wild grass, which grows in the fields that are plowed and sowed by diligent workers of the land to grow nourishment from them. The rain, which God lets fall on the land, is intended for growing good seeds, but in practice it also nourishes bad grass, the wild grass that competes with the good plants and steals their nourishment—the seeds whose source is in the powers of chaos, which are still infiltrating the land. But diligent workers of the land know how to utilize the wild overgrowth and to uproot the wild grass at the root, so that it will not scatter its seeds and not grow in the coming seeding cycle. Likewise, God grows the evil ones through the blessing He bestows upon His creatures in general and upon human beings in particular. But when their evil seeds are disclosed, God punishes them justly and pulls them out at the root. From this comes the assurance that the day will come when all the seeds of evil, which curse the land, will be destroyed. The land will return to be the primordial Garden of Eden—even more, a Garden of Eden in which there is no wild grass, no tree of wickedness, and no snakes. This is the "Psalm for the Sabbath Day," the day that symbolizes the eternal future towards which God strives in His war against evil, with the help of human beings, until it disappears.

To conclude, let us present another psalm representing the idea of providence, in its collective dimension:

Sing forth, O you righteous, to the Lord;
It is fit that the upright acclaim Him.
Praise the Lord with the lyre;
With the ten-stringed harp sing to Him;
Sing Him a new song;
Play sweetly with shouts of joy.
For the word of the Lord is right;
His every deed is faithful.
He loves what is right and just;
The earth is full of the Lord's faithful care.
By the word of the Lord the heavens were made,
By the breath of His mouth, all their host.
He heaps up the ocean waters like a mound,
Stores the deep in vaults.

Let all the earth fear the Lord;
Let all the inhabitants of the world dread Him.
For He spoke, and it was;
He commanded, and it endured.
The Lord frustrates the plans of nations,
Brings to naught the designs of peoples.
What the Lord plans endures forever,
What He designs, for ages on end.

Happy the nation whose God is the Lord,
The people He has chosen to be His own.
The Lord looks down from heaven;
He sees all mankind.
From His dwelling-place He gazes on all the inhabitants of
the earth –
He who fashions the hearts of them all,
Who discerns all their doings.

Kings are not delivered by a large force;
Warriors are not saved by great strength;
Horses are a false hope for deliverance;
For all their great power they provide no escape.
Truly the eye of the Lord is on those who fear Him,
Who wait for His faithful care
To save them from death,
To sustain them in famine.
We set our hope on the Lord,
He is our help and shield;
In Him our hearts rejoice,
For in His holy name we trust.
May we enjoy, O Lord, Your faithful care,
As we have put our hope in You.
(Psalms 33:1–22)

This poem is a look into the past from a certain present in the history of humankind and the nation. It surveys the story of creation, the history of humankind, and the history of Israel among the nations up to the present. Do these offer support to the belief in divine oversight? Are the nation of Israel among the nations, human beings among the living creatures, and all of earthly creations, coming closer to their destiny? The children of Israel, who suffer from the evil of idolatrous nations, are liable to err and think that God left the land and does not oversee it. The psalm therefore repeats and asserts firmly: God looks down upon the world from the great height of His residence in heaven. From there he sees not only the totality. As creator, He knows His creatures individually and from the inside, and judges them, not only according to their open deeds, but also according to their thoughts which are hidden from the sight of others. The poet who knows God knows that He distinguishes between the righteous and the wicked. The poet knows that the power of the wicked is as nothing as compared to God's power to punish them in accordance with their wickedness, while rewarding the pious according to the extent of their piety. The evil ones brazenly ignore this truth, and can do so as long as God lets them thrive in their foolishness, while He prepares their future fall. The pious know the truth and act according to it. They are not seduced and do not behave like the evil ones; they are not jealous of their ephemeral good fortune. It is a test for the pious, and they pass it, and this is the secret of their strength. For even in their suffering, their faith and trust in God is not only their refuge for the coming future, but their wellbeing in the present, for they know that God is with them. "We set our hope on the Lord, He is our help and shield; in Him our hearts rejoice."

The end of the poem changes the gaze infused with faith into praise and prayer. Faith that trusts in divine oversight is not only the basis for the assumption that God expects prayer, hears it and wants to respond to it. Rather, faith is the foundation for the worshipper's feeling that the authority given him to stand before God, to praise Him, and ask for His blessing, is the fulfilled promise of certainty that God hears his cry, and that His hearing anticipates the salvation which is about to come.

The Superiority of the Human Being as a Developing Creature

Let us return to Psalms 8, which describes the status of human beings in the universe. Beyond the explanation of the meaning of the creation of the human in God's image, its message as a song of praise should be examined. We saw how the psalm praises the human being for his humility before God. His humility raises him, because by means of it, God's relationship with him is made into a model to be emulated in the human being's relationship with earthly creation—which humans were chosen to rule over in God's name, even though they are small and ephemeral creatures. Surely they are supported by greatness of God, which simultaneously changes into the greatness of human beings into whom God breathes His spirit. And if so, the greatness of human beings is also expressed in overseeing creatures of creation smaller than they are, for their good. Just like the God who rules in heaven and earth, human beings are to serve those ruled by them who are beneath them—and not to enslave them for his needs. But precisely in this way, human needs are also satisfied in a correct way, bringing about well-being. This complex thought is expressed in the opening of the psalm, which states that the climax of God's greatness is not the creation of heaven and earth and all their hosts, but precisely the fact that "From the mouths of infants and sucklings You have founded strength" (Psalms 8:3). These are the weakest of all creatures, who need love, compassion, and protection until they reach independent status and rule over their lives and what surrounds them. How is one to "have founded strength" from the mouths of the weakest of all creatures, against the strong evil ones who revolt against the ordinances of God and violate His Torah? In what way are the weakest creatures similar to the heavens, which obey God's will and express His glory and the splendor of His rule? The answer to this question lies in the comparison between nurslings and infants, for whom only God's special oversight assures life, growth, and development; and the human species which is counted among the small and weak animals whose nurslings are the weakest and most lacking among all animals. Precisely because of this, God has chosen to "have founded strength" in the weakest creatures.

The psalm points to this comparison without explaining its message. But it is sufficiently explained by the spiritual power exhibited by the hymn. Focus on this: God chose the human being to be His partner in dialogue, because only the human being speaks, intellectualizes, reflects, understands, and knows how to speak the praise of his creator. This is the matter when it comes to the humility in expressing the human being's spiritual ability to evaluate himself in relationship to God and to creation—the ability to know, understand, compare, choose, evaluate, honor, and rule. Unlike all creatures of creation, including heaven, the moon, and stars, the human being, like the babes and infants, is not permanently at the level at which he is born as a physical being. Rather, he keeps in store the attribute for growth, to develop spiritually, to become wise, and to create. With these, his spirit rises to heaven above with all its hosts, and the human being's creativity advances the creation he was chosen to rule. In this way, the babes and infants symbolize the advantage of the human being, as the hope for the future is embodied in them.

The Advantage of the Human Being as Bearer of Spiritual Soul

The second anthropological premise of the Psalms is included in the doctrine of the soul that was adopted from the Pentateuch, but greatly expanded and deepened. The centrality of the doctrine of the soul in the Pentateuch is emphasized in narratives and in commandments concerned with the relation between God and the human being, whether in terms of instruction and education, or in terms of worship. As said, according to the story of creation, all living creatures that walk upon the earth are graced with soul, which is the power of life that pulsates within them in the form of the blood streaming through their veins. The soul is identified with the blood and the beating of the heart, which discharges the blood through the veins. It is the internal mover, which brings out the energy of life that activates the body itself. As the narrative of creation continues, the scripture identifies the soul of animals explicitly with the blood, which streams through the veins of the body. This soul is physical, and its role is to activate all the organs of the body that are in charge of its activities: breathing, nourishment, growth, and reproduction.

Since the human being is also a physical animal, the soul that is identified with his blood is also active in him. But insofar as the human being is created in

God's image, he has been worthy of the additional gift: a spiritual soul, which comes from a higher source. This is the "spirit," which God breathes into the "nostrils" of the human being from His spirit. By means of this act, the human being not only breathes and wails like an animal, but speaks with words. That is, he knows, thinks, understands, and creates. The Torah does not explain how the spirit acts, or what the form of connection and accord between the spirit and the physical soul is. It is nevertheless clear that the spiritual soul is to rule the physical soul and that the physical soul is to serve the spiritual soul, whether by the virtue of its connection to the earthly environment, so that it can know and control it, or by directing the person (*ish*)—who is the unity of body and the soul—to comfortable existence, success, and well-being. From this perspective, body and soul depend upon one another. The success of either one of them means success for the other.

These words refer not only to attributes that define the human species in its entirety, but each individual human being. The spiritual attribute, which emanates from God's spirit, makes each individual conscious of his spiritual soul and of its source in the spirit of God. The individual thus stands before the one and singular God as an individual. From here comes the unique mission, which each human is to fulfill in his lifetime, and which he alone can fulfill. If he does not fulfill it, creation is found to be lacking. Accordingly, each person who reaches the height of knowing himself as bearer of a spiritual soul into which the spirit of God is breathed, and of knowing the moral and spiritual duty that follows from that height, becomes singular and, as said, is made into an individual (*ish*). He stands before God by his own authority and bears responsibility for himself. Let us recall here the statement of Eve upon the birth of her firstborn Cain: "I have gained a male child [*ish*] with the help of the Lord" (Genesis 4:1). In this capacity he is singular, unique, and irreplaceable. With this, we arrive at the depth of the human soul's superiority. In uniting with the erect body and with hands capable of artistic work, the soul elevates the singular humanness of each individual beyond its libidinal existence as an animal, to rise above the animals, to rule them, and become a partner in dialogue with God—who in relation to the soul is not only the king, but also the father who "gives birth" to the soul from His spirit.

This anthropology requires a division of roles between the soul and the body, although they cannot in reality be separated. For as long as the body is alive and serves the spiritual soul by expressing it through the body, they work together. It may be said that the mutual activity defines the essence of the "life" of the human being. Nevertheless, the relationship between the soul and the body is hierarchical. The soul initiates and directs, and the body carries out. Therefore, when the human body says "I," or when others say "you," the reference is to the soul, which is perceptible by means of the body that identifies it. The seed of the "I" as self-consciousness is indeed the spiritual soul that stands uniquely before God. The spiritual soul knows itself and its relation to the body and the world, on the one hand, and to God, on the other. But in this way, a problem is also created for the human being. This problem emerges from the duality of the soul and the body, which harbors the potential for conflict and contradiction. The body of the human being is, on the one side, the instrument suited to serve the spiritual soul. On the other, the body is an entity that has a life distinct from the life of the spiritual soul. The same is the case with the spiritual soul: it too has its independent life. The result is that the individual "I," which is the intellectual ability of the soul in its relationship to the body, does not know the body internally. The proof for this is that the voluntary rule of the human being over the limbs of the body is only partial. But since the spiritual soul is compelled to invest itself in guiding the physical soul in satisfying the needs of its body, it has to divert its attention from the full expanse of the spiritual life, which is bound to its divine source. Only God, creator of the body in His wisdom, who breathes the soul into the body from His spirit, knows them together and judges them together. The "I" discerns and sees what is hidden in the depths of the life of the body only externally, when its inclinations divert the body to activity opposed to the will of its spiritual soul; that is, only when the body "causes" the spiritual soul to "sin" and to turn aside from its true goal. The "I" knows the full depth of the soul only when the inspiration of the "holy spirit" generates the pride, which comes to expression in spiritual creativity: Torah, thought, poetry, and art. They constitute a mirror in which the intellectual "I" of the human being sees the depth of the soul that sustains it.

It is not surprising that these observations about the relations of the soul to the body and those of the physical soul to the spirit are not provided by the prophet, whose soul is filled with the word of God, and who bends his spirit and body to serve Him. Rather, we read about them in the psalms, which express the glory of the soul that the inspiration of the holy spirit generates from within:

> For the leader. Of David. A psalm.
> O Lord, You have examined me and know me.
> When I sit down or stand up You know it;
> You discern my thoughts from afar.
> You observe my walking and reclining,
> And are familiar with all my ways.
> There is not a word on my tongue
> But that You, O Lord, know it well.
> You hedge me before and behind;

You lay Your hand upon me.
It is beyond my knowledge;
It is a mystery; I cannot fathom it.
Where can I escape from Your spirit?
Where can I flee from Your presence?
If I ascend to heaven, You are there;
If I descend to Scheol, You are there too.
If I take wing with the dawn
To come to rest on the western horizon,
Even there Your hand will be guiding me,
Your right hand will be holding me fast.
If I say, "Surely darkness will conceal me,
Night will provide me with cover,"
Darkness is not dark for You;
Night is as light as day;
Darkness and light are the same.
It was You who created my conscience;
You fashioned me in my mother's womb.
I praise you,
For I am awesomely, wondrously made;
Your work is wonderful;
I know it very well.
My frame was not concealed from you
When I was shaped in a hidden place,
Knit together in the recesses of the earth.
Your eyes saw my unformed limbs;
They were all recorded in Your book
In due time they were formed,
To the very last one of them.
How weighty Your thoughts seem to me,
O God,
How great their number!
I count them—they exceed the grains of sand;
I end—but am still with You.

O God, if You would only slay the wicked—
Your murderers away from me!—
Who invoke You for intrigue,
Your enemies who swear by You falsely.
O Lord, You know I hate those who hate You,

And loathe Your adversaries.
I feel a perfect hatred toward them;
I count them my enemies.
Examine me, O God, and know my mind;
Probe me and know my thoughts.
See if I have vexatious ways,
And guide me in ways everlasting.
(Psalms 139:1–24)

"For there is not one good man on earth who does what is best and doesn't err" (Ecclesiastes 7:20)

In creating the human being as a combination of an animal body and the soul into which God breathed His spirit, God's intention was that the body should serve the spiritual soul and the spiritual soul should direct the body to what is good for the body. In doing so, one depends on the other: the human body does not live a human life without its soul, and the spirit cannot express itself by observing the world and creating new things without the body. But on the other hand, tension and conflict emerge from the tendency of the body and the soul to struggle for domination, and dictate longings and goals to each other. When the inclinations of the body overcome, the soul sins and is grieved. When the intellect and spirit overcome, they incite the sinful inclinations of the body to rebel. This is the problem of the human being, who is destined to bridge between the sphere of physical life and the sphere of spiritual life. From the time the human matures and becomes a full-fledged individual, his life is an inner struggle. The struggle extends to the entirety of his relations with other human beings and with creatures of nature, and necessarily also with God who created the man for the good. But he interprets his many lacks and deficiencies as intending to do him harm. Most human beings do not stand up to the trial, and individuals of quality who make the effort to do so are forced to sin from time to time inadvertently, or erroneously, or when their suffering goes beyond the level of their endurance. Therefore, the poet of the Psalms says at the conclusion of the psalm, most of which is cited above:

Who can be aware of errors?
Clear me of unperceived guilt,
And from willful sins keep Your servant;
Let them not dominate me;

Then shall I be blameless
And clear of grave offense.
(Psalms 19:13–14)

But sin lies in wait for every person. Whether inadvertently or in the face of great distress, even the completely pious will sin. "For there is not one good man on earth who does what is best and doesn't err."

Is there, then, a chance that humans will ever succeed in mending their sinful souls while still in the body that enables the soul to act in material reality? The Torah of Moses, as said, deals with that question by offering the act of atonement as a strategy that enables human beings to turn back from sin after they have committed it, and to wipe away their guilt. But at this point, one should pay attention to the fact that atonement does not annul the confrontation between the inclinations of the body and the physical soul. Therefore, atonement does not annul the conflict between the spiritual soul and the physical soul. For were it to do so, the atonement would annul God's intention in creating the human being as a composite creation—an animal body which enables coping with physical-material evils, and a soul emanated from God's spirit which enables restoration. Atonement, therefore, has the following intention: to save the soul, which is forced to cope with evil, from falling captive to the forces of chaos represented by the human being's inclination—which is "evil from his youth" (Genesis 8:21)—and to avert the danger that the human being, who is designated to rule over creation, would defect to the enemy host, who defines good as evil and evil as good, and commit himself to doing evil for its own sake. This is indeed the greatest danger, identified with idolatry. The people of Israel have arisen to conquer this danger, but they, too, were liable to be misled and to fall into its net.

Atonement in the Torah

As we saw, the book of Leviticus attributes central importance to atonement for sins. It erases their impression which defiled the soul of the sinner, in order to rescue the spiritual soul from falling captive to sin and wickedness. If the sins are not erased and prevented from accruing, they are liable to kill the human beings' spiritual souls and their adherence to the good. Even worse, the fall could blacken the soul and transform it into a snakelike, demonic power that adheres to wickedness for its own sake. This is why the book of Leviticus addresses primarily the souls of human beings and not their bodies. It even requires human beings to actually sacrifice their bodies in order to rescue their souls. From this perspective, it is the call of God to sinners to purify their souls and rescue them from death in the moral sense—which in God's eyes is worse than physical death. For this reason, the book of Levitius does not refer to those who study it with the name *ish, adam,* or *ben yisrael* (man, person, Israelite). Rather, it uses the term *nefesh* (soul). In chapter 1 *adam* is said once in order to emphasize that, like all the *mitzvot* of Torah, the *mitzvot* of the book of Leviticus are addressed specifically to the children of Israel: "Speak to the Israelite people and say to them: When any of you [*adam*] present an offering from the herd or from the flock" (Leviticus 1:2). In what follows, the text passes on to the relevant details, and then the term *nefesh* takes the place of the term *adam*: "When a person [*nefesh*] presents an offering of meal to the Lord" (Leviticus 2:1). Other times, the text skips the identification of the commanded individual by addressing him—that is, his soul—directly in "I–You" language: "When you present an offering of meal baked in the oven. . . . If your offering is a meal offering on a griddle" (Leviticus 2:4–5). This way of addressing hints that the "you" who is commanded to bring the sacrifice is the soul by itself, and not in combination with the body—because it is the soul that bears the guilt, is responsible, and requires atonement which only God can grant.

The same distinction is enunciated in the division of roles between the person who offers the sacrifice in his own name and the priest who carries out the sacrifice. The one who offers the sacrifice owns the sacrificial animal. He is commanded to give to God from the best of his possessions, but his active participation consists only in bringing the sacrifice to the Temple and confessing his sins by placing his hands upon the animal's head to symbolically transfer his sins from himself to the sacrificial animal. This action is essentially spiritual. The sacrificial act itself is performed by the priest who is required to sanctify his body and be careful about any kind of defilement coming from material physicality, which is permeated by powers of chaos. In this way the sacrifice is grasped as a symbolic activity. The animal, which is taken from the property of the one who brings the sacrifice, constitutes a symbolic exchange for his body, in the sense that the spiritual soul symbolically sacrifices its sinning body, and washes the blood of its sin. Thus God erases the sins and makes them as if they have never happened.

Sin and Repentance in the Poetry of the Psalms

This, then is the deeper meaning of the *mitzvah* of the sin and guilt sacrifices according to the book of Leviticus. What does the book of Psalms add to the procedure of atonement as described in the book of Leviticus? First, let us emphasize the parallels between the Psalms and Leviticus in how they address the person's soul, apart from the body. In Leviticus, as well as in the book of Psalms, the "I" which prays, discerns, judges, and chastises itself before God, is the spiritual soul which aspires to return to its original character. However, a difference emerges between the soul's stance before God in sacrificial service and its stance in prayer. Offering the sacrifice upon the altar is physical, whereas prayer is spiritual. In prayer, the soul offers itself by coming near to God. It separates itself from the ties to its body and from the influence of the body's inclinations, in order to remove the partition between itself and the spirit of God which enlivens it at its source. By means of this exaltation, the atonement, which God gives to the soul, receives a refined spiritual meaning. The essence of the atonement here is not that the sins are "washed" away with the blood of the sacrifice, but rather that the divine emanation is renewed: God purifies the soul by breathing it anew into the same body, which grants the soul its particular identity—a kind of second spiritual birth.

But the book of Psalms also deepens the understanding of the difficulty which prevents most human beings from turning back in repentance, ceasing their sins, and being redeemed while there is still time. The most difficult experience which humans undergo in their earthly life is their conviction that precisely sinners attain earthly well-being, while the righteous are persecuted and suffer. Most human beings come to doubt the existence of divine oversight or equity. If so, it is not only permitted, but even wise to take the path of sinners and to succeed as they do. Above, we have discussed the answer that the book of Psalms gives to the question about the source of wickedness in the earthly world. Even if this satisfies the mind of the pious questioners, it does not console their aching soul, and it does not dispel the sense of injustice. A consoling answer is found for them only through a deeper understanding of the harm incurred by the sinning soul on account of its sins. This understanding also releases knowledge that the suffering soul, which nonetheless does not divert from its goal, earns spiritual well-being— notwithstanding its physical suffering. Moreover, readiness to suffer without diverging from the righteous path and from the *mitzvot* of Torah increases the worthiness and well-being of the soul, despite the physical suffering.

The book of Psalms gives voice to these meditations about the substance of sin with full clarity. Its hymns illumine the path of the pious person who suffers, and infuses the intellect and reason with the understanding that the wicked who exult in their well-being are deceiving themselves most of all. The sinner's soul is corrupted to the point that it does not know itself. Therefore, it sees the true good as evil, and the evil as good. But this is the harshest of all the punishments that the sinful soul inflicts upon itself. So speaks the prophet Isaiah: "But the wicked are like the troubled sea which cannot rest, whose waters toss up mire and mud" (Isaiah 57:20). The psalms emphasize this truth already in the hymn that opens the book of Psalms:

> Happy is the man who has not followed the counsel of the wicked,
> Or taken the path of sinners,
> Or joined the company of the insolent;
> Rather, the teaching of the Lord is his delight,
> And he studies that teaching day and night.
> He is like a tree planted beside streams of water,
> Which yields its fruit in season,
> Whose foliage never fades,
> And whatever it produces thrives.
> (Psalms 1:1–3)

The danger lurking for the spiritual soul according to the prophets and the book of Psalms, is the adulteration and the perversion of its essence to the point of killing the soul, or its reversal into wickedness. Because of this, the greatest disclosure of God's providential care and benevolence for human beings is the escape hatch He opens for those who revere Him, by way of repentance and atonement. But for this, sacrifices and offerings in the Temple were not enough. Required here is the intention of the soul as expressed in taking responsibility for its sins and regretting them, along with the will to mend what sin perverts and to prevent its repetition. This is the source of the prophet's reservations about sacrifices. It is possible to transform sacrifices into routine and pleasurable activities (eating meat!) on the premise that God will forgive and expiate the sinners because He has been appeased with gifts that "satisfy" Him, as food satisfies the sinners' appetites. The sinners can then go back and sin, and then bring another sacrifice—over and over. In the opinion of the prophets, behavior like this is worshipping God as if He were an idol—and there is no greater sin than that!

Instead, the prophets offer the path of prayer as standing before God for judgment, which brings about repentance as expressed by good deeds that repair the damage caused by sins and justify atonement. But it is the psalms that have paved this path and bequeathed it to the people—to any individual who aspires to purify his soul and to redeem it from enslavement to its drives and from the feelings of guilt bound up with it. In the book of Psalms we find first of all the profound knowledge that the spiritual soul has its own independent life, a life that is not exhausted with intellectual knowing, but rather contains a depth of feeling. It is anchored in the connections of the soul to the body on one hand, and to God on the other—a depth that is not grasped by intellectual knowing. Only in this way can we rightly understand those expressions in which the psalmist distinguishes between the conscious "I" and the spiritual soul that speaks from its lips; or between the speaking "I" and the soul that sustains it—to the point where the "I" turns to the soul, asks it a question, listens to its explanation, argues with it, speaks in its name, or calms and consoles it:

> For the leader. A *maskil* of the Korahites.
> Like a hind crying for water,
> My soul cries for You, O God;
> My soul thirsts for God, the living God;
> O when will I come to appear before God!
> My tears have been my food day and night;
> I am ever taunted with, "Where is your God?"
> When I think of this, I pour out my soul:
> How I walked with the crowd, moved with them,
> The festive throng, to the House of God
> With joyous shouts of praise.
> Why so downcast, my soul,
> Why disquieted within me?
> Have hope in God;
> I will yet praise Him
> For His saving presence.
> O my God, my soul is downcast;
> Therefore I think of You
> In this land of Jordan and Hermon,
> In Mount Mizar.
> (Psalms 42:1–7)

The state of consciousness in which the "I" speaks in the name of its soul and about it, insofar as it views the soul as a being separate from itself, is emphasized where the poem expresses the outpouring of the soul. A wave of feeling, which the person does not foresee and cannot control, wells up from the depths beneath or from above, or from both at once. It brings up thoughts and experiences in the "I," which are formulated in words that the "I" did not think of or invent. Rather, they are "spoken" from within the "I," and the individual knows that they are his thoughts only after he has sounded them to his ears. It may be deduced from this that the spiritual soul by itself, in the depths of its secret place, is pure. Not only when it is in its divine source, but also after it is breathed into the body of a person and connected to his organs. This means that the sinner, as long as he knows and acknowledges that he sins, feels guilty, and is afraid of punishment, is pure in the depths of his soul which is still joined to its source in mystery.

Hiding the Face

This is, therefore, the hatch opened by God for the return of the soul to Him and to itself in repentance—of course, on the condition that the "I," which represents the soul in the body and determines its distinctive particulars, will awaken and recognize that the inner pure seed, which has survived in the soul, is its true self. Only through this awakening can the human being overcome the estrangement between himself and his God, and accept the renewed divine inspiration:

> A psalm of David.
> O Lord, hear my prayer;
> Give ear to my plea, as You are faithful;
> Answer me, as You are beneficent.
> Do not enter into judgment with Your servant,
> For before You no creature is in the right.
> My foe hounded me;
> He crushed me to the ground;
> He made me dwell in darkness
> Like those long dead.
> My spirit failed within me;
> My mind was numbed with horror.
> Then I thought of the days of old;
> I rehearsed all Your deeds,
> Recounted the work of Your hands.
> I stretched out my hands to You,
> Longing for You like thirsty earth. *Selah.*
> Answer me quickly, O Lord;
> My spirit can endure no more.
> Do not hide Your face from me,
> Or I shall become like those who descend into the Pit.
> Let me learn of Your faithfulness by daybreak,
> For in You I trust;
> Let me know the road I must take,
> For on You I have set my hope.
> Save me from my foes, O Lord;

To You I look for cover.
Teach me to do Your will,
For You are my God.
Let Your gracious spirit lead me on level ground.
For the sake of Your name, O Lord, preserve me;
As You are beneficent, free me from distress.
As You are faithful, put an end to my foes;
Destroy all my mortal enemies
For I am Your servant.
(Psalms 143:1–12)

The cruelty of the enemies who pursue the psalmist to oppress his soul is, in his eyes, a sign that his God is hiding His face from him. If so, he has surely sinned before God, and he does not try to deny this. While he is certain of God's justice, he is sure at the same time of God's love for him. For he is certain of his own love for God. They are two facets of the same love, and it is clear from this that the intention of God is not to punish him but to educate him and lead him back to the straight path from which he strayed in error—whether by forgetting or lack of understanding: "Teach me to do Your will, for You are my God" (Psalms 143:10). The psalmist acknowledges his sins before God, as a sinning son before his father. He testifies about himself that he has sinned, he did not intend to sin, for in the depth of his heart he did not turn from God in his love for Him. Here, the prayer that erupts from the depths of the soul testifies to the worshiper's original purity. Let us attend now to the fact that the psalmist's complaint does not relate to his physical suffering, but rather to the suffering of his soul. He accuses his enemies essentially for their desire to oppress his soul and to rob him of confidence in his faith. His soul is therefore in distress, so he is desolate, and he compares his soul to the desert around him. For his soul is, in his eyes, like "parched land," thirsting for water to revive it.

This, then, is the great danger lurking for the soul of the human being. Because of this he seeks the deliverance which affirms that God will not hide His face from him again. In another psalm, the poet affirms that sin is liable to transform human beings into the enemies of their souls, and this is the essential danger:

Who is the man who is eager for life,
Who desires years of good fortune?
Guard your tongue from evil,
Your lips from deceitful speech.
Shun evil and do good,

Seek amity and pursue it. . . .
The Lord is close to the brokenhearted;
Those crushed in spirit He delivers.
(Psalms 34:13–15, 19)

Salvation is first and foremost the very feeling of closeness of the certainty and the purification, which salvation pours into a soul that knows its source. So much so that

Happy is the man whom You discipline, O Lord,
The man You instruct in Your teaching,
To give him tranquility in times of misfortune,
Until a pit be dug for the wicked.
For the Lord will not forsake His people;
He will not abandon His very own.
(Psalms 94:12–14)

The same applies to the following psalm, which describes the sin that oppresses the soul:

Indeed You desire truth about that which is hidden;
Teach me wisdom about secret things.
Purge me with hyssop till I am pure;
Wash me till I am whiter than snow.
Let me hear tidings of joy and gladness;
Let the bones You have crushed exult.
Hide Your face from my sins;
Blot out all my iniquities.
Fashion a pure heart for me, O God;
Create in me a steadfast spirit.
Do not cast me out of Your presence,
Or take Your holy spirit away from me.
Let me again rejoice in Your help;
Let a vigorous spirit sustain me.
I will teach transgressors Your ways
That sinners may return to You.
Save me from bloodguilt,
O God, God, my deliverer,
That I may sing forth Your beneficence.
O Lord open my lips,

And let my mouth declare Your praise.
You do not want me to bring sacrifices;
You do not desire burnt offerings;
True sacrifice to God is a contrite spirit;
God, You will not despise
A contrite and crushed heart.
(Psalms 51:8–19)

These words express the substance of atonement for sins as viewed by the psalmist: the renewal of the soul from its source, the creation of the soul anew in its essential purity. Let us attend to the conclusion of the prayer cited above. In its conclusion, the poet represents the prayer as having its source in the divine inspiration, which has risen up through the channels of his soul. God also is the one who has opened the poet's lips to express what He has emanated to his soul, and this is the poet's praise. The defiled impression of sin is, as such, erased—as if God has replaced the soul that has sinned with a soul that has not sinned. Now that the "I"—identified here with his body—can, by this means, continue its life with a feeling of purity and hope that it will not again fail as it has failed before. Let us also attend to the last sentences of the prayer. They exchange the sacrifice of an animal, which symbolizes the body of the human being, with the voluntary offering of the human soul to God with regret ("contrite spirit") and deep sorrow over its sin ("crushed heart"). Through these, the soul "washes" itself in order to become pure and be worthy of the inspiration to come from God, which renews the "pure heart" in the body, and breathes the "steadfast spirit" into it.

The Psalms: Heralds of the Democratic Ritual Revolution of Prayer

Like the great literary prophets, the psalms do not annul the value of the sacrifices. Rather, the psalms accompany them and enable the assembly of Israel and its individuals to participate with song and prayer in the sacrificial ceremony performed by the priests. Clearly, from the perspective of the poets of the psalms and the pious who use the words of the psalms to pour out their souls before God, the prayer and the praise which are essentially an expression of gratitude that the prayer is heard and answered are most important. With this, a democratic-personal revolution in ritual consciousness comes to expression, shaped by the psalms themselves. This is a part of the emotional revolution, which sets the foundation for the development of prayer in the synagogue and the substitution for sacrificial worship.

Two central aspects of the ritual-democratic revolution are especially important for preparing the transition from sacrificial worship in the Temple to prayer worship in the synagogue. (1) The first is the elevation from physical symbolism to spiritual, reflective, and emotional symbolism—diminishing the dependence upon the Temple priests. (2) The second is the individualization which is involved in this elevation, in terms of the path for realizing the mission in creation, which the people of Israel agreed to carry out. At this level, democratizing the worship of God is expressed in transforming the unified nation's mission as a collective entity, in terms of institutions of administration and the priesthood, into a mission placed upon each individual who voluntarily obeys his King—the King of creation who rules it as the source of laws which He has impressed upon creation. He leads the nation by the power of the Torah ordinances, which He has given to the nation.

Placing the nation's mission upon each individual necessitates a deepening of the social-ethical thought, which relates to the texture of interpersonal, familial, and communal relations—out of which grows the fraternity of human beings. The mission develops the political order out of these relations: not top to bottom as in a hierarchy of rule, but rather from bottom to top—with the expansion of relationships among friends and neighbors. From the perspective of the government, this is not a compulsory process but a representative process which elevates people's delegates to leadership, according to the criterion of loyalty to their values and aims. The arena for the activities of the individuals of the nation, and especially of their delegates, is the assembly of Israel according to families, tribes, and communities. Those in the assembly are commanded to observe the *mitzvot* of loving God and loving the neighbor, in order to elevate their national society to the moral and spiritual height designated for it by God—so as to actually become the "kingdom of priests" and the "treasured people." Towards that end, each individual has to pass the test, to rule over himself and sanctify himself with *mitzvot*. In this way, the essential battlefield in which the commitment to actualization is discovered. There, the great battle led by the "Lord of hosts" against forces of wickedness which permeate creation is actually decided. This is the battlefield of the spiritual soul of each individual against the inclinations of his physical soul and the challenges posed by the frustrating conditions of his earthly life. They include the war of the wicked against the righteous within his nation and the war of idolatrous nations against his own nation.

The responsibility falls upon individuals. Their redemption from enslavement to their inclinations and their overcoming misery; the redemption of the nation from the hostility of its idolatrous enemies, and the liberation of creation from the forces of chaos—all depend upon the actions of each and every individual. Because the final victory will grow from the achievements of each individual within the orbit of their responsibility, narrow or wide. Though the failures of individuals are liable to join into the collective failure of the society, individual successes are likewise liable to join into the collective achievement of subduing evil and enthroning God over the earthly forces of chaos. This is a heavy responsibility, one full of suffering. The path to complete redemption is very long but the reward is great—not only in the future to come but in any present in which the individual and his family, assembly, and people become worthy of spiritual achievement—because any meaningful achievement in the path of redemption, personal and collective, is a holiday in which the envisioned redemption is anticipated, and the people internalize the achievement symbolically with collective pilgrimages to the House of God, where they feel God's closeness and rejoice in worshipping Him.

War of Good against Evil

Let us return to the systematic outline of the worldview in the book of Psalms, especially to its political aspect. Above, we have cited the psalmist's wrestling with the problem of the wickedness which permeates creation. The conclusion that emerged from this encounter is that the war of good against evil is the axis of the collective progress of human activity in creation. This activity continues over the course of human history, from the six days of creation until "the end of days." Then all of creation, heaven and earth, will arrive at the level of achievement about which it was said "God saw that it was good," and the blessing "be fruitful and multiply" was given. The book of Psalms drew this wisdom from the Torah of Moses and the prophets, but deepened and developed it with philosophical consistency whose epistemological basis was the doctrine of the soul expounded above. If we examine the psalms, one after the other, we will find that they are all united by a broad and encompassing common denominator: they place the burden for the war of good against evil upon each individual of Israel as member of the covenant with God, who fights the power of chaos for the well-being of all creation.

Testimony for this is to be found in the first psalm, which constitutes the declarative and pedagogical introduction to the book. We complete the evidence with verses not yet cited:

Not so the wicked;
Rather, they are like chaff that wind blows away.
Therefore the wicked will not survive judgment,

Nor will sinners, in the assembly of the righteous.
For the Lord cherishes the way of the righteous,
But the way of the wicked is doomed.
(Psalms 1:4–6)

These verses summarize the message of the psalm to worshippers of God, who open the book of Psalms so as to serve God with "worship of the heart." God offers two alternative paths to the human beings created in His image—the path of good and the path of evil; the path of life and well-being and the path of death and misery; the path of righteousness and the path of wickedness. Each individual is obliged to choose, but this is not a one-time choice. It is an ongoing test for the entire life of the person who reveres God and walks in His ways. Human beings are judged according to whether they pass or fail the test. The redemption of their nation amid humanity and the redemption of humanity amid creation depends on their success.

The psalm says this in its didactic way. It opens with a series of negative statements intended to assail the erroneous thinking of most human beings who presume that earthly well-being is achieved only in the way of evil ones, the sinners who scorn God. But this is a superficial and false view. If we reflect about what takes place in the depth of the sinners' souls, we will be convinced that their well-being is fiction, and that their security is pretense which covers up vacuity and impotence. The evil ones create nothing, they only take and destroy. And while they exhibit power and pleasure, their well-being is ephemeral. At the end of their life story they leave behind only destruction. And when God will renew creation in the cycle of generations, nothing will remain to testify to, or to remember, their existence. They will be forgotten as if they never were. True well-being, according to the psalmist, is the product of body and spirit that enriches the world. The psalmist states that taking from others does not bring happiness, but rather depression and animosity. The correct path is to create and to give to the world. This is the true well-being of the pious. God knows them. That is, their memory lasts forever, for what they contribute to creation from the fruit of their spirit exists forever, whereas the evil ones will be forgotten as though they never were.

This introductory psalm offers an inclusive perspective. The psalms that follow express the emotions of the impoverished righteous ones who are committed to their mission, struggle, and suffer over it in their different personal life situations and in the face of their people's destiny among the nations. They recount their burdens. They cry out to God about the perversity of their judgment, they seek salvation, they confess to God and praise Him for the coming salvation.

Why, O Lord, do You stand aloof,
Heedless in times of trouble?
The wicked in this arrogance hounds the lowly—
May they be caught in the schemes they devise!
The wicked crows about his unbridled lusts;
The grasping man reviles and scorns the Lord.
The wicked, arrogant as he is,
In all his scheming [thinks],
"He does not call to account;
God does not care."
His ways prosper at all times;
Your judgments are far beyond him;
He snorts at all his foes.
He thinks, "I shall not be shaken,
Through all time never be in trouble."
His mouth is full of oaths, deceit, and fraud;
Mischief and evil are under his tongue.
He lurks in outlying places;
From a covert he slays the innocent;
His eyes spy out the hapless.
He waits in a covert like a lion in his lair;
Waits to seize the lowly;
He seizes the lowly as he pulls his net shut;
He stoops, he crouches,
And the hapless fall prey to his might.
He thinks, "God is not mindful,
He hides His face, He never looks."
Rise, O Lord!
Strike at him, O God!
Do not forget the lowly.
(Psalms 10:1–12)

Most of the optional prayers which the psalmists place on the lips of individuals are prayers of the wretched, the people who suffer because of the difficult conditions of their lives—the impoverished, the destitute, the orphans, the widows, the victims of robbery, the enslaved, and the exploited. They suffer not because of their own wrongdoing, and at times even on account of their righteousness and innocence because the evil attackers see them as the enemy. The psalmist identifies with them and sounds their cry—which is a bill of indictment not only against the evil ones who make them suffer, but also against God. God is obligated to offer help, but His help is apparently delayed—leaving the evil ones to do as they wish. Does this delay take place because of the sin of the wretched? Is God testing those who revere Him in order to refine their faith in Him? At times, it appears so to the psalmist. Then, with a broken heart, he seeks atonement for his sins—and is thus consoled for his suffering. But when his anger over the evil ones greatly increases, he sounds his protest to God—certain that God, who rules His world with justice, will respond to him.

This is, obviously, not a denial of God's providential care or of God's beneficent intention. To the contrary: the poet knows in the depths of his soul that God will not be angry with him and will not abandon him because of his protest. For the God of truth does not desire deception—and the protest is the poet's true praise; it comes only to sound the alarm that the strength of the wretched has been exhausted. That is, the time has come to be rescued. Moreover, in their cry to God the wretched find relief, which consoles them in their suffering and encourages them in their struggle. In the cry to God, the hope that salvation is imminent is also heard. All that is needed is more effort to complete the task of repair, and then the long-suffering will earn double recompense—they will see the fall of the wicked who persecute them, and they will attain their well-being in compensation. Let us remember that the greatest of the psalmists was David, the king of Israel. As the king appointed to defend his nation against its enemies, sometimes it appears that he rejoices over his enemy's fall and the vengeance he will take on account of their evil which is the measure of the size of his victory, no less than he rejoices at achieving tranquility and repose.

> Why do nations assemble,
> And peoples plot vain things;
> Kings of the earth take their stand,
> And regents intrigue together
> Against the Lord and against His anointed?
> "Let us break the cords of their yoke,
> Shake off their ropes from us!"
> He who is enthroned in heaven laughs;
> The Lord mocks at them.
> Then He speaks to them in anger,
> Terrifying them in His rage,
> "But I have installed My king
> On Zion, My holy mountain!"

Let me tell of the decree:
The Lord said to me,
"You are My son,
I have fathered you this day.
Ask it of Me,
And I will make the nations your domain;
Your estate, the limits of the earth.
You can smash them with an iron mace,
Shatter them like potter's ware."
So now, O kings, be prudent;
Accept discipline, you rulers of the earth!
Serve the Lord in awe;
Tremble with fright,
Pay homage in good faith,
Lest He be angered, and your way be doomed
In the mere flash of His anger.
Happy are all who take refuge in Him.
(Psalms 2:1–12)

Thus it is on the political level in the psalm which constitutes the second part of the general introduction to the book of Psalms. So it is also on the personal-representative level:

O Lord, You will not withhold from me Your compassion;
Your steadfast love will protect me always.
For misfortunes without number envelop me;
My iniquities have caught up with me;
I cannot see;
They are more than the hairs of my head;
I am at my wits' end.
O favor me, Lord, and save me;
O Lord, hasten to my aid.
Let those who seek to destroy my life
Be frustrated and disgraced;
Let those who wish me harm
Fall back in shame.
Let those who say "Aha! Aha!" over me
Be desolate because of their frustration.
But let all who seek You be glad and rejoice in You;
Let those who are eager for Your deliverance

> Always say, "Extolled be the Lord!"
> But I am poor and needy;
> May the Lord devise [deliverance] for me.
> You are my help and my rescuer;
> My God, do not delay.
> (Psalms 40:12–18)

Let us reemphasize the political significance of the prayers of individuals who sound the cry of the wretched and the disappointments of the pious. This is the cry of critical complaint against the morality of the society and of the state, where God did not succeed in enforcing the ordinances of His Torah and its *mitzvot*. At the same time, it is the cry of the persecuted nation of Israel against the politics of idolatrous evil, where God did not succeed in enforcing the ordinances of the covenant of Noah and his sons. It is also, in equal measure, the cry of the majority of humans who are slaves and wretched, ruled by tyrants with whom God did not succeed in enforcing the vision of His kingdom (and likewise on all the forces of chaos in creation). Based upon the belief that God indeed fights in the struggle of the wretched of His nation, the struggle of His nation, and the struggle of the wretched of all humanity, this cry is a call for the army of the "Lord of hosts" to tip the scales of the battle. As we will see below, this fighting on behalf of God is the meaning of the concept of ḥasidut (benevolence, piety) which the book of Psalms carries on its banner.

In a number of psalms, these ideas come to expression in a form that unites the prayer for saving the persecuted wretched person with the prayer for the rescue of the entire nation:

> Vindicate me, O God,
> Champion my cause
> Against faithless people;
> Rescue me from the treacherous, dishonest man.
> For You are my God, my stronghold;
> Why have You rejected me?
> Why must I walk in gloom,
> Oppressed by the enemy?
> (Psalms 43:1–2)

Of interest is the identification between strife with "a faithless people" and strife with "the treacherous man." The strife with "a faithless people" is a struggle for the "salvation" of the nation from among nations. The strife with the "treacherous man" is the personal struggle of each individual. In other psalms, this identity is expressed in prayer that is placed on the lips of the nation as a collective entity, or in the language of the first-person plural "we."

For the leader. Of the Korahites. A *maskil*.
We have heard, O God,
Our fathers have told us
The deeds You performed in their time,
In days of old. With Your hand You planted them,
Displacing nations;
You brought misfortune on peoples,
And drove them out.
It was not by their sword that they took the land,
Their arm did not give them victory,
But Your right hand, Your arm, and Your goodwill,
For You favored them.
You are my king, O God;
Decree victories for Jacob!
Through You we gore our foes;
You thwart those who hate us.
In God we glory at all times,
And praise Your name unceasingly. *Selah*.
Yet You have rejected and disgraced us;
You do not go with our armies.
You make us retreat before our foe;
Our enemies plunder us at will.
You let them devour us like sheep;
You disperse us among the nations.
You sell Your people for no fortune,
You set no high price on them.
You make us the butt of our neighbors,
The scorn and derision of those around us.
You make us a byword among the nations,
A laughingstock among the peoples.
I am always aware of my disgrace;
I am wholly covered with shame
At the sound of taunting revilers,
In the presence of the vengeful foe.
All this has come upon us,
Yet we have not forgotten You,

Or been false to Your covenant.
Our hearts have not gone astray,
Nor have our feet swerved from Your path,
Though You cast us, crushed, to where the sea monster is,
And covered us over with deepest darkness.
If we forgot the name of our God
And spread forth our hands to a foreign god,
God would surely search it out,
For He knows the secrets of the heart.
It is for Your sake that we are slain all day long,
That we are regarded as sheep to be slaughtered.
Rouse Yourself; why do You sleep, O Lord?
Awaken, do not reject us forever!
Why do You hide Your face,
Ignoring our affliction and distress?
We lie prostrate in the dust;
Our body clings to the ground.
Arise and help us,
Redeems us, as befits Your faithfulness.
(Psalms 44:1–27)

The King's Prayer

The political message of the psalm that speaks in the name of the nation is very clear. It sounds the cry of the people of Israel to God their king, for Him to disclose His kingship and rescue the nation. For his nation is His army, fighting the powers of wickedness in His name to show the nations the good and the well-being He will provide if they serve Him as do the people of Israel. But this message is identified explicitly as political by the personality and mission of the psalmist to whom most of the psalms are attributed. It is David, king of Israel—the person who established the united kingdom of Israel. Over time, it received exclusive legitimate status, on behalf of the entire nation as one assembly and with the consent of all the institutions of its leadership: the institution representing the authority of the "assembly"—the elders; the institutions, which represented the authority of the Torah—the scribes and sages; and the institutions, which represented the authority of God—the prophets, the priests, and the Levites. Because of this, David is considered to be the founder of the only dynasty worthy to rule over Israel.

What is the role of the king of Israel? How is his kingship different from the kingships of other nations? How is his role different from the role of the elders, the prophets, the priests, and the Levites? Here, let us expand what has been said in earlier chapters with regard to the role of the prophets. According to the basic law of the Torah, the nation of Israel is designated to be a "kingdom of priests" or the "treasured" nation, by means of which God appears as king of earthly creation. The law of the Torah is, as recalled, the law of the covenant enacted by free agreement between the nation of Israel as a collective entity (but with the consent of each and every individual within it) and God its king. This is a mutual obligation between the nation which takes the laws of God and His *mitzvot* upon itself for its benefit, and God who pledges for the benefit of the nation and that of each individual if they keep His *mitzvot*. By means of this, God—the sovereign of all creation overall—becomes the sovereign king of the chosen nation of Israel in particular. The overall kingship of God is expressed in His direct control of the laws embedded in creation, while His particular kingship of Israel is expressed in the granting of the law of the Torah, in punishing sinners, and rewarding the righteous. This is done through God's rule over the powers of creation, and through teaching the way that is communicated by God to His people through His prophets and priests. It is an instinctive fact that from the Mount Sinai theophany onward, God does not intervene directly in the activity of institutions of the nation's governance—the army, the judiciary, the society, the economy. This is because God expects the nation to take responsibility for its life and for its success through its leaders and, as will be seen in what follows, through individuals and mature adults who are fit to take moral responsibility for their lives.

This is the background for the problem of kingship in Israel. Within the framework of the covenant enacted at the foot of Mount Sinai, Israel had no need for a human king, as exemplified by kings of all those nations that worship idols and deities. The one and only king the people were required to obey was the creator God, who ruled the powers of creation and gave Torah to His nation and its leaders through His prophet Moses and His High Priest Aaron, and after that to Joshua and the judges and the sons of Aaron. However in the days of Samuel, who combined the roles of prophet and high priest, it became clear that in its war with its enemies over settlement in its land and establishing order in it, the nation needed a human king like all the nations. In the name of God, Samuel conceded to the people's request, although he wanted to prevent the sin of tyrannical idolatry which was tied to the sovereignty of a human being over the people. The way to do so was by having the human king submit to the divine king, by having the human king submit to the basic law of the Torah, to the instruction of the prophet, and to the signs of leadership signaled by God with the Urim and Thummim under the authority of the high priest and supervised by the elders of the assembly, whose approval was a condition for anointing the king.

From this system of control there resulted the problem that was specific to the kingdom of Israel, and to the king of Israel as a person, as an Israelite, and as a ruler. The king was called upon to fill the roles that were laid on the kings of other nations. For this purpose, he also received from the people the authorizations, the powers, and the necessary instruments. But on the other hand, he was called on to see himself as a member of his people, equal to them before God and before the laws of God's Torah, from which he was not to turn aside, right or left. So, while the kings of the nations were authorized to legislate for their people and they themselves stood above the law, the king of Israel was not permitted to legislate the basic laws of his kingdom but only apply the laws of God's Torah and enforce them through a true and just judicial process. He himself was bound to these laws and was called upon to fulfill them as an example to his people and to their elders who judged them.

This was a very weighty requirement, especially for a king whose role it was to battle and to rule with a high hand. According to the books of Samuel and Kings, only two kings met the requirement with full success: David, and King Solomon at the beginning of his kingship. This was until he deviated from Torah law and from the word of God on the lips of His prophets. And before he caused a split between the kingdom of Israel which became idolatrous, displaced and exiled; and the kingdom of Judah which wavered between opposing propensities that collided within the people until it too was destroyed and exiled. The great test, which the king of Israel had to pass, was to balance the tension between his responsibilities to God and His nation, and sovereign authority. He had to exercise his sovereign authority as the commander-in-chief of a regular professional army, with whose help he protected his people from their enemies and enforced law and order. He also collected taxes and conscripted workers for his great building projects, by means of which he was able to maintain both his army and his ruling administration, and furnish his home with the luxury and splendor proper to a king. On the other hand, he had the duty to receive the approval of the nation as an assembly, and to obey the laws of the Torah and the commands of God from the lips of His prophets and priests.

The failure of Saul to adhere to the criteria for the legal kingship of Israel, the failure of Solomon to do so at the end of his days, and the failure of all the kings of Israel and most of the kings of Judah, point to the seriousness of this problem. In actuality, only David, poet of the Psalms, passed the test, through his reverence for God and his piety (ḥasidut).

But let us not err in understanding the nature of *ḥasidut*, specifically, the *ḥasidut* of a king who is expected by God as well as by those who have elected him, to fight both his enemies abroad and those who resist him at home, and to rule with a firm hand. This *ḥasid*, as said, is a soldier, a king who mobilizes troops and frightens his enemies. He is commanded to be cruel against his foes and to take justified revenge—measure for measure—for their villainy, just as he is to be benevolent to his people who are his brothers in arms. His relationship to God is the same. He sees himself as the son who adores his beloved Father, who knows his loyalty, and recognizes his own weaknesses as a person of flesh and blood. He knows: even when God is angry with him and chastises him, God admonishes him as a loving educator out of concern, and ready to forgive. The attribute of *ḥasidut* is disclosed in the relation of the *ḥasid* to his God, in direct, personal intimacy and unconditional love. Nothing would annul that love or undo its responsibilities. It is obvious that, as a king of flesh and blood, David very often failed in terms of moral sins—even very serious ones. But the sins came from his status and role, and as such they deserved to be forgiven, if only he would regret and repent. And David did indeed hear the rebukes of God's prophet, and he regretted and atoned his sins, for he never betrayed God and never pretended to rule in his own name instead of God's. Rather, in all important decisions he first asked God and he did not disobey God's prophet.

From these matters we learn the depth of the problem, and we understand why most of the kings did not succeed in dealing with it as David did. When a king sits on the throne of his kingship, collects taxes, efficiently mobilizes the machinery of the government, and raises a professional army serving under him which is salaried and over which he is the supreme commander, he accumulates great wealth allowing for a splendid and abundant lifestyle. Consequently, he has the ability to act as an exalted sovereign and to rule his people exactly as any of the kings of nations. He is not to be brought to account: not by priests, not by prophets, and not by his nation's elders. The temptation to act in this way is great, because rivals always rise against the king, and consolidating his money and power appears even necessary for fulfilling his role. Of course, if the king does this, his rule will ultimately degrade into tyranny, and tyranny will lead to resentment and revolt. But until a full-blown rebellion develops, time will pass, and, in the meantime, the despotic king will do whatever suits his fancy. It follows that only the king himself can restrain his base inclinations from taking control. In other words, a legal kingship of Israel, according to Torah, exists only if the king himself is a God-fearing person and a *ḥasid*, a lover of God, and beloved by his people. He makes his entire life as king and private person sacred for the worship of God and service to his nation. According to the testimony of the books of Samuel and Kings, this was the singular trait of David, by merit of which he became the founder of the legal kingdom in Israel. His stature as a deeply religious person, who had reverence and love for God, came to ultimate expression in his genius and talent as a poet who understood prayer. He was a king-poet, upon whom the holy spirit dwelled. By virtue of the holy spirit he reigned as representative of his people before the God who reigned also over him—such that David was but a servant before God like all humans.

Against this background, one may discern the special way in which the king played the role of representative of the nation before God, and representative of God before the people. It is substantially different than the role of representative as played by the priest, the Levite, and the prophet. The king is not an emissary whose task is to bring God's word to the nation. Rather, he is a man of action who is chosen—with the approval of God and the people according to the covenant of the Torah—to stand at the head of the nation in its war against its enemies and in building its civilization. Therefore, God does not reveal Himself to the king as He reveals Himself to His prophets and priests, and the king is not permitted to worship God as the priest and the prophet worship Him. The personal intimacy between God and the king is essentially different. The *ḥasidut* cited above is expressed in the personal-soulful nearness which is special to generational relations between the parent and his children. The basis of these relations is the fact that the person is created in the image of God by means of the breathing of God's spirit into the body of His living creature. This is the soulful-spiritual nearness expressed in inner connection. As the nation of Israel is the firstborn of God among the nations, the king is the firstborn of God among the children of Israel. The king is distinguished by the inspiration of a special holy spirit, which is manifested as a spirit of courage and wisdom, helping him to fulfill his mission; and as a spirit of poetry which pulsates in the king and makes him able to worship his God. But it is clear that the form of the king's worship is different than that of the priest, the Levite, and the prophet. The king worships God as ruler of his nation in God's name, and represents his people as an individual in the name of all individuals under his governance. Indeed, it may be said that in the worship of God the king is but a delegate of the public, which prays to its God.

The relation of soulful intimacy between the king and his God distinguishes the kingdom of Israel as a kingdom of priests over which God reigns. The commonwealth of Israel continued this relation of intimacy, even when the kingdom of the earthly house of David was ravaged, the Temple destroyed, and the nation of Israel exiled. The earthly kingdom was desolate, but the kingdom of heaven situated above it was not destroyed; it was only hidden. In secret, the nation of Israel continued to be a kingdom of priests over whom God was sovereign. Externally, the people of Israel submitted to the governments of idolatrous nations. But in the innermost soul of the dispersed assembly of Israel—and in the innermost soul of each individual loyal to Torah—the assembly congregated in synagogues and continued to worship the true king, king of the nation, king of humanity, king of creation, by keeping the *mitzvot* of His Torah applicable in exile and through worship of God in prayer.

Where, then, does the kingdom of the House of David—the earthly, legal kingdom of the people of Israel—conceal itself? Where does it await the day when it will be renewed on earth? In the book of Psalms. "David, king of Israel, lives and endures" (*Rosh Hashanah* 25a) in the soul and spirit of the children of Israel, and they crown David when they crown God, through David's prayers and psalms.

Personal Political Poetry

This is the essence of the political message of the book of Psalms. Finally, let us briefly examine the poetic genres and the forms of poetic transmission of this political message—all of which have been accepted into the Jewish prayer book, the *siddur*. Let us first recall the psalms attributed personally to David, which reflect the path of his many struggles, his suffering, and trials, until he began to reign, and afterward, when he struggled to maintain his kingdom and defend his nation from its enemies. Let us note that, despite the explicit reminders of events in whose memory the psalms were composed, they are written in personal, private language in a form that can express the distresses and hopes of each individual in the nation who is caught up in trials of this sort.

> A psalm of David when he fled from his son Absalom.
> O Lord, my foes are so many!
> Many are those who attack me;
> Many say of me,
> "There is no deliverance for him through God." *Selah.*
> But You, O Lord, are a shield about me,
> My glory, He who holds my head high.
> I cry aloud to the Lord,
> And He answers me from His holy mountain. *Selah.*
> I lie down and sleep and wake again,
> For the Lord sustains me.

I have no fear of the myriad forces
Arrayed against me on every side.
Rise, O Lord!
Deliver me, O my God!
For You slap all my enemies in the face;
You break the teeth of the wicked.
Deliverance is the Lord's;
Your blessing be upon Your people! *Selah.*
(Psalms 3:1–9)

In addition, let us cite the psalms that reflect decisive events in the history of the people of Israel—the exodus from Egypt, the journey through the desert, settlement in the land, and exile from their land. The uniqueness of these psalms is expressed by their personal style, which revives the lessons of past events in individual memory. When individuals chant one of these psalms, they experience the specific event, placing themselves in the situation of those who actually saw and experienced it. In this way, they place the past into the present and enter into its living reality.

When Israel came forth from Egypt,
The house of Jacob from a people of strange speech,
Judah became His holy one,
Israel, His dominion.
The sea saw them and fled,
Jordan ran backward,
Mountains skipped like rams,
Hills like sheep.
What alarmed you O sea, that you fled,
Jordan, that you ran backward,
Mountains, that you skipped like rams,
Hills, like sheep?
Tremble, O earth, at the presence of the Lord,
At the presence of the God of Jacob,
Who turned the rock into a pool of water,
The flinty rock into a fountain.
(Psalms 114:1–8)

The beginning of this psalm recalls the event in the language of the present referring to the past (*be-tzet*—"in Israel's coming out"—when it went out), but the description continues in the language of the present, so that the individuals who sing this psalm "converse" with the sea, with the Jordan, with the mountains and hills, as they ask and receive an answer. In this way, they participate in an event that embraces heaven and earth, and experience it personally—as if they are now leaving Egypt and God is guiding them to their land.

The following psalm, which commemorates the destruction of Jerusalem and the Temple and going out into exile, works in a similar way:

> By the rivers of Babylon,
> There we sat,
> Sat and wept,
> As we thought of Zion.
> There on the poplars
> We hung up our lyres,
> For our captors asked us there for songs,
> Our tormentors, for amusement:
> "Sing us one of the songs of Zion."
> How can we sing a song of the Lord
> On alien soil?
> If I forget you, O Jerusalem
> Let my right hand wither;
> Let my tongue stick to my palate
> If I cease to think of you,
> If I do not keep Jerusalem in memory
> Even at my happiest hour.
> Remember, O Lord, against the Edomites
> The day of Jerusalem's fall;
> How they cried, "Strip her, strip her
> To her very foundations!"
> Fair Babylon, you predator,
> A blessing on him who repays you in kind
> What you have inflicted on us;
> A blessing on him who seizes your babies
> And dashes them against the rocks!
> (Psalms 137:1–9)

As the previous hymn commemorates the event of the redemption in a personal-actual way, the hymn before us also commemorates the destruction with all its personal-actual pain. The individuals who chanted identified themselves with the Levites who suspended their harps on the weeping willows as a sign of mourning, and by doing so participated in the event as if it was taking place in the present. They took the oath upon themselves to remember Jerusalem and not to rejoice until they were able to return there and reestablish the worship of God in His Temple.

It is likely that these psalms were written in order to be recited on special days of remembrance, the first hymn on Passover and the second on the Ninth of Av. With this, we come to point out the third path of transmitting the political message—that by means of psalms that are intended to be read on the Sabbath and especially on holidays in which the Torah commands pilgrimage to Jerusalem. This pilgrimage is an event bearing very important political meaning. As the nation of Israel gathers in Jerusalem, people are united in their ascent to the capital of the kingdom, and in a symbolic ascent to the Temple of God in the heart of the capital of the kingdom, which is the "palace" of God's kingdom amid His people. "Songs of Ascents" (*shirei hama'alot*) is the name for the poems which the people chanted during their pilgrimage of ascent to the mountain of God, to worship their God with sacrifices and offerings, with poems and praises, to actually become the "kingdom of priests and a holy nation."

> A song of ascents. Of David.
> I rejoiced when they said to me,
> "We are going to the House of the Lord."
> Our feet stood inside your gates, O Jerusalem,
> Jerusalem built up, a city knit together,
> To which tribes would make pilgrimage,
> The tribes of the Lord,
> —As was enjoined upon Israel—
> To praise the name of the Lord.
> There the thrones of judgment stood,
> Thrones of the house of David.
> Pray for the well-being of Jerusalem:
> "May those who love you be at peace.
> May there be well-being within your ramparts,
> Peace in your citadels."
> For the sake of my kin and friends,
> I pray for your well-being;
> For the sake of the house of the Lord our God,
> I seek your good.
> (Psalms 122:1–9)

This is the first "Song of Ascents." It fits together the covenant of the tribes of Israel and the covenant of the House of David and its kingdom, as stairs that lead to the affirmation of the covenant of God's kingship in His Temple, in order for the people to stand before their king, bow before Him, and worship Him. Then God will forgive their trespasses, atone their sins, and have His spirit and blessing dwell upon them.

Let us recall another day which merited special importance in the book of Psalms, the day that marked David's ascent to the throne of the kingdom. This was also the day designated on the annual calendar for the remembrance of the reign of God over Israel, the day that was made into the holiday of Rosh Hashanah after the Babylonian exile. From this follows the importance of this day in the prayer book.

> Of David. A psalm.
> The earth is the Lord's and all that it holds,
> The world and its inhabitants.
> For He founded it upon the ocean,
> Set it on the nether-steams.
> Who may ascend the mountain of the Lord?
> Who may stand in His holy place? –
> He who has clean hands and a pure heart,
> Who has not taken a false oath by My life
> Or sworn deceitfully.
> He shall carry away a blessing from the Lord,
> A just reward from God, his deliverer.
> Such is the circle of those who turn to Him,
> Jacob, who seek Your presence. *Selah.*
> O gates, lift up your heads!
> Up high, you everlasting doors,
> So the King of glory may come in!
> Who is the King of glory!—
> The Lord, mighty and valiant,
> The Lord, valiant in battle.
> Who is the King of glory?—
> The Lord of hosts,
> He is the King of glory! *Selah*
> (Psalms 24:1–8, 10)

The poem speaks in the language of the present, in order to convey its permanent reality. Obviously, the reality cannot be affirmed concretely when the people are in exile. But one can still affirm its moral and spiritual symbolic meaning, which is the essence of the political message of the kingdom of Israel as a kingdom of priests and a holy nation. This psalm is written to be recited by an individual who ascends together with the national congregation of special individuals, children of Jacob, in quest of God, seeking His countenance, clean of hands and pure of heart, loyal to truth and justice, and giving honor with his entire being to God. And God comes down from heaven towards the congregation, towards His earthly Temple, to the mountain of His dwelling, to bless the people in their ascent, morally and spiritually, to grace them with His countenance, and to proclaim His kingship to the nation.

Composed in this spirit is the cluster of psalms designated in the *siddur* as *Hallel*, to be recited on days dedicated to the remembrance of miraculous salvations which disclosed God's kingdom on earth, and which divine intervention alone made possible (Psalms 113–118). The book of Psalms concludes in that same spirit of the perfect kingdom, with several hymns of praise to the God who revealed Himself as God of heaven and earth, Lord of hosts of heaven and creatures of earth, God of all nations, the God of Israel, with David the poet and musical director at its head. The conclusion itself is a trumpet-call of praise with all musical instruments, including the lungs and throat of the person that also make music. The spirit with which they resonate is the soul-breath (*neshamah*) of the person reciting the poem, while the music sweeps through the words. Only the music, which carries the words and elevates the feeling cast in them beyond mere combinations of syllables, can express the perfection of the kingdom and the splendor of its revelation.

> Hallelujah.
> Praise God in His sanctuary;
> Praise Him in the sky, His stronghold.
> Praise Him for His mighty acts;
> Praise Him for His exceeding greatness.
> Praise Him with blasts of the horn;
> Praise Him with harp and lyre.
> Praise Him with timbrel and dance;
> Praise Him with lute and pipe.
> Praise Him with resounding cymbals;
> Praise Him with loud-clashing cymbals.
> Let all that breathes praise the Lord.
> Hallelujah.
> (Psalms 150:1–6)

Hymnal Song for the Sabbath Day. The "Sign" between God and His Treasured Nation and the Isolation from Christianity

As Sons Who Eat at His Table

We pass from the poetry of the Psalms, which adds to the *siddur*'s regular prayer service the dimension of optional prayer, to the poetry of Sabbath and holidays. This poetry is permanently added to the weekday prayers, according to the principle stating that "instead of bulls we will pay [the offerings of] our lips" (Hosea 14:3). The priestly law of the Torah prescribes an additional contingent of sacrifices and offerings for Sabbaths and festivals, designed to increase the joy of people who celebrated these holy days. Correspondingly, a special prayer is arranged which recalls the sacrifices and fills the lack thereof with an expression of longing to renew the days in which the children of Israel are worthy to experience the loftiness of God in His Temple, where He resided amid them as their king. The Sabbath and the holidays are considered to be God's gift to the people of Israel, insofar as they are His "treasure." How does God give His gift? Through His *mitzvot*, through His blessing which enables keeping the *mitzvot* in detail, and through restoring the portion of those who bring sacrifices and offerings designated for strengthening the Temple and its orders of worship, so they could rejoice before Him. This refers to the "daily offerings" (*temidim*), the "additional offerings" (*musafim*), and to sacrifices of "celebration" (*hagigah*) where, in addition to portions of the fat and the blood designated for burning in the fire on the altar—for the "pleasant aroma" (*reaḥ niḥoaḥ*) to please God— the flesh is given to the priests and to people who bring sacrifices and offerings, in order to rejoice before God. The symbolic-poetic meaning of this gesture is that on the Sabbath and festivals, God gives to the children of Israel from the fruit of their labor, which was imparted by His generous blessing, in order to have them rejoice and celebrate at the feast as children eating at His table.

When the Temple stood in its splendor on Mount Zion, the children of Israel performed the *Musaf* (additional) sacrifice on holidays. Each family, along with those who joined in, feasted at the *seudat hamitzvah* (feast of the *mitzvah*) with meat which is originally the "bread of God," and with wine which gladdens the human heart, accompanied by poetry and song. What is the source of this ritual in the scriptural narrative? The poetic feast, which Moses and Aaron, Nadab and Abihu, and seventy of the elders of Israel made before God according to God's command at the height of Mount Sinai. This was after they enacted the covenant with God around the altar, which Moses had set up at the foot of Mount Sinai with the hand of "the youth of Israel" (meaning the eldest sons of all the families who were appointed originally to sanctify themselves to God as priests and thereby to represent the entire nation): "Then Moses and Aaron, Nadab and Abihu, and seventy elders of Israel ascended; and they saw the God of Israel: under His feet there was the likeness of a pavement of sapphire, like the very sky for purity. Yet He did not raise His hand against the leaders of the Israelites; they beheld God, and they ate and drank" (Exodus 24:9–11). The feasting of the people before God, as members of His covenant and as sons eating at the table of their father, symbolizes spiritual ascent and supreme human well-being, through a combination of physical and soulful pleasure, which sates, refreshes, and gladdens. In this sense, the feast by itself is a lofty poetic gesture. In place of sacrifices of the Sabbath and the festivals designated for feasting, additional prayers (*Musafim*) were instituted for Sabbaths and festivals after the destruction of the Temple. The obligatory feasts, with meat and wine, special bread, and songs of praise and thanksgiving, were likewise instituted in place of feasts before God in the Temple. The table around which each family gathered at home with its guests (it was a *mitzvah* of the holiday to invite guests so as to rejoice with collective Israel, and so that no poor person or isolated individual would be left without fulfilling the obligatory feast), was designated to symbolize the altar and the celebratory feast where people ate from the meat of sacrifices and gladdened their hearts before God with wine. God's presence with His people at their Sabbaths in exile was symbolized with poetry and song. The poems and the songs continued without interruption from the days of the Temple, from generation to generation. At the same time, they were renewed and "new songs" were added for each Sabbath and each holiday. The poetry and song are eternal, and yet also new and unique—just as each day of God reflected eternity.

Cyclicality and Singularity of Sabbaths and Festivals

In its collective scope, the *siddur* is a *maḥzor* (cyclical compendium) which reflects the calendar year, whether as a wheel revolving around its axis symbolizing the cycle of the seasons in nature from the beginning of the year to its end, or as a cycle of waymarks of testimony—which were fixed for remembering events that established the nation and charted its path from the Egyptian exodus to Mount Sinai, and from Mount Sinai to Canaan to inherit there the bequest of its land, to establish its government upon it, and to build its Temple at its center. The reference here is to the Sabbaths which have been established "in remembrance of the act of creation" and "in remembrance of the exodus from Egypt"; to the day assigned as the *yom teru'ah* (Day of the Outcry or *Shofar*-blowing) that symbolizes God's reign over His nation and that after the Babylonian exile was designated as Rosh Hashanah—New Year; to the festival that follows it—the Day of Atonement (Yom Kippur) which is the "Sabbath of Sabbaths" (*shabbat shabbaton*); and to the three "pilgrimages": Passover, Shavuot, and Sukkot, when the people are commanded to "ascend by foot" annually to the Temple.

Let us pay attention, that the Jewish calendar is shaped by the interweaving of the cycle of seasons of nature; the cycle of weekly, monthly, and yearly time, and the sequence of foundational events which in their ongoing cycle symbolize the course of life that extends from the time of creation to the time of eternal redemption at the "end of days." This interweaving is accomplished by means of holidays (*mo'adim*) that fix the memories—which help the nation face its future, and thereby establish the memory of foundational events which occurred in the past, within the present of each and every year—and carry their memory into the future. The *mo'ed* (holiday) was created by connecting the marker of the time in which a change is felt in nature with the time in which a foundational event occurred that entered into history as the beginning of a "new day"—a day in which the overall condition of this nation changed, for better or worse, with respect to the nation's progress in realizing its destiny among the nations. The Torah calls it a *mikra kodesh* (holy convocation)—a day when the entire nation remembers its past, understands the obligations implied by it, and looks towards the future—in order that, at the end of the day, the nation returns to the path leading to the next holiday. The holiday is, consequently, a time of rest upon a peak from which we observe the memory of the past behind us and observe the forecast of the future before us. We face the eternal heaven, from which God looks with His view—which includes the beginning and the end of time.

The previous chapters of this book discussed ongoing, permanent prayer, which joins all the days, weekdays and the Sabbath, in their permanent rhythm of alternating between day and night in nature. This is the plane on which the daily life of humans takes place. Its essence is labor, which is designated to satisfy the necessities of human existence by building, maintaining, and operating the civilization necessary for existence on a human level. Let us observe that the Sabbaths and holidays are also implanted into the same level and sequential physical foundation as the universe of time. But they also rise above the foundation, as hills and mountains upon which people ascend to worship God under eternal heaven. The only purpose of this worship is to elevate and exalt God. It is not tied to people's needs. Precisely in this way the nation experiences well-being from coming closer to the realization of its destiny.

Our concern in this chapter is the poetry of the *Musaf* services. But we cannot, nor is there a need, to discuss all of them. Let us separate out one *Musaf* that exemplifies the regularity which unites the *Musafim* (additional services) of all holidays—namely, the *Musaf* of the Sabbath. The Sabbath is repeated—as are the weekdays—in a fixed, uniform rhythm, week after week, over the course of the year. And yet, each and every Sabbath is singular, as it is commanded to be carried out and experienced in the singularity which symbolizes the eternal. On the other hand, all Sabbaths are experienced with reference to the same standard. Thus the uniqueness of each Sabbath by itself is expressed through the experience of the now, and in this respect is singular. But from the perspective of the one who views from the outside, no difference is recognizable from Sabbath to Sabbath—other than differences emerging from the annual seasons and the cycle of Torah readings.

The Sabbath, as said, is the uniform subsoil to which is added the fixed variety of the principal holidays which repeats itself year after year: Rosh Hashanah and Yom Kippur, Pesaḥ, Shavuot, and Sukkot. Incidentally, there are two sequences in the yearly cycle which are connected with one another: the year that begins on the first of Nisan, and the year that begins on the first of Tishrei. But in this chapter, we will discuss only the Sabbath, which defines the fixed, uniform sequence. Those interested in the topics of the structure of the complex Hebrew calendar and the special content of the *Musafim* of the holidays, including those not based on the Sabbath, may turn to my book *The Cycle of Time: The Meaning of the Jewish Holidays.*

"He ceased on the seventh day all the work He had done... He had created to do" (K: 382, *Yom Hashishi*, Genesis 2:2–3)

The Torah of Moses attributes foundational, unique, and supreme importance to the Sabbath. First of all, cosmic status is attributed to it, and in due course historical status is erected upon that. The story of creation testifies to the cosmic significance of the Sabbath. On the seventh day, God rested from His work of creation. The work continued for six days, each distinguished from the other by the single measurement of time: "and there was evening, there was morning, one day" (Genesis 1:5), and after that the second, third, fourth, fifth, and sixth day. No new creation was added on the seventh day. God "finished" (*kilah*) all His work and "completed" (*kalal*) it. This is, as such, a standing still from work, and in this sense the seventh day is a time of rest. But there is a difference between standing still and resting, and idleness. This difference is important from the perspective of the people of Israel. The Sabbath is a day of standing still from sustenance-providing labor of civilization, and of rest from the exertion of this labor. But it is not a day of idleness. The people of Israel are commanded to separate themselves on this day from work that will satisfy their physical needs, and to reserve the fruits of their labor in order to consecrate these fruits and themselves to the creator of the world. In this way the people emulate the creator, God, who sanctified the Sabbath day by settling down to rest, so as to distinguish Himself from His creation and allow creation to be by itself, and maintain itself according to the law that God set for it—and thereby create a mutual relation between Himself and creation like that between a king and his subjects, or between father and son. This relation is expressed from the side of God in His standing back and observing, an act that sums up and unites creation in order to distinguish it from God. This is the meaning of the expression "God finished." God is thereby designated as the owner of the creation. The relation of ownership obligates God to His property and His property to Him. This is the meaning of the expression "and blessed" and "hallowed." The relation of possession and belonging is expressed in the gesture of loving concern, of yearning to be fruitful, to multiply, become complete, and be thankful.

According to the narrative of creation, on the Sabbath day God the creator reached the eternal purpose of His creation, from His own eternal perspective, by distinguishing Himself from creation. With this, God implanted in creation the longing to become complete, beyond the limitations of its character, in order to resemble God. The created world does this in response to the blessing, which flows from God to the world and renews it, advances it, and brings it closer to Him. A poem, in which all creation praises its creator, and which flows from divine inspiration, is the highest expression of this longing for perfection—of independent expression on the one hand, and of mutual commitment on the other.

We learn this from the narrative of creation in Genesis. In the first chapter of this book, there is a poetical abstract that reaches its climax in the passage about the Sabbath. Seven clauses are united in it—six, and one other, which includes them. We recite this poem with a celebratory melody during the *Shemoneh Esrei* prayer and in the *Kiddush* on the eve of every Sabbath.

> (1) And God saw all that He had made, and found it very good.
> (2) And there was evening and there was morning, the sixth day.
> (3) The heaven and the earth were finished, and all their array.
> (4) On the seventh day God finished the work that He had been doing, (5) and He ceased on the seventh day from all the work that He had done. (6) And God blessed the seventh day and declared it holy, (7) because on it God ceased from all the work of creation that He had done. (Genesis 1:31–2:1–3)

These seven clauses are balanced, and joined to one another as a circle— with the end implicitly linked to the beginning. They include the story of creation from its beginning to its end on the seventh day. This structure embodies the idea of completion, implicit in the number seven—which is sanctified as the number representing compound completion. The opening of the seventh clause concludes the documentation of the work of the sixth day. The sixth day is included in the seventh clause, such that it is not pushed into the past as something that was and is no longer. The seventh clause maintains, joins and draws the sixth day into the coming present, and through it into the future.

From the conceptual-literal perspective, this idea is expressed by a mark of the superlative. The activity of each day of creation ends with the summary: "And He saw that it was good," whereas the sixth day ends with "very good." Not because more was done on it than was done on previous days, rather, because the human being is the "very" in creation that longs for its perfection, and because the human being concludes everything done during the six days and completes creation in its longing for "very." This marker points beyond the work of the six days as a preface, which changes the end of the narrative of the sixth day into the opening of the story of the seventh day, a day designed to embody the "very," which is in creation on the one hand, and in God on the other, in the turn to the future.

In terms of the poetic structure, a concatenated connection is created. Each clause flows from the previous one, refers back to it to add detail—and in this way continues it. Without saying so explicitly, the meaning of the "very" is expressed in the form of this structure, which is a movement of thought that goes ahead but also adds a supplement by looking backwards, in order for the progression to be the continuation of the same substance in the same direction. Each clause stands for one day of creation and is perceived as a link that returns to join itself to what has preceded it; it moves forward and joins itself to the "underside" of the next link, which, from its perspective, is joined to the "face" of its predecessor, and thus until the final link, which is joined to the first link—not on the side where the second link joins, but on the opposing side. Thus, clause 7, "all the work of creation that He had done," is joined to clause 1, "and God saw all that He had made, and found it very good. This is repeated. But not as a closed circle. The temporal sequence of creation is rather like a link in a chain, joined to the link after it. Completion is presented as an ongoing effort to leap over the boundary already reached.

The Sabbath of History

The historical meaning of the Sabbath is expressed in the *Kiddush* of the Sabbath, "in remembrance of the exodus from Egypt." The Sabbath in its historical aspect is first mentioned with the exodus of the people of Israel into the desert after the splitting of the Red Sea, in connection with the descent of the manna. The children of Israel were commanded to gather the manna during the six days of the week designated for work to satisfy their needs, each one gathering his portion. Together with this, the people were cautioned that each should take his portion for the day (the portion to which he was rightly entitled)—and no more, for anything remaining would spoil. On the sixth day, by contrast, the people were commanded to gather two portions per person, one for that day and one for the seventh. The manna would not spoil when the day was past. The significance of the distinction between the days is clear. The Sabbath was special, with its *mitzvah* of resting from the work designated for the needs of the person. Accordingly, God grants His blessing of "very" on the sixth day also for the Sabbath, to enable the enjoyment of the Sabbath (Exodus 16). The commandment of the Sabbath itself is not articulated on this occasion, but rather in the Ten Commandments at the Mount Sinai theophany. At the covenant event, which established Israel as a "kingdom of priests," the Sabbath was the foundational and inclusive positive command, in terms of societal order.

> Remember the sabbath day and keep it holy. Six days you shall labor and do all your work, but the seventh day is a sabbath of the Lord your God: you shall not do any work—you, your son or daughter, your male or female slave, or your cattle, or the stranger who is within your settlements. For in six days the Lord

made heaven and earth and sea, and all that is in them, and He rested on the seventh day; therefore the Lord blessed the sabbath day and hallowed it. (Exodus 20:8–11)

This passage commemorates the Sabbath of creation as the reason for the command of resting, and therefore it is a *mitzvah* of remembrance. In light of the remembrance, this passage establishes equality between the rights of the children of Israel and all those dependent upon, and belonging to them before God. God's command applies equally to all of them. They should all rest from work on this day, and in this way become one nation, dedicated to worshipping God and deserving His reward.

The form of this command deserves consideration. The positive command to rest on the Sabbath is given through the negative instruction, which forbids work. The explanation is that God sanctified this day by resting from the work of creation. Therefore, those human beings who are commanded to consecrate themselves to God are bound to sanctify this day in the same way. God emanated to humans, from His spirit, the trait of secondary creativity that they can exercise, using the materials of creation. Resting together from work expresses the positive *zikah* between human beings and God, as members of the covenant.

All this expresses the societal meaning of the *mitzvah* of Sabbath, from the perspective of the people who went out from slavery to freedom. But this meaning is only hinted at in the text of the Ten Commandments in the book of Exodus. It is given more explicit and emphatic statement in the second version of the Ten Commandments, cited in the book of Deuteronomy in preparation for the entry of the children of Israel into Canaan to settle in that land. The prohibition against work receives its full significance and weight there:

> Observe the sabbath day, to keep it holy, as the Lord your God has commanded you. Six days you shall labor and do all your work, but the seventh day is a sabbath of the Lord your God; you shall not do any work—you, your son or your daughter, your male or female slave, your ox or your ass, or any of your cattle, or the stranger in your settlements, so that your male and female slave may rest as you do. Remember that you were a slave in the land of Egypt and the Lord your God freed you from there with a mighty hand and an outstretched arm; therefore the Lord your God has commanded you to observe the sabbath day. (Deuteronomy 5:12–15)

These words make explicit the connection between the *mitzvah* of the Sabbath and the exodus from Egypt. The Sabbath is the day of freedom in the full sense, as defined by the Torah—freedom not only as liberation from oppressive tyranny, and not only as the ability to do what one wants with one's power, but freedom as voluntary acceptance of the *mitzvot* of God, directing the person to the life that is proper for him.

Thus, the Sabbath emphasizes God's selection of the people of Israel to serve Him and be His "treasure" among the nations, as well as the selection of God by the people of Israel, to serve Him as their king, and by doing so become worthy of the true selection designated for human beings who were created in the image of God, and whose soul was emanated from God's spirit. This is the deep meaning of the assertion, which at first glance seems contradictory, that voluntary acceptance of servitude to God is the true freedom designated for human beings, whereas the choice of human beings to do what they want, in opposition to God's command, constitutes their enslavement to the inclinations of the body that rule the soul. Resting on the Sabbath, by observing the severe prohibition against working on it, embodies this paradox with full clarity. The voluntary acceptance of servitude is expressed in restraining oneself from doing whatever arises in the human will to satisfy one's needs—because precisely by doing so, one becomes worthy of a day of freedom from reliance upon the labor which satisfies the needs of life, because this dependence constitutes the essential factor in the servitude of the human being under tyrannical rulers.

The fundamental character of the *mitzvah* of the Sabbath as "remembrance of the exodus from Egypt" is expressed in the many references to this *mitzvah* in the Pentateuch. These references emphasize its singular importance and the absolute obligation to observe it, for the *mitzvah* embodied the paradox of human freedom: Human beings see their benefit in it and want to sanctify it, but they also sense the abnegation the *mitzvah* involves and are tempted to profane it. This became evident already when the nation of Israel first had to deal with the *mitzvah* of keeping the Sabbath, and this event also involved the *mitzvah* of the manna. The Sabbath liberates the children of Israel and redeems them from their labor, but it limits the satisfaction of their physical inclinations and appetites. The human being is inclined to enslave himself to his work so as to satisfy his needs, because he is anxious about his needs not only for this day but also for tomorrow and the day after, so as to assure his future. He is therefore not inclined to rely on supernatural miracles over which he has no control. As creator, God controls nature and His promise is worthy of trust. But from the perspective of routine experience in the world, a very powerful will is required for humans to agree to restrain the urge to take for themselves today what they will need to survive tomorrow and the day after as well—or to abstain from seeking the fixed portion on the sacred day. This illustrates the paradox of enforcing the Sabbath as a day of freedom, in a form that emphasizes that only those who serve God are free—whether in terms of ties to the inclinations that govern their physical nature or from the perspective of their relation to other human beings.

The Sabbath in *Halakhah* and Prayer

Let us introduce the principal passage used in the *Amidah* prayer of the Sabbath *Shaḥarit* and *Musaf*, and in the *Kiddush* recited at the Sabbath table on the afternoon of the Sabbath day:

> And the Lord spoke unto Moses: Speak to the Israelite people and say: Nevertheless, you must keep My sabbaths, for this is a sign between Me and you throughout the ages, that you may know that I the Lord have consecrated you. You shall keep the sabbath, for it is holy for you. He who profanes it shall be put to death; whoever does work on it, that person shall be cut off from among his kin. Six days may work be done, but on the seventh day there shall be a sabbath of complete rest, holy to the Lord; whoever does work on the sabbath day shall be put to death. The Israelite people shall keep the Sabbath, observing the Sabbath throughout the ages as a covenant for all time: it shall be a sign for all time between Me and the people of Israel. For in six days the Lord made heaven and earth, and on the seventh day He ceased from work and was refreshed. (Exodus 31:12–17)

In the Sabbath *Amidah* prayer of *Shaḥarit* and *Musaf*, and in the *Kiddush* in the afternoon we do not, indeed, read this passage in its entirety—only the end. The severity of judgment for profaning the Sabbath is not recited, for it had been eased by the oral Torah. It has retained only the severe punishment for desecrating the Sabbath by the "judgment of heaven" (the judgment of *karet*, being "cut off") and has abolished the threat of being taken out to be killed by human beings. Retaining that would have changed the Sabbath from a day of freedom to a day of shocking tyranny—oppressive and threatening. Nevertheless, the reason behind the singular severity remained. The Sabbath is an eternal "sign" of covenant between God and Israel, and the intention behind it is to symbolize the eternality of the covenant that binds Israel to God, and God to Israel in a form that cannot be annulled by one side. That is, a person who keeps the Sabbath becomes worthy to experience through it the affirmation of God's promise to His nation guaranteeing its freedom and eternity. By contrast, the person who profanes the Sabbath annuls his covenant with God, and his punishment is the annulment of God's obligation to him within the collective people.

The passages cited above, which the *siddur* adopts for Sabbath prayers and the two recitations of the *Kiddush*, on Sabbath eve and Sabbath afternoon, set the basis for the halakhic framework of the oral Torah. The *Halakhah* shaped the Sabbath day with a succession of restrictive *mitzvot* (prohibitions known as *lo ta'aseh*—"do not do") and obligatory positive *mitzvot* (*'asei*—"do so"). Their aim is consecration to God on the one hand, and rest and pleasure on the other. To the sweeping prohibition of any work included in activities to which the human actually dedicates himself during the six days, the Torah adds the severe prohibition against lighting a fire on the Sabbath. Fire is the creative power that God stopped using on the seventh day of creation. The Torah also forbids going out from the settlement in which the children of Israel do their daily work, and where they rest and worship God. This special prohibition, which limits movement and carrying loads on the Sabbath, is derived from, the Torah's prohibiting priests from leaving the Temple's boundaries during the period of their priesthood, because they were obligated to be ready at any time to serve God in His Temple. This means that on the Sabbath day the status of all the children of Israel was disclosed—distinguishing them from other nations— as a "kingdom of priests and a holy nation." But there is a problem emerging from these prohibitions and limitations, each separately and even more when joined together. They are liable to create a prison-like reality, without light when it is dark, warmth when it is cold, without ability to defend oneself during war, troubles, and mishaps, and without the possibility of finding a cure at a time of sickness.

In connection with these matters, one can observe that from the perspective of people not very much in awe before God, and not drawn to the height of holiness as a life-goal, one cannot avoid the feeling of being besieged on the Sabbath—no matter the halakhic solutions invented for all such problems. Even from the perspective of people with reverence for God, who want to sanctify themselves through *mitzvot*, the Sabbath day requires singular self-control, and obliges uninterrupted alertness and care taken to differentiate between what is forbidden, what is commanded, and what is permitted. For without the "permitted," everyone loses the feeling of freedom, which is expressed in the spontaneity of the immediate regular physical responses to various stimuli that cannot be expected in advance. The difficult problem one deals with in oral Torah is how to cope with conflicting opposites encountered in the experience of the Sabbath, from its entry and reception towards the end of the sixth day through its departure and the ceremony of *Havdalah* at the end of the seventh day. It is a day of sequential *mitzvot* of "don't do that" and "do that." But it is also a day of special sanctification by refraining. Not only from moral wickedness and ritual defilement which is always obligatory, but even from very routine activities commanded during weekdays. At the same time, it is a day of higher freedom, a day of rest, celebration, and joy.

In what follows, we will not discuss details of halakhic formulation and resolution of problems. This is not a subject of *Siddur Hatefillah*. In sum: *Halakhah*, which considers the smallest details, has succeeded in transforming the rigid framework of legal prohibition which brings sanctity into an impetus which assists God-revering people who choose to liberate themselves on the Sabbath from the anxieties and distresses which generate a psychological compulsion to commit to labor, that assures material success, and rise to the plane of spiritual life to experience freedom as a covenantal partner of God and participant at God's table. They do so through the sanctification of *mitzvot*. At the same time, the *Halakhah* succeeds in preventing the danger, lest the repose and celebration evoked by the three obligatory feasts of the Sabbath would, God forbid, slide into satisfying gluttonous appetite, or drunkenness, or celebrating idolatrous licentiousness that culminates in lack of restraint and animality. They are rather to be observed within the bounds of morality, purity, and honor proper to a person created in God's image and at His high table, as part of the joy of a *mitzvah*.

Welcoming the Sabbath

The entry of the Sabbath is marked by lighting candles at twilight, towards the end of the sixth day. The source for this ceremonial *mitzvah* is the solution which the rabbis arrived at for the problem of light on the Sabbath eve. We light the candles before the entry of the Sabbath, at a time when it is still permitted to kindle a flame, in order to have illumination during the first customary feast of the Sabbath eve after synagogue prayer—for without light there can be no celebration. But in satisfying the practical need, the symbolic significance breaks through. The *mitzvah* of lighting the candles falls upon the mother. Each woman lights the candles in her home and blesses them in the presence of all family members who live or have gathered together. Symbolically, this ritual concretizes the boundary between the profane time at the end of the sixth day, when the sun is still shining, and the sacred time of the Sabbath eve which begins at sunset. The sun's last rays shine with the departing light through the windows of the house from the outside; and the candle light, which already begins to be felt in the darkness of the house, replaces the sun with an inner light. When the mother lights the candles and raises the candle light in the cup of her blessing hands, the light of the candles illumines her face, and the luster radiating from her face illumines the members of her family. She embraces them in the circle of her love and spreads upon them the comradery of the Sabbath, its calm and peace. This is a poetic gesture that embodies the presence of the Sabbath, which has entered and taken up residence within the home—illuminating it from within.

The Sabbath is experienced around two focal points: the family home whose members gather around the table, symbolizing the altar; and the synagogue, where the congregation gathers around the Holy Ark symbolizing the Tent of Meeting in which God and Moses met. In the synagogue, the entry of the Sabbath is marked by the poetry of *Kabbalat Shabbat* (welcoming the Sabbath) recited before the *Ma'ariv* (evening) prayer. The essence of the *Kabbalat Shabbat* service in the synagogue is the singing of a sequence of psalms (Psalms 95–99) and three additional psalms (Psalms 29, 92, and 93). In the sixteenth century, the reading of the Song of Songs, and the liturgical hymn *Lekhah Dodi* (Come, my beloved) by the poet Rabbi Shlomo Alkabetz of Safed, a student of Isaac Luria, were added. As will be seen below, this added a layer of mystical experience, charged with erotic love, to the layer of congregational experience charged with ethical love.

Let us first consider the concept of "welcoming" (or receiving) the Sabbath. During this ceremony, the people of Israel, according to their families and communities, encounter the day dedicated to worshipping God and resting from labors for human needs. This encounter is transferred from the physical plane of the temporal cycle, which the Sabbath day shares with all days of the week, to the metaphysical plane of sacred time. The expression *Kabbalat Shabbat* is derived from the expression *kabbalat panim* (literally, "receiving the face")—the welcome arranged for an honored personality who comes to visit. We wait for him at the entrance of the household, and the especially devout go out towards him to pay him honor, to bless him, and be blessed by him. In the psalms designated for *Kabbalat Shabbat*, God Himself, with His presence that is felt and at the same time hidden, descends from the height and enters to reside in homes which open themselves for Him to spread His *Shekhinah*.

In this way, the time is dedicated to God. In the course of all the days of the week, God's presence in the world is totally hidden, whereas on the Sabbath, God "reveals His face" to the people of His nation, even in exile—even if secretly. He descends to reside with them in the synagogue, which falls within the definition of the "lesser sanctuary," and lifts the people up to Him. The psalm that opens the ceremony expresses the content of the gesture: the setting out of the hosts and their "walking" towards the guest to pay Him honor and accompany Him as He enters their home.

> Come, let us sing joyously to the Lord,
> Raise a shout for our rock and deliverer;
> Let us come into His presence with praise;
> Let us raise a shout for Him in song!
> For the Lord is a great God,
> The great king of all divine beings.
> In His hand are the depths of the earth;
> The peaks of the mountains are His.
> His is the sea, He made it;
> And the land, which His hands fashioned.
> (Psalms 95:1–5)

In these trumpeting sentences, which go on at length, the hosts who go out towards God recall the Sabbath of creation when God first sat upon His throne to rule over the world. But a welcoming ceremony, especially one bestowing honor to a king, requires that the hosts stand and present themselves before him as deserving and proper to entertain him in their home, as the strong hand of his command is upon them. This dynamic is expressed in the second reading:

> Come, let us bow down and kneel,
> Bend the knee before the Lord our maker,
> For He is our God,
> And we are the people He tends, the flock in His care.
> O, of you would but heed His charge this day:
> (Psalms 95:6–7)

With these words the Sabbath of the Egyptian exodus is remembered, the Sabbath given to the people of Israel when they deserved it. In their going out to receive the king who brought them the gift of His Sabbath, it is incumbent upon the people to prove that they are worthy of His gift on this day as well: to shake off their sins, submit themselves before Him, and to accept the yoke of His *mitzvot* with readiness to serve Him:

> Do not be stubborn as at Meribah,
> As on the day of Massah, in the wilderness,
> When your fathers put Me to the test,

Tried Me, though they had seen My deeds.
Forty years I was provoked by that generation;
I thought, "They are a senseless people;
They would not know my ways."
Concerning them I swore in anger,
"They shall never come to My resting-place!"
(Psalms 95:8–11)

Remembrance of the nation's past sins obliges God's children, who seek to come to the repose of God on the day of His Sabbath, to renew themselves before Him and to sing a new song with the renewal of creation:

Sing to the Lord a new song,
Sing to the Lord, all the earth.
Sing to the Lord, bless His name,
Proclaim His victory day after day.
(Psalms 96:1–2)

And what is the new song? It is the song that announces the kingdom which reveals itself, symbolized by the Sabbath which God bequeathed to His people by bringing them out of the house of slavery, to execute righteous judgment throughout the land:

Declare among the nations, "the Lord is king!"
The world stand firm; it cannot be shaken;
He judges the peoples with equity.
Let the heavens rejoice and the earth exult;
Let the sea and all within it thunder,
The fields and everything in them exult;
Then shall all the trees of the forest shout for joy
At the presence of the Lord, for He is coming,
For He is coming to rule the earth;
He will rule the world justly,
And its peoples in faithfulness.
(Psalms 96:10–13)

These words sum up the conceptual messages of the psalms designated for welcoming the Sabbath as a day on which God sits to rule His kingdom in justice. The proclamation of "the Lord is king" which opens Psalms 96 and

99, and joins with Psalms 29—a singular psalm designated to acclaim God as sovereign over the entire earth. The same proclamation of God's kingship will be heard again at the opening of Psalms 93, which concludes the psalms of *Kabbalat Shabbat* with the declaration of the eternality of God's kingdom in the entire world.

In this connection, the poem already discussed in the previous chapter is included, defined by its heading, "A Psalm. A Song; for the Sabbath day" (Psalms 92:1). It came, as recalled, to resolve the problem of the evil infiltrating earthly creation, against which God, the Lord of hosts, fought after the Sabbath of creation, in order to sanctify creation so as to be worthy of His blessing. Bringing His nation out of Egypt, the house of bondage, constituted a decisive phase in God's war against evil, so as to establish the rule of His true judgment and righteousness over all the earth. His people were commanded, and took it upon themselves, to help God in His great battle until the eternal Sabbath would enter, the Sabbath that would unite the Sabbath of creation with the Sabbath of history. Therefore, God gave His Sabbath to His nation as a sign of the covenant, which is to remain between them forever. In order to be worthy of the Sabbath, the children of Israel are therefore required to live in righteousness, to do justice, and to act justly before God, for only the righteous are worthy to see His face and be seen before Him. We saw above that this is the primary motif of the psalms. The hymnal song for the Sabbath day concludes:

> The righteous bloom like a date-palm;
> They thrive like a cedar in Lebanon;
> Planted in the house of the Lord,
> They flourish in the courts of our God.
> In old age they still produce fruit;
> They are full of sap and freshness,
> Attesting that the Lord is upright,
> My rock, in whom there is no wrong.
> (Psalms 92:13–16)

These psalms express the ethical-metaphysical perspective of the relations of God to His world, to humankind and to His nation, while the liturgical poem *Lekhah Dodi*, which has been accepted by all Jewish congregations, lends a different layer of meaning to the entire ceremony, one related to a mystical-erotic perspective: the love relationship between the congregation of Israel and the Holy One Blessed be He. This aspect is expressed in the repeated refrain, "Come my Beloved to greet the bride; let us welcome the Sabbath" and after that in the closing stanza of the song, "Come in peace, O crown of her husband; Come with joy and jubilation, among the faithful of the treasured people. Enter, O bride! Enter, O bride!" (K:322, *Lekhah Dodi*).

According to the book of the Zohar and the Lurianic *Kabbalah* that followed it, the Sabbath is identified with the *Shekhinah*—and the concept of *Shekhinah* takes on a new meaning: not the hidden presence of God Himself amid His nation, but the spiritual-personal essence emanating from infinite divinity, arranged according to *sefirot*. They infuse a *shefa* (influx), which constitutes, fructifies, and lifts up the universe. The war of the Lord of hosts with the powers of chaos is thereby understood, in a bold flight of thought, as an internal war between the powers of judgment (*din*) and of compassion (*rahamim*) within divinity itself, to correct the essential evil included in the wholeness of divinity. This concept represents the physical-soulful human being, not only as a son of God created in His image, but as the symbol of God Himself—in the sense that the struggle between good and evil, which splits all the divine spheres apart, is reflected in its full force in the human being struggling to correct himself and redeem himself from the evil within him and within the earthly universe that surrounds him and holds him captive.

In the capacity of a *sefirah* of divine emanation, the *Shekhinah* is designated to be a link in the essential passage between God and His people, and by means of it to humanity and the world, for restoring and elevating them. It represents God before His nation on the one hand, and His nation as it ascends and unifies towards God as *keneset yisrael* (the congregation of Israel) on the other. According to the same multivocal symbolism, the Sabbath is also identified with the *Shekhinah*, as it represents God who comes to spread His peace upon the world and to reveal His love for His people. Thus, the metaphorical, symbolic language of the *Lekhah Dodi* hymn translates the welcoming of God in the book of Psalms into the welcoming of the Sabbath itself, as the *Shekhinah* of God on the one hand, and as the mystical essence that embodies the congregation of Israel on the other.

Who is the "friend/lover" (*dod*)? First of all, the Holy One Blessed be He Who descends to unite with His bride, *keneset yisrael*—the congregation of Israel, which unifies itself and ascends with its yearning to unite with God. But along with identifying God as the lover, the nation loyal to God is identified as the "lover" of the Sabbath. Thus, God on the one hand, and the nation on the other, are called to go out towards the Sabbath "bride" and invite her into the "home," which is the synagogue as the miniature sanctuary of God, with the same words, "Enter O bride! Enter O bride!"

This erotic meaning is not articulated in the psalms, which are concerned with God's kingship and with enacting justice and truth. The Safed kabbalists added the recital of the Song of Songs before the *Ma'ariv* prayer on the eve of Sabbath. This poem is the poem of the wedding of King Solomon with his Shulamite wife, and the sages of the *Mishnah* already interpreted it as a poem of the mystical marriage between the Holy One Blessed be He and the congregation of Israel. With respect to the totality of the experience of erotic sanctity, which is expressed in the liturgical poem *Lekhah Dodi*, we recall that on the eve of the Sabbath the women of Israel immersed themselves in the *mikvah* (ritual bath), so as to welcome their husbands on the eves of Sabbath at the ceremonial meal with all the family members and then to be alone and unite with them in sanctity and purity.

The Prayer of the Sabbath Day and Reading the Torah

The welcoming of God as king of the world and as king of His people, enacting justice, truth, and righteousness, takes place on the Sabbath day during the central ceremony of reading the Torah in the synagogue—as a ceremonial renewal of the Sinai covenant. For this purpose, the books of the Pentateuch are divided into "portions" according to the counting of the weeks over the course of the year, a portion for each week, accompanied by the *Haftarah* from the words of the prophets. We have dealt with the meaning of the ceremony as an event that unifies the community before God in the first chapter.

The ceremony of reading the Torah is the center and the climax of the essential celebratory prayer on the Sabbath, which continues from the morning until close to the afternoon of the day. This is the part dedicated to the worship of God. It is composed of two sections: the *Shaharit* (morning) prayer prior to the reading of the Torah and the *Musaf* (additional) prayer after it. The *Shaharit* prayer includes the same components from which the daily morning prayer is comprised: the *Birkhot Hashahar* (morning blessings), *Pesukei Dezimra* (verses of song), the *Keriyat Shema* (the Recitation of the Shema*), and the *Amidah* (standing prayer). But the blessings accompanying the *Shema* are expanded on the Sabbath, filled with festivity by the addition of liturgical hymns that carry a mystical meaning, and the *Amidah* prayer is adjusted for the Sabbath day. This applies to all of the *Amidah* prayers of the Sabbath, namely of the *Arvit* (evening prayer) following *Kabbalat Shabbat*, the *Shaharit*, the *Musaf*, and the *Minhah* (afternoon prayer) of the Sabbath. The adjustment is made by expanding the *Kedushah*, and by replacing six of the blessings following it—which relate to the reality of six days of labor when the community and its individuals cope with the distress of exile and its decrees, with a long poetic blessing dedicated specifically to the Sabbath; also by eliminating the next seven petitions connected to messianic redemption. One of the three Torah passages cited above, which command the Sabbath, is woven into this blessing. Thus, instead of the eighteen (really nineteen) regular blessings—as in the weekday *Shemoneh Esrei*—the Sabbath *Amidah* is composed of seven blessings, corresponding to the seven days of the week which are concluded and sanctified with Sabbath.

The mystical dimension added to the *Shema* blessings and to the *Kedushah* of the Sabbath *Amidah* will be discussed in depth in the coming chapter. In general, this dimension raises the day from the earthly temporal-spatial plane of the days of work to the celestial temporal-spatial plane of the Sabbath day with respect to its cosmic significance. In the expansion of the *Kedushah* (not just in the *Amidah*, but in the first blessing of the Recitation of the *Shema*), the light of the sun, which breaks at dawn and illumines heaven with its brightness and splendor, symbolizes the memory of the first light of creation:

> God said: "Let there be light;" and there was light.
> God saw that the light was good."
> (Genesis 1:3–4)

By remembering the primal light which shines its inner brightness upon the firmament, the similitudes of the higher world beyond the firmament of heaven are imagined. In it, the sun, moon, and stars are set to illumine the world after the light of creation has been concealed from earthly gaze by the firmament itself. On the Sabbath, worshippers of the *Shaḥarit* and *Musaf* prayers envision the heaven opening above them, and God exalted on the throne of His kingdom, surrounded by His heavenly host, with the eyes of their spirit. On the Sabbath day His substantial light, the light of the seven days of creation, shines upon God's angels, and they sing before God and recite His praise. In this pageant, the children of Israel on earth stand with a straightened leg, as the angels do in heaven, to say "Holy! Holy! Holy!" However, on the Sabbath the children of Israel not only do on earth what the angels do in heaven. They also see themselves rising and bowing and reciting praise of their creator with their poetry together with the angels above. The sound of their singing combines with the singing of the angels and of all creatures in the world, which unite, sanctify, and bless the divine Name on the Sabbath. This is the feeling of sublimity, which makes the children of Israel worthy of tasting, while they are on earth in the lands of their exile, the flavor of the Sabbath which reveals the redemption to come in the future at the "end of days".

Interlude: The Theological Stance of the Blessing of the Sabbath

Against the background of the exaltation in the reciting of the *Kedushah* of the *Amidah* prayer, the blessing of the Sabbath in the *Shaḥarit* and *Musaf* prayers is sung, commemorating the specialness of the day:

> Moses rejoiced at the gift of his portion
> When You called him "faithful servant."
> A crown of glory
> You placed on his head
> When he stood before You on Mount Sinai.
> He brought down in his hands two tablets of stone
> On which was engraved the observance of the Sabbath.
> So it is written in your Torah:
> The children of Israel must keep the Sabbath,
> Observing the Sabbath in every generation
> As an everlasting covenant.
> It is a sign between Me and the children of Israel for ever,
> For in six days God made the heavens and the earth,
> But on the seventh day
> He ceased work and refreshed Himself.
> You, O Lord our God, did not give it
> To the other nations of the world,
> Nor did You, our King, give it as a heritage to those who worship idols.
> In its rest the uncircumcised do not dwell,
> For You gave it in love to Israel Your people,
> To the descendants of Jacob whom You chose.
> May the people who sanctify the seventh day
> All find satisfaction and delight in Your goodness,
> For You favored the seventh day and made it holy,
> Calling it the most cherished of days,
> A remembrance of the act of creation.
> Our God and God of our ancestors, find favor in our rest.
> Make us holy through Your commandments

And grant us our share in Your Torah.
Satisfy us with Your goodness, grant us joy in Your salvation,
And purify our hearts to serve You in truth.
In love and favor, Lord our God,
Grant us as our heritage Your holy Sabbath,
So that Israel who sanctify Your name may find rest on it.
Blessed are You, Lord, who sanctifies the Sabbath.
(K:484, 486, *Yismaḥ Mosheh*)

The conclusion of the blessing reverts to the regular form of the *Amidah*'s blessings and the *siddur*'s blessings in general, combining the language of second person ("you") and third person ("He"). But the opening of this blessing, even though a context for it is provided in the extended *Kedushah* blessing, is a surprising exception, and begs for an explanation. Instead of addressing God directly, to praise His benevolence towards His people so as to ask for its continuation, the assembly of worshippers relates to Moses, to whom God bestowed benevolence on one exceptional occasion—whereupon Moses favored his people by bestowing on them the exceptional benevolence that God had rendered to him personally by giving his people the Torah of the covenant, which included the Sabbath as a sign of the covenant. This singled out the children of Israel to be God's treasured people from among all the nations. Because of this, in this blessing in honor of the Sabbath, the people of Israel are called by the name "the people that sanctify the seventh [day]."

We learn from this, first of all, that this exceptional hymn-blessing, which is inserted at the midpoint of the seven blessings to bridge between the first three and the last three, was designed to emphasize the uniqueness of the Sabbath day as an exception to the rule which sheds light on the rule. It does so by referencing a series of singular, exceptional events in which God's unity and uniqueness as creator and king of the universe are revealed: the singularity of the creation; the singularity of the Egyptian exodus; the singularity of the prophecy of Moses; the singularity of the Torah; the singularity of the Sabbath as a sign of the covenant; and the singularity of the election of the nation of Israel as the treasure of God. Let us attend to the fact that in combination with the marking of God's unity and His absolute uniqueness, which all these established events reflect, the singularities rise to the number seven and are included in the sanctification of the seventh day.

Notwithstanding all this, there is the anomaly of the description of Moses standing at the heights of Mount Sinai, with the "crown of splendor" on his head and the symbols of his rule in his hand—the two Tablets of the Covenant, engraved by the "finger of God," on which the commandment of observing the

Sabbath is written—there is nothing like this type of description in any other blessing; not in the *Shemoneh Esrei* and not in the entire *siddur*. We cannot, therefore, overlook the challenging parallel between the status of Moses as a mediator between God and His nation, and the stance of Jesus the "savior." He is the "son of God," mediator between God and all human beings who believe in him through the Christian church. With the crown of thorns upon his head, he is suspended on the cross, symbolizing his sacrifice to atone for the sins of humankind and to save them from the defilement of sin through his resurrection and his ascent to heaven after his crucifixion. And through his promise to return at the "end of days" to redeem all humankind from the slavery of sinking into sinful materialism, and from the wickedness of slavery, sickness, suffering, and death.

The anomaly of this parallel leaps to the eye, especially given the scruples of the Rabbinic sages, on account of which the Passover *Haggadah*, composed after the destruction of the Second Temple, does not mention the name of Moses. The intention was to emphasize the scriptural testimony: that redemption from the Egyptian house of slavery was accomplished by God and not by Moses—in contrast to the Christian expectation that the final redemption would take place through Jesus, who would return to earth a second time. In the Jewish end-of-days scenario as well, the messianic king will be an individual of flesh and blood: "But a shoot shall grow out of the stump of Jesse" (Isaiah 11:1)— who would rise to kingship by God's benevolence. But it is God who rearranges the order of creation, and not the messiah. What, then, explains the position of Moses in the Sabbath *Amidah* prayer as an exalted human figure who mediates between God and His people?

We find the explanation if we turn to differences, emphasized with details, between the church's description of Jesus's character and the description of Moses's character in the Sabbath blessing of the *Amidah*. Moses is not described as a "son of God" in the sense of a personality that is at once divine and human. Rather, he is described as a person of merit who earned his singular rank by virtue of his deeds. Moses is a "faithful servant" who subordinated his will to the will of the one who sent him. The paradox of human freedom, which exists only out of servitude to God, was exemplified with Moses on the highest level. Therefore, he was worthy of being granted rule over the nation that, like him, committed itself to the service of God and deserved the freedom symbolized by the Sabbath: A crown of splendor, not a crown of thorns, was upon his head. The two Tablets of the Covenant, upon which Sabbath is engraved as a sign, are Moses's symbol—not the cross. And it is Moses who gives the Torah of God to his people; the Torah, which is also called by Moses's name, to distinguish and single out the nation from all the nations by its loyalty to the sign of the covenant, as "the people who sanctify the seventh day" (unlike Christians' transfer of the Sabbath day to the first day of the week!).

In this connection, let us emphasize that the *mitzvot* of the Torah of Moses apply to Israel alone, and that only the children of Israel participated in the Sabbath engraved on the Tablets of the Covenant, and not the children of nations to whom Jesus's disciples directed his tidings. It follows from this that, in the future to come as well, when the "Sabbath of creation" will be united with the "Sabbath of history," the children of Israel will be worthy, through the Sabbath, to come to the tranquility of redemption as members of God's covenant—but not the children of the nations, whose flesh is not impressed with the covenantal sign of circumcision. Further, even during their exile under the rule of the idolatrous nations, the children of Israel who sanctify God's name in the sight of all humankind are sheltered under God's wings. On the Sabbath day they serve God according to the *mitzvot* of the Torah, which also apply to them in exile. With this, they declare the obligation of their service and obedience to God alone—sheltered under the wings of His *Shekhinah* and sensing their freedom in their servitude. With this they are uplifted and they celebrate as children of freedom, gathering around their table as if to the altar of God. By virtue of this loyalty, Moses lives forever in his Torah and is remembered forever—from Sabbath to Sabbath. There is no need for him to return to earthly life to save his nation. As stated, God will redeem His people, as in the day they left Egypt.

To summarize: the blessing of the Sabbath represents a theology opposed to the Christian church, and following the Torah—which does not move from its place, will not change, and will never be replaced. In this way, the language of prayer singles out and distinguishes Israel from its Christian surroundings without resorting to the polemical language of the blessing regarding apostates. Such language is necessary for the secular weekdays during the exile, but it is not necessary when the children of Israel experience the Sabbath together. The Sabbath is a sort of redemption in the hidden place of the synagogues and homes where people live, because on this day they climb emotionally beyond the reach of the earthly kingdoms of nations and dwell sheltered under the *Shekhinah* of God.

Feast and Grace after Meals—At First Glance

The afternoon meal of the Sabbath day, which takes place after the *Musaf* prayer, concludes the half-day dedicated to worshipping God and begins the half dedicated to Sabbath rest, as God's recompense to His nation for its worship. The ceremonial name for the grace after the meal is *Birkat Hamazon* (literally, "blessing for nourishment"). It is a complete and fully developed liturgical creation, which stands by itself. The command to bless when eating food applies to the sons and daughters of Israel each and every day, but during the six days of work it is recited briefly and quietly, while on the Sabbaths and holidays we sing all of it together with merriment and joy.

As to its message, the *Birkat Hamazon* is composed of four essential blessings. The first blessing sets the foundation, expressing the gratitude which all men and women of Israel are obliged to acknowledge to God, within the totality of creation insofar as they are its creatures. Their existence, health, and ability to work, create, multiply, and be worthy of happiness depend upon satisfying their needs, especially those of food and drink. The Torah in Genesis teaches that God created all His creatures with the desire to benefit them, and that He was careful to assure them of the resources and conditions necessary for their life and well-being. From this perspective, God took it upon Himself, as king and as father, to satisfy their needs. But the creatures live their own lives by themselves and thereby bear their own responsibility before God, to each other, and to themselves—each creature on its level and according to the abilities developed by it. The kingdom of God is based upon this assumption, and the *Halakhah* defines it as natural justice that exists among all creatures of the divine creation—by means of the equilibrium between their appetites for what they need and the availability of their foodstuff in nature and their ability to attain it. In other words, plants and animals eat and drink until they are contented and satiated, and then stop. They mate so as to be fruitful and to multiply, and they stop. They are not able to draw from resources in creation more than what they themselves provide. They are even unable to control the supplies or to gather produce for themselves in great quantities. Justice is preserved in creation because each creature consumes what is necessary for it according to its requirement for the day, and expects to find tomorrow what it has found today. The psalms cited below document this thought in their descriptions, and the first blessing of the grace after meals epitomizes it by reciting this gratitude to God: "For He is God who feeds and sustains all, does good to all, and prepares food for all creatures He has created" (K:978, *Barukh atah adonai eloheinu melekh ha'olam kulo betuvo*).

"For He is God who feeds and sustains all, does good to all, and prepares food for all creatures he has created" (K:978)

In this respect, the human being created in the image of God is also exceptional. His physical and psychological-emotional needs are infinitely more numerous than those of other living creatures, and his appetite and desire exceed his needs. He is about abundance and is not satisfied with being content and satiated. He needs pleasure for its own sake—and the desire for pleasure knows no satisfaction. Because of this, the inclinations of the ego of the human being direct him to take for himself all he can without thinking of the other. If he were able, he would even use the other and invent tools enabling him to draw from the resources of creation much more than they provide to him by themselves. The human being strives to rule over his surroundings, to overcome his competitors and enslave them for his needs, whose satisfaction he seeks to assure each day of his life with ever greater amounts. By virtue of his excess ability he creates civilization and rules it. But when he crosses the boundary of what is right for him, when he wastes creation's resources, takes for himself alone and enslaves the creatures around him, including his neighbors, to satisfy his needs that have no limit, he destroys the earth from whose resources he draws, and destroys the civilization that he has built with his own hands. The earth is then filled with violence and evil, as happened in the city of Cain, in the Tower of Babel, in Sodom and Gomorrah, and in Pharaonic Egypt. In this way, civilization brings punishment upon itself, inflicted by God through His control of the laws of creation.

Because of limits of character, human beings do not maintain laws of justice, which are vital to their lives and well-being. To the contrary, they are inclined to violate them. This is opposed to the mission for which God created them in His image and granted them governance. For them to fulfill their mission and find their well-being, they are required to submit to the law legislated by God for the civilization created by humans. This law is not impressed upon the humans' substantive souls, but upon their intellect and reason. It is up to human beings to recognize the authority of the God who commands them, and to observe His law and His *mitzvot*—so as to overcome inclinations of egoism and improve their ways in order to become worthy of well-being. The Sabbath, given to Israel as a "sign" of the covenant, testifies to this, as does the Sabbatical year every seventh year, and the Jubilee at the end of every seven Sabbatical cycles.

The connection between the justice in God's distributing gifts and the Sabbath is accentuated in the narrative of the descent of manna in the desert. But the legislation of the Torah emphasizes this also in the ordinances that distinguish the kingdom of Israel from idolatrous kingdoms, which became houses of slavery. The essential provision is that the earth and all its treasures are the absolute property of the God who created it. Creatures that sustain themselves from the earth are also the property of God, including the human being. In this sense, all are God's servants, obliged to do His will. Accordingly, the Torah annuls ownership claims that tyrannical rulers assert over the land and its resources. Human beings retain only the right to obtain from possession of the land the satisfaction of all their needs, with consideration of the needs of their neighbors and the needs of all creatures for which God prepared nourishment in the land. Beyond this, since human beings can control and take for themselves more than their share, they bear responsibility before God to see that their neighbors and all the creatures with whom they live, and whom they need, satisfy their requirements as the humans satisfy theirs. Only in this sense can human beings realize their rights and fulfill their mission as righteous rulers according to the ordinances of God.

Sabbath and "Sabbath of the Land." Assuring that Nourishment Exists for all Earth's Creatures

Let us again recall that, according to the law of the Torah, God distributed possession of the land to all nations, and made their settlement rely on condition of observing the laws of justice, which He legislated in the Noahide covenant. This judgment applied to the children of Israel, who would inherit the possession of Canaan. The sin of Canaan is defined in terms of grave idolatry, which sanctifies cruel and murderous evil. Accordingly, Canaan's right to inherit its land and establish reign over it lapsed. But the children of Israel were bound to pass the test, which the nations of Canaan had failed. If they did not, they would justly lose their right. For this purpose, the Canaanite property was distributed fairly to the tribes of Israel, to clans and families, and their right could not lapse. It was designed to assure each family, clan, and tribe in Israel independent economic-social status vis-à-vis other families, clans, and tribes. In this framework, they were required to pledge to one another before God that none of them would be deprived of their fair share.

But was this order to be maintained forever? The difficulty has to do with the fact that human beings are not equal in talents, abilities, and respective needs, nor in the traits they inherit. These differences create advantages and disadvantages, which need to be balanced for the good through reciprocal relations whereby one compensates for the deficiencies of the other with its advantages. But the tendencies of the egoistic inclination of most human beings direct them to take advantage of the others' deficiencies to rule them, exploit them, and deprive them. The ordinance of the Torah of Moses seeks to assure maintenance of humane relations according to the principle of "love your neighbor as yourself" as applied through the *mitzvah* of *tzedakah* in its various forms. However, since the emergence of inequalities of poverty and wealth cannot be avoided, with the result that the poor lose their property and their economic and societal independence and are liable to be sold into slavery, the Torah instituted the *mitzvot* of the Sabbath, the Sabbatical year, and the Jubilee. During these appointed times, the land and all its resources, including living creatures and human beings, return to God's absolute ownership so that the land rests. At the same time, societal distortions can be corrected and the just distribution of properties of land and its fruits can be restored.

This, therefore, is the societal meaning of the sweeping prohibition against doing any work to satisfy human needs on the Sabbath. On the Sabbath, all temporary ownership given to every son and daughter of Israel over their property, resources, tools, slaves, servants, and cattle lapses. Ownership returns to God. Thus, the harvest of the fields in the seventh year is also given freely to anyone needing it, according to his need—as with the manna in the desert. In this way, the natural justice, which God legislates for His realm is also maintained in human society. All humans go back to being servants of God on the one hand, and free people in reciprocal relations between themselves and other creatures of the land on the other.

At the close of the Sabbath, all return to their status as it was before the Sabbath entered. In order for justice to be preserved also during weekdays, when a person worked for his needs, the Torah added the law of the Sabbatical year. It is considered the "Sabbath of the land," whereby working the land stops for an entire year. The poor who were sold into servitude return to independence. The Torah also added the law of the Jubilee, according to which all properties sold are supposed to be returned to their owners and their owners' heirs. The prophets of Israel required their people, kings, and ministers to implement this ordinance in all its particulars. The fact that their people disobeyed this ordinance, in their view, caused the destruction of the Temple, the city, and the kingdom, and the uprooting of the people from their land. Thus, the land rested because of them against their will. But in gentile lands where they settled, where the *mitzvot* dependent upon the land could not be observed, the *mitzvot* of *tzedakah*—which maintained mutual responsibility within each community and between all dispersed communities—and especially the *mitzvah* of the Sabbath, took their place. By means of the Sabbath, the independent life of the dispersed nation as a nation chosen to worship God—and not worship kings of the gentiles or founders of idolatry-infected religions—came to full-fledged and official expression. This is the meaning of the Sabbath as being a "sign" of the covenant between God and His people. In this way, the Sabbath preserved the existence of the people as one nation, despite dispersion and servitude.

Externally, the people of Israel were enslaved by the kings of the gentiles. From within, the children of Israel experienced their Sabbath as free men.

This double life experience shaped the image of the people in exile. It influenced the morality of justice and righteousness which they followed in their communities, and the way of life which distinguished the people from the gentiles in their worship of God. This did not prevent and did not disturb their striking roots economically and politically in the civilizations in which they made their livelihoods. Thus, there developed the image of the Jew as a householder-businessman who seeks, on the one hand, personal and familial independence in economic terms, and on the other, respected status as contributor to the institutions of the community—the synagogue, the house of learning, the *mikvah*, and charitable institutions. As long as the economic and political conditions which enabled this communal arrangement, its society, and families, to function properly were maintained, Jews lived with a relative feeling of inner freedom. They gave it a celebratory expression in their worship of God and in their rest on the Sabbath.

Three Psalms that Exemplify Concern for All

This message is provided in the *Siddur Hatefillah* in the psalms of *Kabbalat Shabbat* about receiving God's countenance for carrying out righteous justice in the land; in the ceremony of enacting the covenant by ascent to the Torah and the *mitzvot* of charity which accompany it; and in psalms set aside for the *Minḥah* prayer and especially in the grace after meals. Let us first cite three representative passages from the psalms that are set aside for *Minḥah*:

> Your kingship is an eternal kingship;
> Your dominion is for all generations.
> The Lord supports all who stumble,
> And makes all who are bent stand straight.
> The eyes of all look to You expectantly,
> And You give them their food when it is due.
> You give it openhandedly,
> Feeding every creature to its heart's content.
> The Lord is beneficent in all His ways
> And faithful in all His works.
> The Lord is near to all who call Him,
> To all who call Him with sincerity.
> (Psalms 145:13–18)

You make springs gush forth in torrents;
They make their way between the hills,
Giving drink to all the wild beasts;
The wild asses slake their thirst.
The birds of the sky dwell beside them
And sing among the foliage.
You water the mountains from Your lofts;
The earth is sated from the fruit of Your work.
You make the grass grow for the cattle,
And herbage for man's labor
That he may get food out of the earth—
Wine that cheers the hearts of men
Oil that makes the face shine,
And bread that sustains man's life.
The trees of the Lord drink their fill,
The cedars of Lebanon, His own planting,
Where birds make their nests;
The stork has her home in the junipers.
The high mountains are for wild goats;
The crags are a refuge for rock-badgers.
He made the moon to mark the seasons;
The sun knows when to set.
You bring on darkness and it is night,
When all the beasts of the forests stir.
The lions roar for prey,
Seeking their food from God.
When the sun rises, they come home
And couch in their dens.
Man then goes out to his work,
To his labor until the evening.
How many are the things You have made, O Lord;
You have made them all with wisdom;
The earth is full of Your creations.
There is the sea, vast and wide,
With its creatures beyond number,
Living things, small and great.
There go the ships,
And Leviathan that You formed to sport with.
All of them look to You

To give them their food when it is due.
Give it to them, they gather it up;
Open Your hand, they are well satisfied;
Hide Your face, they are terrified;
Take away their breath, they perish
And turn again into dust;
Send back Your breath, they are created,
And You renew the face of the earth.
May the glory of the Lord endure forever;
May the Lord rejoice in His works!
(Psalms 104:10–31)

We cite finally one of the "Songs of Ascents" that is read during the Shabbat *Minḥah* service. It represents the ideal of the Jewish Sabbath-observant family, which is expressed and exemplified by the grace after meals sung around the family table:

A Song of ascents.
Happy are all who fear the Lord,
who follow His ways.
You shall enjoy the fruit of your labors;
you shall be happy and you shall prosper.
Your wife shall be like a fruitful vine within your house;
your sons, like olive saplings around your table.
So shall the man who fears the Lord be blessed.
May the Lord bless you from Zion
may you share the prosperity of Jerusalem
all the days of your life,
and live to see your children's children.
May all be well with Israel!
(Psalms 128:1–6)

Enjoying Life as a Religious Ideal

Having cited these psalms, let us turn to another essential component of the ideal of well-being that is realized on the Sabbath—the ideal's profound earthiness. That is, the war against wickedness coming from the powers of chaos which infiltrate creation does not evoke the Christian reaction of disqualifying earthly life with its sensual pleasures as a basically sinful experience. It does not stir up a longing for pure spiritual happiness—as opposed to earthly enjoyment of this life—achieved through fasting and breaking temptation in this world. Or for the life of the soul purified of physicality in the world to come after death, or for when Jesus will return and redeem humankind from the physicality and materiality into which humanity sunk on account of the "original sin." According to the Torah, the psalms cited above and the grace after meals, physical life, and satisfying its needs, becoming content and satiated, and also enjoying life are all good and proper. Enjoying earthly life does not contradict the spiritual dimension. Instead, it is a vital condition for the development of that dimension (as is said and repeated frequently in the *Ethics of the Fathers*, a tractate of the *Mishnah* that we customarily study on the Sabbath). In other words: the well-being of a person is to be achieved by a proper balance between physical and emotional satisfaction on the one hand, and moral and spiritual satisfaction on the other. It is therefore proper to aspire to well-being and possibly be worthy of it in this world as well—if we walk in God's ways, revere and worship Him in faithfulness, and achieve the needs of life properly while displaying responsibility for the other and for the collective.

The continuity of life is not exhausted by the soul's immortality in heavenly life after death; rather, it is maintained through the chain of generations, as expressed in the "Song of Ascents" cited above and in the *Ethics of the Fathers*. One cannot, obviously, remove the sin and suffering involved in this world. The Jew can experience the well-being with the attribute of perfection that is "like the world to come" only on the Sabbath and the holidays. But also, the oral Torah does not give up hope of recompense for the pious in their physical life in this world, and it distinguishes between pure, soulful recompense in the "world to come" and earthly recompense in the messianic kingdom of justice to be established for Israel in its land at the end of days. On the Sabbath, therefore, the people of Israel experience "a foretaste of the world to come" in the sacred worship of the synagogue, and "a foretaste of the days of the messiah" in the feasts of the Sabbath and in its tranquility.

Grace after Meals: Expression of Earthly Enjoyment and Possession of the Land

The grace after meals gives expression to these two aspects of earthly well-being, which are tied to perpetuating the bond between the people of Israel and their sacred land even when settled in exile. For only in the Land of Israel will they be worthy to serve God by observing all of the *mitzvot* that are dependent on the land on the one hand, and be worthy of perfect rest on the Sabbath and its earthly well-being on the other.

> We thank You, Lord our God,
> For having granted as a heritage to our ancestors
> A desirable, good and spacious land;
> For bringing us out, Lord our God, from the land of Egypt,
> Freeing us from the house of slavery;
> For Your covenant which You sealed in our flesh;
> For Your Torah which You taught us;
> For Your laws which You made known to us;
> For the life, grace and kindness You have bestowed on us;
> And for the food by which You continually feed and sustain us,
> Every day, every season, every hour.
> For so it is written: "You will eat and be satisfied, then you shall bless the Lord your God for the good land He has given you" (Deuteronomy 8:19). Blessed are You, Lord, for the land and for the food.
> (K:978, *Nodeh Lekha*)

A double accentuation distinguishes this blessing from the one preceding it: its relation to the nation of Israel in particular, as the chosen nation; and the gratitude recited in it not only for the food but for the possession of the land. Let us reemphasize that the blessing recited in exile also concerns the Land of Israel conquered by strangers. Hearing the blessing recalls the eternal, never broken bond of the chosen nation to its chosen land, which is a condition for its survival as a chosen nation even when in prolonged exile—as long as the people expect to return to their land. This sentiment is not only a memory. It is now. It generates individual and collective pilgrimages "to cherish the dust" (Psalms 102:15) of the holy land, and it sustains the longing and the yearning to renew the days as of old, with settlement of the nation in its land.

The expectation and hope to return to full earthly life, material and spiritual, is expressed in the third blessing, which concerns the building of Jerusalem. In terms of content, this blessing is connected to the hymn of Psalms 128, cited above: "May the Lord bless you from Zion; may you share the prosperity of Jerusalem" (Psalms 128:5). But it connects with even more power to the psalm that relates to the Babylonian exile:

> By the rivers of Babylon,
> There we sat,

Sat and wept,
As we thought of Zion.
There on the poplars
We hung up our lyres,
For our captors asked us there for songs,
Our tormentors, for amusement:
"Sing us one of the songs of Zion."
How can we sing a song of the Lord
On alien soil?
If I forget you, O Jerusalem
Let my right hand wither;
Let my tongue stick to my palate
If I cease to think of you,
If I do not keep Jerusalem in memory
Even at my happiest hour.
Remember, O Lord, against the Edomites
The day of Jerusalem's fall;
How they cried, "Strip her, strip her
To her very foundations!"
Fair Babylon, you predator,
A blessing on him who repays you in kind
What you have inflicted on us;
A blessing on him who seizes your babies
And dashes them against the rocks!
(Psalms 137:1–9)

The echo of this oath, along with its yearning for revenge against "Edom" (the oral Torah sages identified Edom with pagan Rome and later with the Christian church!) reverberates in the language of the third blessing:

Have compassion,
Please, Lord our God,
On Israel Your people,
On Jerusalem Your city,
On Zion the dwelling place of Your glory,
On the royal house of David Your anointed,
And on the great and holy House that bears Your name.
(K:982, Raḥem Na)

But the blessing is not content with expectation. It demands settling God's obligations in His covenant with Israel, even in exile:

> Our God, our Father,
> Tend us, feed us,
> Sustain us and support us,
> Relieve us and send us relief,
> Lord our God,
> Swiftly from all our troubles.
> Please, Lord our God,
> Do not make us dependent
> On the gifts or loans of other people,
> But only on Your full, open, holy and generous hand
> So that we may suffer neither shame nor humiliation
> For ever and all time.
> (K:982, *Rahem Na*)

Even in exile, God nourishes and sustains His people. He does not let the nations destroy them, despite the advantage of their controlling power. The enemies of Israel endeavor to annihilate Israel, and despite it all there were kings and ministers and other powers among the nations who were interested in the Jews' contribution to their countries, and who defended Jews from the fury of the church and inflamed Christian masses. The Jews regarded this as hidden protection by God, who rescued their souls from the hands of their enemies and their superior earthly power.

We come to the last, inclusive blessing, that of *Hatov Vehameitiv* (who is good and performs good). It relates to the present on earth, with all the changes in the nation's situations while in its land and while in exile. For God is good and His way is to bring about good—so that when He punishes those who revere Him, His intention is to benefit them.

> Blessed are You, Lord our God, King of the Universe –
> God our Father, our King, our Sovereign,
> Our Creator, our Redeemer, our Maker,
> Our Holy One, the Holy One of Jacob.
> He is our Shepherd, Israel's Shepherd,
> The good King who does good to all.
> Every day He has done, is doing, and will do good to us.

He has acted, is acting, and will always act kindly toward us
for ever,
Granting us grace, kindness and compassion, relief and rescue,
Prosperity, blessing, redemption, and comfort,
Sustenance and support, compassion, life, peace, and all
good things,
And of all good things may He never let us lack.
(K:986, *Barukh atah adonai eloheinu melekh ha'olam ha'el avinu*)

The singularity of the prayer's formulation is striking: On the face of it, what it says seems to contradict the life experience of the nation in exile—one full of harsh decrees, persecutions, and discrimination. For it testifies that "every single day" God does good to the children of His nation, and grants them every good. Second, it expresses trust in the God of Israel as the God of truth, the God of mercy, and the powerful King against whom no power can stand when He comes to rescue His people. If so, what is the basis of this certainty? The blessing does not speak of this. It only repeats the truth, returning to it a second and third time, with the intention of fixing it in memory on the one hand, and silencing doubts on the other. The repetition and glorification of God's power for the good, it appears, is to uproot doubt among Jews that is liable to bring despair. The simple and singular logic of faith is this: those who revere God do not doubt that God could save His nation in the twinkle of an eye, and they have no doubt that, were the people of Israel to believe in God and His Torah, and keep His *mitzvot*, God would want to redeem them. Despite the difficulties of the exilic situation, redemption depends upon the will of the people with regard to keeping the *mitzvot* of Torah and on God's response—and not on the goodwill of the nations, their kings, and priests.

The Tranquility of Love

A summary of the same ideas is found in the following prayer, incorporated in the *Amidah* for *Minḥah*:

You are One, Your Name is One;
And who is like Your people Israel,
A nation unique on earth?
Splendor of greatness and a crown of salvation,
Is the day of rest and holiness You have given to Your people.
Abraham will rejoice, Isaac will sing for joy,

Jacob and his children will find rest in it,
A rest of love and generosity,
A rest of truth and faith,
A rest of peace and tranquility,
Calm and trust;
A complete rest in which You find favor.
May Your children recognize and know
That their rest comes from You,
And that by their rest they will sanctify Your Name.
(K:612, *Atah Eḥad*)

This blessing affirms that the second half of the Sabbath day is dedicated to tranquility, and that the essence of Sabbath tranquility is defined as "perfect rest"—as distinct from rest during the days of labor. The opening of the blessing appears to be related to the "sign" of the covenant from the human perspective. Instead of emphasizing the nation's obligation to serve God, the focus is on God's responsibility for His people's tranquility. For as the nation singles out the one God that it serves, God singles out the one nation that serves Him.

This is the perfection of love that is reciprocal and reciprocated. What sets it apart? What is the secret of its perfection as tranquility which is not distorted by distress, anxiety, disturbance, or internal or external anger? The answer is found in the common element of the attributes of "love and generosity," of "truth and faith," of "peace and tranquility"—pairs of descriptions that explain one another and flow from one another. That element is found in the *mitzvah* "Love your neighbor as yourself," which complements the *mitzvah* "love the Lord your God." Complete tranquility is the tranquility of generous lovers—and not the tranquility of egoistic tyrants who take everything for themselves and seek to enjoy their tranquility and well-being by themselves alone. Authentic tranquility is that of giving one to another, which reciprocates one to the other. The advantage of true lovers is, therefore, their ability to rely on one another, and to rely on God who "desires" their tranquility, as they know that God relies on them because of their righteousness towards all their people.

The Ceremony of *Havdalah* (Distinction): Between the Seventh Day of Rest and the Six Days of Activity

The Sabbath enters at the end of the sixth day, and leaves at the end of the seventh day, when darkness prevails as measured by being able to see the light of three stars in the heavenly firmament—which is like a *havdalah* (distinction).

But the ceremonies of *Kiddush* and *Havdalah* are acts of the intelligent will of a knowledgeable person. Such ceremonies, which define the times with their singular content and their profound meaning for the human's orientation in his world, are required to pave a proper path for the human beings to realize their mission. *Havdalah*—the drawing of distinctions—is the basic principle in creating an intelligent and rational world, a world of truth distinct from lie, of good distinct from bad, and of justice distinct from evil. Insofar as the Sabbath is an act of God which obliges the person who serves Him according to His *mitzvot*, even the distinction between light and darkness, between day and night, and between good and bad, is an act of God who established the creation:

> When God began to create heaven and earth—the earth being unformed and void, with darkness over the surface of the deep and a wind from God sweeping over the water—God said, "Let there be light"; and there was light. God saw that the light was good, and God separated the light from the darkness. God called the light Day, and the darkness he called Night. And there was evening and there was morning, a first day. (Genesis 1:1–5)

All the distinctions cited above are included in this introductory passage, which focuses on the work of creation. In order to rule over the earth in the name of his God, the human being, who is created in the image of God, is bound to follow the same principle of distinction. Man learned to implement this principle when God distinguished between man and woman and determined the correlation between them. After that, God taught the man to call all creatures by their names, in order to distinguish among them, to define them, and to rule them with knowledge and reason. Finally, God placed man and his wife before the tree of knowledge, so they would learn to distinguish between true good and true evil, and between truth and falsehood.

The distinction between the six days of activity and the Sabbath is marked by ceremony at both ends. At the Sabbath's entry, it is enacted by lighting the candles, while the day still illumines from the outside and it is still permissible to kindle a fire, so that the light will shine within the homes as night falls. Parallel to this, the *Havdalah* ceremony proper marks the distinction between the departing Sabbath and the coming six days of activity. The main symbolic action during this ceremony is the kindling of a fire that represents the opposition between weekdays, during which kindling fire is necessary for observing the *mitzvah* of the person's labor for his needs, and the Sabbath, during which labor is forbidden. In this way, kindling the flame of the *Havdalah* candle amid darkness resembles God's act of creation. It demonstrates the difference between the light of the day which is now past, and the darkness of night which prevails; and between the light of the candle and the darkness of night. This ceremony grants the children of Israel, still immersed in their tranquility, the fortitude needed to go out to greet the six days of labor, with all their difficulties, darknesses, anxieties, and disappointments:

> Behold, God is my salvation. I will trust and not be afraid. The Lord, the Lord, is my strength and my song.
> He has become my salvation.
> With joy you will draw water from the springs of salvation.
> Salvation is the Lord's; on Your people is Your blessing, *Selah*.
> The Lord of hosts is with us,
> The God of Jacob is our stronghold, *Selah*.
> Lord of hosts: happy is the one who trusts in You.
> Lord, save! May the King answer us on the day we call.
> For the Jews there was light and gladness, joy and honor—so may it be for us.
> I will lift the cup of salvation and call the name of the Lord.
> (K:724, *Hinei El Yeshuati*)

These are calls of encouragement to rely on God and go out to the coming days of labor with a heart full of hope. Next, the blessing over wine, which gladdens the heart, is recited; then a blessing on the various species of spices which strengthen the human heart with their good aroma; then another essential blessing over the light of the flame, with which the candle glows and illumines the eyes, enabling them to distinguish darkness from light, as a symbol of all distinctions. It appears that all these symbolic acts are designed to instill in the human heart—after drawing the distinction between light and darkness, day and night, sacred and profane, and Israel and the nations—the vigor and hope to succeed in the coming days for the good. Kindling the flame, drinking the wine, smelling the spices, looking at the light that the person knows to illumine for himself—all these strengthen self-assurance. Again, we see here the positive relation of the *siddur* to the earthly life of the human beings, for which it is intended—a life that is worthwhile as long as they remain faithful to their mission: to do the good that God wants from them.

But despite the optimism, which warms the heart, the departure from the Sabbath is sad. Still, we escort the Sabbath with a heart stirred by longing, and after the *Havdalah* we sing a liturgical poem of yearning and consolation. How so? With the memory of the image of the person who was zealous for God, who battled idolatry with great commitment, who fought the king of Israel who oppressed and afflicted his people. For all this, he was worthy of the wonderful recompense of ascending to heaven in his living body, to be an advocate for the good of Israel, to suddenly appear as a savior for the pious of his people who suffer, and to become the messenger who will announce to his people when the authentic messiah will come from the House of David (as distinct from the false mission of Jesus, the Messiah in whom Christians believe). The messiah of the House of David will be a human being and not a god, but God will help him to return His nation to its land and renew His kingdom on earth.

The days have lengthened. The measure of exile is full. The right of the nation of Israel is abundant, together with the fullness of the measures of suffering which has purified the people. Because of this, the believers and loyal followers of God, who revere God and rely on His righteousness, know that the announcement on the lips of the wondrous messenger of truth, none other than the prophet Elijah who "will come to us speedily with the Messiah son of David," may come at any moment. The people of Israel are commanded every day to expect Elijah to come and give his announcement. But even if the path lengthens, hope does not stop. For when another six days pass, Israel will again be worthy to sanctify and rejoice before God on its Sabbath.

Breaking the Boundary of Mystery between the Kingdom of Heaven and the Earth: Praying with *Devekut* (Adherence) and with *Kavanah* (Intention)

Prayer as Prerequisite for Success of a Person's
Actions for Achieving His Objectives

Throughout the chapters of this book our concern has focused on the intellectual contents of prayer and the emotional poetry that expresses these contents. As to its reception and response, we saw that prayer, as a poetic genre, creates through its expression the experience of closeness to God, the awesome king and loving father, who judges justly and has compassion for those who serve Him and for His children. The soul fills itself with the experience of this intimate relation with the certainty that the prayer is not only heard but receives a positive response. Prayer affirms the swell of feelings with words of gratitude, exaltation, and praise of God.

> Who is like the Lord our God,
> Who, enthroned on high,
> Sees what is below,
> In heaven and on earth?
> He raises the poor from the dust,
> Lifts up the needy from the refuse heap
> To set them with the great,

With the great men of His people.
He sets the childless woman among her household
As a happy mother of children.
Hallelujah.
(Psalms 113:5–9)

During normal times, when the life of the people, the life of the community, and the life of its individual children proceeds on its natural path—without encountering extraordinary troubles, which call for powers of soul that transcend those of ordinary flesh and blood—the response itself which believers who serve God experience in their worship and prayer is sufficient. Their daily life experience proves to them that God oversees His world and leads it as best as possible in the earthly world—as expected of Him—while contending with the powers of chaos that oppose God's laws and constitute a source of the unavoidable wickedness and misery disclosed in the cycles of earthly life. These mishaps are offset by feeling the nearness and love which people experience in prayer, and by the faith that a good reward is expected for them in the world to come. However, in extreme situations of crises in personal life (crises of health, poverty, and major disappointments in family life), and all the more in catastrophic crises in the nations' fate (wars against cruel nations that prevail, destruction, decrees, persecution, violence, expulsion), the basis of faith in God as just ruler and savior of those who revere and love Him is liable to be upset. At such times, prayer expresses more explicitly the expectation that God will hear and respond, and that in addition to the experience of personal closeness to God, prayer will change the objective situation of the worshipping individual, of his family, his community, and his nation for the good—that, as a consequence of the prayer, at least a sign will come heralding hope that the path of personal and group life is about to turn for the better.

From the halakhic perspective it is forbidden "to rely on the miracle"—which is a direct intervention of God by forcing the natural order. Every Jew is commanded to do everything on his part to extricate himself from crisis conditions. If he does or does not succeed, it is up to him to justify the judgment for himself—perhaps he has sinned and this is his punishment; perhaps the moment was not right—for it is up to him to remember that there is a wide gap between his limited judgment and the all-inclusive judgment of his creator, so that any identification between the thought of God and the thought of the human being is impossible. However, since it is impossible to overcome situations of such extreme crisis without heavenly help, and even repentance for sins requires heavenly help (as in Jeremiah's words at the end of the scroll of Lamentations,

"Turn us unto Thee, O Lord, and we shall be turned; renew our days as of old"—Lamentations 5:22), prayer is considered to be a prerequisite for human beings' successful deployment of practical steps taken to succeed in their paths.

In other words: according to the *Halakhah*, prayer also is a kind of activity that each Jew, and the nation of Israel in its entirety, are commanded to carry out for the sake of their success and salvation. The sages of the oral Torah learned this principle through the narrative about our patriarch Jacob's encounter with Esau's threat during his return to Canaan, when Esau came towards him at the head of a great army. Amid his distress, Jacob took three steps: he prepared a defense; he sent gifts to appease his brother who was furious over his being denied, and, most importantly, he prayed to God to bless his endeavor with success (Genesis 32:4–32). From Jacob's perspective, the counsel and insight disclosed by his practical wisdom, through which he extricated himself from the troubles and turned failure into success, were products of the inspiration he received from God in his dreams. In his eyes, all this was concrete proof that God was watching over him and that at the end of all his troubles his path would be successful. To sum up: the halakhic position that prohibits reliance on miracles, is the recommendation not to sin by putting God to a test. A person is required to trust that, if he observes the *mitzvot* of God, including prayer, he will succeed and have well-being—even if he is to have patience in expecting this. It is forbidden to put God to the test; this is a serious sin both against God and against the person himself. Against God, because it places doubt in God's righteousness and capability. Against the person himself, lest he become disappointed and lose the support of his faith. In this connection, we need to remember that faith is the soul's most important resource in crisis situations—for it is on the basis of faith that a person discovers hidden strengths in himself, whose existence in his daily life was unknown to him. These strengths can determine outcomes in his struggles and encounters with crises for the good. This disposition is basically optimistic, and we should also recognize that opposition to testing God does not come to annul faith in the power of prayer to effectuate objective change for the good in situations of individual and national prayer. Rather the opposite—to strengthen that faith. For if this faith is denied, prayer would lose its meaning as a *zikah* of mutual obligation between the human being and God.

The Position of the Human Being before God—Standing at the Gates of Mystery

The premise of mutual responsibility anchored in the covenant is the ultimate basis of the Torah of Moses. It emerges from the basic premises of the doctrine of creation: God the creator is the king over His creation and the father of all His creatures, and especially the human being. He oversees human beings, commands them, judges them, recompenses the good with goodness, and the evil with evil. God's goodness means being good to the good, and that anyone who causes evil to them is His enemy. According to the doctrine of the prophets, this is at once an intellectual-rational truth (the intellect and reason, which God implanted in the human being from His intellect and reason, necessitate that God the creator will be identified as the sovereign power of wisdom and as the one who does good in all His actions) and a trans-intellectual and trans-rational stipulation. For the human being does not have the ability to know and to understand the power of God, His wisdom, His will, and the wondrous way in which God knows the situation of every creature, every individual, every community, and every nation—whereby He is concerned with all the needs of His creatures and recompenses each according to its deeds. That power and those abilities, and the way they are disclosed in the actual reality experienced by human on earth, are a great mystery—both from the perspective of their being grasped in themselves, and from the perspective of their existence in reality.

On the one hand, human beings see themselves as part of the totality of the universe, and on the other, as particular personalities of intrinsic importance. Against the background of expectations anchored in their own evaluation, humans sense a wide gap between the wisdom and good will disclosed to them when they objectively examine the wondrous cyclical character of life in nature and the mutual relations revealed in it, and their subjective evaluation of the necessity of their personal destiny as ephemeral individuals who conclude their lives with old age, sickness, and death. From this perspective, Solomon, wisest of all men said: "For as wisdom grows, vexation grows; to increase learning is to increase heartache" (Ecclesiastes 1:18).

We saw that this gap arouses the great question: How does the totality of human experience reconcile with the earthly reality in which people conduct their lives with the faith in divine leadership that is righteous and benevolent for all? Regarding our discussion of prayer, we should add that the theoretical answers discussed above, which are anchored in God's war with powers of chaos infiltrated into His creation, are suitable to respond to this objective conundrum. But they leave behind those who encounter poverty, sickness, and death as individuals before the mystery of suffering, which is so difficult to make one's peace with, let alone justify. Even completely pious individuals, like Job, would revolt when they faced troubles of exceptional intensity, because they did not feel that, given their righteousness, they deserved such recompense.

From all these perspectives, the position of the human being before God is, therefore, that of standing in front of the gates of mystery which surround a person's life on earth as a physical creature. When it is joined to the body, which is filled with deficiencies and pains, the soul becomes limited in its ability to know the secret of creation (referred to by sages of the oral Torah as *ma'aseh bereshit*) and the secret of the ruling hierarchy of God in His world (called by the scholars of oral Torah *ma'aseh merkavah*, the work of the chariot). Accordingly, the human being is not entitled to rely on his intellect and reason alone in conducting his relations with God. He needs instruction, upon the revelation of God's word from behind the veil of mystery between Himself and His universe, to accompany him and show him the path mediated by the prophets.

Now we can define the central question with which we need to deal, when it comes to defining the requests made in prayer and in shaping the proper way to pray in order for the request to be granted. It concerns the proper form of the relationship to the mystery of the reciprocal *zikah* between God and all creation with all its components, and especially between God and the human being created in His image. More crucially, it concerns the relation between God and the nation of Israel and all its members.

The basic premise of the doctrine of the prophets, as said, is that prayer is possible only on the basis of that doctrine's instruction and command. As a created creature, whose spirit is implanted in the body of an animal, the human being is unable, for his part, to bridge over the mystery between himself and the God who is absolutely separate from the universe. Nevertheless, the person finds himself with God in the reciprocal *zikah* of creator and creature. From the person's perspective, the separateness of God (the sacred) is a matter of mystery imposing awe, whereas God's *zikah* to him is a matter of mystery awakening love. This is a gap that only God, who creates the universe with His power over all forces of chaos, can bridge with His all-embracing wisdom and His universally benevolent will. That is, God bridges the gap between the creatures and Himself with the initiative of His governance, which parallels the initiative of His creation and perpetuates it. God commands the human being to serve Him, pray to Him, thank Him, and praise Him. God Himself determines the *mitzvot* and the rituals with which to worship Him, and He enables prayer to Him by revealing the name with which those humans who serve Him and are committed to His *mitzvot* can address Him, so as to remind themselves of His oversight, to be remembered by Him, and to stir His attributes of benevolence to overcome the attributes of His judgment.

"Do not come closer" (Exodus 3:5)

In this way, the Torah sets the procedure for shaping the proper encounter between God and the human beings with their needs, who are in distress and cry out to God to help, turn to them, and relate to them. In His response to the people's turn to Him, God discloses to them His revelation. This norm is exemplified in the encounter at the burning bush, which was not consumed, before the eyes of Moses; and after that, in the revelation that Moses experienced in the "cleft of the rock" after the sin of the golden calf, when Moses was commanded to lead his people by his own authority as a wise leader who knew God's *mitzvot*. In order to be able to carry out his assignment properly, Moses asked God on that occasion to be granted knowledge of God as proof of leadership.

In these two events, Moses expressed his desire to decipher the secret of divine leadership: with the appearance of the angel in the flame burning by itself in the bush, Moses rushed to get closer and see "why the bush is not burnt" (Exodus 3:3); and when God revealed Himself to him at the height of Mount Sinai to speak with him, Moses asked, "Now if I have truly gained Your favor, pray let me know Your ways that I may know You and continue in Your favor" (Exodus 33:13). On these two occasions, God did not invalidate the substance of Moses's desire to see what appeared before his eyes, to know, and to understand it. The angel was sent to appear to Moses to stir his curiosity; and had it not been stirred, Moses would not have accepted his mission. The same applies to God's revelation to Moses in the cleft of the rock (Exodus 33–34). God, who appointed Moses to lead the nation in His name, wanted Moses to take interest in knowing the aspects of his leadership. But in order to respond to Moses's request as much as possible, God proceeded to set the boundary beyond which His power as creator of the universe and His sovereign control would remain unchallenged—by the strength of mystery that could not be deciphered by a human being insofar as he was human. The human being needs to experience mystery, to know its power and its influence, and from this to know that he cannot know the mystery itself. Therefore, despite Moses's justified desire to know, he was forbidden to try to decipher it. When he tried to look inside the flame burning in the bush, he was told, "Do not come closer" (Exodus 3:5). When he asked, "Pray let me know Your ways, that I may know You" (Exodus 33:13), he was told, "For man may not see Me and live" (Exodus 33:20). Accordingly, what God actually revealed to Moses as he faced the bush burning with fire was the name *Ehyeh-Asher-Ehyeh* (Exodus 3:14), with which Moses and the children of his nation, the seed of Abraham, Isaac, and Jacob, could call upon God with His name, for Him to rescue them. In the cleft of the rock,

Moses was given to see the "goodness" of God, defined as God's "back"—that is, the deeds that flowed from God and that Moses could emulate in his conduct as leader of his people, but not the secret of His power as creator and sovereign ruler of all powers of creation. Moses was thus required to reconcile himself to the boundary placed before him, and to refrain from any attempt—intellectual, rational, emotional, or magical—to cross this boundary. Any such attempt is defined as grave, idolatrous sin; as a revolt against God out of the desire to have control over His power, to use it, and to transfer it to human control. This is the idolatrous dream that manifested itself in the building of the Tower of Babel, whose top reached toward heaven in order to conquer the sovereign position of god; or in the sorcery of the magicians of Egypt who pretended to rule with divine powers and to compete with god by demonstrating their control of powers of creation.

In these episodes, the Torah defined the intellectual-rational norm for "humility" in relationship to God and the mystery surrounding God whether as creator, as king, or as father who loves the person and draws him near to Him. Moses was considered "a very humble man, more so than any man on earth" (Numbers 12:3), precisely because of his greatness as a prophet "whom the Lord singled out face to face" (Deuteronomy 34:10). The character of service to God that is commanded according to Torah within the bounds of human intellect and reason is defined on the basis of the norm of humility. This also applies to keeping its *mitzvot* and norms, whose purpose is to remind that the human being is bound to obey God's will eagerly and for its own sake—and not for the sake of utility or for greater satisfaction of the needs of his existence. God is to be served with service for its own sake, to express recognition of His greatness and benevolence—for even the sort of *mitzvot* that are included in sacrificial worship have no foundation in magic.

The Mysteries of the Name

In this connection, it is proper to reexamine the use of the name of God entrusted to Moses to place on the lips of his people. What is the nature of the mystery inherent to this name? Is its use intellectual, and not a matter of magic? At the encounter of the burning bush, the answer to these questions is given by comparing and distinguishing between the use of names of the deities in Pharaonic ritual, against whom Moses went to war, and the use of the name of God on the lips of Moses in that same war, in order to vanquish the magicians of Egypt. The magicians attributed the supernatural signs that they wrought (changing water to blood, bringing frogs out of the Nile, changing staffs into snakes) to their own powers, while Moses attributed the infinitely grander signs, which he announced only after they arrived, to God above. This means, that according to the Torah of Moses, knowledge of the name of God enables one to address God and commands attention. But it does not bestow control and does not force God to act according to the will of the person who uses it. This is opposed to using the name of God in the idolatrous manner of the Egyptian magicians, where knowledge of the name bestows control over the being invoked by it even if this is one of the deities, because blind fate also controls the deities. The calling of the divine Name activates memory. It reminds God about the duty He accepted upon Himself in His covenant with His servants who are His children—to whom He revealed His name and assured that if they observed His *mitzvot* and accepted His leadership, He would "be God for them." The response coming from God to His servants who call out His name is the awakening of His will, which is anchored in His goodness and love. The meaning of the name *Ehyeh-Asher-Ehyeh* also testifies to this—as discussed above. Added to this is the title "the God of Abraham, the God of Isaac, and the God of Jacob," which recalls the covenant that bound God to the patriarchs, to rescue them and their seed.

In order to enter into *zikah* with humans, God takes the initiative to traverse the boundary of mystery that separates heaven, His place of "residence" as king of the universe, from earth where He appointed the humans to rule in His name. Only in this way is the mystery "revealed"—not by departing from mystery in terms of the human ability to know and comprehend His essence, but rather in terms of human awareness of His power, of His influence, of the direction towards which He strives. Since the mystery remains in full force, the human is required to show a gesture of withdrawal, expressing respect and reverence before the power of holiness upon which his life depends. He is to stand afar, and maintain the mutual relation between himself and God, who reveals Himself from His mystery, by means of people serving Him with His *mitzvot* that are known to human beings through God's prophets. In the sacrificial ritual in the Tabernacle and in the Temple, the same boundary is signified in practice by the prohibition of offering "strange fire"—that is, natural fire lit by human beings—on the altar of God. The boundary is clear. The "eternal fire" which burns on the altar is the same wondrous fire that descended from heaven in the sight of Moses. It is the same amazing fire that blazed upon Mount Sinai behind the smoke and clouds, which covered God from the people's sight. It is also the same fire that descended from heaven with the dedication of the Sanctuary in the desert, in order to take the sacrifices to God. In this way, God Himself accepts the sacrifices to Himself when they are burned. God does not need the sacrifices themselves, but rather the psychological readiness of His servants to offer them to Him. Therefore, the Torah strictly forbids the lighting of natural fire with human hands on the altar—even if the benevolent intention is to assure the acceptance of the sacrifice and avoid disgrace, should the miracle of the fire's falling from heaven not occur at the right moment. The clear reason is that the human being is forbidden from doing by himself that which God needs to do. By doing so, he changes God into an idol made by the humans, and no sin is more serious. Because of this, the two sons of Aaron, who kindled a "strange fire" on the altar on the day of dedication of the Sanctuary of God in the desert, were punished immediately with conflagration, and their father was not permitted to mourn over them (Leviticus 10:1–10). The same applies to prayer. The only way to assure God's response to His nation is for the worshippers to commit themselves to the ethical and ritual *mitzvot* and to pray with a pure heart and clean hands, according to the form they are commanded to pray, and to trust that the prayer will fulfill its function according to God's will.

"Mending from Below"—the Destiny of Israel after the Destruction

This is, accordingly, the norm for worshipping God following the Torah of Moses. It was sufficient during the days of the Sanctuary and also during the Temple, when the children of Israel could make pilgrimages so as to be seen before God, perform their sacrifices and feel the response promised them by virtue of the covenant and by means of the *Shekhinah* of God amid His people. But it is clear that the destruction of the Temple and the Jewish commonwealth and going into exile created a new situation. The destruction of the Temple severed the tie that God Himself made between heaven and earth, and His *Shekhinah* was removed from amid His people—that is, God's face was now hidden from His people. It also meant that the customary rituals collapsed. It was no longer possible to worship God with sacrifices, because the commandment to offer them applied only to the Temple in Jerusalem. The Temple was the place dedicated to the sacrifices, and there was no other. Prayer came in exchange for sacrificial worship, with *mitzvot* that were not dependent upon the land and remained in effect also in exile. But it is understood that the situation of the hiding of God's face raised the great question: what power does prayer have to remind God about the worshipping nation and to stir Him to remember His obligation to Abraham, Isaac, and Jacob, the patriarchs of the nation, concerning their seed, and His eternal obligation to the covenant made at Sinai?

These matters reveal the depths of the problem of exile under the rule of tyrannical regimes, idolaters, people who deny God, His kingdom, and His Torah, and either worship stars and constellations, or invent "other gods" and "other doctrines" so as to enthrone themselves in the land and justify their tyranny. The rule of idolatrous sovereignties across the earth, including the Land of Israel, is the success of powers of dark chaos that have risen from the depths in order to rule over civilizations built by human hands, and to take control of the earth away from God. So, at least from the human perspective of the children of Israel, it appeared that despite their sins they remained faithful to the covenant and to its *mitzvot*, while the powers of chaos pursued them to destroy them.

On this point it is proper to take note of the upheaval that took place in the situation and consciousness of the people of Israel between the time they were judged for their sin during settlement on their land—punished justly, according to the prophets, with the destruction of the Temple and the kingdom and leaving for exile—and the time they were punished and exiled under a regime of a tyrannical, idolatrous nation, a nation that sinned against God with sins greater than those of Israel; not only sins of cruel, tyrannical idolatry, but of the destruction of the Temple of God and His city, and exiling the nation appointed to be God's treasure among the nations. These matters apply especially after the first generation of exiles died and the generation of their children rose in their place. The children were innocent of all trespass, and suffered the pains of exile for no sin of their own. The quality of Israel's relative loyalty to God and His Torah became clear against this background, even though the people had sinned while residing in the land. Beyond this, it is striking that the people of Israel did not suffer in exile on account of their sin against God, but to the contrary, on account of their righteousness and loyalty to God and His Torah which stirred hatred against them on the part of the ruling enemy idolaters. That is the complexity of the dilemma with which the nation of Israel in exile had to cope. The heavier and deeper the exile, the heavier and deeper the feeling that God also abandoned the land, hid His face from His nation, abandoned it to its fate, and let their enemies rule and do whatever they wanted. This means that the ongoing hiding of God's face was an unbearable injustice with regard to Israel. It was impossible to attribute this injustice to God. Or, perhaps it testified that not only was the nation defeated at the hand of the enemy, but that God Himself was defeated by idolatrous powers of chaos who rose to rule the earth. Could one consider such an explanation, without surrendering to idolatrous thinking? Surely not. But if so, the only explanation, enveloped in mystery, is tied to the mission of the nation of Israel. Possibly, Israel went into exile not as punishment for its sins but rather to penetrate the realm of idolatrous evil and fight it from within, to bring about restoration from below, from the subsoil of the earth and from the depths of darkness hidden beneath it. By doing so, the nation would effectuate the transformation of evil into good, to be revealed upon completion of its endeavor.

In any case, the situation of the nation in exile and its prolongation, without any signs of redemption on the horizon, was a crisis of despair that was liable to bring about the collapse of the nation, assimilation, and ruin. The sole source of faith and hope was the Torah of God, regarding the truth of which we have the testimony of the trustworthy ancestral tradition. Even the nations that enslaved Israel recognized it as true. To the people of Israel, the Torah is the official writ of commitment by the sovereign of heaven and earth, whose word is true and whose promise is true.

Against this background, it is possible to discern something wondrous, which has no explanation in terms of the way of the world. When we consider the situation of the nation of Israel in exile, observed inclusively over time, it becomes clear that, despite the nation's weakness and its dependence on governments that enslave it, and despite its dispersion among the nations making it impossible to unify its power as could a people dwelling in its land, the nation nevertheless has stood fast. Its collective identity, based upon its language, its societal institutions, its laws, and ways of life, has remained firmly in place—perhaps even more so than it was when the nation was settled on its soil. There were, of course, cases of individual assimilation, and sometimes assimilation was widespread. But still, "the oak, of which stumps are left even when they are felled: its stump shall be a holy seed" (Isaiah 6:13) remained standing forever—standing the test with zealous stubbornness. Despite the hatred of enemies who worship other deities, the attempts to bring the people of the stock to change their Torah or nullify its *mitzvot* do not succeed. After every such attempt, the enemy regimes despair and let the communities live according to the laws of Torah and the *mitzvot* that do not depend upon the land of Israel. According to the scholars of oral Torah, this is not according to the path of nature, but in fact, some hidden power restrains the will of the gentiles who attempt to purge Israel out of their midst. This power overcomes all the "sectarians" who rise up against Israel to destroy it. As said in the Passover *Haggadah*: "In every generation there are those who rise against us to destroy us. But the Holy One, blessed be He, has delivered us out of their hands." This wondrous fact testifies, as a hundred witnesses, that despite their apparent enslavement, the children of Israel who choose to serve God with His Torah are still free, and have not returned to Egyptian slavery. For indeed, as stated in the Passover *Haggadah*: "God drew us close to worship Him." Punishment for the people's sins is not the explanation for the ongoing exile. To the contrary: the exile is explained by the righteousness of Israel. There is something secret in it, the secret of the mission that Israel carries out in exile through the testimony it provides with its loyalty to Torah despite its suffering. Namely, that God is the true king, and not the kings of gentiles or their deities whose power can terrorize for a time but soon passes because it is ephemeral.

The fate of the nation in exile is the mystery of divine oversight, which does not cease even for a moment despite the outward hiding of God's face. This fact is striking—especially since the Christian church, which proclaimed that it superseded the inherited birthright of Israel as the chosen nation, has achieved rule in the gentile lands into which Israel was exiled. A wondrous paradox discloses itself in this situation: the Christians denied that Israel was the chosen nation in the present by confirming its chosenness in the past; and denied the authority of the Sinai covenant in the present by affirming that it was obligatory as an eternal covenant. The result was the absolute desire of the Christian church that the nation of Israel change its religion and disappear as a nation. At the same time, the church needed the nation of Israel to affirm the birthright of the church, which would be acceptable only if the people of Israel changed their religion willingly and without force. This is the secret as to why the church refrained from destroying the nation of Israel, despite its absolute desire to do so. There is no doubt: the church's awe for the God who chose the nation of Israel according to the testimony of God's Torah is the impediment! It is clear from this that the hiding of God's face is not absolute, that it can be changed at any time into a hidden revealing of the face—into testimony that God acts in mysterious ways to defend His nation. In this way, one can find reinforcement for the belief that the exile is not punishment but rather the mission of the nation of Israel for the sake of God's war against idolatry— whether by the mending (*tikkun*) which the nation performs by observing the *mitzvot* of Torah on the soil of gentiles, or by means of "sanctifying God's name" (*Kiddush hashem*—that is, martyrdom) in their midst.

These matters also hint at another secret: the severity of the decrees of the oppressive and ongoing exile does not, as gentile idolaters think, testify to their victory. To the contrary, it testifies to the hidden victory of the nation of Israel in its war against the powers of evil and chaos that have rendered it captive, from their fortified realm. In other words, the severity of the cruel hatred against Israel does not testify to the strengthening of the power of ruling idolatry, but to its gradual weakening. The idolatry, which seems to be victorious, senses that its control is collapsing from within, and falling apart more and more. Its defeat is imminent—and therefore it increases its hopeless war against God, His nation, and Torah. The consoling conclusion is clear: the increasing severity of the darkness of exile does not testify to God's defeat in the war against the powers of chaos, but rather to God's imminent victory. The worse the misery, the closer the victory; and when the persecution reaches its peak, God will be revealed as the head of His host, He will win the decisive battle, and His kingdom will be established in heaven and in earth.

But until the moment when the kingdom of the House of David will be established in the Land of Israel and the Temple will be built for the third time, the nation of Israel will need an alternative leadership that would know how to unite the people around the Torah, to illumine their vision, to show them the light amid the increasingly abominable darkness, and envision the harbinger of salvation amid the depths of suffering. Since the authority of prophecy was annulled with the destruction of the commonwealth and the Temple, the alternative leadership needed to forge its own path to God who was hidden in heaven. This mysterious path was opened to the new leaders of Israel on the basis of their merit, righteousness, and holiness, and on the basis of knowledge they acquired in their research into the realm of mystery and the way of reaching God, so as to bring the people's needs before God and influence God's decisions about them.

The Development of the "Secret Wisdom"

As said, the people of Israel in exile organized themselves into societal strongholds. Their communities were bequeathed with conducting life according to *mitzvot* of Torah, its laws and judgements which did not depend upon the Land of Israel. The leadership that adapted itself to the communal organization was the leadership of the "scribes," Torah scholars who studied in, and were ordained by authorized schools ("yeshivot"). The degrees of ordination they received were "Rabbi" and "Rabban." These degrees had a measure of social and political authority representing the true king of Israel whose kingdom remained hidden. This was obvious: under the yoke of gentile kingdoms, the authority of the scribes could be manifested in its spiritual-instructional dimension, in the halakhic, moral, and legal sense. In this way, they played both the role of the "scribes" of the kingdom of the House of David, and the prophets, as they represented the word of God to His nation. But since the authority of the prophets was conditioned upon the existence of the kingdom of the House of David on the one hand, and the functioning of the Temple in Jerusalem on the other, the new leadership was required to fulfil its role as representative of the nation and not as emissary of God. This was so, not only as to the legal decisions that shaped the ways of life of the community in exile, but also as to representation of the nation before God in order to work for His favor. For that purpose they needed *hokhmat harazim*, the "wisdom of secrets." By means of it, the leaders took the initiative to break into the arena of mystery. They ascended towards heaven in their visions, and negotiated with the angels of God and even God Himself about increasing His compassion for Israel. The exemplary image, which they imitated in their double role, was that of Daniel, the legendary mysterious personality who became a model for his people and taught them the prayer which exalted them to the sphere of spirituality, beyond the darkness of exile and its sufferings. He delved deeply into his hidden wisdom in order to know how to direct the prayer so that it would achieve its aims efficiently.

The "secret wisdom," like the *Halakhah* that was debated according to the oral Torah, developed over the course of generations as instruction which required deep learning. It also had a tradition of being passed from teachers to worthy students. The students passed moral, ritual, and spiritual tests, although in secret and not openly—for this was about "secrets" of which not every person was suitable or worthy of knowing and using—lest one fail and cause others to fail, leading to ruin rather than improvement. The subject of this wisdom is delineated into two secret disciplines: *ma'aseh bereshit* (the work of creation), whose subjects are secrets of creation, and *ma'aseh merkavah* (the work of the chariot), whose subjects are secrets of the kingship of God as revealed in visions of the prophets. In particular, *ma'aseh merkavah* is tied to the vision of consecration of the prophet Isaiah son of Amoz in the Temple in Jerusalem, and to that of Ezekiel, to whom God appeared upon the chariot of His angels, on the Kebar river during the Babylonian exile.

Our subject in this chapter is the influence of the mystical lore on prayer, especially on the formulation of the prayer's recitation, as part of changes made in the attempt to produce a prayer that will be heard, receive a response, cause the objective conditions of the nation to change for the good, and bring the time of redemption nearer. Accordingly, we will not delve deeper into the further development of the mystical lore over the course of the generations, and will only point out the essential topics that it discusses: the secret of the first light of creation and the secret of the influence of the sun, the moon, and the stars over life on earth; the secret of God's spirit that shaped creation; the secrets of the human soul that received emanation from the spirt of God; the secret of the rain that descends from heaven to saturate the land and grow its seeds; the secret of the angels, the host of heaven, who are God's messengers carrying out His word on earth, and who stand up to praise and glorify God in heaven;

the secret of the position of the human being as created in God's image; and the secret of the human being's mission as ruler in God's name over the creatures of the earth. Also, the secret of Israel's selection to be God's treasure in the world; the secret of prophecy as revelation of God's word to humanity; and the secret of God's *Shekhinah* amid His people in His sanctuary—which is also the secret of the sanctity of Mount Moriah, which is open and standing before the "gate" through which the angels of God go and come. Through that gate, God listens to the prayers of His people; through it, He looks at earth. Therefore, through this gate, human beings who have sanctified themselves through *mitzvot*, and delved into knowledge of the secret wisdom, are also able to ascend to heaven. The paradigmatic example is the prophet Elijah. According to what is said in the book of Kings, he ascended bodily to heaven. But during the time of exile he began to visit the earth often as a hidden angel, in order to reveal to the spiritual leaders of the nation of Israel the secrets he heard from "behind the curtain of the *Shekhinah*," so they would know how to act for the good of their people. From then on, Elijah became the secret embodiment of the mystery, the source of useful knowledge about the mystery, and especially the great proclaimer of the Messiah's appearance, precisely at a time when troubles of Israel in exile reached their climax.

The Renewal of Creation as an Answer to the Hiding of God's Face

The influence of these secrets on the prayer intended to reach God who hides His face from His nation in exile, and to influence change in the nation's situation for the good, is seen in three ways.

First, the mystic lore gives expression to the experience of spiritual elation, testifying that, despite the divine hiddenness in exile, God's presence in the world, or that of His *Shekhinah*, is ongoing and constant, and recognizable in the cycles of life on earth and in their eternal renewal. From this perspective, creation does not conclude on the seventh day. It rather renews itself at every moment, every hour, every day, every week, every month, and every year. Were the creative presence to disappear for but one moment, creation would not be maintained by itself, but revert to primal chaos and darkness. Because the light that illumines our eyes; the warmth and the spirit that enliven us; the rain that refreshes the living creatures and the earth, all flow continuously from the essence of God and from the expression of His will. From this perspective, God's presence expands beyond creation (for He indeed preceded it) and is also within it; and there is no place empty of it. Moreover, God is also present internally within the human being, in the spirit that God has breathed into the human body, so as to emanate the intellectual, expressive and creative life into him which are expressions of God's inspiration. The extension of God's presence into all of creation brings creation within God. This does not suppress and does not conceal the separate existence of creation on the one hand and of God on the other. That is, from the one side there is no place without God and from the other side no place is set apart for God. God resides in the mystery of His presence in creation, through isolation from it; and the presence of creation for Him through its self-isolation. The scholars of oral Torah pointed to this mystery by calling God "the Place," as in their statement, "God is the place of the world and His world is not His place" (*Midrash Bereshit Rabbah* 68a). In other words, God includes the universe within Himself, but the universe does not include God within itself. From His perspective, God is present in every place, while from the perspective of the human being God vanishes beyond all places. These are two dimensions of one mystery.

The author of the Psalms expresses this mystical experience of the presence of God, who is found in every place and vanishes beyond all place, in a psalm that we have already cited above. Here it is interpreted in depth:

> If I ascend to heaven, You are there;
> If I descent to *Sheol*, You are there too.
> If I take wing with the dawn
> To come to rest on the western horizon,
> Even there Your hand will be guiding me,
> Your right hand will be holding me fast.
> If I say, "Surely darkness will conceal me,
> Night will provide me with cover,"
> Darkness is not dark for You;
> Night is as light as day;
> Darkness and light are the same.
> (Psalms 139:6–12)

The same experience comes to expression in the *siddur*, in the *piyyut* (liturgical poem) *El Adon* that has been added to the regular prayer in the celebratory blessing of God as creator of the lights, which is added to the Sabbath *Shaḥarit* service:

> God, Lord of all creation,
> The Blessed, is blessed by every soul.
> His greatness and goodness fill the world;

Knowledge and wisdom surround Him.
Exalted above the holy Ḥayot,
Adorned in glory on the Chariot;
Merit and right are before His throne,
Kindness and compassion before His glory.
Good are the radiant stars our God created,
He formed them with knowledge,
Understanding and deliberation.
He gave them strength and might
To rule throughout the world;
Full of splendor, radiating light,
Beautiful is their splendor throughout the world;
Glad as they go forth, joyous as they return,
They fulfil with awe their Creator's will.
Glory and honor they give to His name,
Jubilation and song at the mention of His majesty.
He called the sun into being and it shone with light.
He looked and fashioned the form of the moon.
All the hosts on high give Him praise;
The Seraphim, Ophanim and holy Ḥayot
Ascribe glory and greatness.
(K:460, *El Adon*)

The subject of this beautiful *piyyut* is the mystical symbolism of the light of the sun, which shines at dawn and illumines the eyes of the human being who sees the wonders of creation. The poem opens by recalling the attributes of God as creator of the universe and as Lord over His creation. With these titles, God rules and leads His world from beyond it, while being concealed from it. The *piyyut* proceeds to describe God's being borne on the "chariot" envisioned by Ezekiel in his consecration-vision as a prophet. The chariot is God's *Shekhinah* within His heavenly realm. The third rank in the hierarchy of the divine kingdom is that of the luminaries in the firmament of heaven—the sun, the moon, and the stars—established to rule the earth. This rank is revealed to the creatures of the earth, and speaks of God's glory, without saying so in words, to the upright human beings whose eyes are lifted towards heaven, and whose intellect sees the spiritual light beyond the sensual light.

The poem concludes, therefore, with a description of the sight seen by the worshipper's physical eyes at dawn: the light of the sun which shines and drives the darkness away, revealing the vault of the shining firmament and the beauty of renewed earth. It is as if only now is the sun called into existence by God. It obeys, and deserves the affirmation, "It is good." From the perspective of the worshipper, the physical light which shows heaven in its brilliance and the earth in its splendor, is the first rung on a ladder. The worshipper rises on it and ascends from sensual sight to intellectual contemplation, to rational reflection about God's threefold appearance as creator, ruler, and king upon the chariot, and to descriptions of the attributes with which God creates and rules—which are His mystery. In body, the worshipper is riveted to the earth; but in spirit he is carried to the heavens and sees himself partnering with the angels of heaven in singing praise to God. With his voice, he sounds the voice of angels to himself, and with his sight he visualizes the light of the seven days, which angels see directly but which he sees by means of the sun that symbolizes the primal light. With this, he praises and thanks God for creating the eternal kingdom of heaven:

> May You be blessed,
> Our Rock, King, and Redeemer, Creator of the holy beings.
> May Your name be praised forever,
> Our King, Creator of maintaining ministry angels,
> All of whom stand in the universe's heights,
> Proclaiming together,
> In awe, aloud,
> The words of the living God, the eternal King.
> (K:462, 464, *Tishbarakh Tzureinu*)

With this, the worshipper is renewed as the creation is renewed, and he sounds a new song, which announces the vision of the renewal of the first light that will be revealed in the era of redemption on earth as well: "May you shine a light on Zion, and may we all speedily merit its light" (K:94, *Le'el Barukh*).

So it is also in the *piyyut* that expands the third blessing, "You are holy," in the *Amidah* prayer of Sabbaths and holidays. There are a number of versions parallel to the *piyyut*'s expansion, but they are identical in content—which flows from joining Isaiah's vision of the chariot (Isaiah 6) with that of Ezekiel (Ezekiel 1–3). Here is one of them:

> We will sanctify Your name on earth,
> As they sanctify it in the highest heavens,
> As is written by Your prophet,

"And they [the angels] call to one another saying:
Holy, holy, holy is the Lord of hosts
The whole world is filled with His glory."
Then with a sound of mighty noise, majestic and strong,
They make their voice heard, raising themselves
Toward the Seraphim, and facing them say" "Blessed . . .
"Blessed is the Lord's glory from His place."
Reveal Yourself from Your place, O our King, reign over us, for
we are waiting for You. When will You reign in Zion?
May it be soon in our days, and may You dwell there for ever
and all time. May You be exalted and sanctified in the midst of
Jerusalem, Your city from generation to generation for evermore.
May our eyes see Your kingdom, as is said in the songs of Your
splendor, written by David your righteous anointed one:
"The Lord shall reign for ever. He is your God, Zion,
From generation to generation, Hallelujah!"
From generation to generation we will declare Your greatness,
And we will proclaim Your holiness for evermore.
Your praise, our God, shall not leave our mouth forever,
For You, God are a great and holy King.
Blessed are You, Lord, the holy God.
(K:482, *Nekadesh Et Shimekha*)

This *piyyut* is a drama which imitates—in the synagogue on earth and in the reality of exile—the pageant of the angels' worship before God around the throne of His glory and His chariot, as the angels appear to the prophets Isaiah and Ezekiel. After the Temple was destroyed, it was impossible for the chariot and the throne upon it to descend to earth. They are permanent in heaven above the "gate" through which Mount Moriah, upon which the Temple stands, is seen. But we are inclined to an opposite meaning, that of the symbolic ascent of the worshipper, which is expressed in the emulation of the event of worship on high by human beings worshipping below. The prophecies of Isaiah and Ezekiel testify to the initiative of God to reveal Himself to them and consecrate them to a mission—either in the Temple in Jerusalem (to Isaiah) or on the Kebar River in exilic Babylon (to Ezekiel). But in the *Kedushah,* that initiative is a symbolic one and it comes from the worshipper. The conversation between God and His servants is conducted in the worshipper's voice. The *shaliah hatzibur* (the representative of the congregation, that is, the cantor) turns simultaneously to God in the name of his assembly, and to the assembly in the name of God. He describes what is happening on high, and the worshippers answer and are answered. In this way the worshippers raise themselves to the height to which their symbolic gesture elevates them—their body in the synagogue and their soul in the congregation of heavenly angels amid whom God resides. The exalting experience is symbolic, and to this extent is real from the emotional-ideational perspective. Again, the body of the worshipper is rooted in the earth, but the spirit is carried to heaven and has the worshipper associate with the angels—with God's presence among them symbolizing the spirit's elevation above heaven and earth. The angels are also rooted in this place, and as such represent the glory of God whose "presence fills all the earth" (Isaiah 6:3)—above which He is present, concealed in mystery.

God's Ongoing War with Powers of Chaos

The second manner of expressing the breakthrough into the area of mystery in prayer is through knowledge acquired by secret wisdom. God's oversight as creator, as the "master over all works" who rules creation from beyond it, does not disappear on account of the exile—for exile does not depend upon civilization and its history but rather upon creation itself. As stated in the first blessing of the *Shema*, God renews the act of creation every day, and forever. This means that, every day, the command "let there be" of Genesis renews itself. The orderly succession of the laws of nature does not emerge by itself, but rather from the divine will that imposes its laws on the forces of chaos. From this substantive-essential perspective, God's war with evil, identified with powers of chaos, continues without respite—and without any connection to exile. Also, God's war against idolatry continues on the level of God's control of powers of nature—which are deified by worshippers of gods and idols. Human beings are given a choice between observing God's *mitzvot* and refusing to do so. But they are not given control over the results of their deeds. God rules human beings by imposing laws of nature according to His will. Accordingly, enacting God's *mitzvot* achieves its good aim right away or over time, while doing evil in God's eyes does not bring the benefit intended by the evil ones; the end, rather, is that they are punished. That is, God's laws and His *mitzvot* are intended for the benefit of all His creatures together, and insofar as God cares for all of them and intends to transform evil powers to good, His work is ongoing—especially because God provides latitude to the evil ones for them to return in repentance, and puts up with their sins until their wickedness and evil finally become clear.

This is the source of Israel's suffering in exile, although it is disclosed and known to the suffering nation that God's victory is assured from the outset. God is the true king, and the war is conducted as He wants. If God wanted to suppress the forces of chaos and annihilate them, He could have done so immediately. But His desire is to correct them and elevate them to the good, as stated in the *Aleinu* prayer recited at the end of the weekday *Shaḥarit* prayer and at the conclusion of the *Musaf* prayer on Sabbaths and holidays. Its subject is that of proclaiming the kingdom of heaven, which exists and stands forever, and will be disclosed speedily in the future to the sight of all flesh—as it is disclosed to the angels of heaven and to the children of Israel on earth:

> He is our God; there is no other.
> Truly He is our King, there is none else,
> As it is written in His Torah:
> "You shall know and take to heart this day that the Lord is God,
> In heaven above and on earth below.
> There is no other" (Deuteronomy 4:39).
> Therefore, we place our hope in You, Lord our God,
> That we may soon see the glory of Your power,
> When You will remove abominations from the earth,
> And idols will be utterly destroyed,
> When the world will be perfected under the sovereignty of the
> Almighty,
> When all humanity will call Your name,
> To turn all the earth's wicked toward You.
> All the world's inhabitants will realize and know that to You
> every knee must bow and Every tongue swear loyalty.
> Before You, Lord our God, they will kneel and bow down
> And give honor to Your glorious name.
> They will all accept the yoke of Your kingdom,
> And You will reign over them soon and for ever.
> For the kingdom is Yours,
> And to all eternity You will reign in glory,
> As is written in Your Torah: "The Lord will reign for ever and
> ever." [Exodus 15:18]
> And it is said: "then the Lord shall be King over all earth;
> On that day the Lord shall be One and His name One."
> [Zechariah 14:9]
> (K:562, 564, *Aleinu Leshabeaḥ*)

These words provide an explanation for the misery which the nation of Israel is required to endure for God's sake. Undoubtedly, this brings about an injustice to the nation of Israel, which each and every individual feels—especially when the decrees and persecutions increase in severity. The students of the scribes, the scholars, and the poets who composed the prayers are cognizant of this. They are also aware that philosophical understanding of the cause of the suffering contains nothing to console, or to silence rightful protest, because the suffering exceeds the endurance of normal human beings of flesh and blood. How, then, does the prayer wrestle with this suffering? By sounding the protest and by forceful expression of the belief that God Himself justifies the protest, shares in His nation's troubles and sufferings, and credits the people with standing the test, so as to reward the nation for the righteousness that it renders to God in its struggle. The reward will surely come. It will be expressed with vengeance, measure for measure, against the enemies of the nation who are enemies of God, and with distinguishing God's people for endless good, at the head of all the nations, which will now acknowledge Israel's righteousness!

This idea is expressed in the *siddur* on two levels. The first is the level of prayers of the individual, who sins as an individual on account of human weaknesses residing in every person, and, consequently, is in need of repentance, forgiveness, and atonement. But as a member of the nation of Israel loyal to Torah, the merit of his forefathers and that of his nation stand him in good stead, and he is distinguished for the good when judged before God. This is found in all prayers of the *siddur* that are dedicated specifically to repentance, such as the *Taḥanun* and *Avinu Malkeinu*.

On the level of wrestling with the fate of the nation, on the other hand, we see the protest and outcry voiced to see vengeance against the enemies, as well as reward of the pious who have sanctified the name of God in their life and death. The prayer *Av Haraḥamim* is such a prayer, dedicated to the memory of those who sanctified the name of God. It is included in the prayers following the reading of the Torah:

> Father of compassion, who dwells on high: may He remember in His compassion the pious, the upright and the blameless— holy communities who sacrificed their lives for the sanctification of God's name. Lovely and pleasant in their lives, in death they were not parted. They were swifter than eagles and stronger than lions to do the will of their Maker and the desire of their Creator. O our God, remember them for good with the

other righteous of the world, and may He exact retribution for
the shed blood of His servants, as it is written in the Torah of
Moses, the man of God: "O nations acclaim His people, for He
will avenge the blood of His servants, wreak vengeance on His
foes, and make clean His people's land." [Deuteronomy 32:43]
(K:528, Av Haraḥamim)

Following this memorial prayer there is a succession of scriptural texts, in which
God promises His people vengeance against idolaters for having persecuted
His nation. What is the purpose of recalling these texts? To remind the nation
of that promise, so as to encourage and strengthen the nation in its suffering;
and to remind God of the promise, which He is to literally keep. But in practice
this is a protest expressed in positive language. The people of Israel stand
before God as lenders stand before debtors who delay paying debts—leaving
the lenders impoverished. They show God the debt-certificate in their hand.
They justly claim payment from God, who is required to be a righteous judge of
Himself, as He is when he judges His creatures.

The Righteousness of Israel and Its Readiness to Die "in Sanctification of the Name" (Al kiddush hashem) Guarding the World from Chaos

These words are also recited in confronting the harshest suffering, which appears
so wicked as to be without justification in any moral way. Because of this, the fact
that God permits it under His reign is a matter of shocking mystery. The reference,
as said above, is to the victory of Christianity, which has separated itself from
the people of Israel with the claim that the ecclesiastical institution applies to all
human beings and therefore inherits the position of Israel as the "chosen nation."
How can any member of Israel comprehend why God allowed those who spread
this idolatrous untruth to achieve rule over many nations and to oppress the
truly chosen nation in order to pressure it into acknowledging the tidings of
Christianity and affirm its claim by joining it? How can anyone comprehend that
God, who rules heaven and earth, has imposed upon His nation—the smallest
of all nations, dispersed and weaker than all in terms of earthly power—the
necessity of proving, for His sake and for that of the existence of His kingdom on
earth, that the church's claim was idolatrous and false? How could the persecuted
nation prove this? Or perhaps the torment was intensified so the people would
acknowledge that the church's claim was false; and demonstrate readiness to

sanctify the name of heaven and die and not annul God's Torah—this would provide the proof needed proof? If so, how possibly justify the God who decreed such a terrible decree—one which could be decreed only for a righteous nation, as a sinful nation could obviously not withstand it?

We will see that only a revolutionary change in Israel's self-image as a "treasured nation," and in the definition of relations between Israel and its God, would justify an ideational revolution—one which included a kind of internalization of the original Christian claim so as to refute it. If Christianity earned victory over the idolatrous Roman Empire through the readiness of Jesus and that of the martyrs who followed his path to sanctify the name of heaven publicly, now—when the Christian church joins the idolatrous empire, persecutes the nation of Israel, and compels it to sanctify the name of heaven publicly—it demonstrates its untruth by its action, its tyranny, its betrayal of the nation from which it was born and of the God whom it supposedly worships. The church thereby demonstrates that the nation of Israel, which has remained true to its destiny, to Torah, and God, is the chosen nation—claiming by itself to observe the decree of God for His sake, in order to remove the last impediment to its redemption!

This way of thinking is expressed with special power in the *Eleh Ezkerah* ("These [things] I remember") prayer, recited on the Days of Awe in memory of the ten martyrs, to remind God of the worthiness of the people of Israel who are prepared to give their souls in sanctification of His name and for their keeping the *mitzvot* of His Torah—and of the great debt God owes the people, according to His promise. There is a close connection between the recital of *Eleh Ezkerah* hymn on the Days of Awe and the commemoration of the binding of Isaac in the prayers read on those days. The liturgical poem *Eleh Ezkerah*, which was written in medieval times and actually commemorates the death of Jewish scholars in sanctification of God's name during the Crusades in Germany, emphasizes the source of this connection—the confrontation with the ruling Christian church, which puts the nation of Israel to repeated tests of martyrdom.

To understand this, note that the *siddur* attributes a special meaning to the entire episode of the binding of Isaac, a meaning that is derived directly from Christian martyrology. This meaning is explicit in *Eleh Ezkerah*. The story about the ten rabbis martyred by the ancient Romans is narrated against the background of the confrontation between Jewish scholars and the church, after Christianity became the religion of the Roman Empire. The Roman emperor prosecuted the Jewish scholars, as told in the *piyyut*, for the sin of Joseph's brothers selling him into slavery. In his eyes, this was the collective sin of the nation of Israel, committed by the patriarchs of their tribes. It was similar to the sin of the people of Israel against Jesus of Nazareth—who, according to

New Testament testimony, was handed over by the Sanhedrin elders to the Roman governor, who sentenced him to death. The Torah states "He who kidnaps a man—whether he has sold him or is still holding him—shall be put to death" (Exodus 21:16). But Joseph's brothers were not punished for their crime. Because of this, the emperor regarded the great Jewish scholars of his generation as bearing responsibility for the collective crime of the Jewish nation. The scholars knew that this was malicious libel. But did God issue a decree against the Jews, for them to be handed over to the emperor? The scholars of Israel engaged with this, and prevailed upon the great mystical sage, Rabbi Ishmael, to ascend to heaven with a "question of a dream," to ascertain whether this was a decree of God. Rabbi Ishmael received the answer that it was indeed an irrevocable decree—even though this was not explained. It was God's will for the pious scholars of Israel, innocent of all sin, to voluntarily accept this decree upon themselves. If they refused, God would return the world to chaos, and, together with the entire nation, the collective human species would disappear. What did this mean? In God's view, the evil of humanity (which also found expression in church rule) had increased by this point to an unbearable degree. Again, God repented over the creation of the human being, because He concluded that there no longer was any possibility that humankind would overcome its evil inclination and corruption, so as to fulfill the destiny set for it at creation. As in the days of Noah, only one thing could rescue the human species: if "the pious of this generation," whose piety balanced out all the triumphant evil, could be found. This would tip the scales of justice once again in favor of the human species, and give it further respite. Who then, were likely to be these pious—other than the holy and pure scholars of Israel who were not only "pious in their generation," as Noah was in his time, but perfectly pious? If they would be prepared to accept upon themselves death in sanctification of the name with terrible sufferings—even though in their view such a requirement was a terrible injustice—God the righteous judge would annul His decision and retreat from His destructive activity. Because of this, God issued the terrible decree for His pious ones—while acknowledging that their protest was just. From their perspective this was totally arbitrary—"So it arose in thought before me"—without any explanation!

The scholars of Israel protested, but they accepted the judgment upon themselves in order to rescue their people, and God Himself, from the destruction of His work! This is the wondrous, charitable act that they rendered to God and their people. By doing so they prevented the disastrous decrees, being carried out in the world, and they rescued all of humankind. The tragic paradox is that, in doing so, the Jewish scholars, out of an inverted motive, were doing what Christianity attributed to the Jewish Jesus, whom they thought of as the son of God: sacrificing themselves in order to rescue humankind. However, they were not moved by the false claim that the death of a person innocent of sin was likely to atone for the sins of evil ones who did not repent by themselves. Rather, by offering opposing testimony: the Christian Church was the true transgressor, by its sacrificing innocent scholars of Israel; whereas the Jewish people were not only innocent of all sin—for all its sins were atoned by exilic suffering—but ready to ascend voluntarily to the "*Akeidah*" in order to bear witness to the victory of the kingdom of God in His world! Thus, the earthly victory of the persecuting church changes into a terrible moral and spiritual failure—while the disaster of the exiled nation of Israel changes into a most lofty spiritual-moral victory!

Devekut (Adherence) and *Kavanah* (Intentionality) of Prayer

The third way in which prayer breaks into the arena of mystery relates not to the contents of prayer, but to its manner—in answer to the question: how does one pray properly, in order to achieve the goal of prayer? Two topics are interconnected in the *siddur*'s encounter with this question: *devekut* (achieving attachment or intimacy with God) and *kavanah* (intentionality of the act). *Devekut* is a *mitzvah* of the Torah, which touches upon the general relation required of the Israelites in their *zikah* to God as their king: "Follow none but the Lord your God, and revere none but Him; observe His commandments alone, and heed only His order; worship none but Him, and hold fast to Him [*u-vo tidbak*]" (Deuteronomy 13:5). This passage explains the meaning of *devekut* to God in its context—total commitment, and firm hold by followers onto their one leader; a leader who unites in Himself all the aspects of leadership needed by a person for his life on earth, without conditions and without restrictions. To be precise: the attachment (*devekut*) commanded in the Torah is not a passive reliance of being dragged, nor the folly of the ignorant, and also not the blindness of the blind who is forced to be paired together with a seeing person ready to lead him. It is rather an active choice, anchored in intellectual knowledge and in the understanding that the path led by God is the only good path for realizing one's destiny and well-being.

Let us recall that the literal meaning of the word "*devekut*" is a physical concept: a close pairing of two bodies, which by themselves are separate from each other, both in definition and essence. The Torah transfers this physical concept to the *zikot* between the spiritual soul and God as a spiritual entity. The soul (*nefesh*) is the spirit, which God breathes into the body of the person.

Because of this, the soul is itself distinct. But as bodies are able to adhere to one another by means of compatible material, spirits are able to adhere to one another through spiritual activity. This means that adherence of the soul to God is expressed in actions that bring it closer to God in terms of moral activity and the spiritual quest for truth.

For this, it is not enough to observe *mitzvot* in a mechanical way. One needs to study and reflect upon them in order to do God's will by means of them. The concept of *kavanah* is born out of the concept of *devekut*, in this way: adherence exists only when the intention is correct—namely, to attain what God commands as good. If not, the activity would not be a matter of keeping the command of God, but rather of enacting a person's instinctual desire, with pretense of observing God's command. This is a sin, in its original sense of the word—missing the divine aim and, simultaneously, the aim appropriate to the person. Accordingly, authentic adherence requires intentionality based upon deep knowledge and well-considered reason. These matters are the foundation of *Halakhah* as determined by the oral Torah in its broadest sense. We may define *Halakhah* as the applied discipline of adherence to God out of correct intentionality in all the areas to which the Torah relates. From this perspective, scholars of oral Torah have viewed prayer as the *mitzvah* in which *devekut* and *kavanah* express themselves in direct relations between the human being and God. Therefore, they have defined prayer as a mode of action with independent value, a *mitzvah* to be observed for its own sake, or as an expression of love for God. In such a capacity, the *mitzvah* of adherence to God is comparable to the adherence of a person to his wife, as he is commanded to fructify her and to be one flesh with her—and as the wife is commanded to adhere to her husband and be fructified by him. As it is written: "Hence a man leaves his father and mother and clings to his wife, so that they become one flesh" (Genesis 2:24). When we apply this concept of the "clinging," which brings about the blending and unification of the partners who cling to each other, to the relations between a person's spiritual soul and the spirit of God that is the soul's source—the person ascends and the concept of intention ascends with him to the realm of mystery.

Devekut in this sense expresses itself with symbolic actions. The most meaningful action in terms of *devekut* is the placing of *tefillin*, of the head and the arm, which is understood as a ceremony of engagement between the worshipping soul, as a "bride" and wife, and God, as a "bridegroom" and husband. Other actions that can be instilled with important symbolic meaning include gestures of sitting and standing, bending and bowing, kissing the Torah as it is carried from the Holy Ark to the reading table and back, saying specific words, whether quietly or out loud with precise emphasis, and the like.

Kavanah, as a soulful gesture, intentionality continues successively from *devekut* and expresses itself especially in the *Keriyat Shema*, when the worshipper stretches out the *Shema*—as explained in chapter 7, dedicated to the *Keriyat Shema* and its blessings. Correct *kavanah* is implemented by accompanying the words "The Lord our God, the Lord is one" with reflection upon each divine name and the idea that develops in transitioning from the meaning of one name to the following, until they are all united in the adjectival word "one" (*eḥad*). This word is pronounced letter by letter: the beginning, the middle, and the end, which sets the boundary of one (*ḥad*). This operation of thought is a mimetic process that imitates the meaning of the pronounced words. It unifies several ideas, joins them, and blends them together into complete wholeness. Note that this is the only way to present the "one" as a general concept, for it is not definable positively by itself: we experience the idea of unity in the thought that aspires to it, without defining it! In this way, the worshipper conceives the existence of the "one" that is unique to itself, and distinct in relation to the other. The reflection on unity (*aḥdut*) implements a transition from the concept in a person's thought to what stays forever in the realm of a mystery upon which his entire life depends: the singular mystery that sets the person apart, the mystery to which he is commanded to adhere. This is the attainment of mutuality, whereby the person influences God who remains in *zikah* with him by means of the person's openness and longing to receive God's emanation. In this way, prayer with mindful intentionality (*kavanah*) brings about the response expected by the worshipper.

This understanding of the activity of affirming the unity (*iḥud*) and singularity (*yiḥud*) of God's name in prayer adds an additional dimension to the intentionality of prayer of the "person of mystery." The *kavanah* is comprehended by him as an intellectual-voluntary action based upon knowledge that God has revealed to him. Its concern is the ability to awaken God to implement specific activities that will satisfy appropriate requests of interest to the worshipper. For this *kavanah*, every divine name, every appellation and attribute which is pronounced with understanding and intention, brings about a special emanation from the divine source for the earthy world. When we activate this attribute, we cause the requests which we intend to satisfy to be satisfied. With the spread of the *Kabbalah* of Rabbi Isaac Luria in the sixteenth century, *kavanah* in this sense changed into the technical expertise of the "master of secrets," the kabbalist, as an expert, professional prayer-master. There is, indeed, a legal basis to this kind of *kavanah* in the doctrine of the divine names from the Bible. But in its later development, especially in the area of "practical *kabbalah*," it is difficult to distinguish it from idolatrous acts of magic—and this is a warning sign. Generally, the scholars of Israel prefer to heed this warning.

The Holy of Holies: Pronunciation of the Tetragrammaton

Let us return to the subject of addressing God with the names that God revealed to His loyal worshippers, and especially to the use of the "divine name according to its letters" given to Moses to transmit to the members of his people so that they would have confidence in His help when they turned to Him. After establishing the sanctuary and appointing priests and Levites to the order of worship, the name was pronounced solely by the high priest on the Day of Atonement, when he entered the Holy of Holies to offer the prayers of Israel to God—who would respond to them, forgive the sins of His people, pardon them, and judge them as worthy. Much preparation was required of the high priest for this. He had to purify and sanctify himself of any stain or sin, and from every kind of defilement, and atone for his transgressions—those of his family, his tribe, and his nation—with special sacrifices, requiring utmost precision in all details of execution, for them to be directed as *mitzvot* of God. The high priest was also required to learn how to pronounce the divine name in the correct form, as preserved in tradition and transmitted secretly from high priest to high priest. The correct form was considered to be one of the most sacred mystical secrets, because tremendous power was attributed to the name. Imprecision in activating it was liable to bring disaster akin to what happened to the sons of Aaron who had kindled strange fire on the altar.

At the fateful hour the high priest entered the Holy of Holies. Its curtain was sprinkled with the blood of sacrifices. He bowed down in prostration before the Ark of the Covenant, and articulated the letters of the sanctified name. It was a moment of highest anxiety. All the priests, the Levites, and all the people gathered in the courtyard, tensely following after the high priest. They prostrated themselves on the ground, and answered *"Amen"* after him. When the priest emerged healthy and whole from the Holy of Holies, the people knew that his prayer had been accepted. They erupted with great joy, replacing the anxiety.

The Day of Atonement was considered to be the holiest day of the year, the day when the fate of the entire nation and each of its individuals was sealed for the coming year. The moment of pronouncing the sacred name by its letters was the holiest moment of all. There was no anxiety like its anxiety, and no joy as its joy. After the destruction of the Temple, the liturgical poem *(piyyut)* of the *avodah* (order of worship) replaced the pronunciation of the sacred name in the synagogue service. The *piyyut* refers to that moment. Not with a description of the past, but with its symbolic dramatization in the synagogue. There, through this drama, we also strive to achieve a kind of mysterious experience, one of sublime *devekut* through *kavanah* that unifies the worshippers' thought with absolute concentration on their aim to surrender themselves to their creator. We experience a moment of great anxiety as we bow down prostrate to the ground, and when we stand up we experience the return to life—out of trust that the prayers recited with complete heart and pure intentions are received.

Epilogue

The Universality and Perpetuity of Moving from
Slavery to Freedom and from Exile to Redemption

The communal synagogue is a small sanctuary and the *siddur*—the Jewish
prayer book—replaces the worship of God with sacrifices, which took place in
the Tabernacle in the desert and the Temple in Jerusalem. The synagogue and
the prayer book are creations of the era which began with the destruction of the
First Temple and the Babylonian exile. The consciousness of being situated in
exile is expressed in prayers, which are gathered in the *siddur*. This is especially
prominent in the *Shemoneh Esrei* prayer (the Eighteen Benedictions), which
is recited, with various adjustments, three times every day of the year on
weekdays, on Sabbath days, on holidays, and festivals. After its establishment in
the Babylonian exile, the communal synagogue carried out the role of the "lesser
sanctuary" also in the Land of Israel—even after the building of the Second
Temple. The process of creation and consolidation of the central prayers which
compose the *siddur*, is the work of scribes, rabbis, and scholars of oral Torah in
the Land of Israel. This work began in the days of return to Zion and continued
into the reign of the Hasmonean family. In this context, let us recall that the
ceremony instituted at the event of renewing the covenant—reading the
Torah and having it explained at the gathering of the assembly of Israel, which
is renewed every Sabbath and holiday in the contemporary synagogue—was
carried out in the public square that served as a synagogue outside the Temple,
even though the Temple had already been built, and sacrificial worship had
been renewed. Moreover, already in those days the leaders of the majority of
the children of Israel—scribes, rabbis, and scholars of the oral Torah—held
the view that renewal of the kingdom of the House of David, the legitimate
kingdom from the legal perspective of the nation of Israel, which God as the
supreme king of the nation had selected, was a vision for the end of days. The
end of days might be drawing near, but it would be entirely realized only as a
result of God's supernatural intervention, in which the "kingdom of heaven" on

earth will be revealed. Let us reemphasize: this vision is the union of two forms of redemption: (1) the political, earthly redemption, in which the nation will reside in peace among all the nations and be regarded by them as first among equals; and (2) spiritual redemption from all causes of suffering in human life on earth: death and sickness, poverty, starvation in war—a redemption that is both communal and individual-existential. The scholars of oral Torah distinguished the materialization of the lofty vision as a future reality, which they called "the world to come," from the reality of the present, which they called "this world." All of humankind, with the nation of Israel at its head, were commanded to do all they could to bring the era of the appearance of God's kingdom in the "world to come" near, by observing God's *mitzvot* of the "covenant of the children of Noah" and the "covenant of Sinai." But the phenomenon of God's kingdom could only be experienced through its symbolic materialization on Sabbath and festivals, the times sanctified to worshipping God.

These matters sum up the basic assumptions of the *siddur*. But each generation is commanded to interpret and apply the assumptions to its present circumstances. The following question certainly arises in the heart of the readers of this book, who are concerned with the situation of the Jewish people in our generations: Do the prayers which express the existing and political experience of the exile suit the emotional and conceptual needs of the nation which has returned to its birthplace and capital, has established its government there, and lives there as a sovereign nation as do all free peoples? With the establishment of the State of Israel, the people of Israel no longer dwell in exile. The same considerations apply also to most diaspora Jews, for the gates of *aliyah* to their state are wide open to them. Are these Jews not commanded to pray and sing a "new song," as redeemed people, and not as exiled?

To answer this question, let us first recall that the Jewish prayer book is an open creation which has not been finished, and will not be finished as long as there are still worshippers for whom the prayer, from their perspective, is not only an obligation but a need of the soul—whether of individuals wrestling with their life's destiny or a nation confronting its destiny among the nations. Every generation impresses its signature on the *siddur*—whether by adding blessings, prayers, and liturgical poems, or by amending its texts. In particular, the understanding of the significance and emphasis of the intentions of prayer changes with each generation. There have been generations in which the need to add, subtract, and renew has been dominant, and generations when there was less of this. Our generation is among those that feel the need to add, subtract, interpret, and renew with particular force, because of all the great upheavals that have taken place in its history. This refers not only to the establishment of the

State of Israel, which arose after the Holocaust, the most terrible destruction our nation has undergone. To this is added the ongoing wrestling of the nation of Israel over the shape of its independent identity and over its integration as a free nation among the nations. The fact that shaping an independent identity and integration as one nation, peacefully within the family of nations, is far from becoming a certain and complete achievement, requires no proof. Divisions, internal struggles, and war with enemies are a daily reality for us. Especially bitter is the fact that the State of Israel is still fighting not only over the existence of the nation in its land as a free people, but also over international recognition of its right to exist as a free nation in its land. This is a warlike encounter with difficult ramifications both for Israel's internal unity and for Israel's ability to deal with societal distresses, which upset the camaraderie of the people. On account of this complex of reasons, including disputes over the nation's essential identity—and not only by reason of its emigration from the diaspora—many Jews in various religious movements feel a need to renew the Jewish prayer book, to add much and to remove much—especially the laborious repetitions and the liturgical poems which do not express the feelings and thinking of the people. Lamentations and prayers have been added in memory of victims of the Holocaust and in memory of those slain in Israel's wars; and prayer for peace of the state, its success and its improvement—which are recited in many synagogues on Sabbaths and festivals; mourning ceremonies on the Day of Remembrance of the Holocaust and Heroism, and Day of General *Kaddish*; and ceremonies of thanksgiving on Israel's Independence Day and Jerusalem Day. It should be added that, in the various religious movements which have arisen in the nation of Israel in modern times, a broad-based effort has been underway to adapt the *siddur* to the culture of the time, its new societal and political values, and the changes that have taken place in the social and political hierarchy. The innovation based in the struggle of women for equal rights in the synagogue has been especially conspicuous. In this connection, it would be proper to note that the trend for renewal is sweeping. It expresses itself not only in the prayer books of the Reform and Conservative movements and their leadership, but in the prayer of Orthodoxy and even ultra-Orthodoxy.

The trend of expansion and renewal connected directly to Zionism as a redemptive national, socio-economic, cultural, and political movement is expressed in the shaping of the annual calendar with its holidays and festivals. Two of the essential forms in which the expansion and renewal are expressed regarding these subjects are: (1) enrichment of the conceptual and emotional-artistic content (including music and dance) of holidays and traditional days of remembrance, and (2) addition of new holidays and days of remembrance, including those with a traditional source, and those that mark the history of the nation in modern times.

The first form is notable principally with respect to the *Haggadah* of Passover, but the same applies to the holidays of Shavuot, Sukkot, Hanukkah, and Purim. The second form is that of additions of holidays on the 15th of Shevat, 15th of Av, and the 33rd day of the Omer, as well as the institution of the Day of Remembrance on the 9th of Tevet—where the source is traditional, but the content is entirely new; and new days of remembrance: Day of Remembrance of the Holocaust and Heroism, Remembrance Day of the Slain of the Israel Defense Forces, Independence Day, and Jerusalem Day. Great creative activity is recognizable in all these directions, which has also stirred controversies, in the name of heaven—all as customary for the people of Israel over the generations. In this book I did not analyze these innovations, because to do so properly, relevantly, and in detail would necessitate an additional book. Those who are interested can turn to my earlier book *The Jewish Experience of Time: Philosophical Dimensions of the Jewish Holy Days*, which discusses the new festivals.

Along with acknowledging the necessity, the importance, and even the urgency of changes and additions, it is appropriate to emphasize their limitations, and the established, definite, and ongoing importance of the permanent prayers in the traditional Jewish prayer book. To be sure, they have been added at certain historical moments, but not for those moments only but for the generations, just as the written Torah is given for the generations. In the present, the heritage of the written Torah and the prayer book are important not only by virtue of the authority of the past which is sanctified by the religious institution, but because the people of Israel recognize that the circumstances of their living among the nations do not yet allow for the realization of the kingdom of God on earth without God's supernatural intervention to change the order of creation. That is, perfect redemption is not possible in this world—not for humankind in its entirety, and not for the nation of Israel within it. Humankind and the nation of Israel are therefore still commanded to forge ahead with all their ability to mend the world, and the "end of days" is a vision for the very distant future, whose wondrous realization will be in eternity, which is beyond all times.

The formal halakhic basis for this conclusion regarding the State of Israel is simple, although it includes the dimensions of experiential and conceptual depth that are discussed in this book. The Chief Rabbinate of Israel has formulated the basic concept in a prayer for the peace of the state. The state is defined in this prayer as the "beginning of the sprouting of our redemption."

This definition is singular. The state changed the relative situation of the Jewish people among the nations, as it made the socio-economic, cultural, and political situation of the Jewish nation equal to the "normal" situation of free nations of our time. But this is still not the complete redemption, not in terms of the relative situation of the Jewish nation among the nations, and certainly not in terms of the aspects of life in which even mighty powers are very far from perfect redemption. Humankind is still wrestling with the distresses of the existence of civilization in nature—and especially with the distresses that humankind itself causes on account of the evil that permeates it.

From the religious-legal perspective, the absence of perfection is expressed both on the ritual and the socio-political level. On the ritual level: the Temple remains destroyed, and it is impossible to rebuild it. A boundary was created, which cannot be removed *bazeman hazeh* (in the present time). On the one hand, the Temple Mount is occupied by two Muslim houses of prayer; on the other, pilgrimage to the Temple Mount is now forbidden to Jews due to special laws of purity, which are impossible to observe under the present conditions. It should be stressed in this regard, that losing the possibility of worshipping God with sacrifices is not the essence of the religious-legal problem. From the perspective of most Jews today, renewing sacrificial worship of God is not at all desirable, and the worship of God that suits the moral and cultural notions of most Jews is the spiritual exaltation of prayer. The religious-legal problem has rather to do with the symbolic significance of the fact that God's direct tie to His people, His *Shekhinah's* presence amid His nation, and His conduct towards the people with a "revealed face," ceased with the destruction of the First Temple of the kingdom of the House of David. There is no path in sight to restore them through actions of which the Jewish people is capable.

The social and political perspective frames the significance of the distance between the people and their God through ideas about maintaining the covenant made between God and His people according to the Torah, which is the book of the covenant. The kingdom of David was elevated in the eyes of the exiled generations to the level of myth, reflecting the relation between God and earthly reality from the perspective of eternity—which is the trans-human view. In this sense, the kingdom of the House of David is larger than life and can be established only through a divine intervention that will raise earthly time to heavenly eternity. This is because in the kingdom of the pious King David, servant of God and composer of the psalms, royal sovereignty bowed to the kingdom of God as embodied by God's Torah and the guidance of His prophets. But already in the last days of Solomon, son of David, the covenant was transgressed and the sovereign kingdom set ordinances and laws in the sinful manner of all nations, which were not in accordance with the ordinances, *mitzvot*, and morality of the Torah of Moses and the prophets. Thus began the decline and fall, which concluded with the destruction of Jerusalem and the Temple, the uprooting of the kingdom of the House of David, and the Babylonian exile. One must keep the religious-legal significance of this historical myth in mind. The kingdom in which the nation would be worthy of total redemption would, from now on, be the kingdom that fulfills the laws of justice and equity, that assures freedom for all members of the nation and peace among the nations—as the prophet Isaiah envisioned for the messianic end of days:

> For instruction shall come forth from Zion
> The word of the Lord from Jerusalem.
> (Isaiah 2:3)

And:

> Zion shall be saved in the judgment;
> Her repentant ones, in the retribution.
> (Isaiah 1:27)

This, then, is the reason why the reality of exile—in general as a metaphor for human existence, and in particular as the situation of the people of Israel—was not annulled either during the return from Babylonia to Zion, or during the reign of the Hasmonean dynasty. The Hasmoneans began by breaking the yoke of the kingdom of Greece and restoring obligatory authority of the basic law of the Torah, but quickly turned into a dynasty subordinate to Greco-Roman rule and effectively serving its aims, which were those of imperial rule that only strove towards gaining more and more power. The Hasmonean dynasty thereby enacted and enforced laws of a tyrannical kingdom instead of the just ordinances, laws, and judgments of the Torah. It became clear that the establishment of the Hasmonean dynasty quickly exhausted its justification and lost the path to progress. The dynasty regressed, together with the Greco-Roman empires that sought world domination, into a new tyrannical degradation—a degradation deeper than that into which the kingdom of Judah sunk together with the kingdom of Babylon. This is an old story, according to the testimony of the biblical narrative, which traces God's repeated efforts to perfect His goals in creation—with the help of humankind and, after that, with the help of Israel. It thus became clear that after returning to Zion in the days of Cyrus, Ezra, and Nehemiah, the process of reformation submerged all humanity and the nation of Israel in particular into a progressively deeper evil—in terms of descent necessitating ascent—and, in the meantime, darkness increased more and more. Only when it reached its climax would redemption illumine from above, with all the power of its light.

This pattern came to expression in the *siddur*, with the tension between the expressions "who redeemed Israel" (*Ga'al yisrael*) at the conclusion of the *Keriyat Shema* and "who redeems Israel" (*Go'el yisrael*) in the *Shemoneh Esrei* prayer. Let us recall the *midrash* of the sages in the *Haggadah* of Passover:

> Originally our ancestors were idolators, but at present the Lord hath brought us near to His worship. . . .

> And it is this same promise which has been the support of our ancestors and of ourselves for not one only has risen up against us, but in every generation some have arisen against us to anni-hilate us, but the Most Holy, blessed be He, hath delivered us out of their hands. . . .

> In every generation each individual is bound to regard himself as if he personally had gone forth from Egypt, as is said "and thou shalt relate to thy son that day, saying, this is on account of what the Eternal did for me, when I went forth from Egypt" [Exodus 13:8]. It was not our ancestors alone whom the most Holy, blessed be He, redeemed from Egypt, but us also did he redeem with them.[1]

Let us probe further and recall what was said to Abraham with the command "Go forth" (Genesis 12:1) and to Moses at the event of the bush burning with fire that was not consumed, which is echoed in Moses's words in the book of Deuteronomy and especially in the *Ha'azinu* song—all of which are recalled in the *Shemoneh Esrei* prayer. The God of Israel is the God of the future, whose promise is not enacted in the present. Rather, it is enacted when we act in the present and aim to reach the future despite the overwhelming suffering, which we make efforts to overcome. The more we approach the future, the more it distances itself. Humans can experience the future only when they succeed in progressing in realizing the vision of the righteousness and justice in their society, and on the symbolic level when they sit together on Sabbaths and festivals for the worship of God as free people who are pledged to one another. This is the deeper meaning of the statement that the state is the "beginning of the sprouting of our redemption," as Israel's Declaration of Independence says—if we take it upon ourselves to view the governing order not as the end, but as the instrument that enables us to pursue the improvement of individual and group life with greater vigor. The state is obliged to adopt the eternal book of books as the source of the nation's identity, thereby realizing social justice in light of the vision of the prophets of Israel, and by doing so, advance the cause of peace among ourselves and our neighbors. Only by achieving this peace will redemption sprout and reach its perfection. Following the establishment of the State of Israel, have we reached that level of complete redemption of humankind and of the Jewish nation within humanity, whereby the requests and expectations of the *Shemoneh Esrei* prayer are fulfilled—including the requests for the ideal ingathering of exiles, uniting people in their land, and restoring justice and righteousness there, as commanded abundantly in the Torah of Israel? The simple answer is that not all worshippers, even in the most innovative religious movements who believe in human progress, raise this question. It appears that the existing version is enough for them, simply because human personal and collective life experience, as humankind in its totality and of the nations within it, is still very distant from the feeling of perfect redemption. Moreover, most of us have already arrived at the recognition that the end of days, in which redemption is completed, is a vision that is not to be realized in the future, because a change in the orders of creation is not to be expected, and humankind will only be redeemed to the extent that it will use its powers to rule over nature for the good, and not for the bad. Beyond that, we think that those who deceive themselves stating that the vision of perfect redemption has already been realized in our time, or is about to actually be realized tomorrow, have exempted themselves from dealing with the obstacles and difficult moral problems of the present, and because of this have pushed back the vision's fulfillment instead of striving to diligently realize it.

An additional question: Is humankind, and the Jewish nation within it—as it is found today, seventy-seven years after the Second World War and the Holocaust, and seventy-four years after the establishment of the State of Israel by agreement of the United Nations—in a process of advancement in the moral, societal, cultural and political, national and international senses, or the opposite? After one step of advance that was required for reconstructing humankind after its destruction in the war, and for reconstruction of the Jewish nation out of its destruction in the Holocaust, humankind finds itself again in a process of moral decline, which is likely to conclude with a grievous disaster of even greater destruction on account of the technological power accumulated today in human hands. Is this power itself a guarantee of human progress, or perhaps the opposite—perhaps the danger of absolute downfall is embodied in it? These questions are controversial. But it is impossible to deny or hide the dangers and the great distresses, and it is impossible to deny or hide the fact that the Jewish nation and the State of Israel are threatened today, internally and externally, concerning both their existence and their self-identity. There is only one subject connected to the *Shemoneh Esrei* prayer, where, it is thought, the time has come for change, and it is the matter of relations between Judaism and Christianity. But while a change has truly taken place for the good in relations between Judaism and Christianity after the Holocaust, the establishment of the State of Israel has caused great animosity, ever intensifying, between Judaism and Islam.

From all the personal and national perspectives outlined above, the two basic prayers of the Jewish prayer book—the *Keriyat Shema* and the *Shemoneh Esrei*—express both the obligations imposed on the people of Israel for their redemption and that of humankind, and their anticipations, hopes, and longings. Moreover, in order to effectuate these hopes in life, the people need communities and synagogues in which the covenant that has established the people as a nation is renewed—and within the framework of which the people realize the covenant in their way of life. This is a pressing need, because modern civilization, materialistic and egoistic, is shattering the ties of the covenant and its modes of life; shattering the community and the family; and casting the morality of loving of God and loving neighbors, which is at the foundation of the morality of the covenant, into oblivion. From this perspective, before any progress can be achieved, to a limited extent, by means of the state, the people of Israel, in their state need, redemption—in the sense of "return to the days as of old" (Lamentations 5:2). As we conclude our words, let us remember that the event of prayer, as an experience of faith, love, and sanctification, is not only education for redemptive spiritual and moral ascent. The event of prayer is also the symbolic gesture of prayer as anticipation of the future.

Endnotes

1   Ze'ev Raban, ed., *Haggadah: With an English Translation and Explanatory Notes* (Tel Aviv: Sinai, 1961), 21–22, 41.

Glossary

Adon Olam "Lord of the World"—a medieval poem added to the liturgy, which expresses God's transcendence and nearness to the believer

Afikomen A portion of matzah eaten as the last item in the Passover feast (from Greek *epi-kommos*, after the meal)

Ahavah Rabbah "Abundant love"; the second blessing in the Recitation of the *Shema*. Its theme is God showing His love for Israel through revelation of the Torah

Aliyah Ascent: (a) going up to the Torah reading table in the synagogue to recite the blessings over the reading of the Torah; (b) immigration to the Land of Israel

Amen "So be it." An affirmation of agreement with a prayer someone else has said

Amidah "Standing [prayer]"—the Eighteen Benedictions recited on weekdays, or the corresponding seven-benediction prayer recited on Sabbaths or Festivals, which comprises the principal part of the service

Ani "I." (See *Anokhi*, I–Thou)

Anokhi "I" (especially of God)

Ark (or Holy Ark) (a) A ceremonial box in the Tabernacle to hold the Tablets of the Covenant (Exodus 25:10–16). (b) A ceremonial chest or alcove with a decorative curtain, in the front of the synagogue sanctuary, to hold the Torah scrolls

Arvit (or Ma'ariv) The daily evening prayer service

Atah "You," "Thou" (as in Buber's I–Thou)

Attribute[s]	(a) In medieval philosophy and theology, any descriptive term, especially of God, such as "wise," "loving," "powerful." (b) In rabbinic theology, specifically the thirteen attributes of mercy described in Exodus 34:6–7: "The Lord! The Lord! A God compassionate and gracious, etc."
Av Haraḥamim	"Father of mercy"—a prayer in memory of Jewish victims of religious persecution, recited especially on Sabbaths
Avdut	Servitude; the status of being an *eved* (servant) and performing *avodah* (service). (See *avodah*)
Avinu Mal-keinu	"Our Father, our King"—a penitential litany recited on fast days and during the Days of Awe
Avodah	Service: (a) the status of being a servant (*eved*); (b) service to God (worship), either sacrificial (in the ancient Temple) or in the form of prayer (in the synagogue); (c) labor (especially manual); (d) the *Avodah* service—a section of the Yom Kippur *Musaf* prayer describing and partially emulating the service of the high priest in the Temple on Yom Kippur
Avodah zarah	Idolatry
Avot	Patriarchs. (a) The biblical patriarchs, Abraham, Isaac, and Jacob, as figures invoked in the prayers. (b) *Avot*—the first benediction of the *Shmoneh Esrei*, with the theme of God of the patriarchs being also the God of the worshipper.
Ba'al [ha] bayit	Householder, a responsible (generally male) member of the Jewish community (pl. *ba'alei batim*)
Ba'al [ha] kore	Torah reader in the synagogue service
Beit keneset	House of gathering; synagogue
Beit midrash	House of study (for adolescents and adults)
Ben berit	A "son" (that is, party) of the covenant (pl. *benei berit*, or Bnai Brith)
Beshem umalkhut	"Name and kingship"—the liturgical formula invoking God by name and also acknowledging God's kingship, specifically, the formula *Barukh atah adonai eloheinu melekh ha'olam*: "Blessed are You, O Lord, King of the universe"
Birkat Hamazon	"Blessing for sustenance"—grace after meals

Birkhot Hashahar	"Morning blessings" or "blessings of the dawn"; the first introductory portion of the public morning service in the synagogue
Devekut	Adherence, attachment, cleaving (see Deuteronomy 10:20 and 13:5: "and hold fast to Him")
Edah	Assembly, especially of Israel (see Leviticus 8:3–5 and elsewhere)
Eden, Garden of	(a) The garden described in Genesis, chapters 2–3 as the original abode of Adam and Eve. (b) Paradise, conceived as the abode of the righteous with which they are rewarded in the end of days. In this connection, the Garden of Eden is invoked in the memorial prayer for the departed
Ehyeh	(a) Hebrew: "I will be." (b) The divine name related to *Yod-Hay-Vav-Hay* and revealed to Moses according to Exodus 3:13–15: "*Ehyeh-Asher-Ehyeh*—I will be as I will be"
Eleh Ezkerah	"These [things] I remember"—a martyrology recited on Yom Kippur
Elohim	(a) God, especially in the impersonal sense of the generic or philosophical God, and in contrast to the personal God called by name. (b) Plural of *el*: gods (along the line of thinking that the Israelite God takes the place of the pagan gods; see Psalms 82)
Epicurean	(Hebrew: *apikoros*.) (a) A follower of the ancient Greek philosopher Epicurus, who taught that the world is subject to chance and the gods do not care about human destiny. (b) By extension, in Jewish thought, any heretic
Gabbai	(a) Treasurer, fundraiser, or financial officer of a Jewish community. (b) A participant serving a supporting role in the Torah service, who stands at the reading table as the Torah is read
Gevurot	(a) Might, manifestations of divine power. (b) The second benediction of the *Shemoneh Esrei*, with the theme of God's power over life and death
Ha'azinu	(a) The poem traditionally recited by Moses before his death (see Deuteronomy 32). (b) The Torah portion containing the poem

Haftarah	A passage from the prophetic books of the Bible, read after the Torah reading for the day in the synagogue on Sabbaths and holidays (from root PTR, "to take one's leave"; pl. *haftarot*)
Haggadah	"Telling," specifically the canonical order of the home service on the night of Passover, telling the story of the Exodus from Egypt
Hagiogra-pha	The third division of the Hebrew Bible, comprising Psalms, Proverbs, Job, Song of Songs, Ruth, Lamentations, Ecclesiastes, Daniel, Ezra, Nehemiah, and Chronicles.
Halakhah	Codified Jewish law, especially deriving from the Talmudic tradition (pl. *halakhot*; adj. halakhic). This word is spelled in this book with a capital H when it refers to the Jewish law as a system, and with a lowercase h when it refers to a specific clause of this law
Hallel	"[Hymns of] Praise"—the cycle of Psalms 113–118, recited on festivals of rejoicing
Ḥalutz	Zionist pioneer (pl. *ḥalutzim*, adj. *ḥalutzic*)
Ḥasid	(a) An adherent of Hasidism, a popular Jewish pietistic movement in the eighteenth–twentieth centuries. (b) A pious or spiritual individual. (Pl. *ḥasidim*; adj. *ḥasidic*)
Havayah	(a) Being. (b) Allusion to the name of God, *Yod-Hay-Vav-Hay*, which is related to the Hebrew verb HVH, "to be"
Ḥavayah	Living experience (from *ḥai*, living), a term coined by Aaron David Gordon
Havdalah	"Separation" or "distinction"; specifically, the ceremony over wine, candle, and spices performed at the close of the Sabbath to mark the distinction between the Sabbath and the secular weekdays following it.
Ḥeder	"[Class]room"; traditional elementary religious school
Hester panim	Hiddenness of [God's] face (see Deuteronomy 31:18)
Ḥokhmat harazim	"Wisdom of secrets"—secret wisdom, esoteric lore
Ḥukkim	Law, especially with the connotation of an arbitrary law (sing. *ḥok*)

Hoda'ah	Acknowledgement; hence, thanksgiving or confession. (Related to *todah* and *vidui*)
I–Thou	Genuine person-to-person dialogue; a key term in Martin Buber's philosophy of dialogue, elaborated in his book *I and Thou*
Jubilee	Every fiftieth year when, by the Levitical law, release from all personal servitude and land mortgages is enacted (see Leviticus 25)
Kabbalah	Jewish mystical tradition, especially the *Zohar* and its associated literature and traditions (adj. kabbalistic)
Kabbalat Shabbat	"Welcoming the Sabbath." A series of psalms and hymns recited before the formal evening service on Friday night, at the onset of the Sabbath
Kaddish	(a) Sanctification; a prayer occurring in various longer or shorter forms, generally at the end of sections of the service. (b) The Mourner's *Kaddish*, recited at the end of the service by mourners as part of their observation of their period of mourning
Karet	The punishment of "being cut off" by divine decree ("that person shall be cut off from his kin," Leviticus 19:8 and elsewhere)
Kavanah	Intention, intentionality, mindfulness, especially in prayer
Kedushah	"Sanctification." The third benediction of the *Shemoneh Esrei*, with the theme of God's holiness, recited in a short version (in individual worship) and in a long version (when said by the entire congregation together)
Keneset yisrael	The congregation of Israel. (See *klal yisrael*)
Keriyat Shema	"Recitation of the *Shema*": (a) biblical passages Deuteronomy 6:4–9, 11:13–21, and Numbers 15:37–41, as a unit of the liturgy; (b) these together with the benedictions recited before and after them in the Jewish liturgy
Ketubim	"Writings," Hagiographa. (See Hagiographa)
Kibbutz	A farming collective, especially in the early Zionist movement
Kiddush	Sanctification; the short prayer recited at home or in synagogue, usually over wine, inaugurating the Sabbath or other holy day

Kiddush hashem	"Sanctification of the Name," specifically, martyrdom
Klal yisrael	The collectivity of Israel
Kohen	Priest, specifically, in Judaism, a member of the priestly clan traditionally descended from Aaron
Lekhah Dodi	"Come, my beloved." A hymn composed in sixteenth-century Safed, included in the *Kabbalat Shabbat* service on Friday night at the onset of the Sabbath
Levite	A member of the clan traditionally descended from Levi, who in Temple times served as assistants to the priest
Ma'ariv	Evening prayer. (See *Arvit*)
Ma'aseh bereshit	"The work of creation"—the mystical doctrine of the orders of creation, based on study of the opening chapters of Genesis
Ma'aseh merkavah	"The work of the chariot"—the mystical doctrine of God and the heavenly mysteries, based on study of the opening chapters of Ezekiel
Maḥzor	Compendium, especially the prayer book for High Holy Days, which contains many added prayers. More generally, any similar compendium (such as the *siddur*)
Mezuzah	A cylinder containing a small scroll with the Hebrew paragraphs Deuteronomy 6:4–9 and 11:13–21 in observance of the command "You shall write them on the doorposts of your house" (pl. *mezuzot*)
Midrash	(a) The rabbinic art of exegesis, finding layers of interpretation in the words of the written scriptures. (b) A literary work composed in this style (such as *Midrash Rabbah*, *Midrash Tanḥuma*). (c) A single teaching, interpretation, or tradition in the midrashic style
Mikdash me'at	"Small sanctuary." This term reflects the concept that the synagogue is a miniature substitute for the original Temple in Jerusalem
Minḥah	The afternoon prayer service (from *minḥah*, the meal offering in the Temple)
Minyan	Quorum, especially a quorum of ten Jews assembled in public prayer (from *manah*, "to count")

Mi Shebei- *rakh*	"Who has blessed . . . may He bless. . . ." A prayer recited on behalf of an individual or group for several different purposes, incluing celebration and request for healing
Mishnah	(a) *Mishnah*—the code of Jewish law compiled in the second century CE, the basis of the Talmud. In this sense, this word is spelled in this book with a capital M. (b) *Mishnah*—a paragraph of the *Mishnah*, as a unit of study (pl. *mishnayot*). In this sense, this word is usually spelled here with a lowercase m
Mishneh *Torah*	(a) A copy of the Torah, specifically, for the Israelite king to keep in his possession (Deuteronomy 17:8). (b) The rabbinic name for the book of Deuteronomy. (c) A legal code by Maimonides, deliberately taking as its title the ancient name of Deuteronomy
Mishpat	Justice; equity; jurisprudence
Mitnaged	An opponent of Hasidism, especially among Orthodox east-European Jews (pl. *mitnagdim*; adj. mitnagdic)
Mitzvah	(a) Commandment; any of the rules of Jewish behavior as conceived as commanded by God. (b) By extension, all the behavioral norms, ethical or ritual, formal or informal, of the Jewish tradition (pl. *mitzvot*).
Mitzvah feast	A feast to celebrate the performance of a *mitzvah*
Mizmor	In the Temple worship, a poem sung with instruments, a psalm. *Mizmor* is the standard Hebrew term for "psalm" in the singular; however, the Hebrew title for the book of Psalms as a whole is *Sefer Tehillim*
Modeh Ani	"I give thanks." The prayer recited by an individual at home on first waking up
Mo'ed	Appointed time; festival (pl. *mo'adim*)
Modim	"We give thanks." The second of the three concluding benedictions of the *Amidah* on all days
Musaf	(a) An additional sacrifice offered in the Temple on Sabbaths and holidays. (b) An additional section of the synagogue prayer service on mornings of Sabbaths and holidays, corresponding to the ancient *musaf* sacrifice
Nefesh	Soul (from a root meaning "breath")
Neshamah	Soul (from *nasham*, "to breathe")

Oral Torah	The tradition of Jewish law passed down orally until its canonization in the *Mishnah* and Talmud, and by some accounts, developing continually
Parnas	Lay executive of a Jewish community, especially in early modern Polish Jewry
Pesukei Dezimra	"Verses of song"; the second introductory part of the public daily service, consisting of psalms and similar prayers
Pidyon haben	Redemption of the firstborn (see Exodus 13:11–13)
Piyyut	Liturgical poem (pl. *piyyutim*)
Priestly benediction	The benediction prescribed in the Torah (Numbers 6:22–27) for the priests to bless the people, and incorporated toward the end of the public *Amidah* in the morning service on weekdays, Sabbaths, and holidays
Prophets	(a) The inspired spiritual leaders of ancient Israel, from Moses through Malachi. (b) Prophets—the second division of the Hebrew Bible, comprising Joshua, Judges, Samuel, Kings, and the books of the literary prophets (Isaiah, Jeremiah, Ezekiel, and "the Twelve")
Recitation of the Shema	See *Keriyat Shema*
Retzei Adonai	"Have favor"—the first of the three concluding benedictions of the *Amidah*, on weekdays and Sabbaths and holidays, with the themes of restoration of worship in the Temple and God favorably accepting Israel's prayer
Ruaḥ	(a) Spirit, soul. (b) Wind
Sabbatical year	The seventh year of the seven-year cycle, during which the land was to lie fallow. (See Leviticus 25:1–7)
Sefirot	Emanations of God according to the doctrine of Zoharic kabbalah (sing. *sefirah*)
Segulah	Special treasure; special cohort. A term applied to the Jewish people as God's chosen nation
Shaḥarit	The daily morning prayer service (from *shaḥar*, dawn)
Shaliaḥ [ha] tzibur	Emissary of the community; the prayer-leader capable of praying on behalf of the other members of the congregation

Shekhinah	(a) God's presence or immanence (from *shakhan*, "to dwell," applied to God's dwelling amidst His people, especially in the Tabernacle, or *mishkan*; see Exodus 25:8). (b) In Zoharic kabbalah, the tenth *sefirah*, closest to the created world and identified with *keneset yisrael*
Shema	(a) The Recitation of the *Shema* (see *Keriyat Shema*); (b) the verse 6:4: "Listen, O Israel, the Lord is our God, the Lord is One"
Shema Koleinu	"Hear our voice." (a) The sixteenth benediction of the *Shemoneh Esrei*, concluding the middle petitionary section for the weekday prayer. (b) Part of the *Seliḥot* prayers for High Holy Days
Shemitah	(a) The release of debts in the seventh year (see Deuteronomy 15:1–11). (b) By extension, the totality of rules for the seventh year, including letting the land lie fallow (see Leviticus 25:1–7)
Shemoneh Esrei	(a) The Eighteen Benedictions (actually nineteen), also called the *Amidah* (standing prayer). This, together with the Recitation of the *Shema*, comprises the core of the daily service. (b) By extension, the *Amidah* of Sabbath and festivals, even though these comprise only seven benedictions
Sheol	In the biblical worldview, the underworld; the realm of the dead; comparable to Hades in Greek mythology
Siddur	(a) Order; arrangement. (b) *Siddur hatefillah*—the "order of prayer," that is the Jewish prayer book, embodying the liturgical rite of traditional Judaism
Sim Shalom	"Grant peace." The final benediction in the *Amidah*, in the longer version used in the morning service (the shorter version *Shalom Rav* is used in the afternoon and evening services)
Simḥat Torah	"Rejoicing of the Torah," a Jewish holiday on the 23rd of Tishrei, concluding the week-long Sukkot festival
Tabernacle	The large tent dedicated to the worship of God by the Israelites during the years of wandering in the wilderness. (See Exodus 25ff.)
Taḥanun	"Supplication"; penitential prayers recited in the weekday morning service after the *Amidah*

Tallit	Prayer shawl with ritually prescribed fringes on the four corners, worn in observance of the command to "make fringes on the corners of their garments" (Numbers 15:38)
Talmid ḥakham	"A student of the wise," a Jewish scholar of Talmudic law
Talmud	The repository of Jewish legal discussion and religious lore, compiled as a commentary on the *Mishnah* and written down in the fifth and sixth centuries CE.
Tefillah	Prayer (from the root PLL with the meaning of litigation, suggesting that, in prayer, one enters into a kind of judgment with God)
Tefillin	"Phylacteries"; black leather ornaments worn on the arm and head during prayer, containing scriptural verses, in observance of the command "You shall bind them as a sign upon your hand, and they shall be as a symbol on your forehead" (Deuteronomy 6:8)
Tehillim (pl.)	"Praises"; the Hebrew title of the book of Psalms (sing. *tehillah*)
Temple	The central worship site of ancient Israel, especially (a) First Temple, built by Solomon in 937 BCE and destroyed by the Babylonians in 586 BCE; (b) Second Temple, built by the Jewish returnees from exile around 516 BCE and destroyed by the Romans in 70 CE. Since then, Jewry has been without a temple, properly speaking; the synagogue (called "temple" by some Jews) is a substitute for it. The restoration of the Temple is a part of the Messianic scenario and a theme of many Jewish prayers
Terumah	(a) "Heave offering"—an in-kind contribution of agricultural produce from the Israelites to the priests (see Numbers 15:18–19). (b) Any contribution by the laity to the sanctuary (see Exodus 25:2–7)
Teshuvah	(a) Turning or return; see Lamentations 25:21. (b) Repentance, conceived as the turn, or return, of the sinner to God
Tetragrammaton	The divine Name consisting of four letters: *Yod-Hay-Vav-Hay* (see entry below)
Thirteen principles	A credo formulated by Maimonides, summarizing the content of Jewish faith in thirteen affirmations.

Tikkun olam   Mending or repairing the world, especially in the Lurianic kabbalistic tradition, according to which the brokenness of the world, requiring reparative response, is an essential part of the cosmic narrative

Tishah b'Av   9th of Av (Ab); a fast observed in commemoration of destruction of the First and Second Temples, and, by extension, of many tragedies in Jewish history

Todah   (a) Thanksgiving, as in prayer. (See *Hoda'ah, Modeh Ani.*) (b) In ancient Temple worship, a thanksgiving-offering

Torah   (a) All Jewish religious teaching. (b) The canonized Jewish religious literature, comprising Written Torah (Genesis, Exodus, Leviticus, Numbers, Deuteronomy) and Oral Torah (*Mishnah* and Talmud). (c) A Hebrew scroll of the Written Torah (Genesis through Deuteromy), read ceremonially in synagogue on certain weekdays and on all Sabbaths and holidays

Tree of life   (a) A poetic figure for Torah as a source of spiritual sustenance (see Proverbs 3:18, K:512). (b) Colloquially, one of the wooden spindles around which the scroll of the Torah is rolled (pl. *atzei ḥayyim*)

Tzedek   Justice

Tzedakah   (a) Righteousness, justice. (b) Alms, money contributed for the support of the poor and other communal charitable purposes

Tzelem   Image (as in "God created man in His image")

Twelve, the   The twelve minor prophets: Hosea, Joel, Amos, Obadiah, Jonah, Micah, Nahum, Habakkuk, Zephaniah, Haggai, Zechariah, and Malachi

Vidui   Confession. (See *Hoda'ah*)

Written Torah   (a) The books Genesis through Deuteronomy. (b) The laws contained therein

YHVH   The English equivalent of *Yod-Hay-Vav-Hay* (see entry below)

Yigdal   "May [God] be great"—a medieval poem added to the liturgy, poetically summing up Maimonides's thirteen principles of faith

Yizkor   (a) A memorial service for departed family and friends, held on the last or next-to-last days of certain holidays. (b) An individual memorial prayer that is part of the *Yizkor* service. (c) A similar memorial prayer, for instance on behalf of martyrs, not necessarily during the holiday *Yizkor* service

Yod-Hay-   The four Hebrew letters of the personal name of God accord-
Vav-Hay   ing to the Hebrew Bible (see Exodus 6:3). English equivalent YHVH. Generally substituted by *Adonai* ("the Lord") in sacred contexts such as prayer, or *Hashem* ("the Name") in more casual contexts

Yotzer   "Creator of heavenly lights." The first blessing in the Recita-
hame'orot   tion of the *Shema,* with the theme of God as creator

Zekhut   (a) A legal right. (b) Merit (as in *zekhut avot,* the merit of the patriarchs counted for the benefit of their latter-day descendants)

Zikah   Link, relation, connection, bond. In Hermann Cohen's philosophy, correlation (especially between God and humanity or between person and person). Related to the root ZKK, from which comes the word *zakuk*—"needing, depending on"

Index

INDEX LOCORUM

CPSIA information can be obtained
at www.ICGtesting.com
Printed in the USA
BVHW012327021022
648528BV00002B/53